Dear Joan
Thanks for the inspiration!
Ash 3/2012

Sep 3—

The Logic of Pronominal Resumption

Oxford Studies in Theoretical Linguistics

Recent titles

15 A Natural History of Infixation
by Alan C. L. Yu

16 Phi-Theory
Phi-Features Across Interfaces and Modules
edited by Daniel Harbour, David Adger, and Susana Béjar

17 French Dislocation: Interpretation, Syntax, Acquisition
by Cécile De Cat

18 Inflectional Identity
edited by Asaf Bachrach and Andrew Nevins

19 Lexical Plurals
by Paolo Acquaviva

20 Adjectives and Adverbs
Syntax, Semantics, and Discourse
edited by Louise McNally and Christopher Kennedy

21 InterPhases
Phase-Theoretic Investigations of Linguistic Interfaces
edited by Kleanthes Grohmann

22 Negation in Gapping
by Sophie Repp

23 A Derivational Syntax for Information Structure
by Luis López

24 Quantification, Definiteness, and Nominalization
edited by Anastasia Giannakidou and Monika Rathert

25 The Syntax of Sentential Stress
by Arsalan Kahnemuyipour

26 Tense, Aspect, and Indexicality
by James Higginbotham

27 Lexical Semantics, Syntax, and Event Structure
edited by Malka Rappaport Hovav, Edit Doron, and Ivy Sichel

28 About the Speaker Towards a Syntax of Indexicality
by Alessandra Giorgi

29 The Sound Patterns of Syntax
edited by Nomi Erteschik-Shir and Lisa Rochman

30 The Complementizer Phase
edited by E. Phoevos Panagiotidis

31 Interfaces in Linguistics
New Research Perspectives
edited by Raffaella Folli and Christiane Ulbrich

32 Negative Indefinites
by Doris Penka

33 Events, Phrases, and Questions
by Robert Truswell

34 Dissolving Binding Theory
by Johan Rooryck and Guido Vanden Wyngaerd

35 The Logic of Pronominal Resumption
by Ash Asudeh

For a complete list of titles published and in preparation for the series, see pp 464–5.

The Logic of Pronominal Resumption

ASH ASUDEH

OXFORD
UNIVERSITY PRESS

OXFORD
UNIVERSITY PRESS

Great Clarendon Street, Oxford OX2 6DP

Oxford University Press is a department of the University of Oxford.
It furthers the University's objective of excellence in research, scholarship,
and education by publishing worldwide in

Oxford New York

Auckland Cape Town Dar es Salaam Hong Kong Karachi
Kuala Lumpur Madrid Melbourne Mexico City Nairobi
New Delhi Shanghai Taipei Toronto

With offices in

Argentina Austria Brazil Chile Czech Republic France Greece
Guatemala Hungary Italy Japan Poland Portugal Singapore
South Korea Switzerland Thailand Turkey Ukraine Vietnam

Oxford is a registered trade mark of Oxford University Press
in the UK and in certain other countries

Published in the United States
by Oxford University Press Inc., New York

First published 2012

British Library Cataloguing in Publication Data
Data available

Library of Congress Cataloging in Publication Data
Data available

Typeset by SPI Publisher Services, Pondicherry, India
Printed in Great Britain
on acid-free paper by
MPG Books Group, Bodmin and King's Lynn

ISBN 978–0–19–920642–1 (Hbk)
978–0–19–920643–8 (Pbk)

1 3 5 7 9 10 8 6 4 2

For my family

Contents

Part V: Other Kinds of Resumption

Part VI: Appendices

General Preface

The theoretical focus of this series is on the interfaces between subcomponents of the human grammatical system and the closely related area of the interfaces between the different subdisciplines of linguistics. The notion of 'interface' has become central in grammatical theory (for instance, in Chomsky's recent Minimalist Program) and in linguistic practice: work on the interfaces between syntax and semantics, syntax and morphology, phonology and phonetics, etc. has led to a deeper understanding of particular linguistic phenomena and of the architecture of the linguistic component of the mind/brain.

The series covers interfaces between core components of grammar, including syntax/morphology, syntax/semantics, syntax/phonology, syntax/pragmatics, morphology/phonology, phonology/phonetics, phonetics/speech processing, semantics/pragmatics, and intonation/discourse structure as well as issues in the way that the systems of grammar involving these interface areas are acquired and deployed in use (including language acquisition, language dysfunction, and language processing). It demonstrates, we hope, that proper understandings of particular linguistic phenomena, languages, language groups, or inter-language variations all require reference to interfaces.

The series is open to work by linguists of all theoretical persuasions and schools of thought. A main requirement is that authors should write so as to understood by colleagues in related subfields of linguistics and by scholars in cognate disciplines.

In the current volume, Ash Asudeh examines resumptive pronouns as a challenge to the fundamental idea that natural languages, unlike classical logics, are constrained by the following principle: the meaning of each part of an expression is used exactly once in computing the meaning of the expression as a whole. This property of language appears in the theoretical constructs of many versions of generative grammar, but resumption constitutes a prima facie challenge to it. Asudeh's approach implies the existence of special lexical elements which will act to 'consume' the meanings of resumptives, and he show how this theory explains the interpretation and syntax of a number of kinds of resumption. In addition, he develops a processing model for intrusive resumptives, showing how these can be integrated with the system as a whole.

David Adger
Hagit Borer

Preface

This book is a substantially revised version of my doctoral thesis. The core of the theory, which rests on resource-logical semantic composition, has not changed considerably, but there are several new ideas, principally concerning syntactic distinctions between the two major classes of grammatically licensed resumptive pronouns, the grammatical encoding of resumptive licensing in terms of lexical templates and morphological features, and the analysis of copy raising, particularly variation between speakers.

The chapter on copy raising has been particularly influenced by my continuing collaboration with Ida Toivonen on this topic, which began very shortly after the thesis was completed. This collaboration has given me a much richer understanding of the phenomenon than I could have had on my own. Ida and I have also collaborated on other topics and these collaborations have substantially informed my view of syntax and its relationship to other parts of the language system.

Many people and several institutions were thanked in the acknowledgements to the doctoral thesis and I remain thankful to them, without exception, although only some are also explicitly acknowledged here, along with some new people and places. My thesis committee—in various guises, David Beaver, Richard Crouch, Mary Dalrymple, James McCloskey, and Peter Sells—provided me with outstanding support and advice and contributed greatly to many of the good results and none of the bad. Chris Potts and I have had many enjoyable discussions about linguistics and much else over the years. The title of this book is in part a tribute to Chris's book in the same series. Jim McCloskey's work has been tremendously influential on my understanding of resumption, and I am also grateful to Jim for being so personally accessible. Mary Dalrymple's work also forms an important basis for the theory developed here. I thank Mary for this, as well as for our many informative discussions of linguistics and for her comments on a draft of the book. Louisa Sadler also provided comments on some chapters, which I appreciate greatly. I would also like to thank my supportive colleagues at the Institute of Cognitive Science and the School of Linguistics and Language Studies at Carleton University, at the Faculty of Linguistics, Philology and Phonetics at the University of Oxford, and at Jesus College. I would particularly like to thank my current and recent research assistants at Carleton, who considerably facilitated this research: Crystal Bruce, Elizabeth Christie, Mark Fortney,

Marzieh Mortazavinia, Stephanie Needham, and Asaf Parush. Dag Haug very kindly, and serendipitously, provided the LaTeX code for the blobs in chapter 3. Last, but not least, John Davey and Julia Steer, my editors at Oxford University Press, have provided continued, patient support. They have my heartfelt thanks for piloting this thing to shore.

This book was partly written in Svartsmara, Åland, over several summers and some other seasons besides. I remain grateful to all the denizens of that remarkable village, but especially Gun, Karl-Johan, Ruby, Matts, Göran, Kickan, Sune, Maria, and Elin. The book was also written in Ottawa and Oxford, under the auspices of two institutions: Carleton University and the University of Oxford. The accent colour on the cover is a polychromatic sign of my appreciation—it is a mixture of Carleton Red and Oxford Blue.

This research has been supported by a Research Award from the Faculty of Arts and Social Sciences, Carleton University, by an Early Researcher Award from the Ministry of Research and Innovation of the Province of Ontario, by the Natural Sciences and Engineering Research Council of Canada (Discovery Grant 371969), and by the Social Sciences and Humanities Research Council of Canada (Standard Research Grant 410-2006-1650).

Turning back to the subject of my collaborations with Ida Toivonen, our most important collaboration is our children, Thora, Isak, Alfred, and Harald. This book would not have been possible without Ida's support and sacrifices, for which I could never adequately express my gratitude, and the children's perplexed indulgence of my physical and mental absences. My parents and sister and Ida's parents, brothers, aunt, uncle, cousins, and late grandmothers were also tremendously supportive, despite often being nearly as perplexed as the children. Ida and I essentially started our family in Christchurch, New Zealand, which, as I write this, has just suffered a terrible disaster. This book is also dedicated to Christchurch.

Ash Asudeh
Oxford, 2011

List of Figures

List of Tables

List of Symbols, Glosses, and Abbreviations

$\multimap$	Linear implication
$\otimes$	Linear conjunction (multiplicative)
$\multimap_{\mathcal{E}}$	Implication elimination
$\multimap_{\mathcal{I},n}$	Implication introduction, discharge assumption *n*
$\otimes_{\mathcal{E}}$	Conjunction elimination
$[\alpha]^n$	Assumption, flagged *n*
$[\alpha/\beta]$	Substitute α for β
$\exists\varepsilon$	Existential closure of eventuality variable
$\sim$	Adapted example, in gloss, or Similarity operator, in meaning language
$\Rightarrow_\beta$	β-reduction
*	Kleene star
+	Kleene plus
>	Relational grammaticality marker ('better')
<	Relational grammaticality marker ('worse')
_	Gap
{A | B}	Disjunction, A or B
+COMP	COMP morphological feature
+WH	WH morphological feature
1PL	First person plural
1SG	First person singular
2SG	Second person singular
3PL	Third person plural
3SG	Third person singular
<u>abc</u>	Resumptive pronoun 'abc'
ACC	Accusative case
ADJ	ADJUNCT, grammatical function
ANT	ANTECEDENT, semantic structure attribute
C	Complementizer
C-REL	Relative complementizer
CF	Complement function, COMP or XCOMP grammatical function

COMP	Complementizer, gloss, or Closed complement, grammatical function
COMP	Left periphery of CP (SpecCP or C)
COND	Conditional mood
COP	Copula
CR	Copy raising template
DECL	Declarative
DEF	Definite, gloss, or DEFINITE, f-structure attribute
FEM	Feminine gender, gloss or f-structure value
FIN	Finite
FOCUS	FOCUS, information structure attribute
FUTURE	Future tense
GEN	Genitive case
GEND	GENDER, f-structure attribute
GF	Grammatical Function
HSR	Highest Subject Restriction
INF	Infinitive
IRREALIS	Irrealis mood
LOW	Low tone, prosodic structure feature
MASC	Masculine gender, gloss or f-structure value
MID-HIGH	Mid-high tone, prosodic structure feature
MR	Manager resource template
NEG	Negative
NOM	Nominative case
NUM	NUMBER, f-structure attribute
OBJ	OBJECT, grammatical function
OBL	OBLIQUE, grammatical function
$\underline{p}$	Parasitic gap
PART	Participle
PASS	Passive
PAST	Past tense
PERS	PERSON, f-structure attribute
PL	PLURAL, f-structure value
PRED	PRED feature (semantic form)
PRES	Present tense

PROG	Progressive aspect
PRON	Pronoun
QUEST	Question particle
RAISING	Raising template
REL	Relative pronoun/relativizer
RELABEL	Dependency relabelling template
RELσ	Relative clause meaning constructor
REL.PRON	Relative pronoun
RESTR	RESTRICTION, semantic structure attribute
Rpro	Resumptive pronoun
RMTR	Resource Management Theory of Resumption
RSH	Resource Sensitivity Hypothesis
SELF	Simplex reflexive
SG	SINGULAR, f-structure value
SPEC	SPECIFIER, f-structure attribute
SUBJ	SUBJECT, grammatical function
@T	Invocation of template T
TOPIC	TOPIC, information structure attribute
UD	Unbounded dependency marker, placeholder f-structure feature
UDF	UNBOUNDED DEPENDENCY FUNCTION, grammatical function
VAR	VARIABLE, semantic structure attribute
WH	Question particle
XCOMP	Open complement, grammatical function

1

Introduction

This book is an exploration of the theoretical hypothesis in (1), in light of the phenomenon of resumption, as exemplified by the underlined pronoun in the Irish example, (2).

(1) **The Resource Sensitivity Hypothesis (RSH)**
Natural language is resource-sensitive.

(2) an ghirseach ar ghoid na síogaí í (Irish)
the girl COMP.PAST stole the fairies her
'the girl that the fairies stole (her) away' (McCloskey, 2002: 189, (9b))

The hypothesis is briefly investigated with respect to phonology and syntax, but the heart of the exploration concerns the syntax–semantics interface and semantic composition, in particular. I will return to the issue of resumption shortly, but let us first explore RSH further.

With respect to semantics, the hypothesis is that the meaning of each part of a linguistic expression is used exactly once in the computation of the meaning of the expression. For example, the sentence in (3) can be interpreted as in (4), but not as in (5) or (6).

(3) Kim fooled Sandy.

(4) *fool*(*kim*, *sandy*)

(5) *fool*(*kim*, *kim*)

(6) *fool*(*sandy*, *sandy*)

This may seem trivial, but it is not. As explored in chapter 5, quite a large variety of theoretical proposals, from a variety of theories, can be eliminated once RSH is taken seriously as a foundational aspect of semantic composition (also see Moortgat, 1999).

RSH is ultimately derived from the use of a resource logic for semantic composition. In this case, the resource logic is linear logic (Girard, 1987), as used for semantic composition in Glue Semantics (Dalrymple et al., 1993;

Dalrymple, 1999, 2001, among others). Resource sensitivity has also been investigated in a number of works in the type-logical tradition of Categorial Grammar, such as van Benthem (1991), Moortgat (1997), and Jäger (2005), and in various papers in Bouma et al. (1999) and Kruijff and Oehrle (2003*b*).

RSH is tested by empirical phenomena that exhibit either 'resource deficit', where there are apparently too few meaning resources to satisfy all consumers, or 'resource surplus', where there are apparently more meaning resources than required. VP-coordination is an example of resource deficit. In example (7), there is a single meaning resource contributed by the shared subject *Kim*, but there are two consumers of this resource, the meanings of *sang* and *danced*.

(7) Kim sang and danced.

The solution to this kind of resource deficit is the general polymorphic approach of treating the coordination as a consumer of the two VP resources, such that a single, conjoined consumer of the subject is produced (Steedman, 1985; Emms, 1990; Carpenter, 1997; Asudeh and Crouch, 2002*a*). This illustrates the basic intuition behind treating resource deficit in resource-sensitive semantic composition: where there is apparent resource deficit, in order for RSH to be maintained, there must be a possible reduction of multiple consumers of a resource to a single consumer.

Resumption exhibits the opposing problem of resource surplus. If the pronoun in (2) is an ordinary pronoun, then it saturates the scope of the relative operator, such that the relative clause cannot compose with the relative head. There is very good reason to assume that resumptive pronouns indeed are ordinary pronouns. McCloskey (2002: 192) observes that, cross-linguistically, resumptive pronouns are not morphologically or otherwise distinct from non-resumptive pronouns. This observation is enshrined in the following independently motivated assumption of the theory developed here:

(8) **McCloskey's Generalization**
Resumptive pronouns are ordinary pronouns.

As ordinary pronouns, resumptive pronouns are surplus resources for semantic composition. If the Resource Sensitivity Hypothesis is to be maintained, then there must be some other consumer of the resumptive pronoun's resource. I postulate such a consumer and argue that it is these consumers that license all sorts of resumption. Resumption is then fundamentally a problem of semantic composition, as observed in early generative work (McCloskey, 1979), but subsequently largely disregarded. The resulting theory is the Resource Management Theory of Resumption (RMTR).

The paradigmatic cases of resumption are resumptive pronouns in unbounded dependencies, as in the Irish example above. But there is another intuitively resumptive-like use of pronouns that does not involve an unbounded dependency, namely copy raising:

(9) Alfred seems like he's sick.

The following related example provides evidence for the fact that this is a raising verb and that *Alfred* is not interpreted as an argument of the matrix verb:

(10) It seems like Alfred's sick.

Alternation with an expletive subject is normally taken to be a key piece of evidence that the subject of a verb is not a semantic argument of the verb. Moreover, for most speakers, the copy pronoun *he* in (9) is obligatory:

(11) *Alfred seems like Harry's sick.

If *seems* in (9) is a raising verb, as evidenced by (10), then the pronoun in the complement would seem to be blocking the position where the subject *Alfred* should be integrated into the interpretation. The obligatory nature of the pronoun is explained if it is a kind of resumptive pronoun that allows composition of the subject in its place while also satisfying the independent constraint that an English finite clause must have a subject. There is also variation between speakers with respect to certain details of copy raising. This variation is taken seriously here and is explained as lexical variation.

Another resumptive puzzle concerns the differential syntactic behaviour of unbounded dependency resumption in various languages (McCloskey, 2006). For example, while resumptive pronouns in Irish do not create weak crossover violations and are not island-sensitive (McCloskey, 1990), the resumptive pronouns of Swedish (Zaenen et al., 1981; Engdahl, 1982, 1985) and Vata (Koopman, 1982; Koopman and Sportiche, 1986) have been reported to create weak crossover violations and, at least in the latter case, are island-sensitive. Similarly, there can be differences with respect to parasitic gaps, reconstruction, and across-the-board extraction. Pretheoretically, it seems that one kind of resumptive, as in Swedish and Vata, behaves in some ways like gaps, whereas the other kind of resumptive, as in Irish, does not. I will argue that, despite syntactic differences between the two kinds of resumptive, at heart they equally constitute a problem for semantic composition and require the same licensing mechanism (Asudeh, 2011*c*).

The Resource Management Theory of Resumption thus achieves two significant unifications:

1. The kind of unbounded dependency resumptive that is gap-like and the kind that is not gap-like are unified by a common licensing mechanism based on semantic composition.
2. Resumptive pronouns in unbounded dependencies and copy pronouns in copy raising are unified as a case of pronominal resource surplus and are licensed by the same mechanism.

In addition to these unifications, it will also be shown that RMTR also explains several other aspects of the grammar of resumption.

Lastly, RMTR forms the basis for a processing theory for another kind of unbounded dependency resumptive, as found in English (Sells, 1984; McCloskey, 2006), which is not grammatically licensed, but which is instead some kind of processing artefact:

(12) *This is the man who Ida said Thora is fond of <u>him</u>.

As indicated by the asterisk, speakers find these examples ungrammatical. This has also been independently confirmed by a number of controlled studies (e.g., Alexopoulou and Keller, 2007). Nevertheless, English speakers do produce such examples, as shown by attested examples (Prince, 1990) and, moreover, they do so even in controlled conditions (Ferreira and Swets, 2005). The processing theory that I present treats this kind of resumption as a consequence of incremental production of locally well-formed structures, at the potential expense of global well-formedness (Asudeh, 2011*b*). That is, sentences like (12) are uttered during incremental production, but they are perceived as globally ill-formed, because English does not have the grammatical licensing mechanism for true resumption in unbounded dependencies. The processing theory also considers parsing and interpretation of English unbounded dependency resumptives, and investigates how, under certain conditions, ungrammatical utterances containing these resumptives may receive informative, partial interpretations.

1.1 Outline of the Book

The book is divided into six parts. The first part provides background on (1) the empirical phenomenon of resumption, including copy raising and processing-based resumptives, (2) the syntactic theory that is assumed (Lexical-Functional Grammar), and (3) the semantic theory (Glue Semantics). The second part presents the theoretical heart of the book, divided into chapters on the Resource Sensitivity Hypothesis and on the Resource Management Theory of Resumption. The third and fourth parts apply the theory to the two kinds of grammatically licensed unbounded dependency resumptives. The third part, which concerns true resumptives that do not pattern syntactically like gaps, applies the theory to Irish in detail, followed by a shorter analysis of Hebrew. The fourth part, which concerns true resumptives that do pattern syntactically like gaps, applies the theory to Swedish in detail, followed by a shorter expansion to the analysis of Vata. The fifth part of the book considers other kinds of resumption, in particular resumptive pronouns in processing and copy pronouns in copy raising. The sixth part consists of three appendices: an appendix on the logic of composition, a fragment of Irish, and a fragment of Swedish.

Part I
Background

2

Resumption

This chapter reviews the different resumption phenomena that are analysed in subsequent chapters, focusing principally on data. The first part of the chapter, section 2.1, concerns resumptive pronouns in unbounded dependencies in languages where they are fully grammatically licensed. This is the central kind of resumption, at least in terms of the amount of theoretical attention that it has received. The data mainly comes from Irish, Hebrew, Swedish, and Vata, which are the languages that receive individual attention in chapters 7 to 10. Section 2.1.1 examines the form of resumptive pronouns and presents a typological generalization that I call 'McCloskey's Generalization' (McCloskey, 2002, 2006). Section 2.1.2 looks at the interpretation of resumptive pronouns as bound pronouns and establishes that resumptives are interpreted like non-resumptive pronouns and unlike gaps. The data on the form and interpretation of resumptives strongly indicates that resumptive pronouns are just ordinary pronouns. Section 2.1.3 looks at the distribution of resumptive pronouns in various kinds of unbounded dependencies. Section 2.1.4 looks at the similarities and differences between resumptive pronouns and gaps and proposes that there are two kinds of resumptive pronoun, following McCloskey (2006).

The second part of the chapter, section 2.2, examines English resumptive-like pronouns, which are not grammatically licensed, but are rather some kind of processing effect. Data is reviewed that reveals an interesting puzzle: English resumptives are judged to be ungrammatical, but are nevertheless produced, as confirmed by both attested examples and elicitations in controlled experiments.

The third part of the chapter, section 2.3, examines copy raising, a phenomenon in which a pronominal copy of a matrix subject is required, for most speakers, in the complement to a raising verb. Copy raising is thus apparently a kind of resumption phenomenon, but one that involves a local dependency similar to raising, rather than an unbounded dependency.

2.1 Resumptive Pronouns in Unbounded Dependencies

2.1.1 *Form*

McCloskey (2002: 192) identifies a crucial yet rarely discussed morphological property of resumptive pronouns:

> A remarkable but little commented on property of resumptive pronouns is that they simply *are* pronouns. I know of no report of a language that uses a morphologically or lexically distinct series of pronouns in the resumptive function. (emphasis in original)

This is captured in the following typological generalization:

(1) **McCloskey's Generalization**:
Resumptive pronouns are ordinary pronouns.

McCloskey's Generalization has both morphological and lexical consequences, which theories of resumptive pronouns should predict.

The morphological consequences are as follows:

1. Resumptive pronoun languages do not have resumptive-specific morphological paradigms.
2. Resumptive pronoun languages do not have certain pronouns that are only resumptive or have a resumptive-specific usage to the exclusion of other pronouns.

The first consequence is that languages do not have pronominal paradigms that are reserved exclusively for resumption. Any pronoun that is used resumptively will also be used in other morphosyntactic contexts. For example, Adger (2011) discusses 'bare resumptives' in colloquial Skye Gaelic and São Tomense Creole (Adger and Ramchand, 2005), which are required to have only default agreement features, but these pronouns are not used exclusively resumptively (Asudeh, 2011*c*). The second consequence is that languages do not have a particular pronoun or pronouns reserved for resumption. This is best understood in light of expletive pronouns. It is quite usual for a language to allow only certain pronominals to serve as expletives. For example, in English, the only expletives are the pronominals *it* and *there*. These pronouns are not solely expletives, but they have expletive-specific usages to the exclusion of other pronouns. In contrast, there do not seem to be distinguished resumptives like there are distinguished expletives.

In light of McCloskey's Generalization we can classify theories of resumption into two kinds (Asudeh, 2011*c*):[1]

[1] The distinction applies equally in theories that reject the traditional notion of a lexicon, such as Distributed Morphology (Halle and Marantz, 1993; Embick and Noyer, 2007; Siddiqi, 2009). In such a

(2) **Ordinary Pronoun Theory of Resumption**:
There is no lexical/morphological/featural/syntactic difference between resumptive pronouns and referential or bound pronouns.

(3) **Special Pronoun Theory of Resumption**:
There is some lexical/morphological/featural/syntactic difference between resumptive pronouns and referential or bound pronouns

Ordinary pronoun theories uphold McCloskey's Generalization. Special pronoun theories are incompatible with the generalization and must either show that the generalization is not true or else provide a precise theory as to why resumptives are apparently ordinary pronouns despite being underlyingly special. Thus, not only do general considerations of parsimony favour ordinary pronoun theories, since special pronoun theories by definition postulate something additional in order to capture resumption, there is also a typological generalization that favours ordinary pronoun theories of resumption over special pronoun theories.

Irish provides a compelling demonstration of McCloskey's Generalization. The following examples show that free-standing Irish resumptive pronouns are just the normal forms of the pronouns that would occur in the same positions. Compare the pronouns in the resumptive examples (4a), (5a), and (6a) with those in the corresponding non-resumptive examples (4b), (5b), and (6b):

(4) a. an fear ar dhúirt mé go dtiocfadh sé
the man COMP said I COMP would.come he
'the man that I said (he) would come'
(McCloskey, 1990: 214, (41))

b. dúirt mé go dtiocfadh sé
said I COMP would.come he
'I said he would come'

(5) a. an scríbhneoir a molann na mic léinn é
the writer COMP praise the students him
'the writer whom the students praise (him)'
(McCloskey, 1979: 6, (5))

theory, the claim that a resumptive pronoun is an ordinary pronoun due to its lexical specification can instead be understood as the claim that a resumptive pronoun accrues the same set of features as an ordinary pronoun.

b. molann na mic léinn é
praise the students him
'the students praise him'

(6) a. an fear a bhfuil a mháthair san otharlann
the man COMP is his mother in.the hospital
'the man whose mother is in the hospital'
(McCloskey, 1979: 6, (4))

b. tá a mháthair san otharlann
is his mother in.the hospital
'his mother is in the hospital'

In each case the resumptive pronoun is identical to the corresponding non-resumptive.

The most significant evidence comes from 'incorporated' pronouns in Irish, i.e. pronominal information borne by inflection, which is discussed at length by McCloskey and Hale (1984), McCloskey (1986), and Andrews (1990). Irish verbal paradigms consist of forms that are traditionally called *synthetic* and *analytic* (McCloskey and Hale, 1984: 489). The analytic form does not exhibit subject agreement and is the form used with non-pronominal lexical subjects, with subject gaps, and with pronominal subjects under certain limited circumstances that will be specified shortly. The synthetic form bears person and number subject agreement information. The crucial facts are:

1. The synthetic form cannot be used in conjunction with the appropriate pronominal (McCloskey and Hale, 1984: 489–490).

   (7) a. chuirfinn (Ulster)
   put.CONDITIONAL.1SG
   'I would put'

   b. *chuirfinn mé
   put.CONDITIONAL.1SG 1SG

2. The analytic form generally cannot be used in conjunction with the appropriate pronominal if a synthetic form with the relevant person–number information exists[2] (McCloskey and Hale, 1984: 491–492, ~(89)).

[2] This is only generally, not universally, the case, because certain paradigm slots in certain dialects are exceptional in allowing the analytic form with an independent pronoun, despite having a synthetic form for the corresponding paradigm slot; e.g. the Connacht third person plural conditional (McCloskey and Hale, 1984: 491).

(8) a. chuirfinn
put.CONDITIONAL.1SG
'I would put'

b. *chuirfeadh mé
put.CONDITIONAL 1SG

(9) a. —
put.CONDITIONAL.3PL

b. chuirfeadh siad
put.CONDITIONAL 3PL
'they would put'

McCloskey and Hale (1984), working in Principles and Parameters Theory, analyse the synthetic form as contributing a null pronominal argument (i.e., *pro*). Andrews (1990), working in Lexical-Functional Grammar (LFG), analyses the synthetic form as contributing the PRED of its argument at functional structure. In both cases, the impossibility of using the synthetic form with an independent pronoun follows from the fact that the synthetic form itself contributes pronominal information.

What is crucial for present purposes is that the pronominal information contributed by the synthetic form can function as a resumptive pronoun:

(10) na daoine aN raibh mé ag dúil goN gcuirfidis isteach ar
the people COMP was I expect PROG COMP put.COND.3PL in on
an phost sin
that job
'the people that I expected (that they) would apply for that job'
(McCloskey and Hale, 1984: 498, (23))

There are two reasons to conclude that the subject agreement on *gcuirfidis* is functioning as a resumptive. First, the relative clause exhibits the classic Irish resumptive complementizer pattern (McCloskey, 1979, 1990, 2002), which consists of a resumptive-sensitive complementizer *aN* (identified by the nasalization mutation it triggers on the following word) immediately following the relative head and neutral complementizers *go* introducing each clause until the clause containing the resumptive pronoun:

(11) $\mathrm{NP}_i\ [_{\mathrm{CP}}\ \mathrm{aN} \ldots [_{\mathrm{CP}}\ \mathrm{go} \ldots [_{\mathrm{CP}}\ \mathrm{go} \ldots \mathit{Rpro}_i \ldots]]]$
(McCloskey and Hale, 1984: 498, ~(22))

If the subject of the synthetic form were a gap, there would be a different pattern of complementizers. Second, McCloskey and Hale establish independently that subject gaps occur with the *analytic* verb form, "even in those cases where the binder of the trace is a pronoun with person-number features for which the verb in question has a synthetic form" (McCloskey and Hale, 1984: 490):

(12) Chan mise a chuirfeadh tisteach ar an phost sin.
COP.NEG me COMP put.COND in on that job
'It's not me that would apply for that job.'
(McCloskey and Hale, 1984: 490, (5))

Taken together, the complementizer pattern in (10) and the fact that subject gaps, in contrast, occur with the analytic form constitute strong evidence that the synthetic form can function resumptively.

The data from Irish underscores the fact that resumptive pronouns are ordinary pronouns. Free-standing resumptives have the features and form of a non-resumptive pronoun in the same position. Even more strikingly, the synthetic forms reveal that inflectional pronominal information on a head can function resumptively. This last point is further underscored by several resumptive examples in section 2.1.3, where the pronominal information is contributed by an inflected preposition.

Resumptive pronouns in Hebrew and Swedish are similarly ordinary pronouns, but Vata presents an apparent challenge to McCloskey's Generalization, because, upon initial inspection, the language seems to have a special paradigm for resumptives. Resumptives are segmentally identical to the non-resumptive pronouns but bear different tone marking. For example, the normal third person pronoun is ɔ̆, with mid-high tone, and the resumptive form is ɔ̀, with low tone (Koopman, 1982: 128–129).[3] However, as discussed further in chapter 10, the tonal distinction is a general reflex of *wh*-binding and is not specific to resumption. Even non-resumptive pronouns that are indirectly *wh*-bound bear the low tone.

2.1.2 *Interpretation*

2.1.2.1 *Bound Pronouns* Resumptive pronouns are interpreted as bound pronouns (McCloskey, 1979, 1990; Sells, 1984) and gaps are interpreted as bound variables. This allows a general understanding of unbounded dependencies, whether binder-resumptive or filler-gap dependencies, as variable-binding relations (McCloskey, 2006: 105). Chao and Sells (1983) argue

[3] All page references to work by Koopman or by Koopman and Sportiche are to reprints in Koopman (2000).

that the criterion that resumptives are interpreted as bound pronouns distinguishes true, grammatically licensed resumptive pronouns from superficially resumptive-like pronouns, which Sells (1984: 17) calls 'intrusive pronouns'. Intrusive pronouns were first discussed by Ross (1967: 432–434), who called them 'returning pronouns', following the tradition of the Classical Arabic grammarians. Intrusive pronouns cannot receive bound interpretations. The interpretation of intrusive pronouns is discussed further in chapter 11.

Chao and Sells (1983) and Sells (1984) present three binding-related tests for distinguishing true resumptive pronouns from intrusive pronouns: (1) true resumptives permit binding by a quantifier that resists an E-type interpretation, (2) true resumptives support a list answer to a constituent question, and (3) true resumptives support a functional answer to a constituent question. Each test shows that an intrusive pronoun does not support the bound reading that a gap in the same position supports. The first test concerns binding by a quantifier that does not license a coreferential or E-type reading (Evans, 1980), such as quantifiers built around the quantificational determiners *every*, *each*, *no*, or *any*.[4] The only available reading for a pronoun that takes an E-type-resistant quantifier as its antecedent is a bound reading. A sentence with a quantifier-bound pronoun in an unbounded dependency should therefore be grammatical if the pronoun is a resumptive pronoun and ungrammatical if it is an intrusive pronoun. The ungrammaticality of the following English sentences indicates that the pronouns are intrusive pronouns—at least in standard varieties—and are not true resumptive pronouns:

(13) *I'd like to review every book that Mary couldn't remember if she'd read it before. (Chao and Sells, 1983: 49, ~(5c))

(14) *I've watched no movie that Mary couldn't remember if she liked it or not.

(15) *I wouldn't make any recipe that Mary couldn't remember if she'd gotten it to work before.

These judgements are somewhat subtle, since the corresponding examples with gaps instead of the resumptive are also degraded, due to islands.

[4] Quantifiers built from *every* are perhaps not ideal candidates, since they can license E-type readings so long as the pronoun is plural (Evans, 1980).

The other two tests that Chao and Sells (1983) present concern answers to *wh*-questions. The first of these tests shows that an English intrusive pronoun does not support a list answer to a *wh*-question, which should be possible for a bound pronoun:

(16) Which of the linguists do you think that if Mary hires him then everyone will be happy? (Sells, 1984: 13, ~(10b))

a. Chris

b. #Chris, Daniel, or Bill

The fact that the intrusive pronoun requires the answer to be about a particular individual indicates that the pronoun is not receiving a bound interpretation.

The second *wh*-test concerns functional answers to questions (Engdahl, 1986), which a bound pronoun supports, as shown in (17):

(17) Which exam question does no professor believe will be tough enough?

a. The one her students aced last year (functional)

b. Question 2A (individual)

(Chao and Sells, 1983: 50, ~(8a))

The pronoun *her* in the functional answer is bound and covaries with the professors in the domain of discourse. The individual answer specifies a particular question that no professor believes will be tough enough. An analogous question with an intrusive pronoun, as shown in (18), disallows the bound, functional reading and allows only the individual reading:

(18) Which exam question does no professor even wonder if it will be tough enough?

a. #The one her students aced last year (functional)

b. Question 2A (individual)

(Chao and Sells, 1983: 51, ~(10a))

The three tests by Chao and Sells show that resumptive-like intrusive pronouns in English cannot be true resumptives, since they do not pattern like bound variables. Chapter 11 explains intrusive pronouns, which I include in the broader class of *processor resumptives*, as a processing artefact. Processor resumptives are also briefly reviewed in section 2.2 below.

2.1.2.2 *Resumptives are Interpreted as Ordinary Pronouns* Doron (1982) observes that an opaque verb such as the equivalent of *seek* in Hebrew allows a non-specific or *de dicto* reading for its object if the object is a gap, but not if its object is a resumptive pronoun (Doron, 1982: 26, (49–50)):

(19) dani yimca et haʔiša še hu mexapes __
Dani will-find ACC the.woman that he seeks __
'Dani will find the.woman that he seeks.'

(20) dani yimca et haʔiša še hu mexapes <u>ota</u>
Dani will-find ACC the.woman that he seeks her
'Dani will find the woman that he seeks (her).'

The second sentence only allows a reading that can be paraphrased as 'There is a woman that Dani seeks and Dani will find this woman'.

The observation that pronouns block non-specific readings was in fact made quite early in the development of formal semantics (Partee, 1970; Montague, 1973). The contrast above would therefore follow naturally if a resumptive pronoun just is an ordinary pronoun semantically. Given a proper analysis of the general resistance by pronominals to non-specific readings, nothing further needs to be said about the lack of such readings for resumptive pronouns. This line of reasoning is pursued by Sells (1984, 1987), who relates the impossibility of the non-specific reading to the general impossibility of pronominal reference to concepts. He therefore calls the non-specific reading the 'concept reading'. Following Doron (1982), he assumes that the resumptive pronoun, like pronouns in general, forces its antecedent to be extensional. The inability to take a concept as an antecedent then follows, since concepts are intensional.

Support for this line of reasoning comes from the following contrasting sentences. The one with the gap allows three readings, represented below, whereas the one with the resumptive pronoun does not have the third, concept reading (Sells, 1984, 1987):

(21) kol gever yimca ʔet haʔiša še hu mexapes __
every man will-find ACC the.woman that he seeks __
'Every man will find the woman that he seeks.'

(Sells, 1987: 288, (48a))

a. There is a particular individual woman (e.g., Lauren Bacall) that every man is looking for and will find.

b. Each man is looking for a woman particular to that man (e.g., Sam is looking for Susie and Jay is looking for his mother and Will for Anne ...).

c. Each man is looking for a woman with certain properties, but does not know who such a woman might be (e.g., Sam is looking for a woman the same size as his wife, Jay needs a woman who can milk goats, and Will is looking for someone to act in his movie.)

(22) kol gever yimca ʔet haʔiša še hu mexapes ota
every man will-find ACC the.woman that he seeks her
'Every man will find the woman that he seeks (her).'
(Sells, 1987: 288, (48b))

a. As in (21a)

b. As in (21b)

c. #Each man is looking for a woman with certain properties, but does not know who such a woman might be (e.g., Sam is looking for a woman the same size as his wife, Jay needs a woman who can milk goats, and Will is looking for someone to act in his movie.)

Sells (1984, 1987) argues that the inability to take concept readings follows if resumptive pronouns are treated as ordinary pronouns, since pronouns in general do not take concept readings. This is illustrated by the contrast between the following sentences:

(23) Dani owns a unicorn. It is tall. (Sells, 1987: 290, ∼(52a))

(24) Dani seeks a unicorn. # It is tall. (Sells, 1987: 290, ∼(52b))

Sells (1984, 1987) goes on to show that apparent counterexamples that seem to show pronouns taking concept antecedents actually involve them taking individual kinds (Carlson, 1977) as antecedents and, furthermore, that pronouns cannot take concept kinds as antecedents (Sells, 1987: 290–292).

Sharvit (1999) provides further evidence and argumentation supporting the claim that Hebrew resumptive pronouns are interpreted like ordinary pronouns. Her argument is two-fold. The first part shows that both resumptive pronouns and non-resumptive pronouns generally do not allow pair-list answers to *wh*-questions that contain a quantifier (Engdahl, 1980). This is straightforwardly shown for resumptive pronouns by the inability to answer a question containing a resumptive with a pair-list answer, although a pair-list answer is available for the corresponding question with a gap:

(25) ezyo iša kol gever hizmin __
which woman every man invited
'Which woman did every man invite?' (Sharvit, 1999: 594, (16))

a. et Gila
ACC Gila
'Gila'

b. et im-o
ACC mother-his
'His mother'

c. Yosi et Gila; Rami et Rina
Yosi ACC Gila; Rami ACC Rina
'Yosi, Gila; Rami, Rina'

(26) ezyo iša kol gever hizmin ota
which woman every man invited her
'Which woman did every man invite (her)?' (Sharvit, 1999: 594, (17))

a. As in (25a)

b. As in (25b)

c. *Yosi et Gila; Rami et Rina
Yosi ACC Gila; Rami ACC Rina
'Yosi, Gila; Rami, Rina'

The pair-list answer is not possible if the question is formed with a resumptive.

Sharvit goes on to show that both the individual answer (25a) and the natural function answer (25b) can provide the antecedent for a non-resumptive pronoun, but that the pair-list reading cannot. Thus, only (25a) and (25b) can be followed by a sentence like:

(27) hi gam ha-iša še kol gever baxar
she also the-woman that every man chose
'She is also the woman that every man chose'

There is, once again, a correlation between non-resumptive pronominal interpretation and resumptive pronominal interpretation and this interpretation stands in contrast to the interpretation of a gap. The second part of Sharvit's argument brings the correlation out further by showing that pair-list readings are possible for pronouns in specificational (equative) clauses and that these readings appear for resumptive pronouns in the same environment (Sharvit, 1999: 596). In sum, the evidence from Doron (1982), Sells (1984, 1987), and Sharvit (1999) shows that (1) there is a strong correlation between the interpretation of non-resumptive pronouns and resumptive pronouns and (2) gaps show interpretive possibilities that are distinct from both non-resumptive and resumptive pronouns.

2.1.3 *Distribution*

Resumptive pronouns, narrowly defined to exclude copy pronouns in copy raising, occur in unbounded dependencies. In Irish there are no restrictions on which unbounded dependencies host resumptives. McCloskey

(1990: 208, (25)) notes that "resumptive pronouns appear in every WH-construction". He provides a comprehensive appendix of the distribution of Irish resumptive pronouns (McCloskey, 1990: 238–242). Here is a subset of the relevant examples:

1. **Restrictive relative clauses**

(28) an ghirseach a-r ghoid na síogaí í
the girl COMP-PAST stole the fairies her
'the girl that the fairies stole away' (McCloskey, 2002: 189, (9b))

(29) an fear a dtabharann tú an tairgead dó
the man COMP give you the money to.him
'the man to whom you give the money' (McCloskey, 1979: 6, (3))

2. **Nonrestrictive relative clauses**

(30) Tháinig an saighdiúir eile, nach bhfaca mé roimhe é,
came the soldier other NEG.COMP saw I before him,
aníos chugainn.
up to.us
'The other soldier, whom I hadn't seen before, came up to us.'
(McCloskey, 1990: 238, (97a))

3. **Questions**

(31) Céacu ceann a bhfuil dúil agat ann?
which one COMP is liking at.you in.it
'Which one do you like?' (McCloskey, 2002: 189, (10b))

(32) d'inis siad cén turas a raibh siad air
told they what journey COMP be.PAST they on.3SG.MASC
'they told what journey they were on (it)'
(McCloskey, 1990: 238, (98a))

4. **Clefts**

(33) Is tú a bhfuil an deallramh maith ort.
COP.PRES you COMP is the appearance good on.2SG
'It is you that looks well.' (McCloskey, 1990: 239, (99a))

5. **'Reduced' Clefts**

(34) Teach beag seascair a-r mhair muid ann.
house little snug COMP-PAST lived we in.it
'It was a snug little house that we lived in.'
(McCloskey, 2002: 189, (11b))

6. **Comparatives**

(35) Do fuair sé leaba chó math agus ar lui sé riamh uirthi.
get PAST he bed as good as COMP lie.PAST he ever on.3SG.FEM

'He got a bed as good as he ever lay on (it).'
(McCloskey, 1990: 239, (100b))

In all of these examples but (28) and (30), the pronominal is incorporated as an argument to an inflected preposition. It is generally agreed in the literature that these prepositions are best analysed as contributing full pronominal information, just as if the pronoun were a prepositional object (McCloskey 1979: 47, fn.2, McCloskey and Hale 1984: 506ff., McCloskey 1986: 252ff., Sells 1984: 111–112), as discussed above. For further examples of Irish unbounded dependencies containing resumptive pronouns see McCloskey (1979, 1985, 2002) and especially McCloskey (1990).

In other resumptive pronoun languages, the unbounded dependencies which allow resumptive pronouns may be further restricted. For example, it was initially claimed of Hebrew that resumptives are ungrammatical in questions (Borer, 1981: 114) and this is apparently supported by the following data:

(36) *mi ra?iti oto?
who I.saw him?
(Sells, 1984: 63, (58b))

(37) *mi nifgašta ito
who you.met with.him
(Sharvit, 1999: 591, (8b))

However, Sells (1984: 64) shows that resumptive pronouns are possible in Hebrew questions if the resumptive follows a complementizer:

(38) eyze xešbon kol maškia lo zoxer im hu noten ribit
which account every investor not remembers if it gives interest
tova?
good
'Which account does every investor not remember if (it) gives good interest?' (Sells, 1984: 64, (61))

Thus, a resumptive can be used in a 'COMP-trace' environment.[5,6]

[5] Shlonsky (1992: 448, fn.3) disputes this data. This is discussed further in chapter 8.

[6] Throughout out this book, I use the term 'COMP-trace' pretheoretically, as a label for the phenomenon. There are no traces in the version of Lexical-Functional Grammar that is assumed here; see chapter 3.

Additionally, Sharvit (1999: 591) notes that *which*-questions in dialectal Hebrew do allow resumptives:

(39) eyze student nifgašta ito?
which student you.met with.him
'Which student did you meet with?' (Sharvit, 1999: 591, (9))

Sharvit (1999: 591) attributes the grammaticality of resumptives in *which*-questions to the fact that *which*-phrases are "almost" D(iscourse)-linked (Pesetsky, 1987) and tentatively concludes that "resumptive pronouns are sensitive to D-linking in a way that traces are not". However, the implication that traces are insensitive to D-linking is problematic, since D-linking was in fact initially proposed as part of an explanation of *wh*-superiority effects (Pesetsky, 1987: 107ff.). Pesetsky's explanation of the superiority effects depends on traces somehow being sensitive to D-linking. The D-linking explanation of the Hebrew data is thus somewhat tenuous.

Swedish similarly disallows resumptive pronouns in simple questions:

(40) *Vem såg du honom?
who see.PAST you him

Like Hebrew, Swedish allows resumptives in questions when a subject gap is not licensed (Engdahl, 1982):

(41) Vilket konto vet inte varje investerare om det ger bra ränta?
which account knows not every investor if it gives good interest
'Which account does every investor not remember if (it) gives good interest?'

However, unlike Hebrew, resumptives in relative clauses are also restricted to this kind of 'COMP-trace' environment:

(42) Det var den fången som läkarna inte kunde avgöra om han verkligen var sjuk.
it was that prisoner that doctors.DEF not could decide if he really was ill
'This is the prisoner that the doctors couldn't determine if (he) really was ill.' (Engdahl, 1985: 7, ~(8))

(43) *Jag känner mannen som Maria träffade honom.
I know man.DEF that M. met him

The difference between (40) and (41) is a reflection of the broader generalization that Swedish resumptives are only licensed following material at the left periphery of CP (Engdahl 1982: 156, Sells 1984, 1987: 267, McCloskey 1990: 235).

Further evidence for the generalization comes from the fact that, again unlike Hebrew, resumptives in simple Swedish *which*-questions are ungrammatical:

(44) *Vilken elev hade du möte med henne?
which student had you meeting with her

(45) *Vilken elev träffade du honom?
which student met you him

In sum, Swedish does not really distinguish between resumptives in relative clauses and questions, whereas Hebrew allows resumptives more freely in relative clauses than in questions. In the theory developed here, the distributional restrictions on resumptives in Swedish and the distinctions between Swedish and Hebrew are a consequence of how the licensing mechanism for resumption is realized, not of restrictions on the resumptive pronouns per se (see chapters 8 and 9).

There is thus cross-linguistic variation as to which unbounded dependencies allow resumptives and under what circumstances. Irish allows resumptives in every kind of unbounded dependency. Hebrew allows resumptives in relatives, but their distribution in questions is more limited. Swedish allows resumptives in only a very specific circumstance—immediately following lexical material in the left periphery of CP—but does not distinguish between unbounded dependencies that meet the requisite requirement.

The role of a resumptive pronoun in a binder-resumptive dependency, as the base of the unbounded dependency, is analogous to that of a gap in a filler-gap dependency. However, resumptive pronouns and gaps generally have non-identical distribution with respect to the syntactic positions or grammatical functions that they can fill, although there can be substantial overlap.

Initial examination of Irish, Welsh, and Hebrew points to the possibility of a rough characterization in terms of the accessibility/obliqueness hierarchy of Keenan and Comrie (1977), as noted by both McCloskey (1979: 5) and Sells (1984: 20–21), such that resumptives become obligatory in more oblique positions. However, the distribution of resumptives in Swedish and Vata shows that any hierarchical generalization is untenable, unless one is willing to claim that in some languages only the *least* oblique arguments can be resumptives (Swedish, Vata), while in others only the *most* oblique arguments can be resumptives (Irish, Welsh, Hebrew), in which case the utility of the hierarchy in a theory of resumptive pronouns is quite questionable. Having made the initial tentative connection to the hierarchy, neither McCloskey nor Sells incorporates it into his actual theory; they derive what effects it accounts for in other ways.

McCloskey (1990: 209) notes that, in Irish, "within each WH-construction, resumptive pronouns can appear in every clausal position but one". The one clausal position in which they cannot appear is the subject position immediately following the relative head (the "highest subject"):

(46) a. *an fear a raibh sé breoite
the man COMP be.PAST he ill
'the man that (he) was ill' (McCloskey, 1990: 210, (29a))

b. *na daoine a rabhadar breoite
the people COMP be.PAST.3PL ill
'the people that (they) were ill' (McCloskey, 1990: 210, (29b))

McCloskey (1990: 210) calls this the *Highest Subject Restriction* (HSR). The restriction applies only to the highest subject; resumptives are licensed in the embedded subjects of both finite and non-finite clauses:

(47) a. an t-ór seo ar chreid corr-dhuine go raibh sé ann
this gold COMP believed a few people COMP was it there
'this gold that a few people believed (it) was there'
(McCloskey, 1990: 210, (30a))

b. cúpla muirear a bhféadfaí a rá go rabhadar bocht
a.few families COMP one.could say.INF COMP be.PAST.3PL poor
'a few families that one could say (they) were poor'
(McCloskey, 1990: 210, (30b))

Resumptive pronouns are obligatory when a possessor or prepositional object is extracted (McCloskey 1979: 6, McCloskey 1990: 209), as demonstrated here for the object of the preposition *le* ('with'):

(48) a. an fear a raibh mé ag caint leis
the man COMP was I talk.PROG with.3SG.MASC
'the man that I was talking to him' (McCloskey, 1990: 209, (28a))

b. *an fear a bhí mé ag caint le _
the man COMP was I talk.PROG to _
'the man that I was talking to' (McCloskey, 1990: 209, (28b))

A natural account of Irish is thus that resumptives can appear anywhere, subject to additional restrictions, in particular the HSR (McCloskey, 1990).

The HSR is typically accounted for by an anti-locality requirement between the binder and the resumptive, defined in such a way that it applies to subjects, but not objects or other arguments (Borer, 1984; McCloskey, 1990: 212–224).[7] The apparent obligatoriness of certain resumptives stems from gaps not being licensed in the relevant positions due to conditions on extraction. For example, in terms of Principles and Parameters Theory, extraction of a possessor is a subjacency violation and it is assumed that extraction of a prepositional object is an Empty Category Principle (ECP) violation, due to prepositions in Irish not being proper governors (Sells, 1984; Chung and McCloskey, 1987).

Welsh is similar to Irish with respect to the HSR, except that in Welsh the highest object is also inaccessible to resumptive pronouns, as shown by the following examples:

(49) a. y car a werthodd Gareth __
the car COMP sold Gareth __
'the car that Gareth sold' (Willis, 2000: 533, (4))

b. *y llyfr y darllenais i ef
the book COMP read I it
'the book that I read' (Sells, 1984: 133, (27))

In Welsh, an unbounded dependency terminating in a highest direct object gap is grammatical, but one terminating in a highest direct object resumptive is apparently not.[8]

Sells (1984: 143ff.) argues that there is a further difference between Welsh and Irish: filler-gap dependencies into embedded clauses are grammatical in Irish but ungrammatical in Welsh. The empirical claim is that resumptive pronouns are obligatory in embedded clauses in Welsh, but not in Irish. However, Willis (2000) argues that filler-gap dependencies in Welsh can also access embedded positions. This issue clearly requires further empirical and theoretical investigation, but I will follow Willis (2000) in assuming that embedded clauses in Welsh can host both gaps and resumptives. The key difference between Irish and Welsh is that the former allows resumptives as highest objects, while the latter does not.

[7] McCloskey's work on this anti-locality condition, essentially an extension of Principle B of the binding theory to A′-binding, dates to the early eighties but was first published in McCloskey (1990).

[8] Louisa Sadler (p.c.) has pointed out to me that this claim depends in part on the analysis of clause types in Welsh, since in certain analytic tense/aspect combinations a pre-head object pronominal clitic may be analysable as a resumptive pronoun. I leave this matter aside here, but it would be an interesting topic for future work, since it would bring Welsh in line with the other languages for which a Highest Subject Restriction has been observed and avoid the peculiarity of a Highest Object Restriction. A barrier to a potentially deeper understanding of the HSR would thus be removed.

Shlonsky (1992: 445–446) notes that Hebrew and Palestinian Arabic are like Irish in disallowing a resumptive as the highest subject, as shown respectively in (50) and (51):

(50) ha-ʔiš še __ / * še-hu ʔohev ʔet Rina
the-man that __ / * that-he loves ACC Rina
'the man who loves Rina' (Shlonsky, 1992: 445, (6))

(51) l-bint ʔilli __ / * hiy raayḥa ʕal beet
the-girl that __ / * she going to house
'the girl that is going home' (Shlonsky, 1992: 446, (12))

The distribution of gaps and resumptives in Hebrew and Palestinian Arabic is otherwise quite distinct (Shlonsky, 1992: 444–446). In Palestinian Arabic relative clauses, gaps and resumptives are in complementary distribution: gaps are licensed only in the highest subject, where resumptives may not occur, and pronouns are obligatory in every other position (Shlonsky, 1992: 444). In contrast, in Hebrew the distribution of gaps and resumptives overlaps in embedded subject and all direct object positions. Resumptives are blocked only in highest subject position and are obligatory in possessor and oblique positions. The HSR in Hebrew is also accounted for by an anti-locality condition on A′-binding (Borer, 1984: 251ff.). Both the proposals of Borer (1984) and McCloskey (1990) essentially extend Principle B of binding theory to A′-binding of pronouns, such that pronouns must be both A-free and A′-free in their governing categories.

Table 2.1 summarizes the distribution of gaps and resumptives in Irish, Welsh, Hebrew, and Palestinian Arabic. Overlapping distribution is identified by bold and the HSR column further highlights the fact that all four languages obey this restriction (with Welsh further disallowing resumptives in highest object position). The information in the table is compiled from McCloskey (1979, 1990), Sells (1984), Shlonsky (1992), and Willis (2000).

Table 2.1 reveals that there is no position that is categorically unavailable to resumptive pronouns in these languages. The highest subject and object may be unavailable, but none of the languages block resumptives from subject and object position in general. There is therefore no categorical statement that one can make in terms of a hierarchy of grammatical functions or syntactic positions to the effect that grammatical functions that are more oblique than X must be realized as a resumptive pronoun. Any such statement would in addition have to minimally refer to level of embedding. In fact, all of the languages except Palestinian Arabic show some overlap in the distribution of gaps and pronouns.

TABLE 2.1. Distribution of gaps and resumptives in Irish, Hebrew, Welsh, and Palestinian Arabic.

	Gap	Resumptive	HSR
Irish	Highest subject		Yes
	Embedded subject	**Embedded subject**	
	Direct object	**Direct object**	
		Possessor	
		Oblique	
Hebrew	Highest subject		Yes
	Embedded subject	**Embedded subject**	
	Direct object	**Direct object**	
		Possessor	
		Oblique	
Welsh	Highest subject		Yes
	Highest object		
	Embedded subject	**Embedded subject**	
	Embedded object	**Embedded object**	
		Possessor	
		Oblique	
Palestinian Arabic	Highest subject		Yes
		Embedded subject	
		Direct object	
		Possessor	
		Oblique	

A simpler generalization about the distribution of resumptive pronouns in Irish, Welsh, Hebrew, and Palestinian is that they can appear anywhere, except where independent constraints block them (McCloskey, 1990). In this case, the independent constraint is the HSR (extended appropriately for Welsh), however it is implemented. Similarly, extending the observation of McCloskey (1990: 209) about Irish, the basic generalization about the distribution of gaps in the four languages is that they are permitted everywhere, except where they are blocked by independent constraints, such as subjacency and the Empty Category Principle or whatever handles their work in other theories. This way of looking at things is in contrast to Last Resort theories of resumptive pronouns (Shlonsky, 1992; Pesetsky, 1998; Aoun et al., 2001), which hold that resumptives are only inserted in order to rescue derivations that would fail due to ungrammatical filler-gap dependencies.

The HSR is potentially all one has to say about the distribution of resumptive pronouns in Irish, Hebrew, Welsh, and Palestinian Arabic with respect to syntactic position or grammatical function. If the grammars of these languages freely generate resumptive pronouns and the HSR blocks them from the highest subject (and object, for Welsh), then the correct distribution is generated. Other constraints could also block resumptives altogether in certain environments. For example, we saw above that Hebrew resists resumptives in questions, except in certain specific circumstances.

However, the distribution of resumptive pronouns in Vata is strikingly different from that of Irish, Hebrew, Welsh, and Palestinian Arabic. Resumptive pronouns in Vata are obligatory *only* in subjects, highest or embedded, as shown in (52). The resumptive system of Vata is described in work by Hilda Koopman and Dominique Sportiche (among others, Koopman, 1982; Koopman and Sportiche, 1982, 1986).

(52) a. **Highest subject**
àlɔ́ ɔ̱ / * __ lē sa̍ká la̍
who he / * __ eat rice *wh*
'Who is eating rice?' (Koopman, 1982: 128, (1a))

b. **Embedded subject**
àlɔ́ ǹ gūgū nā ɔ̱ / * __ yì la̍
who you think that he / * __ arrive *wh*
'Who do you think arrived?' (Koopman, 1982: 128, (4a))

c. **Highest object**
yī kòfi le̍ __ / * mí̱ la̍
what Kofi eat __ / * it *wh*
'What is Kofi eating?' (Koopman, 1982: 128, (1b))

d. **Embedded object**
àlɔ́ ǹ gūgū nā wa̍ yɛ̍` __ / * mɔ̱̀ yé la̍
who you think that they see __ / him PART *wh*
'Who do you think they saw?' (Koopman, 1982: 128, (4b))

Koopman and Sportiche (1986: 154) note that resumptive pronouns are also barred for indirect objects and subcategorized PPs. Unbounded dependencies terminating in these positions are grammatical, but must terminate in gaps. Koopman (1982: 128) notes that all unbounded dependencies in Vata—*wh*-questions, focus constructions (roughly, clefts), and relative clauses—fall under the same generalization: resumptives are obligatory in subject position and prohibited elsewhere. The Vata facts indicate that the HSR should not be treated as a general linguistic principle, although it could potentially be parameterized.

2.1.4 *Resumptives and Gaps*

An important theoretical question is whether binder-resumptive dependencies can be reduced to filler-gap dependencies or whether languages have resumptive strategies that are distinct from filler-gap unbounded dependencies. A weaker reductionist stance is that resumptives and gaps are theoretically distinct, but that the binder-resumptive and filler-gap relations are nevertheless the same. A stronger reductionist stance is that resumptive pronouns are actually underlyingly gaps. McCloskey (1990, 2002), Sells (1984, 1987), and Merchant (2001) all take the position that binder-resumptive dependencies cannot be reduced to filler-gap dependencies and that resumptive pronouns cannot be gaps in the syntax. The position that binder-resumptive dependencies are reducible to filler-gap dependencies, or at least arise from the same mechanism, and that resumptive pronouns are essentially gaps in the syntax has been held by, among others, Zaenen et al. (1981), Engdahl (1985), Kayne (1994), Noonan (1997), and Boeckx (2001, 2003).

In a survey of resumption, McCloskey (2006) argues that there is, in fact, reason for distinguishing between two kinds of grammatically licensed resumptive pronouns, so that both views of resumption are, at least in part, correct. The reason is that resumptives cross-linguistically do not behave uniformly with regard to the following syntactic diagnostics for gaps and filler-gap dependencies: islands, weak crossover, across-the-board extraction, parasitic gaps, and reconstruction. McCloskey (2006: 109) nevertheless sees theoretical progress in this division:

> The two sets of properties (properties of movement-derived constructions and properties of non-movement-derived constructions) still line up in neat opposition. In Swedish, Vata, and Gbadi, those A-bar-binding relations which terminate in a pronoun show the complete constellation of properties associated with A-bar-movement. In Irish and similar languages, resumptive pronoun constructions show none of those properties. As long as we can make sense of the idea that a pronoun can be the 'spell-out' of a trace (as in the former group of languages), the larger conceptual architecture is not severely threatened.

The key point here is that binder-resumptive dependencies in some languages, for example Swedish and Vata, are like filler-gap dependencies, whereas binder-resumptive dependencies in other languages, for example Irish, are not.

However, it is problematic to attempt to unify binder-resumptive dependencies cross-linguistically based on "[making] sense of the idea that a pronoun can be the 'spell out' of a trace". The particular method that McCloskey

(2006) sketches for this in terms of the copy and delete theory of movement is criticized in detail in Asudeh (2011*c*). The general problems are that (1) resumptive pronouns are not interpreted completely equivalently to gaps, (2) resumptive binders do not receive the case of their base position, as discussed in 2.1.4.6 below, and (3) copies of moved constituents do not have the same features as pronouns. These are substantial empirical and theoretical problems in their own right. Moreover, the featural differences, in particular, mean that an appeal to a resumptive pronoun as an underlying gap/trace/copy is actually tantamount to treating resumptive pronouns in languages with gap-like resumptives as special pronouns, since these resumptives are distinct in their featural composition from other pronouns. This is then problematic in light of the typological generalization that resumptives are ordinary pronouns, which applies equally to Swedish and Vata.

In chapter 6, I present an analysis of the two kinds of resumption in which both kinds of resumptive are underlyingly ordinary pronouns (see also Asudeh, 2011*c*). This correctly predicts that both kinds of resumptive are interpreted like ordinary pronouns and are not distinct in their form from ordinary pronouns, maintaining McCloskey's Generalization. The essence of the analysis is that the gap-like kind of resumptive pronoun is licensed in a grammar where the filler-gap relationship is modified such that it also applies to resumptive pronouns, but the resumptive itself is not underlyingly like a gap. The effect of this is that gap-like resumptive pronouns make the same semantic contribution as ordinary pronouns and are present in LFG's syntactic level of constituent structure. However, gap-like resumptives are absent in LFG's syntactic level of functional structure (f-structure); I therefore call the gap-like resumptives 'syntactically inactive resumptives'. The similarity between syntactically inactive resumptives and gaps is thus captured in f-structure. In contrast, the resumptives that do not have gap-like properties are fully present in f-structure; I therefore call these resumptives 'syntactically active resumptives'. The distinction between syntactically active and syntactically inactive resumptives is thus captured at f-structure, which is independently the level at which the relevant diagnostic properties are analysed in LFG syntax. In the remainder of this section, I review these properties and how they classify resumptives.

2.1.4.1 *Islands* The first diagnostic concerns islands (Ross, 1967). It seems clear that islands are not a monolithic phenomenon and that in addition to syntactic factors there are semantic, pragmatic, and processing factors involved (see, e.g., Cinque, 1990; Rizzi, 1990; Deane, 1991; Kluender, 1991, 1998,

2004; Kluender and Kutas, 1993; Goodluck and Rochemont, 1992; Hofmeister and Sag, 2010; Sag, 2010). This does not substantively affect the use of these phenomena as diagnostics. The phenomena in question can serve the function of classifying resumptives and gaps together or apart whether the phenomena are grammatical or extra-grammatical, in part or in whole.

McCloskey (1979) discusses two island constraints in Irish: the Complex NP Constraint and an Irish correlate of the *Wh*-Island Constraint. The latter constraint is descriptively characterized as follows: "no item can be extracted from an embedded question" (McCloskey, 1979: 31, (81)). A filler-gap dependency, as signalled by use of the direct relative marker *aL*, is ungrammatical in either case. This is shown for both relative clause formation and *wh*-question formation in the following examples:

(53) a. *an fear aL phóg mé an bhean aL phós
the man COMP kissed I the woman COMP married
'the man who I kissed the woman who married'
(McCloskey, 1979: 30, (78))

b. *Cén fear aL phóg tú an bhean aL phós?
which man COMP kissed you the woman COMP married
'Which man did you kiss the woman who married?'
(McCloskey, 1979: 30, (80))

(54) a. *fear nachN bhfuil fhios agam cén cineál mná aL phósfadh
a man COMP.NEG I know what sort of a woman COMP would marry
'a man who I don't know what woman would marry'
(McCloskey, 1979: 32, (87))

b. *Cén sagart nachN bhfuil fhios agat caidé aL dúirt?
which priest COMP.NEG you know what COMP said
'Which priest don't you know what said?'
(McCloskey, 1979: 32, (88))

c. *Cén sagart aL d'fhiafraigh Seán díot arL bhuail tú?
which priest COMP asked John of.you QUEST hit you
'Which priest did John ask you if you hit?'
(McCloskey, 1979: 32, (89))

In contrast, a binder-resumptive dependency, signalled by the indirect relative marker *aN*, can freely cross these islands, as shown for a complex NP island in (55) and for an embedded question island in (56):

(55) Sin teanga aN mbeadh meas agam ar duine ar bith aL tá
that a.language COMP would be respect at me on person any COMP is
ábalta í a labhairt
able it to speak
'That's a language that I would respect anyone who could speak it.'
(McCloskey, 1979: 34, (95))

(56) Sin fear nachN bhfuil fhios agam cén cineál mná aL
that a man COMP.NEG I know what sort of a woman COMP
phósfadh é
would marry him
'That's a man who I don't know what kind of woman would marry him.' (McCloskey, 1979: 33, (91))

Thus, Irish filler-gap dependencies are island-sensitive, but binder-resumptive dependencies are not. This is strong evidence that the two kinds of dependencies are distinct and that the resumptive dependency cannot be reduced to the filler-gap dependency.

Borer (1984: 221, (3–4)) shows that Hebrew binder-resumptive dependencies are similarly island-insensitive. Such dependencies can reach into complex NP islands and coordinate structure islands:

(57) raʔiti ʔet ha-yeled she-/asher dalya makira ʔet ha-ʔisha she-
saw-I ACC the-boy that Dalya knows ACC the-woman that
ʔohevet ʔoto
loves him
'I saw the boy that Dalya knows the woman who loves him.'
(Borer, 1984: 221, (3))

(58) raʔiti ʔet ha-yeled she-/asher dalya makira ʔet ha-ʔisha
saw-I ACC the-boy that Dalya knows ACC the-woman
she-xashva ʔalav
that-thought about-him
'I saw the boy that Dalya knows the woman who thought about him.'
(Borer, 1984: 221, (3))

(59) raʔiti ʔet ha-yeled she-/ʔasher rina ʔohevet ʔoto ve- ʔet ha-xavera
saw-I ACC the-boy that Rina loves him and- ACC the-friend
shelo
of.his
'I saw the boy that Rina loves him and his girlfriend.'
(Borer, 1984: 221, (4))

If the resumptive were a gap, then example (59) would be a violation of the Coordinate Structure Constraint (Ross, 1967).

Swedish is less revealing with respect to islands than Irish and Hebrew, since it generally allows island violations quite freely (Engdahl, 1982). The only islands it seems to partially respect are left-branch islands and subject islands. However, Engdahl (1982: 163–165) shows that, in certain circumstances, even these islands can be extracted from. Engdahl (1985: 10) points out that island violations that are judged ungrammatical (for whatever reason) are not improved by insertion of a resumptive:

(60) ?* Vilken bil$_j$ åt du lunch med [$_{NP}$ någon$_i$ [$_{S'}$ som t_i körde t_j /
which car ate you lunch with someone that drove __ /
* den]]?
* it
'Which car did you have lunch with someone who drove it?'
(Engdahl, 1985: 10, (16))

It is a little unclear what this example indicates about islands and resumptives, since its unacceptability likely has to do with processing difficulty. In addition to a complex NP island violation, it is a garden path sentence that makes no sense on the first pass (*Which car did you have lunch with?*). One could therefore only cautiously conclude that Swedish does not distinguish between filler-gap and binder-resumptive dependencies with respect to islands.

Resumptive pronouns in Vata are island-sensitive (Koopman and Sportiche, 1986), as shown by the ungrammaticality of the following examples:

(61) *àIÓ ǹ nİ̍ [zĒ mĒmĖ̀ gbU̍̇ Ò dİ̍̀ -ɓȮ̍ *t* mÉ] yì lá̍
who you NEG-A reason it-it for he-R cut REL it know WH
'Who don't you know why he cut it?'
(Koopman and Sportiche, 1986: 161, (19a))

(62) *àIÓ ǹ nylá̍ nyni̍ nā Ò dİ̍ mÉ lá̍
who you wonder NA he-R cut it WH
'Who do you wonder whether he cut it?'
(Koopman and Sportiche, 1986: 161, (19b))

2.1.4.2 *Weak Crossover* The status of weak crossover as a narrowly syntactic phenomenon is also controversial (see, e.g., Shan and Barker, 2006). Once again, though, this does not preclude its being used as a diagnostic for categorization of resumptives together or apart from gaps.

McCloskey (1990, 2006) shows that weak crossover effects hold for Irish in filler-gap dependencies:

(63) a. *fear a d'fhág a bhean _
man COMP left his wife
'a man that his wife left'

b. *an fear so a mhairbh a bhean féin _
this man COMP killed his own wife
'this man that his own wife killed'

(McCloskey, 1990: 237, (95a–b))

The corresponding examples with the gap replaced by a resumptive pronoun are grammatical:

(64) a. fear ar fhág a bhean é̲
man COMP left his wife him
'a man that his wife left'

b. an fear so ar mhairbh a bhean féin é̲
this man COMP killed his own wife him
'this man that his own wife killed'

(McCloskey, 1990: 236–237, (94a–b))

Whatever the analysis of weak crossover, Irish filler-gap dependencies and binder-resumptive dependencies behave differently with respect to the phenomenon and it therefore constitutes evidence that the two kinds of dependency are distinct.

Resumptive pronouns do not result in weak crossover in Hebrew either (Doron, 1982; Sells, 1984, 1987; Shlonsky, 1992). The situation for Swedish is a little more subtle and I will return to it in chapter 9. In contrast to Irish and Hebrew, Vata resumptive pronouns pattern like gaps with respect to weak crossover (Koopman and Sportiche, 1982). Resumptive pronouns give rise to weak crossover effects:

(65) *àlɔ́$_i$ ɔ̍$_i$ nɔ́ gùgù nā $\underline{\text{ɔ̀}}_i$ mlì là̍
who$_i$ his$_i$ mother think that he$_i$ left WH
'Who did his mother think left?'

(Koopman and Sportiche, 1982: 22, (10a))

(66) *àlɔ́$_i$ ǹ yrà̍ ɔ̍$_i$ nɔ́ nā $\underline{\text{ɔ̀}}_i$ mlì là̍
who$_i$ you tell his$_i$ mother that he$_i$ left WH
'Who did you tell his mother left?'

(Koopman and Sportiche, 1982: 22, (10b))

The lower pronoun in these examples must be the resumptive, because resumptives in Vata only occur in subject position.

2.1.4.3 *Reconstruction* Zaenen et al. (1981) argue that Swedish resumptive pronouns allow what is now commonly called 'reconstruction' (Barss, 1986; Chomsky, 1993). This term refers both to an empirical phenomenon and to certain theoretical treatments of the phenomenonon in work originating in transformational grammar, particularly in Principles and Parameters Theory and the Minimalist Program; see Barss (2001) and Sportiche (2006) for overviews of reconstruction in the theoretical sense and for further references. I use the term only pretheoretically, in reference to the empirical phenomenon in which the top of an unbounded dependency behaves as if it were in its base position for the purpose of binding or scope.

Zaenen et al. (1981) examine reconstruction of a phrase containing a reflexive in place of a resumptive pronoun. They first show that reflexive possessors in Swedish must be in the proper subordinate configuration to their antecedents and that they must take an antecedent within the sentence. They then note that the following sentence is grammatical, even though the reflexive is in a fronted constituent:

(67) Vilken av sina$_i$ flickvänner tror du att Kalle$_i$ inte längre träffar __?
which of his girlfriends think you that Kalle no longer sees
'Which of his girlfriends do you think that Kalle no longer sees?'
(Zaenen et al., 1981: 680, (6))

The reflexive must be bound in its base position; otherwise the sentence should be ungrammatical, contrary to fact. In movement-based theories of unbounded dependencies, the fronted material must be reconstructed in its base position. In theories of filler-gap dependencies based on equality, as in LFG (Kaplan and Zaenen, 1989), or structure sharing, as in Head-Driven Phrase Structure Grammar (Bouma et al., 2001) or Sign-Based Construction Grammar (Sag, 2010), the fronted material simultaneously serves two syntactic functions—as the top of the unbounded dependency and the object of the clause containing the subject binder—without any operation of reconstruction.

Reconstruction should be blocked by the presence of a resumptive pronoun, but it is apparently not:

(68) Vilken av sina$_i$ flickvänner undrade du om det att Kalle$_i$ inte längre
which of his girlfriends wondered you if it that Kalle no longer
fick träffa <u>henne</u>$_i$ kunde ligga bakom hans dåliga humör?
sees her could lie behind his bad mood
'Which of his girlfriends do you think the fact that Kalle no longer gets to see (her) could be behind his bad mood?'
(Zaenen et al., 1981: 680, (6))

Zaenen et al. (1981: 679) therefore conclude that Swedish resumptives are "syntactically bound", which essentially means that they are gaps in the syntax.

However, the resumptive pronoun in this example is arguably not a true resumptive, but rather a processing-based resumptive. Engdahl (1982) argues that true grammatically licensed resumptives in Swedish occur only in embedded subject position after material in the left periphery of CP. The resumptive is in fact optional:

(69) Vilken av sina$_i$ flickvänner undrade du om det att Kalle$_i$ inte längre
which of his girlfriends wondered you if it that Kalle no longer
fick träffa __$_i$ kunde ligga bakom hans dåliga humör?
sees __ could lie behind his bad mood
'Which of his girlfriends do you think the fact that Kalle no longer gets to see could be behind his bad mood?'

Informants varied as to whether they considered this sentence completely well-formed or somewhat ill-formed, but no informant rejected it outright. The pronoun arguably makes the sentence easier to process, and this will in fact form the basis of the explanation of this kind of example in chapter 11.

Reconstruction of reflexives is thus actually not a viable test for the status of Swedish resumptives, if the only grammatically licensed resumptives are embedded subjects following left-peripheral material in CP, because reflexives cannot be subjects for independent reasons. I return to the question of reconstruction in Swedish in chapter 9, where I examine scope reconstruction. Anticipating that discussion, the results are uncertain. It does not seem that resumptives allow scope reconstruction either, but this may be due to independent interpretive constraints on the pronoun. Swedish reconstruction thus does not provide as good evidence for the status of resumptives as has previously been thought.

Aoun et al. (2001) note that Lebanese Arabic allows reconstruction at the site of resumption if the resumptive is not in an island, as in (70), but resumptives in islands do not allow reconstruction, as in the adjunct island example (71).

(70) təlmiiz-[a]$_i$ l-kəsleen ma baddna nχabbir [wala mʕallme]$_i$ ʔənno
student-her the-bad NEG want.1PL tell.1PL no teacher that
huwwe zaʕbar b-l-faħṣ.
he cheated.3SG.MASC in-the-exam
'Her bad student, we don't want to tell any teacher that he cheated on the exam.' (Aoun et al., 2001: 381, ~(25b))

(71) *təlmiiz-[a]$_i$ l-kəsleen ma ħkiina maʕ [wala mʕallme]$_i$ ʔabl-ma
student-her the-bad NEG talked.1PL with no teacher before
huwwe yuuṣal
he arrive.3SG.MASC
'Her bad student, we didn't talk to any teacher before he arrived.'
(Aoun et al., 2001: 381, ~(27b))

This correlation between lack of an island and reconstruction immediately follows if Lebanese Arabic has both resumption strategies (McCloskey, 2006; Asudeh, 2011*c*). In an island, only a syntactically active resumptive—the kind of resumptive that is not like a gap—could be grammatical. But this kind of resumptive does not allow reconstruction. Outside an island, either strategy is grammatical, but reconstruction is observable only if the gap-like, syntactically inactive resumptive is employed. I return to these facts in chapter 6, where I will explain why the two kinds of resumptive are nevertheless identical in form, which McCloskey (2006: 113) points to as a puzzling open question.

2.1.4.4 *Across-the-Board Extraction* Swedish normally respects the condition that extraction from a coordinate structure must be across-the-board (Williams, 1978), i.e. must extract from all conjuncts. However, extraction out of a single conjunct is allowed if the other conjunct contains a resumptive pronoun (Zaenen et al., 1981; Sells, 1984; Engdahl, 1985):

(72) Där borta går en man som jag ofta träffar _ men inte minns
There goes a man that I often meet _ but not remember
vad han heter.
what he is called
'There goes a man that I often meet but don't remember what he is called.' (Zaenen et al., 1981: 681, (9))

This resumptive pronoun is the subject of a clause with left-peripheral material in CP, so this is a true grammatically licensed resumptive (Engdahl, 1982). The sentence is ungrammatical if the pronoun is not a resumptive and is instead meant to refer freely.

2.1.4.5 *Parasitic Gaps* Swedish resumptive pronouns license parasitic gaps. Engdahl (1985) presents examples like the following for Swedish:

(73) Det var den fången$_i$ som läkarna inte kunde avgöra om han$_i$
it was that prisoner that the.doctors not could decide if he
verkligen var sjuk utan att tala med P$_i$ personligen.
really was ill without to talk with _ in person
'(This is the prisoner that the doctors couldn't detemine if he really was ill without talking to in person.)' (Engdahl, 1985: 7, (8))

The English translation is ill-formed, even though a weak island is a position where English allows intrusive pronouns (Sells, 1984). The resumptive pronoun is a true resumptive, since it occurs immediately following a complementizer. The fact that the resumptive licenses a parasitic gap,[9] together with the across-the-board extraction evidence, leads Engdahl (1985) to propose that Swedish resumptive pronouns are variables at S-structure; i.e. they are spelled out gaps.

The status of parasitic gaps in Hebrew is more controversial (Sells, 1984; Shlonsky, 1992; Ouhalla, 2001). Sells (1984: 79ff.) and Shlonsky (1992: 462–463) are in agreement that parasitic gaps in adjuncts cannot be licensed by a resumptive pronoun, as shown in (74), even though they can at least marginally be licensed by a gap, as shown in (75).

(74) *ʔelu ha-sfarim$_i$ še-Dan tiyek <u>otam</u>$_i$ bli likro <u>p</u>$_i$
these the-books that-Dan filed them without reading __
'These are the books that Dan filed without reading.'
(Shlonsky, 1992: 462, (32c))

(75) ??ʔelu ha-sfarim$_i$ še-Dan tiyek __$_i$ bli likro <u>p</u>$_i$
these the-books that-Dan filed __ without reading __
'These are the books that Dan filed without reading.'
(Shlonsky, 1992: 462, (32b))

Sells (1984: 82) notes that the grammaticality of a parasitic gap licensed by a resumptive pronoun is improved if there is a further level of embedding, in particular a tensed clause, between the binder and the resumptive. Shlonsky (1992: 462, fn.19) points out that distance in general improves the acceptability of otherwise ungrammatical resumptive pronouns (see also Erteschik-Shir, 1992). The embedding/distance facts indicate that the resumptive pronoun in question is likely a complexity resumptive, which is a subclass of the processor resumptives discussed in chapter 11. We can therefore conclude that Hebrew resumptive pronouns in base position do not license classic parasitic gaps in adjuncts. The fact that Hebrew resumptives do not robustly license parasitic gaps has been related to a Leftness Condition by, among others, Sells (1984) and Demirdache (1991).

[9] We can tell this is a parasitic gap, because it is only licensed by another gap or a resumptive pronoun.

Shlonsky (1992: 463) observes that if the resumptive pronoun is fronted and cliticized to the relative pronoun then a parasitic gap is permitted in an adjunct clause:

(76) ʔelu ha-sfarim$_i$ še-otam$_i$ Dan tiyek bli likro p$_i$
these the-books that-them Dan filed without reading _
'These are the books that Dan filed without reading.'
(Shlonsky, 1992: 463, (33))

Borer (1984) argues that this process involves movement. It is therefore not surprising that pronoun-fronting licenses a parasitic gap, since there is a non-parasitic gap in object position. Shlonsky (1992: 463) reaches a similar conclusion.

Parasitic gaps inside subjects, however, seem to be licensed by resumptive pronouns in Hebrew even without pronoun-fronting (Sells, 1984):

(77) zo-hi ha-iša še ha-anašim še šixnati levaker p$_i$
this-is the-woman that the-people that I-convinced to-visit _
teʔaru ota$_i$
described her
'This is the woman who the people who I convinced to visit described (her).'
(Sells, 1984: 79, (86a))

Shlonsky (1992: 462, fn.19) observes that it is not obvious that parasitic gaps in subjects are licensed in the same manner as parasitic gaps in adjuncts, although there have been attempts to unify the two (Nissenbaum, 2000). These could be processing-based resumptives, as discussed in section 2.2 below, rather than grammatically licensed resumptives.

2.1.4.6 *Form-Identity Effects* Merchant (2001: 128–146) identifies another diagnostic that potentially cuts across the two kinds of resumption. He notes that a filler and its gap show form-identity effects for case-marking, whereas a resumptive binder and its resumptive do not. Merchant (2001: 132) observes that

> The basic point of the argument is simple: while moved wh-phrases always take their case from their base position, wh-phrases linked to resumptives need not do so, and in general cannot, appearing instead in some default case if possible.

This observation extends to English intrusive pronouns and accounts for the following pattern:

(78) a. Who did the police say that finding his car took all morning?
b. *Whose did the police say that finding his car took all morning?
(Merchant, 2001: 133, (65a–b))

Merchant (2001: 146, (99)) offers the following generalization:

(79) **Case and resumptive-binding operator generalization**
No resumptive-binding operator can be case-marked.

Merchant (2001: 146) notes that "this follows directly if resumptive-binding operators are base-generated in SpecCP and can never check their Case feature".

A more theory-neutral formulation is that a resumptive binder never occupies the argument position of the resumptive, where case is assigned, and therefore cannot receive the case appropriate to that position. A filler does occupy the position of its gap, whether by originating there and moving away or via simultaneous occupation of two grammatical functions/positions through equality or structure sharing. The filler therefore receives the case of the gap position. If the binder-resumptive dependency were to be completely reduced to a filler-gap dependency, this contrast would be unexplained, since the resumptive-binder should also occur in the resumptive position. This constitutes another important argument against attempts to treat even gap-like resumptives as a spelled out trace or copy.

It is not possible to test the generalization for Irish, because the relevant case marking does not exist (which means that Irish vacuously satisfies the generalization). However, Hebrew behaves as predicted. Hebrew allows resumptives in topicalization, as shown in (80a), but the topicalized element cannot bear case if a resumptive is used, as shown in (80b). If the topic bears case, only a gap is grammatical, as shown in (80c).[10]

(80) a. Dani, Miriam raʔata ʔoto.
Dani Miriam saw him
'Dani, Miriam saw.'

b. *ʔet Dani, Miriam raʔata ʔoto.
ACC Dani Miriam saw him

c. ʔet Dani, Miriam raʔata __ .
ACC Dani Miriam saw __
'Dani, Miriam saw.'

[10] I thank Itamar Francez (p.c.) for these judgements.

If the topicalized element is case-marked, then the resumptive pronoun cannot be case-marked. The facts for Swedish are a little more subtle, since grammatically licensed resumptives necessarily occur in the default nominative case; this is discussed further in chapter 9.

2.2 Processing-Based Resumptive Pronouns

English resumptive pronouns are not grammatically licensed resumptives, since they are not intepreted as bound pronouns, as shown by Chao and Sells (1983) and Sells (1984). English resumptives, which Sells (1984) calls 'intrusive pronouns', will here be called 'processor resumptives', because they are an instance of a processing strategy that is generally available cross-linguistically: a resumptive element, typically but not necessarily a pronoun, is inserted where a gap would lead to ungrammaticality or processing difficulty (Kroch, 1981; Erteschik-Shir, 1992; Dickey, 1996; McDaniel and Cowart, 1999; Alexopoulou and Keller, 2002, 2007; Creswell, 2002; Swets and Ferreira, 2003; Ferreira and Swets, 2005; Heestand et al., 2011). Processor resumptives have been claimed to occur in three main circumstances: (1) when there is sufficient complexity or 'distance' between the top of the unbounded dependency and its base, as in (81); (2) in islands, as in (82); and (3) to avoid 'COMP-trace' effects, as in (83).

(81) This is the girl that Peter said that John thinks that yesterday his mother had given some cakes to her. (Erteschik-Shir, 1992: 89, (4))

(82) a. I'd like to meet the linguist that Mary couldn't remember if she had seen him before. (Sells, 1984: 11, (9a))

b. I'd like to meet the linguist that Peter knows a psychologist that works with her.

(83) This is a donkey that I wonder where it lives. (Ferreira and Swets, 2005: (4a))

For each of these examples, the claim is that the sentence is even worse with a gap than with the processor resumptive. These processor resumptives can be subclassified as 'complexity resumptives', 'island resumptives', and 'COMP resumptives', respectively.

Experimental work has supported some theoretical claims about resumptives and has cast doubt on others. On the one hand, controlled experimental studies have shown that speakers indeed find resumptive pronouns in English to be unacceptable in questions and relative clauses (McDaniel and Cowart,

1999; Alexopoulou and Keller, 2002, 2007; Swets and Ferreira, 2003; Ferreira and Swets, 2005; Heestand et al., 2011):

(84) *Who does Harry like her?

(85) *the woman who Harry likes her is here.

On the other hand, the same experimental studies have failed to show an ameliorating effect for complexity resumptives or island resumptives over gaps.

Alexopoulou and Keller (2002, 2007) studied resumptive pronouns in islands using Magnitude Estimation (Stevens, 1956, 1975; Bard et al., 1996). This technique allows subjects to construct their own scale and to rate items relationally. Alexopoulou and Keller first established that islands have a significant effect on grammaticality of filler-gap extraction, as expected (Alexopoulou and Keller, 2007: 118–119). However, they also found that resumptives do not improve the grammaticality of extraction from islands—neither weak islands nor strong islands. Lastly, Alexopoulou and Keller found that level of embedding (single or double) did not improve grammaticality of resumptives. McDaniel and Cowart (1999) also studied resumptive pronouns in islands using Magnitude Estimation. They similarly found no significant improvement of grammaticality of resumptive pronouns over gaps. Heestand et al. (2011) have recently replicated these results for complex noun phrase islands and relative clause islands. McDaniel and Cowart (1999) did, however, find an improvement of pronoun over gap in 'COMP-trace' configurations.

Ferreira and Swets (2005) ran two grammaticality judgement experiments on island resumptives. Stimuli were presented visually in one experiment and auditorily in the other. Participants were asked to rate sentences like (86), which contains an island resumptive, and corresponding control items like (87) on a forced scale of 1 (perfect) to 5 (awful) for acceptability in English.

(86) This is a donkey that I don't know where it lives.

(87) This is a donkey that doesn't know where it lives.

In both the auditory and visual presentations, resumptive sentences like (86) were rated as significantly worse than control sentences.

The most puzzling thing about English resumptives is that, although speakers find them ungrammatical even in regions of processing difficulty, they nevertheless produce them. This is a long-standing observation in the theoretical literature (Kroch, 1981; Prince, 1990) that has subsequently been confirmed experimentally (Swets and Ferreira, 2003; Ferreira and Swets, 2005). Prince (1990) presents examples like the following, which are attested examples from native speakers:

(88) You get a rack that the bike will sit on it. (Prince, 1990: (15d))

(89) I have a friend who she does all the platters. (Prince, 1990: (4c))

Kroch (1981) observed that the inserted element need not be a resumptive pronoun, but could be a definite description, as in the following example:

(90) There was one prisoner that we didn't understand why the guy was even in jail. (Kroch, 1981: 129, (13a))

Prince (1990) presents other attested examples that confirm this:

(91) I had a handout and notes from her talk that that was lost too. (Prince, 1990: (34a))

(92) He's got this lifelong friend who he takes money from the parish to give to this lifelong friend. (Prince, 1990: (34b))

(93) You assigned me to a paper which I don't know anything about the subject. (Prince, 1990: (34d))

Prince's attested examples are all the more remarkable, because they are not particularly complex and would not be ungrammatical with a gap instead of the resumptive element, perhaps with the exception of (91), at least on the apparently intended interpretation.

These attested productions could, however, be speech errors, so it is important to see whether English resumptives are produced under controlled circumstances. Ferreira and Swets conducted two experiments that tested production of English resumptives (Swets and Ferreira, 2003; Ferreira and Swets, 2005). In one experiment, participants were under pressure to begin speaking quickly due to a deadline procedure (Ferreira and Swets, 2002). In the other experiment, participants were not under pressure to begin quickly. The expectation was that, if English resumptives are produced due to lack of planning in production (Kroch, 1981) or are errors, then speakers could plan their utterance in the no-deadline experiment to avoid the resumptive pronoun and any island violation. For example, a participant could construct something like (94) instead of the resumptive sentence in (86) above, repeated in (95).

(94) This is a donkey and I don't know where it lives.

(95) This is a donkey that I don't know where it lives.

Instead, participants overwhelmingly produced island resumptive sentences like (95) in both the no-deadline and the deadline experiments.

In sum, speakers of varieties of English that lack resumptives reliably judge resumptive sentences to be ungrammatical, as expected by the theory. However, speakers of English nevertheless produce resumptive elements, as found both in attested examples and in controlled experiments. There is thus a very puzzling disconnect between the grammar and the processing system (Asudeh, 2004, 2011*a*,*b*). This and other aspects of processor resumptives are the subject of chapter 11.

2.3 Copy Raising

Copy raising is a phenomenon in which a raising verb takes a non-expletive subject and an apparently finite complement containing a pronominal 'copy' of the subject, as in the following English example:

(96) Alfred seems like he is happy.

Copy raising is not typologically uncommon and has been studied in a number of languages other than English, including Greek (Joseph, 1976; Perlmutter and Soames, 1979), Haitian Creole (Déprez, 1992), Hebrew (Lappin, 1984), Igbo (Ura, 1998), Irish (McCloskey and Sells, 1988), Persian (Darzi, 1996; Ghomeshi, 2001), Samoan (Chung, 1978), and Turkish (Moore, 1998). I will focus on copy raising in the grammar of English (Rogers, 1971, 1972, 1973, 1974; Postal, 1974; Horn, 1981; Heycock, 1994; Gisborne, 1996, 2010; Gisborne and Holmes, 2007; Bender and Flickinger, 1999; Potsdam and Runner, 2001; Asudeh, 2002*b*, 2004; Asudeh and Toivonen, 2007, 2012; Fujii, 2005, 2007; Landau, 2009, 2011).

The copy raising verbs in English are *seem* and *appear* with complements introduced by *like*, *as if*, or *as though*, as illustrated in this expanded version of (96):[11]

(97) Alfred seems/appears like/as if/as though he is happy.

Seem and *like* will stand in for the other possibilities in the rest of this section. Complements introduced by *like/as if/as though* will be called '*like*-complements'.

[11] Many authors include similar subcategorizations of the perception verbs *look*, *sound*, *smell*, *taste*, and *feel* in copy raising, but these 'perceptual resemblance verbs' are distinct from true copy raising verbs (Asudeh, 2002*b*, 2004; Asudeh and Toivonen, 2007, 2012).

Asudeh and Toivonen (2012) report results of questionnaire surveys of 110 native English speakers, which found that speakers can be divided into four dialects. About 6% of speakers did not accept copy raising sentences. Another 6% accepted the copy raising subcategorization, e.g. ... *seems like* ..., with a non-expletive subject but with no copy pronoun in the complement, as in the following:

(98) Alfred seems like Harry is hurt.

A third group, comprising about 45% of speakers, accepted copy raising sentences only if the copy pronoun is the highest subject in the complement, as in (96) and (97). The fourth and final group, comprising about 42% of speakers, accepted copy raising sentences only if the complement contained a copy pronoun, but did not require that the pronoun be the highest subject. The copy pronoun could be an embedded subject or an object, as in the following examples:

(99) Alfred seems like Thora decided that he could join in.
(100) Alfred seems like Harry hurt him.

In sum, some 88% of a large number of English speakers surveyed require that a copy raising verb with a non-expletive subject have a complement that contains a pronominal copy of that subject. In short, it seems that the grammars of these speakers treat copy raising as a kind of resumption.

The copy raising verbs *seem* and *appear* can also take an expletive *it* subject, in which case the complement does not require a copy pronoun.

(101) It seems like Alfred is happy.

(102) It appears as if Harry is hurt.

Sentences of this kind were accepted by all speakers who were surveyed.

Perhaps most interestingly, copy raising verbs are able to 'raise' expletives from the finite complement introduced by *like/as if/as though*. Horn (1981: 353–356) argues, based on *de dicto* versus *de re* readings in comparatives, that the expletive subject in (103) is the 'weather *it*' from the complement and not the independently available expletive seen in (101).

(103) It seems like it's raining.

Even more interestingly, some speakers allow expletive *there* as an expletive subject of a copy raising verb, as in (104), even though the copy raising verb cannot otherwise take a *there* expletive subject, as shown in (105).

(104) %There seems like there's a fly in my soup.

(105) a. *There seems like Harry's jumping.
b. *There seems like it's raining.

The grammars of these speakers, together with the arguments from Horn (1981), show conclusively that there is some kind of relation between the higher and lower expletive subjects. In chapter 12, I provide an explanation for this and argue that there is no direct relation of raising between the higher expletive subject and the lower expletive subject, but rather an indirect relation in which there is an intervening subject function.

Lastly, copy raising verbs cannot take scope over their subjects (Horn, 1981; Lappin, 1984; Potsdam and Runner, 2001; Asudeh, 2002*b*, 2004; Asudeh and Toivonen, 2012), as shown in (106), even though the raising verbs involved can normally take scope over a raised subject, as shown in (107).

(106) Many children seemed like they had eaten chocolate.
⇒Many children were such that they seemed like they had eaten chocolate.
(*many children* > *seem*)
⇏It seemed to be the case that many children had eaten chocolate.
(*seem* ≯ *many children*)

(107) Many children seemed to have eaten chocolate.
⇒Many children were such that they seemed to have eaten chocolate.
(*many children* > *seem*)
⇒It seemed to be the case that many children had eaten chocolate.
(*seem* > *many children*)

If the copy pronoun in copy raising is treated as a kind of resumptive pronoun in the Resource Management Theory of Resumption, then the lack of scope ambiguity for the copy raising example follows from resource-sensitive semantic composition (Asudeh, 2004; Asudeh and Toivonen, 2012), as discussed further in chapter 12.

2.4 Conclusion

This chapter reviewed three kinds of resumption phenomena: resumptive pronouns in unbounded dependencies, processing-based resumptives, and copy raising. Resumptives in unbounded dependencies were shown to have the form and interpretation of non-resumptive pronouns, which indicates that they are ordinary pronouns. If resumptive pronouns are just ordinary pronouns, then the term 'resumptive pronoun' is just a descriptive term and resumptive pronouns are eliminated as theoretical constructs. In contrast, unless a special pronoun theory can show that the special pronouns in question have some kind of independent justification outside a theory of resumption, then the special pronoun theory is admitting 'resumptive pronoun' as a theoretical construct. Therefore, theoretical considerations of parsimony, in addition to empirical considerations, favour ordinary pronoun theories of resumption.

Distinctions and similarities between binder-resumptive unbounded dependencies and filler-gap unbounded dependencies were examined that indicate that there are two distinct kinds of grammatically licensed resumptive pronouns: syntactically inactive resumptives, which are roughly gap-like, and syntactically active resumptives, which are not. Resumptives in Irish and Hebrew seem to be of the syntactically active variety, while resumptives in Swedish and Vata seem to be of the syntactically inactive variety.

The last two parts of the chapter presented data from English on processing-based resumptives and copy raising. Data from experimental studies confirms the theoretical finding that English resumptives are considered ungrammatical by native speakers, but generally fails to confirm the theoretical claim that resumptive pronouns are better than gaps in case of sufficient complexity or distance between the top and bottom of the unbounded dependency and in islands. There is, however, some evidence that resumptives are preferred over gaps in 'COMP-trace' environments.

Copy raising shows some variation, but the great majority of speakers require a copy pronoun in the complement of the raising verb. This suggests that copy raising is a kind of resumption, but one that involves a local dependency between a verb's subject and a grammatical function in the verb's complement, much like standard raising. However, for many speakers the grammatical function in the complement does not have to be the highest subject, unlike standard raising. Lastly, English copy raising involves some kind of relation between an expletive subject of a copy raising verb and an expletive subject of the verb's complement. The key piece of evidence for this stems from speakers who allow an expletive *there* as the subject of the copy raising verb, so long as the expletive is licensed in the complement.

3

Lexical-Functional Grammar

This chapter is a brief introduction to Lexical-Functional Grammar (LFG), the syntactic framework and grammatical architecture that is assumed in this work. Section 3.1 introduces the 'Correspondence Architecture', the grammatical architecture of LFG. Sections 3.2–3.4 introduce the most relevant components of the architecture: constituent structure, functional structure, and semantic structure. Section 3.5 introduces templates, which allow grammatical generalizations to be captured compactly, with inheritance of information by more specific descriptions from more general descriptions. Section 3.6 outlines syntactic aspects of anaphora and binding. Section 3.7 introduces the non-transformational, trace-less treatment of unbounded dependencies. Section 3.8 outlines the treatment of raising, which will be relevant to the analysis of copy raising in chapter 12.

There are many sources for further information on Lexical-Functional Grammar. Bresnan (1978) provides much of the theory's foundational linguistic motivation and argumentation, but the paper is not cast in LFG per se. The key foundational LFG paper is Kaplan and Bresnan (1982), which is the initial presentation and formalization of the theory. This and other important early papers are collected in Bresnan (1982*b*) and Dalrymple et al. (1995); another collection of influential early papers is Butt and King (2006). Kaplan (1987, 1989) are two foundational papers on the Correspondence Architecture and also provide compact formal presentations of the framework. Dalrymple (2001) is a reference work on LFG. Bresnan (2001) and Falk (2001) are advanced and introductory textbooks, respectively; the latter provides numerous comparisons between LFG and Government and Binding Theory. Dalrymple (2006) is a short encyclopedia article. Asudeh and Toivonen (2009) is a handbook introduction to the LFG framework and theory and contains pointers to further references and resources.

3.1 Grammatical Architecture

The original grammatical architecture of LFG, presented in Kaplan and Bresnan (1982), consisted of two syntactic levels: constituent structure (c-structure) and functional structure (f-structure). C-structure is represented as a standard phrase structure tree. It represents syntactic information about precedence, dominance, and constituency. F-structure is represented as a feature structure (also known as an 'attribute-value matrix'). It is also a syntactic representation, but represents more abstract aspects of syntax, such as grammatical functions, predication, subcategorization, and local and non-local dependencies. C-structure and f-structure are projected from lexical items, which specify their c-structure category and f-structure feature contributions. The two syntactic representations are present in parallel, with the structural correspondence or projection function ϕ establishing the relationship between c-structure and f-structure by mapping c-structure elements (i.e., nodes in a tree) to f-structure elements (i.e., feature structures). The basic grammatical architecture can be schematized as in Figure 3.1.

An LFG representation of a sentence, on this view, is a triple consisting of a c-structure, an f-structure, and a ϕ correspondence function that maps the c-structure to the f-structure: $\langle c, f, \phi \rangle$. C-structures and f-structures are constructed by simultaneous constraint satisfaction—LFG is a declarative, constraint-based, non-transformational theory. The fact that c-structure and f-structure are represented using distinct data structures (trees and feature structures) demonstrates that LFG uses mixed data structures related by structural correspondence, rather than a single monolithic data structure. This distinguishes LFG from the majority of both transformational theories and non-transformational theories. For example, Principles and Parameters Theory, a transformational theory, represents all syntactic information in a tree, and Head-Driven Phrase Structure Grammar (HPSG; Pollard and Sag, 1994), a non-transformational theory, represents all grammatical information in a directed acyclic graph.

The LFG architecture was subsequently further generalized (Kaplan, 1987, 1989; Halvorsen and Kaplan, 1988) and became known as the 'Parallel Projection Architecture' or the 'Correspondence Architecture'. I use the latter term in order to avoid potential confusion with the similar but distinct 'Parallel

$$\text{constituent structure} \xrightarrow{\phi} \text{functional structure}$$

FIGURE 3.1. The original LFG architecture.

Architecture' of Jackendoff (1997, 2002, 2007). The Correspondence Architecture postulates various levels of linguistic representation that are present simultaneously. Each level is governed by its own rules and representations. This separation of levels permits simple theoretical statements to capture the linguistic generalizations modelled at the level in question. The architecture also permits systematic mismatches between levels. For example, null pronouns are not represented at c-structure, because they are unmotivated by the syntactic phenomena represented at that level, but are represented at f-structure, where they can participate in agreement, binding, and other syntactic processes that are captured at that level.

The distinct levels in the Correspondence Architecture are related by structural correspondences, formally captured by correspondence functions that map elements of one level into elements of another. C-structure and f-structure remain the most deeply investigated levels, but they are now two among several levels of representation and the correspondence function ϕ is now one of many. For example, f-structures are mapped into semantic structures by the σ correspondence function (Dalrymple, 1993; Dalrymple et al., 1999*b*; Dalrymple, 2001). Even the correspondence function π from the string to syntax can be useful for capturing linguistic generalizations, as in the linearization-based analysis of 'COMP-trace' effects in Asudeh (2009).

The Correspondence Architecture represents the decomposition, via the correspondence functions, of a mapping Γ from form to meaning. The domain of each correspondence function is the range of the previous one; so the mapping Γ is the composition of the intermediate correspondence functions. Composition of correspondence functions yields important modularity for the Correspondence Architecture. It means that new levels can be proposed while preserving old mappings as the composition of new correspondence functions. Similarly, old levels can be moved within the architecture without losing previous mappings, since these can be recovered from the composition of the new arrangement of correspondence functions.

Kaplan (1987, 1989) proposed the architecture in Figure 3.2 as a programmatic example of the Correspondence Architecture. This has given rise to much subsequent work, such that the modern Correspondence Architecture realizes much of the architecture in Figure 3.2, although not in that exact configuration. First, anaphora have been analysed in semantic structure (Dalrymple, 1993, 2001), rather than in a separate level of anaphoric structure. Second, discourse structure has mainly been investigated under the rubric of 'information structure', although some work has sought to maintain a distinction between the two (O'Connor, 2006). Some other relevant LFG references for discourse/information structure are Bresnan and Mchombo

(1987), King (1995, 1997) Butt and King (1996, 2000), Choi (1999), King and Zaenen (2004), Mycock (2006), and Dalrymple and Nikolaeva (2011). Third, some other levels have been proposed for the architecture: morphological structure (Butt et al., 1996; Butt et al., 1999; Frank and Zaenen, 2002), prosodic structure (Butt and King, 1998; Mycock, 2006; O'Connor, 2006; Bögel et al., 2008, 2009, 2010), and argument structure (Butt et al., 1997). This last proposal is a demonstration of the architectural modularity derived from composition of correspondence functions. Butt et al. (1997) propose that argument structure should be interpolated between c-structure and f-structure with the ϕ correspondence function broken up into the α correspondence function from c-structure to argument structure and the λ correspondence function from argument structure to f-structure. The ϕ function is then the composition of these two new functions: $\phi = \lambda \circ \alpha$.

The addition of these levels was initially done in such a way that the architecture fans out at some point, like the programmatic architecture in Figure 3.2, as discussed by Asudeh (2006) and Asudeh and Toivonen (2009). However, there have been recent proposals that the levels are instead arranged in a 'pipeline' (Bögel et al., 2009, 2010). Bögel et al. (2009) propose that prosodic structure maps to c-structure, and thus indirectly to f-structure (through the ϕ mapping from c-structure to f-structure). This is in opposition to the original proposal of Butt and King (1998), in which prosodic structure is mapped from c-structure (and, as a result, does not map to f-structure). The Bögel et al. (2009) proposal thus postulates a pipeline from the phonological string to a prosodic structure to c-structure. Dalrymple and Nikolaeva (2011) propose that semantic structure maps to information structure, thus postulating a pipeline from c-structure to f-structure to semantic structure to information structure.

Assuming that argument structure is still interpolated between c-structure and f-structure (Butt et al., 1997), a question remains regarding the place of morphology in a pipeline arrangement of the Correspondence Architecture.

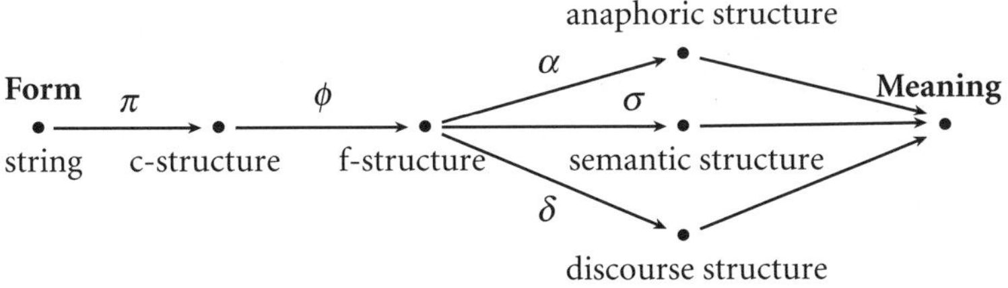

FIGURE 3.2. An early, programmatic version of the Correspondence Architecture (Kaplan, 1987, 1989).

There is reason to place morphology between the phonological string and prosodic structure.[1] It is standardly assumed, at least in computational treatments of LFG (Crouch et al., 2011), that there is a finite state morphology (Beesley and Karttunen, 2003) that analyses the string and feeds the syntax.[2] This means that morphological structure should follow the phonological string and precede c-structure. In addition, syntactic categories, which are part of the morphological information associated with a word, have prosodic effects, as in the opposition between *prótest*$_N$ and *protést*$_V$. This means that morphological structure should precede prosodic structure. The resulting pipeline version of the Correspondence Architecture is shown in Figure 3.3. The architecture is shown as a mapping from form to meaning, but the reverse mapping is definable by taking the composition of the relations that are the inverses of the correspondence functions.

The Correspondence Architecture facilitates investigation of certain levels and their interfaces in isolation from other aspects of linguistic representation. In this work, I am primarily concerned with the syntax–semantics interface and semantic composition. The relevant parts of the architecture are thus constituent structure, functional structure, semantic structure, and the mapping from semantic structure to meaning, as modelled by linear logic proofs. Information structure is not directly relevant to the investigation, so the ψ correspondence function is defined as a direct mapping from semantic structure to meaning, circumventing information structure, just as the ϕ function is a direct mapping from c-structure to f-structure, circumventing argument structure.

Lastly, let us consider the nature of the mappings between structures from different subsystems. The Correspondence Architecture does not in itself determine how the mappings are specified (Kaplan, 1989). Two principal methods for specifying the correspondence mappings have been explored in the LFG literature. In the first method, known as *codescription*, a single description jointly describes several structures. For example, a lexical item generally minimally contains the following information, which codescribes c-structure, f-structure, and compositional semantics:

(1) *Item*, C-STRUCTURE CATEGORY f-structure description
semantic structure meaning constructor

[1] This means that the motivating factors for placing morphological structure later in the architecture (Butt et al., 1996; Butt et al., 1999; Frank and Zaenen, 2002) will have to be revisited.

[2] Finite state morphology is quite a general framework. Many other theories of morphology can be equivalently expressed in a finite state morphology, even apparently more powerful theories like that of Stump (2001); see Karttunen (2003).

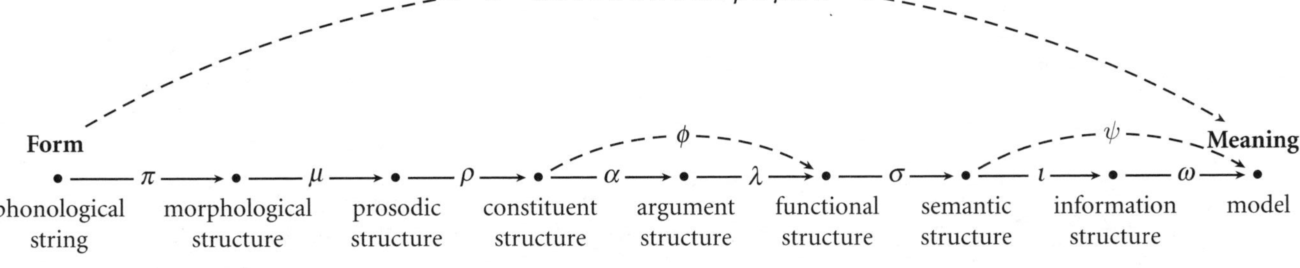

FIGURE 3.3. The Correspondence Architecture, pipeline version.

Item is the unique lexical identifier of the lexical item, typically represented as the corresponding word that would appear as the terminal node in the c-structure. The C-STRUCTURE CATEGORY is the category of the pre-terminal node, e.g. N^0. The f-structure description specifies the information that the item contributes to the f-structure of the pre-terminal node and any f-structural constraints it places on this f-structure. The last part of the entry provides the meaning constructor for semantic composition, which is instantiated through the mapping from f-structure to semantic structure. Codescription is the method for defining the relation between structures that is implicit in the original theory developed by Kaplan and Bresnan (1982) and it is the prevalent method in LFG theory (Dalrymple, 2001: 185–187). It is this method that I assume. This will be important in the analysis of the class of grammatically licensed resumptives that I call 'syntactically inactive resumptive pronouns', which pattern syntactically like gaps but semantically like pronouns, as discussed in chapter 6.

In the second method, known as *description by analysis* (Halvorsen, 1983), a structure is analysed in order to yield the description of another structure. For example, in the semantic theory developed by Halvorsen (1983), an f-structure is systematically analysed to yield a semantic structure and an interpretation, as exemplified in detail by Dalrymple (2001: 187–189). Description by analysis is directly inspired by the translational system in Montague Semantics (Montague, 1974), in which particular syntactic rules are paired with particular semantic rules. This is essentially equivalent to interpreting a certain kind of syntactic structure in a certain way. The modern reflex of this can be seen in the kind of interpretation method developed for Logical Form semantics by Heim and Kratzer (1998).

Although description by analysis is perhaps a reasonable approach to semantics in LFG (also see Crouch and King, 2006), it is difficult to see how it could provide a general method for relating structures in the Correspondence Architecture. For example, consider the nature of a description by analysis mapping from c-structure to f-structure. The mapping would have to be specified such that an f-structure is defined by a c-structure configuration. This would effectively mean, for example, that grammatical functions are defined configurationally. But this is completely antithetical to the core assumptions of the framework (Bresnan, 2001: 44–46), which holds that grammatical functions are not reducible to c-structure configurations. This sort of consideration favours the codescription method, quite apart from the work that codescription does in the theory of resumption.

3.2 Constituent Structure

Constituent structure is modelled using non-tangled phrase structure trees. It represents precedence, dominance, and constituency. The nodes in the tree are syntactic categories, so c-structure also encodes categorially determined syntactic distribution. C-structures are defined by phrase structure rules.

LFG commonly adopts an X-bar theory (Chomsky, 1970; Jackendoff, 1977) approach to phrase structure (Bresnan, 2001; Falk, 2001; Toivonen, 2001, 2003). I adopt Toivonen's (2001; 2003) theory of c-structure, which is motivated by extensive data from Swedish and other Germanic languages. Toivonen proposes a theory of non-projecting words within a general X-bar theory of phrase structure. Terminal categories in this theory of phrase structure can either be of the projecting category X^0 ('X-zero') or of the non-projecting category $\hat{X}$ ('X-roof'). In Toivonen's theory, X^0 categories must project a medial X' category which in turn must project a maximal XP category. In contrast, $\hat{X}$ categories are non-projecting and cannot be immediately dominated by an X'. Toivonen (2003: 63–65) takes the strong position that a non-projecting word must be head-adjoined; i.e. a non-projecting $\hat{X}$ not only cannot be inserted under X', a medial category of the same kind, it also cannot be inserted under Y', a medial category of a different kind, or any maximal category (XP or YP). Non-projecting words will be used in the analysis of the complementizer system of Irish in chapter 7.

Toivonen (2003: 62), following Bresnan (2001: 100), proposes that the following syntactic categories are universally available, although a given language may use only a subset of these:[3]

(2) F(unctional): C, I, D
    L(exical): V, A, P, N

The functional categories C(omplementizer), I(nflection), and D(eterminer) are the only functional categories commonly used in LFG, although the functional category K for case (Lamontagne and Travis, 1987, 1986; Bittner and Hale, 1996) has been used in some work (Butt and King, 2004*b*). Falk (2001: 37ff.) argues that the theory should only admit functional categories that exhibit head-like properties and that are realized as independent words.

In addition to these endocentric categories, Bresnan (2001) and Toivonen (2001, 2003) allow the exocentric category S, which dominates a nominal

[3] Bresnan and Toivonen do not include a category for adverbs, but this could easily be amended.

category and a predicative XP, as in the following slightly amended form of their proposals:

(3) S $\longrightarrow$ NomP, XP

NomP is a generalization over DP and NP, based on the idea that the functional category D shares features of the lexical category N (Grimshaw, 1998). Bresnan and Toivonen specify the nominal as an NP, but given the adoption of the category D, presumably a DP should also be allowed in this position.

Given the distinction between non-projecting and projecting categories, the full set of categories is (Toivonen, 2003: 63):

(4) X^0: V^0, P^0, A^0, N^0, C^0, I^0, D^0 **Projecting categories**
$\hat{X}$: $\hat{V}$, $\hat{P}$, $\hat{A}$, $\hat{N}$, $\hat{C}$, $\hat{I}$, $\hat{D}$ **Non-projecting categories**
S **Exocentric category**

Toivonen (2003: 22) generalizes over non-projecting $\hat{X}$ categories and projecting X^0 categories with a plain X category. The category X is theoretically justified based on the fact that both projecting and non-projecting categories are terminal nodes that dominate lexical material (Toivonen, 2003: 64). It is empirically justified based on lexical items that behave ambiguously as both projecting and non-projecting words (Toivonen, 2003: 22ff.). One such lexical item is Swedish *dit* ('there.DIRECTIONAL'), which is either of the projecting category P^0, in which case it projects a full PP and occurs at the end of the verb phrase, or of the non-projecting category $\hat{P}$, in which case it is a verbal particle adjoined to V^0 (Toivonen, 2003: 90–91).

Basic X-bar structures in Toivonen's theory are defined by the following general schemas (Toivonen, 2003: 61):

(5) a. $XP \longrightarrow X', YP^*, \; X \neq S$

b. $X' \longrightarrow X^0, YP^*, \; X \neq S$

Specifiers and complements in these schemas are annotated with the Kleene star. Multiple specifiers and non-binary complementation structures are thus permitted by these general schemas, although they may be ruled out by independent specific constraints. Also, the constraints explicitly state that the exocentric category S cannot serve as X.

In addition to the X-bar structures defined by (5), Toivonen (2003: 63) assumes that adjunction structures described by the following schemas are allowed:

(6) a. $XP \longrightarrow XP, YP^*$

b. $X^0 \longrightarrow X^0, \hat{Y}^*$

Toivonen (2003: 62) proposes that adjunction to X′ is not permitted and that the following generalization holds:

(7) **Adjunction Identity**:
Same adjoins to same.

X^0 and $\hat{X}$ categories count as the same for adjunction identity, for the reasons that justify the generalized category X.

Adjunction identity only affects the analyses in this book in a peripheral way. In particular, it means that restrictive relative clauses are adjoined to NP within a DP:

(8)

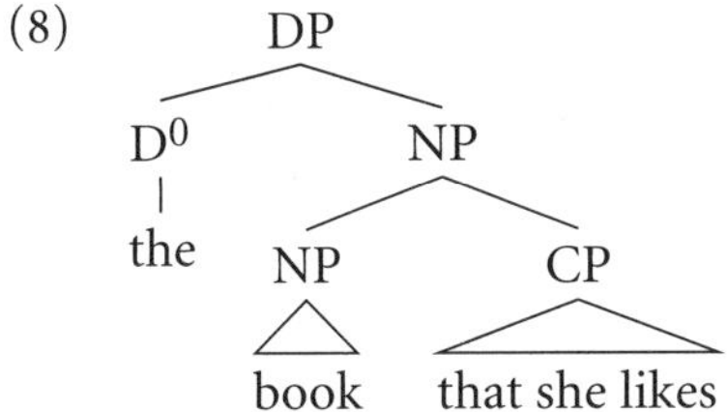

This structure is adopted for relative clauses in order to be consistent with Toivonen's overall theory.

There is no deep theoretical commitment in this book to either the DP analysis of nominals (Brame, 1982; Abney, 1987) or to adjunction identity, though. Such a commitment is unnecessary, given the overall theory, since the main interest is the syntax–semantics interface and semantic composition. The determiner is a co-head of the NP, which means that material in D and N ultimately map to the same f-structure. Since Glue Semantics works with semantic structure, which is projected from f-structure, the attachment site of the relative clause in c-structure does not affect compositional semantics, providing it is attached to a reasonable place in DP or NP. The semantics only sees the f-structure that all the head material in the nominal projects to. This also means that certain semantic considerations that have been key to deciding relative clause attachment (Partee, 1975; Bach and Cooper, 1978) do not arise. In particular, if the DP hypothesis is not pursued and nominals receive the traditional category NP, it would be possible to adjoin the relative to NP. However, this would not require the addition of a relative clause variable, as in Bach and Cooper (1978). Alternatively, if both the DP hypothesis and adjunction identity are given up, then the relative clause could adjoin at the N′ level, which is effectively the modern update of Partee (1975). In sum, relative clause attachment, in this theory, is not decided by c-structurally determined facts of semantic composition, but rather by syntactic facts about constituency. This is a desirable result in a grammatical architecture that attempts to properly distinguish syntactic and semantic generalizations.

Finally, as in much LFG work, all constituent structure positions are optional (Kroeger, 1993; King, 1995; Bresnan, 2001; Dalrymple, 2001; Toivonen, 2003).[4] In some cases this will lead to non-endocentric structure, but LFG adopts a theory of extended projection in which various c-structure positions project as a single f-structure head (Bresnan, 2001). Thus, a notion of endocentric head is definable by referring to c-structures and f-structures together, using the ϕ correspondence function (Bresnan, 2001: 131–134). However, the lack of c-structure endocentrity resulting from optionality of c-structure material is not a violation of LFG-theoretic X-bar theory. LFG separates the formal objects of the theory, such as trees, from constraints on and descriptions of those objects, such as phrase structure rules. Thus, X-bar theory in LFG is a theory of phrase structure rules, not of phrase structures (Asudeh and Toivonen, 2009).

3.3 Functional Structure

Functional structure is a level of syntactic representation that encodes more abstract syntactic information—essentially, everything apart from categorial status, precedence, dominance, and constituency. Information represented at f-structure includes: grammatical functions, subcategorization, predication, case, agreement, tense, mood, aspect, syntactic restrictions on anaphoric binding, local dependencies (e.g., control and raising), and unbounded depedencies. Much of the information represented in f-structures corresponds to information that, in Principles and Parameters Theory and the Minimalist Program, is encoded in VP and *v*P (subcategorization, grammatical functions) and in the functional projections above VP (case, agreement, tense, aspect, unbounded dependencies).

An f-structure is a finite set of attribute-value pairs called 'features'. The attributes are symbols. Possible values are: (1) symbols (e.g., FEMININE or +), (2) semantic forms—values of PRED features, which are potentially complex symbols in single quotes, (3) f-structures, and (4) sets. F-structures are represented as feature structures, also known as attribute-value matrices. For

[4] In some LFG work, this optionality is not stipulated, but is rather derived from the principle of Economy of Expression (Bresnan, 2001; Toivonen, 2001, 2003), which removes excess c-structure material. The main effect of Economy of Expression for Bresnan (2001: 91ff.) is to tightly circumscribe the distribution of traces in c-structure. I assume a trace-less version of LFG, so this motivation for Economy does not apply. Toivonen (2001, 2003) has a more narrowly empirical motivation for Economy of Expression, which is used to derive certain aspects of the distribution of Swedish particles (Toivonen, 2003: 101ff.). I set these issues aside here.

example, the relative clause example in (8) has the f-structure in (9), leaving aside for the moment the unbounded dependency of relativization.

(9)

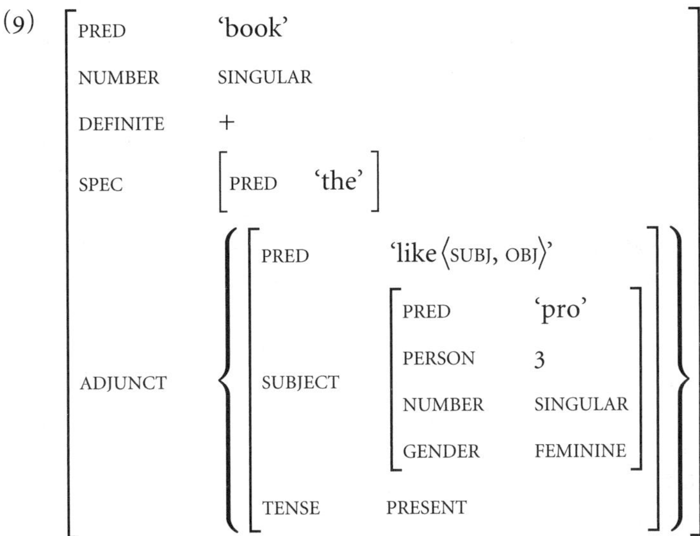

This f-structure demonstrates all four possible attribute values. The features DEFINITE, PERSON, NUMBER, and GENDER all have symbols as their values. The features SPEC(IFIER) and SUBJECT have f-structures as their values. The value for the feature ADJUNCT is a set, which contains as a member the f-structure of the relative clause. This illustrates the use of sets to gather all of the modifiers of a given f-structure, since a head can have indefinitely many modifiers. Another typical use for sets is in coordination, where there can be indefinitely many conjuncts or disjuncts. Lastly, there are several instances of the feature PRED, which has a special value called a *semantic form*, indicated by single quotes. The term 'semantic form' is no longer such an apt description of the role of PRED, since the semantic contributions it made in the original treatment by Kaplan and Bresnan (1982) have largely been taken over by other aspects of the theory, such as Lexical Mapping Theory (Bresnan and Kanerva, 1989) and Glue Semantics (for discussion, see Dalrymple, 2001: 219–221). But the term has stuck.

3.3.1 *The C-structure to F-structure Mapping*

C-structures are mapped to f-structures via the correspondence function ϕ. F-structures are constrained by specifications called *functional descriptions*, *f-descriptions* for short. Functional descriptions, in general, are sets of equations and constraints that define linguistic structures in the Correspondence

Architecture, but a key role of f-descriptions is to define f-structures.[5] F-descriptions are specified in lexical entries and in phrase structure rules.

F-descriptions consist of two parts: (1) some designator for the linguistic structure being described and (2) some description of the designated structure. In f-descriptions for f-structure, these two parts are the f-structure metavariables $\uparrow$ and $\downarrow$, which designate f-structures, and regular expressions that describe f-structure paths. The metavariables denote f-structures and f-structures can be thought of as functions that are applied to attributes to yield values. For example, the expression ($\uparrow$ SUBJECT), which is typically abbreviated as ($\uparrow$ SUBJ), is equivalent to $\uparrow$(SUBJ) and denotes the value of the SUBJ attribute of the f-structure designated by $\uparrow$. This kind of application can be iterated. For example, ($\uparrow$ SUBJ NUM) abbreviates (($\uparrow$ SUBJ) NUM) and designates the value found by applying to NUM the function designated by ($\uparrow$ SUBJ), which itself is the value of the SUBJ attribute of $\uparrow$. The expression SUBJ NUM can equivalently be considered a path expression, such that ($\uparrow$ SUBJ NUM) refers to the value reached by following the path SUBJ NUM from the f-structure designated by $\uparrow$.

The f-structure metavariables are constructed from two c-structure variables and the ϕ function. The c-structure variables are $*$, which refers to the c-structure node that it annotates, and $\hat{*}$ (sometimes represented as $\mathcal{M}(*)$), which refers to the c-structure node that immediately dominates the annotated node (i.e., its mother). The f-structure metavariables are thus defined as follows:

(10) $\downarrow := \phi(*)$ the annotated node's f-structure
$\uparrow := \phi(\hat{*})$ the annotated node's mother's f-structure

For example, the f-description ($\uparrow$ SUBJ) refers to the SUBJ of the f-structure corresponding to the mother of the c-structure node that bears the f-description.

The phrase structure rules that construct c-structures are annotated with f-descriptions. These f-descriptions describe the f-structures that the c-structure node maps to. For example, leaving aside irrelevant X-bar theoretic details, the annotated rules in (11) could be used for the relative clause example (8). In (12) below, I present a more detailed version of (8) in its annotated form together with the partial f-structure that the annotations describe and an explicit representation of the ϕ function.

[5] In fact, it is common in the LFG literature to use the term 'functional description' only with respect to descriptions of f-structures, but I follow Dalrymple et al. (2004*b*) in using the term more generally.

(11) a. $\text{DP} \longrightarrow \underset{\uparrow = \downarrow}{\text{D}^0} \quad \underset{\uparrow = \downarrow}{\text{NP}}$

b. $\text{NP} \longrightarrow \underset{\uparrow = \downarrow}{\text{NP}} \quad \underset{\downarrow \in (\uparrow \text{ ADJ})}{\text{CP}}$

c. $\text{NP} \longrightarrow \underset{\uparrow = \downarrow}{\text{N}'}$

d. $\text{N}' \longrightarrow \underset{\uparrow = \downarrow}{\text{N}^0}$

(12)

DP
↑ = ↓ D⁰ the
↑ = ↓ NP
↑ = ↓ NP
↑ = ↓ N′
↑ = ↓ N⁰ book
↓ ∈ (↑ADJ) CP that she likes
φ
[ADJ {[ ]}]
φ

The f-description ↑ = ↓ indicates equality between two f-structures and is how LFG expresses the notion of headedness at f-structure: all of the c-structure nodes projecting from the head *book* map to the same f-structure, as does the c-structure node projecting from *the*. The f-description ↓ ∈ (↑ ADJ) indicates that the f-structure contributed by the CP is a member of the set that constitutes the NP's ADJUNCT.

The rest of the information shown in the fuller f-structure (9) above comes from the lexical entries in the structure, which also contribute f-descriptions:

(13) *the*, D^0 (↑ SPEC PRED) = 'the'
(↑ DEFINITE) = +

(14) *book*, N^0 (↑ PRED) = 'book'
(↑ NUMBER) = SINGULAR

(15) *she*, D^0 (↑ PRED) = 'pro'
(↑ PERSON) = 3
(↑ NUMBER) = SINGULAR
(↑ GENDER) = FEMININE

(16) *likes*, V^0 (↑ PRED) = 'like⟨SUBJ,OBJ⟩'
(↑ TENSE) = PRESENT
(↑ SUBJECT PERSON) = 3
(↑ SUBJECT NUMBER) = SINGULAR

I have assumed that the complementizer *that* makes no contribution to the f-structure. This illustrates that there can be elements at one level of structure that have no correspondent at another level. Another example of this is null pronouns. These are represented at f-structure, but there is no null pronominal in the c-structure.

F-structures are constructed by instantiating the f-description metavariables in the annotated tree to f-structure labels. The f-descriptions of the terminal nodes of the tree are also instantiated. The instantiated version of (12) is the following, where only the lexical information from *the* and *book* is shown:

(17)

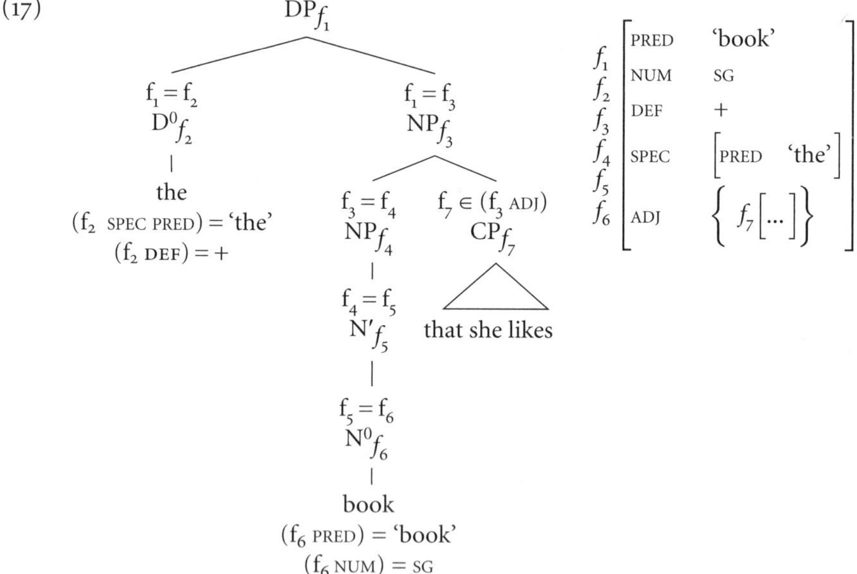

Details of the instantiation mechanism for the c-structure to f-structure mapping can be found in Bresnan (2001: 56–60) and Dalrymple (2001: 122–125).

In the remainder of the book, the instantiation step will be skipped. I will instead assume the convention that f-structures are labelled mnemonically with the first letter of their PRED. I will also abbreviate features where there is no danger of confusion; this includes leaving out the subcategorization information in PRED values. The f-structure in (9), given these conventions, would be as follows:

(18)
$$b\begin{bmatrix}\text{PRED} & \text{`book'}\\ \text{NUM} & \text{SG}\\ \text{DEF} & +\\ \text{SPEC} & \begin{bmatrix}\text{PRED} & \text{`the'}\end{bmatrix}\\ \text{ADJ} & \left\{ l\begin{bmatrix}\text{PRED} & \text{`like'}\\ \text{SUBJ} & p\begin{bmatrix}\text{PRED} & \text{`pro'}\\ \text{PERS} & 3\\ \text{NU M} & \text{SG}\\ \text{GEND} & \text{FEM}\end{bmatrix}\\ \text{TENSE} & \text{PRES}\end{bmatrix}\right\}\end{bmatrix}$$

F-structure labels are arbitrary up to identity. If more than one f-structure would get the same label, they are differentiated using numerals (e.g., *p1* and *p2*) or one is assigned an arbitrary distinct label.

Functional descriptions are a set of constraints, some members of which are equations. There are two main kinds of functional equations: *defining equations* and *constraining equations*. Defining equations, which are the sort we have seen so far, add information to an f-structure. For example, suppose a lexical entry for a verb has the following defining equation:

(19) $(\uparrow \text{ SUBJ NUM}) = \text{SG}$

Whether the subject of the verb adds this information or not, the f-structure will contain it, due to the verb's defining equation. This contrasts with a constraining equation, indicated with a subscript $_c$ on the equal sign. A constraining equation checks the f-structure to make sure the equation holds, but does not itself add the information. For example, suppose the verb instead had the following constraining equation:

(20) $(\uparrow \text{ SUBJ NUM}) =_c \text{SG}$

Now the verb itself does not add the information—it checks to see if it is has been added by something else. The constraining equation cannot be satisfied if the f-structure does not contain the information.

Three other kinds of constraints, which function similarly to constraining equations in checking the presence of independently added information, are *existential constraints*, *negative existential constraints*, and *negative equations*. An existential constraint checks that a certain attribute or path of attributes exists in the f-structure but does not state anything about its value. For example, the expression (↑ SUBJ) indicates that the f-structure designated by ↑ must have a SUBJ feature, regardless of its value. The negative version of this, ¬ (↑ SUBJ), indicates that ↑ cannot have a SUBJ feature, regardless of its value. A negative equation, such as (↑ NUM) ≠ SG, indicates that the feature cannot have the given value, but allows the feature to exist with any other value. Boolean connectives other than negation can also be used in functional equations and have the expected interpretations (for details, see Bresnan, 2001: 62).

F-descriptions are stated using regular expressions over f-structure paths. The regular language supports the usual operations, including Kleene star (*) and Kleene plus ($^+$), disjunction (|), and conjunction, which is normally implicit, but is sometimes indicated by ∧ or &. Kaplan and Zaenen (1989) use the regular language—in particular, the notion of sets of strings defined by regular expressions—to provide *functional uncertainty* for f-descriptions with regular expressions over paths. Dalrymple (2001: 143) gives the following definitions:

(21) $(f\ \alpha) = v$ holds if and only if f is an f-structure, α is a set of strings, and for some s in the set of strings α, $(f\ s) = v$.

(22) $(f\ as) \equiv ((f\ a)\ s)$ for a symbol a and (possibly empty) string of symbols s.
$(\mathrm{f}\ \epsilon) \equiv f$, where ϵ is the empty string.

This kind of functional uncertainty is typically called *outside-in* functional uncertainty and is used in unbounded dependencies, as we will see below. Outside-in descriptions do not need to invoke uncertainty, though; if there is no uncertainty in the expression, it is just outside-in functional application. We have already seen examples like the following:

(23) (↑ SUBJ NUM) = SG

Any f-description that starts with an f-structure and works its way in counts as an outside-in functional application.

The opposite cases of *inside-out* functional application and functional uncertainty (Halvorsen and Kaplan, 1988; Dalrymple, 1993) are also defined.

These are f-descriptions which have one or more attributes before the metavariable, e.g.:

(24) (SUBJ ↑)

This is an inside-out existential equation that states that the ↑ is the SUBJ of some f-structure. Dalrymple (2001: 145) gives the following definitions for inside-out functional uncertainty:

(25) $(\alpha\ f) \equiv g$ if and only if g is an f-structure, α is a set of strings, and for some s in the set of strings α, $(s\ f) \equiv g$.

(26) $(\epsilon\ f) \equiv f$, where ϵ is the empty string.
$(s a\ f) \equiv (s\ (a\ f))$ for a symbol a and a (possibly empty) string of symbols s.

One last feature of the regular language for f-descriptions should be mentioned. The set membership symbol ∈ can be used to state that a certain f-structure is in a certain set, as we have already seen above, but it can also be used as in attribute in a regular expression (Dalrymple, 2001: 154). For example, the following f-description states that the f-structure ↑ is in some adjunct set:

(27) (ADJUNCT ∈ ↑)

The set membership symbol thus serves two functions: it states membership and it allows traversal in and out of sets in path descriptions. The interpretation is always contextually clear.

3.3.2 *Well-Formedness Criteria*

There are three principal well-formedness criteria for f-structures: *Completeness*, *Coherence*, and *Consistency* (also known as *Uniqueness*). Completeness requires that all subcategorized arguments represented in a PRED feature must be present in the f-structure. Coherence requires that all arguments that are present in the f-structure must be subcategorized by a PRED. Formal definitions of Completeness and Coherence can be found in Dalrymple (2001: 35–39) and in section 5.3.2 of chapter 5.

For example, consider the verb *like* in the following two f-structures:

(28)
$$\begin{bmatrix} \text{PRED} & \text{`like}\langle\text{SUBJ, OBJ}\rangle\text{'} \\ \text{SUBJ} & \begin{bmatrix} \ \end{bmatrix} \end{bmatrix}$$

(29) 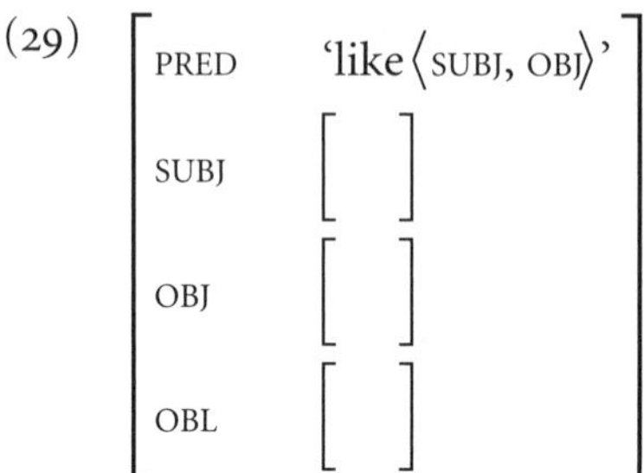

The first f-structure is incomplete: it is missing a subcategorized OBJECT. The second f-structure is incoherent: it contains an unsubcategorized OBLIQUE. As mentioned above, I adopt the convention of abbreviating PRED features without the subcategorized grammatical functions, on the assumption that the f-structure is complete and coherent unless otherwise indicated. For example, the PRED for *likes* would just be 'like'. I also adopt the further convention of abbreviating the information inside an f-structure using the word that contributes the f-structure. For example, the f-structure to which *like* contributes would be abbreviated as ["like"].

Consistency, or Uniqueness, is the requirement that each f-structure attribute have at most one value, which ensures that f-structures are functions from attributes to values. PRED features are special in this regard as semantic forms. Semantic forms are always unique. This means that two f-structures cannot be equated if they each have a PRED, even if the PRED values are identical.

3.4 Semantic Structure

Semantic structure is projected from functional structure via the σ correspondence function. Semantic structures are used as resources in linear logic proofs in Glue Semantics. The level of semantic structure—as a representational level, as opposed to as a resource pool for proofs in Glue Semantics—has not received nearly as much attention as constituent structure and functional structure. An exception to this is the LFG theory of anaphora, as initially put forward by Dalrymple (1993). Dalrymple argues that binding relations should be represented at semantic structure. Since semantic structure is projected from f-structure, this allows a treatment of anaphora that takes both syntactic and semantic factors into account. This approach has been pursued in the Glue Semantics theory of anaphora, where binders are represented at semantic structure using the feature ANTECEDENT (Dalrymple, 2001); this is reviewed in the next chapter. The role of semantic structure in binding is also pursued in Asudeh (2005*b*). Two other semantic structure features in Glue Semantics are VARIABLE (VAR) and RESTRICTION (RESTR). These are used in providing common noun meanings and in the treatment of generalized quantifiers; this is also reviewed in the next chapter.

3.5 Templates

An LFG template is a label for a functional description—a set of equations and constraints that describes linguistic structures, such as the functional descriptions that describe f-structures (Dalrymple *et al.*, 2004*b*; Asudeh et al., 2008; Crouch et al., 2011). Template invocation is denoted by the prefix '@' in a functional description. The semantics of template invocation is substitution. Any occurrence of a template in a lexical entry or rule can be equivalently replaced by the grammatical description that the template is associated with. Templates are therefore purely abbreviatory devices, but can nevertheless capture linguistic generalizations, since associating a grammatical description with a template treats the description as a natural class. Thus, a grammar with templates is extensionally equivalent to the same grammar with all templates replaced by their associated grammatical descriptions, but the first grammar might express generalizations that the second grammar does not.

Templates can also encode information hierarchically, since template definitions may refer to other templates. This is reminiscent of the type hierarchies of HPSG (Pollard and Sag, 1987, 1994) and Sign-Based Construction Grammar (SBCG; Michaelis, 2010, Sag, 2010). There are nonetheless some important differences between template hierarchies and type hierarchies. Type hierarchies represent relations between structures, while template hierarchies represent relations between descriptions of structures. Unlike types, templates do not appear in grammatical structures, but only in descriptions that the structures must satisfy. Type hierarchies in HPSG and SBCG represent inheritance in an *and/or* semilattice. The daughters of a type represent disjoint sub-types (*or*) and a sub-type may be a sub-type of multiple mothers, which are conjoined super-types (*and*). In contrast, template hierarchies represent inclusion, rather than inheritance. If template B is a sub-template of template A, then the description that A labels is included in the description that B labels.

The template for English agreement in (30) is a simple illustration of how templates can encode linguistic generalizations.

(30) 3SG = $(\uparrow \text{SUBJ PERS}) = 3$
$(\uparrow \text{SUBJ NUM}) = \text{SG}$

Verbs with third singular agreement, such as *smiles*, would invoke this template as follows:[6]

(31) *smiles* (↑ PRED) = 'smile⟨SUBJ⟩'
@3SG

Since the template is just an abbreviation, the lexical entry in (31) is completely equivalent to an entry in which the template invocation is replaced with the equations that it labels. However, use of the template explicitly generalizes across the verbs in question—they all call the @3SG template—whereas the generalization is only implicit in the version without the template.

Functional descriptions in LFG may contain the boolean operations of conjunction, disjunction, and negation. Templates therefore also support boolean operations. For example, the @3SG template can be negated in a lexical entry:

(32) *smile* (↑ PRED) = 'laugh⟨SUBJ⟩'
¬@3SG

This further underscores the ability of a template to capture generalizations, since now another set of verbs is identifiable as the set that calls the 3SG template but negates it.

The lexical entries for *smiles* and *smile* are both 'daughters' of the template 3SG, because both entries include the template, although one negates it and the other does not. This is captured in the following small hierarchy:

(33) 3SG
smiles *smile*

This hierarchy illustrates the difference between a hierarchy that represents inclusion, as in LFG template hierarchies, and a hierarchy that represents inheritance, as in HPSG or SBCG type hierarchies. Both *smiles* and *smile* include the information in the 3SG template, but it would not make sense in an inheritance hierarchy for *smile* to inherit from a *3sg* type.

Templates can also take arguments. For example, a template for intransitive verbs can be defined as in (34). The lexical entry for *smiles* is accordingly revised as in (35).

(34) INTRANS(P) = (↑ PRED) = 'P⟨SUBJ⟩'

(35) *smiles* @INTRANS(smile)
@3SG

[6] This is a simplification: the morphology would in fact associate the agreement information with the suffix, rather than this information being repeated across the present tense verbal paradigm.

This lexical entry is equivalent to the following template-free lexical entry:

(36) *smiles* $(\uparrow \text{PRED}) = \text{`smile}\langle\text{SUBJ}\rangle\text{'}$
$(\uparrow \text{SUBJ PERS}) = 3$
$(\uparrow \text{SUBJ NUM}) = \text{SG}$

Another way in which templates express generalizations is by allowing the lexical entry, as in (34), to contain only the idiosyncratic information of the root, i.e. that this is the verb 'smile', as opposed to some other intransitive verb. The entry for *frowns* would differ only in the argument to the parametrized INTRANS template, which would be 'frown' instead of 'smile'. A final, notational point: In Dalrymple *et al.* (2004*b*) and in the implemented version of templates (Crouch et al., 2011), multiple arguments to templates with arity of greater than one are separated by spaces, as in @T(f g). I will instead separate arguments to templates with commas, as in @T(f,g).

3.6 Anaphora and Syntax

Anaphoric binding in LFG is mediated by *binding equations* (Dalrymple, 1993: 120), which are used in LFG's binding theory (Dalrymple, 1993, 2001; Bresnan, 2001). Binding equations state syntactic constraints on binding and relate bound elements and their binders. The following is an example of a binding equation:

(37) $(\uparrow_\sigma \text{ANTECEDENT}) = ((\text{GF}^* \text{ GF} \uparrow) \text{ GF})_\sigma$

This equation identifies the binder of the pronominal in question using the semantic structure feature ANTECEDENT. The semantic structure of the f-structure designated by $\uparrow$ is $\uparrow_\sigma$, the σ projection of $\uparrow$.

The binding relation may be stated by co-indexation (see, for example, the expository binding theory of Bresnan, 2001: 212–235), as it is in much of the Principles and Parameters binding literature. Co-indexation is a symmetric relation: if A is co-indexed with B, then B is co-indexed with A. The binding relations employed here are asymmetric: if A is the ANTECEDENT of B, then B is not the ANTECEDENT of A. Higginbotham's 'linking' theory (Higginbotham, 1983, 1985) is a similarly asymmetric binding theory (also see Safir, 2004*a*,*b*).

The left-hand side of the binding equation (37) identifies a semantic structure. The semantic structure is the value of the attribute ANTECEDENT in the semantic structure of the pronoun. The right-hand side of the equation also identifies a semantic structure, as indicated by the subscripted σ correspondence function. The equation therefore equates two semantic structures, but is otherwise similar to defining equations that have already been encountered for f-structures.

The right-hand side of the equation specifies (1) the domain in which the antecedent can occur, (2) the path from the antecedent to the pronoun, and (3) the grammatical function of the antecedent. The latter is unrestricted, in this case, but could be further constrained to, e.g., SUBJECT (if the anaphor is subject-oriented). This information can be schematized as follows (Dalrymple, 1993: 120):

(38) ((DomainPath ↑) AntecedentPath)

The expression (DomainPath ↑), also known as the binding domain (Dalrymple, 2001: 283–291), is an inside-out functional equation. The expression specifies where the antecedent can occur. It specifies an f-structure from which there is a path, DomainPath, to ↑. AntecedentPath is the path from the f-structure identified by the DomainPath expression to the f-structure of ↑'s antecedent.

The binding domain may be suitably restricted through off-path constraints, such as ¬ (→ SUBJ); off-path constraints are discussed further in the next section. The expression → is an f-structure variable (like ↑ and ↓); it refers to the value of the f-structure attribute which it annotates. For example, the f-structure equation in (39) is suitable for the binding domain of English reflexives (Dalrymple, 2001: 279–287).

(39) (GF* GF ↑)
¬ (→ SUBJ)

The off-path constraint states that for each f-structure *f* identified by the regular expression GF*, *f* cannot contain a SUBJECT grammatical function. Notice that the off-path constraint does not apply to the f-structure in which the pronoun occurs, (GF ↑), which is embedded one level further than the first f-structure to which the off-path constraint applies. This restricts the binding domain of the reflexive to the smallest f-structure that contains the reflexive and a SUBJECT grammatical function, the "Minimal Complete Nucleus" of the reflexive (see, e.g. Dalrymple, 2001: 281). The binding domain in (39), with the off-path constraint given, effectively captures Principle A.

Returning to the specific binding equation in (37), we see that the binding domain is (GF* GF ↑). The f-structure variable ↑ specifies the f-structure of the anaphor. The expression (GF ↑) identifies the f-structure, call it *g*, of the predicate that takes the anaphor as an argument. The expression GF* uses Kleene star to identify an f-structure, call it *f*, that is found by moving zero or more GFs out from *g*. The f-structure identified by (GF* GF ↑) is thus either *g*, the f-structure in which the anaphor occurs, or an f-structure that can be found by following a series of GF attributes outward from *g*. The binding domain expression, (GF* GF ↑), thus specifies the possible f-structures within which the anaphor finds the f-structure that maps to its antecedent at semantic structure. The binding domain in this equation is completely unrestricted; this is the "Root Domain" (Dalrymple, 2001: 284).

The inside-out binding equation in (37) is appropriate as part of the lexical entry for a syntactic anaphor, such as a reflexive, and suitably restricts the anaphor's relationship to its antecedent. For further details of such binding equations, see Dalrymple (1993, 2001) and Bresnan (2001). However, the binding relation in binder-resumptive dependencies is not associated with the resumptive pronoun, which is not necessarily a syntactic anaphor. Instead, it is associated with the binder in the dependency and is stated at the top of the binder-resumptive dependency using an outside-in equation like the following:

(40) $(\uparrow \text{GF})_\sigma = ((\uparrow \text{GF}^+)_\sigma \text{ ANTECEDENT})$

This particular equation states that one of the grammatical functions in the f-structure identified by ↑ is the ANTECEDENT of a grammatical function that is found in the same f-structure or in any embedded f-structure. The grammatical function that gets bound may have its own inside-out binding equation that further restricts the binding.

3.7 Unbounded Dependencies

Unbounded dependencies in LFG have traditionally been analysed in terms of the grammaticized discourse functions TOPIC and FOCUS in f-structure (Bresnan and Mchombo, 1987; Kaplan and Zaenen, 1989; King, 1995; Bresnan, 2001; Dalrymple, 2001). For example, the topicalized constituent or relative pronoun that is the top of a topicalization or relative clause dependency respectively, is a TOPIC, whereas the *wh*-phrase at the top of a constituent question dependency is a FOCUS. However, this conflates the syntactic role of the top of the unbounded dependency with its information structure role (King, 1997; Alsina, 2008; Asudeh, 2011*c*). This is against the spirit of the Correspondence Architecture, since part of the motivation of the architecture is to avoid conflation of grammatically distinct information in a single representation.[7]

[7] For some languages, the grammatical function that represents the top of the unbounded dependency may be a set-valued feature, because there are potentially multiple fronted elements (Bresnan, 2001; Dalrymple, 2001).

I posit a single grammatical function in f-structure for unbounded dependencies (Asudeh, 2011*c*), where this function can be mapped to either information structure TOPIC or FOCUS (King and Zaenen, 2004; Dalrymple and Nikolaeva, 2011), as appropriate. This avoids complicating syntactic generalizations that are neutral to the TOPIC/FOCUS distinction, but allows relevant distinctions to be made where necessary. The f-structure grammatical function for unbounded dependencies is UDF, short for UNBOUNDED DEPENDENCY FUNCTION. Alsina (2008) also assumes a single f-structure function, but he calls it OP. However, the name 'OP' conflates the syntax and semantics of unbounded dependencies and is perhaps not appropriate for all unbounded dependencies.

Unbounded dependencies are integrated into syntactic representations according to the Extended Coherence Condition, or ECC (among others, see Zaenen, 1980; Bresnan and Mchombo, 1987; Fassi-Fehri, 1988). Bresnan and Mchombo (1987: 746) formulate the condition as follows:

(41) **Extended Coherence Condition**
FOCUS and TOPIC must be linked to the semantic predicate argument structure of the sentence in which they occur, either by functionally or by anaphorically binding an argument.

Filler-gap unbounded dependencies satisfy the ECC through functional equality: the UDF is equated with some subcategorized grammatical function. Binder-resumptive unbounded dependencies satisfy the ECC through anaphoric binding, in the case of syntactically active resumptives, or through functional equality, in the case of syntactically inactive resumptives. This syntactic difference is the essential distinction between the two kinds of binder-resumptive dependency. Binder-resumptive dependencies are discussed in detail in chapter 6. The following discussion of the general LFG approach to unbounded dependencies concerns just the simpler filler-gap case.

The UDF grammatical function of a filler is functionally equated with some subcategorized grammatical function in order to satisfy the ECC. I assume a trace-less theory of unbounded dependencies, following Kaplan and Zaenen (1989) and Dalrymple (2001). Integration of a filler, in this theory, is accomplished by an outside-in functional uncertainty equation that is associated with the filler or a c-structural position. For example, the following functional uncertainty states that the UDF is equated to a GF embedded in zero or more COMP f-structures:

(42) $(\uparrow \text{UDF}) = (\uparrow \text{COMP}^* \ \text{GF})$

This would account for sentences like the following:

(43) Who did you see?

(44) Who did Mary say that you saw?

(45) Who did Mary claim that John alleged that you saw?

There is nothing that identifies gaps as such in this theory, neither a trace nor any other gap-specific grammatical device (e.g., the *gap-synsem* of Bouma et al. 2001). The filler-gap dependency is analysed as a single f-structure simultaneously serving as the value of both the UDF grammatical function and the subcategorized, base grammatical function.

The functional uncertainty path above is clearly inadequate. For example, it does not handle extraction from an adjunct, as in the following sentence:

(46) What do you play records on?

Dalrymple (2001: 396, 404, 407) gives the following path for English filler-gap dependencies (adapted to UDF, instead of TOPIC/FOCUS):

(47)
$$(\uparrow \mathrm{UDF}) = (\uparrow \{\mathrm{XCOMP} \mid \underset{(\rightarrow\ \mathrm{UD}) \neq -}{\mathrm{COMP}} \mid \underset{(\rightarrow\ \mathrm{TENSE})}{\mathrm{OBJ}}\}^{*}\ \{(\mathrm{ADJ}\ \underset{\neg(\rightarrow\ \mathrm{TENSE})}{\in})\ (\mathrm{GF}) \mid \mathrm{GF}\})$$

According to this equation, the UDF can be equated with a grammatical function that is arbitrarily deeply embedded in any number of XCOMP, COMP, or OBJ grammatical functions. The UDF can also be equated with (1) an adjunct of or (2) an argument of an untensed ADJUNCT of one of these grammatical functions (Dalrymple, 2001: 396). The feature UD −, where UD stands for 'unbounded dependency', marks f-structures that the path cannot reach into, such as complements of non-bridge verbs like *whisper*. The expression (47) is intended here mainly as an illustration. It shows that a wide range of possible unbounded dependency paths can be captured in a single, complex functional uncertainty expression.

The equation also illustrates the use of *off-path constraints* (Dalrymple, 1993: 128–131) to further restrict the unbounded dependency. Off-path constraints can be defined as follows (Dalrymple, 2001: 151):

(48) In an expression $\underset{(\leftarrow\ s)}{a}$, '←' refers to the f-structure of which *a* is an attribute.

(49) In an expression $\underset{(\rightarrow\ s)}{a}$, '→' refers to the value of the attribute *a*.

The off-path metavariables refer to the f-structure that has the annotated attribute as its value (←) or the f-structure that is the value of the annotated attribute (→). For example, in the above expression, the off-path constraint ¬ (→ TENSE) entails that there cannot be extraction from a tensed adjunct. The constraint blocks sentences such as the following:

(50) *John is the man who we laughed when we saw.

The specification of the grammatical functions in the functional uncertainty together with the off-path constraints constrain possible unbounded dependencies and extraction sites. It may be that the unbounded dependency path can be substantially simplified, given arguments that some constraints on extraction are extra-grammatical (Cinque, 1990; Rizzi, 1990; Deane, 1991; Kluender, 1991, 1998, 2004; Kluender and Kutas, 1993; Goodluck and Rochemont, 1992; Hofmeister and Sag, 2010; Sag, 2010).

I do not use complex functional uncertainties in much of what follows, although off-path constraints will become relevant in some discussion of constraints on extraction in subsequent chapters. The c-structure rule in (51) for introducing unbounded dependency functions suffices. The unbounded dependency path in the right-hand side of equation (47) is here abbreviated as 'UDFPATH'.

(51)
$$\text{CP} \longrightarrow \left\{ \begin{array}{c} \text{XP} \\ (\uparrow \text{UDF}) = \downarrow \\ (\uparrow \text{UDF}) = (\uparrow \text{UDFPATH}) \end{array} \middle| \begin{array}{c} \epsilon \\ (\uparrow \text{UDF PRED}) = \text{'pro'} \\ (\uparrow \text{UDF}) = (\uparrow \text{UDFPATH}) \end{array} \right\} \begin{array}{c} \text{C}' \\ \uparrow = \downarrow \\ \end{array}$$

This rule allows an XP to be generated in SpecCP that maps to UDF at f-structure. It also allows for the generation of a relative clause without a relative pronoun (e.g., *a guy I know*). This is accomplished by using the empty string to introduce material into f-structure without anything being present in c-structure. The material that is introduced is the specification that the UDF's PRED has the value 'pro', which is appropriate for a missing relative pronoun. The rule is both unconstrained and not general enough, but rather than adding details that would distract attention from more relevant points, I just assume that the methods outlined by Dalrymple (2001: 400ff.) can be applied appropriately.

The f-structure for the relative clause *the book that she endorses*, with the unbounded dependency properly integrated, is shown in (52); the c-structure is shown in (12) above.

(52)

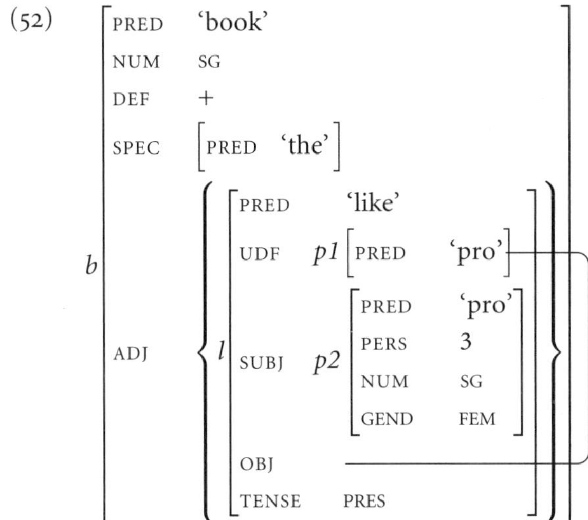

3.8 Raising

Raising is represented as functional equality between a grammatical function of the raising verb and the subject of its open complement (Bresnan, 1982*a*), which is a predicative or infinitival complement. An open complement is represented as the grammatical function XCOMP and lacks a subject of its own. The XCOMP must have its subject specified by the predicate that selects the XCOMP, through a local functional equality called a 'functional control' equation (Bresnan, 1982*a*). The nomenclature is perhaps somewhat misleading, because these equations are used in the analysis of both control and raising. The raising equation for subject raising is:

(53) $(\uparrow \text{SUBJ}) = (\uparrow \text{XCOMP SUBJ})$

The matrix and subordinate subjects are identified at f-structure and share a single, token-identical value.

For example, the f-structure for (54) is shown in (55)

(54) Thora seems happy.

(55)

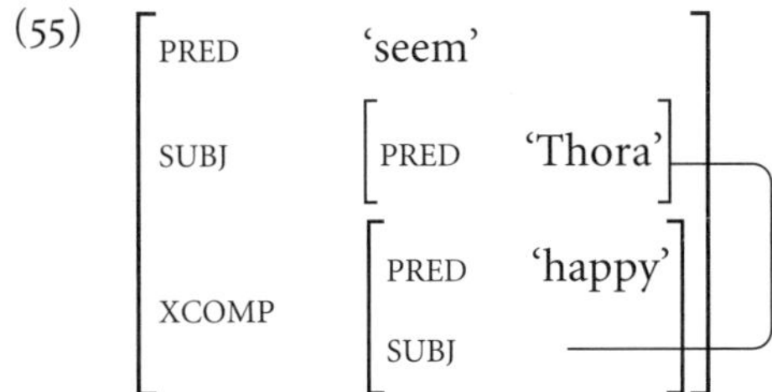

An infinitival raising complement is handled similarly:

(56) Thora seems to enjoy cookies.

(57) 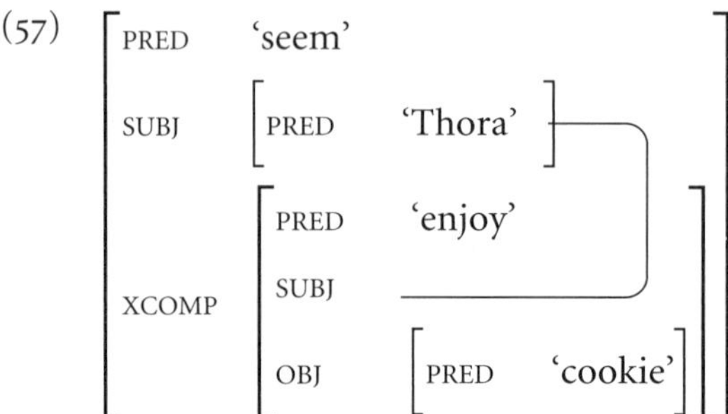

Raising is thus a lexically controlled local dependency and involves simultaneous instantiation of two grammatical functions to a single f-structure value. There is no movement involved in raising and the target of raising in the complement is not represented in c-structure. For further details, including c-structures, and references for the LFG analysis of raising, see Dalrymple (2001), Asudeh (2005*a*), and Asudeh and Toivonen (2009).

4

Glue Semantics

This chapter is a brief introduction to Glue Semantics (Glue) for Lexical-Functional Grammar, the approach to semantic composition and the syntax–semantics interface that is assumed in this work. Section 4.1 introduces the basic theory of composition and interpretation. Section 4.2 introduces the variable-free treatment of anaphora that is standard in Glue Semantics. Section 4.3 introduces the underspecified treatment of scope-taking operators.

There are several further sources for information on Glue Semantics, of which I list only a selection here. A general introduction is provided by Dalrymple (2001). The foundational paper is Dalrymple et al. (1993) and several other key papers can be found in Dalrymple (1999), especially Dalrymple et al. (1999*a*,*b*,*c*), Crouch and van Genabith (1999), and van Genabith and Crouch (1999*a*). Lev (2007) uses Glue as the basis for detailed meaning representations in a computational semantics system. Kokkonidis (2008) reformulates Glue as a first-order logical system, in lieu of the partly second-order system assumed here and in much other work on Glue. The relationship between Glue Semantics and Lexical-Functional Grammar is also explored in a number of papers by Andrews (2004, 2007, 2008, 2011). Crouch and van Genabith (2000) is an unpublished introduction to linear logic for linguists and also features a good technical introduction to Glue. Some linguistically oriented references on linear logic are provided in the appendix of the present volume. Lastly, sketches of Glue Semantics for other frameworks are provided for Head-Driven Phrase Structure Grammar by Asudeh and Crouch (2002*c*) and for Tree-Adjoining Grammar by Frank and van Genabith (2001).

4.1 Composition and Interpretation

The elements of semantic composition in Glue Semantics are *meaning constructors*. Meaning constructors are mainly associated with lexical items, although they can also be associated with non-terminal nodes in c-structure. Each constructor has the following form:

(1) $\mathcal{M} : G$

$\mathcal{M}$ is a term from some representation of meaning, a *meaning language*, paired by the uninterpreted colon symbol with G, a term of the *glue logic*. The glue logic performs composition by 'sticking meanings together'. A fragment of linear logic (Girard, 1987) serves as the glue logic (Dalrymple et al., 1993, 1999*a*,*b*).

The meaning constructors are used as premises in a linear logic proof that produces a sentential meaning. A successful Glue proof of sentential semantics proves the following sequent (following Crouch and van Genabith, 2000: 117), where Γ is the set of premises and G_t is a linear logic term of type t:

(2) $\Gamma \vdash \mathcal{M} : G_t$

Alternative derivations from the same set of premises result in semantic ambiguity, such as scope ambiguity (Dalrymple, 2001; Asudeh, 2006). The logics for $\mathcal{M}$ and G are presented in appendix A.1.

The fragment of linear logic that is assumed here is a limited modality-free, multiplicative fragment of intuitionistic linear logic, MILL$_l$. The logic MILL$_l$ does not have existential quantification or negation. The logic has universal quantification, but it is not fully higher order, since the quantification is strictly limited to universal quantification over t-type atoms of the linear logic (Crouch and van Genabith, 2000: 124). Although the logic is quite weak from a proof-theoretic perspective (there are many statements it cannot prove), it is sufficient to capture linguistic phenomena, such as basic composition of functors and arguments, anaphora, and scope. See appendix A for further details of MILL$_l$.

Three proof rules of MILL$_l$ are dominant in the analyses in this book: conjunction elimination for the multiplicative linear conjunction, $\otimes$, and implication introduction and elimination for linear implication, $\multimap$.[1] These are shown in (3), in natural deduction format.

(3) a. Implication Elimination

$$\cfrac{\begin{matrix}\vdots \\ A\end{matrix} \qquad \begin{matrix}\vdots \\ A \multimap B\end{matrix}}{B} \multimap_{\mathcal{E}}$$

[1] Other common terms for the implication rules are 'abstraction' or 'hypothetical reasoning', for implication introduction, and 'modus ponens' for elimination.

b. Implication Introduction

$$\frac{\begin{array}{c}[A]^1\\ \vdots\\ B\end{array}}{A \multimap B}\multimap_{\mathcal{I},1}$$

c. Conjunction Elimination

$$\frac{\begin{array}{c}\vdots\\ A \otimes B\end{array} \quad \begin{array}{c}[A]^1\ [B]^2\\ \vdots\\ C\end{array}}{C}\otimes_{\mathcal{E},1,2}$$

The bracket notation in (3b) and (3c) indicates an assumption. The numerical flags keep track of which assumptions have been withdrawn and which are active.

Proof rules for linear logic are paired with proof terms by the Curry–Howard isomorphism (also known as 'formulas-as-types'; Curry and Feys, 1958, 1995; Howard, 1980). The isomorphism establishes a formal correspondence between natural deduction and terms in the lambda calculus. These terms have useful applications, such as stating identity criteria for proofs. These identity criteria can be used to determine if two proofs are equivalent. Term reduction is thus related to proof normalization (Prawitz, 1965), as discussed by Gallier (1995). The basic insight behind the isomorphism is that implications correspond to functional types. Implication elimination therefore corresponds to *functional application* and implication introduction corresponds to *abstraction*. The basic isomorphism was discovered by Curry (Curry and Feys, 1958, 1995). Howard (1980) extended the isomorphism for other types.

The Curry–Howard term assignments for the three rules in (3) are:

(4) a. Application : Implication Elimination

$$\frac{\begin{array}{c}\vdots\\ a : A\end{array} \qquad \begin{array}{c}\vdots\\ f : A \multimap B\end{array}}{f(a) : B}\multimap_{\mathcal{E}}$$

b. Abstraction : Implication Introduction

$$\frac{\begin{array}{c}[x : A]^1\\ \vdots\\ f : B\end{array}}{\lambda x.f : A \multimap B}\multimap_{\mathcal{I},1}$$

c. Pairwise substitution : Conjunction Elimination

$$\frac{a : A \otimes B \qquad \begin{array}{c}[x : A]^1 \ [y : B]^2 \\ \vdots \\ f : C\end{array}}{\mathsf{let}\ a\ \mathsf{be}\ x \times y\ \mathsf{in}\ f : C} \otimes_{\mathcal{E},1,2}$$

Implication elimination corresponds to functional application. Implication introduction corresponds to abstraction. A variable is assumed and then abstracted over when the assumption is discharged. A multiplicative conjunction $A \otimes B$ corresponds to a tensor product $a \times b$, where a is the proof term of A and b is the proof term of B. The term constructor, let, prevents projection into the individual elements of the tensor pair and therefore enforces pairwise substitution (Abramsky, 1993; Benton et al., 1993; Crouch and van Genabith, 2000: 88). A let expression β-reduces as follows:

(5) $\mathsf{let}\ a \times b\ \mathsf{be}\ x \times y\ \mathsf{in}\ f \ \Rightarrow_\beta \ f[a/x, b/y]$

The substitution of the pair is simultaneous and does not involve projection into the members. The let term is a slightly more structured form of functional application.

The Curry–Howard term assignments determine operations in the meaning language, but they do not themselves constitute the meaning language. The term assignments constructed by rules of proof for linear logic result in *linear* lambda terms (Abramsky, 1993), in which every lambda-bound variable occurs exactly once, not permitting vacuous abstraction or multiple abstraction. The proof terms therefore satisfy resource sensitivity. However, lexically contributed meanings need not contain only linear lambdas (for a similar point about the Lambek Calculus, see Moortgat, 1997: 122ff.). This is not a violation of the isomorphism though, because the isomorphism says nothing about the internal structure of the functions that correspond to rules of proof. The relationship between proof terms and the meaning language, however, means that the meaning language must support the operations determined by the Curry–Howard isomorphism.

The meaning language therefore must support application and abstraction, as well as product pairs for the multiplicative conjunction. This is straightforward if the meaning language is a lambda calculus of some kind. The meaning language can be construed as simply being a convenient representation for the model theory itself, as discussed by Jacobson (1999: 122). The lambda calculus is one convenient way to describe the functions in the model, but it is not the only one, as discussed in detail in Asudeh (2005*b*: 392–393). The meaning language for Glue is therefore variable-free in the usual sense of variable-free semantics (Jacobson, 1999): all variables are bound, so there is no crucial use of variables. This is underscored by the fact that the combinators of combinatory logic (Curry and Feys, 1958; Hindley and Seldin, 1986), which dispense with the variables of the lambda calculus, could be used to represent the meaning language instead (Asudeh, 2005*b*: 393). However, combinatory logic is harder to read than the lambda calculus. It is common even in Combinatory Categorial Grammar to adopt the more easily readable lambda calculus for meaning representations (Jacobson, 1999: 122), even though the combinators form the heart of the theory. The meaning language is presented in appendix A.1, where I assume a simple extensional semantics.

There are two further proof rules for MILL$_l$, conjunction introduction ($\otimes_{\mathcal{I}}$) and universal elimination ($\forall_{\mathcal{E}}$).[2] The rule for conjunction introduction corresponds to pair formation in the meaning language:

(6) Product : Conjunction Introduction

$$\frac{\begin{matrix}\vdots & & \vdots \\ a : A & & b : B\end{matrix}}{a \times b : A \otimes B}\otimes_{\mathcal{I}}$$

The rule for universal elimination is trivial and is used only implicitly; it is provided in appendix A.

The universal quantifier symbol ∀ occurs only in the glue logic side of meaning constructors. The universal ∀ is interpreted as 'any', not 'all', in linear logic (Crouch and van Genabith, 2000: 89), since linear logic is a resource logic. The universal states that some property holds of all relevant resources, but it does not consume all resources that it quantifies over. Rather, any one resource in the domain of quantification can be consumed. This contrasts with the existential quantifier (which is absent in this fragment). In the case of the existential quantifier, the property holds of some resource, but we cannot arbitrarily pick just any resource, since the property may not hold of that resource. That the linear logic universal is a true universal is further underscored by the fact that the universal introduction and elimination rules are identical to those of intuitionistic logic (Gamut, 1991; van Dalen, 2001).

[2] In the version of the linear logic fragment presented in Asudeh (2005*b*: 440–441), I also provided a rule for universal introduction, for a fully balanced logical fragment in which there were introduction and elimination rules for all logical connectives and operators. However, the universal introduction rule is not used, since the only occurrence of universal quantifiers in meaning language terms are in meaning constructors for scope-taking elements. In other words, the universal is never introduced in proof, occurring only in underlying functions in the basic premise set. Therefore, I adopt a more limited version of the linear logic fragment here, without a universal introduction rule.

Meaning constructors are instantiated relative to a particular syntactic parse. The assumption of a syntax separate from the syntax of proof theory allows the logic of composition to be commutative. I am assuming an LFG syntax and grammatical architecture. The linear logic resources for semantic composition in Glue-LFG are nodes in semantic structure, instantiated by the σ projection function. Meaning constructors are thus defined by σ projections on f-structure equations, which are commonly called functional descriptions or f-descriptions. For example, the proper name *Alfie* provides the meaning constructor in (7a) and the intransitive verb *chuckled* the one in (7b).

(7) a. $alfie : \uparrow_{\sigma_e}$

b. $chuckle : (\uparrow \textsc{subj})_{\sigma_e} \multimap \uparrow_{\sigma_t}$

If we had the f-structure (8), with labels as indicated, then the f-descriptions in (7) would get instantiated as in (9):

(8) $f\begin{bmatrix} \textsc{pred} & \text{`chuckle'} \\ \textsc{subj} & g\begin{bmatrix} \textsc{pred} & \text{`Alfie'} \end{bmatrix} \end{bmatrix}$

(9) a. $alfie : g_{\sigma_e}$

b. $chuckle : g_{\sigma_e} \multimap f_{\sigma_t}$

The lexical item *Alfie* contributes the resource that is the σ-projection of its f-structure. The lexical item *chuckled* contributes a resource that is an implication from the σ-projection of its subject to the σ-projection of the verb, where $(f\ \textsc{subj}) = g$ in (8). However, it is often useful to name meaning constructors mnemonically and to suppress the σ and type subscripts. Under these conventions, the normal abbreviation for the resources contributed by *Alfie* and *chuckled*, when the former is the subject of the latter, would be a and $a \multimap c$. This convention provides a schematic presentation of meaning constructors that brings the compositional semantics into focus, by abstracting away from how the meaning constructors are derived from the syntax.

The lexically contributed meaning constructors for the sentence *Alfie chuckled* are then as follows:

(10) 1. $alfie : a$ Lex. **Alfie**

2. $chuckle : a \multimap c$ Lex. **chuckled**

I adopt the general covention of providing the meaning constructors together with their contributors, and a gloss of the contributor if this is appropriate. The fact that the meaning constructor is provided by a lexical item is indicated by 'Lex'. I often suppress the meaning terms in both premise lists and proofs, since the meanings follow from the Curry–Howard isomorphism.

The premises above construct the following proof:

(11)
$$\frac{alfie : a \qquad chuckle : a \multimap c}{chuckle(alfie) : c} \multimap_{\mathcal{E}}$$

The proof tree is annotated with the proof rule that was used ($\multimap_{\mathcal{E}}$). Proof trees will not normally be annotated for implication elimination, because its application is obvious. I will sometimes provide the proof twice, first without the meaning terms, except in the conclusion, and then with the meaning terms. This maximizes ease of readability, since the first pass shows the structure of the proof, which determines the meanings.

Proofs are abstract objects that can be represented in various ways, so there is no privileged status for these proof trees. It makes no more sense to think of proof trees as special than it does to think of '0' as a special representation of zero. The proof above could equivalently be provided in a list style:

(12)
1. $alfie : a$ — Lex. **Alfie**
2. $chuckle : a \multimap c$ — Lex. **chuckled**
3. $chuckle(alfie) : c$ — E$\multimap$, 1, 2

Nevertheless, proof trees are easier to read for larger proofs and that is how proofs will be presented.

4.2 Anaphora

The treatment of anaphora in Glue Semantics is variable-free: pronouns are functions on their antecedents. Variable-free analyses of anaphora in Glue Semantics (Dalrymple et al., 1999*c*) developed independently of variable-free treatments in Categorial Grammar (CG), such as that of Jacobson (1999) in the combinatory tradition and those of Hepple (1990) and Jäger (2003, 2005) in the type-logical tradition. The commutativity of the glue logic, linear logic, is the basis for the difference. In CG, the pronoun's function cannot apply to the antecedent directly. The pronoun does not occur adjacent to its antecedent in the string and the non-commutative logic of CG does not allow arbitrary reordering for direct application of the pronominal function to the antecedent. This necessitates either a series of function compositions such that a function that has composed with the pronoun applies to the antecedent (Jacobson, 1999) or a special implication connective for pronominals and a corresponding proof rule (Jäger, 2003, 2005: 121). In contrast, the pronoun can directly apply to its antecedent in Glue Semantics, because the glue logic is commutative. This in turn means that the variable-free treatment in Glue is an immediate option, since there are no complications caused by intervening material between the pronoun and its antecedent. There is thus no need for either the additional complication of assignment functions or the additional complications of type-shifts or special connectives and proof rules.

The meaning constructor for a pronoun uses multiplicative conjunction, $\otimes$, as shown here:

(13) $\lambda z.z \times z :$
$(\uparrow_\sigma \text{ ANTECEDENT})_e \multimap ((\uparrow_\sigma \text{ ANTECEDENT})_e \otimes \uparrow_{\sigma_e})$

The feature ANTECEDENT is a semantic structure feature, not a f-structure feature.

The pronoun's meaning constructor can be schematically represented as follows, where A is the antecedent's resource and P is the pronoun's resource:

(14) $A \multimap (A \otimes P)$

The pronoun's meaning constructor consumes its antecedent's resource to produce a conjunction of the antecedent resource and the pronoun's resource. The pronoun has a functional type, $\langle e, e \times e \rangle$, from type e to the product type $e \times e$. The antecedent's resource must be replicated in the output of the pronominal function, because consumption of the antecedent in a formula like $A \multimap P$ would result in the antecedent being unavailable for consumption in its role as an argument to a predicate. In other words, if the pronoun were to consume the antecedent without reproducing it, a resource deficit problem would occur. The possible values of ANTECEDENT at semantic structure are constrained by syntactic factors (Dalrymple et al., 1999c: 58), including LFG's binding theory, which is stated using f-structural relations and the mapping from f-structure to semantic structure (Dalrymple 1993; Bresnan 2001; see chapter 3).

The proof in (16) is constructed for the simple example (15), where p indicates 'pronoun' and '$\Rightarrow_\beta$' indicates β-reduction of a lambda term.

(15) Thora said she giggled.

(16)

$$\dfrac{\dfrac{\dfrac{\begin{array}{l} thora : \\ t \end{array} \quad \begin{array}{l} \lambda z.z \times z : \\ t \multimap (t \otimes p) \end{array}}{thora \times thora : t \otimes p} \quad \dfrac{\dfrac{[x : t]^1 \quad \begin{array}{c} \lambda u \lambda q.say(u, q) : \\ t \multimap g \multimap s \end{array}}{\begin{array}{l} \lambda q.say(x, q) : \\ g \multimap s \end{array}} \quad \dfrac{[y : p]^2 \quad \begin{array}{c} \lambda x.giggle(x) : \\ p \multimap g \end{array}}{\begin{array}{l} giggle(y) : \\ g \end{array}}}{say(x, giggle(y)) : s}}{\text{let } thora \times thora \text{ be } x \times y \text{ in } say(x, giggle(y)) : s} \otimes_{\mathcal{E},1,2}}{say(thora, giggle(thora)) : s} \Rightarrow_\beta$$

There is nothing special about the predicate *giggle*. It has not undergone a type-shift or been modified in any way to accommodate the pronoun. The resource corresponding to the pronoun is the right-hand member of the conjunction pairing the antecedent and the pronoun. The pronoun is a type *e* atomic resource. However, the proof rule for conjunction elimination requires simultaneous substitution of the terms of the product pair and does not permit separate projection into either member of the pair. Lastly, the pronoun does not correspond to a free variable, since the corresponding variable is lambda-bound.

The pronoun in example (15) can also refer deictically or be discourse bound. It does not need to be bound by the intra-sentential antecedent. There are a number of options for handling inter-sentential anaphora in Glue Semantics. It is possible to adopt Jacobson's (1999: 134–135) approach, which assumes that free pronouns are left unresolved, such that a sentence need not denote a proposition, but can instead denote a function from the type of a pronominal antecedent to the type of a proposition. Jacobson (1999: 135) notes that it is no worse for a sentential meaning to be dependent on a nominal meaning for saturation then it is for it to be dependent on an assignment function. In the context of resource-logical composition, it might, however, be difficult to ensure that the right proof conditions hold. A proof must be allowed to terminate in a functional type of type $\langle e,t \rangle$, but it must be ensured that the input type *e* is the type of a pronominal antecedent from previous discourse. This is complicated by the fact that the type $\langle e,t \rangle$ is also the type for an unsaturated predicate. In addition, a method has to be established for generalizing to an unbounded number of free pronouns. These complications also apply to Jacobson's approach.

The second option is to move to a dynamic semantics. There are two fundamental methods for making Glue Semantics dynamic. The most straightforward method is to use a dynamic meaning language that supports lambda abstraction, such as Lambda DRT (Bos et al., 1994), as suggested briefly by Dalrymple et al. (1999*b*) and pursued in detail by Kokkoridis (2005), or Compositional DRT (Muskens, 1994), as developed by van Genabith and Crouch (1999*a*). Another method is to keep the meaning language static and to allow the glue logic to also handle contextual update. This effectively moves the dynamics into the linear logic side of Glue terms. This approach was initially developed by Crouch and van Genabith (Crouch and van Genabith, 1999; van Genabith and Crouch, 1999*b*) and was further developed by Dalrymple (2001: 291ff.), but it has not been fully generalized.

I set the issue of inter-sentential anaphora aside here, because a resumptive pronoun is by definition bound within its sentence. Discourse anaphora will be briefly revisited in chapter 11, when the interpretation of certain resumptive-like discourse pronouns is considered.

4.3 Scope

Quantifiers and *wh*-operators are analysed as generalized quantifiers. The following is an example of a lexical entry for a quantifier:

(17) *most*, D^0 $(\uparrow \text{SPEC PRED}) = \text{'most'}$
$\lambda R \lambda S.most(R, S)$:
$[(\uparrow_\sigma \text{VAR})_e \multimap (\uparrow_\sigma \text{RESTR})_t] \multimap \forall X.[(\uparrow_{\sigma e} \multimap X_t) \multimap X_t]$

The c-structure category D^0 is a co-head: its f-structure is identified with the f-structure of its nominal complement. The type of the meaning constructor is the generalized quantifier type $\langle\langle e,t\rangle,\langle\langle e,t\rangle,t\rangle\rangle$.

The restriction of the quantifier, which it consumes as its first argument, is an implication from the common noun's VAR(IABLE) to the noun's RESTR(ICTION), which are semantic structure features contributed by common nouns. The following is an example of a meaning constructor for an ordinary common noun:

(18) *president* : $(\uparrow_\sigma \text{VAR})_e \multimap (\uparrow_\sigma \text{RESTR})_t$

The common noun has type $\langle e,t\rangle$.

The second argument for the generalized quantifier is its scope. The scope-taking part of the quantifier is represented by the expression $\forall X.[(\uparrow_{\sigma e} \multimap X_t) \multimap X_t]$. The universal quantification in the linear logic—which is used by all scope-taking elements and which does not entail an interpretation with universal force—means that the meaning constructor for a quantifier can consume any $\langle e,t\rangle$ implication that depends on the resource of the quantified DP. Universal quantifaction over X allows the quantifier to take wide scope by introducing a hypothesis on the resource instantiating X, discharging the dependency on this resource locally, and then reintroducing it at a later point in the derivation.

Using the mnemonic convention for the glue logic and suppressing σ and type subscripts, the lexically contributed premises in (20) are obtained for sentence (19). The term *president** represents the denotation of the plural common noun.

(19) Most presidents speak.

(20)
1. $\lambda R \lambda S.most(R, S) : (v \multimap r) \multimap \forall X.[(p \multimap X) \multimap X]$ Lex. **most**
2. $president^* : v \multimap r$ Lex. **presidents**
3. $speak : p \multimap s$ Lex. **speak**

From these premises we construct the proof in (21).

(21)
$$\dfrac{\dfrac{\lambda R \lambda S.most(R, S) : (v \multimap r) \multimap \forall X.[(p \multimap X) \multimap X] \quad president^* : v \multimap r}{\lambda S.most(president^*, S) : \forall X.[(p \multimap X) \multimap X]} \quad speak : p \multimap s}{most(president^*, speak) : s} \multimap_{\mathcal{E}}, [s/X]$$

The quantifier takes its scope by finding an appropriate dependency and consuming it through implication elimination. Universal elimination is implicit and the elimination step is annotated with the appropriate substitution.

The following example illustrates the Glue approach to scope ambiguity:

(22) Most presidents speak some language.

Here are the lexically contributed premises:

(23)
1. $\lambda R \lambda S.most(R, S) : (v1 \multimap r1) \multimap \forall X.[(p \multimap X) \multimap X]$ Lex. **most**
2. $president^* : v1 \multimap r1$ Lex. **presidents**
3. $\lambda x \lambda y.speak(x, y) : p \multimap l \multimap s$ Lex. **speak**
4. $\lambda P \lambda Q.some(P, Q) : (v2 \multimap r2) \multimap \forall Y.[(l \multimap Y) \multimap Y]$ Lex. **some**
5. $language : v2 \multimap r2$ Lex. **language**

This single set of premises leads to two Glue proofs, corresponding to the two readings. The surface scope reading is represented in Figure 4.1 and the inverse scope reading is represented in Figure 4.2.

The verb has been curried in Figure 4.2. Currying can be executed in the proof, by making a series of assumptions followed by discharging the assumptions in the order they were made:

(24)
$$\dfrac{\dfrac{\dfrac{\dfrac{\lambda y \lambda x.f(x, y) : b \multimap a \multimap c \quad [v : b]^1}{\lambda x.f(x, v) : a \multimap c} \multimap_{\mathcal{E}} \quad [u : a]^2}{f(u, v) : c} \multimap_{\mathcal{E}}}{\lambda v.f(u, v) : b \multimap c} \multimap_{\mathcal{I},1}}{\lambda u \lambda v.f(u, v) : a \multimap b \multimap c} \multimap_{\mathcal{I},2}$$

$$\frac{\lambda P\lambda Q.some(P,Q) : (v2 \multimap r2) \multimap \forall Y.[(l \multimap Y) \multimap Y] \qquad language : v2 \multimap r2}{\lambda Q.some(language, Q) : \forall Y.[(l \multimap Y) \multimap Y]}$$

$$\frac{\lambda x\lambda y.speak(x,y) : p \multimap l \multimap s \qquad [z : p]^1}{\lambda y.speak(z,y) : l \multimap s}$$

$$\frac{\lambda Q.some(language, Q) : \forall Y.[(l \multimap Y) \multimap Y] \qquad \lambda y.speak(z,y) : l \multimap s}{some(language, \lambda y.speak(z, y)) : s}\;[s/Y]$$

$$\frac{some(language, \lambda y.speak(z, y)) : s}{\lambda z.some(language, \lambda y.speak(z, y)) : p \multimap s}\;\multimap_{\mathcal{I},1}$$

$$\frac{\lambda R\lambda S.most(R,S) : (v1 \multimap r1) \multimap \forall X.[(p \multimap X) \multimap X] \qquad president^* : v1 \multimap r1}{\lambda S.most(president^*, S) : \forall X.[(p \multimap X) \multimap X]}$$

$$\frac{\lambda S.most(president^*, S) : \forall X.[(p \multimap X) \multimap X] \qquad \lambda z.some(language, \lambda y.speak(z, y)) : p \multimap s}{most(president^*, \lambda z.some(language, \lambda y.speak(z, y))) : s}\;[s/X]$$

FIGURE 4.1. Example of a surface scope quantifier proof.

$$
\dfrac{
\dfrac{
\begin{array}{l}\lambda P \lambda Q.some(P,\ Q) : \\ (v2 \multimap r2) \multimap \forall Y.[(l \multimap Y) \multimap Y]\end{array}
\qquad
\begin{array}{l}language\ : \\ v2 \multimap r2\end{array}
}{
\begin{array}{l}\lambda Q.some(language,\ Q) : \\ \forall Y.[(l \multimap Y) \multimap Y]\end{array}
}
\qquad
\dfrac{
\dfrac{
\dfrac{
\begin{array}{l}\lambda R \lambda S.most(R,\ S) : \\ (v1 \multimap r1) \multimap \forall X.[(p \multimap X) \multimap X]\end{array}
\quad
\begin{array}{l}president^{*} : \\ v1 \multimap r1\end{array}
}{
\begin{array}{l}\lambda S.most(president^{*},\ S) : \\ \forall X.[(p \multimap X) \multimap X]\end{array}
}
\quad
\dfrac{
\begin{array}{l}\lambda y \lambda x.speak(x,\ y) : \\ l \multimap p \multimap s\end{array}
\qquad [z : l]^{1}
}{
\begin{array}{l}\lambda x.speak(x,\ z) : \\ p \multimap s\end{array}
}
}{
most(president^{*},\ \lambda x.speak(x, z)) : s
}\ [s/X]
}{
\lambda z.most(president^{*},\ \lambda x.speak(x, z)) : l \multimap s
}\ {\multimap}_{\mathcal{I},1}
}{
some(language,\ \lambda z.most(president^{*},\ \lambda x.speak(x,\ z))) : s
}\ [s/Y]
$$

FIGURE 4.2. Example of an inverse scope quantifier proof.

Throughout this work, I assume a curried alternative where appropriate and suppress this sub-proof.

In sum, scope in Glue Semantics is calculated on linear logic proofs. Scope ambiguity is represented as multiple possible proofs from the same set of premises. There is no need to posit any syntactic ambiguity. There is also no need for any type-shifting mechanism. Further details can be found in Dalrymple et al. (1999*c*), Crouch and van Genabith (1999), Dalrymple (2001), and Asudeh (2006).

4.3.1 *Unbounded Dependencies*

The unbounded dependencies that are typically discussed in the literature on resumptive pronouns are restrictive relative clauses and *wh*-questions. This section illustrates the Glue Semantics treatment of these unbounded dependencies, as shown in Figures 4.3 and 4.4, respectively. There are several more examples of proofs of unbounded dependencies in subsequent chapters.

Restrictive relative clauses are handled by the following kind of meaning constructor:

(25) $\lambda P \lambda Q \lambda x. Q(x) \wedge P(x) :$
$[(\uparrow \text{UDF})_{\sigma_e} \multimap \uparrow_{\sigma_t}] \multimap$
$[[((\text{ADJ} \in \uparrow)_\sigma \text{VAR})_e \multimap ((\text{ADJ} \in \uparrow)_\sigma \text{RESTR})_t] \multimap$
$[((\text{ADJ} \in \uparrow)_\sigma \text{VAR})_e \multimap ((\text{ADJ} \in \uparrow)_\sigma \text{RESTR})_t]]$

Restrictive relative clauses are inside a set-valued ADJUNCT grammatical function at f-structure. This meaning constructor states that the scope of the relative clause is a $\langle e,t \rangle$ dependency on the relative head and that the relative clause restricts the relative head by modifying its common noun meaning constructor.

The schematic form of the relative clause meaning constructor is as follows, where *rel-head* is the semantic structure of the relative head, *pred* is the semantic structure of the predicate that takes the relative head as an argument, and v and r are the VAR and RESTR of the relative head:

(26) $\lambda P \lambda Q \lambda x. Q(x) \wedge P(x) : (\textit{rel-head} \multimap \textit{pred}) \multimap (v \multimap r) \multimap (v \multimap r)$

The relative clause meaning constructor is a common noun modifier of type $\langle\langle e,t \rangle,\langle\langle e,t \rangle,\langle e,t \rangle\rangle\rangle$.

The relative clause meaning constructor can be contributed by the relative pronoun, but it can also be associated directly with the appropriate c-structure rule element in the case of relative clauses that lack overt pronouns:

$$
\dfrac{\begin{array}{l}\lambda R\lambda S.every(R,S) : \\ (v \multimap r) \multimap \forall Y.[(b \multimap Y) \multimap Y]\end{array} \quad \dfrac{\begin{array}{l}book : \\ v \multimap r\end{array} \quad \dfrac{\begin{array}{l}\lambda P\lambda Q\lambda x.Q(x) \wedge P(x) : \\ (b \multimap l) \multimap (v \multimap r) \multimap (v \multimap r)\end{array} \quad \dfrac{\begin{array}{l}isak : \\ i\end{array} \quad \begin{array}{l}\lambda x\lambda y.like(x, y) : \\ i \multimap b \multimap l\end{array}}{\begin{array}{l}\lambda y.like(isak, y) : \\ b \multimap l\end{array}}}{\begin{array}{l}\lambda Q\lambda x.Q(x) \wedge like(isak, x) : \\ (v \multimap r) \multimap (v \multimap r)\end{array}}}{\begin{array}{l}\lambda x.book(x) \wedge like(isak, x) : \\ (v \multimap r)\end{array}}}{\lambda S.every(\lambda x.book(x) \wedge like(isak, x), S) : \forall Y.[(b \multimap Y) \multimap Y]}
$$

FIGURE 4.3. Example of a relative clause proof.

$$\dfrac{\lambda S.\mathcal{Q}(thing, S) : \forall X.[(w \multimap X) \multimap X] \quad \dfrac{isak : i \quad \lambda x \lambda y.like(x,y) : i \multimap w \multimap l}{\lambda y.like(isak, y) : w \multimap l}}{\mathcal{Q}(thing, \lambda y.like(isak, y)) : e}\,[l/X]$$

FIGURE 4.4. Example of a *wh*-question proof.

(27) CP ⟶ ϵ / (↑ UDF PRED) = 'pro' / (ADJUNCT ∈ ↑) / REL_σ — C′ / ↑ = ↓

(27)	CP ⟶	ϵ	C′
		(↑ UDF PRED) = 'pro'	↑ = ↓
		(ADJUNCT ∈ ↑)	
		REL_σ	

The relative clause meaning constructor has been abbreviated as REL_σ.

As an example of relative clause composition, consider example (28) and the premises it contributes, shown in (29).

(28) every book that Isak likes

(29)
1. $\lambda R \lambda S.every(R, S) : (v \multimap r) \multimap \forall Y.[(b \multimap Y) \multimap Y]$ — Lex. **every**
2. $book : v \multimap r$ — Lex. **book**
3. $\lambda P \lambda Q \lambda x.Q(x) \wedge P(x) : (b \multimap l) \multimap (v \multimap r) \multimap (v \multimap r)$ — Lex. **that**
4. $isak : i$ — Lex. **Isak**
5. $\lambda x \lambda y.like(x, y) : i \multimap b \multimap l$ — Lex. **likes**

These premises construct the proof in Figure 4.3 for the relativized DP. The proof terminates in a nominal type, not a propositional type. Further details of relative clause composition in Glue Semantics can be found in Dalrymple (2001: 415–422).

For *wh*-questions, I assume that the *wh*-word is a generalized quantifer, represented by the operator $\mathcal{Q}$. The treatment is illustrated by the following example:

(30) What did Isak like?

The contributed premises for the example are as follows:

(31)
1. $\lambda S.\mathcal{Q}(thing, S) : \forall X.[(w \multimap X) \multimap X]$ — Lex. **what**
2. $isak : i$ — Lex. **Isak**
3. $\lambda x \lambda y.like(x, y) : i \multimap w \multimap l$ — Lex. **like**

These premises construct the proof in Figure 4.4.

Part II
Theory

5

The Resource Sensitivity Hypothesis

The guiding principle of this work is the following:

(1) **The Resource Sensitivity Hypothesis (RSH):**
Natural language is resource-sensitive.

The overview of Glue Semantics in the previous chapter began the presentation of the formal theory behind the Resource Sensitivity Hypothesis. This chapter continues the investigation and focuses on resource logics, in particular *linear logic* (Girard, 1987), and their relationship to the hypothesis. I consider several theoretical proposals in linguistic theory which can either be reduced to resource sensitivity or can at least be understood in new terms based on RSH.

Section 5.1 presents the notions of Logical Resource Sensitivity and Linguistic Resource Sensitivity. I present a hierarchy of substructural logics and illustrate their linguistic relevance with respect to the combinatorics of three principal grammatical subsystems: phonology, syntax, and semantics. I motivate linear logic as the appropriate logic for the syntax–semantics interface and semantic composition and discuss the consequences of its adoption for grammatical architecture. I consider how the choice of logic affects the relationship between Logical and Linguistic Resource Sensitivity.

Section 5.2 begins with a brief consideration of certain explicit discussions of resource accounting in the literature (van Benthem, 1991; Dalrymple et al., 1993; Moortgat, 1997; Dalrymple et al., 1999*b*; Dalrymple, 2001; Bouma et al., 1999; Kruijff and Oehrle, 2003*b*). I then proceed to a detailed examination of the relationship between Logical and Linguistic Resource Sensitivity. Despite initial appearances, Logical Resource Sensitivity is generally insufficient on its own to guarantee a useful notion of Linguistic Resource Sensitivity, although Logical Resource Sensitivity does form the foundation for Linguistic Resource Sensitivity. A linguistically useful notion of resource sensitivity is demonstrated to require coupling of Logical Resource Sensitivity to a theory of natural language.

Section 5.3 considers various proposals in the theoretical linguistics literature which I argue to be implicit appeals to resource sensitivity. The proposals considered are: bounded closure in type-driven translation (Klein and Sag, 1985), Completeness and Coherence (Kaplan and Bresnan, 1982), the Theta Criterion (Chomsky, 1981), the Projection Principle (Chomsky, 1981, 1982, 1986), the ban on vacuous quantification (Chomsky, 1982, 1995; Kratzer, 1995; Kennedy, 1997; Heim and Kratzer, 1998; Fox, 2000), the Principle of Full Interpretation (Chomsky, 1986, 1995), and numerations and the Inclusiveness Condition (Chomsky, 1995). Linguistic Resource Sensitivity not only captures the important insights behind these proposals, but also solves certain empirical and theoretical problems. The Resource Sensitivity Hypothesis thus paves the way to a new understanding of these proposals and their potential elimination.

5.1 Substructural Logics and Linguistic Theory

Characterizing the syntax–semantics interface and semantic composition in logical terms is the predominant view in linguistic theory, stemming from the work of Montague (1970, 1973). Similar logical approaches to syntax and phonology have not been as influential, although such approaches to syntax have been available at least as long as generative approaches (Bar-Hillel, 1953; Lambek, 1958) and have earlier precursors (Ajdukiewicz, 1935). Categorial Grammar has contributed greatly to understanding the logical underpinnings of syntax (see Morrill, 1994, 2009, 2011; Moortgat, 1997; Steedman, 2000, 2007, for overviews and references and Wood, 1993, for a general introduction) and, to a lesser degree, phonology (Wheeler, 1988). Categorial Grammar investigations in the type-logical, or Lambek Calculus, tradition (van Benthem, 1991; Morrill, 1994, 2009, 2011; Carpenter, 1997; Moortgat, 1997) are instances of the logical approach based on *substructural logics*, which I apply in this section to the combinatorics of phonology, syntax, and semantics, but based on a different theoretical perspective.

Restall (2000: 1–2) offers the following characterization of substructural logics:

> Substructural logics focus on the behaviour and presence—or more suggestively, the *absence*—of *structural rules*. These are particular rules in a logic which govern the behaviour of collections of information. (emphasis in original)

The basic insight behind substructural logics is that, by carefully manipulating the structural rules that characterize a logic, we can home in on a logic that precisely characterizes the informational system under consideration. A unifying guiding principle of modern linguistics has been the characterization

Weakening	*Contraction*	*Commutativity*
$\dfrac{\Gamma \vdash B}{\Gamma, A \vdash B}\,\mathsf{K}$	$\dfrac{\Gamma, A, A \vdash B}{\Gamma, A \vdash B}\,\mathsf{W}$	$\dfrac{\Gamma, A, B \vdash C}{\Gamma, B, A \vdash C}\,\mathsf{C}$

FIGURE 5.1. Three key structural rules.

of language as information, whether from a logical perspective (e.g., van Benthem, 1991) or from a cognitive perspective (e.g., Chomsky, 1986).

There are many structural rules that have been explored (Restall, 2000). The three that are particularly relevant here are weakening, contraction, and commutativity. These rules are shown in Figure 5.1. The intuitions behind the rules can be summarized as follows:

1. **Weakening:** Premises can be *freely added.*
2. **Contraction:** Additional occurrences of a premise can be *freely discarded.*
3. **Commutativity:** Premises can be *freely reordered.*

Restall (2000) names these rules in terms of the associated combinators from *Combinatory Logic* (Curry and Feys, 1958): K, W, and C.

Weakening and contraction are of particular interest here, because a substructural logic that lacks these rules is a *resource logic.* Lack of these structural rules means that premises cannot be freely added or discarded. This has the effect that premises in a proof in the logic in question are resources that require strict accounting. Weakening and contraction therefore form the basis for Logical Resource Sensitivity, which is a property of logics, as opposed to Linguistic Resource Sensitivity, which is a property of natural language:

(2) **Logical Resource Sensitivity**:
In a resource logic, premises in proofs cannot be freely *reused* or *discarded.*

(3) **Linguistic Resource Sensitivity**:
Elements of combination in grammars cannot be freely *reused* or *discarded.*

Linguistic Resource Sensitivity is the property at the core of the Resource Sensitivity Hypothesis. Throughout this work, the term 'Resource Sensitivity' concerns these substantive claims about language.

This is already enough background on substructural logics to see how they yield a useful perspective on phonology, syntax, and semantics. There are two simple but fundamental points that I want to make about these grammatical subsystems. The first is that phonology, syntax, and semantics vary as to how important the order of the elements to be combined is. Order is very important in phonology and not important at all in semantics, with syntax falling somewhere in between. The second point is that all of these grammatical subsystems require tight control of their combinatorics. In particular, in all three cases elements of combination cannot be freely discarded or reused: the three grammatical systems are equally resource-sensitive.

Let us see how these two points play out for each grammatical subsystem, beginning with phonology:

(4) **Phonology**

a. Order very important:

XY $\not\equiv$ YX

b. Elements of phonological combination cannot be freely discarded or reused:

XY $\not\equiv$ X
XY $\not\equiv$ XXY

Phonological sequences cannot be freely reordered: a sequence XY of phonemes X and Y is (generally) not equivalent to a sequence YX. For example, no language allows a three-phoneme word to be represented in all of the six possible orderings. Metathesis may at first seem to be an exception to the generalization, but no language allows free metathesis of any two phonemes. Rather, metathesis is a phonological rule or constraint that applies under certain specific conditions. The second point is that no language allows free dropping or adding of just any phoneme. There may be specific rules of deletion or epenthesis, but again these will apply to particular phonemes in particular environments. Phonology is therefore highly order-sensitive and also resource-sensitive.

The combinatorics of syntax with respect to these two points can be summarized as follows:

(5) **Syntax**

a. Order important in some languages, less important in others:

WORD1 WORD2 $\Diamond\equiv$ WORD2 WORD1

b. Elements of syntactic combination cannot be freely discarded or reused:

WORD1 WORD2 $\not\equiv$ WORD1
WORD1 WORD2 $\not\equiv$ WORD1 WORD1 WORD2

Word order is less universally strict than phoneme order. In many languages, two alternative word orders may be equivalently allowed.[1] This is indicated in (5a), where it is noted that the order WORD1 WORD2 is possibly equivalent ($\Diamond \equiv$) to the order WORD2 WORD1. Certain languages, such as English, have quite strict word order. Nevertheless, under certain circumstances even such strictly ordered languages may allow some freedom:

(6) a. i. Thora looked the number up.
 ii. Thora looked up the number.

 b. i. In the room stood a smiling baby.
 ii. A smiling baby stood in the room.

Other languages, such as German, Dutch, and Persian, allow fairly free word order due to scrambling (Karimi, 2003). Still other languages, such as Warlpiri, allow even more free word order, with even elements of the same noun phrase being separable and reorderable. Yet even extremely free word order languages make certain word order requirements. For example, Warlpiri roughly requires that the second position in the clause be occupied by the auxiliary (Hale, 1980, 1983; Simpson, 1983, 1991; Austin and Bresnan, 1996). Although freedom of word order is a major locus of variation among languages (and hence a major focus of syntactic research), no language allows free deletion or addition of syntactic material. Once again, as in phonology, there may be specific processes that meet this characterization; perhaps pro-drop could be considered a candidate, for example. However, no language allows completely indiscriminate addition or deletion of syntactic material. Syntax is therefore order-sensitive to varying degrees across languages but is universally resource-sensitive.

Semantic combinatorics with respect to order and resource sensitivity can be characterized as follows:

(7) **Semantics**

 a. Order unimportant:

$$\left[\!\left[\textbf{argument} \quad \textbf{functor} \right]\!\right] \equiv \left[\!\left[\textbf{functor} \quad \textbf{argument} \right]\!\right]$$

 b. Elements of semantic combination cannot be freely discarded or reused.

[1] Notice that we are discussing syntactic order alone, leaving semantics aside. The alternative orders may have different semantic or information-theoretic content, but they are all syntactically valid under some interpretation.

Semantic composition has long been understood in terms of functor-argument combination, with the idea often being traced back to Frege (1891/1952). Order is irrelevant to this sort of composition: a functor can equally well combine with an argument to its left or to its right. There can of course be syntactic constraints on the distribution of the syntactic realizations of functors and arguments, but this is semantically irrelevant. For example, an intransitive verb in English always follows the subject. If the subject has a lower type, e.g. if it is a proper name, then the verb is the functor and the subject is the argument; in this case we have right–left functor-argument order. However, if the subject has a higher type, e.g. if it is a quantifier, the subject consumes the verb as an argument. In this case we have left–right functor-argument order. Another way to think about it is that it is the types of the expressions that determine functor-argument combination, not their order. For example, in their rule for Functional Application, Heim and Kratzer (1998: 44, 95) simply state that the functor applies to the argument, regardless of order.

Despite its lack of sensitivity to order, semantics is resource-sensitive. We cannot just disregard contentful expressions or use single occurrences of contentful expressions more than once. This is demonstrated by examples such as the following:

(8) Kim fooled Sandy.

(9) This innocent man is allegedly guilty, according to some.

The meanings of the words *Kim*, *Sandy*, and *fooled* in (8) can each be used to produce the meaning in (10), but it is not possible to disregard the meaning of *Sandy* and to use the meaning of *Kim* twice to derive the meaning in (11).

(10) *fool*(*kim*, *sandy*)

(11) *fool*(*kim*, *kim*)

Similarly, we cannot use the single occurrence of the adverb *allegedly* twice to give (9) a meaning equivalent to that of (12).

(12) This allegedly innocent man is allegedly guilty, according to some.

The two sentences are truth-conditionally distinct, since (9) entails that the man is innocent, whereas (12) does not. In sum, semantics is not order-sensitive but is resource-sensitive.

Phonology, syntax, and semantics are thus order-sensitive to differing degrees, with phonology being highly order-sensitive and semantics being order-insensitive, but all three grammatical subsystems are resource-sensitive.

This picture indicates that the logical understanding of grammar should focus on resource logics—i.e. logics that lack weakening and contraction and thus satisfy Logical Resource Sensitivity. Order-sensitivity can then be handled in various ways, as discussed shortly.

A resource logic that is of central interest in proof theory and substructural logic is linear logic (Girard, 1987, 1989). An aspect of linear logic that makes it especially interesting to logicians and proof theorists, in particular, is its very articulated and controlled use of logical connectives and modalities. These aspects of the logic are not relevant to us here, and indeed a surprising amount of linguistic work can be done by the very impoverished and logically weak modality-free, multiplicative fragment presented in the appendix. This fragment currently seems to be sufficient for characterizing natural language semantics. Certain analyses of coordination and right-node raising in Glue Semantics (Kehler et al., 1999; Dalrymple, 2001) have used a logically stronger fragment of linear logic with the *of course* modality (!), but these phenomena have also been successfully analysed using the weaker multiplicative modality-free fragment adopted here (Asudeh and Crouch, 2002*a*). It is important in maintaining a strong version of the Resource Sensitivity Hypothesis that the linear modalities be kept out of the logical fragment, because it is precisely these modalities that allow a controlled relaxation of resource accounting in linear logic. A premise that is prefixed with the of course modality, e.g. $!A$, can be reused an unlimited number of times.

Tables 5.1 and 5.2 (Asudeh and Crouch, 2002*c*) contrast two well-known non-resource-sensitive logics—classical logic and intuitionistic logic—with linear logic. In each table, premises are separated by a semicolon. Table 5.1 shows that in non-resource-sensitive logics we can use a premise in deriving some conclusion and then reuse the premise. In this case a conditional and its antecedent yield the conditional's conclusion (by modus ponens) and the

TABLE 5.1. Logical Resource Sensitivity: no reuse of premises/resources.

Classical/Intuitionistic Logic	Linear Logic
$A;\ A \rightarrow B \vdash B$	$A;\ A \multimap B \vdash B$
Premise A is used to derive conclusion B	Premise A is consumed to produce conclusion B
$A;\ A \rightarrow B \vdash B \wedge A$	$A;\ A \multimap B \nvdash B \otimes A$
Premise A is reused, conjoined with conclusion B	Premise A is consumed to produce conclusion B, no longer available for conjunction with B

TABLE 5.2. Logical Resource Sensitivity: no discarding premises/resources.

Classical/Intuitionistic Logic	Linear Logic
$A; B \vdash A$ Can ignore premise B	$A; B \not\vdash A$ Cannot ignore premise B

antecedent is then conjoined with the conclusion. This is not possible in linear logic: the antecedent premise is used up in deriving the conclusion and cannot be reused to be conjoined with the result; recall that $\multimap$ is linear implication and $\otimes$ is multiplicative linear conjunction.

Table 5.2 shows the opposite situation. In classical or intuitionistic logic, if we have two premises we can ignore one and just conclude the other. This is not possible in linear logic: we cannot just leave one premise aside. It must be used in the proof.

Classical logic is characterizable as a logic of truth and intuitionistic logic as a constructive logic of consequence or proof (Gamut, 1991; van Dalen, 2001), whereas linear logic captures the intuitionistic notions of constructions, proofs, and consequence but is also a resource logic that requires strict accounting of resources.

We can make more precise the fit between particular substructural logics and modules of grammar by looking at a hierarchy of substructural logics characterized by the structural rules of weakening, contraction, and commutativity,[2] as shown in Figure 5.2. The top of the hierarchy is occupied by the logic **L**, the simple non-commutative Lambek Calculus (Lambek, 1958; see van Benthem, 1991 and Moortgat, 1997), which lacks weakening, contraction, and commutativity. We get logics on the hierarchy below **L** by adding the structural rule that labels the transition. By adding commutativity, we get the commutative Lambek Calculus **LP** (van Benthem, 1991; Moortgat, 1997), which is roughly equivalent to linear logic. A proof theorist might balk at this characterization, since the points of divergence between **LP** and linear logic are potentially logically important. Nevertheless, if we are keeping things simple by sticking to a consideration of just the three structural rules of weakening, contraction, and commutativity, adding commutativity to the simple Lambek Calculus basically gets us linear logic. The next two logics on the hierarchy are captured by adding either contraction or weakening. If we add contraction to linear logic we get relevance logic (Anderson and Belnap, 1975; Read, 1988).

[2] The logics discussed here additionally all share the rule of associativity (B), but this rule is not really relevant to our considerations of order sensitivity and resource sensitivity.

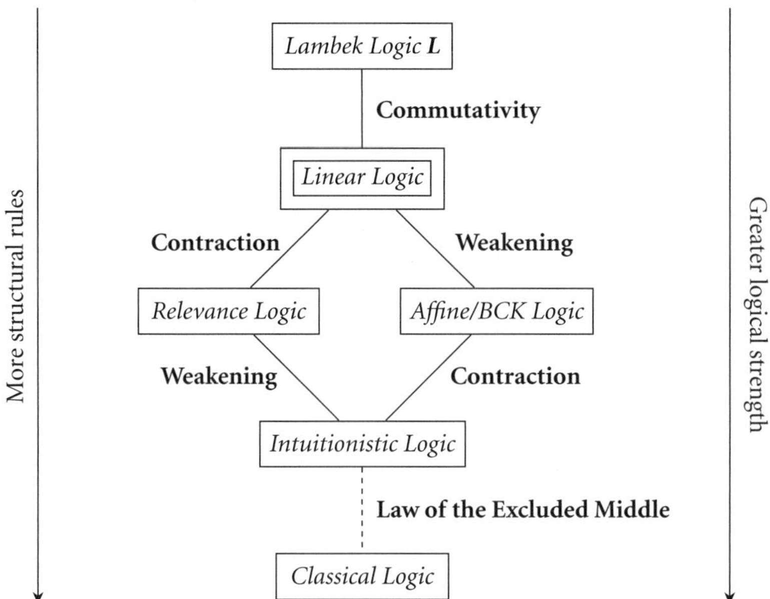

FIGURE 5.2. Hierarchy of logics related by structural rules.

Relevance logic lacks weakening: a premise cannot be freely added while maintaining validity, because every premise in the premise set must be used in reaching the conclusion—i.e. every premise must be *relevant*. Contraction obtains though: multiple instances of the same premise may be discarded, since a single occurrence is sufficient to establish relevance. Thus, relevance logic allows reuse of premises but does not allow premises to be discarded. Each premise must be used in reaching the conclusion, since weakening is absent. Gregory (2001, 2002) has applied relevance logic to linguistic analyses. Affine/BCK logic, on the other hand, lacks contraction but has weakening. In affine logic, the condition of relevance does not hold: not every premise need be used in reaching the conclusion. However, premises cannot be reused. In other words, relevance logic allows reuse of premises but not discarding, whereas affine logic allows discarding of premises but not reuse. Linear logic allows neither: each premise must be used exactly once; i.e. no premise may go unused and no premise may be reused. By adding the last of the three proof rules—either weakening to relevance logic or contraction to affine logic—we arrive at intuitionistic logic (Gamut, 1991; van Dalen, 2001). Finally, classical logic (Gamut, 1991; Shapiro, 2001; Hodges, 2001) can be obtained by adding the Law of the Excluded Middle (LEM), which states that either a proposition or its negation must hold ($\phi \vee \neg \phi$); this is related to *reductio ad absurdum* (reasoning from contradiction) and double negation ($\neg\neg\,\phi \vdash \phi$). Intuitionistic logic is based on Brouwer's denial of the validity of LEM, based on a constructive notion of proof (Gamut, 1991; van Dalen, 2001). The relationship between intuitionistic logic and classical logic is represented with a dashed line because the Law of the Excluded Middle is not a structural rule.

With this hierarchy of substructural logics at hand, let us turn back to the consideration of grammatical subsystems. I argued above that phonology, syntax, and semantics are all equally resource-sensitive. This means that the logics that characterize their combinatorics should lack weakening and contraction. In terms of the hierarchy in Figure 5.2, this requirement picks out linear logic and the Lambek logic **L**. With respect to the three structural rules we have been considering, these two logics differ only on commutativity. The logic **L** does not have commutativity and is therefore appropriate for modelling rigid order. It is the logic that is appropriate for phonology, where order is quite important. It is possible to take into account phonological processes such as metathesis, deletion, and epenthesis. These phonological processes can be enriched by adding modalities to **L** to obtain a Multimodal Type Logic (Moortgat, 1997; Baldridge, 2002). For syntax, where freedom of word order is fairly variable among languages, there are two basic options. One option is to model syntax with a non-commutative resource logic, which models strict word order well, and to add modalities for controlled relaxation of order, as in Multimodal Type Logic. The second option is to characterize syntactic combination using a commutative resource logic, which models free word order, and to add controlled non-commutativity.

Semantic composition, in contrast, is resource-sensitive but order-insensitive. This means that linear logic is an appropriate choice for modelling semantic composition, for a number of reasons. First, it is a logic of resources and therefore models the apparent resource sensitivity of natural language semantics. Second, it is a pure logic of composition for semantics, since it lacks commutativity. A different option is to use a non-commutative resource logic with controlled commutativity, as in Multimodal Type Logic, to simultaneously model syntax and semantic composition. This option faces the danger of conflating properties of syntactic and semantic combination by failing to separate syntax, where order is relevant, from semantics, where order is irrelevant. There may be complexities that arise in controlling syntactic or semantic combination, but these will not be localized in syntax or semantics and will instead infect the system as a whole. Using linear logic for semantic combination, in contrast, keeps syntax and semantics separate and therefore quarantines one from the other. Finally, the use of linear logic for semantic composition forms a bridge between linguistics and proof theory, a field at the intersection of logic, theoretical computer science, and mathematics. Linear logic was devised largely as an investigation into properties of proofs (Girard, 1987), rather than as a logic of resources per se, and has led to a productive and influential research programme in proof theory (see Girard, 1989, for a classic presentation and Girard, 1995, for an overview).

There are consequences for grammatical architecture in choosing linear logic for semantic composition. The main consequence is that there must be some separate level of syntax, otherwise the commutative logic will wildly overgenerate word orders. Glue Semantics is an instantiation of this kind of architecture: semantic composition is handled by linear logic and syntax is handled by a separate syntactic theory. The bulk of Glue work, as in this book, adopts Lexical-Functional Grammar as the syntactic theory (Dalrymple et al., 1993; Dalrymple, 1999, 2001; Asudeh, 2000, 2002*a*, 2004, 2005*a*,*b*; Asudeh and Crouch, 2002*a*, *b*; Andrews, 2004, 2007, 2008, 2011). Glue based on LFG syntax has been implemented as part of the LFG implementation at Palo Alto Research Center (Crouch et al., 2011). There has also been work that couples Glue Semantics to Tree-Adjoining Grammar (Frank and van Genabith, 2001) and Head-Driven Phrase Structure Grammar (Asudeh and Crouch, 2002*c*).

5.1.1 *Summary*

Phonology, syntax, and semantics all require tight control of their elements of combination, i.e. resource accounting. Their combinatorics are thus best modelled with a resource logic, i.e. a logic that satisfies Logical Resource Sensitivity. Consideration of these grammatical subsystems in terms of resource logics naturally leads to Linguistic Resource Sensitivity, according to which elements of combination in grammar cannot be freely discarded or reused. Linguistic Resource Sensitivity forms the basis for the Resource Sensitivity Hypothesis. To investigate this hypothesis we need to look for cases where there is apparent reuse (resource deficit) or non-use (resource surplus). Resumptive pronouns constitute an apparent case of resource surplus. If cases of apparent resource deficit or surplus yield to analysis in terms of full resource use, then the Resource Sensitivity Hypothesis is maintainable. If the cases in question crucially require controlled relaxation of resource accounting through the use of linear modalities (*of course*, !, and *why not*, ?), then the hypothesis cannot be maintained in a strong form. If not even controlled resource reuse or non-use is adequate for a satisfactory analysis and the phenomenon requires complete relaxation of resource accounting, then Linguistic Resource Sensitivity and the Resource Sensitivity Hypothesis must be rejected.

5.2 Logical and Linguistic Resource Sensitivity

Logical Resource Sensitivity concerns properties of logics, whereas Linguistic Resource Sensitivity is a substantive hypothesis about natural language as characterized by linguistic theory. There has been some explicit investigation of issues of resource accounting in the literature. Van Benthem (1991) and Moortgat (1997) discuss resource sensitivity, but principally with respect to properties of the logics that they are concerned with. These works are essentially investigations of Logical Resource Sensitivity in logics that have linguistic applications. Dalrymple et al. (1993, 1999*b*) discuss Linguistic Resource Sensitivity explicitly, noting that the use of linear logic for semantic composition mirrors the apparent resource accounting of natural language, but do not pursue the matter in any depth. In-depth investigations of both Logical and Linguistic Resource Sensitivity are found in the volumes edited by Bouma et al. (1999) and Kruijff and Oehrle (2003*b*), which primarily address the issues from a Categorial Grammar perspective. The latter volume concentrates specifically on resource issues raised by anaphora, but also considers Linguistic Resource Sensitivity more broadly construed, particularly in the contributions by Kruijff and Oehrle (2003*a*) and Oehrle (2003).

This section considers Logical and Linguistic Resource Sensitivity in more detail. The main goal is to establish a fairly simple point: the relationship between Logical and Linguistic Resource Sensitivity is real but potentially complex.[3] Properties of the resource logic, in particular which connectives it contains, affect the relationship between Logical and Linguistic Resource Sensitivity. The key point is that Linguistic Resource Sensitivity is based on Logical Resource Sensitivity together with constraints derived from linguistic theory.

In order to establish this point, some further aspects of the linear logic approach to semantic composition must be reviewed. The following observations apply equally to type-logical approaches to semantic composition (van Benthem, 1991; Morrill, 1994, 2009, 2011; Carpenter, 1997; Moortgat, 1997). Let us first assume a fragment of linear logic which contains only the implication connective, $\multimap$. In a natural deduction presentation, we need a rule for introducing the connective and one for eliminating the connective. The rules are identical to the more familiar rules for implication introduction and elimination in classical and intuitionistic logic (see, e.g., Gamut, 1991: 131ff.). The rule for elimination is just *modus ponens*:

[3] This section has benefited greatly from discussions with Dick Crouch and Valeria de Paiva, who are not responsible for any errors.

(13) Implication Elimination

$$\frac{\begin{matrix}\vdots \\ A\end{matrix} \qquad \begin{matrix}\vdots \\ A \multimap B\end{matrix}}{B} \multimap_{\mathcal{E}}$$

According to the Curry-Howard isomorphism (Curry and Feys, 1958; Howard, 1980), implication elimination corresponds to functional application:

(14) Functional Application : Implication Elimination

$$\frac{\begin{matrix}\vdots \\ a : A\end{matrix} \qquad \begin{matrix}\vdots \\ f : A \multimap B\end{matrix}}{f(a) : B} \multimap_{\mathcal{E}}$$

If the premises consist of lexically specified meaning terms coupled with appropriate linear logic formulae, then implication can do a lot of the work necesary for semantic composition (for much more detailed exposition of this point, see van Benthem, 1991). Suppose we have the lexical meanings *thora* and *laugh* from the words *Thora* and *laughs*. We can then perform the following derivation for the sentence *Thora laughs*:

(15) $$\frac{thora : A \qquad laugh : A \multimap B}{laugh(thora) : B} \multimap_{\mathcal{E}}$$

If the only connective we have is implication, there is a tight fit between Logical Resource Sensitivity and Linguistic Resource Sensitivity. Logical Resource Sensitivity, which is captured formally through the absence of the structural rules of weakening and contraction, requires that each premise is used exactly once. If we have a premise $thora : A$ and a premise $laugh : A \multimap B$, then the only way to use both premises, given only the implication connective, is the proof shown in (15).[4]

Now suppose that we have conjunction in our logical fragment. Like implication, conjunction has rules for introduction and elimination. The introduction rule for multiplicative linear conjunction is straightforward and corresponds to a product type via the Curry–Howard isomorphism:

[4] More precisely, any other proof that involves only introduction and elimination of implication is provably equivalent to (15).

(16) Product : Conjunction Introduction

$$\frac{\begin{array}{cc}\vdots & \vdots \\ a : A & b : B\end{array}}{a \times b : A \otimes B} \otimes_{\mathcal{I}}$$

The type of the product is $\sigma \times \tau$, where σ is the type of the first conjunct and τ is the type of the second. This logical conjunction does not necessarily conjoin like types; a product may be formed of any two types. The like-types restriction seems to be valid for linguistic conjunction (e.g., English *and*), but it is not a feature of the conjunction connective in the purely logical sense.

With the inclusion of conjunction, Logical and Linguistic Resource Sensitivity diverge. The following proof on the premises $thora : A$ and $laugh : A \multimap B$ satisfies Logical Resource Sensitivity by using each premise exactly once in an instance of conjunction introduction:

(17) $$\frac{thora : A \qquad laugh : A \multimap B}{thora \times laugh : A \otimes (A \multimap B)} \otimes_{\mathcal{I}}$$

This proof is linguistically unilluminating but logically impeccable. Thus, conjunction drives a wedge between Logical and Linguistic Resource Sensitivity by allowing satisfaction of the former in a way that we intuitively feel should not satisfy the latter.

Two questions naturally arise. The first is: do we need a conjunction connective? The second is: if we do need conjunction, how do we regain a notion of Linguistic Resource Sensitivity? The answer to the first question is that there is indeed ample linguistic motivation for a conjunction connective. One application is in a variable-free treatment of pronouns. Jacobson (1999) provides extensive theoretical and empirical arguments in favour of such a variable-free theory.

Recall that a pronoun is represented as follows in Glue Semantics, where A is the antecedent resource and P is the pronominal resource:

(18) $A \multimap (A \otimes P)$

The pronoun consumes its antecedent to compute pronominal reference but must then replicate the antecedent, since the antecedent is also an argument to some functor; a simple implication of the form $A \multimap P$ would therefore result in resource deficit with respect to the antecedent. The conjunction is thus necessary for the pronoun to output its own meaning together with a copy of its antecedent's meaning. The necessity of conjunction is evident if we also look at the meaning language side of the meaning constructor:

(19) $\lambda y.y \times y : A \multimap (A \otimes P)$

The meaning of the antecedent is applied once and becomes both the meaning of the copy of the antecedent and of the pronoun. The conjunction is necessary in order for the meaning to get distributed properly and for proper binding.

There are yet other reasons to pick a logical fragment containing conjunction. Crouch and van Genabith (1999) and van Genabith and Crouch (1999*a*) define a method of context update for Glue Semantics which involves contexts as linear logic resources. This effectively shifts the dynamics of dynamic semantics from the meaning language to the linear logic that performs semantic composition. With context update handled in the linear logic, conjunction is necessary to bundle together the sentential semantics with the updated context. The result of a Glue derivation for a sentence *s* is then represented as follows (Crouch and van Genabith, 1999: 122):

(20) $\Gamma, \Delta_1 \vdash \ \phi : s \ \otimes \ \Delta_2$

The input context is Δ_1, the updated output context is Δ_2, and the meaning assignment for the sentence is $\phi : s$.[5] Thus, the conjunction is necessary to derive a single premise that represents the static and dynamic aspects of sentential meaning.

A third use of conjunction that is similar in spirit to the context update use is motivated by Potts's (2005) multidimensional semantics for conventional implicature. As discussed by Potts (2003, 2005: 85–87), the logic $\mathcal{L}_{\mathrm{CI}}$ that he uses to represent at-issue meanings (i.e., normal sentential semantics) and conventional implicatures can be translated into Glue Semantics by using premises that consist of at-issue type resources conjoined with CI-type meanings.

There is thus plenty of motivation for conjunction. The question is how Linguistic Resource Sensitivity can be regained. The basic method is to set some linguistically motivated goal for the resource logic proof that models the system in question. In Glue Semantics, the standard goal is the following:

(21) $\Gamma \vdash \phi : s_t$

[5] Crouch and van Genabith actually present a slightly more complex picture involving sets of contexts (Crouch and van Genabith, 1999; van Genabith and Crouch, 1999*a*), represented as conjoined individual contexts, but the details of their presentation are peripheral to the main point, which is just that at least one conjunction is necessary.

From a premise set Γ, the goal is to establish a type t conclusion s that corresponds to the semantics of the sentence, represented as ϕ. If the goal condition of the semantic proof is constrained in this manner, then proof (17) for *Thora laughed*, which has a conclusion $thora \times laugh : A \otimes (A \multimap B)$, is a valid linear logic proof but not a valid Glue proof. Although (17) satisfies Logical Resource Sensitivity, it does not satisfy Linguistic Resource Sensitivity.

We can accommodate the innovations of Crouch and van Genabith (1999), van Genabith and Crouch (1999*a*), and Potts (2005) by further articulating the goal condition. The conjunctive goal condition for Crouch and van Genabith's context update was shown in (20). Similarly, if we are dealing with conventional implicature using the types discussed by Potts (2005), then the goal condition can be defined as:[6]

(22) $\Gamma \vdash \phi : s^a_t \otimes \psi : s^c_t$

Here $\phi : s^a$ is an at-issue meaning and $\psi : s^c$ a conventional implicature. Providing we make the necessary adjustments so the logic can handle all the required types, we can even put together Crouch and van Genabith's context update approach with Potts's conventional implicature approach by having the following as a goal condition:

(23) $\Gamma, \Delta_1 \vdash \phi : s^a \otimes \psi : s^c \otimes \Delta_2$

The rest of this work does not deal with context update or conventional implicature, so the simple goal condition in (21) is sufficient and will be adopted here.

In sum, Linguistic Resource Sensitivity is based on Logical Resource Sensitivity, but requires that proofs are further constrained in a manner motivated by linguistic theory.

5.3 Resource Sensitivity and Linguistic Theory

This section considers various implicit appeals to Resource Sensitivity in the linguistics literature. By adopting a resource logic, such as linear logic, for semantic composition and thus obtaining a notion of Linguistic Resource Sensitivity, we point the way to elimination of the various heterogeneous proposals by capturing them directly in semantic composition. This would

[6] Potts's logic allows multiple conventional implicature types. This could be represented using conjoined CI-types, on analogy with the conjoined contexts of Crouch and van Genabith (1999) (see footnote 5), but I set this complication aside.

not only achieve theoretical simplification by eliminating unnecessary additional principles, it would also provide a bridge between the different theories in which the proposals have been made. Moortgat (1999) makes related points with respect to resource logics and linguistic theory, but in light of Categorial Grammar.

5.3.1 *Bounded Closure*

An early appeal to resource accounting in the linguistic literature and the one which Dalrymple et al. (1993, 1999*b*) mention explicitly is bounded closure in Klein and Sag's (1985) influential type-driven translation. As a preliminary to defining bounded closure, Klein and Sag (1985: 171) note that:

> Translation rules in Montague semantics have the property that the translation of each component of a complex expression occurs exactly once in the translation of the whole.

The property mentioned in this quotation just is resource accounting: the components to be translated are resources that must be used exactly once. The implicit claim is that natural language semantics is resource-sensitive. It should be noted that Klein and Sag (1985) were writing before the linguistic implications of linear logic and other resource logics were well understood.

Klein and Sag (1985: 171ff.) define an operation of *functional realization* which is a mapping from a set of expressions of Montogovian intensional logic to a set of the expressions that can be built out of the input set. They note that functional realization must preserve the resource accounting property of translation in Montague semantics that is mentioned in the quote above. They write:

> This property must be preserved by functional realization. That is to say, we do not want the set *S* mentioned above to contain all meaningful expressions of IL [Intensional Logic—AA] which can be built up from the elements of *S* [a set of expressions of IL—AA], but only those which use each element of *S* exactly once. For example, suppose that *S* = {*walk′*, *quickly′*}, where *walk′* is of type VP and *quickly′* is of type ⟨VP, VP⟩. Then *S′* should contain the expression *quickly′*(*walk′*), but not *quickly′*(*quickly′*(*walk′*)), or any other of the infinite number of expressions constructed in this way. Consequently, we shall take the preliminary step of defining the bounded closure of a set under a binary operation *h*. By contrast to the standard notion of the closure of a set under some operation, bounded closure obeys the restriction just discussed, namely that each element in the initial set is employed exactly once.
> (Klein and Sag, 1985: 172)

The bounded closure of a set is thus set closure with the added restriction that each item in the initial set must be used and no item can be used more than once. It is clear that this is resource accounting. Since this notion was not available to Klein and Sag (1985), the best they could do was to stipulate a special kind of closure. If we adopt a resource logic for semantic composition, not only do we capture the effects of bounded closure without ad hoc stipulations, we do so in a manner that ties into a substantial body of work in the neighbouring disciplines of substructural logic and proof theory.

5.3.2 *Completeness, Coherence, and Semantic Forms*

The principles of Completeness and Coherence are well-formedness constraints on LFG's f(unctional)-structures (Kaplan and Bresnan, 1982). The following are the standard precise formulations of the principles:

(24) **Completeness**
An f-structure is *locally complete* if and only if it contains all the governable grammatical functions that its predicate governs. An f-structure is *complete* if and only if it and all its subsidiary f-structures are locally complete. (Kaplan and Bresnan, 1982: 65 [211–212])

(25) **Coherence**
An f-structure is *locally coherent* if and only if all the governable grammatical functions that it contains are governed by a local predicate. An f-structure is *coherent* if and only if it and all its subsidiary f-structures are locally coherent. (Kaplan and Bresnan, 1982: 65 [211–212])

Completeness demands that every grammatical function required by a predicate is found in the f-structure. Coherence demands that every grammatical function that is found in the f-structure is required by some predicate. The two principles, taken together, perform analogous roles to the Theta Criterion, the Projection Principle, and Full Interpretation in Principles and Parameters Theory, which are discussed below. A key difference between Completeness and Coherence and these other principles is that Completeness and Coherence are defined recursively in strictly local terms.

It is easy to see how Resource Sensitivity can take over the role of Completeness and Coherence. If an f-structure does not satisfy Completeness, then there is at least one semantic argument whose resource is missing. This means that the consumer of this resource cannot be satisfied and its premise cannot be properly used in the proof. Similarly, if an f-structure does not satisfy Coherence, then there is at least one semantic resource that has no consumer. This resource cannot be used properly in the proof and Linguistic

Resource Sensitivity is not satisfied. In a version of LFG that is coupled to Glue Semantics, it may be that Completeness and Coherence are not necessary as separate grammatical statements. It is nonetheless still convenient to use them as descriptive labels, especially for local realization of grammatical functions.

One potential challenge to taking over the roles of Completeness and Coherence with Linguistic Resource Sensitivity comes from expletives. If expletives are semantically contentless, then their presence will not be ensured by the resource sensitivity of the semantics. There are a number of potential responses to this challenge. First, expletives might not be semantically empty (Bolinger, 1977). Second, semantics is not the only component of grammar that is resource-sensitive. I argued in section 5.1 that syntax is also resource-sensitive. It is possible that a resource-sensitive perspective on syntactic combination could capture the expletive cases. Categorial Grammar would constitute a good starting point for such an investigation, since its syntax can be characterized by a resource logic (at least in the type-logical approach). The Resource-Based LFG (R-LFG) approach of Johnson (1999*a*,*b*)—which treats LFG syntax as directly resource-sensitive rather than derivatively resource-sensitive off the semantics, as in the present theory—is another potential avenue.

LFG's semantic forms, i.e. PRED features, are another instance of an implicit appeal to Linguistic Resource Sensitivity. Kuhn (2001) points out that in the current state of LFG the only function that PRED features seem to play that is not redundant with other aspects of the grammar (see Dalrymple, 2001: 220) is unique instantiation. This is the property that prevents distinct f-structures with the same PRED from being equated. This property can be reduced to Resource Sensitivity on the assumption that, in the general case, if multiple compatible predicates each contribute resources that are looking for the same arguments there will not be enough arguments to go around. Kuhn (2001) observes that there are several benefits to taking over the uniqueness role of PRED features with Resource Sensitivity. First, since this role is the last remaining role for PRED features in the syntax, they can be eliminated entirely. Second, it would remove the distinction between equatable and unequatable features from the theory. This potential benefit is somewhat weakened by the introduction of *instantiated symbols* in Kaplan and Maxwell (1996). Instantiated symbols are not semantic forms but have the uniqueness property: equality between instantiated symbols fails. Third, Kuhn (2001) notes that removal of unequatable features results in an architecture where all resource accounting is performed by the semantics and the syntax is free to engage in acts of multiple exponence quite freely. Fourth, he notes that there are empirical reasons to suppose that there can be multiple exponence of PRED, just like other features. The case he looks at is split NPs in German, as shown in the following example:

(26) Bücher sieht Anna drei.
books sees Anna three
'As for books, Anna can see three.' (Kuhn, 2001: (1.1))

Despite the apparent elliptical nature of the second NP, the two NPs behave as complete NPs with respect to marking of declension class and determiner selection. It seems that this constitutes a case where two NPs with independent but compatible PRED features need to map to the same f-structure.

Although reduction of Completeness, Coherence, and the resource accounting aspect of semantic forms to Linguistic Resource Sensitivity is appealing, Andrews (2008) has argued that PRED features are nevertheless necessary and has proposed an alternative version of Glue Semantics as a consequence. In the rest of this work, I assume an LFG syntax that has the usual notions of Completeness, Coherence, and semantic forms, because reduction of these principles to Resource Sensitivity is a major architectural change to the theory that requires more careful consideration than is possible here.

5.3.3 *The Theta Criterion*

The Theta Criterion of Principles and Parameters (P&P), as first adopted in the Government and Binding Theory of Chomsky (1981) and also in early versions of its successor, the Minimalist Program (Chomsky, 1995), is another implicit appeal to Resource Sensitivity. A standard formulation of the Theta Criterion is:[7]

(27) **Theta Criterion**
Each argument bears one and only one θ-role and each θ-role is assigned to one and only one argument. (Chomsky, 1981: 36)

[7] Chomsky (1986) subsequently reduces the Theta Criterion in terms of movement chains:

Each argument α appears in a chain containing a unique visible θ-position P, and each θ-position P is visible in a chain containing a unique argument α. (Chomsky, 1986: 97)

This is then further refined:

A CHAIN has at most one θ-position; a θ-position is visible in its maximal CHAIN. (Chomsky, 1986: 135)

A CHAIN is either a movement chain or an expletive-associate pair (e.g., $\langle$there$_i$, a book$_i\rangle$ in *There is a book here.*).

Once again we see that a notion of resource accounting is at play: theta roles must be assigned exactly once and each argument must bear exactly one theta role.

A serious shortcoming of the Theta Criterion is that it actually conflicts with the larger theory of theta roles in which it is couched. Theta roles were originally proposed to make generalizations about event participants in related sentence types (Gruber, 1965; Jackendoff, 1972). Chomsky (1981: 139, fn.14) notes that this original motivation for theta roles is at odds with the Theta Criterion. For example, *John* in the following sentence is both agent and theme (Jackendoff, 1972):

(28) John deliberately rolled down the hill.

This sentence violates the Theta Criterion because there is an argument, *John*, that bears two theta roles. The problem is that the notion of theta role is being overloaded. Chomsky's (1981: 139) proposal is to reformulate theta role assigment to deal with such problems. But why should theta role assignment be complicated rather than abandoning the Theta Criterion? In fact, this was exactly the move that was made subsequently, as discussed below in light of Full Interpretation.

If the Theta Criterion is reduced to Linguistic Resource Sensitivity then the problem does not arise in the first place. Resource Sensitivity achieves the goals of the bijective Theta Criterion with respect to arguments and predicates (ensuring a one-to-one match) while allowing theta roles as originally motivated. In the specific case of (28), for example, the intransitive version of *rolled* requires one resource, which is contributed by *John*.[8] The fact that *John* is assigned two theta roles does not impinge on the fact that the lexical item provides a single resource.

A related problem has to do with coordination. In a VP-coordination like the following, each of the verbs has a subject theta role to assign, but there is only one recipient:

(29) Kim sang and danced.

The subject *Kim* receives two theta roles and this should therefore be a violation of the Theta Criterion. In contrast, it has been demonstrated that theories that propose resource-sensitive analyses of coordination, such as Categorial Grammar and Glue Semantics, can handle such cases without giving up Resource Sensitivity (Steedman, 1985; Asudeh and Crouch, 2002*a*).

[8] I am assuming for the sake of argument that *down the hill* is an adjunct, not an argument. The point I am making is not affected if it is in fact analysed as an argument and *rolled* therefore takes two resources.

5.3.4 *The Projection Principle*

The Projection Principle (Chomsky, 1981, 1982, 1986) requires that lexical properties must be preserved throughout the derivation: "the θ-marking properties of each lexical item must be represented categorially at each syntactic level" (Chomsky, 1982: 8). The Projection Principle is thus deeply related to the Theta Criterion and essentially ensures that the actions of the latter are syntactically realized. Although the Projection Principle is not as clearly an appeal to Resource Sensitivity as the cases examined so far, it inherits Resource Sensitivity from the Theta Criterion. In addition, there is a resource accounting interpretation of the Projection Principle that is independent of the Theta Criterion.

The Projection Principle has not been well defined formally; intuitive definitions like the following are typical:

> In general, the phrase structure rules expressing head-complement structure can be eliminated apart from order by recourse to a projection principle, which requires that lexical properties be represented by categorial structure in syntactic representations. (Chomsky, 1986: 82)

> The projection principle requires that complements of heads must be represented at each syntactic level (D-structure, S-structure, LF), so that, in particular, objects must be represented, but it says nothing about subjects. (Chomsky, 1986: 116)

If we assume that the lexical properties in question are resources that must be accounted for, the intuitions behind the principle are captured precisely. If the complement is a resource, then it must be properly licensed (i.e., consumed) and cannot be freely discarded or inserted in the course of the derivation. Thus, the Projection Principle is reducible to Resource Sensitivity quite apart from its relationship to the Theta Criterion.

As indicated by the second quote above, the Projection Principle does not apply to subjects. Chomsky (1982: 10) notes that θ-marked subjects cannot be required by the Projection Principle, citing as evidence nominalizations that lack subjects, passives with suppressed (logical) subjects, and expletive subjects:

(30) a. I do not find the claim that the earth is flat compelling.
b. That passive is NP-movement has been questioned.
c. It is virtually conceptually necessary that the earth is round.

The nominalization and passive sentences indicate that what would be the subject's theta role in the corresponding active declarative need not be realized. The expletive sentence indicates that, even in the absence of a subject theta role, there must be a syntactically realized subject. There is thus some separate subject condition that cannot be reduced to the Projection Principle.

The Projection Principle and this subject condition together constitute the Extended Projection Principle (Chomsky, 1982, 1986), which has been a central research topic in the Minimalist Program under the guise of the EPP feature (Svenonius, 2002). Resource Sensitivity gives a new perspective on the Extended Projection Principle and the EPP feature, particularly with respect to expletives. If expletives have no semantic content, they presumably contribute no resources for semantic composition. This means that semantic resource accounting will not guarantee their presence. This leaves the options discussed in section 5.3.2.

5.3.5 *No Vacuous Quantification*

There have been appeals in the linguistic literature to a syntactic principle that bans vacuous quantification (Chomsky, 1982, 1995; Kratzer, 1995; Kennedy, 1997; Heim and Kratzer, 1998; Fox, 2000). The ban on vacuous quantification, which I will henceforth refer to as No Vacuous Quantification (NVQ), following Potts (2002*b*), has been used to account for the ungrammaticality of a number of examples. Chomsky (1982: 11, (6–7)) uses it to bar double quantification over the same restriction, as in (31), and to bar relative clauses and matrix and embedded questions with saturated scopes, as in (32).

(31) *all some men

(32) a. *the man who John saw Bill
b. *Who did John see Bill?
c. *I wonder who John saw Bill.

Kratzer (1995: 129ff.) uses NVQ to block certain examples involving adverbial quantification, such as (33), which contrasts with (34).

(33) *When Mary knows French, she knows it well.
(Kratzer, 1995: 129, (15a))

(34) When a Moroccan knows French, she knows it well.
(Kratzer, 1995: 129, (15b))

Kennedy (1997) assumes that NVQ governs extraction of the null operator *OP*. Potts (2002*b*: (2a–b)) notes that NVQ should presumably similarly govern variable-binding by *OP*, explaining the following contrast:

(35) the soup OP_1 Martha prepared t_1

(36) *the soup OP_1 Martha prepared dinner

Fox (2000) builds his account of the Coordinate Structure Constraint (Ross, 1967; Grosu, 1973) on NVQ.

Kratzer (1995: 131) offers the following formulation of No Vacuous Quantification:

(37) **Prohibition against Vacuous Quantification**
For every quantifier Q, there must be a variable x such that Q binds an occurrence of x in both its restrictive clause and its nuclear scope.

Potts (2002*b*) points out that the requirement that the quantifier binds a variable in both its restriction and its scope fails to extend to empty operator (*OP*) cases like (36), because the empty operator has no restriction. He offers an alternative formulation of NVQ in terms of lambda abstraction. The following formulation from Heim and Kratzer (1998: 126, (11)) similarly captures all of the intended cases:

(38) Each variable binder must bind at least one variable.

The main points are that NVQ bans vacuous quantification and that it has been appealed to as a condition on syntactic well-formedness. The last point is not necessarily obvious, given the formulations we have looked at, but it follows since variables and their binders are represented at Logical From (see, e.g., Heim and Kratzer, 1998) and LF is a level of syntax—the only level of syntax in the Minimalist Program.

Potts (2002*b*) argues that NVQ should not be adopted as a syntactic costraint in the grammar based on both theoretical and empirical considerations. He argues, following Marsh and Partee (1984), that the complexity of NVQ is such that it probably requires a grammar more powerful than an indexed grammar. Indexed grammars are normally thought to be the most powerful class of grammar required for natural language (Partee et al., 1993), since they are sufficient for generating dependencies that fall outside the generative capacity of context-free grammars (Shieber, 1985). The complexity of NVQ is thus quite bad. Furthermore, Potts (2002*b*) shows that data that has been thought to motivate NVQ can be reanalysed in a simple Generalized Phrase Structure Grammar (GPSG; Gazdar et al., 1985). It is an established result that GPSGs are context-free and therefore cannot represent phenomena requiring indexed grammars. By providing an adequate analysis of NVQ phenomena in GPSG, Potts thus demonstrates that these phenomena cannot require NVQ as a syntactic constraint, since GPSG could not capture such a constraint.

Lastly, Potts presents several attested examples that violate NVQ as a condition on syntax and also provides contexts for examples like Kratzer's (33) which render them well-formed. He concludes that NVQ should not be an axiomatic statement of the grammar, although it could be a theorem, or consequence, of the grammar.

NVQ is in fact a consequence of Resource Sensitivity. It is sufficient to just look at the types of the expressions involved to establish this. Linguistic Resource Sensitivity requires Logical Resource Sensitivity plus some linguistically motivated goal condition for the proof. Let us assume the goal condition is of type t. Let us also assume that operators are generalized quantifiers of type $\langle\langle e,t\rangle,\langle\langle e,t\rangle,t\rangle\rangle$. The empty operator lacks a restriction and is of type $\langle\langle e,t\rangle,t\rangle$. Thus, the restriction and scope of operators are $\langle e,t\rangle$ types. Making the standard move of representing functional types by implication (van Benthem, 1991), which is valid given the Curry–Howard isomorphism, a successful semantic derivation involving an operator looks like this:

(39)
$$\frac{\dfrac{(e \multimap t) \multimap ((e \multimap t) \multimap t) \qquad (e \multimap t)}{(e \multimap t) \multimap t}\multimap_{\mathcal{E}} \qquad (e \multimap t)}{t}\multimap_{\mathcal{E}}$$

If the variable in the restriction is missing, this means that the restriction is not a $\langle e,t\rangle$ type. Representing the restriction's type as R and keeping $(e \multimap t)$ for the scope (annotated as 'S' for clarity), we get the following proof, which does not satisfy Resource Sensitivity:

(40)
$$\frac{\dfrac{(e \multimap t) \multimap ((e \multimap t) \multimap t) \qquad S : (e \multimap t)}{(e \multimap t) \multimap t}\multimap_{\mathcal{E}} \qquad R}{((e \multimap t) \multimap t) \otimes R}\otimes_{\mathcal{I}}$$

The proof does not terminate in a type t and is therefore not well-formed.[9]

Similarly, if the variable in the scope is missing, we get the following invalid proof, where S represents the type of the scope and the restriction has its usual $(e \multimap t)$ type:

(41)
$$\frac{\dfrac{(e \multimap t) \multimap ((e \multimap t) \multimap t) \qquad R : (e \multimap t)}{(e \multimap t) \multimap t}\multimap_{\mathcal{E}} \qquad S}{((e \multimap t) \multimap t) \otimes S}\otimes_{\mathcal{I}}$$

[9] Given the possibility of contextual update and conventional implicature discussed in section 5.2, we might want to generalize the stopping condition to an appropriate product of t types, but the above proof would still be ill-formed.

The proof once again fails to terminate in a type t and therefore does not satisfy Linguistic Resource Sensitivity.

A concrete example of this kind of proof failure is given by Chomsky's example in (31) above, which is repeated here with a scope:

(42) *All some men laughed.

The quantifier *some* will take the restriction and scope, leaving *all* without either. The proof we get for this is:

(43)
$$\cfrac{\cfrac{\cfrac{\overset{\textbf{some}}{(e \multimap t) \multimap ((e \multimap t) \multimap t)} \quad \overset{\textbf{men}}{(e \multimap t)}}{(e \multimap t) \multimap t)} \multimap_{\mathcal{E}} \quad \overset{\textbf{laugh}}{(e \multimap t)}}{t} \multimap_{\mathcal{E}} \quad \overset{\textbf{all}}{(e \multimap t) \multimap ((e \multimap t) \multimap t)}}{t \otimes ((e \multimap t) \multimap ((e \multimap t) \multimap t))}$$

This proof does not satisfy Resource Sensitivity, since it does not terminate in a type t, but rather in the monstrous type $\langle t \times \langle \langle e,t \rangle, \langle \langle e,t \rangle, t \rangle \rangle \rangle$.

In sum, given Resource Sensitivity there is no requirement for NVQ as a separate statement of the grammar. It is instead a consequence of the grammar and we avoid the pitfalls that Potts (2002*b*) outlines while still capturing the effect of NVQ.

5.3.6 *Full Interpretation*

Chomsky (1986) describes the Principle of Full Interpretation (FI) as follows:

> We might express many of these ideas by saying that there is a principle of full interpretation (FI) that requires that every element of PF [Phonetic Form—AA] and LF [Logical Form—AA], taken to be the interface of syntax (in the broad sense) with systems of language use, must receive an appropriate interpretation—must be licensed in the sense indicated. None can simply be disregarded. (Chomsky, 1986: 98)

This is unfortunately rather vague and open to conflicting interpretations, as discussed further below.

Chomsky (1986) gives the following as examples of the kind of sentences that FI blocks due to improper LF licensing:

(44) a. I was in England last year [the man]
b. John was here yesterday [walked]
c. [who] John saw Bill
d. [every] everyone was here

The postulation of a Principle of Full Interpretation is perhaps compelling but was in fact completely redundant with other principles that were active in the theory at the time. The Theta Criterion blocks the first two sentences. In the first, *the man* is not assigned a theta role. In the second, *walked* cannot properly assign its one theta role (assuming this is intransitive *walk*). The only potential recipient of the theta role is *John*, but if it were to receive *walk*'s theta role then the subject would bear two theta roles, violating the Theta Criterion. The last two examples are blocked by the ban on vacuous quantification, NVQ: the *wh*-operator *who* and the quantifier *every* do not have variables that they can bind. There was thus a point of considerable redundancy between various principles in the theory.

This redundancy was subsequently addressed by early work in the Minimalist Program. It was realized from quite early on in the Minimalist Program that Full Interpretation could subsume and eliminate both the Theta Criterion and the Projection Principle:

> Let us now look more closely at the economy principles. These apply to both representations and derivations. With regard to the former, we may take the economy principle to be nothing other than FI: every symbol must receive an "external" interpretation by language-independent rules. There is no need for the Projection Principle or θ-criterion at LF. A convergent derivation might violate them, but in that case it would receive a defective interpretation. (Chomsky 1993: 32, Chomsky 1995: 200)

Although all the Full Interpretation examples in (44) involve extra material, if Full Interpretation is to subsume the Theta Criterion and the Projection Principle, then FI must be understood in a completely resource-sensitive manner: it must not only block extra, unrequired material, but also enforce lexical requirements that certain material is obligatorily present.

Chomsky (1995: 151) also reduces No Vacuous Quantification to Full Interpretation:

> One consequence [of FI at LF—AA] is that vacuous quantification should be forbidden.

All of the P&P/Minimalist principles reviewed up to this point have ultimately been reduced to FI.

Full Interpretation is very obviously just an informal formulation of Linguistic Resource Sensitivity. Proponents of FI may then feel that its reduction to Resource Sensitivity is unwarranted or trivial. I do not think this is so, for several reasons. First, Full Interpretation is vague, unformalized, and hence open to conflicting interpretations. It can lead to many potentially wasteful and misguided debates based on its lack of precision. Resource Sensitivity is by contrast strongly formalized in terms of resource logics, proof theory, and type theory. Second, if Full Interpretation is such a robust and pervasive property of language, there is no sense in stipulating it as a separate principle, a kind of theoretical appendage. Resource Sensitivity, in contrast, is part of the formal system that performs composition. It is embedded as an integral part of the theory. Third, as an economy condition, Full Interpretation is transderivational (Potts, 2002*b*). Resource Sensitivity is not transderivational: it is a condition on a single structure (a proof). Given the worrying complexity properties of transderivational constraints and the theoretical and empirical arguments against them (Jacobson, 1998; Johnson and Lappin, 1997, 1999; Potts, 2001, 2002*a*; Pullum and Scholz, 2001), if FI and Resource Sensitivity are equivalent but the latter is not transderivational, this is reason enough to adopt it instead of FI. Fourth, to the extent that its precise content can be divined, FI seems to be a claim about contentful elements in semantics. In contrast, Resource Sensitivity is a claim about semantic composition, whatever the nature of the meanings that are being composed. This means that Full Interpretation has nothing to say about the necessity of words that seem to have no semantic content, such as do-support *do*, the complementizer *that*, expletive pronouns, and certain subcategorized prepositions, such as *of* (Potts, 2002*b*). However, it is possible for semantically contentless elements to contribute bleached identity functions together with resources for composition. In that case, Resource Sensitivity covers these cases while FI does not.

5.3.7 *Numerations and the Inclusiveness Condition*

The Minimalist Program introduces the notion of *numeration* for the multiset of lexical items from which a syntactic derivation is computed. Chomsky (1995: 228) notes that a 'perfect language' should meet the "condition of inclusiveness":[10]

> Any structure formed by the computation (in particular, π and λ) is constituted of elements already present in the lexical items selected for N; no new objects are added in the course of the computation apart from rearrangements of lexical properties …

Chomsky (1995: 228) goes on to note that the inclusiveness condition is not fully met, which would seem to be a weakness of the framework.

It is clear that Resource Sensitivity, in contrast, entails a version of the inclusiveness condition that is fully met. The multiset of lexically obtained premises

[10] The inclusiveness condition is also discussed in relation to Resource Sensitivity by Potts (2003, 2005: 85).

(the 'numeration') must be exhaustively used up. Furthermore, Resource Sensitivity is a stronger condition than the inclusiveness condition. Not only can no items be entered into computation during derivation, the existing items cannot be reused and all existing items must be used up. Lastly, if Resource Sensitivity holds, then there is no room—in the weak, modality-free version of linear logic assumed here (see the appendix)—for even slight departures from the inclusiveness condition. If such departures from the condition are strictly necessary in Minimalist terms, then they can still potentially be understood using the linear logic modalities, but that would come at the cost of weakening Resource Sensitivity.[11]

5.4 Conclusion

This chapter presented the formal theory behind the guiding hypothesis of this work:

(45) **The Resource Sensitivity Hypothesis**:
Natural language is resource-sensitive.

This hypothesis is based on the property of Linguistic Resource Sensitivity, which is in turn based on the property of Logical Resource Sensitivity of resource logics, although Logical Resource Sensitivity alone is insufficient to capture the intuitions behind Linguistic Resource Sensitivity.

I explored several proposals in the linguistic literature and showed how they can be construed as implicit appeals to Linguistic Resource Sensitivity. However, this is no reason to conclude that the Resource Sensitivity Hypothesis is an established aspect of linguistic theory and is therefore not a new idea worthy of exploration. In every case, I showed that Resource Sensitivity leads to a new understanding of the theoretical principle, offers new avenues of research, yields new interpretations of established results, or addresses theoretical or empirical problems with the principle in question.

[11] An entire issue of the journal *Research on Language and Computation* focuses on understanding the Minimalist Program in resource logical terms (Retoré and Stabler, 2004). Also see Vermaat (2005).

6

The Resource Management Theory of Resumption

The Resource Management Theory of Resumption (RMTR) is based on two key assumptions:

1. **The Resource Sensitivity Hypothesis (RSH)**
   Natural language is resource-sensitive.
2. **McCloskey's Generalization**
   Resumptive pronouns are ordinary pronouns.

The logic behind the theory is as follows. If a resumptive pronoun is an ordinary pronoun, then it constitutes a surplus resource. If the Resource Sensitivity Hypothesis is to be maintained, then there must be an additional consumer of the pronominal resource present. The additional consumer is a *manager resource*, which licenses the resumptive pronoun by managing the resource surplus constituted by the resumptive. Manager resources are thus at the heart of RMTR.

Section 6.1 shows that an ordinary pronoun theory of resumptives leads to resource surplus and that resumptive pronouns therefore pose a problem for semantic composition. Section 6.2 presents manager resources in detail. Section 6.3 shows how manager resources are integrated into an LFG architecture. Section 6.4 presents the analysis of gap-like resumptives, which require an additional syntactic mechanism. Section 6.5 is a consideration of the theoretical implications and empirical predictions of the theory.

6.1 The Problem of Resumptives as Resource Surplus

Consider the English sentence in (1), which contains a resumptive pronoun in a relative clause and is therefore ungrammatical, since the grammars of standard varieties of English do not license resumptive pronouns.

(1) *Every clown who Thora knows <u>him</u> laughed.

It is sufficient to look at the linear logic resources to reveal the problem for composition, since the meaning terms follow by the Curry-Howard isomorphism.

The linear logic sides of the meaning constructors that are contributed by the lexical items for example (1) are shown in (2). All resources are named mnemonically, as per the conventions outlined in chapter 4.

(2)
1. $(v \multimap r) \multimap \forall X.[(c \multimap X) \multimap X]$ Lex. **every**
2. $v \multimap r$ Lex. **clown**
3. $(p \multimap k) \multimap [(v \multimap r) \multimap (v \multimap r)]$ Lex. **who**
4. t Lex. **Thora**
5. $t \multimap p \multimap k$ Lex. **knows**
6. $c \multimap (c \otimes p)$ Lex. **him**
7. $c \multimap l$ Lex. **laughed**

For further details on meaning constructors and what kinds of meaning constructors are contributed by different lexical items, refer to chapter 4. A brief review should be sufficient for present purposes. The common noun *clown* contributes a type $\langle e,t \rangle$ resource, an implication from its semantic structure VARIABLE (v) to its RESTRICTION (r). The quantifier *every* contributes a generalized quantifier resource of type $\langle\langle e,t\rangle,\langle\langle e,t\rangle,t\rangle\rangle$ that consumes the resource of the common noun to find its restriction and, in this case, consumes the resource contributed by the matrix verb to find its scope.[1] The name *Thora* refers to an individual and contributes a type e resource. The pronoun consumes its antecedent's resource and reproduces it along with its own resource. In this case, the antecedent is the DP headed by the common noun *clown*. I am adopting a DP analysis of nominal phrases in order to be consistent with Toivonen's phrase structure theory (Toivonen, 2001, 2003), but an NP analysis would not affect any crucial aspect of the semantic theory. The verb *know* contributes a resource that needs to consume two arguments, its pronominal object and its subject, a proper name. The intransitive matrix verb *laughed* contributes a resource that needs to consume one argument, the matrix subject. Lastly, the relative pronoun contributes a resource that performs modification of the relative head by the relative clause. The first argument is the resource corresponding to the relative clause it introduces, i.e. the scope of the relative operator. This is a type $\langle e,t \rangle$ implication from the relativized argument's resource to the resource corresponding to the head of the relative clause. In this case, the relativized argument is the embedded object and the

[1] The linear universal is used in calculating scope and has nothing to do with the denotational semantics of the scope-taking element in the meaning side. In other words, all scope-taking elements have such a universal in their linear logic. See chapter 4.

first argument of the modificational resource is therefore $p \multimap k$, which is the resource corresponding to the embedded transitive once it has combined with its subject. The second argument of the relative modifier is the resource being modified, which is that of the head noun, $v \multimap r$.

A Glue proof for the semantics of a sentence S succeeds if and only if there is a proof from the premises contributed by the lexical items in S that uses each premise exactly once and terminates in a linear logic atom corresponding to the semantic projection of the sentence. Given the premises in (2), a proof for (1) must terminate in the linear logic atom l, because l is the consequent of the premise contributed by the matrix verb *laughed*. The attempted proof in Figure 6.1 shows that there is no such proof from the premises in (2) that uses all of the premises.[2] The pronominal resource is identified as the culprit. There are other proofs that could be constructed, but none of them could get rid of the pronominal resource p. The only consumer of p is the premise $t \multimap p \multimap k$ contributed by the verb *know* in the relative clause. The resource p is the resource corresponding to the relativized object. In order for the body of the relative clause to compose with the relative pronoun, this argument of *know* must not be saturated. Therefore, there is in fact no consumer for the resource p and there is no valid proof for this sentence from the premises in (2). The resumptive pronoun's resource is a surplus resource that leads to proof failure. In other words, the resumptive pronoun saturates its position in the relative clause and semantic composition of the relative clause with the rest of the sentence is blocked.

The resource logic perspective reveals that a resumptive pronoun is a surplus resource. The notion of resource surplus allows us to give a unified theory of resumption which encompasses both syntactically active and syntactically inactive resumptive pronouns on the one hand (Asudeh, 2011*c*) and copy raising on the other (Asudeh, 2002*b*; Asudeh and Toivonen, 2007, 2012). The theory basically works as follows. If a resumptive pronoun is a surplus resource then the pronoun constitutes a barrier to the basic compositional requirements of the sentence in which it occurs. This would normally lead to ungrammaticality. If the sentence is nonetheless grammatical, then the Resource Sensitivity Hypothesis entails that there must be something that in fact consumes the resumptive pronoun's resource. The consumer of the resumptive is an additional resource of the appropriate type to consume a pronominal resource. These resumptive consumers are called manager resources, because they manage an otherwise unconsumable pronominal resource. A language

[2] The lexically contributed premises are decorated with the corresponding word solely for added readability; this is not an integral part of the proof.

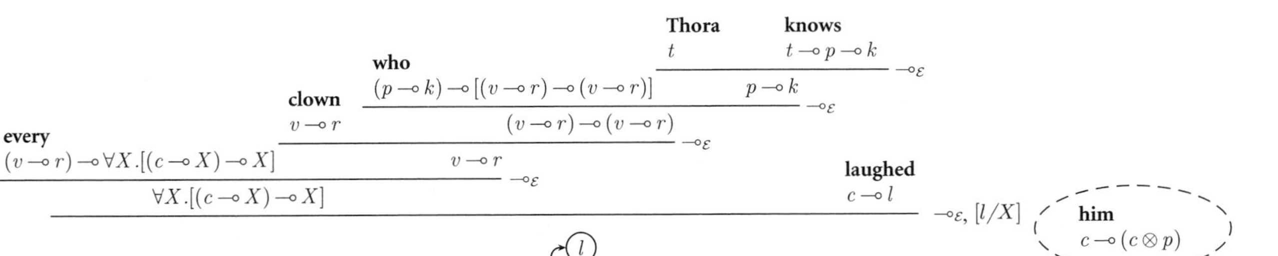

FIGURE 6.1. Proof failure due to a surplus resumptive pronoun resource.

with grammatically licensed resumptive pronouns has such manager resources in the portion of its lexical inventory or grammar that concerns unbounded dependencies. A language that does not license resumptive pronouns in unbounded dependencies lacks manager resources in its grammar. A language may have manager resources in some environments without having them in others. This is exemplified by English, which exhibits copy raising and therefore has a subset of raising verbs that contribute manager resources, but which lacks resumptive pronouns in unbounded dependencies and therefore lacks manager resources in the portion of the grammar that concerns such dependencies.

6.2 Manager Resources

A manager resource is a lexically contributed premise that consumes a pronominal resource. Manager resources are the licensing mechanism for resumption in general, both for resumptive pronouns and for copy raising pronouns. In the specific case of resumptive pronouns, manager resources are contributed through the part of a language's lexical inventory that concerns unbounded dependencies. More specifically, resumptive-licensing manager resources are contributed by complementizers, and perhaps also other material that occurs in the left periphery of CP.

Manager resources have the following general compositional schema, where P is some pronoun that the lexical contributor of the manager resource can access and A is the antecedent or binder of P:

(3) $(A \multimap A \otimes P) \multimap (A \multimap A)$

The antecedent of the main implication is a pronominal-type meaning constructor. The consequent is a function on the binder.

The resources corresponding to the manager resource, the resumptive pronoun and the binder of the resumptive pronoun together yield just the binder. Suppose we have the following lexically contributed premises:

(4)
1. A Lex. **(antecedent)**
2. $A \multimap (A \otimes P)$ Lex. **(pronoun)**
3. $[A \multimap (A \otimes P)] \multimap (A \multimap A)$ Lex. **(manager resource)**

The antecedent is a simple type *e* nominal, such as a name, in this case. Figure 6.2 shows the linear logic proof that is constructed from these premises. The proof terminates in the antecedent resource. The manager resource has removed the pronoun from composition. The consequent of the main implication in the manager resource must be an implication on the pronoun's

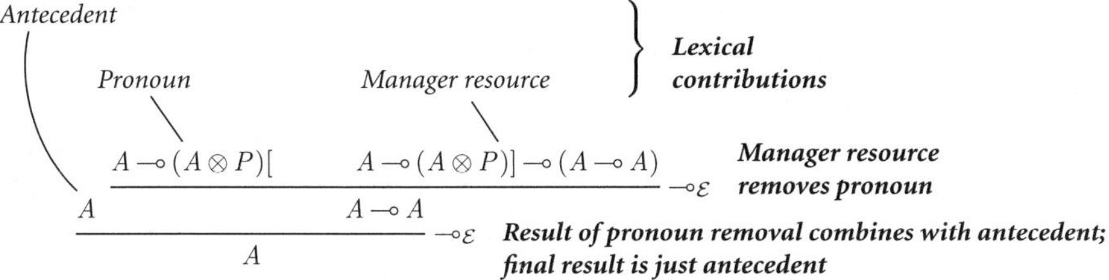

FIGURE 6.2. A manager resource in action (lower type antecedent).

binder ($A \multimap A$), not just another instance of the binder's resource (A). In the latter case, there would be a new copy of the resource A introduced into the proof. This would lead to a new resource surplus problem, since there would be two copies of A where only one is required.

If the binder of the resumptive is a higher type nominal, such as a quantifier, we would instead get the following schematic meaning constructors:

(5) 1. $\forall X.[(A \multimap X) \multimap X]$ Lex. **(quantificational binder)**
2. $A \multimap (A \otimes P)$ Lex. **(pronoun)**
3. $[A \multimap (A \otimes P)] \multimap (A \multimap A)$ Lex. **(manager resource)**

The premise marked *Antecedent* in Figure 6.2 is replaced by an assumption of a type *e* resource on which the quantificational binder's scope depends. The manager resource consumes the pronoun and then modifies the assumption. The resulting resource, A, is taken as an argument by the scope of the quantificational binder. The assumption is then discharged and the scope can compose with the quantifier. This is sketched in Figure 6.3. The boxed proof chunk in Figure 6.3 is equivalent to Figure 6.2.

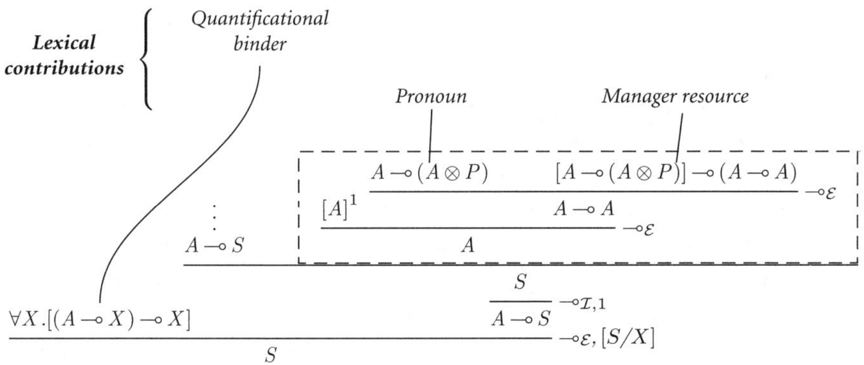

FIGURE 6.3. A manager resource in action (higher type antecedent).

The basic function of the manager resource is to remove the pronoun from composition. A resumptive pronoun that is licensed by a manager resource behaves syntactically exactly like a non-resumptive pronoun—the resumptive is an ordinary pronoun—but behaves like a gap with respect to semantic composition: the semantic argument position corresponding to the pronoun gets saturated by the pronoun's antecedent or bound by the pronoun's binder, rather than being saturated by the pronoun. The fact that a manager resource removes a pronoun from semantic composition is reflected in the meaning side of the manager resource's meaning constructor by vacuous lambda abstraction over the pronoun's function, as shown in (6). The function in the meaning language that corresponds to the modification on the antecedent resource is an identity function.

(6) $\lambda P \lambda x.x : (A \multimap A \otimes P) \multimap (A \multimap A)$

A manager resource is therefore a type $\langle\langle e,\langle e \times e\rangle\rangle,\langle e,e\rangle\rangle$ function. Its role is exclusively to remove a pronoun from semantic composition, without affecting the rest of the composition.

The proof in (8) shows the meaning language side of Figure 6.2. The proof is constructed from the lexically contributed premises in (7), which are just the premises in (4) with the meaning side of the meaning constructors added.

(7)
1. $a : A$ — Lex. **(antecedent)**
2. $\lambda y.y \times y : A \multimap (A \otimes P)$ — Lex. **(pronoun)**
3. $\lambda P \lambda x.x : [A \multimap (A \otimes P)] \multimap (A \multimap A)$ — Lex. **(manager resource)**

(8)
$$\dfrac{a : A \qquad \dfrac{\lambda y.y \times y : A \multimap (A \otimes P) \qquad \lambda P \lambda x.x : [A \multimap (A \otimes P)] \multimap (A \multimap A)}{\lambda x.x : (A \multimap A)} \multimap_{\mathcal{E}}}{a : A} \multimap_{\mathcal{E}},\ \Rightarrow_{\beta}$$

It is worth reiterating that the effect of a manager resource is to remove a pronoun from semantic composition but that there is no underlying syntactic or semantic difference between resumptive and non-resumptive pronouns. The resumptive pronoun is an ordinary pronoun that makes a normal lexical contribution in all grammatical aspects, including syntax and semantics.

At this stage, it is useful to look at the derivation for a grammatical sentence containing a resumptive in order to see in some detail how resumptives work according to this theory. I will abstract away from language-particular details by using English words for expository purposes. This should not be taken as an implicit claim that English has grammatically licensed resumptive pronouns.

(9) Every clown who$_{pro}$ Thora knows him laughed.

Let us suppose that *who*$_{pro}$ is a relative pronoun that licenses a resumptive pronoun.

Making certain simplifications, we get the meaning constructors in (10) from the lexical items in this example. The precise manner in which manager resources are integrated into the larger Glue and LFG theories is the subject of section 6.3. For now it suffices to use the usual mnemonic convention in naming the resources.

(10)
1. $\lambda R \lambda S.every(R, S)$:
   $(v \multimap r) \multimap \forall X.[(c \multimap X) \multimap X]$ — Lex. **every**
2. $clown : v \multimap r$ — Lex. **clown**
3. $\lambda Q \lambda P \lambda z.P(z) \wedge Q(z)$:
   $(p \multimap k) \multimap [(v \multimap r) \multimap (v \multimap r)]$ — Lex. **who**$_{pro}$
4. $\lambda P \lambda x.x : [c \multimap (c \otimes p)] \multimap (c \multimap c)$ — Lex. **who**$_{pro}$ **(MR)**
5. $thora : t$ — Lex. **Thora**
6. $\lambda x \lambda y.know(x, y) : t \multimap p \multimap k$ — Lex. **knows**
7. $\lambda z.z \times z : c \multimap (c \otimes p)$ — Lex. **him**
8. $laugh : c \multimap l$ — Lex. **laughed**

Note in particular that the relative pronoun *who*$_{pro}$ is contributing two meaning constructors. The first is the normal meaning constructor for a restrictive relative clause, a modifier on the relativized noun's meaning. The second meaning constructor is the manager resource.

The proof in Figure 6.4 shows how the meaning of the sentence is composed from the lexically contributed Glue resources in (10). The operations in the meaning language follow straightforwardly by the Curry-Howard isomorphism, but are also shown in detail in Figure 6.5. The manager resource removes the pronoun from composition, clearing the way for the argument corresponding to the pronoun in the semantics to be bound by the pronominal binder, *every clown*, just as if the relative clause had contained a gap in lieu of a resumptive pronoun. In sum, a manager resource removes a pronoun from composition, which proceeds as if the pronoun had been a gap.

6.2.1 *Summary*

The basic idea behind the Resource Management Theory of Resumption is that the problem of resumption is a problem of resource surplus in semantic composition: the resumptive pronoun's resource apparently goes unconsumed. The consumer of the resource is a manager resource and it is the presence of a manager resource that licences a resumptive use of a pronoun.

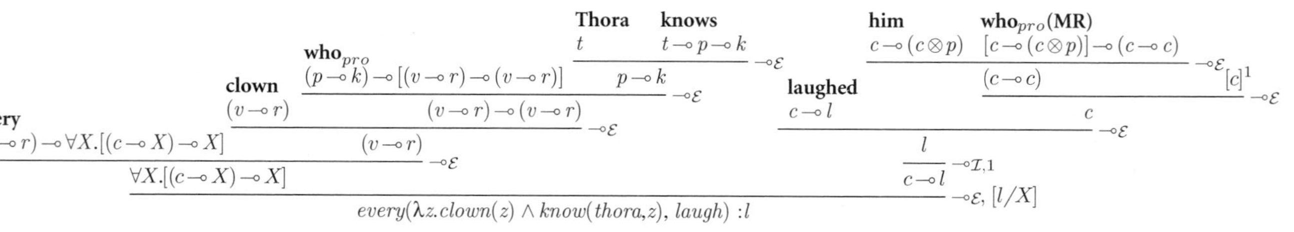

FIGURE 6.4. Proof for the expository resumptive example, *Every clown who$_{pro}$ Thora knows him laughed.*

$$
\dfrac{
\dfrac{
\begin{array}{l}\textbf{every}\\ \lambda R\lambda S.\, every(R,S) :\\ (v \multimap r) \multimap \forall X.[(c \multimap X) \multimap X]\end{array}
\quad
\dfrac{
\begin{array}{l}\textbf{clown}\\ clown:\\ (v \multimap r)\end{array}
\quad
\dfrac{
\begin{array}{l}\textbf{who}_{pro}\\ \lambda Q\lambda P\lambda z.P(z) \wedge Q(z) :\\ (p \multimap k) \multimap [(v \multimap r) \multimap (v \multimap r)]\end{array}
\quad
\dfrac{
\begin{array}{l}\textbf{Thora}\\ thora:\\ t\end{array}
\quad
\begin{array}{l}\textbf{knows}\\ \lambda x\lambda y.\, know(x,y) :\\ t \multimap p \multimap k\end{array}
}{
\begin{array}{l}\lambda y.know(thora,y) :\\ p \multimap k\end{array}
}
}{
\begin{array}{l}\lambda P\lambda z.P(z) \wedge know(thora,z) :\\ (v \multimap r) \multimap (v \multimap r)\end{array}
}
}{
\begin{array}{l}\lambda z.clown(z) \wedge know(thora,z) :\\ (v \multimap r)\end{array}
}
}{
\begin{array}{l}\lambda S.every(\lambda z.clown(z) \wedge know(thora,z),S) :\\ \forall X.[(c \multimap X) \multimap X]\end{array}
}
\quad
\dfrac{
\dfrac{
\begin{array}{l}\textbf{laughed}\\ laugh:\\ c \multimap l\end{array}
\quad
\dfrac{
\dfrac{
\begin{array}{l}\textbf{him}\\ \lambda z.z \times z:\\ c \multimap (c \otimes p)\end{array}
\quad
\begin{array}{l}\textbf{who}_{pro}\textbf{(MR)}\\ \lambda P\lambda x.\, x:\\ [c \multimap (c \otimes p)] \multimap (c \multimap c)\end{array}
}{
\lambda x.x : (c \multimap c)
}
\quad
[y: c]^{1}
}{
y: c
}
}{
\begin{array}{l}laugh(y) :\\ l\end{array}
}
\multimap_{\mathcal{I},1}
}{
\begin{array}{l}\lambda y.\, laugh(y) :\\ c \multimap l\end{array}
}
}{
every(\lambda z.\, clown(z) \wedge know(thora,z), laugh) : l
}
[l/X]
$$

FIGURE 6.5. Proof for the expository resumptive example, *Every clown who$_{pro}$ Thora knows him laughed*, with meaning language.

Manager resources are lexically specified and operate at the syntax–semantics interface. The result is a theory of resumptives that treats resumptive pronouns as ordinary pronouns in the syntax and ties their occurrence to the presence of a manager resource, which licenses the resumptive pronoun by dealing with the resource surplus.

The specification of manager resources presented here is an attempt to present their resource consumption role in the most conceptually clear fashion. Kokkonidis (2006) presents an alternative specification of manager resources that is more logically elegant than the one presented here. However, the compactness of Kokkonidis's presentation means that the role of the manager resource in the theory is perhaps not as clear as it is here.

6.3 Integrating Resource Management in LFG

6.3.1 *The Lexical Specification of Manager Resources*

In the previous section, the meaning constructors for manager resources were given in only schematic form. In this section, I show how manager resources are integrated into an LFG architecture. In particular, I show how manager resources are lexically specified using functional descriptions and the σ correspondence function from f-structure to semantic structure. I also discuss the interaction of an ordinary pronoun theory of resumptives with LFG's theory of unbounded dependencies, in particular the Extended Coherence Condition. Finally, I discuss how the ordinary pronoun theory necessitates an auxiliary mechanism of dependency relabelling, given the usual method for handling anaphora and resource mapping in Glue Semantics.

The generalized form of a manager resource's meaning constructor is shown in (11), where I have abbreviated the feature ANTECEDENT as ANT after its first occurrence.

(11) $$[((\uparrow \text{ GF}^{+})_{\sigma} \text{ ANTECEDENT})_{e} \multimap [((\uparrow \text{ GF}^{+})_{\sigma} \text{ ANT})_{e} \otimes (\uparrow \text{ GF}^{+})_{\sigma_e}]] \multimap [((\uparrow \text{ GF}^{+})_{\sigma} \text{ ANT})_{e} \multimap ((\uparrow \text{ GF}^{+})_{\sigma} \text{ ANT})_{e}]$$

The meaning constructor has two constituent functional descriptions, $((\uparrow \text{ GF}^{+})_{\sigma} \text{ ANTECEDENT})$ and $(\uparrow \text{ GF}^{+})_{\sigma}$. The feature ANTECEDENT is proper to semantic structures and therefore does not need to be σ-mapped. The feature GF is short for any f-structural grammatical function and the specification $(\uparrow \text{ GF}^{+})_{\sigma}$ uses Kleene plus to indicate that it can be satisfied by the σ-projection of a grammatical function in the f-structure of the manager resource's contributor (designated by $\uparrow$) or by a grammatical function arbitrarily deeply embedded in the manager resource's contributor's f-structure.

The instantiation of the two component functional descriptions $((\uparrow \text{GF}^+)_\sigma \text{ ANTECEDENT})$ and $(\uparrow \text{GF}^+)_\sigma$ results in the following schematic meaning constructor.

(12) $(A \multimap A \otimes P) \multimap (A \multimap A)$

This is just the schematic form of the manager resource from (3) above.

The meaning constructor in (11) is rather unconstrained. There is no guarantee that the instances of $(\uparrow \text{GF}^+)$ get instantiated to the same f-structure, such that the instances of $(\uparrow \text{GF}^+)_\sigma$ get instantiated to the same semantic structure. It would in principle be possible to satisfy a manager resource by constructing its antecedent through the linear logic proof rules of conjunction introduction (to get the conjunction, ⊗) and implication introduction (to get the implication into the conjunction) applied to resources that satisfy the component functional descriptions of $((\uparrow \text{GF}^+)_\sigma \text{ ANTECEDENT})$ and $(\uparrow \text{GF}^+)_\sigma$. We therefore need to exercise more control over the realization of separate instances of $(\uparrow \text{GF}^+)_\sigma$. From a computational perspective, this additional control also has the desirable effect of preventing some attempts to construct proofs that are bound to fail, thus reducing the proof space.

We therefore use *local names* (Kaplan and Maxwell, 1996), which are f-structure variables that have scope only in the lexical item or rule element in which they occur (Dalrymple, 2001: 146–148), to ensure that distinct instances of $(\uparrow \text{GF}^+)$ refer to the same f-structure. Using a local name, %RP, we would break up (11) as follows:

(13) $\%\text{RP} = (\uparrow \text{GF}^+)$
$[(\%\text{RP}_\sigma \text{ ANT}) \multimap ((\%\text{RP}_\sigma \text{ ANT}) \otimes \%\text{RP}_\sigma)]$
$\multimap [(\%\text{RP}_\sigma \text{ ANT}) \multimap (\%\text{RP}_\sigma \text{ ANT})]$

The local name %RP is set to the f-structure of the resumptive pronoun. Every instance of %RP in the scope of the lexical item that contributes the manager resource refers to the same f-structure.

The specification of manager resources can be further simplified if we take into account the fact that a manager resource is a device for eliminating resumptives and copy pronouns. Both kinds of pronoun are bound pronouns (McCloskey, 1979; Lappin, 1983; Sells, 1984). The lexical contributor of the manager resource will therefore specify binding of the resumptive pronoun that is to be removed in terms of some local GF, as follows:

(14) $(\uparrow \text{GF})_\sigma = ((\uparrow \text{GF}^+)_\sigma \text{ ANTECEDENT})$

Given this equality, the expression $((\uparrow \text{GF}^+)_\sigma\ \text{ANTECEDENT})$ in the manager resource's meaning constructor can be replaced by $(\uparrow \text{GF})_\sigma$. The resulting meaning constructor is shown in (15). For extra readability, the GF local to the manager resource's f-structure is underlined and the resumptive pronoun's GF, which is an unbounded distance away, is double underlined.

(15) $[\underline{(\uparrow \text{GF})_\sigma} \multimap (\underline{(\uparrow \text{GF})_\sigma} \otimes \underline{\underline{(\uparrow \text{GF}^+)_\sigma}})] \multimap [\underline{(\uparrow \text{GF})_\sigma} \multimap \underline{(\uparrow \text{GF})_\sigma}]$

Thus, if we take into account the function of a manager resource—the removal of a bound, resumptive pronoun—the theory allows a completely local statement of manager resources, except for the part that concerns pronominal binding, which is independently known to be a non-local process.[3]

Local names can again be used to constrain realization of the various instances of GF and the instance of GF$^+$. The lexical contributor of the manager resource would then contain the following information:

(16) $\%\text{GF} = (\uparrow \text{GF})$
$\%\text{RP} = (\uparrow \text{GF}^+)$
$\%\text{GF}_\sigma = (\%\text{RP}_\sigma\ \text{ANTECEDENT})$
$[\%\text{GF}_\sigma \multimap (\%\text{GF}_\sigma \otimes \%\text{RP}_\sigma)] \multimap [\%\text{GF}_\sigma \multimap \%\text{GF}_\sigma]$

The theory therefore allows a compact, controlled, and local specification of manager resources.

6.3.1.1 *Summary* Manager resources can be specified in a highly general form, as shown above. The resource logic tightly constrains how the generalized manager resource may be realized: a manager resource must remove a resumptive pronoun and it can remove only a resumptive pronoun,[4] or else there is no valid Glue proof from lexically contributed premises. The use of local names provides further control over the specification of manager resources. Lastly, the theory allows specification of manager resources in local terms. This follows from the fact that a resumptive pronoun is a bound pronoun and the fact that the lexical contributor of the manager resource will in general require anaphoric binding of the resumption pronoun by a local grammatical function, i.e. one that is found in the f-structure of the lexical contributor of the manager resource. The actual binding of the resumptive pronoun is non-local, but pronominal binding is non-local in general.

[3] I mean 'non-local process' in a descriptive sense here: a pronoun may be bound by a binder that occurs an arbitrarily long distance away. The point at hand is not affected if pronominal binding is broken down into a series of local bindings, as in, e.g., Kratzer (2009).

[4] More precisely, a manager resource must remove a pronoun that is a surplus resource, whether a resumptive pronoun in an unbounded dependency or a copy pronoun in copy raising.

A manager resource thus acts (principally) locally, but has a non-local effect, through pronominal binding.

6.3.2 *Satisfaction of the ECC and Integration of the Binder*

Unbounded dependencies in LFG are traditionally represented by the features TOPIC and FOCUS, depending on the kind of unbounded dependency. I instead use the single grammatical function UDF, which is short for UNBOUNDED DEPENDENCY FUNCTION. This function can be mapped to either i(nformation)-structure TOPIC or FOCUS as appropriate (Dalrymple and Nikolaeva, 2011), through the use of the ι correspondence function in the Correspondence Architecture, as discussed in chapter 3.

The Extended Coherence Condition (ECC) requires an unbounded dependency to be integrated into the grammatical representation (Zaenen, 1980; Bresnan and Mchombo, 1987; Fassi-Fehri, 1988):

(17) **Extended Coherence Condition**
A UDF must be linked to the semantic predicate argument structure of the sentence in which it occurs, either by being functionally equated with or by binding an integrated grammatical function.

An 'integrated grammatical function' is a grammatical function that independently satisfies Completeness and Coherence or an ADJUNCT, which does not need to satisfy Coherence and is essentially automatically integrated (for further details, see chapter 4 of Bresnan, 2001, and Bresnan et al., 2012).

One way to satisfy the ECC is through functional equality. Functional equality occurs when there is a functional equation that equates the UDF (TOPIC or FOCUS) with some GF, resulting in two grammatical functions with a single, shared f-structure as their value. This is sketched in (18).

(18)
$$\begin{bmatrix} \text{PRED} & `\ldots' \\ \text{UDF} & \begin{bmatrix} \text{PRED} & `\ldots' \end{bmatrix} \\ \text{GF} & \text{———} \end{bmatrix}$$

Some lexical entry or rule element must provide the functional equation that integrates the UDF into the f-structure (Kaplan and Zaenen, 1989; Dalrymple, 2001).

The second way to satisfy the ECC is through binding, which involves the semantic structure feature ANTECEDENT. This is sketched in (19):

(19)

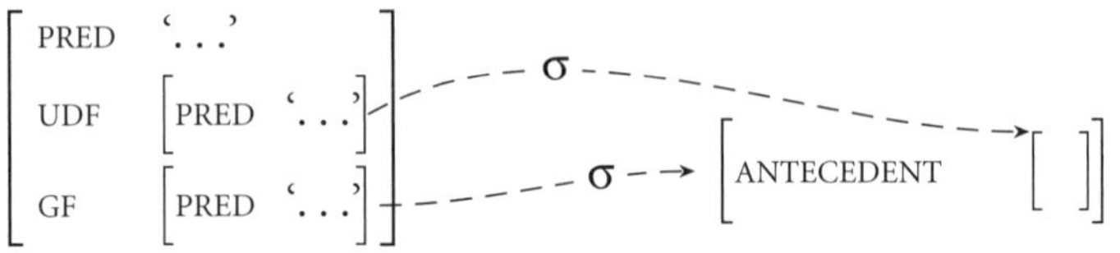

$$\left[\begin{array}{ll}\text{PRED} & \text{`...'} \\ \text{UDF} & \left[\text{PRED `...'}\right] \\ \text{GF} & \left[\text{PRED `...'}\right]\end{array}\right] \quad \begin{array}{l} \text{UDF} \xrightarrow{\sigma} [\;] \text{ (in ANTECEDENT)} \\ \text{GF} \xrightarrow{\sigma} \left[\text{ANTECEDENT } [\;]\right]\end{array}$$

The UDF is integrated into the grammatical representation by binding an argument.

Independent aspects of the theory presented here entail that a resumptive binder must satisfy the ECC through the binding option, unless an additional syntactic mechanism mediates the functional equality option. The resumptive pronoun itself contributes a PRED, on the assumption that it is an ordinary pronoun. The top of the unbounded dependency, i.e. the binder in the binder-resumptive dependency, will also contribute a PRED feature. The value of the feature PRED is a semantic form (Kaplan and Bresnan, 1982: 32–35[177–180]). Each instance of a semantic form is unique (Kaplan and Bresnan, 1982: 124–125[274]).[5] This means that even two semantic forms that bear the same information, e.g. 'pro', cannot be equated. If two different sources attempt to specify an f-structure's PRED value, there is therefore a violation of Consistency (Kaplan and Bresnan 1982: 58[204], Dalrymple 2001: 39), also known as the Uniqueness Condition. Consistency requires that each f-structure has only one value for a particular attribute, but since semantic forms cannot be equated there would be two values for the attribute PRED. If a resumptive pronoun is an ordinary pronoun that contributes a PRED feature and the top of the unbounded dependency (e.g., a *wh*-phrase) also contributes a PRED feature, then there cannot be an unmediated functional equality between the resumptive pronoun's f-structure and the f-structure of the UDF, since this would result in a Consistency/Uniqueness violation.

Syntactically active resumptives (SARS) and syntactically inactive resumptives (SIRS), which were introduced in chapter 2, are distinguished according to these criteria. The grammar of SARS involves only pronominal binding between a binder and a resumptive pronoun. The grammar of SIRS involves functional equality between the binder and the resumptive, where an extra operation of restriction (Kaplan and Wedekind, 1993) mediates the functional equality such that there is no Consistency violation (Asudeh, 2011*c*). The two

[5] In chapter 5, I discussed the possibility of dispensing with the uniqueness of PRED, since this seems to follow from Resource Sensitivity. As mentioned in that chapter, though, such a large-scale architectural change to the underlying syntactic theory is beyond the scope of this book. However, if the change in question were made, the analysis of syntactically inactive resumptives could potentially be greatly simplified.

kinds of resumption are nevertheless unified by manager resources, which in both cases use the mechanisms underlying pronominal binding to consume the resumptive pronoun. We return to this distinction between SARS and SIRS in section 6.4 below.

A resumptive pronoun's binder is an unbounded dependency function, UDF.[6] We can use this to further refine the lexical specification of manager resources. The binding equation in (14) can therefore be rewritten as:

(20) $(\uparrow \text{UDF})_\sigma = ((\uparrow \text{GF}^+)_\sigma\ \text{ANTECEDENT})$

We can then replace the manager resource (15) with the one shown in (21).

(21) $[(\uparrow \text{UDF})_\sigma \multimap ((\uparrow \text{UDF})_\sigma \otimes (\uparrow \text{GF}^+)_\sigma)] \multimap [(\uparrow \text{UDF})_\sigma \multimap (\uparrow \text{UDF})_\sigma]$

We thus get a version of the manager resource that is specified locally to the UDF that binds the resumptive pronoun. The local name specification in (16) is essentially unaffected, except that we replace %GF = (↑ GF) with %GF = (↑ UDF).

We can in fact take advantage of the projection architecture and use inside-out functional uncertainty at semantic structure to define a completely local version of the manager resource. Observe that the local UDF is the ANTECEDENT of GF^+ at semantic structure , given the binding equation in (14). The following inside-out equality therefore holds:

(22) $(\uparrow \text{GF}^+)_\sigma = (\text{ANTECEDENT}\ (\uparrow \text{UDF})_\sigma)$

The right-hand side of the equation picks out the node at semantic structure that has a feature ANTECEDENT whose value is the semantic structure node corresponding to the local UDF. We know by (14) that the UDF is the ANTECEDENT of the resumptive pronoun, which is the GF^+ in question. In other words, another way to identify $(\uparrow \text{GF}^+)_\sigma$ is as the semantic structure node that has the ANTECEDENT feature with $(\uparrow \text{UDF})_\sigma$ as its value.

Given the equality (22), we can replace (15) with the following:

(23) $[(\uparrow \text{UDF})_\sigma \multimap ((\uparrow \text{UDF})_\sigma \otimes (\text{ANTECEDENT}\ (\uparrow \text{UDF})_\sigma))] \multimap$
$[(\uparrow \text{UDF})_\sigma \multimap (\uparrow \text{UDF})_\sigma]$

This is a completely local specification of the manager resource. However, its specification depends on the binding equation (14), which is non-local, since pronominal binding is not bounded. The inside-out functional uncertainty in (23) may be difficult for readers unfamiliar with LFG. I therefore do not

[6] This is only the case for resumptive pronouns narrowly construed to exclude copy pronouns. We will return to this issue in chapter 12.

use this formulation and instead specify manager resources as in (15) and (21). However, it is important to realize that (23) is a possible local specification for manager resources. In particular, the fact that the specification uses the feature ANTECEDENT is important, as discussed further in section 6.5.

6.3.3 *Dependency Mismatch and Relabelling*

There is a final complication that must be dealt with to fully integrate manager resources into Glue Semantics for LFG. The issue is best highlighted if we consider another 'resumptive' sentence, this time with a *wh*-phrase binder (again using English purely for expository purposes):

(24) Who did Thora see <u>him</u>?

For (24), we obtain the mnemonically labelled f-structure and semantic structure in (25).

(25)
$$s\left[\begin{array}{ll} \text{PRED} & \text{`see'} \\ \text{UDF} & w\left[\text{PRED}\ \text{`pro'}\right] \\ \text{SUBJ} & t\left[\text{PRED}\ \text{`Thora'}\right] \\ \text{OBJ} & p\left[\text{PRED}\ \text{`pro'}\right] \end{array}\right] \xrightarrow{\sigma} \left[\text{ANTECEDENT}\ \left[\ \right]\right]$$

The manager resource will remove the pronominal resource contributed by the resumptive pronoun *him*, clearing the way for the dependency on the resumptive, $p \multimap s$, to serve as the scope of the *wh*-phrase.

There is now a slight hitch that has to do with how resource mapping and naming work. The binder in the binder resumptive dependency is a scopal element that needs to find its scope. The generalized meaning constructor for the *wh*-word *who* is shown in (26) and the instantiated version, in terms of node labels from the f-structure above, is shown in (27):

(26) $\forall X.[(\uparrow_\sigma \multimap X)] \multimap X]$

(27) $\forall X.[(w \multimap X) \multimap X]$

The scope of the binder is specified in terms of its local f-structure label, which is *w*. But the dependency which it actually needs to consume—the one left by removal of the resumptive pronoun—is not a dependency on *w*. It is a dependency on *p*, the resumptive pronoun's label. That is, the dependency available is $p \multimap s$, but the *wh*-word needs something of the form $w \multimap X$. The predicate that locally selects for the resumptive does not 'know' that it is in a resumptive environment and the binder does not 'know' that it is in a binder-resumptive dependency. The top and the bottom of the binder-resumptive dependency are completely locally specified and blind to what is happening elsewhere in the structure.

This local/blind specification holds for filler-gap dependencies too, but the crucial difference is that these are integrated through functional equality. The situation is sketched in the following f-structure:

(28)
$$s\left[\begin{array}{ll} \text{PRED} & `\ldots\text{'} \\ \text{UDF} & w\left[\text{PRED} \quad `\ldots\text{'}\right] \\ \text{GF} & \underline{\qquad\qquad} \end{array}\right]$$

The f-structure of the filler is the same f-structure as that of the gap and the scope of the filler will therefore match the dependency that is missing the gap. In this case, the scope of the filler will be specified as $\forall X.[(w \multimap X) \multimap X]$ and the dependency on the functionally bound GF will be $w \multimap s$.

The dependency mismatch problem does not have the same status as the resource surplus problem that manager resources solve. The latter problem stems from an assumption that resumptives are ordinary pronouns and the Resource Sensitivity Hypothesis. The resource surplus problem concerns the whole enterprise of using a resource logic at the syntax–semantics interface. In contrast, the dependency mismatch problem is essentially a bookkeeping problem. It concerns how resources are labelled based on the regular mapping from the syntax to the linear logic proofs. A valid linear logic proof could easily be constructed from the relevant premises so long as the resource labels could be made to match. There are various ways one could think of doing this. One way would be to have pronouns output a multiplicative conjunction that has as conjuncts two instances of the antecedent-labelled resource, rather than an antecedent-labelled conjunct and a pronominal-labelled conjunct. Another option would be to state that unbounded dependency functions that are integrated into the grammatical representation by binding an argument that bears the resource identifier of the argument. Either option would effectively mean that a pronominal resource has the form $b \multimap (b \otimes b)$. The dependency mismatch would not arise, then, because the dependency on the resumptive pronoun would be stated in terms of the binder's resource identifier.

A simpler option than modifying the basic resource-mapping conventions is available, though. The licensers of resumptive pronouns not only contribute manager resources, they also perform *resumptive dependency relabelling* by contributing an additional meaning constructor of the following general form:

(29) $\lambda P.P : ((\uparrow \text{GF}^{+})_{\sigma} \multimap \uparrow_{\sigma}) \multimap ((\uparrow \text{UDF})_{\sigma} \multimap \uparrow_{\sigma})$

This meaning constructor takes a dependency on a resumptive pronoun and returns a dependency on the unbounded dependency function that binds it, without affecting the semantics (the meaning language is just an identity function). This meaning constructor can be further controlled by using local names:

(30) $\lambda P.P : (\%\text{RP}_{\sigma} \multimap \uparrow_{\sigma}) \multimap (\%\text{GF}_{\sigma} \multimap \uparrow_{\sigma})$

With this meaning constructor, the problematic resumptive dependency $p \multimap s$ for (25) is consumed and the dependency $w \multimap s$ is produced. The resulting dependency can serve as the scope for the *wh*-phrase that is the resumptive's binder. The same dependency relabelling will properly adjust a relative clause predicate. Dependency relabelling is a general lexical mechanism for renaming dependencies at the top and bottom of binder-resumptive dependencies that are mismatched due to the normal resource naming conventions. The alternative specification of manager resources presented by Kokkonidis (2006) incorporates dependency relabelling into the meaning constructor for the manager resource. I will continue to present relabelling as a separate premise from the manager resource, in order to separate these distinct concepts.

6.4 Syntactically Inactive Resumptive Pronouns

McCloskey (2006) identifies two kinds of grammatically licensed resumptive pronouns,[7] which I call 'syntactically active resumptives' (SARS) and 'syntactically inactive resumptives' (SIRS). The division of resumptives into these two kinds is based on a number of diagnostics, which were examined in detail in chapter 2 and which are summarized in Table 6.1.[8] As made plain by the discussion in chapter 2, the facts are somewhat messier than indicated in the summary table. Some of the complexities are discussed further in chapter 9 (see also McCloskey, 2006, and Asudeh, 2011*c*).

[7] He also discusses a third kind of resumptive, as found in English. These I set aside as not properly integrated into the grammar (Chao and Sells, 1983; Sells, 1984). I argue in chapter 11 that so-called resumptives in English are actually an artefact of the processing system.

[8] The fact that some of these diagnostics have been claimed to involve non-syntactic factors, as mentioned in chapter 2, does not invalidate them in establishing categories of resumptive pronouns, since categorization does not depend on the source of the distinction, but only the distinction itself.

TABLE 6.1. Some properties of syntactically active and syntactically inactive resumptive pronouns (idealized).

	Syntactically Active RPs	Syntactically Inactive RPs
Grammatically Licensed	Yes	Yes
Island-Sensitive	No	Yes
Weak Crossover Violation	No	Yes
Licenses Reconstruction	No	Yes
Licenses ATB Extraction	No	Yes
Licenses Parasitic Gaps	No	Yes

The basic difference between syntactically inactive resumptives and syntactically active resumptives is that SIRS pattern like filler-gap dependencies with respect to certain diagnostics, whereas SARS do not. Syntactically inactive resumptives are nevertheless subject to McCloskey's Generalization—they are morphologically ordinary pronouns. In sum, the problem is that syntactically inactive resumptives are apparently ordinary pronouns, just like syntactically active resumptives, but behave like gaps, while SARS do not.

One solution to this impasse is to treat syntactically inactive resumptives as ordinary pronouns that contain the same morpholexical information as the corresponding non-resumptive pronouns of the language in question, but to modify the regular filler-gap relation such that these resumptives and their antecedents receive a filler-gap analysis in some part of the grammar. One way to do this is to analyse syntactically inactive resumptives as fully contributing to c-structure, but to treat the binder-resumptive dependency using a modified functional equality. The difference between syntactically active and syntactically inactive resumptives is then analysed as a difference in satisfaction of the Extended Coherence Condition: syntactically active resumptives satisfy the ECC through binding, whereas syntactically inactive resumptives satisfy the ECC through functional equality.

This entails that SARS binder-resumptive dependencies and SIRS binder-resumptive dependencies have different representations at f-structure. A syntactically active resumptive and its binder are distinct entities at f-structure—the grammatical functions that represent the binder and the resumptive have distinct values. In contrast, a syntactically inactive resumptive and its binder are not distinct entities at f-structure—the grammatical functions that represent the binder and the resumptive share a single value. Table 6.2 shows the SARS and SIRS f-structures for the target sentence (31) (English is used solely for exposition).

(31) Who did Thora see <u>him</u>?

TABLE 6.2. F-structures for syntactically active and syntactically inactive resumptive analyses of the expository example, *Who did Thora see him?*

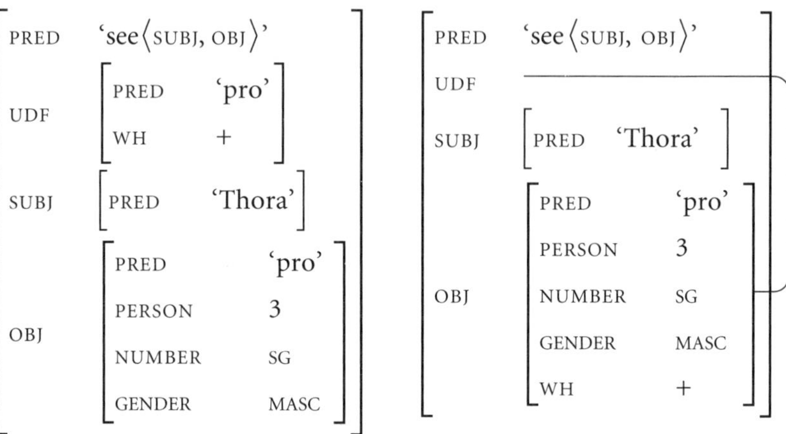

The pronoun in the SIRS analysis of this sentence is an ordinary pronoun underlyingly and is present in c-structure, but it is not present as an independent entity in f-structure.

Despite the difference at f-structure, syntactically active and syntactically inactive resumptives are equally ordinary pronouns in terms of their lexical specifications and contributions to c-structure. This also means that they contribute pronominal meaning constructors to the semantics. The pronominal meaning constructor is the point of theoretical unification between the two kinds of resumptive pronouns (Asudeh, 2011*c*): both kinds of resumptive equally constitute a resource surplus and both must therefore be licensed by manager resources, given the Resource Management Theory of Resumption.

The representation of the relation between the binder and the resumptive is the point of divergence between syntactically active and syntactically inactive resumptives. The binder-resumptive relation for syntactically active resumptives is pronominal binding, which explains why they do not display diagnostic properties of gaps, since pronominal binding is a distinct mechanism from the functional equality involved in filler-gap dependencies. In contrast, the binder-resumptive relation in the syntactically inactive resumptive f-structure involves functional equality at f-structure. The relation between the binder and the resumptive in the SIRS f-structure in Table 6.2 is precisely the same relation of functional equality that would have obtained for the corresponding filler-gap sentence (32).

(32) Who did Thora see _?

The functional equality at f-structure that holds between the syntactically inactive resumptive and its binder explains its gap-like behaviour with respect to relevant diagnostic properties, since these constraints standardly hold of f-structures (see Dalrymple, 2001, and further references therein).[9] This is explored in detail with respect to Swedish and Vata in chapters 9 and 10.

However, treating the pronoun as an ordinary pronoun in terms of its lexical specifications means that the pronoun contributes a PRED feature with value 'pro' to the f-structure. The SIRS resumptive pronoun is therefore unlike a gap in certain respects. In this theory, gaps are not lexical items and are not represented at c-structure; as a consequence, gaps do not contribute a PRED feature to f-structure. Functional equality between a filler, which does contribute a PRED to f-structure, and the grammatical function corresponding to the gap is therefore unproblematic. In contrast, if the syntactically inactive resumptive is an ordinary pronoun and is contributing a PRED 'pro', then functional equality between the resumptive pronoun and the binder would cause a Consistency violation. If this is to be avoided, something must mediate the functional equality. An appropriate option is the f-structure operation of restriction (Kaplan and Wedekind, 1993). The next section introduces the operation and sketches its application to syntactically inactive resumptives.

6.4.1 *Functional Equality in Resumption via Restriction*

Restriction is a set-theoretic operation on an f-structure. The restriction of some f-structure f by an attribute a, designated $f \backslash a$, is the f-structure that results from deleting the attribute a and its value v from f-structure f (Kaplan and Wedekind, 1993: 198); the pair $\langle a,v \rangle$ is removed from the set of pairs that constitutes the f-structure in question. The input and output f-structures are thus in a subsumption relation: the output of restriction subsumes the input.[10]

Kaplan and Wedekind (1993: 198) formally define restriction as follows:

(33) **Restriction**

If f is an f-structure and a is an attribute:

$$f \backslash a = f|_{\mathrm{Dom}(f)-\{a\}} = \{ \langle \mathrm{s}, \mathrm{v} \rangle \in f \mid s \neq a \}$$

[9] The explanation goes through even if there are extra-grammatical processing factors involved in islands and weak crossover: if the structures that underly processing are the same for gaps and syntactically inactive resumptives, the same processing factors should apply to both.

[10] Restriction is implemented such that the input and output are both delivered in the result (Kaplan and Wedekind, 1993; Crouch et al., 2011); the operation is thus not quite non-monotonic, because the information in the input f-structure is not lost.

The operation can be iterated, because the restriction of an f-structure is itself an f-structure. Iterated restriction is not order-sensitive, since the operation is associative and commutative in its attribute argument: $[f\backslash a]\backslash b = [f\backslash b]\backslash a = f\backslash\{a\ b\}$ (Kaplan and Wedekind, 1993: 198). Restriction of an f-structure by an attribute that the f-structure does not contain vacuously succeeds, since restriction is defined in terms of set complementation. It is therefore not necessary to know in advance whether an f-structure actually contains the restricting attribute. Kaplan and Wedekind (1993: 199) also provide a generalization of the operator to attributes whose values are sets, so the operator is defined for all types of f-structure feature values. The extension to sets is straightforward, but will not be considered further here.

Restriction by the attribute PRED is exemplified in (34).

(34) a. $f = \begin{bmatrix} \text{PRED} & \text{'pro'} \\ \text{PERSON} & 3 \\ \text{NUMBER} & \text{SG} \\ \text{GENDER} & \text{MASC} \end{bmatrix}$

b. $f\backslash\text{PRED} = \begin{bmatrix} \text{PERSON} & 3 \\ \text{NUMBER} & \text{SG} \\ \text{GENDER} & \text{MASC} \end{bmatrix}$

This example illustrates that the restriction of an f-structure never contains more information than the input f-structure: $f\backslash a$ subsumes f ($f\backslash a \sqsubseteq f$).

Restriction can be combined with equality in the expected manner (Kaplan and Wedekind, 1993: 198):

(35) If f and g are f-structures, then $f\backslash a = g\backslash a$ is true if and only if f and g have all attributes and values in common other than a; they may or may not have values for a and those values may or may not be identical.

This provides another perspective on the operation. Standard, unrestricted equality at f-structure designates which attributes and values two f-structures necesarily have in common. Restricted equality designates which attributes two f-structures necessarily do not have in common.

The puzzlingly gap-like properties of syntactically inactive resumptive pronouns are explained if we assume that the filler-gap functional equality in these languages contains a restriction of the PRED feature, which allows them to also apply to ordinary pronouns without causing a violation of Consistency due to the uniqueness of PRED values. This is sketched here:[11]

[11] I assume that the personal pronoun is not specified for the feature WH, such that the WH feature of the UDF does not need to be restricted out; see Table 6.2. If PRONTYPE features are assumed (Butt et al., 1999; Dalrymple, 2001), these would also need to be restricted out, but I leave this aside here.

(36) $$(\uparrow \mathrm{UDF})\backslash\mathrm{PRED} = (\uparrow \underset{\textit{Constraints}}{\mathrm{GF}^*}\ \mathrm{GF})\backslash\mathrm{PRED}$$

The right-hand side of the equality allows the dependency to pass through zero or more grammatical functions (GF*), which captures the unboundedness of the dependency in the usual way. The notation *Constraints* stands for whatever constraints normally apply to filler-gap unbounded dependencies (Dalrymple, 2001: 390–408). These constraints will also apply to binder-resumptive unbounded dependencies, because they are subject to the same equation. There are some further factors that we will return to in the detailed discussion of syntactically inactive resumptives in part IV, but this captures the basic idea: restriction allows the functional equality involved in the filler-gap dependencies to be extended to binder-resumptive dependencies. This yields representations like the one shown in the right-hand side of Table 6.2 above.

However, both lexically and at c-structure, the resumptive pronoun is nothing but an ordinary pronoun. The pronoun therefore contributes a pronominal meaning constructor that a manager resource must consume. Otherwise, the syntactically inactive resumptive would equally give rise to a resource surplus. The Resource Management Theory of Resumption thus provides a unification of syntactically active and syntactically inactive resumptives in semantic composition, as discussed in more detail in Asudeh (2011*c*). The remaining difference between the two kinds of grammatically licensed resumptives concerns their syntax: SIRs require restriction in their syntax, but SARs do not. Syntactically inactive resumptives thus involve an additional mechanism that syntactically active resumptives do not require (Asudeh, 2011*c*).

This work assumes a version of LFG based on codescription (Kaplan, 1989; Dalrymple, 2001: 185–187), as discussed in chapter 3. This means that a lexical entry simultaneously contributes information to all relevant levels of the architecture, including semantic information, phonological information, categorial information, and f-structural information. Crucially, these contributions are made independently of each other: the f-structure is not 'interpreted' to obtain semantic information, as it is in the alternative, description by analysis approach (Halvorsen, 1983; Crouch and King, 2006). Thus, even if the unbounded dependency equation impacts on some of the syntactic information contributed by the pronoun, the phonological specifications and, most importantly, semantic specifications are left untouched.

6.5 Conclusion

The Resource Management Theory of Resumption treats resumptive pronouns as ordinary pronouns that constitute surplus resources. The licensing mechanism for resumption is manager resources. A manager resource consumes the surplus resumptive pronoun resource, allowing the composition of the unbounded dependency to proceed as if the resumptive had been absent. The fact that the pronoun is treated as an ordinary pronoun means that the pronoun is syntactically and lexically distinct from a gap, which in this theory is literally nothing. That is, a gap is not a trace, a copy, or any other kind of special gap object, but is rather an unrealized syntactic argument that is integrated into the grammatical representation by being functionally equated with an unbounded dependency function.

The manager resources that license resumptives are lexically contributed meaning constructors and are therefore specified in particular lexical entries. The theory thus predicts that resumption must be licensed through the presence of lexically specified licensers in lexical inventories. The RMTR theory is thus a lexicalist theory. Theories as otherwise disparate as Lexical-Functional Grammar, Head-Driven Phrase Structure Grammar, and Categorial Grammar, as well as the Minimalist Program framework and recent Principles and Parameters Theory, have converged on the desirability of locating language variation in the lexicon (i.e., in underlying featural distinctions).

Given the uncontroversial premise that lexical specification affects morphological exponence, the theory further predicts that resumptive licensers may be distinguished by morphology or lexical class. The first part of this prediction is verified by the complementizer system of Irish (McCloskey, 1979), as discussed in chapter 7. The second part of the prediction is verified by copy raising in English, which is restricted to a certain class of raising verbs, as discussed in chapter 12.

Finally, the theory offers an answer to what must be one of the central questions about resumption: Why are only pronouns used for resumption? The answer to this question in this theory is that the Glue specification of the linear logic term for a pronoun and the way in which pronouns take their antecedents are such that pronouns are the only lexical items that can be consumed by manager resources. A manager resource consumes a type $\langle e, e \times e \rangle$ expression that is specified in terms of the feature ANTECEDENT. Pronouns are the only expressions that both have the correct type and are correctly specified for the feature ANTECEDENT; the latter is discussed in detail in Asudeh (2005*b*).

The first answer to the question of why only pronouns are used for resumption is thus that pronouns are the only things that have the correct form, given the grammar and the resource logic, to be consumed by manager resources. Why do pronouns have this form? They have this form because, on a variable-free theory of anaphora such as the one assumed here, a pronoun is a function on its antecedent. Pronouns are therefore used in resumption because of how they receive their meanings. Why do pronouns receive their meanings in this manner? Pronouns receive their meanings in this manner because they lack inherent meaning and are dependent for their interpretation on their antecedents. In other words, pronouns are the only items used for resumption because they lack inherent meaning. It is unsurprising that pronominal elements can be consumed by manager resources, because it is precisely these elements whose interpretation is recoverable from elsewhere in the interpretation of the sentence.

Chapter 2 presented a descriptive overview of resumptive pronouns and identified several key empirical characteristics:

1. Resumptive pronouns are ordinary pronouns. (McCloskey's Generalization)
2. Resumptive pronouns are interpreted as bound pronouns.
3. Resumptive pronouns display restrictions on their interpretation. These restrictions are shared with ordinary pronouns, but not with gaps.
4. Syntactically active resumptives occur in unbounded dependencies, but do not share syntactic properties with gaps.
5. Syntactically inactive resumptives occur in unbounded dependencies, and do share syntactic properties with gaps.
6. Resumptive pronouns and gaps have distinct syntactic distributions.

The Resource Management Theory of Management explains these characteristics.

McCloskey's Generalization is one of the two key assumptions in RMTR, along with the Resource Sensitivity Hypothesis, so it is explained to the extent that the theory is independently successful. McCloskey's Generalization is captured as follows in the theory. The only way in which syntactically active resumptives resemble gaps is in semantic composition. This has nothing to do with the information that is lexically specified for the resumptive pronoun and is rather the effect of a manager resource. There is no special lexical specification or resumptive 'feature' that marks a resumptive pronoun in distinction to other pronouns: resumptive pronouns are just ordinary pronouns. This is equally true for syntactically inactive resumptives—they are lexically and c-structurally just ordinary pronouns—even though they are integrated in syntax through functional equality, as gaps are.

The analysis therefore predicts that both syntactically active and syntactically inactive resumptive pronouns are morpholexically identical to non-resumptive pronouns with the same case and agreement features. For example, if the third person object pronoun in some language is *foo* and the language has resumptives, then the third person object resumptive pronoun will also be *foo*. In fact, manager resources consume components of pronominal *meanings* (resources for composition) and are completely insensitive to the form of the pronoun. This means that a manager resource licenses all instances of pronominal information, whether instantiated by a free-standing pronoun or incorporated into a head (such as certain Irish verbs and prepositions). It equally means that syntactically active resumptives and syntactically inactive resumptives receive a unified compositional analysis, despite their syntactic differences.

For both kinds of unbounded dependency resumptive, SARS and SIRS, the manager resource identifies the resumptive in terms of an unbounded dependency function and binds the resumptive to the UDF. Well-formedness of the result depends on something consuming the dependency on the resumptive pronoun that has been left behind by the manager resource's consumption of the pronoun, since that dependency can no longer consume the pronoun itself—the pronoun has been removed. It is the top of the unbounded dependency that consumes the vacated dependency as its scope. The result is that these resumptives are licensed only in unbounded dependencies. Their interpretation as bound pronouns also follows, because in terms of semantic composition, the resumptive pronoun is a bound argument, just like a gap. Chapter 12 extends RMTR to copy pronouns in copy raising, which do not occur in unbounded dependencies, by parametrizing manager resources for copy raising such that they consume the copy raising verb's subject. This once again correctly predicts that a copy pronoun is interpreted as a bound pronoun.

Nevertheless, the fact that resumptive pronouns are interpreted as bound arguments, just like gaps, does not mean that they cannot place further restrictions on interpretation. Gapped objects of intensional verbs like *seek* allow both *de re*/specific and *de dicto*/non-specific readings, whereas corresponding resumptives allow only specific readings (Doron, 1982; Sells, 1984, 1987). Zimmermann (1993) has argued against the classic quantifier scope analysis of the specific/non-specific difference for certain intensional verbs, including *seek*. He has shown that properties of the quantified DP are relevant to whether the ambiguity arises, as are properties of the particular verb. He notes in particular that the class of quantifiers that induce *de dicto* readings in opaque verbs are those that can be characterized as existential (Zimmermann, 1993: 163). The opaque verb takes as an object the relativizing property of the quantifier (Zimmermann, 1993: 164–165). Sells (1984, 1987) has shown that the relevant kind of non-specific reading, which he calls a *concept* reading, is similarly unavailable for pronouns in general. For example, the mini-discourse in (37) can only mean that Dani is looking for a particular unicorn that is tall. It cannot mean that Dani is looking for something or other that is a unicorn and is tall.

(37) Dani seeks a unicorn. It is tall (Sells, 1987: 290, ~(52b))

Sells (1984) argues that the object of *seeks* denotes an individual concept. The general conclusion that Sells (1984, 1987) comes to is that the restriction on interpretation for resumptives hold for non-resumptive pronouns too and is explained if resumptive pronouns are ordinary pronouns.

Even though manager resources remove resumptive pronouns from composition, these pronouns can still place lexically specified conditions on their antecedents, which must be met for the antecedent–pronoun relation to be established. I have been assuming a simple extensional semantics, but it would be straightforward to define an intensional version of the semantics that handles individual concepts (Dalrymple et al., 1999*c*). Zimmermann's (1993) treatment is also, at base, compatible with this. If a pronoun takes only a type *e* antecedent, following Sells (1984, 1987), then the pronoun can only be of type $\langle e, e \times e \rangle$. Since an individual concept is of type $\langle s, e \rangle$, a pronoun cannot take it as an antecedent, due to a type mismatch. Resumptive pronouns on this theory are ordinary pronouns, which means they have the same type as ordinary pronouns and therefore have the same restrictions on their antecedents. It thus follows without further ado that resumptive pronouns have the same restriction on interpretation as ordinary pronouns, since resumptive pronouns just are ordinary pronouns in terms of their meanings and other lexical specifications.

Furthermore, the interpretation of resumptives provides yet more evidence for an ordinary pronoun theory of resumptives over a special pronoun theory that postulates that resumptives are underlyingly gaps. The form of the argument is simple. If resumptive pronouns are just 'spelled out' gaps, then their morphological form is perhaps predictable given certain modern assumptions about morphological realization. The language that has constituted the best case for an analysis of resumptives as spelled out gaps is Swedish. In chapter 9, I present data on Swedish that shows that the putatively spelled out gaps are also *interpreted* like pronouns and not like gaps. In particular, the same lack of non-specific reading that Doron (1982) identifies for Hebrew holds robustly for Swedish. This would be completely unpredicted if resumptives are underlyingly gaps. They should then be intepreted like gaps, whatever their surface form.

Turning now to the syntactic distinctions between syntactically active and syntactically inactive resumptives pronouns, it was observed in chapter 2 that syntactically active resumptive do not display certain key characteristics of gaps; in particular, island sensitivity and form-identity effects. The lack of island-sensitivity follows directly from the Extended Coherence Condition and the fact that the theory presented here treats resumptives as ordinary pronouns. The ECC requires that an unbounded dependency function be integrated into the grammatical representation either through functional equality or through binding. The ordinary pronoun theory means that the pronoun contributes full syntactic information to f-structure, including a PRED feature. The top of the unbounded dependency will also contribute a PRED feature. It is impossible to functionally equate two grammatical functions that each have a PRED feature, because the value of PRED is a unique semantic form and the result of the attempted functional equality will necessarily violate Consistency. The only option available is binding, unless an extra syntactic mechanism mediates the functional equality. Syntactically active resumptives do not involve any such extra mechanism, in constrast to syntactically inactive resumptives. Therefore, syntactically active resumptives involve only a relation of pronominal binding between binder and resumptive. Pronominal binding is not sensitive to islands. It therefore follows that binder-resumptive dependencies for syntactically active resumptives are not island-sensitive, because the mechanism that integrates them—pronominal binding—is not island-sensitive.

Form-identity effects concern features of the unbounded dependency function that could only be assigned to the argument with which it is integrated, such as case (Merchant, 2001: 128–146). The observation is that such form-identity effects routinely arise for filler-gap dependencies but not for binder-resumptive dependencies. This is predicted by the theory. The ordinary pronoun theory of resumptives and the ECC requires that the grammatical function of the resumptive and the unbounded dependency function at the top of the dependency have distinct f-structures as values. Therefore, whatever features occur in the f-structure of the resumptive will not be transmitted to the f-structure of the binder, since it is a distinct f-structure. In contrast, filler-gap dependencies are realized via functional equality. The filler and the gap share the very same f-structure. Therefore, whatever features are added at the gap site will necessarily be borne by the filler. Furthermore, even though syntactically inactive resumptives are integrated through functional equality, they do not necessarily integrate all features with the UDF. As explained in section 6.4, the restriction operation that applies for syntactically inactive resumptives sets aside only the features that are specifically mentioned in the operation. Since the purpose of the restriction operation, in this case, is only to integrate the top of the unbounded dependency and the syntactically inactive resumptive, the only feature that is restricted is PRED. There is no reference to the feature CASE in the restriction operation. Therefore, the form-identity effect holds equally of both SARS and SIRS.

However, syntactically inactive resumptive pronouns do share certain properties of gaps. This is potentially problematic for ordinary pronouns theories of resumption like RMTR. If resumptives are ordinary pronouns, it is somewhat surprising that they behave like gaps in certain respects. This characteristic is obviously not surprising if resumptives are not ordinary pronouns and, in contrast, are like gaps at some underlying level, as in special pronoun theories (see chapter 2).

Even though syntactically inactive resumptives are not underlyingly gaps in RMTR and are just ordinary pronouns, the restriction operation enables the use of functional equality for syntactically inactive binder-resumptive dependencies. The upshot of this is that—although SIRS are lexically pronouns and are present at c-structure—in f-structure, a SIRS unbounded dependency looks like a filler-gap dependency and, moreover, the mechanism that integrates a UDF and a syntactically inactive resumptive is the very same mechanism that integrates a UDF and a gap, i.e. functional equality. The phenomena that have indicated gap-like status for SIRS can then be captured straightforwardly. This will be investigated further in chapters 9 and 10.[12]

Lastly, in each resumptive language, there are normally at least some positions or grammatical functions that resumptives can fill but not gaps, and vice versa. The Resource Management Theory of Resumption does not specify specific positions in which resumptives may not appear or in which they must appear. Rather, like the theory of McCloskey (1979, 1990), resumptives appear to be obligatory where gaps are blocked by independent factors and similarly resumptives can be blocked from certain positions or grammatical functions for independent reasons. For example, in Irish, resumptives are obligatory as objects of prepositions. This is not hardwired into the lexical entry for the manager resources, the resumptive-licensing complementizer, *aN*, or any other aspect of the analysis. The obligatoriness arises because the

[12] Alternatively, it is possible to capture the phenomena in question in semantic composition (i.e., Glue proofs), where similarities between gaps and resumptives are unproblematic on this theory, as explored in Asudeh (2004). However, that treatment arguably leads to a less clear typological picture of resumptive properties (McCloskey, 2006) than the view adopted here.

complementizer that licenses gaps, *aL*, independently cannot reach prepositional objects, since these are necessarily embedded in an OBL or other inaccessible grammatical function. In other words, the resumptive only appears obligatory by virtue of the fact that the gap is independently ungrammatical. This is explored further in the next chapter.

Part III

Syntactically Active Resumptives

7

Irish

This chapter applies the Resource Management Theory of Resumption to data from Irish. Section 7.1 presents the basic clausal structure of Irish that I am adopting, based on work by McCloskey (1979, 1996), Chung and McCloskey (1987), and Sells (1984). I adapt these proposals to LFG using Toivonen's (2003) theory of phrase structure. Section 7.2 presents the data to be analysed. Section 7.3 presents detailed analyses of core Irish filler-gap and binder-resumptive dependencies. Section 7.4 extends these analyses to deal with the difficult "mixed chain" cases discussed by McCloskey (2002). I conclude with a discussion of some further empirical predictions of the analysis of Irish, some directions for further research, and an extended comparison to the Minimalist analysis of McCloskey (2002). Appendix B is a fragment of Irish; it presents some of the analyses in this chapter in more detail.

7.1 Irish Clausal Structure

The clausal structure of Irish has been described in detail by McCloskey (1979, 1990), Chung and McCloskey (1987), Sells (1984, 1987), and Duffield (1995), among others. In this section, I review an LFG-theoretic analysis of the syntax of Irish complementizers (Asudeh, 2002*c*) and I present the basic structure that I assume for Irish clauses, essentially adapting the proposals of Chung and McCloskey (1987) to LFG. The upshot of the analysis is that it reconciles two seemingly incompatible analyses of Irish complementizers, one by Sells in his dissertation (Sells, 1984) and the other by McCloskey in various publications, but principally in McCloskey (1979) and McCloskey (1996).

The Irish complementizer system morphologically registers filler-gap and binder-resumptive dependencies (McCloskey, 1979). Unbounded dependencies in Irish may terminate in a gap or a resumptive pronoun, subject to certain restrictions in both cases. The complementizers of Irish are sensitive to the two kinds of unbounded dependency: roughly, there is a complementizer that registers gaps and another complementizer that registers resumptive pronouns. The complementizers are morphophonologically identical in the non-past

Table 7.1. Irish complementizers (McCloskey, 1979).

	Non-past	Past
go		
Affrmative	***goN***	***gurL***
Negative	***nachN***	***nárl***
aN		
Affirmative	***aN***	***arL***
Negative	***nachN***	***nárL***
aL		
Affirmative	***aL***	***aL***
Negative	***nachN***	***nárL***

form—as shown in Table 7.1, which is based on McCloskey (1979: 11, (18))—but trigger different mutations on following words. The complementizer that is associated with gaps triggers a lenition mutation; it is therefore often written as *aL* in the generative literature, following McCloskey (1979). The complementizer that is associated with resumptives triggers a nasalization mutation; it is therefore often written as *aN* in the generative literature, again following McCloskey (1979). The neutral complementizer *go* is used when there is no unbounded dependency, in a sense to be made more precise shortly.

There is strong evidence that the Irish particles of particular interest here—*aL*, *aN*, and *go*—are indeed complementizers and not *wh*-words or relative pronouns (McCloskey, 1979, 2001). First, they occur left-peripheral to the clause they introduce. Second, they co-occur with *wh*-words in questions, which indicates that they themselves are probably not *wh*-words. Third, they bear no inflection for case, animacy, number, or gender, despite the fact that the pronouns of Irish normally inflect for one or more of these features (McCloskey, 1979: 11). Fourth, the complementizers do inflect for properties of the clause they introduce, in particular tense and mood, as summarized in Table 7.1. Based on this sort of evidence, McCloskey has consistently treated these particles as complementizers. McCloskey (2001) gives a thorough overview of arguments for the complementizer status of the particles.

However, Sells (1984: 127–131) has explicitly argued that the particles are not complementizers and that they are actually head-adjoined to the verb. In particular, he proposes that the preverbal particles are base-generated as adjuncts to the verbal head:

(1)

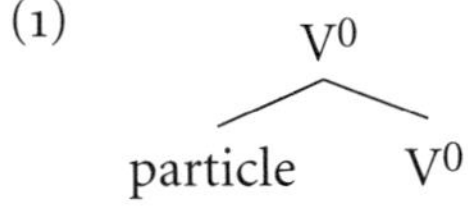

As adjuncts to V^0, the preverbal particles are still within the verbal domain. In fact, they are part of the core verbal domain, rather than the extended functional domain of the verb that complementizers appear in. The evidence that McCloskey gives for the complementizer status of the preverbal particles (that they are left-peripheral, register extraction phenomena, and register tense and negation information) is therefore compatible with Sells's position that they are head-adjoined to the verb.

Two pieces of evidence that Sells presents for his position are that no material can separate the particle from the verb, and that, in VP-coordination structures, the particle must occur in each conjunct, as shown here:

(2) a. an fear aL cheannaionn agus aL dhíolann tithe
the man *aL* buys and *aL* sells houses
'the man that buys and sells houses' (Sells, 1984: 131, (25a))

b. *an fear aL cheannaionn agus d(h)íolann tithe
the man *aL* buys and sells houses
(Sells, 1984: 131, (25b))

If the particles were complementizers, then the obligatory repetition of the particle in VP-coordination would be unexplained.

The claim that the particles are head-adjuncts to the verb is incompatible with the claim that they are complementizers if the complementizers project X-bar structure. For independent reasons having to do with adjunction, McCloskey (1996) proposes that there is complementizer lowering in Irish. He effectively ends up with a similar structure to (1), but by lowering of the complemenizer from CP to adjoin to I^0:

(3)

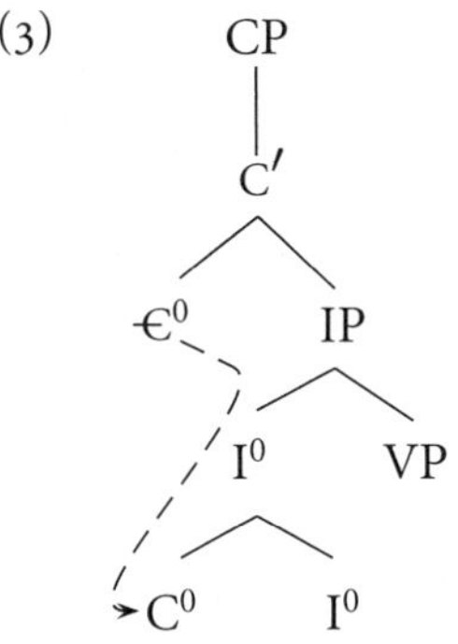

The C^0 does project a CP, but it is lowered and head-adjoined to I^0. The lowered C^0 under current transformational assumptions would leave a deleted copy at its extraction site.

In Asudeh (2002*c*), I present a base-generated LFG analysis that reconciles the head-adjunction analysis of Sells (1984) with the complementizer analysis of McCloskey (1996). Rather than lowering a complementizer, the analysis builds on Toivonen's theory of non-projecting words (Toivonen, 2001, 2003). Toivonen argues for a revised X-bar theory which accommodates heads that do not project any X-bar structure. These are non-projecting words, represented as $\hat{X}$ ('X-roof'). Projecting heads are annotated X^0. In Toivonen's X-bar theory, non-projecting heads are head-adjoined to an X^0. The proposal in Asudeh (2002*c*) is that the Irish complementizers are base-generated as non-projecting adjuncts to I^0:

(4) 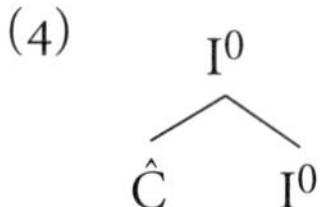

This structure is generated by the following c-structure rule:

(5) $I^0 \longrightarrow \quad \underset{\uparrow = \downarrow}{\hat{C}} \qquad \underset{\uparrow = \downarrow}{I^0}$

Part of the motivation for McCloskey's (1996) complementizer-lowering analysis was the explanation of certain facts about adjunction in Irish which motivate the presence of a CP node above IP. In Asudeh (2002*c*), I show how the base-generated non-projecting word analysis can ensure the presence of such a CP node even though it is not projected by the non-projecting $\hat{C}$. Here I will make the simplifying assumption that all sentential complements (COMP grammatical functions) in Irish are CPs in c-structure and that the c-structure rules generate CP nodes appropriately. The LFG theory of endocentricity and extended heads (Zaenen and Kaplan, 1995; Bresnan, 2001) will again ensure that the CP has a head (in this case $\hat{C}$ and I^0 are co-heads of both IP and CP).

The basic clausal structure of Irish is VSO in finite matrix and subordinate clauses (McCloskey, 1979, 1990; Chung and McCloskey, 1987). The order in non-finite clauses is subject-initial and generally SOV, although SVO order occurs in certain dialects under certain conditions (Chung and McCloskey, 1987: 211–212, 230–232). Chung and McCloskey (1987) argue that the complement of Infl in both finite and non-finite clauses is a small clause, yielding a structure like the following:

(6)

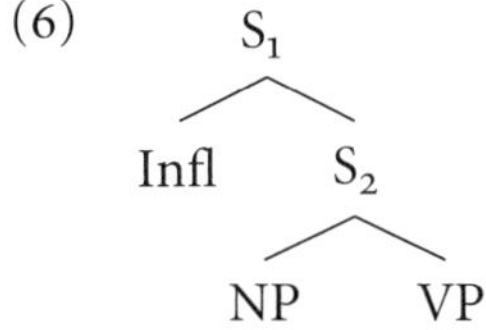

This structure accounts for the word order facts as follows on the Chung and McCloskey analysis. The finite verb moves from V to Infl (see also McCloskey, 1996), with the subject in the NP position of the small clause and the object in the VP. This derives VSO order. The non-finite verb does not occupy Infl. It occupies V in the VP. This derives SV order. Base-generation of the object in a preverbal position would derive the correct word order in both finite and non-finite clauses: in finite clauses the verb moves to Infl, leaving the subject and object in place, and in non-finite clauses nothing moves and the correct SOV order is derived. However, Chung and McCloskey (1987: 230) argue against this sort of analysis based on the fact that Irish is "an overwhelmingly regular head-initial language" and the fact that there are other kinds of VPs that have VO order. They instead propose an analysis on which the object moves and left-adjoins to the VP dominating the non-finite V. A final general property of Irish clause structure that bears mentioning is that pronominal direct objects tend to occur at the right edge of their clause (Chung and McCloskey, 1987: 195). That is, even though full objects immediately follow the subject and precede obliques and adverbials, pronominal objects follow obliques and adverbials and occur clause-finally.

I adopt the structures that Chung and McCloskey propose for both finite and non-finite clauses. However, since LFG is a non-transformational framework, there will be no head movement from V to finite Infl, no leftward movement for adjunction of an object to the VP that contains non-finite V, and no rightward movement in postposing of a pronoun. Everything will instead be base-generated by c-structure rules and controlled by appropriate functional descriptions on these rules, as is standard in LFG. Following King (1995) and Bresnan (2001: 127–131), I derive the effect of head movement of V to I through lexical category specification. Finite verbs in Irish will have the category I^0 and non-finite verbs will have the category V^0. I will adopt Chung and McCloskey's small clause structure for the complement of I^0. I assume that full clauses in Irish have the category CP. The basic structures generated for finite and non-finite clauses are as follows:[1]

[1] This distribution of the feature FINITE is probably not quite sufficient for periphrastic clauses, as pointed out to me by Louisa Sadler (p.c.), but I leave this complication aside here.

(7) Finite clause

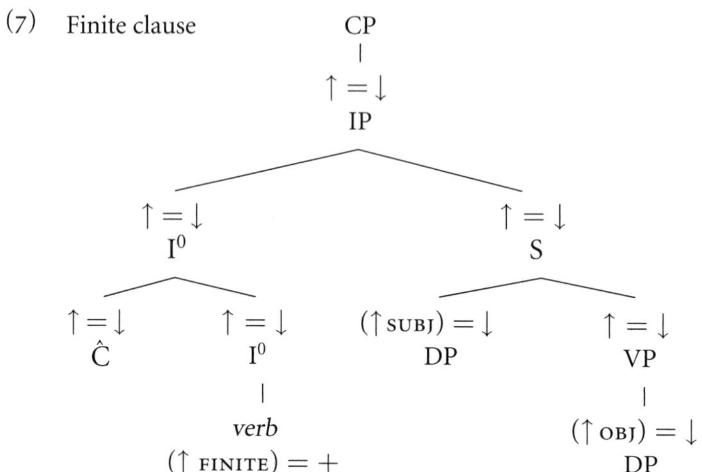

(8) non-Finite clause

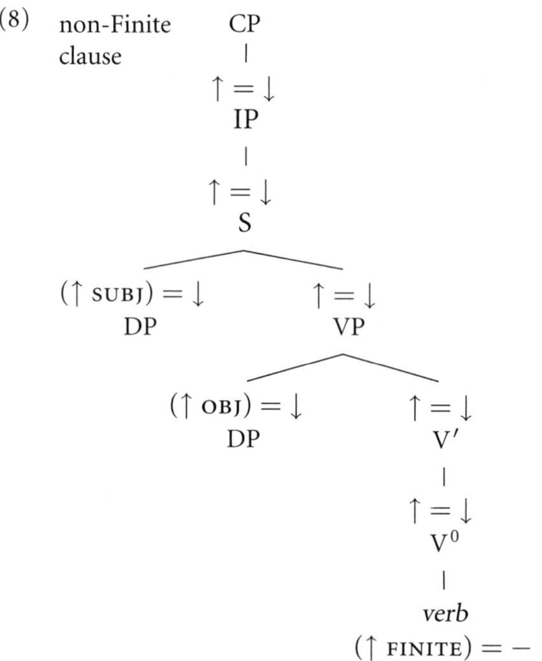

These c-structures presuppose the theory of phrase structure developed by Bresnan (2001) and Toivonen (2001, 2003). I^0 in (7) counts as an extended head for the VP, satisfying the LFG version of endocentricity (Zaenen and Kaplan, 1995: 221, Bresnan, 2001: 132–134). The equation on the verb in (8),

($\uparrow$ FINITE) = $-$, will introduce this specification into the f-structure for the whole CP. Therefore, a finite verb could not appear elsewhere in the c-structure material contributing to the matrix CP's f-structure.

7.1.1 *Summary*

The structures for finite and non-finite clauses in (7) and (8) are based on the structures motivated by Chung and McCloskey (1987) and the theory of non-projecting heads developed by Toivonen (2001, 2003). The analysis of the I^0 adjunction structure and the theory of non-projecting Irish complementizers is further developed in Asudeh (2002*c*). The LFG theory of endocentricity and extended heads (Zaenen and Kaplan, 1995; Bresnan, 2001) is also instrumental to the analysis.

7.2 Unbounded Dependencies in Irish

This section presents the commonly occurring core patterns for unbounded dependencies in Irish, as well as three patterns that are much less frequent, but which nevertheless do occur in both spontaneous speech and text. The latter patterns are what McCloskey (2002) calls "mixed chains". I also adopt this terminology, for the sake of continuity with McCloskey's work, but the term 'chain' is purely a descriptive one in this analysis and has no theoretical status.

The basic patterns for one-clause cases are shown in (9) and (10) (McCloskey, 1979, 1990, 2002).

(9) [$_{CP}$ *aL* ... _ ...]

a. an scríbhneoir a mholann na mic léinn _
   the writer *aL* praise the students _
   'the writer whom the students praise' (McCloskey, 1979: 6, (6))

b. Céacu ceann a dhíol tú _?
   which one *aL* sold you _
   'Which one did you sell?' (McCloskey, 2002: 189, (10a))

(10) [$_{CP}$ *aN* ... *Rpro* ...]

a. an scríbhneoir a molann na mic léinn é
   the writer *aN* praise the students him
   'the writer whom the students praise (him)' (McCloskey, 1979: 6, (5))

b. Céacu ceann a bhfuil dúil agat ann?
   which one *aN* is liking at.you in.it
   'Which one do you like (it)?' (McCloskey, 2002: 189, (10b))

The resumptive pronoun need not be a free-standing pronoun. The pronominal information can be contributed by inflection on a head, as illustrated by (10b).

The core multi-clause patterns show an interesting divergence between the two unbounded dependency types. The filler-gap dependency is marked by an instance of *aL* on every clause from the filler to the gap. This is strong evidence for some kind of successive-cyclicity in the filler-gap dependency (McCloskey, 1990, 2002), although it is not necessarily evidence of successive-cyclic *movement*, as demonstrated by Zaenen (1983) and Bouma et al. (2001), who offer non-transformational accounts of successive-cyclic unbounded dependency marking. In contrast, the common pattern for the binder-resumptive dependency marks only the top of the dependency (e.g., the first clause modifying a relative head). Intervening complementizer positions are marked by the neutral complementizer *go*. Thus, there is no evidence of successive cyclicity in binder-resumptive dependencies. The two patterns are shown here:

(11) $[_{CP}$ *aL* ... $[_{CP}$ *aL* ... $[_{CP}$ *aL* ... _ ...]]]
an t-ainm a hinnseadh dúinn a bhi _ ar an áit
the name *aL* was-told to-us *aL* was _ on the place
'the name that we were told was on the place'
(McCloskey, 2002: 190, (13a))

(12) $[_{CP}$ *aN* ... $[_{CP}$ *go* ... $[_{CP}$ *go* ... *Rpro* ...]]]
fir ar shíl Aturnae an Stáit go rabh siad díleas do'n Rí
men *aN* thought Attorney the State *go* were they loyal to-the King
'men that the Attorney General thought were loyal to the King'
(McCloskey, 2002: 190, (16))

Any analysis of Irish unbounded dependencies must minimally explain these two patterns.

McCloskey (2002) identifies three further multi-clause patterns, which he calls "mixed chains". These are somehow peripheral but nevertheless part of the grammar of Irish, as clarified by the following passage from McCloskey (2002: 195):

> Examples of both [core multi-clause] patterns turn up with great frequency in published texts and in speech, formal and informal. But many other examples turn up as well in written and oral usage. Many of these examples seem to represent only "noise"—errors of production, the consequence of ill-informed copy-editing, or nonce productions which aren't replicable. Others, however, represent patterns which recur and which can be investigated in a systematic way with native speaker consultants ... Although these constructions turn up in speech and writing, they are rarer than

the two [core multi-clause patterns]. The patterns are real, but are liminal parts of the language, lying at the edge of people's competence and at the edge of their experience.

It is clear, then, that a fully explanatory account of Irish unbounded dependencies must extend to mixed chains, because they are real parts of the grammar, although peripheral. McCloskey (2002: 195) goes on to note that:

> What the patterns have in common is that they all involve a resumptive pronoun, but they also have a "successive-cyclic" character in the sense that they involve distinctive morphosyntactic marking of intermediate positions.

I will follow McCloskey's (2002) usage and simply refer to the three mixed chain patterns as Patterns 1, 2, and 3.

Pattern 1 concerns the Complex NP Constraint. The key to understanding the pattern lies in the fact that complex NPs, unlike other islands, have an internal clause that can host an unbounded dependency. McCloskey (2002: 195–196) notes that the "commonest way to realize" complex NPs is the core resumptive pattern (12):

(13) achan rud a rabh dóchas aca go dtiocfadh sé
every thing *aN* was hope at-them *go* come.COND it
'everything that they hoped (that it) would come'
(McCloskey, 2002: 196, (26a))

Pattern 1 is an alternative way to realize complex NPs, with *aL* marking the NP-internal complementizer, rather than *go*. This gives rise to the mixed chain shown in (14).[2]

(14) [$_{\text{CP}}$ *aN* ... [$_{\text{NP}}$ N [$_{\text{CP}}$ *aL* ... _ ...]]]
a. rud a raibh coinne aige a choimhlíonfadh _ an aimsir
thing *aN* was expectation at-him *aL* fulfil.COND _ the time
'something that he expected time would confirm'
(McCloskey, 2002: 196, (28))
b. biseach ... a raibh súil agam a bhéarfá _
recovery *aN* was hope at-me *aL* get.COND.2SG _
'a recovery that I hoped you would stage'
(McCloskey, 2002: 196, (29))

McCloskey (2002: 196–197) notes that a filler-gap dependency internal to the complex NP, signalled by *aL*, is unsurprising. It arises through the normal filler-gap mechanism, since there is a filler position free within the embedded clause (SpecCP on both his theory and this theory) and there is no island

[2] These examples and others provided by McCloskey (2002: 196) are attested examples.

constraint violation in relating a gap to a filler in this position. However, given that *aN* normally signals the presence of a resumptive pronoun, the question is: where is the resumptive pronoun (McCloskey, 2002: 197)?

Pattern 2 is the inverse of Pattern 1. In Pattern 2, a resumptive pronoun in the lower clause occurs in a position that is inaccessible to a filler-gap dependency (for independent reasons) and is signalled by the resumptive complementizer *aN*. The complementizer in the higher clause is the complementizer *aL*, which signals a filler-gap dependency:

(15) $[_{CP}$ *aL* ... $[_{CP}$ *aN* ... *Rpro* ...]]

a. aon duine a cheap sé a raibh ruainne tobac aige
any person *aL* thought he *aN* was scrap tobacco at-him
'anyone that he thought had a scrap of tobacco'
(McCloskey, 2002: 198, (34))

b. Cé is dóigh leat a bhfuil an t-airgead aige?
who *aL*.COP.PRES likely with-you *aN* is the money at-him
'Who do you think has the money?'
(McCloskey, 2002: 198, (35))

c. an galar a chuala mé ar cailleadh bunadh an oileáin leis
the disease *aL* heard I *aN* died people the island [GEN] by-it
'the disease that I heard that the people of the island died of (it)'
(McCloskey, 2002: 198, (36))

McCloskey (2002: 198) notes that this pattern is explained (in the transformational terms he is working in) if there is binding of the resumptive by an operator in the lower SpecCP, with subsequent movement of the operator to the higher SpecCP, as suggested by Finer (1997) for similar Selayarese data. The lower dependency in the chain is a binder-resumptive dependency, while the higher dependency is a filler-gap dependency.

Pattern 3 is a mix of Patterns 1 and 2. As in Pattern 2, a resumptive pronoun in the lower clause occurs in a position that is inaccessible to a filler-gap dependency and is signalled by the resumptive complementizer *aN*. But, as in Pattern 1, the higher clause is also introduced by the resumptive-sensitive complementizer:

(16) $[_{CP}$ *aN* ... $[_{CP}$ *aN* ... *Rpro* ...]]

a. an bhean a raibh mé ag súil a bhfaighinn uaithi é
the woman *aN* was I hope.PROG *aN* get.COND.1SG from-her it
'the woman that I was hoping that I would get it from (her)'
(McCloskey, 2002: 199, (41))

b. san áit ar dúradh leis a bhfaigheadh sé Jim ann
in-the place *aN* was-told with-him *aN* find.COND he in-it
'in the place where he was told that he would find Jim'
(McCloskey, 2002: 199, (43))

c. na cuasáin thiorma ar shíl sé a mbeadh contúirt ar bith
the holes dry *aN* thought he *aN* would-be danger any
uirthi tuitim síos ionnta
on-her fall.[−FIN] down into-them
'the dry holes that he thought there might be any danger of her falling down into them' (McCloskey, 2002: 199, (44))

It appears that there are two binders for the single resumptive pronoun. This is problematic for the resource logic account, since there is apparently only one pronominal resource and two consumers for it, but it is also problematic on an operator-binding approach such as McCloskey's (2002), for reasons that will be clarified below. The basic question for both kinds of theory boils down to the same question that Pattern 1 raises: where's the (other) resumptive pronoun?

In the following two analysis sections, we will see how the Resource Management Theory of Resumption accounts for the data outlined in this section. The analysis accounts for all the data types presented here, as well as the descriptive characteristics presented in chapter 2. The analysis of Irish is tightly constrained on the one hand by the dictates of the theory, in particular the Resource Sensitivity Hypothesis, and on the other hand by empirical observations and generalizations about the language. The heart of the analysis is the lexical specifications for the complementizers.

7.3 Analysis of Core Patterns

7.3.1 *Filler-Gap Dependencies*

Let us first consider a simple filler-gap dependency signalled by *aL*:

(17) $[_{\mathrm{CP}}$ *aL* … _ …]

(18) an scríbhneoir a mholann na mic léinn _
the writer *aL* praise the students _
'the writer whom the students praise' (McCloskey, 1979: 6, (6))

The crucial c-structure rules for the analysis of unbounded dependencies are the rules for CP and relative clause modifiers of nominals in (19) and (20):

(19)
$$\text{CP} \longrightarrow \left\{ \begin{array}{c|c} \text{XP} & \epsilon \\ (\uparrow \textsc{udf}) = \downarrow & (\uparrow \textsc{udf pred}) = \text{`pro'} \\ & (\textsc{adjunct} \in \uparrow) \\ & REL_\sigma \end{array} \right\} \quad \begin{array}{c} \text{C}' \\ \uparrow = \downarrow \end{array}$$

(20)
$$\text{NP} \longrightarrow \begin{array}{c} \text{NP} \\ \uparrow = \downarrow \end{array} \quad \begin{array}{c} \text{CP} \\ \downarrow \in (\uparrow \textsc{adjunct}) \end{array}$$

The NP rule adjoins a CP to NP; the f-structure of the CP is an ADJUNCT of the NP's f-structure. This generates binary branching relativized NPs. An alternative analysis with a flat structure is presented in Asudeh (2004: 181).[3]

The CP rule realizes SpecCP, if it is present, as one of two options.[4] If CP is a *wh*-question or cleft, SpecCP is realized as the left option, an XP that serves as the UDF of the clause. This XP will dominate the *wh*-constituent or clefted material, which will add further information to the clause's functional structure through lexical specifications. If CP is a relative clause, SpecCP is not phonetically realized, signified by the empty string 'ϵ', since Irish systematically lacks relative pronouns. The rule specifies that the relative clause has a UDF with a PRED 'pro'. This is analogous to the situation for an English relative clause that lacks a relative pronoun. The proposal is thus similar to McCloskey's (2002) proposal that the relative operator is itself a little *pro*. However, there is no null constituent proposed, since ϵ is by definition not realized in c-structure. In addition, when the CP is a relative clause (i.e., it is an ADJUNCT) the rule contributes a meaning constructor, abbreviated as REL_σ. This meaning constructor performs the modification of the relative head, integrating the relative clause semantics (Dalrymple, 2001: 417–419). This semantic function would be performed by relative pronouns in languages where they are obligatory (see Dalrymple, 2001, for an analysis of English, where the relative pronoun can be optional).[5]

The last ingredient for the analysis of simple filler-gap dependencies is the lexical entry for *aL* in (21):

(21) *aL*, $\hat{\text{C}}$ $\quad (\uparrow \textsc{udf}) = (\uparrow \textsc{gf})$

[3] It is not clear to me at this point that there are reasons to prefer one c-structural analysis over the other.

[4] Since all c-structure nodes are optional, as discussed in chapter 3, it follows that a CP need not have a specifier at all.

[5] One could equivalently propose a null relative pronoun that contributes the PRED 'pro' and REL_σ.

The lexical entry assigns the category Ĉ, a non-projecting complementizer, to *aL*. The only f-structural information that *aL* specifies is that the UDF of its clause is identified with some grammatical function in its clause.

The c-structure in (22) is constructed for the relative clause example (18). I have abbreviated irrelevant parts of the c-structure; see section 7.1 and the fragment in appendix B for further details.

(22)

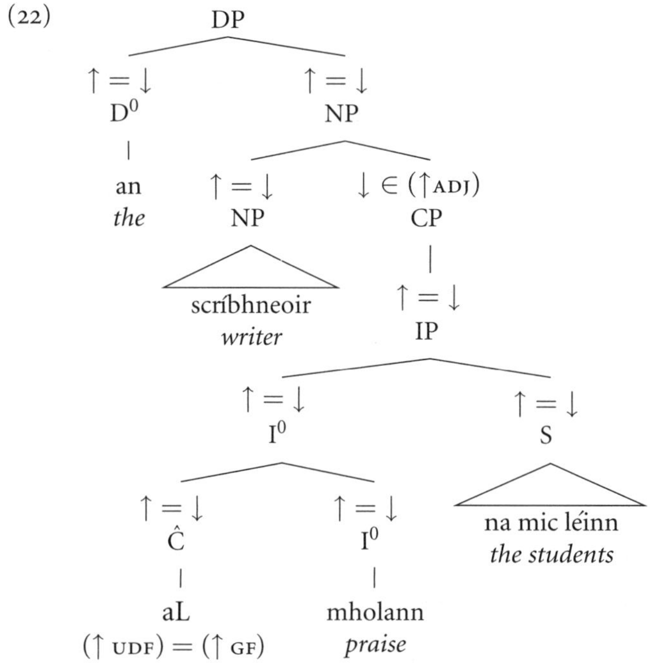

Instantiating GF in the lexical entry for *aL* to OBJ constructs the following f-structure:

(23)

$$\left[\begin{array}{ll} \text{PRED} & \text{`writer'} \\ \text{SPEC} & \left[\text{PRED} \;\; \text{`the'}\right] \\ \text{ADJ} & \left\{\left[\begin{array}{ll} \text{PRED} & \text{`praise'} \\ \text{UDF} & \left[\text{PRED} \;\; \text{`pro'}\right] \\ \text{SUBJ} & \left[\text{``the students''}\right] \\ \text{OBJ} & \rule{4em}{0.4pt} \end{array}\right]\right\} \end{array}\right]$$

(The UDF value is linked to the OBJ.)

There is an interaction between the CP rule (19) and the lexical entry for *aL*. The CP rule provides the PRED of the relative clause's UDF and the complementizer ensures that the UDF is integrated with the rest of the f-structure. The contribution of the complementizer ensures that the f-structure satisfies the Extended Coherence Condition (i.e., integration of the UDF at f-structure by functional equality). I will refer to this role of the complementizer *aL* as *filler grounding*, because it grounds the bottom of a filler-gap dependency by integrating it into the grammatical representation. The CP rule ensures that resulting shared UDF/OBJECT has a PRED value. If this were not the case, the f-structure of 'praise' would not meet the condition of Completeness, which requires that all arguments that are selected by a predicate be realized in the predicate's f-structure and that all semantic arguments (i.e., non-expletives) must have their own PRED. In sum, the relative clause formation rule and the entry for the complementizer jointly ensure the proper construction of the relative clause.

The role of filler grounding that *aL* performs explains the ungrammaticality of marking a filler-gap clause with *go*:

(24) *[$_{\text{CP}}$ *go* ... __ ...]

The neutral complementizer *go* only contributes information about mood (negation) and tense (past/non-past) to its clause. Without the contribution of *aL*, the relative clause is not well-formed, since the UDF is not integrated into the f-structure. This results in an Extended Coherence Condition violation by the unintegrated UDF and a Completeness violation by the OBJECT, since it must be identified with the UDF to receive a PRED.

A question might arise about ensuring that cleft and *wh*-question CPs cannot be substituted for the relative clause CP, resulting in an ungrammatical DP consisting of a relative head followed by a non-relative CP:

(25) *an scríbhneoir teach beag a cheannaigh muid
the writer house little *aL* bought we
'the writer it was a little house that we bought'

In fact, nothing more needs to be said to block such ill-formed nominals. Their ungrammaticality follows from the resource logic itself. Clefts and *wh*-questions have sentential semantics and the linear logic proof of their semantics will terminate successfully in an atomic linear logic term. However, the resulting resource is not integrated into the semantics for the nominal and as a result the larger proof for a sentence containing the DP above will not terminate successfully, because the resource corresponding to the cleft or question will be left over. In other words, sentence (25) is ungrammatical because there is no successful proof of its semantics: it fails for reasons of semantic composition. The syntax does not need to repeat the work of the semantics and ensure that such sentences are blocked syntactically.

Let us now turn to the core pattern for multi-clause filler-gap dependencies:

(26) $[_{\text{CP}}$ *aL* … $[_{\text{CP}}$ *aL* … $[_{\text{CP}}$ *aL* … _ …]]]

(27) an t-úrscéal aL mheas mé aL thuig mé _
the novel *aL* thought I *aL* understood I _
'the novel that I thought I understood'
(McCloskey, 1979: 17, (42c))

The NP and CP rules above are sufficient for multi-clause cases. The embedded CP is a sentential complement (COMP) of the verb *mheas* ('thought').

As things stand now, each *aL* will contribute a filler-grounding equation, as shown schematically here:

(28) an t-úrscéal $[_{\text{CP}}$ *aL* mheas mé *aL* thuig mé _]
aL: (↑ UDF) = (↑ GF)
aL: (↑ UDF) = (↑ GF)

From the contributions of the NP and CP rules in (19) and (20) and other necessary rules, the following partial f-structure is constructed, setting aside the contributions of the complementizers for now:

(29)
$$\left[\begin{array}{ll}
\text{PRED} & \text{`novel'} \\
\text{SPEC} & \left[\begin{array}{ll}\text{PRED} & \text{`the'}\end{array}\right] \\
\text{ADJ} & \left\{ t\left[\begin{array}{ll}
\text{PRED} & \text{`think'} \\
\text{UDF} & \left[\begin{array}{ll}\text{PRED} & \text{`pro'}\end{array}\right] \\
\text{SUBJ} & \left[\begin{array}{ll}\text{PRED} & \text{`pro'} \\ \text{PERS} & 1 \\ \text{NUM} & \text{SG}\end{array}\right] \\
\text{COMP} & u\left[\begin{array}{ll}\text{PRED} & \text{`understand'} \\ \text{SUBJ} & \left[\text{“I”}\right] \\ \text{OBJ} & [\ ]\end{array}\right]
\end{array}\right] \right\}
\end{array}\right]$$

As things stand, this f-structure is ill-formed. The UDF of *t* is unintegrated and the OBJ of *u* does not have a PRED.

The information contributed by the two complementizers has not been added yet, but there is in fact no way to do this. The higher *aL* attempts to identify the UDF of its clause with some GF in its clause, but the only such GFs are SUBJ and COMP. Both of these GFs have their own PRED and, since each semantic form is unique, equating the UDF to either of them would result in a Consistency violation (i.e., multiple values for the same attribute). The lower *aL* can satisfy its equation by introducing a UDF into the COMP and equating it to the OBJ. However, the resulting structure would still lack a PRED.

Intuitively, the problem is that the filler is not being linked to its extraction site. The fact that *aL* marks each clause between the filler and the gap is a strong indication that it is the complementizer that performs the integration (McCloskey, 1990, 2002). The lexical entry for the complementizer is therefore preliminarily refined as follows:

(30) *aL*, $\hat{\mathrm{C}}$ $\{ (\uparrow \text{UDF}) = (\uparrow \text{COMP UDF}) \mid (\uparrow \text{UDF}) = (\uparrow \text{GF}) \}$

The revised lexical entry for *aL* now has the complementizer performing one of two roles. The right-hand option performs filler grounding as before: it identifies a UDF with a GF in its f-structure. The left-hand option performs *filler passing*: it identifies an unbounded dependency function in its clause with one in its complement clause.

The general pattern for multi-clause filler-gap dependencies in Irish will be marking of the CP containing the gap with *aL* in its filler grounding capacity and marking of each higher CP until the filler is reached with *aL* in its filler passing capacity. This is shown schematically in (31):

(31) $[_{\text{CP}}$ *aL* ... $[_{\text{CP}}$ *aL* ... $[_{\text{CP}}$ *aL* ... _ ...]]]
└ - - - pass - - - ┘ └ - - - pass - - - ┘ └ ground ┘

According to this analysis, the complementizer *aL* not only marks filler-gap dependencies, it is also instrumental in relating the top of the dependency to the bottom.

Rather than the ill-formed f-structure in (29), the revised lexical entry for *aL* constructs the following well-formed f-structure for example, (27):

(32) 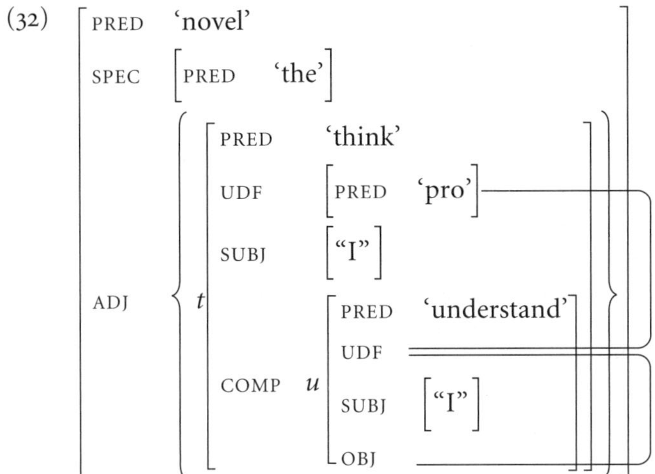

The CP rule introduces a UDF with PRED 'pro' into the f-structure marked by the top *aL*. The top *aL* equates the UDF of its f-structure, *t*, with that of its COMP, *u*. The bottom *aL* equates the UDF of its f-structure with the OBJECT corresponding to the gap. All constraints on f-structure well-formedness are therefore satisfied.

Cann *et al.* (2005*b*: 158) criticize the disjunctive nature of the lexical entry in (30), as originally presented in Asudeh (2004: 186). However, this disjunction is not a necessary feature of the analysis; rather, it clarifies the dual roles of *aL*. The passing and grounding functions of the complementizer can instead be captured by the following equation (Asudeh, 2011*c*):[6]

(33) *aL*, $\hat{\mathrm{C}}$ $(\uparrow \textsc{udf}) = (\uparrow \underset{(\rightarrow \textsc{udf}) = (\uparrow \textsc{udf})}{\textsc{comp}^*} \textsc{gf})$

This lexical entry captures both the passing and grounding roles simultaneously. The unbounded dependency must be grounded in GF to satisfy the equation. The off-path equation furthermore equates the UDF of each intervening complement (if there are any) with the UDF of *aL*'s f-structure.

This equation in itself does not guarantee the successive-cyclic pattern (i.e. *aL* ... *aL* ... *aL* ... __) and also allows intervening *go* complementizers, overgenerating **aL* ... *go* ... *go* __. The two problems are both solved if the lexical entry for *go* includes the following negative constraint:

(34) *go*, $\hat{\mathrm{C}}$ $\neg(\uparrow \textsc{udf})$

[6] In fact, the analysis of Cann *et al.* (2005*b*) is itself disjunctive, since their generalizations are stated in terms of conditionals, which are logically equivalent to disjunctions; see Asudeh (2011*c*) for further discussion.

The constraint states that the f-structure of the clause in which *go* occurs cannot contain a UDF. This rules out an occurrence of *go* intervening between *aL* and the gap. It also guarantees successive-cyclic marking by *aL*, since the alternative results in an unintegrated UDF. The constraint in (34) is equivalent to the assumption in McCloskey (2002: 203) that *go* is the realization of C that bears neither the Op-feature nor the EPP-feature, which has the effect, in his theory, that *go* is the realization of a C whose specifier is unfilled. The latter is equivalent in LFG-theoretic terms to a C whose f-structure contains no UDF.

The analysis already captures two key characteristics of Irish filler-gap dependencies. The first characteristic is the successive marking of CPs from the filler to the gap with the complementizer *aL*. This was achieved without postulating empty pronouns in c-structure, traces, or movement. The spirit of the analysis is close to that of Bouma et al. (2001), although the details are quite different. In particular, there is no postulation of a special kind of gap object (*gap-synsem*) and no special mechanism for passing of such objects (the DEPENDENTS list).

The analysis also already goes a long way to accounting for the island-sensitivity of Irish filler-gap dependencies. The Complex NP Constraint simply falls out of the equation for filler passing. The equation passes an unbounded dependency through a series of COMPS. A complex NP will necessarily be embedded in at least one further grammatical function, such as SUBJECT or OBJECT. The unbounded dependency would therefore stall in a non-COMP f-structure and could not be passed further. The result would be an f-structure that is ill-formed, due to lack of integration of the UDF. The *Wh*-Island Constraint is also derivable from the analysis presented here, if reasonable auxiliary assumptions are made. This will be discussed in section 7.6.

The remainder of this section brings the different threads together and provides examples of relative clause and *wh*-question formation. C-structures and f-structures will be abbreviated quite freely, with only relevant parts shown. In order to avoid unnecessary clutter, the meaning language side of the Glue proofs will not be presented. The operations on these meanings that correspond to proof rules follow from the Curry-Howard isomorphism. More details of the syntax and semantics can be found in appendix B.

Example (27), repeated here, serves as a relative clause example. Its c-structure and f-structure are shown in (36) and (37):

(35) an t-úrscéal aL mheas mé aL thuig mé _
the novel *aL* thought I *aL* understood I _
'the novel that I thought I understood' (McCloskey, 1979: 17, (42c))

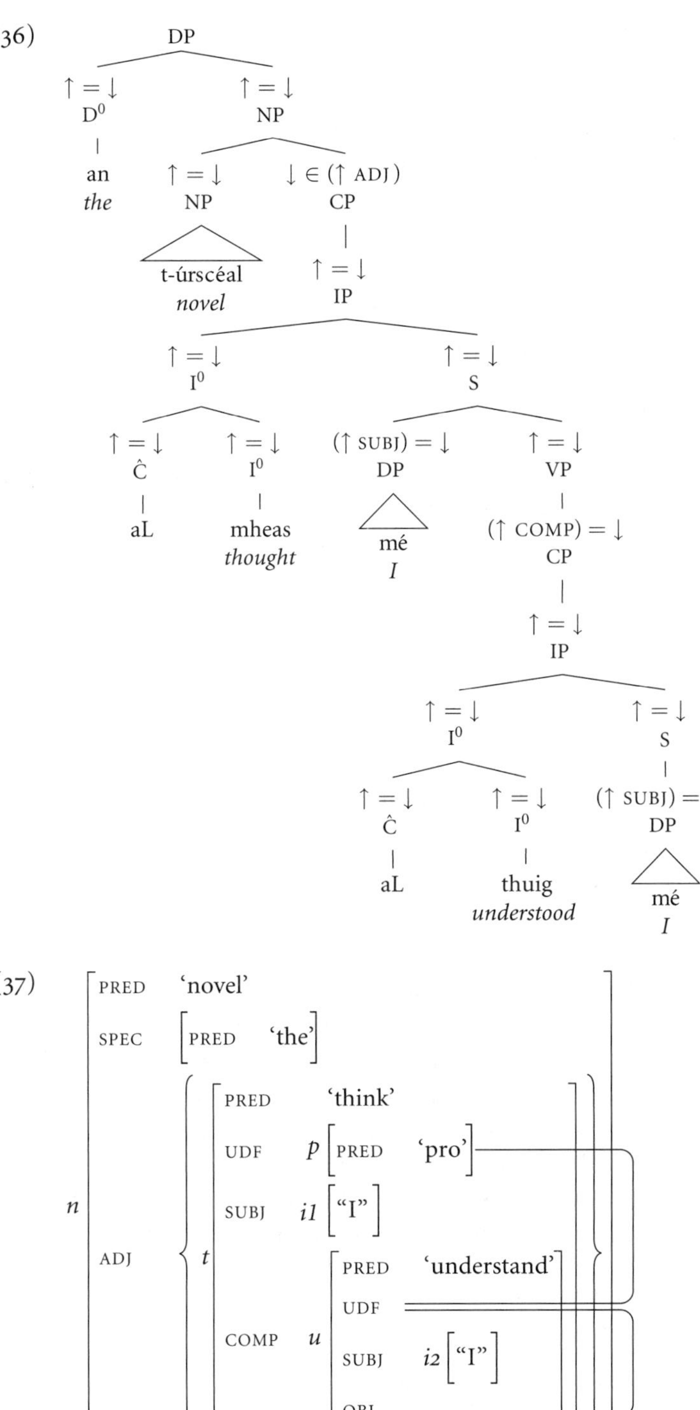
(36)
DP
↑ = ↓
D0
an
the
↑ = ↓
NP
↑ = ↓
NP
t-úrscéal
novel
↓ ∈ (↑ ADJ)
CP
↑ = ↓
IP
↑ = ↓
I0
↑ = ↓
Ĉ
aL
↑ = ↓
I0
mheas
thought
↑ = ↓
S
(↑ SUBJ) = ↓
DP
mé
I
↑ = ↓
VP
(↑ COMP) = ↓
CP
↑ = ↓
IP
↑ = ↓
I0
↑ = ↓
Ĉ
aL
↑ = ↓
I0
thuig
understood
↑ = ↓
S
(↑ SUBJ) = ↓
DP
mé
I
(37)
n
PRED 'novel'
SPEC
PRED 'the'
ADJ
t
PRED 'think'
UDF
p
PRED 'pro'
SUBJ
i1
"I"
COMP
u
PRED 'understand'
UDF
SUBJ
i2
"I"
OBJ

The CP rule (19) contributes the meaning constructor that composes the restrictive relative modifier with the relative head, abbreviated as REL_σ. The full version of this meaning constructor is as follows:

(38) $REL_\sigma :=$
$\lambda P \lambda Q \lambda x. Q(x) \wedge P(x)$:
$[(\uparrow \text{UDF})_\sigma \multimap \uparrow_\sigma] \multimap$
$[[((\text{ADJ} \in \uparrow)_\sigma\ \text{VAR}) \multimap ((\text{ADJ} \in \uparrow)_\sigma\ \text{RESTR})] \multimap$
$[((\text{ADJ} \in \uparrow)_\sigma\ \text{VAR}) \multimap ((\text{ADJ} \in \uparrow)_\sigma\ \text{RESTR})]]$

This is just the usual sort of meaning constructor for composing a restrictive relative clause with a relative head in Glue Semantics (Dalrymple, 2001).

The f-structure (37) instantiates the lexically contributed meaning constructors for (35) and REL_σ as follows:[7]

(39)

1.	$(v \multimap r) \multimap \forall X.[(n \multimap X) \multimap X]$	Lex. **an ('the')**
2.	$v \multimap r$	Lex. **t-úrscéal ('novel')**
3.	$i1 \multimap u \multimap t$	Lex. **mheas ('thought')**
4.	$i1$	Lex. **mé ('I')**
5.	$i2 \multimap p \multimap u$	Lex. **thuig ('understood')**
6.	$i2$	Lex. **mé ('I')**
7.	$(p \multimap t) \multimap [(v \multimap r) \multimap (v \multimap r)]$	REL_σ

These premises construct the proof in Figure 7.1 for the relative clause. Notice that the proof terminates in a nominal type, not a sentential type, since it is a proof for a DP containing a relative clause modifier (i.e., the DP's scope is yet to be provided).

The complementizer *aL* does not play a direct role in the semantics in terms of contributing a meaning constructor. However, the filler grounding and passing role it fulfils is instrumental in the well-formedness of the linear logic proof. In other words, the role that *aL* plays in the syntax is necessary for proper semantic composition. In particular, the UDF of the relative clause must be identified with the gapped object of *thuig* ('understood'). The dependency that *thuig* forms on the semantic structure node corresponding to the shared UDF/OBJ is satisfied by assumption of the corresponding resource. This assumption is subsequently discharged to form the relative clause predicate on

[7] I make the simplifying assumption that the first person pronoun always refers to a speaker index and therefore does not have a functional type like that of pronouns that pick up their reference from an antecedent. Second person pronouns similarly pick out the hearer index. The dependency $v \multimap r$ is based on semantic structure features of the common noun (VAR and RESTR).

(35) an t-úrscéal aL mheas mé aL thuig mé __
the novel *aL* thought I *aL* understood I __
'the novel that I thought I understood'

$$\dfrac{(v \multimap r) \multimap \forall X.[(n \multimap X) \multimap X] \qquad \dfrac{\dfrac{\dfrac{\dfrac{\dfrac{\dfrac{i2 \quad i2 \multimap p \multimap u}{p \multimap u}\multimap_{\mathcal{E}} \quad [p]^1}{u}\multimap_{\mathcal{E}} \quad \dfrac{i1 \quad i1 \multimap u \multimap t}{u \multimap t}\multimap_{\mathcal{E}}}{t}\multimap_{\mathcal{E}}}{p \multimap t}\multimap_{\mathcal{I},1} \quad (p \multimap t) \multimap [(v \multimap r) \multimap (v \multimap r)]}{(v \multimap r) \multimap (v \multimap r)}\multimap_{\mathcal{E}} \quad v \multimap r}{v \multimap r}\multimap_{\mathcal{E}}}{\lambda S.the(\lambda x.novel(x) \wedge think(s, understand(s,x)), S)) : \forall X.[(n \multimap X) \multimap X]}\multimap_{\mathcal{E}}$$

FIGURE 7.1. Proof for an Irish relative clause filler-gap dependency.

mheas ('thought'). The dependency is then consumed by the modifier premise REL_σ. It is therefore vital that the resource corresponding to the gapped OBJ and the UDF be identical. Otherwise there would be no way to integrate the relative clause. The premise REL_σ would be left over and the proof would fail, since all resources must be consumed.

Let us now look at a closely related *wh*-question, shown in (40). Its c-structure and f-structure are shown in (41) and (42):

(40) Cén t-úrscéal aL mheas mé aL thuig mé _
which novel *aL* thought I *aL* understood I _
'Which novel did I think I understood?'
(McCloskey, 1979: 54, ∼(10))

(41)

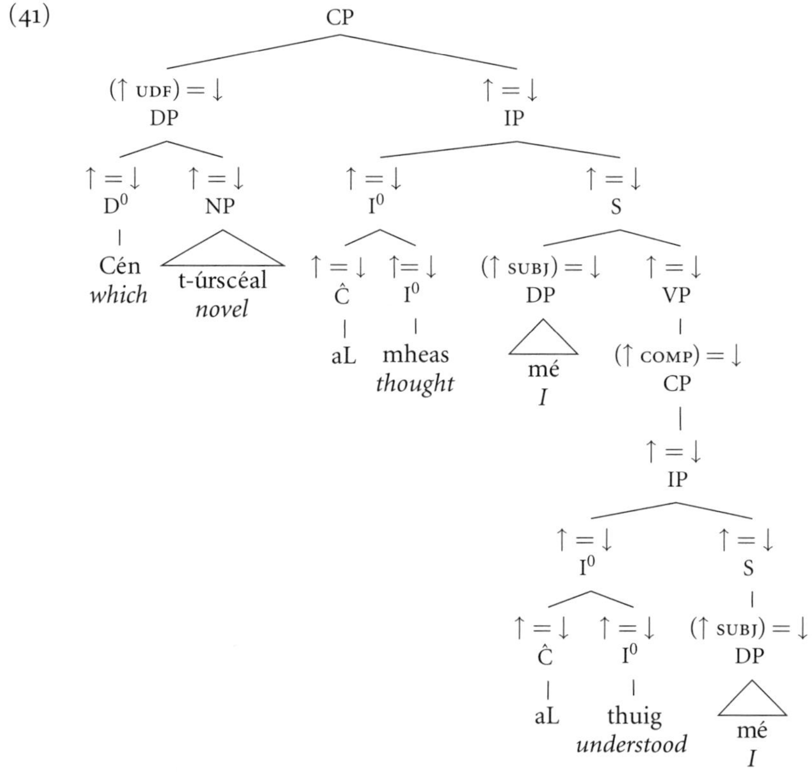

(42)

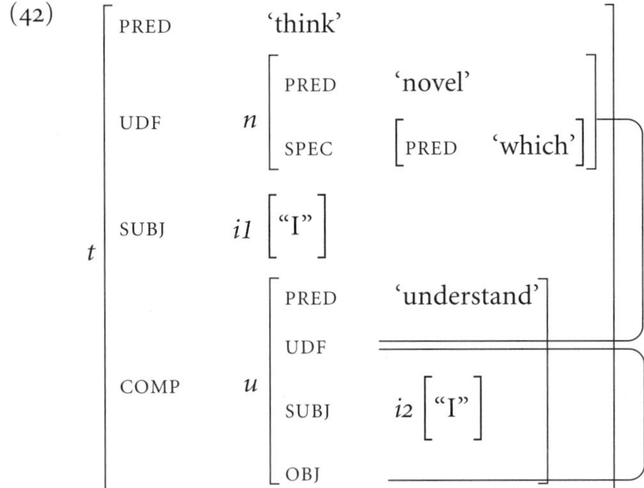

The presence of an XP in SpecCP means that the CP does not contribute a REL_σ meaning constructor; see (19).

The *wh*-determiner contributes a meaning constructor that has a question operator in the meaning language, as shown in (43). The question operator takes the determiner's noun as its restriction and finds its scope by consuming a dependency on the noun. The linear logic term for the *wh*-determiner is therefore like that of a quantificational determiner.

(43) *cén*: $\lambda R \lambda S.\mathcal{Q}(R, S) :$
$[(\uparrow_\sigma \text{VAR}) \multimap (\uparrow_\sigma \text{RESTR})] \multimap$
$\forall X.[(\uparrow_\sigma \multimap X) \multimap X]$

The essential thing is that the *wh*-phrase is a scope taking element.

The f-structure (42) instantiates the lexically contributed meaning constructors for (40) as follows (I have taken a shortcut by combining the *wh*-determiner with its noun):

(44)
1. $\forall X.[(n \multimap X) \multimap X]$ Lex. **Cén t-úrscéal ('which novel')**
2. $i1 \multimap u \multimap t$ Lex. **mheas ('thought')**
3. $i1$ Lex. **mé ('I')**
4. $i2 \multimap n \multimap u$ Lex. **thuig ('understood')**
5. $i2$ Lex. **mé ('I')**

These premises construct the proof in Figure 7.2 of the *wh*-question's semantics. Again the role of *aL* in linking the head of the unbounded dependency

$$\dfrac{\forall X.[(n \multimap X) \multimap X] \qquad \dfrac{\dfrac{\dfrac{\dfrac{i2 \quad i2 \multimap n \multimap u}{n \multimap u}{\multimap_{\mathcal{E}}} \quad [n]^1}{u}{\multimap_{\mathcal{E}}} \qquad \dfrac{i1 \quad i1 \multimap u \multimap t}{u \multimap t}{\multimap_{\mathcal{E}}}}{t}{\multimap_{\mathcal{E}}}}{n \multimap t}{\multimap_{\mathcal{I},1}}}{\mathcal{Q}(novel, \lambda x.\,think(s, understand(s, x))) : t}{\multimap_{\mathcal{E}}, [t/X]}$$

FIGURE 7.2. Proof for an Irish *wh*-question filler-gap dependency.

to the gap site is instrumental. By identifying the f-structure of the *wh*-phrase with that of the embedded OBJECT, *aL* allows the *wh*-phrase to find its scope.

7.3.1.1 *Summary* The lexical entry of the filler-gap complementizer *aL* is repeated here:

(45) *aL*, Ĉ (↑ UDF) = (↑ COMP* GF)
(→ UDF) = (↑ UDF)

The functional schema captures the *filler passing* and *filler grounding* roles of the complementizer. This constraint, together with the constraint for *go* in (34), ensures 'successive-cyclic' marking of the filler-gap dependency.

The complementizer does not contribute any premises to the proof, but filler grounding and filler passing are crucial to proper integration of the filler into the grammatical representation and hence proper semantic composition. The mechanism for both filler passing and grounding is functional equality. The filler passing role accounts for the strongly successive cyclic nature of filler-gap marking in Irish and derives the Complex NP Constraint on Irish filler-gap dependencies. Table 7.2 summarizes the contribution of *aL*.

TABLE 7.2. The role of the Irish complementizer *aL* in filler-gap dependencies.

	Role Relative to Position			
	Not bottom	**Bottom**	**Method**	**Cyclic**
aL	passing	grounding	Functional equality	Yes

7.3.2 *Binder-Resumptive Dependencies*

The core single-clause pattern for a binder-resumptive dependency is marked by the complementizer *aN*:

(46) $[_{CP}$ *aN* ... *Rpro* ...]

(47) an scríbhneoir a molann na mic léinn é
the writer *aN* praise the students him
'the writer whom the students praise (him)'
(McCloskey, 1979: 6, (5))

The core multi-clause pattern reveals that only the highest complementizer needs to be realized as *aN*. Lower complementizers are realized as the neutral complementizer *go*:

(48) $[_{CP}$ *aN* ... $[_{CP}$ *go* ... $[_{CP}$ *go* ... *Rpro* ...]]]

(49) fir ar shíl Aturnae an Stáit go rabh siad díleas do'n Rí
men *aN* thought Attorney the State *go* were they loyal to-the King
'men that the Attorney General thought were loyal to the King'
(McCloskey, 2002: 190, (16))

This pattern of marking indicates that the binder-resumptive dependency is not successive-cyclic (McCloskey, 2002). This is explained if the binder-resumptive relationship is just normal pronominal binding, since such binding is never successive-cyclic.

The complementizer *aN* plays a similar role to the complementizer *aL* in integrating the UDF into the grammatical representation. The Extended Coherence Condition allows for two methods for doing this: functional equality or binding. Irish resumptive pronouns are syntactically active resumptives and therefore must be integrated by binding, since functional equality between the binder and the resumptive would result in a Consistency violation in the f-structure. The complementizer *aN* is the licenser of the resumptive pronoun and it specifies that a UDF in its clause is the ANTECEDENT of the resumptive at semantic structure, binding the pronoun. The preliminary lexical entry for *aN*, which will be revised shortly, is therefore as follows:[8]

(50) *aN*, $\hat{C}$ $(\uparrow \text{UDF})_\sigma = ((\uparrow \text{GF}^+)_\sigma\ \text{ANTECEDENT})$

[8] There is a general constraint that only pronominals directly have the semantic structure feature ANTECEDENT, as discussed briefly at the end of chapter 6 and in more detail in Asudeh (2005*b*).

Like the entry for *aL*, the entry for *aN* depends on the introduction of the PRED of its UDF via material in SpecCP or via the CP rule itself. The entry states that there is a UDF in *aN*'s f-structure that binds a grammatical function, which will be the resumptive pronoun. The grammatical function is found by following a path of grammatical functions of length one or longer (indicated by Kleene plus). Thus, the UDF of *aN*'s clause binds (is the ANTECEDENT of) a grammatical function that is an unlimited distance away. The binding is accomplished in one step (it is not successive-cyclic) and is unbounded. The binder-resumptive dependency is an unbounded dependency, but the mechanism of integrating the head of the dependency with the foot is (1) pronominal binding, and (2) distinct from the filler-gap mechanism. Since *aN* integrates a UDF without passing it steadily through successive intervening clauses, any clauses occurring between the *aN*-marked clause and the resumptive can be marked by the neutral complementizer *go*.

I will refer to the integration of the UDF that *aN* performs via pronominal binding as *binder grounding*. Thus, both *aL* and *aN* have a role in grounding an unbounded dependency. *AL* grounds the filler in a filler-gap dependency through functional equality. *AN* grounds the binder in a binder-resumptive dependency through pronominal binding. Each complementizer is instrumental in integrating a UDF and satisfying the Extended Coherence Condition. The mechanisms of functional equality and binding are precisely those that have been independently proposed for ECC satisfaction by Bresnan and Mchombo (1987). The fact that *aN* performs binder grounding through pronominal binding—which is the only option that the theory allows—and the fact that pronominal binding is a non-local, unbounded process account for the multi-clausal marking pattern with a single *aN* at the top of the binder-resumptive dependency and successive neutral *go*-marking up to and including the clause containing the resumptive.

Before turning to a multi-clausal example, let us see how the analysis handles a single-clause case like (47), which I repeat here:

(51) an scríbhneoir a molann na mic léinn <u>é</u>
the writer *aN* praise the students him
'the writer whom the students praise (him)'

The relevant parts of the c-structure, f-structure, and semantic structure for (51), as constructed by the rules in (19) and (20) and the lexical entry for *aN* in (50), are as follows (ANTECEDENT is abbreviated as ANT):

(52)

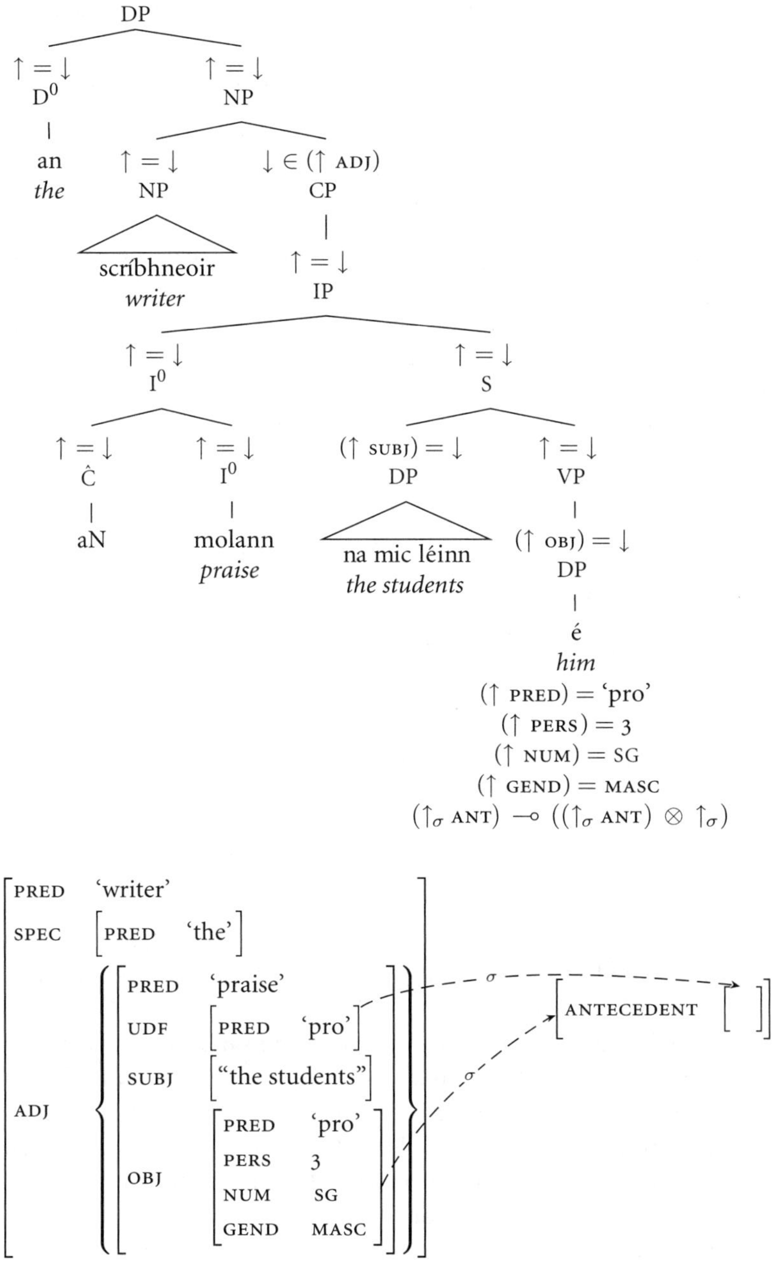

DP
- $\uparrow = \downarrow$ D^0: an *the*
- $\uparrow = \downarrow$ NP
  - $\uparrow = \downarrow$ NP: scríbhneoir *writer*
  - $\downarrow \in (\uparrow$ ADJ$)$ CP
    - $\uparrow = \downarrow$ IP
      - $\uparrow = \downarrow$ I^0
        - $\uparrow = \downarrow$ Ĉ: aN
        - $\uparrow = \downarrow$ I^0: molann *praise*
      - $\uparrow = \downarrow$ S
        - $(\uparrow$ SUBJ$) = \downarrow$ DP: na mic léinn *the students*
        - $\uparrow = \downarrow$ VP
          - $(\uparrow$ OBJ$) = \downarrow$ DP: é *him*

$(\uparrow$ PRED$) =$ 'pro'
$(\uparrow$ PERS$) = 3$
$(\uparrow$ NUM$) =$ SG
$(\uparrow$ GEND$) =$ MASC
$(\uparrow_\sigma$ ANT$) \multimap ((\uparrow_\sigma$ ANT$) \otimes \uparrow_\sigma)$

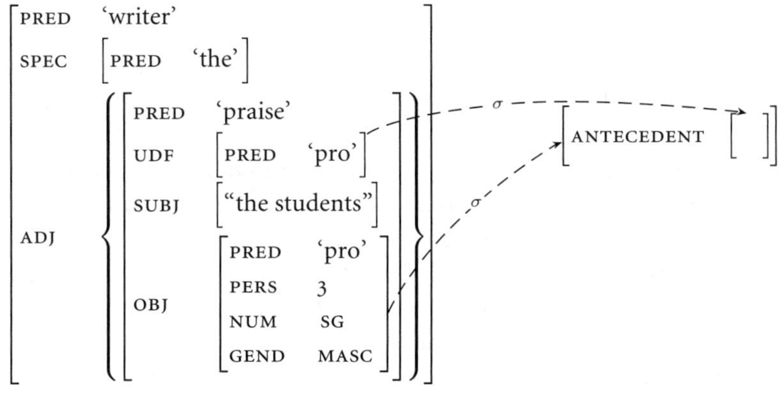

The UDF is integrated by pronominal binding. The binding is mediated by the complementizer *aN*.

The multi-clausal pattern exemplified by (49) is sketched here:

(53) fir [$_{\text{CP}}$ ar shíl Aturnae an Stáit [$_{\text{CP}}$ go rabh
$(\uparrow \text{UDF})_\sigma = ((\uparrow \text{GF}^+)_\sigma \text{ ANT})$
siad díleas do'n Rí]]

The relevant parts of the f-structure and semantic structure of this example are shown in (54). I have made the simplifying assumption that the copula is providing only tense and agreement information and that the head of the subordinate S is the AP. It may be that the relationship is better analysed as the copula taking the AP as an XCOMP, but this complication does not affect the analysis of the binder-resumptive dependency.

(54)
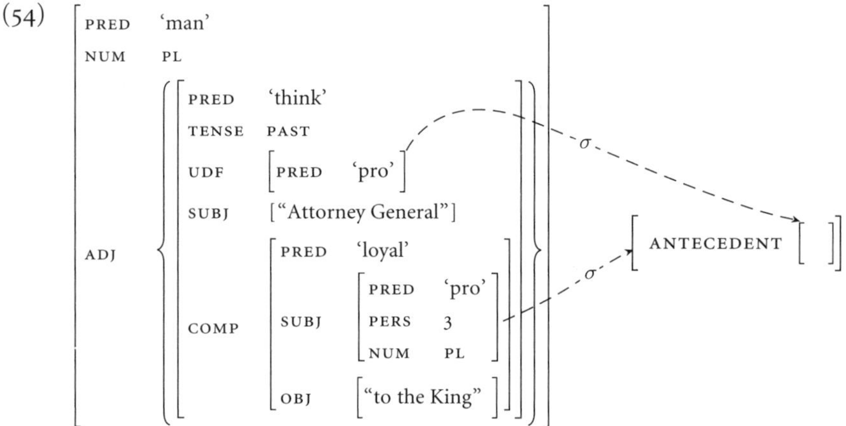

The path GF$^+$ in the lexical entry for *aN* is set to COMP SUBJ in this case. The UDF is integrated into the grammatical representation through pronominal binding in semantic structure.

The lexical entry for *aN* integrates the unbounded dependency into the grammatical representation, satisfying the ECC, but does not deal with the resumptive pronoun. Resumptive pronouns, in this theory, are just ordinary pronouns and therefore make the lexical contribution of ordinary pronouns. In particular, they contribute pronominal meaning constructors, as shown in the c-structure in (52). As things stand, the meaning constructor for the resumptive will result in ungrammaticality due to resource surplus. The lexical entry for *aN* so far does nothing about this.

The licensing mechanism for resumptive pronouns is an extra pronominal consumer, a manager resource. Therefore, a manager resource needs to be added to the lexical entry for *aN*. In addition, a meaning constructor for relabelling the resumptive dependency is contributed. The lexical entry for *aN* is revised as follows, using the templates in (56) and (57):

(55) *aN*, $\hat{\mathrm{C}}$ $\%\mathrm{RP} = (\uparrow \textsc{gf}^{+})$
$(\uparrow \textsc{udf})_{\sigma} = (\%\mathrm{RP}_{\sigma}\ \textsc{antecedent})$
@MR(%RP)
@RELABEL(%RP)

(56) $\mathrm{MR}(f) \;=\; \lambda P \lambda y.y : [(\uparrow \textsc{udf})_{\sigma} \multimap (\uparrow \textsc{udf})_{\sigma} \otimes f_{\sigma})] \multimap [(\uparrow \textsc{udf})_{\sigma} \multimap (\uparrow \textsc{udf})_{\sigma}]$

(57) $\mathrm{RELABEL}(f) = \lambda P.P : (f_{\sigma} \multimap \uparrow_{\sigma}) \multimap ((\uparrow \textsc{udf})_{\sigma} \multimap \uparrow_{\sigma})$

The local name %RP is used in the first line of (55) to identify the grammatical function of the resumptive pronoun. Subsequent instances of the local name are all instantiated alike within the scope of the lexical entry. For example, if the resumptive pronouns's f-structure, $(\uparrow \textsc{gf}^{+})$, is instantiated as an f-structure *g* and equated to %RP, then all subsequent occurrences of %RP also stand for *g* on this instantiation of the lexical entry. The complementizer states that the UDF of its clause is the antecedent of the resumptive pronoun. The resumptive pronoun's f-structure is also passed as an argument to the MR template, which is the manager resource, and the RELABEL template, which performs dependency relabelling. With the addition of a manager resource, *aN* now licenses a resumptive pronoun.

Let us look at how the analysis deals with the relative clause example (49), repeated here:

(58) fir ar shíl Aturnae an Stáit go rabh siad díleas do'n Rí
men *aN* thought Attorney the State *go* were they loyal to-the King
'men that the Attorney General thought were loyal to the King'
(McCloskey, 2002: 190, (16))

The c-structure for this example, shown in (59), holds no surprises. In its gross structure it is very similar to the c-structure in (36) for the multi-clause filler-gap relative (35). The key differences are in the embedded S. The predicate of the embedded S is an AP, not a VP, and it has an embedded subject that is a resumptive pronoun. Recall that I have made the simplifying assumption that the copula just provides tense and agreement information. The complementizer *ar*, the inflected version of *aN*, bears a constraining equation that checks for past tense in its f-structure, but which does not add this information itself.

(59)

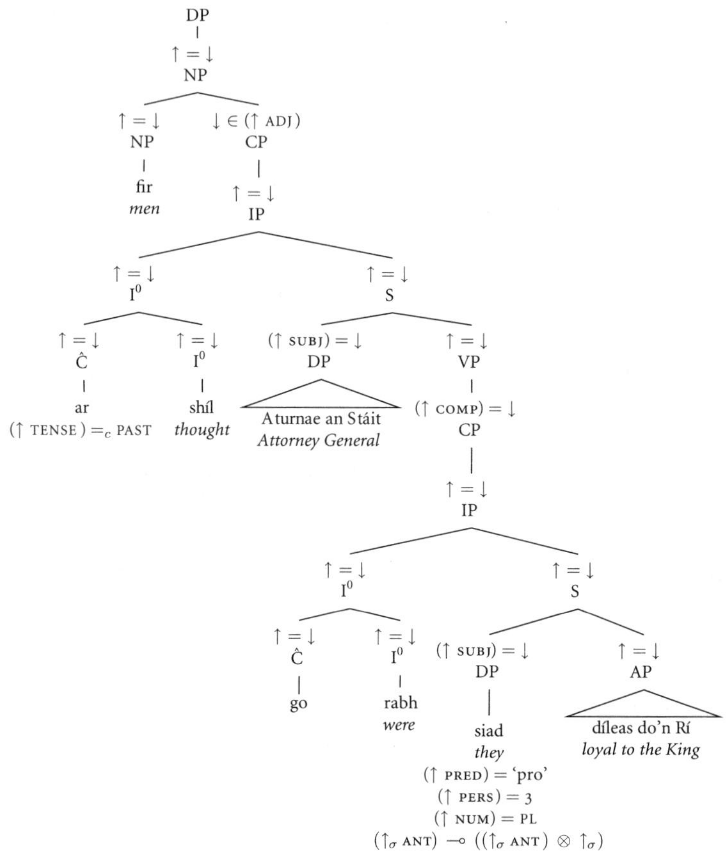

DP
$\uparrow = \downarrow$ NP
$\uparrow = \downarrow$ NP — fir *men*
$\downarrow \in (\uparrow$ ADJ$)$ CP
$\uparrow = \downarrow$ IP
$\uparrow = \downarrow$ I^0
$\uparrow = \downarrow$ Ĉ — ar — $(\uparrow$ TENSE$) =_c$ PAST
$\uparrow = \downarrow$ I^0 — shíl *thought*
$\uparrow = \downarrow$ S
$(\uparrow$ SUBJ$) = \downarrow$ DP — Aturnae an Stáit *Attorney General*
$\uparrow = \downarrow$ VP
$(\uparrow$ COMP$) = \downarrow$ CP
$\uparrow = \downarrow$ IP
$\uparrow = \downarrow$ I^0
$\uparrow = \downarrow$ Ĉ — go
$\uparrow = \downarrow$ I^0 — rabh *were*
$\uparrow = \downarrow$ S
$(\uparrow$ SUBJ$) = \downarrow$ DP — siad *they*
$(\uparrow$ PRED$) =$ 'pro'
$(\uparrow$ PERS$) = 3$
$(\uparrow$ NUM$) =$ PL
$(\uparrow_\sigma$ ANT$) \multimap ((\uparrow_\sigma$ ANT$) \otimes \uparrow_\sigma)$
$\uparrow = \downarrow$ AP — díleas do'n Rí *loyal to the King*

The f-structure and semantic structure for (58) are repeated here with appropriate labels:

(60)

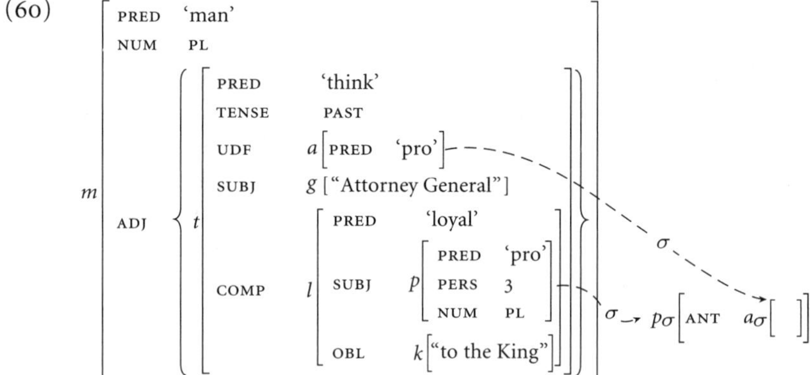

The complemenizer *aN* does three things. First, it integrates the UDF, which is contributed by the CP rule, through pronominal binding. The complementizer specifies that its f-structure's UDF—the UDF of f-structure *t* in this case—is the semantic structure ANTECEDENT of a grammatical function in its clause or in an embedded clause, GF^+. In this case GF^+ is *t* COMP SUBJ. The description $(\uparrow \text{ UDF})_\sigma$ in *aN*'s lexical entry is therefore instantiated to the same resource as $(\uparrow \text{ ANTECEDENT})_\sigma$ in the generalized meaning constructor for the pronoun, which is shown in (61). The instantiated version is shown in (62), with labels from the structures above.

(61) $(\uparrow_\sigma \text{ANTECEDENT}) \multimap ((\uparrow_\sigma \text{ANTECEDENT}) \otimes \uparrow_\sigma)$

(62) $a_\sigma \multimap (a_\sigma \otimes p_\sigma)$

In binding the resumptive to the UDF in its clause, the complementizer grounds the binder in the binder-resumptive dependency. Second, the complementizer contributes a manager resource that licenses the resumptive pronoun by removing its surplus resource. Third, the complementizer relabels the dependency vacated by the pronoun in terms of the resumptive's binder.

The lexically contributed premises for (58) and the relative clause premise REL_σ that is contributed by SpecCP are shown in (63). I have made the simplifying assumption that the OBLIQUE *díleas do'n Rí* ('to the King') just contributes a type *e* resource and that *díleas* ('loyal') is translated as *loyal-to*.

(63)

1.	$v \multimap r$	Lex. **fir ('men')**
2.	$(a \multimap t) \multimap [(v \multimap r) \multimap (v \multimap r)]$	REL_σ
3.	$[a \multimap (a \otimes p)] \multimap (a \multimap a)]$	Lex. **ar (aN, MR)**
4.	$(p \multimap t) \multimap (a \multimap t)$	Lex. **ar (aN, RELABEL)**
5.	$g \multimap l \multimap t$	Lex. **shíl ('thought')**
6.	g	Lex. **Aturnae an Stáit ('Attorney General')**
7.	$a \multimap (a \multimap p)$	Lex. **siad ('they')**
8.	$k \multimap p \multimap l$	Lex. **díleas ('loyal')**
9.	k	Lex. **do'n Rí ('to-the King')**

Figure 7.3 shows a succesful proof for (49), given the lexical entry for *aN* in (55) and the premises in (63).[9] The manager resource contributed by the complementizer solves the resource surplus problem that the resumptive pronoun poses by consuming the resumptive. The second meaning constructor contributed by the complementizer relabels the dependency on the pronoun so that it is instead a dependency on the complementizer's unbounded

[9] The denotation of the plural common noun *fir* ('men') is represented as *man**.

(58) fir ar shíl Aturnae an Stáit go rabh <u>siad</u> díleas do'n Rí
men *aN* thought Attorney the State *go* were they loyal to-the King
'men that the Attorney General thought were loyal to the King'

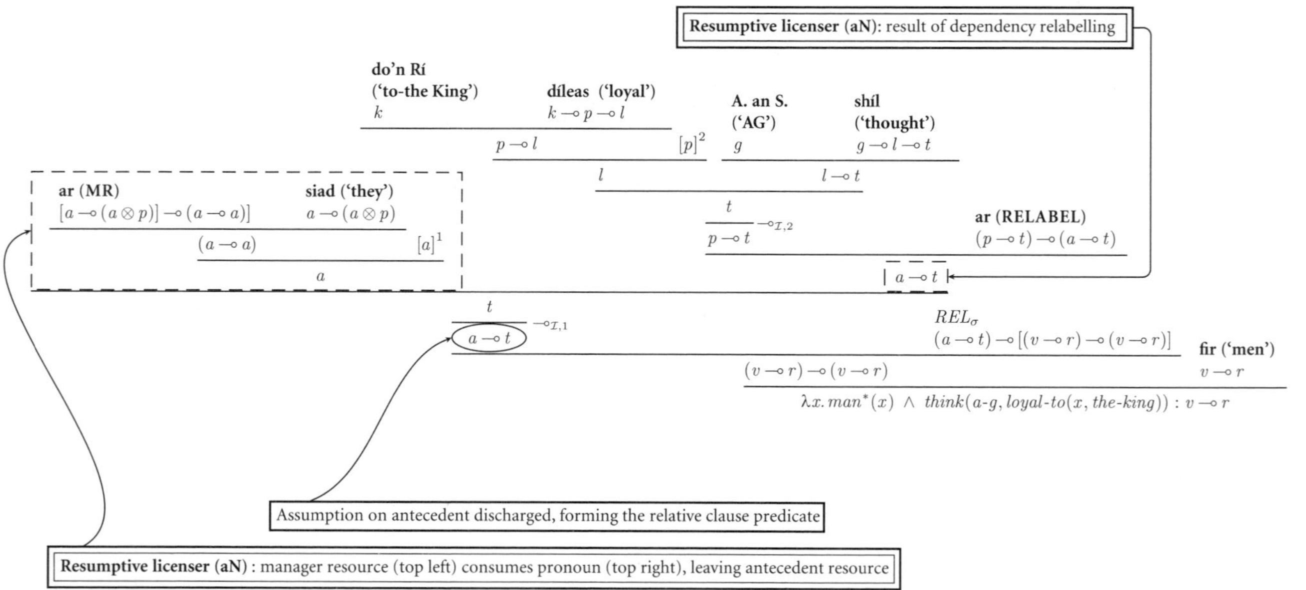

FIGURE 7.3. Proof for a core multi-clause Irish binder-resumptive dependency.

dependency. With these adjustments made, the proof goes through just as if the resumptive pronoun had not been there. The meaning language follows by the Curry-Howard isomorphism; also see appendix B. Like *aL*, the resumptive-sensitive complementizer *aN* is instrumental in grounding the unbounded dependency. But whereas *aL* uses the mechanism of functional equality, *aN* uses binding.

The crucial thing in licensing the resumptive pronoun is the contribution of the manager resource. Without this contribution, the pronoun will result in failure of the linear logic proof due to a surplus resource. The analysis predicts the impossibility of a resumptive pattern without the complementizer *aN*:

(64) $^{*}[_{\mathrm{CP}}$ go ... *Rpro* ...]

(65) $^{*}[_{\mathrm{CP}}$ aL ... *Rpro* ...]

Neither the lexical entry for *go* nor the one for *aL* contributes a manager resource and these complementizers therefore do not license resumptives.

The analysis does not currently predict the possibility of Patterns 1 or 3 of the mixed chains:

(66) Pattern 1
$[_{\mathrm{CP}}$ *aN* ... $[_{\mathrm{NP}}$ N $[_{\mathrm{CP}}$ *aL* ... _ ...]]]

(67) Pattern 3
$[_{\mathrm{CP}}$ *aN* ... $[_{\mathrm{CP}}$ *aN* ... *Rpro* ...]]

Pattern 1 has an instance of *aN*, which contributes a manager resource, but there is no resumptive pronoun to be consumed. In this case, it is the manager resource that would not be discharged, resulting in proof failure. Pattern 3 has two instance of *aN* but only one resumptive pronoun. One of the two manager resources that the complementizers contribute will be satisfied, but the other one will necessarily be left over, since the resumptive has been consumed by the first manager resource, and there will once again be proof failure.

The solution to this problem is shown in the next section. It involves adding a kind of binder passing capacity to the entry for *aN*. The result is an appealing symmetry between the lexical entries for the filler-gap complementizer *aL* and the binder-resumptive complementizer *aN* along independently motivated theoretical dimensions. Both complementizers engage in unbounded dependency passing and grounding, but *aL* does it through functional identity, whereas *aN* does it through pronominal binding. Both of these mechanisms are independently motivated in the grammatical theory in general and in the analysis of unbounded dependencies in particular.

7.4 Analysis of Mixed Chains

7.4.1 *Pattern 2*

Let us first look at Pattern 2 of the mixed chains, because the theory already successfully deals with this:

(68) Pattern 2
$[_{CP}$ *aL* ... $[_{CP}$ *aN* ... *Rpro* ...]]

(69) aon duine a cheap sé a raibh ruainne tobac aige
any person *aL* thought he *aN* was scrap tobacco at-him
'anyone that he thought had a scrap of tobacco'
(McCloskey, 2002: 198, (34))

(70) Cé is dóigh leat a bhfuil an t-airgead aige?
who *aL*.COP.PRES likely with-you *aN* is the money at-him
'Who do you think has the money?'
(McCloskey, 2002: 198, (35))

This pattern is analysed as an instance of binder grounding by *aN* and filler passing by *aL*.

The CP rule, in (19) above, specifies that SpecCP contributes the UDF at the top of the 'mixed chain'. In the particular case of (69) both the UDF and its PRED are contributed by the right SpecCP option of the CP rule, since there is no relative pronoun. In the case of (70) the *wh*-word that realizes the left option of SpecCP is the UDF of the outermost f-structure. The complementizer *aL* in its filler passing role equates this UDF with the UDF of its COMP, such that the UDF that is introduced through SpecCP occurs in the COMP. The result is two UDFs that are functionally equated. There is no directionality to the passing: the UDF is not 'passed up' or 'passed down'. This subordinate f-structure is the one that *aN* contributes to. The lower complementizer performs the same functions as we saw in the previous section. It integrates the shared UDF by binding the resumptive pronoun, thus grounding the binder-resumptive dependency. It also licenses the resumptive through contribution of a manager resource and relabels the resumptive's dependency appropriately.

The overall analysis of a Pattern 2 mixed chain is shown schematically in (71), where GF is the resumptive pronoun:

(71)

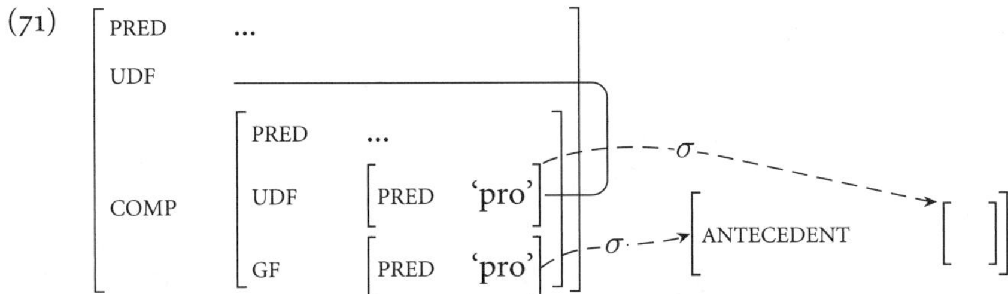

Pattern 2 is thus licensed by binder grounding by the lower complementizer *aN* and filler passing by the higher complementizer *aL*. The only mechanisms necessary are the ones that explained the core multi-clause patterns.

This may seem counterintuitive, since there is in fact no filler for *aL* to pass. However, 'filler' is just a convenient descriptive term and is not reified in the analysis. All *aL* really needs to do in its filler passing capacity is to identify the unbounded dependency function in its clause with an unbounded dependency function in the complement of its clause (COMP). *AL* does not actually distinguish the case where the embedded UDF is functionally equated to a gap (i.e., the embedded UDF is a filler) and the case where the embedded UDF binds a resumptive (i.e., the embedded UDF is a binder). *AL* just functionally equates its UDF with that of its COMP. In order for the complementizer to accomplish this in a well-formed way, there must be some ultimately grounded UDF in the COMP. Such a function is introduced by the lower complementizer *aN* and grounded by binding the resumptive pronoun.

In sum, Pattern 2 follows from the analysis developed for core multi-clause unbounded dependencies. Although the notion of 'chain' and hence the notion of 'mixed chain' has no theoretical status in this theory, it is interesting to note that there is a certain parallel here. The bottom of the dependency is grounded via binding and then passed by functional equality. Both of these mechanisms are independently motivated in LFG theory, in general, and thus in the particular theory of Irish unbounded dependencies developed here. The result is mixed handling of the unbounded dependency. There is thus some theoretical convergence between this analysis and the analysis of McCloskey (2002), despite the fact that the analyses are based on quite different assumptions and come at the problem from distinct directions. Both analyses require mixed mechanisms.

7.4.2 *Patterns 1 and 3*

Pattern 1 is the inverse of Pattern 2 in terms of complementizer marking. The higher complementizer is the binder-resumptive complementizer *aN* and the lower complementizer is the filler-gap complementizer *aL*:

(72) $[_{CP}$ *aN* ... $[_{NP}$ N $[_{CP}$ *aL* ... _ ...]]]

(73) rud a raibh coinne agam a choimhlíonfadh _ an aimsir
thing *aN* was expectation at-me *aL* fulfil.COND _ the time
'something that I expected time would confirm'
(McCloskey, 2002: 196, ~(28))

This mixed chain is one possibility for marking an unbounded dependency out of a complex NP. The more common realization is the standard multi-clause resumptive pattern: *aN ... go ... Rpro*. McCloskey (2002: 195–197) notes that the *aL*-marking of the CP inside the NP is to be expected, given that that this CP can host a filler-gap dependency within the NP. The thing that is surprising about the pattern is the presence of the resumptive complementizer in the upper CP, because there is no resumptive pronoun for it to bind.

Pattern 3 shares aspects of Patterns 1 and 2. The lower clause is marked by the resumptive complementizer *aN*, as in Pattern 2. But, the higher clause is also marked by the resumptive-sensitive complementizer, as in Pattern 1:

(74) $[_{CP}$ *aN* ... $[_{CP}$ *aN* ... *Rpro* ...]]

(75) na cuasáin thiorma ar shíl sé a mbeadh contúirt ar bith
the holes dry *aN* thought he *aN* would-be danger any
uirthi tuitim síos ionnta
on-her fall.[−FIN] down into-them
'the dry holes that he thought there might be any danger of her falling down into them'
(McCloskey, 2002: 199, (44))

The resumptive pronoun in the lower clause once again occurs in a position that is inaccessible to a filler-gap dependency, as in Pattern 1. Notice in particular that the resumptive site in example (75) is in a kind of complex NP, but one with a prepositional complement. This NP does not have an inner CP to host a filler-gap dependency.

The crucial feature that Patterns 1 and 3 have in common in terms of the Resource Management Theory of Resumption is that each pattern contains more instances of *aN* than there are resumptive pronouns. Pattern 1 contains one *aN* and no resumptive and Pattern 3 contains two *aN*s but only one resumptive. The lexical entry of *aN* will be extended in a way that addresses this commonality and thus simultaneously explains both patterns. The result of the extension is further parallelism between the roles of *aL* and *aN* in licensing Irish unbounded dependencies.

The proposal is to add a *binder passing* specification to the lexical entry for *aN*, on a par with the *filler passing* specification in the entry for *aL*. The binder passing specification is the following binding equation:

(76) $(\uparrow \text{UDF})_\sigma = ((\uparrow \text{GF}^+ \text{ UDF})_\sigma \text{ ANTECEDENT})$

The complementizer thus fulfils both its binder passing and grounding roles through pronominal binding. This binding can occur non-locally, just as it does in *aN*'s binder grounding guise (see (55) above). In both cases there is an unbounded path of length 1 or more specified by GF^+. However, the binder passing requires the path to eventually terminate in a UDF. The result is that the binder passing option for *aN* is realizable only if there is an unbounded dependency below the complementizer. This lower unbounded dependency must in turn be licensed either by *aL* or *aN*. The binder passing *aN* is thus an integral part of a larger unbounded dependency. It does not itself provide a meaning constructor and add a resource to the proof, but it serves an important function in semantic composition: to connect the top of the unbounded dependency to the bottom. If it did not fulfil this function, then semantic composition would fail. In sum, *aN* in its binder passing role is integral to semantic composition, despite not contributing a semantic resource itself.

The crucial aspect of the analysis is that the binder passing *aN* does not contribute a manager resource. In passing a dependency, *aN* needs to rely on it being grounded further down. It is the binder grounding guise of *aN* that therefore licenses a resumptive pronoun through the contribution of a manager resource. The revised and final lexical entry for *aN* is as follows:

(77) *aN*, $\hat{\text{C}}$ $\quad$ %Bound = $(\uparrow \text{GF}^* \; \{ \; \text{UDF} \; | \; [\text{GF} - \text{UDF}] \; \})$
@MR($\rightarrow$)
$(\uparrow \text{UDF})_\sigma = (\%\text{Bound}_\sigma \text{ ANTECEDENT})$
@RELABEL(%Bound)

The first line instantiates a local variable, %Bound, to some f-structure. The attribute GF ensures that the f-structure in question can be an unbounded distance away, since %Bound is subsequently used as part of a binding equation in the second line. The final part of the equation in the first line performs binder passing and binder grounding. If %Bound is instantiated to a UDF, then this is *aN* in its binder passing guise: the UDF of *aN*'s clause binds a subordinate UDF (per the binding equation in the second line of the lexical entry). If %Bound is instantiated to a GF other than UDF (formalized by the regular language complementation operator), then this is *aN* in its binder grounding guise: the UDF of *aN*'s clause binds a resumptive pronoun. In its binder grounding guise, *aN* contributes a manager resource. The argument passed to the manager resource template is the f-structure that is the grounding grammatical function (i.e., the f-structure of the resumptive pronoun). The third line of the entry ensures that each instance of *aN*, whether passing or grounding, relabels the resumptive dependency appropriately.

The picture that emerges for *aL* and *aN* in two-clause cases is the following:

(78) a. $[_{CP}$ *aL* ... $[_{CP}$ *aL* ... _ ...]]] Core *aL* multi-clause
└ – – pass – – ┘ └ ground ┘

b. $[_{CP}$ *aN* ... $[_{CP}$ *aL* ... _ ...]]] Pattern 1
└ – – pass – – ┘ └ ground ┘

c. $[_{CP}$ *aL* ... $[_{CP}$ *aN* ... *Rpro* ...]]] Pattern 2
└ – – pass – – ┘ └ ground ┘

d. $[_{CP}$ *aN* ... $[_{CP}$ *aN* ... *Rpro* ...]]] Pattern 3
└ – – pass – – ┘ └ ground ┘

Longer mixed chains are hard to find, since they test the limits of speakers' competence (McCloskey, 2002: 195). The predictions of the theory for longer mixed chains are discussed in section 7.6. I will end this subsection by showing in a little more detail how the theory accounts for Patterns 1 and 3. I will leave out the c-structures and present only the relevant parts of the f-structures and semantic structures.

Consider first the following Pattern 1 example:

(79) rud a raibh coinne agam a choimhlíonfadh _ an aimsir
thing *aN* was expectation at-me *aL* fulfil.COND _ the time
'something that I expected time would confirm'
(McCloskey, 2002: 196, ~(28))

The relevant parts of the f-structure and semantic structure for this example are as follows:[10]

[10] I have been fairly free in my assumption about the internal structure of the complex NP and the role of the copula, because these considerations are quite peripheral to the point at hand. I have also assumed that the inflected PP *agam* ('at-me') is the SUBJ of *coinne* ('expectation'). Again, this is peripheral to the main concern.

(80)

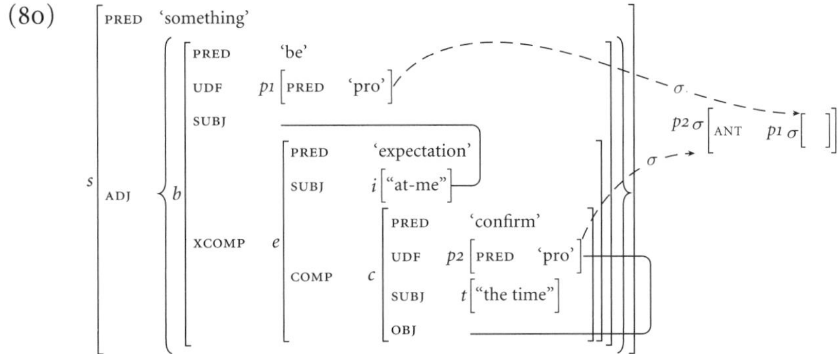

The lower SpecCP contributes the embedded UDF and its PRED. The complementizer *aL* grounds this filler to the object gap through functional equality. This integrates the UDF, satisfying the ECC, and gives the OBJ a PRED, satisfying Completeness. The lower SpecCP does not contribute the meaning constructor REL_σ, because this CP is not in a relative clause. The upper SpecCP similarly contributes a UDF with PRED 'pro'. This cannot be a UDF that is passed by *aL*, because *aL* can only functionally equate its UDF with that of its COMP. The lower UDF is too far embedded for *aL* to pass it up—hence the Complex NP Island. The upper complementizer can be realized as *aN* in its binder passing capacity. *AN* integrates the upper UDF by anaphorically binding the lower UDF, thus 'passing' it from the lower clause to the upper clause.

Example (79) contributes the following meaning constructors, instantiated to (80):

(81)

1.	$(v \multimap r) \multimap \forall X.[(s \multimap X) \multimap X]$	Lex. **rud ('thing')**
2.	$v \multimap r$	Lex. **rud ('thing')**
3.	$(p1 \multimap b) \multimap [(v \multimap r) \multimap (v \multimap r)]$	REL_σ
4.	$(p2 \multimap b) \multimap (p1 \multimap b)$	Lex. **a (aN, RELABEL)**
5.	$e \multimap b$	Lex. **raibh ('was')**
6.	$i \multimap c \multimap e$	Lex. **coinne ('expectation')**
7.	i	Lex. **agam ('at-me')**
8.	$t \multimap p2 \multimap c$	Lex. **choimhlíonfadh ('confirm')**
9.	t	Lex. **an aimsir ('the time')**

These premises construct the the proof in Figure 7.4 for the relative clause (79).

Lastly, consider the following Pattern 3 example:

(79) rud a raibh coinne agam a choimhlíonfadh __ an aimsir
thing *aN* was expectation at-me *aL* fulfil. COND __ the time
'something that I expected time would confirm'

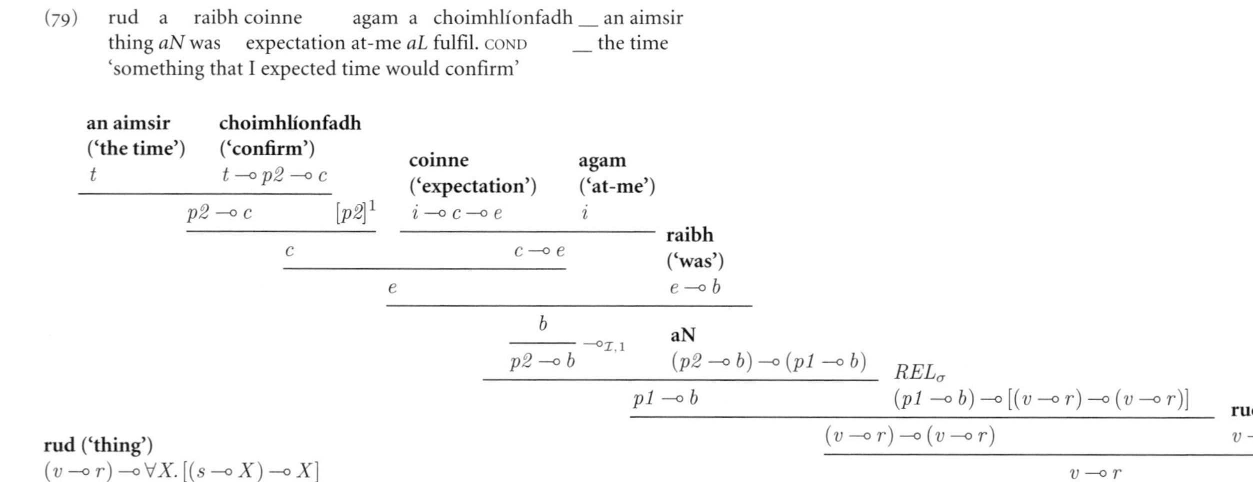

FIGURE 7.4. Irish Pattern 1 proof.

(82) an bhean a raibh mé ag súil a bhfaighinn an t-airgead
the woman *aN* was I hope.PROG *aN* get.COND.1SG the money
uaithi
from-her
'the woman that I was hoping that I would get the money from (her)'
(McCloskey, 2002: 199, ~(41))

The relevant parts of the f-structure and semantic structure for this example are as follows:[11]

(83)
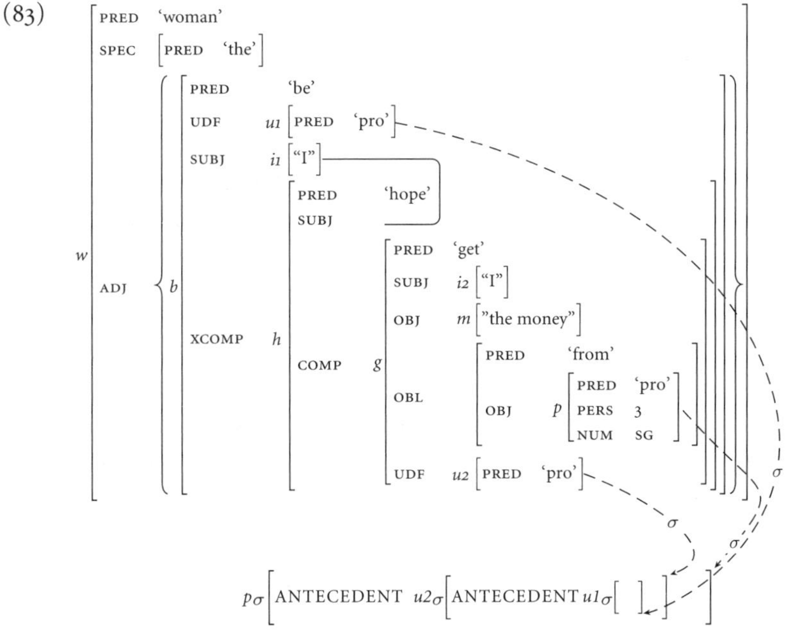

The lower SpecCP contributes the lower UDF and its PRED 'pro'. Again, the lower SpecCP does not contribute the meaning constructor REL_σ, because the lower CP is not a relative clause. The lower UDF is grounded by *aN* in its binder grounding capacity. The lower UDF binds the resumptive pronoun OBJECT at semantic structure. The higher SpecCP contributes the higher UDF and also the relative clause meaning constructor REL_σ, since this CP is a relative clause. The higher UDF is integrated by *aN*, but this time in its binder passing capacity. Notice that *aL* is again ruled out at the top of this mixed chain, because the

[11] I have assumed that the preposition that incorporates the resumptive pronoun as its OBJ is just a case-marking preposition. This allows simplification of the proof, but the analysis does not depend on this assumption.

lower UDF is too far embedded (in XCOMP COMP) for it to be integrated by *aL* in its filler passing capacity.

The following meaning constructors, instantiated to (83)are contributed for example (82):

(84)

1.	$(v \multimap r) \multimap \forall X.[(w \multimap X) \multimap X]$	Lex. **an ('the')**
2.	$v \multimap r$	Lex. **bhean ('woman')**
3.	$(u1 \multimap b) \multimap [(v \multimap r) \multimap (v \multimap r)]$	REL_σ
4.	$(u2 \multimap b) \multimap (u1 \multimap b)$	Lex. **a (aN, RELABEL)**
5.	$h \multimap b$	Lex. **raibh ('was')**
6.	$i1$	Lex. **mé ('I')**
7.	$i1 \multimap g \multimap h$	Lex. **ag súil ('hope')**
8.	$[u2 \multimap (u2 \otimes p)] \multimap (u2 \multimap u2)$	Lex. **a (aN, MR)**
9.	$(p \multimap g) \multimap (u2 \multimap g)$	Lex. **a (aN, RELABEL)**
10.	$i2 \multimap m \multimap p \multimap g$	Lex. **bhfaighinn ('get')**
11.	$i2$	Lex. **bhfaighinn ('get')**
12.	m	Lex. **an t-airgead ('the money')**
13.	$u2 \multimap (u2 \otimes p)$	Lex. **uaithi ('from-her')**

These premises construct the proof shown in Figure 7.5. The lower *aN* anaphorically binds the pronoun, thus grounding the binder-resumptive dependency, and contributes a premise for relabelling the resumptive's dependency. The lower *aN* crucially also contributes a manager resource to license the resumptive. The higher *aN* binds the lower UDF, thus passing the binder-resumptive dependency, and contributes a dependency relabelling premise for the bound UDF.

7.5 Summary

The previous sections presented a detailed application of the Resource Management Theory of Resumption in an analysis of Irish unbounded dependencies that has accounted for both filler-gap and binder-resumptive dependencies.

In addition to the Resource Management Theory of Resumption, the analysis of Irish consisted of the rule for CP formation and lexical entries for the Irish complementizers. These are repeated here:

(85)

CP ⟶	{	XP	|	ϵ	}	C′
		(↑ UDF) = ↓		(↑ UDF PRED) = 'pro'		↑ = ↓
				(ADJUNCT ∈ ↑)		
				REL_σ		

(82) an bhean a raibh mé ag súil a bhfaighinn an t-airgead <u>uaithi</u>
the woman *aN* was I hope. PROG *aN* get.COND 1SG the money from-her
'the woman that I was hoping that I would get the money from (her)'

bhfaighinn ('get') $i2 \multimap m \multimap p \multimap g$; **bhfaighinn ('get')** $i2$ ⟹ $m \multimap p \multimap g$

$m \multimap p \multimap g$; **an t-airgead ('the money')** m ⟹ $p \multimap g$

$p \multimap g$; **aN (RELABEL)** $(p \multimap g) \multimap (u2 \multimap g)$ ⟹ $u2 \multimap g$

$u2 \multimap g$; $[u2]^1$ ⟹ g

mé ('I') $i1$; **agsúli ('hope')** $i1 \multimap g \multimap h$ ⟹ $g \multimap h$

$g \multimap h$; g ⟹ h

h ; **raibh ('was')** $h \multimap b$ ⟹ b

b ⟹ $u2 \multimap b$ ($\multimap_{\mathcal{I},1}$)

uaithi ('from-her') $u2 \multimap (u2 \otimes p)$; **aN (MR)** $[u2 \multimap (u2 \otimes p)] \multimap (u2 \multimap u2)$ ⟹ $u2 \multimap u2$

$[u2]^2$; $u2 \multimap u2$ ⟹ $u2$

$u2 \multimap b$; $u2$ ⟹ b

b ⟹ $u2 \multimap b$ ($\multimap_{\mathcal{I},2}$)

aN (RELABEL) $(u2 \multimap b) \multimap (u1 \multimap b)$; $u2 \multimap b$ ⟹ $u1 \multimap b$

$u1 \multimap b$; REL_σ $(u1 \multimap b) \multimap [(v \multimap r) \multimap (v \multimap r)]$ ⟹ $(v \multimap r) \multimap (v \multimap r)$

bhean ('woman') $v \multimap r$; $(v \multimap r) \multimap (v \multimap r)$ ⟹ $v \multimap r$

an ('the') $(v \multimap r) \multimap \forall X.[(w \multimap X) \multimap X]$; $v \multimap r$ ⟹

$\lambda S.the(\lambda x.woman(x) \wedge be(hope(s, get\text{-}from(s, the\text{-}money, x))), S) : \forall X.[(w \multimap X) \multimap X]$

FIGURE 7.5. Irish Pattern 3 proof.

(86) *aL*, $\hat{C}$ $(\uparrow \text{UDF}) = (\uparrow \quad \text{COMP}^* \quad \text{GF})$
$(\rightarrow \text{UDF}) = (\uparrow \text{UDF})$

(87) *aN*, $\hat{C}$ $\%\text{Bound} = \ (\uparrow \text{GF}^* \ \{ \ \text{UDF} \ | \ [\text{GF} - \text{UDF}] \ \})$
$@\text{MR}(\rightarrow)$
$(\uparrow \text{UDF})_\sigma = (\%\text{Bound}_\sigma \ \text{ANTECEDENT})$
$@\text{RELABEL}(\%\text{Bound})$

(88) *go*, $\hat{C}$ $\neg(\uparrow \text{UDF})$

The analysis not only explains the core Irish data, it also explains the difficult 'mixed chains', Patterns 1, 2, and 3.

The basic generalization that emerges about the Irish unbounded dependency complementizers *aL* and *aN* is that they are instrumental in integrating unbounded dependencies into the grammatical representation. They share the fundamental role of satisfying the Extended Coherence Condition. Two methods for integrating unbounded dependencies and satifying the ECC have been independently proposed in the LFG literature (Zaenen, 1980; Bresnan and Mchombo, 1987; Bresnan, 2001; Dalrymple, 2001): functional equality and binding. These are precisely the methods used by *aL* (functional equality) and *aN* (binding). The complementizers further share the twin roles of *passing* and *grounding* unbounded dependencies. *AL* performs filler passing and filler grounding via functional equality. *AN* performs binder passing and binder grounding via pronominal binding. The different mechanisms explain why filler-gap dependencies are marked successive-cyclically by *aL* in the core case, whereas binder-resumptive dependencies are not cyclic, since pronominal binding is not marked successive-cyclically. The functional equality specified in the off-path constraint in *aL*'s lexical entry identifies the UDF of *aL*'s clause with a UDF in each intervening complement function to the bottom of the dependency. The binding mechanism, in contrast, grounds the binder-resumptive dependency through binding of a pronoun that is arbitrarily deeply embedded. The complementizer system for unbounded dependencies is summarized in Table 7.3.

7.6 Discussion

This section presents some further predictions of this theory with respect to Irish and some directions for further research. The analysis presented here is also compared to the Minimalist analysis of McCloskey (2002).

TABLE 7.3. The role of the Irish complementizers *aL* and *aN* in unbounded dependencies.

	Role Relative to Position			
	Not bottom	**Bottom**	**Method**	**Cyclic**
aL	Passing	Grounding	Functional equality	Yes
aN	Passing	Grounding Resumptive licensing	Binding	No

7.6.1 *Predictions and Directions for Future Work*

I mentioned in section 7.3.1 that the Complex NP Island facts are derived from the analysis of *aL* and the Extended Coherence Condition. The complementizer *aL* either grounds a filler to a GF in its clause or it passes the filler by identifying the UDF in its clause with that of its COMP. The complex NP will correspond to an f-structure that is itself the value of a grammatical function other than COMP. This is sketched here:

(89)

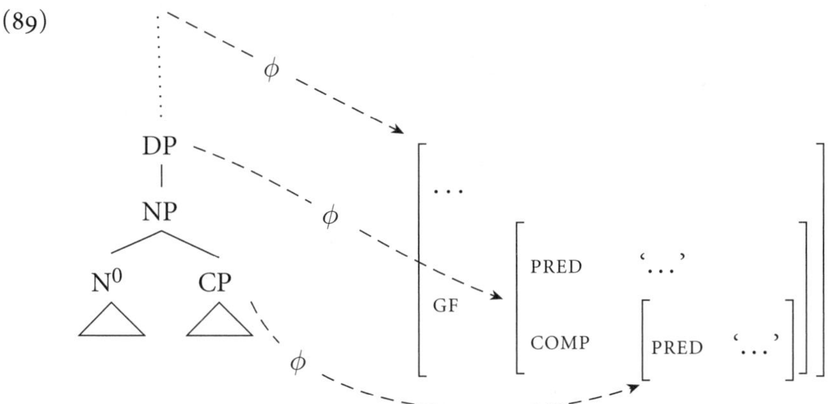

There is thus no way for the filler-gap complementizer to pass information out of a complex NP, because the filler will be trapped in the complex NP's GF. This is a direct result of the functional equalities in the complementizer's lexical entry.

The very same reasoning accounts for the impossibility of gaps in various other positions. McCloskey (1979: 8) notes that gaps are not licensed in prepositional objects, possessive NPs and objects of comparison. All of these positions are further embedded in some grammatical function. A PP maps to grammatical functions such as OBLIQUE, ADJUNCT, and SUBJECT. Its object will necessarily be too far removed for the paths in *aL*'s equations to reach. Possessive NPs and objects of comparison will likewise map to grammatical functions inside other NPs. The outer nominal will again trap the filler.

It therefore seems that if we take the successive cyclicity of *aL*-marking seriously then many of the facts about gap distribution in Irish follow. No auxiliary statements about the inability of prepositions to properly govern or otherwise license gaps seem necessary (Sells, 1984; McCloskey, 1990). The aspect of the analysis that captures the successive cyclicity is filler grounding and passing by functional equality. It may be that the path specified in the particular lexical entry for *aL* that I have presented is not quite right (i.e., it wrongly excludes or includes some cases), but the general strategy seems promising. A direction for further research is to examine the distribution of gaps in Irish carefully in light of this kind of analysis. One particular adjustment that seems likely to be neccessary is to allow *aL* to pass a filler through an open complement XCOMP as well as a closed COMP.

The fact that path specifications in the lexical entries for *aL* and *aN* can capture some of the distributional facts about gaps and pronouns does not mean that they must capture all of them. Some distributional facts might be better stated separately. For example, embedded questions are also islands for filler-gap dependencies in Irish (McCloskey, 1979). One way to capture this would be to add an off-path constraint, $(\rightarrow \textsc{mood}) \neq \textsc{interrogative}$, to the filler-passing capacity of *aL* that states that the COMP that is passed through cannot have interrogative mood. The off-path metavariable $\rightarrow$ picks out the value of the f-structure attribute with which it is associated on the path, in this case COMP. The equation states that the COMP that *aL* passes the UDF through cannot be a question. The means are therefore there to capture the embedded question constraint in *aL*'s lexical entry.

Alternatively, we could refrain from complicating *aL*'s lexical entry in this manner and depend on a general theory of *wh*-islands to account for the facts instead. It may be that the ultimate theory makes use of path equalities too. For example, it could state that the a UDF path cannot terminate in a question clause:

(90) $(\uparrow \textsc{mood}) = \textsc{interrogative} \;\Rightarrow\; ((\textsc{gf}^{+}\ \uparrow)\ \textsc{udf}) \neq (\uparrow\ \textsc{gf})$

The equation on the right hand side is similar to the equations used in LFG's binding theory (Dalrymple, 1993, 2001; Bresnan, 2001). It states that there cannot be an f-structure g that is found by going out one or more f-structures from $\uparrow$ such that g's UDF is functionally equated with a grammatical function in $\uparrow$.

Another independent constraint is the Highest Subject Restriction (McCloskey, 1990), which blocks a resumptive pronoun from the highest subject of an unbounded dependency (e.g., the subject in the clause immediately following the relative head). Only a gap may appear in this position. One possibility is to adopt McCloskey's (1990) position that there is an anti-locality effect on binding of a subject resumptive pronoun by a UDF in its own clause. The restriction can be stated as follows:

(91) $(\uparrow_\sigma \text{ANTECEDENT}) \neq ((\text{SUBJECT} \uparrow) \text{ UDF})_\sigma$

This equation means that a subject cannot be locally bound by an unbounded dependency function in its clause. It is stated in terms of the binding equations used in LFG for pronominal binding (Dalrymple, 1993). This formulation of the HSR is therefore a binding-theoretic formulation, like McCloskey's.

As it stands, the equation makes a certain prediction about Patterns 2 and 3. In each of these patterns there is binder grounding of a UDF by *aN* in an embedded clause. This is done through pronominal binding. The HSR equation above therefore predicts that even in an embedded clause the subject cannot be locally grounded by *aN*. That is, the restrictions sketched here hold as well as the HSR:

(92) *[$_{CP}$ *aL* ... [$_{CP}$ *aN* ... SUBJ ...]] Pattern 2
  |– – – pass – – –| └ * ground ┘

(93) *[$_{CP}$ *aN* ... [$_{CP}$ *aN* ... SUBJ ...]] Pattern 3
  |– – – pass – – –| └ * ground ┘

The prediction in (93) is correct. McCloskey (1990: 219) notes that despite speakers' "uncertainty and insecurity" about judgements for Pattern 3 in general, they share the firm intuition that a resumptive in the subject of a lower CP marked by *aN* is ungrammatical (also see McCloskey, 1979: 168, and McCloskey, 2002: 202):

(94) *an fear ar shíl mé a raibh sé breoite
the man *aN* thought I *aN* was he ill
'the man that I thought (he) was ill'

(McCloskey, 1990: 219, (54))

It remains to be seen what the status of the embedded subject is in the Pattern 2 example (92). The theory predicts that it will be equally ungrammatical.

Finally, let us turn back to mixed chains. The analysis makes predictions about longer instances of these. The predictions are hard to verify, since the mixed chains test the limits of speakers' competence (McCloskey, 2002), but the predictions are there nonetheless. The first prediction is that the bottom of Patterns 2 and 3, which are grounded by *aN*, can be extended as per the core multi-clause patterns for binder-resumptive dependencies:

(95) *aL* ... *aN* ... *go* ... *go* ... *Rpro* Pattern 2

(96) *aN* ... *aN* ... *go* ... *go* ... *Rpro* Pattern 3

The binder grounding function of *aN* anaphorically binds the resumptive and is therefore non-local. The binder passing function of *aN* is similarly non-local, but requires a subordinate UDF to bind. The prediction is that the top of Pattern 1 and 3 can also be stretched out with intervening instances of *go*, so long as there is an *aL* or *aN* below:

(97) *aN* ... *go* ... *go* ... *aL* ... _ Pattern 1

(98) *aN* ... *go* ... *go* ... *aN* ... *Rpro* Pattern 3

Lastly, the *aL*-marking can also be stretched out successive cyclically, so long as the general conditions on filler passing can be satisfied:

(99) *aN* ... *aL* ... *aL* ... _ Pattern 1

(100) *aL* ... *aL* ... *aN* ... *Rpro* Pattern 2

Mixed chains occur infrequently, but Jim McCloskey (p.c.) has informed me that he has previously collected examples like the following, which are of the extended-*aL* Pattern 2 form in (100):

(101) an fear a dúirt tú a shíl siad a raibh saibhreas mór aige
the man *aL* said you *aL* thought they *aN* was wealth great at-him
'the man that you said they thought was very wealthy'

In sum, the analysis makes several specific predictions with respect to extended mixed chains. The predictions are difficult to test, but some are corroborated by existing data.

7.6.2 *A Comparison to an Alternative Analysis*

McCloskey's (2002) analysis of the unbounded dependency system of Irish is formulated in terms of concurrent work in the Minimalist Program (Chomsky, 2000, 2001). The analysis is simple and elegant and explains a wide array of data. It sets a benchmark for analyses of Irish unbounded dependencies. However, a potential Achilles heel of McCloskey's analysis is that it has trouble ensuring proper semantic composition, a problem that McCloskey (2002: 219) acknowledges. The present analysis derives the entire licensing mechanism for resumptives from considerations of semantic composition and therefore, unsurprisingly, does not have this problem.

Although issues of semantic composition distinguish this theory and McCloskey's, there are other points of divergence, as well as points of convergence, between the two theories. McCloskey (2002) first shows that there are certain problematic assumptions in his earlier theory of Irish unbounded dependencies (McCloskey, 1990). In the earlier theory, it is assumed that successive-cyclic *wh*-movement to SpecCP results in *aL*-marking of each CP. Binder-resumptive dependencies are licensed by a null operator in the highest SpecCP that anaphorically binds the resumptive. There is no successive-cyclic movement through intermediate SpecCPs and therefore no marking of the intermediate CPs (which are marked by *go*). The crucial assumption that allows the analysis to predict the form of the complementizers is that the operator that licenses resumptives must have distinct properties from the *wh*-operator that determines *aL*-marking. Furthermore, whatever these properties are, they must be such that the complementizer can be sensitive to them (McCloskey, 2002: 192). McCloskey proposes and explores two options (McCloskey, 2002: 192, (i–ii)):

1. There is an intrinsic, lexically-specified difference between the element that determines the form *aL* and the element which determines the form *aN*.
2. The operator that binds resumptives inherits features from the resumptive pronoun that are distinct from features of the *wh*-operator that determines the form *aL*.

The second option is basically the one taken by McCloskey (1990).

The first option seems at first to be equivalent to the lexicalist position taken here, in the context of the Resource Management Theory of Resumption. This is a spurious similarity. Option 1 is about lexically specified differences between the element that determines the form *aL* and *aN*—that is, lexically specified differences between the two kinds of *operators*. The equivalent on the present theory might be if the mechanism of functional equality or binding were to determine the form of the complementizer. This is not what happens though: it is lexical differences between the complementizers *themselves* that determines their form. In other words, RMTR is an even more strongly lexicalist theory than that countenanced in McCloskey's first option.

McCloskey (2002: 192–193) presents two arguments against the second option of feature inheritance from resumptives to *aN*-marking operators. The first concerns the lack of viable features to make the distinction, and the second concerns the non-locality of the mooted feature inheritance. The feature in question cannot be a feature associated with pronouns in their resumptive capacity, because this would distinctively mark resumptive pronouns as special pronouns, contra McCloskey's Generalization. McCloskey (2002: 192) notes that resumptive pronouns are overwhelmingly morphologically realized like ordinary pronouns and he wants to maintain an ordinary pronoun theory of resumption. The question then becomes whether some of the normal formal features that mark pronouns (e.g., person, number, gender) can be inherited by the resumptive-binding operator. McCloskey concludes that this is unlikely, based on data that shows non-agreement between the relative head and the resumptive pronoun:

(102) A Alec, tusa a bhfuil an Béarla aige
you *aN* is the English at-him
'Hey, Alec–you that know(s) English'
(McCloskey, 2002: 192, (20a))

(103) Is sinne an bheirt ghasúr a-r dhíol tú ár lóistín.
COP.PRES we the two boy *aN*-PAST paid you our lodging
'We are the two boys that you paid our lodging.'

McCloskey (2002: 193) notes that the agreement features on these resumptives "fail to match the person-number features of their (ultimate) binders. If person-number features are inherited from bound pronouns by the elements which bind them, such mismatches are unexpected". McCloskey is here making a claim about *inheritance* of features from a resumptive pronoun by the null operator in SpecCP that binds the resumptive, not just about agreement between a binder and the element that it binds.

The agreement itself is interesting, though. It is worth taking a slight detour at this point to see how the current theory fares with the data above. The binder of the resumptive pronoun in relative clauses such as the ones above is a UDF that has PRED 'pro', i.e. a kind of null pronominal. This null pronominal does not have inherent person–number–gender features, although it is the right sort of element to enter into agreement relations. The UDF is the ANTECEDENT of the resumptive at semantic structure. The distribution of agreement features is explained if the UDF itself has an ANTECEDENT which is found elsewhere in the sentence. This is in most cases the relative head itself, but it can also be something else—*Alec* in (102) and *sinne* ('we') in (103). Based on the usual assumption that there must be agreement between an antecedent and the element it is the antecedent of, there is agreement between the element outside the relative clause and the UDF and in turn agreement between the UDF and the resumptive. By transitivity of agreement, the resumptive agrees with the element outside the relative clause. The theory does not require the relative head to agree with the UDF in the relative clause, though, so it is left out of the loop. Normally there is no opportunity to observe any potential mismatch, since the UDF is a null pronominal, but in this case we do get to observe the lack of agreement, albeit indirectly. So the agreement possibilities above are predicted by the current theory, at least for relative clauses. In *wh*-constructions there is no wiggle room, since there is no equivalent of the relative head: the binder of the resumptive pronoun must agree with the pronoun, where such featural distinctions occur (e.g., the binder may be underspecified for the relevant agreement features).

I noted above that the proposal in option 2 is that the resumptive-binding operator actually inherits features from the resumptive, not just that the operator agrees with features of the resumptive. The second argument that McCloskey (2002) gives against such an inheritance mechanism is that it would have to be completely non-local, potentially reaching into all kinds of sentential nooks and crannies, such as positions inside PPs, possessors, islands, and deeply embedded clauses, to mention a few. Furthermore, the search for the pronoun to inherit from can skip several closer, potentially more accessible pronouns. McCloskey (2002: 193) notes that such non-local inheritance of morphosyntactic features would be unprecedented. He therefore rejects the second of the two options above.

The remaining option is that the lexical specification in the operator in SpecCP determines the form of the complementizer (option 1). McCloskey rejects this option based on the mixed chain patterns. The basic reasoning goes like this. Assume that the operator that undergoes successive-cyclic movement to SpecCP (marked by *aL*) is itself a null pronominal, following earlier work (Browning, 1987). Now consider what happens in Pattern 1, which consists of *aL*-marking of a CP inside a complex NP and *aN* marking of the CP that contains the complex NP. If the *wh*-operator that determines movement is itself a pronominal, then it can move to the lower SpecCP and then be bound by the upper SpecCP as a resumptive (McCloskey, 2002: 197, (32)):

(104) $[_{\text{CP}}\ \text{XP}_j\ aN\ [_{\text{TP}}\ \ldots\ [_{\text{DP}}\ (\text{D})\ [_{\text{NP}}\ \text{N}\ [_{\text{CP}}\ pro_j\ aL\ [_{\text{TP}}\ \ldots\ t_j\ \ldots]]]]]]$

The crux of the problem is that the lower SpecCP needs to have certain features that determine *aL*, but it needs to pass up to the higher SpecCP features that determine *aN*. These are features which the lower SpecCP itself does not bear (since it determines *aL*).

Now consider Pattern 2, which is the inverse of Pattern 1 (*aL* … *aN* … *Rpro* …). McCloskey (2002: 198) notes that this pattern can be understood if the operator in the lower SpecCP that binds the resumptive and results in *aN*-marking subsequently moves to the higher

SpecCP, resulting in *aL*-marking. The problem is clear: the very same element must through its featural properties determine *aN*-marking in the lower CP and *aL*-marking in the higher SpecCP.

Based on these considerations, McCloskey (2002) rejects the option of having the lexical specifications of the operator in SpecCP determine the realization of C as *aL* or *aN*. McCloskey (2002: 201) suggests instead that the assumption that *aL* is associated with *wh*-movement and that *aN* signals the absence of movement leads to a hypothesis based on the independently postulated tree-formation mechanisms of the Minimalist Program (Chomsky, 1993). The effect of the proposal is the following (McCloskey, 2002: 201, (47)):

(105) C whose specifier is filled by Move is realized as *aL*.
C whose specifier is filled by Merge is realized as *aN*.
C whose specifier is not filled is realized as *go*.

It would be quite a novel proposal if the mode of introduction of syntactic material were to affect its morphological exponence, but this is just the effect of the proposal, not the actual proposal.

What McCloskey (2002: 203, (50)) actually proposes is the following, based on the theory of phases and feature-checking of Chomsky (2000, 2001):

(106) C which bears both the *Op*-feature and the EPP-feature is realized as *aL*.
C which bears only the EPP-feature is realized as *aN*.
C which bears neither the *Op*-feature nor the EPP-feature is realized as *go*.

The '*Op*-feature' is assumed to be a feature that identifies operators. It is assumed to appear on both *wh*-operators and null pronominal operators. It is interpretable, meaning that it has a semantic effect and need not be erased from the derivation to prevent Crash.

The *Op*-feature also occurs on C, to check the matching feature of the operator in SpecCP. The complementizer *aL* has the *Op*-feature and enters into an agreement relation with a null pronominal *pro* operator bearing the *Op*-feature. *AL* also bears the EPP-feature, which means that its specifier must be filled (Chomsky, 2001). The EPP-feature of *aL* can be checked by Merge of the null operator into its SpecCP. However, independent aspects of the theory entail that the *Op*-feature on C cannot be checked by Merge. The *Op*-feature on C is assumed to be uninterpretable (unlike the *Op*-feature on the operator, which is interpretable) and the derivation would crash. Thus, the *Op*-feature and EPP-feature on C jointly force the null pronominal operator to Move to

SpecCP of *aL*'s CP. *AL* realizes C with an *Op*-feature and an EPP-feature and therefore marks *wh*-movement.

AN realizes a C with the EPP-feature, but with no *Op*-feature. The EPP-feature means that SpecCP of C must be filled to check the feature. This could happen by either Move or Merge, but economy conditions of the theory dictate that it must be Merge, since Move is considered to be more complex than Merge. *AN* is therefore associated with Merge and the absence of movement. McCloskey (2002: 204–205) shows that the mixed chains follow if at each point a local decision is made to either Move or Merge.

Despite their quite different theoretical assumptions and mechanisms, several points of convergence can be identified between McCloskey's (2002) theory and the Resource Management Theory:

1. Both theories postulate a null pronominal in unbounded dependencies. In McCloskey's theory, the null pronominal operator is present in all unbounded dependencies. In the Resource Management Theory, the null pronominal occurs only in the absence of overt syntactic material.
2. Both theories account for successive cyclicity or lack thereof locally. In McCloskey's theory this arises from local application of Move or Merge. In the present theory this arises from local application of filler or binder grounding at the bottom of the dependency and local application of filler or binder passing in each intermediate position.
3. Both theories treat resumptive pronouns as ordinary pronouns and derive distinctions between resumptives and gaps from this assumption.
4. Both theories are strongly lexicalist. It is the presence of an item that bears the relevant lexical information borne by *aN*—the EPP-feature but no *Op*-feature in McCloskey's theory or a manager resource in the present theory—that "distinguishes languages which have a productive and grammaticized resumptive pronoun strategy from those which do not" (McCloskey, 2002: 205). As McCloskey (2002) notes, the difference between languages that have resumptive pronouns and those that do not reduces to the availability of a particular lexical item.

This much convergence is heartening. The two theories are based on quite different assumptions and employ quite different mechanisms. Any convergence between them is potentially indicative of true progress.

This is not to say that there are no points of divergence, though. One key difference between the two theories is that the present theory ties the presence of *aN* to a resumptive pronoun in a way that McCloskey's theory does not. McCloskey (2002: 205) notes that "A third feature of the proposal is that it does not in any direct way force the appearance of a resumptive pronoun within a clause headed by *aN*". Any material that is Merged into SpecCP of *aN* can potentially check its EPP-feature.

The pattern of complementizer marking in adjunct unbounded dependencies is relevant to this point. McCloskey (2002: 206–212) shows that adjunct extraction often results in *aN*-marking, even though there is no overt resumptive:

(107) Siúd an áit a bhfuair mé é
that the place *aN* got I it
'that's the place that I got it' (McCloskey, 2002: 208, (60b))

Based on data from dialect variation, McCloskey (2002: 207) shows that this is the same *aN* as in binder-resumptive dependencies. He shows that for locatives, manner adverbials, and temporals, there is free alternation between *aL*- and *aN*-marking. McCloskey (2002: 209) argues that there is reason to believe that there are pronominal elements corresponding to temporal and locative adverbials and that—given the general availability of null pronominals, or incorporated pronominal information, in Irish—it is reasonable to assume that there are null pronominals corresponding to these adverbials. The proposal is therefore that *aN*-marked temporal, locative, and manner unbounded dependencies contain null resumptive pronouns. If I am granted the same assumptions, then *aN*-marking also follows in this theory. *AL*-marking is also possible, on the assumption that the null adverbial pronominal is not obligatory (and there is no indication that it is), because ADJUNCT is a grammatical function and *aL* can ground the filler appropriately. McCloskey (2002: 208–209) notes that frequency and durative adverbials can only be marked by *aL* and assumes that there are no null pronouns corresponding to these adverbials. The lack of *aN*-marking follows on both theories.

The crucial case has to do with reason adverbials. These can only occur with *aN*-marking:

(108) Cén fáth a-r dhúirt tú sin?
what reason *aN*-PAST said you that
'Why did you say that?' (McCloskey, 2002: 209, (67a))

(109) *Cén fáth a dúirt tú sin?
what reason *aL* said you that
'Why did you say that?' (McCloskey, 2002: 209, (67b))

McCloskey (2002: 210) follows Rizzi (1990, 1996) in treating the interrogative form of reason adverbials as being base-generated in SpecCP. It then follows that the only C that can appear is *aN*, the one that has only the EPP-feature and whose SpecCP must be filled by Merge.

This is certainly a neat result that stems from the fact that *aN* on McCloskey's theory signals filling of SpecCP by Merge rather than presence of a resumptive pronoun. In contrast, on the theory presented here *aN*-marking is strongly tied to the presence of a resumptive pronoun, except where there is an embedded unbounded dependency that undergoes binder passing. There is no such UDF in the example above, though. I would have to postulate an obligatory null resumptive pronoun for reason adverbials or else argue that it is not the same *aN*, in which case the pattern of dialect variation would be hard to account for. I will leave this as an open problem for the Resource Management Theory, but I want to make a couple of final observations about adjunct extractions.

The reason that McCloskey (2002: 209) gives for positing null pronouns for temporal and locative adverbials is that they are fairly easily extracted from weak islands and such extraction has been connected to the availability of corresponding pronouns (often null). However, manner adverbials in Irish also allow *aN*-marking but these are notoriously difficult to extract from even weak islands and also tend not to have corresponding pronominal forms. Thus, whatever it is that allows manner adverbials to have null pronominals cannot be justified in the same terms as temporal and locative adverbials. If manner adverbials can help themselves to null pronouns—for a reason that is basically unknown at this point—then perhaps reason adverbials can, too. Whatever the ultimate explanation is, it must also explain why manner adverbial extraction is only optionally *aN*-marked whereas reason adverbial extraction is obligatorily *aN*-marked. The only proposal that I can make at this point is an explanatorily unsatisfactory but descriptively adequate one: manner adverbials optionally contribute a null pronominal, whereas reason adverbials obligatorily do so. However, I will argue shortly that McCloskey's proposal for *aN* leads to problems with semantic composition in the reason adverbial case and therefore ultimately fails to explain the facts, despite initial appearances.

This brings us to semantic composition, which is the second key difference between the two theories, where the resource management theory arguably fares better than McCloskey's theory. McCloskey (2002: 205–206) proposes that the *Op*-feature on an operator in SpecCP is interpretable and that the effect on semantics of the null operator is Functional Abstraction over the variable that it binds. The variable in question is either a resumptive pronoun or the trace of the null pronominal operator *pro*. McCloskey (2002: 206) assumes that the tree below has the semantic effect indicated (based on the theory of Heim and Kratzer, 1998):

(110)

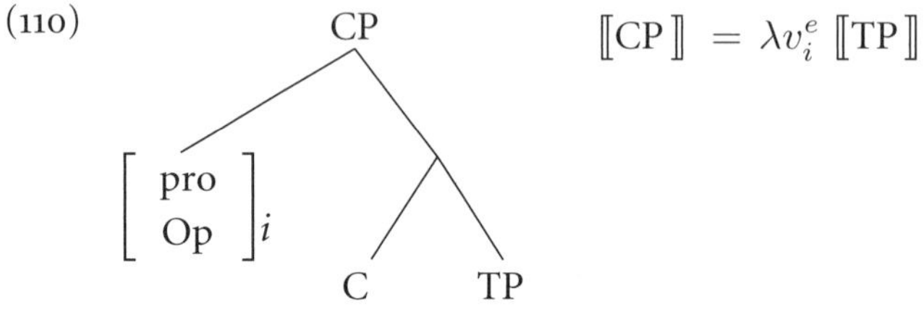

The operator results in abstraction over the *i*-th variable of type *e*, which is co-indexed with the operator. The operator thus forms a predicate out of the clause that it is attached to, allowing it to serve as a scope or a relative clause predicate.

McCloskey (2002: 219) notes the problem for semantic composition that this causes:

> This operation will apply appropriately at the "top" of A′–dependencies. But if it applies in intermediate positions, the result will be uninterpretable (the embedded CP will denote a predicate, rather than the proposition which the embedding verb expects to encounter in its complement position).

Application of the operation at intermediate positions will lead to improper variable-binding, resulting in the wrong intepretation. Consider a case where there is successive-cyclic movement of an operator through two complementizer positions. The resulting structure is sketched here:

(111) $[_{CP}$ Op_i *aL* ... $[_{CP}$ ~~Op_i~~ *aL* ... t_i]]

The lower operator performs abstraction over its variable, as specified by (110), and results in the lower CP denoting a predicate. The upper operator then needs to perform the same operation. There are two potential variables for it to bind: the lower operator and the trace at the foot of the chain. The lower operator performs lambda abstraction over a type *e* variable and must therefore be a functional type on *e*. Therefore, the lower operator cannot itself be a type *e* variable. It is then the wrong type to be bound by the upper operator. This means that the upper operator must attempt to bind the trace. However, this variable is already bound by the lower operator and is no longer free for binding. The lower operator has thus rendered functional abstraction at the top of the chain impossible. Thus, the intermediate position is apparently problematic.

The problem of intermediate positions has been the focus of a criticism of the analysis in McCloskey (2002) by Levine and Sag (2003: 171–219), as part of a larger critique of *wh*-movement theories. After citing McCloskey's (2002) discussion of the problem of intermediate trace interpretation, Levine and Sag (2003) note:

> The problem, of course, is that the intermediate traces left by successive-cylic movement in the transformational analysis of extraction UDCs do no work at all that would justify having them in the representation.

It could be argued that this criticism ignores the fact that intermediate traces are a necessary effect of what *determines* the successive-cyclic effects. Although the traces themselves may not be doing any work, their place in the representation is justified by the mechanism that does the work of successive *aL*-marking, according to the theory being criticized.

The mixed chains are still problematic, however. In mixed chains there are invariably multiple instances of abstraction, and some of them will, as McCloskey observes, lead to uninterpretability, for the reasons discussed above. Consider Pattern 1 (*aN* ... *aL* ... __). An operator Moves to the lower SpecCP and an operator is Merged into the higher SpecCP. The lower operator performs abstraction over its variable and results in the complement CP in the complex NP denoting a predicate, rather than a proposition. Meanwhile, the upper SpecCP binds the null pronominal operator in the lower SpecCP. However, if the lower SpecCP is an operator, it cannot also be a type *e* variable. The upper operator's predicate abstraction should therefore fail due to a type mismatch. Furthermore, even if somehow binding of an operator could be made to follow, the wrong variable would be abstracted over. The upper operator needs to abstract over the variable that the lower operator binds. But the variable is within the scope of and is bound by the lower SpecCP operator. The upper SpecCP operator therefore cannot bind the requisite variable because it is not free within the scope of the upper operator. The other two mixed chain patterns give rise to exactly the same set of problems.

The problem is that the functional abstraction mechanism is necessary for proper integration of the core cases and works for these cases if some kind of deletion mechanism is assumed, but it cannot successfully handle the mixed chains. McCloskey (2002: 219) speculates tentatively about three possible solutions, but they are either implausible, as McCloskey himself notes about the first one, or they will not work. First, he proposes and rejects the possibility of Functional Abstraction being optional. He notes that "the concept of 'optional' rules of semantic composition is not obviously a coherent one" (McCloskey, 2002: 219). The second solution considered is that perhaps "the offending element is deleted by some mechanism from the structures that semantic composition operates on" (McCloskey, 2002: 219). One question that arises is how to ensure deletion of only the lower complementizers. A second potential problem is the resulting complication in the feature theory of the Minimalist Program. What does it mean for something to be Merged in or Moved to SpecCP for reasons of interpretation (and checking of an interpretable feature) only to be deleted for reasons of interpretation? The third problem, which McCloskey (2002: 223, fn.29) notes, is that the theory would then lose its explanation of why the Highest Subject Restriction applies to an embedded subject if it is in a clause introduced by *aN* (see McCloskey, 2002: 202). The third solution proposed is that perhaps some kind of Cooper storage (Cooper, 1975, 1983) can be used to postpone interpretation of the operator until a point at which it can be successfully integrated. But there is no such point in the structure: no matter where integration of the 'extra' operator is attempted composition will fail for reasons discussed above.

In contrast, semantic composition is not problematic for the Resource Management Theory, because the manager resources that license resumptive pronouns do so precisely by addressing the problem of composition. The points of similarity between the two theories are numerous and show a welcome theoretical convergence. The two key differences between the theories have to do with semantic composition, where the resource management theory is to be preferred, and certain adjunct extractions concerning reason adverbials, where the feature-checking theory initially seems to fare better.

However, the problem of semantic composition also ultimately undermines McCloskey's appealing account of reason adverbials. The account was based on the assumption that there is no resumptive pronoun in this case and that the *aN* marking arises due to Merge of the interrogative form of the reason adverbial into SpecCP. This means that an operator is Merged into SpecCP. The operator performs Functional Abstraction and there must therefore be a variable in the clause in which the reason adverbial is interpreted. This variable cannot be a trace, because then the reason adverbial would have had to Move to SpecCP, wrongly predicting *aL*-marking, which is ungrammatical, as shown in (109) above (see McCloskey, 2002: 209, (67b), (68b)). The only option is for there to be a null resumptive pronoun to serve as the variable. Therefore, based on its assumptions about semantic interpretation, McCloskey's (2002) theory also needs to have a null resumptive pronoun in these cases and thus fares no better than the present theory, which ties *aN*-marking to the presence of a resumptive.

7.7 Conclusion

The Resource Management Theory of Resumption has been applied to a detailed analysis of resumptive pronouns in Irish. The analysis was driven by lexical properties of the Irish complementizers, as summarized in Table 7.3, repeated here.

The role of the Irish complementizers *aL* and *aN* in unbounded dependencies

	Role Relative to Position			
	Not bottom	**Bottom**	**Method**	**Cyclic**
aL	Passing	Grounding	Functional equality	Yes
aN	Passing	Grounding Resumptive licensing	Binding	No

The complementizer *aL* either passes or grounds an unbounded dependency function. Neither the passing or grounding role are reified in the analysis, but rather express the inuition that the complementizer mediates the unbounded dependency in a 'successive-cyclic' manner (McCloskey, 1990, 2002). The off-path constraint that captures this is stated in terms of functional equality between the UDF function that hosts the top of the dependency and intervening UDF functions in subordinate clauses. As such, no passing or grounding function plays a role in the analysis. The functional equality in the lexical entry for *aL* thus explains the successive-cyclic marking of *aL* and derives a large part of the distribution of gaps in Irish.

The lowest instance of the complementizer *aN* performs binder grounding, analogously to the filler grounding of *aL*. However, the mechanism used is pronominal binding and the binder grounding is therefore not successive-cyclic. Higher instances of *aN* perform binder passing, again through pronominal binding. Thus, each complementizer performs unbounded dependency passing and grounding using the mechanisms of functional equality and binding, which have independently been proposed as the two ways to satisfy LFG's condition on unbounded dependency integration, the Extended Coherence Condition (Bresnan and Mchombo, 1987). The analysis not only deals with the core Irish unbounded dependencies, but also extends to the difficult mixed chain cases discussed by McCloskey (2002). The analysis was shown to make several further predictions and suggests various directions for future work. A detailed comparison was made to McCloskey's (2002) analysis, which is couched in the Minimalist Program. There were several points of theoretical convergence, which is heartening given the quite different starting points of the analyses. A key point of divergence, though, had to do with ensuring proper behaviour at the syntax–semantics interface, particularly proper interpretation. McCloskey's (2002) theory has problems ensuring proper interpretation, especially in the mixed chain cases, whereas the Resource Management Theory of Resumption does not have such problems. RMTR is ultimately founded on a solution to the problem of resumptive pronouns as surplus resources for semantic composition; ensuring proper composition and interpretation forms the heart of the theory.

8

Hebrew

The resumptive pronoun system of Hebrew is similar to that of Irish. With respect to distribution, resumptive pronouns occur in every position except the highest subject. This chapter extends the analysis of Irish to Hebrew. The main difference between the two languages concerns the realization of the licensers for resumptive pronouns. In Irish, the information is associated with the complementizer *aN*. In Hebrew, the information is associated with complementizers in general, i.e. with the complementizer system.

Section 8.1 presents some basic Hebrew unbounded dependency data, focusing on resumptive pronouns. Section 8.2 presents the lexical licensing mechanism for resumptives. Section 8.3 provides an analysis of the data. I also consider dialectal variation in Hebrew with respect to resumptive pronouns in questions and suggest how the lexical licensing mechanism can be adjusted for Hebrew dialects that disallow resumptives in questions. Section 8.4 concludes with a comparison of the Irish and Hebrew resumptive pronoun systems.

8.1 Resumptive Pronouns in Hebrew

I will focus on the direct object grammatical function in Hebrew, since both gaps and resumptives occur in that function. Borer (1984: 220, (1)) gives the following data on the distribution of direct object resumptives and gaps:

(1) a. raʔiti ʔet ha-yeled she/ʔasher rina ʔohevet ʔoto
saw.I ACC the-boy COMP/COMP Rina loves him
'I saw the boy that Rina loves (him).' (Borer, 1984: 220, ~(1a))

b. raʔiti ʔet ha-yeled she/ʔasher ʔoto rina ʔohevet
saw.I ACC the-boy COMP/COMP him Rina loves
'I saw the boy that Rina loves (him).' (Borer, 1984: 220, ~(1b))

c. raʔiti ʔet ha-yeled ʔoto rina ʔohevet
saw.I ACC the-boy him Rina loves
'I saw the boy Rina loves (him).' (Borer, 1984: 220, ~(1c))

d. raʔiti ʔet ha-yeled she/ʔasher rina ʔohevet _
saw.I ACC the-boy COMP/COMP Rina loves _
'I saw the boy that Rina loves.' (Borer, 1984: 220, ~(1d))

Examples (1a) and (1b) show the co-occurrence of either the complementizer *she* or the more formal complementizer *ʔasher* with a resumptive pronoun. The pronoun is in its standard position in (1a) and in a fronted position in (1b). Example (1c) is particularly interesting because there is a fronted resumptive pronoun but no apparent licenser. Example (1d) has a gap in object position rather than a resumptive pronoun.

Borer (1984: 225) notes that there is a general process in Hebrew whereby a pronoun is fronted through an unbounded filler-gap dependency to what she calls a topic position:

(2) ʔamarti le-kobi she-ʔoto rina ʔohevet _
said.I to-Kobi COMP-him Rina loves _
'I told Kobi that it is him that Rina loves.' (Borer, 1984: 225, (11a))

(3) ʔamarti le-kobi she-ʔoto dalya xoshevet she-rina ʔohevet _
said.I to-Kobi COMP-him Dalya thinks that-Rina loves _
'I told Kobi that it is him that Dalya thinks that Rina loves.'
(Borer, 1984: 225, (11b))

Borer (1984: 228–237) argues that the fronted pronoun in (1b) and (1c) is not in the topic position, but has rather moved to COMP. She notes that Hebrew does not block multiple overt elements in COMP (Borer, 1984: 234, 240); i.e., the 'Doubly-Filled COMP Filter' (Chomsky and Lasnik, 1977) does not apply in Hebrew.

The Hebrew data is challenging for a couple of reasons. First, there is no one element like the Irish complementizer *aN* that correlates with a resumptive pronoun. The complementizers *she* and *ʔasher* occur with resumptives in (1a) and (1b), but these same complementizers also occur with a gap in (1d). Second, as shown in (1c), a resumptive pronoun can occur without either of these complementizers. The challenge is to identify a licenser for resumptives in Hebrew and to do so in a way that connects to the grammar of Irish resumption. The next section meets this challenge, following a conjecture by McCloskey (2002: 205) that a general theory of resumptive licensing should be based on lexical specifications of some element in the environment of the resumptive pronoun.

8.2 Licensing Resumptives Lexically

One of the points of convergence that was identified between the analysis of Irish binder-resumptive dependencies in the Resource Management Theory of Resumption and the Minimalist analysis presented by McCloskey (2002) is that both theories are lexicalist. In particular, both theories depend on lexical specification of the complementizer *aN* to drive resumptive-licensing in Irish. McCloskey (2002: 205) makes a conjecture that forms the basis for a promising hypothesis about why some languages have productive resumptive strategies while others do not:

> [W]e might assume that the presence of a lexical form corresponding to the Irish complementizer *aN* is the property which distinguishes languages which have a productive and grammaticized resumptive pronoun strategy from those which do not. Irish, Hebrew, Arabic and so on would possess such a lexical item; English would not. This is surely too crude a proposal as it stands (more distinctions are required than are provided by this simple binary choice), but it might be a place to start. It has the advantage of letting us understand what is otherwise a truly mysterious difference among languages (whether or not they deploy resumptive pronouns as a grammatical device) in terms of the availability or unavailability of a particular morphosyntactic form. The proposal thus assimilates this parametric difference to others which have yielded to similar kinds of understanding.

The key proposal is that the difference between grammars that allow resumptive pronouns and those that do not is a matter of lexical inventories. A language that has a lexical item (or lexical items) that corresponds in its specifications to the Irish complementizer *aN*—in a relevant manner to be determined—will have a resumptive pronoun strategy, while a language that lacks the requisite lexical item(s) will not. There are two quite appealing aspects to the proposal. The most important aspect is that it attempts to reduce variation with respect to resumptive pronoun licensing to lexical variation. In the current state of linguistic theory, lexical variation is an irreducible feature of our theoretical understanding of language. It is hard to even imagine what it would mean to claim that all languages have the same lexicon. Theories as otherwise disparate as Lexical-Functional Grammar, Head-Driven Phrase Structure Grammar, Principles and Parameters Theory (including the Minimalist Program), and Categorial Grammar have converged on the desirability of locating language variation in the lexicon to the greatest extent possible.

The second appealing aspect of McCloskey's conjecture is related to the first and concerns the notion of "parametric difference". There are theory-independent and theory-dependent notions of parameter that need to be separated here and the conjecture implicitly concerns them both. The theory-independent notion of parameter is some specific dimension of variation among languages, however it is captured, that has a finite range of options. In this case, the 'parameter' that is identified is binary, as McCloskey notes, and consists of whether a language has a lexical item with a particular property or not. As discussed in the previous paragraph, this is a notion that makes sense cross-theoretically. The theory-dependent notion of parameter is the one postulated in Principles and Parameters Theory. In that sense, possession of a lexical item is not really a 'parameter'. However, part of the theory-internal import of McCloskey's conjecture is that there has been a failure within P&P Theory to identify a 'resumptive pronoun parameter'. One of the main arguments of Sells (1984, 1987) is that there is no single parameter that can be identified as governing resumptive pronouns and there has been no P&P account in the intervening time that successfully refutes his conclusion. When considered in modern terms, Sells's analysis basically postulates that languages differ with respect to lexical properties of their resumptive-licensing operators and their pronouns.

Returning to RMTR, the Hebrew data indicates that the manager resource that licenses resumption ought to be associated with the complementizer system as a whole, rather than with a particular complementizer like Irish *aN*. The LFG correspondence architecture, presented in chapter 3, posits a level of morphological structure that interfaces with the c-structure. The morphological analysis yields features that provide a morphological parse of words in the string. For example, the words *banged* and *sang* would be morphologically analysed as bang+PAST and sing+PAST. Morphological structure can be formalized as a finite state morphology (Beesley and Karttunen, 2003), as in the main computational implementation of LFG, the Xerox Linguistic Environment (Crouch et al., 2011). One role of morphological features is to identify classes of lexical items, such as complementizers, with features, such as +COMP. Lexical information and templates, which abbreviate lexical information, are then associated with the morphological feature. All information that is common to complementizers would be associated with +COMP, with particular complementizers adding further features. For example, in English, the feature +COMP could be associated with the constraining equation (COMP ↑), which indicates that complementizers must occur in subordinate clauses, correctly blocking ungrammatical matrix occurrences, such as * *That the boy likes the cat* and * *Whether the boy likes the cat*. Particular complementizers would automatically inherit any information associated with the feature +COMP and could add further information of their own. For example, the English complementizer *whether* could add the information that it contributes interrogative mood to its clause with the equation ($\uparrow$ MOOD) = INTERROGATIVE.

The important point is that information associated with morphological features is lexical information, so a lexicalist analysis of resumption, following McCloskey (2002), can be maintained for Hebrew by associating resumptive-licensing information with the morphological feature +COMP:

(4)
$$+\textsc{comp},\quad C^0 \quad \left(\begin{array}{l} \%RP = (\uparrow \textsc{gf}^{+}) \\ (\uparrow \textsc{udf})_{\sigma} = (\%RP_{\sigma}\ \textsc{antecedent}) \\ @MR(\%RP) \\ @RELABEL(\%RP) \end{array}\right)$$

The lexical information in this entry is identical to that provided for *aN* in (55) of chapter 7. In the first line, a local name, %RP, is associated with a grammatical function in the complementizer's clause or with a GF that is more deeply embedded; this is the resumptive pronoun. In the second line, the unbounded dependency function of the complementizer's f-structure binds the resumptive pronoun. The third line contributes the manager resource that deals with the resumptive pronoun's resource surplus, thus licensing the resumptive. The last line is the dependency relabelling premise. All of the information is optional (indicated by parentheses). The lexical information must be realized if there is a resumptive pronoun to be licensed, as in (1a) and (1b), but can be ignored if there is no resumptive pronoun, as in (1d).

Example (1c) remains a challenge, because it contains a resumptive pronoun but no overt complementizer. The challenge can be met if we assume that Hebrew has a null complementizer, Ø+COMP. This complementizer would then automatically be associated with the lexical information in (4).

Null categories are to a great extent anathema to monostratal theories like LFG, HPSG, and Categorial Grammar, but this has been partly a side effect of distinguishing these theories from transformational theories. In the latter theories, null elements have played such a central role in transformations that their use elsewhere is easily justified on at least theory-internal grounds. However, even in monostratal theories there are general grounds for accepting the possibility of some null elements. In monostratal and transformational theories alike, a lexical item is an association of a form (or features that determine a form) with a meaning. The theories allow for a form with no meaning (e.g., expletives, *do*-support *do*, the complementizer *that*). It seems that the opposite situation of a meaning without a form should be theoretically possible and that it could, in fact, only be excluded by fiat.

Turning to LFG in particular, the null elements that are typically rejected are syntactic arguments. In particular, the 'big PRO' and 'little *pro*' of Principles and Parameters Theory are not theoretical postulates of LFG. The null pronoun represented by *pro* is not present in c-structure, since it does not correspond to a lexical item. The pronominal information is rather represented at f-structure, where it is added by the head that bears the pronominal inflection. The cases covered by PRO are either handled through functional equality (Bresnan, 1982*a*) or binding of pronominal information that is again represented only at f-structure (arbitrary control and also obligatory control in some analyses; e.g. Zec 1987, Dalrymple 2001). Some LFG analyses have postulated traces to mark the bottom of filler-gap dependencies (Bresnan, 1995, 2001; Falk, 2001, 2007). However, possible occurrences of traces are tightly controlled by Economy of Expression in these analyses (Bresnan, 2001: 90–94). In general, null elements that represent subcategorized arguments are either absent from the theory entirely or appear as a last resort (in some versions of the theory).

A null complementizer is a different proposition, though. First, it is a c-structure co-head (annotated $\uparrow = \downarrow$) and not an argument. Second, it is a functional category, not a lexical category. LFG does not treat the two sorts of category in a uniform manner (Bresnan, 2001). The c-structure to f-structure mapping theories postulated by Bresnan (2001) and Toivonen (2003) distinguish functional categories from lexical categories. C-structure complements of functional categories are co-heads, whereas c-structure complements of lexical categories are argument functions (Bresnan, 2001: 102). The theoretical considerations that allow elimination of null syntactic arguments (i.e., null lexical categories) in c-structure therefore do not readily extend to null functional categories.

8.3 Analysis

I will adopt Borer's proposal that the fronted pronoun is in COMP, but adapt it to Toivonen's (2003) X-bar theory and theory of non-projecting words. Pronouns in Hebrew will be assigned the category D. This means that they can be realized as either $\hat{\text{D}}$ or D^0. Fronted pronouns must be realized as $\hat{\text{D}}$ and will head-adjoin to C^0. Non-fronted pronouns will have the standard category of D^0. In this analysis, there is no movement or dislocation that fronts pronouns. The fronted position is just another position where a pronoun can be generated, local in the f-structure to the head that subcategorizes for the pronoun's grammatical function. Any information-structural effects associated with the fronted pronoun are handled by the mapping of the fronted position to information structure (Choi, 1997, 1999; King, 1997; King and Zaenen, 2004; Dalrymple and Nikolaeva, 2011).

A sample lexical entry for *ʔoto* ('him') is shown here:

(5) *ʔoto*, D $(\uparrow \text{PRED}) = \text{`pro'}$
$(\uparrow \text{PERS}) = 3$
$(\uparrow \text{NUM}) = \text{SG}$
$(\uparrow \text{GEND}) = \text{MASC}$

The head adjunction rule that generates the fronted pronoun is as follows:

(6) $C^0 \longrightarrow \underset{\uparrow = \downarrow}{C^0} \quad \underset{(\uparrow \text{GF}) = \downarrow}{\hat{D}}$

The fronted pronoun in example (1c) is generated as a $\hat{D}$ bearing the OBJECT grammatical function.

Lexical entries for the complementizers *she* and *ʔasher* are shown in (7). The complementizer *she* can be used in both relativization and in complement clauses, whereas *ʔasher* is only a relative complementizer (Borer, 1984: 235). This difference is captured lexically through the existential constraint in *ʔasher*'s lexical entry, which requires it to appear in an ADJUNCT clause and therefore restricts its appearance to relatives (complement clauses will have the grammatical function COMP).

(7) a. *she*+COMP, C^0
b. *ʔasher*+COMP, C^0 $(\text{ADJUNCT} \in \uparrow)$

Example (1d) is straightforward: the complementizer occurs in C^0 and there is a gap corresponding to the relativized object. The basic structure of (1a) is also straightforward: a complementizer occurs in CP and the pronoun is in its base position as a D^0 projecting a DP.

The relativized DP, *ʔet ha-yeled she-/ʔasher ʔoto rina ʔohevet*, of example (1b) is shown here:

(8)

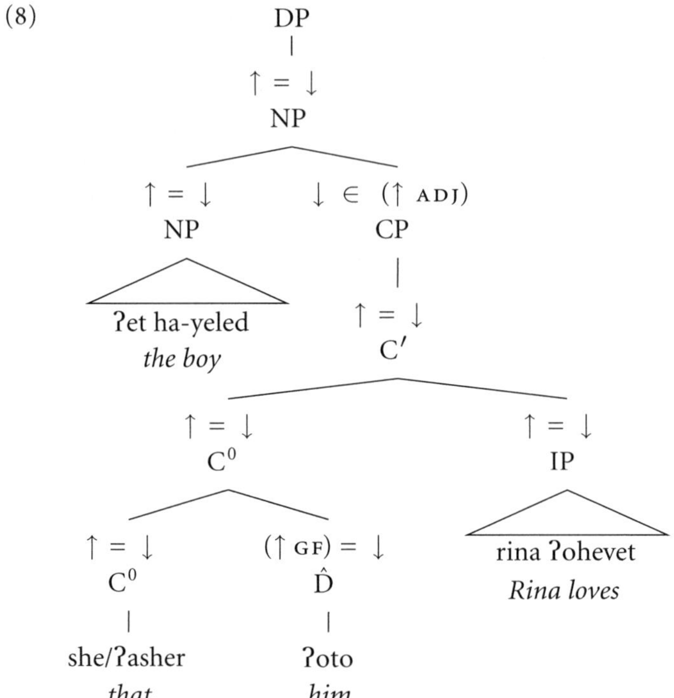

The fronted pronoun is adjoined to the complementizer as a non-projecting word. The functional uncertainty GF in the annotation (↑ GF) = ↓ on the fronted pronoun must be instantiated as OBJECT in order for the corresponding f-structure to satisfy Completeness and Coherence, since *ʔohevet* ('loves') requires a SUBJECT and an OBJECT.

The phrase structure rule for CP is the same as in Irish (and English), since the grammar of Hebrew generates relative clauses without relative pronouns:

(9) CP ⟶ { XP | ϵ } C′
(↑ UDF) = ↓ | (↑ UDF PRED) = 'pro' | ↑ = ↓
(ADJUNCT ∈ ↑)
REL_σ

The rule allows for an XP in the SpecCP to contribute the UDF function or for it to be contributed in the absence of overt material, in which case the CP is a relative clause. The material in SpecCP is optional, since all c-structure nodes are optional (Bresnan, 2001).

The analysis yields the following structures for the relativized DPs in (1), which are repeated as necessary:

(10) a. raʔiti ʔet ha-yeled she/ʔasher rina ʔohevet ʔoto
saw.I ACC the-boy COMP/COMP Rina loves him
'I saw the boy that Rina loves (him).'

b.

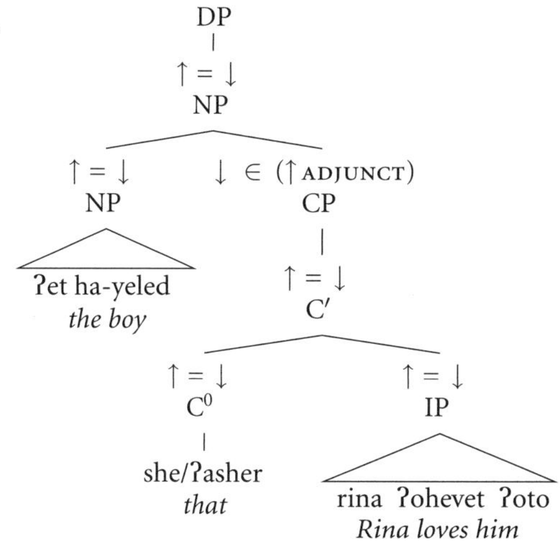

(11) a. raʔiti ʔet ha-yeled she/ʔasher ʔoto rina ʔohevet
saw.I ACC the-boy COMP/COMP him Rina loves
'I saw the boy that Rina loves (him).'

b.

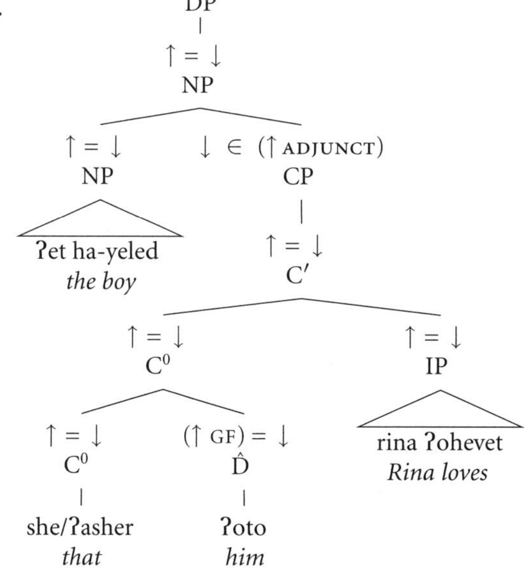

(12) a. ra?iti ?et ha-yeled ?oto rina ?ohevet
saw.I ACC the-boy him Rina loves
'I saw the boy that Rina loves (him).'

b.

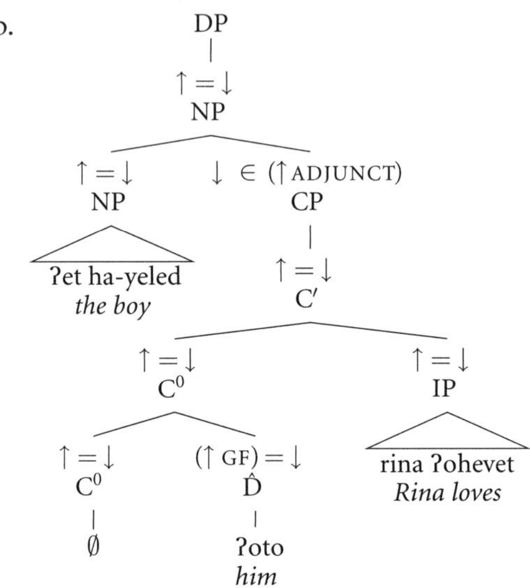

(13) a. ra?iti ?et ha-yeled she/?asher rina ?ohevet __
saw.I ACC the-boy COMP/COMP Rina loves __
'I saw the boy that Rina loves.'

b.

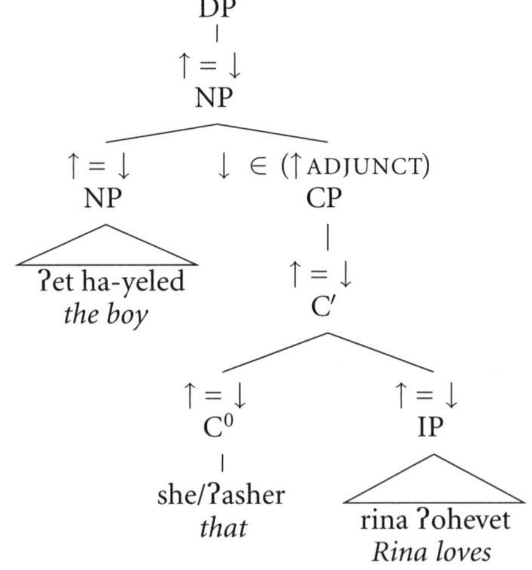

The three resumptive pronoun structures in (10)–(12) have identical functional structures and semantic structures. The common f-structure and semantic structure are shown here:

(14)

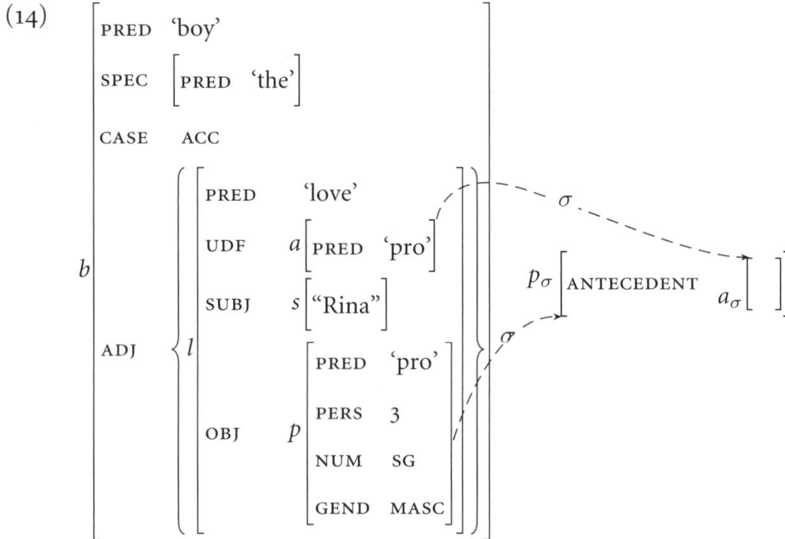

Binding of the resumptive pronoun by the UDF is established by the complementizer, as per (4). The complementizer also contributes a manager resource and performs required dependency relabelling.

The following premises are contributed by the lexical items, as instantiated by (14):

(15)

1.	$(v \multimap r) \multimap \forall X.[(b \multimap X) \multimap X]$	Lex. **ha ('the')**
2.	$v \multimap r$	Lex. **yeled ('boy')**
3.	$(a \multimap l) \multimap [(v \multimap r) \multimap (v \multimap r)]$	REL_σ
4.	$[a \multimap (a \otimes p)] \multimap (a \multimap a)$	Lex. **+comp (MR)**
5.	$(p \multimap l) \multimap (a \multimap l)]$	Lex. **+comp (RELABEL)**
6.	s	Lex. **rina**
7.	$s \multimap p \multimap l$	Lex. **ʔohevet ('loves')**
8.	$a \multimap (a \otimes p)$	Lex. **ʔoto ('him')**

These premises can be compared to those in (63) of chapter 7 for a similar Irish relative clause example. The proof that they construct is shown in Figure 8.1.

The analysis offered here is by no means a complete account of resumptives in Hebrew. The main aim has been to show that the mechanisms that have been used in the analysis of Irish can readily deal with Hebrew. However, the analysis already captures some further facts about Hebrew grammar. Hebrew

(1) a. raʔiti ʔet ha-yeled she/ʔasher rina ʔohevet ʔoto
saw.I ACC the-boy COMP/COMP Rina loves him

b. raʔiti ʔet ha-yeled she/ʔasher ʔoto rina ʔohevet
saw.I ACC the-boy COMP/COMP him Rina loves

c. raʔiti ʔet ha-yeled ʔoto rina ʔohevet
saw.I ACC the-boy him Rina loves

'I saw the boy that Rina loves (him).'

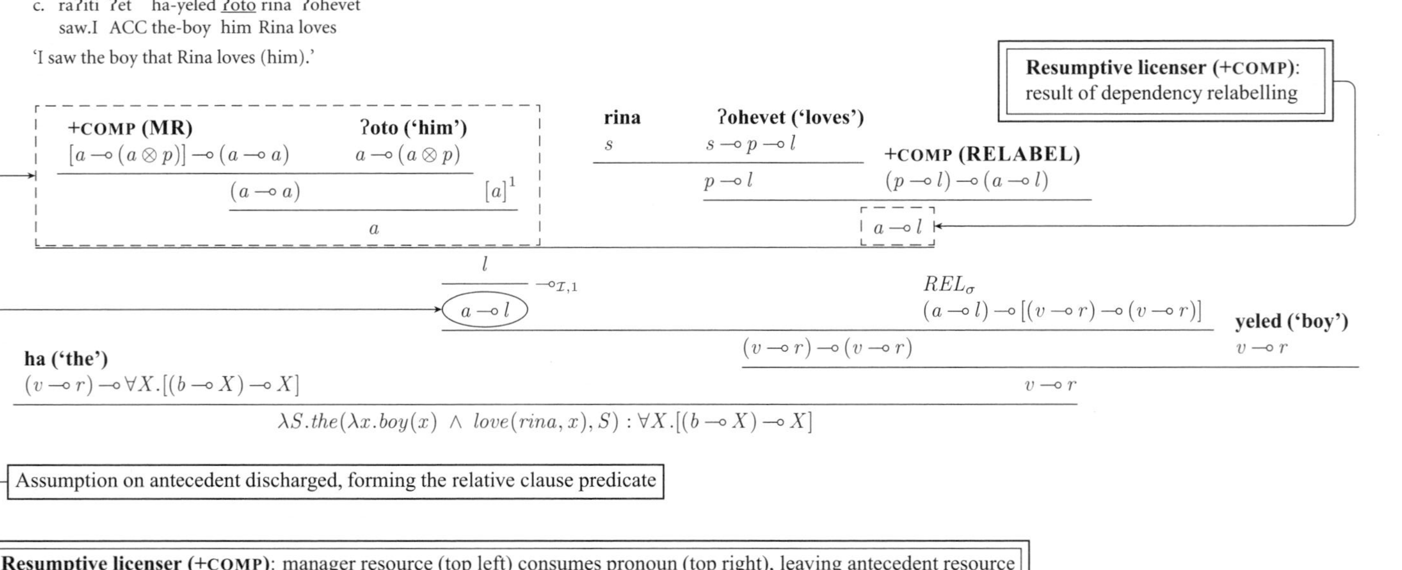

FIGURE 8.1. Proof for a Hebrew binder-resumptive dependency.

has prepositional forms that bear pronominal inflection, like in Irish. These prepositional forms set up a parallel resumptive paradigm to the direct object paradigm that was shown in (1), as in the following:

(16) a. raʔiti ʔet ha-yeled she/ʔasher rina xashva ʔalav
saw.I ACC the-boy COMP/COMP Rina thought about.him
'I saw the boy that Rina thought about (him).'
(Borer, 1984: 220, (2a))

b. raʔiti ʔet ha-yeled she/ʔasher ʔalav rina xashva
saw.I ACC the-boy COMP/COMP about.him Rina thought
'I saw the boy that Rina thought about (him).'
(Borer, 1984: 221, (2b))

c. raʔiti ʔet ha-yeled ʔalav rina xashva
saw.I ACC the-boy about.him Rina thought
'I saw the boy Rina thought about (him).' (Borer, 1984: 221, (2c))

The corresponding gap example is impossible: Hebrew does not allow prepositional object gaps (Borer, 1984; Shlonsky, 1992).

Borer (1984) analyses a fronted inflected preposition as movement into COMP, assimilating the analysis of fronted prepositions to her analysis of fronted pronouns. I maintain her insight by treating the inflected preposition similarly to the pronoun in assigning it the category P, which can be realized as P^0 or as $\hat{P}$.

(17) *ʔalav*, P (↑ PRED) = 'about'
(↑ OBJECT PRED) = 'pro'

As a P^0, the preposition is realized in the non-fronted position, where PPs normally appear. As a $\hat{P}$, the preposition is realized in the fronted position, provided the C^0 rule is amended as follows:

(18) $C^0 \longrightarrow \underset{\uparrow = \downarrow}{C^0} \quad \underset{(\uparrow \text{GF}) = \downarrow}{\{\hat{D} \mid \hat{P}\}}$

The inflected preposition contributes a pronominal resource, just like in Irish. Nothing more needs to be said to derive the examples in (16). The preposition is either generated in a non-fronted position as a P^0 or in a fronted position as a $\hat{P}$. The complementizer system licenses the resumptive pronominal information contained in the preposition by realizing GF^+ in (4) as OBLIQUE OBJECT.

8.3.1 *Dialectal Variation: Questions*

There has been some dispute in the literature about whether Hebrew allows resumptive pronouns in questions or not. Borer (1981: 114) claims that resumptive pronouns are not possible in Hebrew questions. However, subsequent work claimed that Hebrew does allow resumptives in questions in restricted circumstances. Sells (1984) noted that, while simple *wh*-questions like (19) are ungrammatical, a resumptive pronoun in a question is grammatical in a 'COMP-trace' environment:

(19) *mi raʔiti oto?
who saw-I him
'Who did I see (him)?' (Sells, 1984: 63, (58b))

(20) eyze xešbon kol maškia lo zoxer im hu noten ribit tova?
which account every investor not remembers if it gives good interest
'Which account does every investor not remember if (it) gives good interest?' (Sells, 1984: 64, (61))

Erteschik-Shir (1992) subsequently argued that what she calls "ECP resumptives", like the one in (20), must be distinguished from true resumptives in Hebrew, which she calls "syntactic resumptives" or "restrictive resumptives". However, Sharvit (1999: 591) has subsequently argued that at least some dialects of colloquial Hebrew allow resumptives in *which*-questions:

(21) eyze student nigashta ito?
which student you.met with.him
'Which student did you meet with (him)?' (Sharvit, 1999: 591, (9))

Sharvit (1999: 591) analyses the distinction between grammatical examples of resumptives in questions, like (21), and ungrammatical examples, like (19), in terms of *D-linking* (Pesetsky, 1987). She notes that *which*-questions can qualify as D-linked more readily than *who*-questions. Based on the distinction, she argues that resumptive pronouns are sensitive to D-linking.

The analysis given in the previous section captures the dialect that allows resumptive pronouns in questions. It does not address the D-linking distinction, but if Sharvit's (1999)'s assumptions about D-linking are adopted, the lack of non-D-linked *wh*-questions will follow for independent reasons. In order to syntactically capture the dialect that does not allow resumptives in questions at all, not even in D-linked questions, the only thing that needs to be done is to add an equation to the lexical entry for the resumptive-licensing

TABLE 8.1. A comparison of the resumptive pronoun systems of Irish and Hebrew.

	Resumptive licenser					Binding	
	HSR	Form	Category	C-structure Position	Local to	Antecedent	Resumptive
Irish	Yes	*aN*	$\hat{C}$	Top	UDF	UDF	GF^+
Hebrew	Yes	+COMP	C^0	Top	UDF	UDF	GF^+

+COMP morphological feature such that it cannot co-occur with a UDF that maps to FOCUS at information structure, since this is the information structure role of *wh*-phrases (King, 1997; Dalrymple and Nikolaeva, 2011):

(22)
$$+\text{COMP},\quad C^0 \quad \left(\begin{array}{l} (\uparrow \text{UDF})_\sigma \not\in (\uparrow_{\sigma\iota}\ \text{FOCUS}) \\ \%\text{RP} = (\uparrow \text{GF}^+) \\ (\uparrow \text{UDF})_\sigma = (\%\text{RP}_\sigma\ \text{ANTECEDENT}) \\ @\text{MR}(\%\text{RP}) \\ @\text{RELABEL}(\%\text{RP}) \end{array}\right)$$

It remains to be seen whether this simple solution is restrictive enough. Further work should also be done to see whether the distribution of resumptives can be reduced to solely semantic differences between relative clauses and questions and whether any such differences can explain the variation.

8.4 Conclusion

The lexical analysis of Irish, in terms of the Resource Management Theory of Resumption, has been extended to Hebrew. The resulting picture is summarized in Table 8.1. Both languages license resumptive pronouns through their complementizer systems. The licensing information is associated with a particular complementizer, *aN*, in Irish, but is associated with complementizers in general in Hebrew, through a morphological feature that marks complementizers. Both languages license ordinary pronouns as resumptive pronouns through binding of a resumptive pronoun that is arbitrarily deeply embedded, subject to the Highest Subject Restriction, by the unbounded dependency function at the top of the binder-resumptive dependency. The theory has thus achieved a unified analysis of resumptives in the two languages. This was done following McCloskey's conjecture (McCloskey, 2002: 205), which states that the difference between languages with respect to whether they license resumptive pronouns, and also with respect to how they do so, is a matter of lexical specification. English, unlike Irish and Hebrew, does not have the required kind of complementizer and therefore lacks grammatically licensed resumptives.

Part IV

Syntactically Inactive Resumptives

9

Swedish

It has been suggested in the literature that Swedish resumptive pronouns are actually underlyingly gaps (Zaenen et al., 1981; Engdahl, 1985; McCloskey, 2006). This would seem to explain their gap-like behaviour with respect to certain diagnostic phenomena, which were discussed in chapters 2 and 6 and which will be investigated further in this chapter. Based on some of the same sort of evidence, this claim has also been made for resumptives in Vata (Koopman, 1982, 1984; McCloskey, 2006), which are the subject of the next chapter. McCloskey (2006) notes that the behaviour of Swedish (and other) resumptives can nevertheless be reconciled with the theoretical understanding of unbounded dependencies. He writes (McCloskey, 2006: 109):

> The two sets of properties (properties of movement-derived constructions and properties of non-movement derived constructions) still line up in neat opposition. In Swedish, Vata, and Gbadi, those A-bar-binding relations which terminate in a pronoun show the complete constellation of properties associated with A-bar-movement. In Irish and similar languages, resumptive pronoun constructions show none of those properties. As long as we can make sense of the idea that a pronoun can be the 'spell-out' of a trace (as in the former group of languages), the larger conceptual architecture is not severely threatened.

Setting aside the theory-internal notions in the passage, the point is that, although there are a set of properties associated with filler-gap unbounded dependencies that are exhibited by resumptive pronouns in certain languages, if the resumptive pronouns in question can be successfully analysed as gaps, in some sense, then their properties are not surprising.

I have argued elsewhere (Asudeh, 2011*c*) against the kind of analysis that McCloskey (2006: 110–111) briefly sketches for Swedish, as an exemplar of the notion of 'spelling out' a gap, for two main reasons. First, in order to maintain McCloskey's Generalization—that resumptive pronouns are ordinary pronouns cross-linguistically—the pronoun must bear the same pronominal information as it would were it not in an unbounded dependency. In other words, if the pronoun is underlyingly a gap, the fact that it surfaces exactly like the corresponding non-resumptive personal pronoun in the given argument position is a mere coincidence. Second, there are interpretive differences between gaps and pronouns in Swedish that would be unexplained if the pronouns are underlying gaps. We will return to the matter of interpretation below.

However, McCloskey's main point in this passage is compelling: if Swedish resumptives could, in some sense, be analysed like gaps, then their gap-like properties could be subsumed under the general explanations for the properties in question. In Asudeh (2011*c*), where I present an analysis of Vata resumptives, which is developed further in the next chapter, I argue that it is the binder-resumptive relation in languages like Swedish and Vata that undergoes a further, syntactic operation, such that it is equivalent in effect to a filler-gap dependency. The resumptive pronouns are, however, completely ordinary pronouns. It is the relation between the binder and the resumptive that is exceptional, not the resumptive. The formal mechanism that accomplishes this is restriction (Kaplan and Wedekind, 1993), as outlined in chapter 6. The restriction operator allows two f-structures to be equated, setting specified features aside. It allows the functional equality for filler-gap dependencies to be used in resumption, which would normally be impossible due to the uniqueness of PRED features. Aside from the modification of the filler-gap functional equality, resumptives in Swedish (and Vata) are licensed exactly as in Irish and Hebrew. As ordinary pronouns, they contribute pronominal meaning constructors that are consumed by manager resources, which remove the resource surplus created by the pronouns, thus allowing successful composition and licensing the pronoun.

Section 9.1 presents key data and generalizations about Swedish resumptives. Some important variation in the dialect of Swedish spoken on the Åland Islands in Finland is considered in section 9.1.1. Evidence for the syntactically inactive status of Swedish resumptives is reviewed in section 9.1.2. Section 9.1.3 presents semantic evidence against treating Swedish resumptives as underlying gaps. Section 9.2 concerns the licensing and integration of syntactically inactive resumptives. The licensing mechanism is the same as that for syntactically active resumptives—manager resources—but the integration mechanism is distinct. Section 9.3 presents the analysis. Section 9.4 is a discussion of some implications of the theory and section 9.5 concludes.

9.1 Resumptive Pronouns in Swedish

Swedish resumptive pronouns have been investigated principally in four environments (Engdahl, 1982, 1985; Maling and Zaenen, 1982: 235–239; Sells, 1984: 55–57), which are listed here with relevant examples.

1. Sentential subjects

(1) [Vilken skådespelare]$_i$ var det att publiken inte kände igen _$_i$
which actor was it that audience.DEF not recognize _
/ honom$_i$ ganska konstigt?
/ him rather strange
'Which actor was the fact that the audience did not recognize (him) rather strange?' (Engdahl, 1982: 165, (58))

2. Crossing dependencies

(2) [Den här presenten]$_i$ kan du säkert aldrig komma på vem$_j$ jag fick
this here present.DEF can you surely never come on who I got
den$_i$ / * _$_i$ av _$_j$.
it / _ from _
'This present you'll never guess who I got (it) from.'
(Maling and Zaenen, 1982: 236, ~(13a))

3. Deep embedding (at least two clauses)

(3) I går såg jag [en film]$_i$ [$_{CP}$ som jag undrar om någon
yesterday saw I a film that I wonder if anyone
minns [$_{CP}$ vem som regisserat _$_i$ / den$_i$]].
remembers who that directed _ / it.
'Yesterday I saw a film that I wonder if anyone knows who directed (it).' (Engdahl, 1982: 154, ~(12))

4. Following material at the left periphery of CP

(4) [Vilket ord]$_i$ visste ingen [$_{CP}$ [hur många *M*]$_j$ [$_{C'}$ det$_i$ stavas
which word knew nobody how many *M*s it is.spelled
med _$_j$]]?
with _
'Which word did nobody know how many *M*s (it) is spelled with?'
(Engdahl, 1985: 8, ~(11))

(5) [Vilket ord]$_i$ visste ingen [$_{CP}$ [$_{C'}$ om det$_i$ stavas med ett *M*]]?
which word knew nobody if it is.spelled with an *M*
'Which word did nobody know if (it) is spelled with an *M*?'
(Engdahl, 1985: 8, ~(11))

Engdahl (1982) argues that the pronouns found in the first three environments are either governed by processing constraints (environments 2 and 3) or are problematic for other reasons (environment 1). I follow Engdahl in treating only the last kind as true, grammatically licensed resumptives in Swedish. In standard varieties of Swedish, a gap is ungrammatical in the corresponding positions. I will return to the first three environments in chapter 11, where I will argue that they should be treated as a processing effect, outside the grammar proper.

Engdahl (1982) offers the following generalization about grammatically licensed resumptives in Swedish (Engdahl, 1982: 154, (18)):[1]

(6) Associate a preposed WH phrase with a pronoun which agrees in number, gender, and person in the context COMP __ .
[+LEX]

The standard theoretical assumption at the time was that both *wh*-phrases and complementizers occurred in COMP. Engdahl's generalization therefore effectively captured the necessity of a resumptive pronoun after lexical material at the left periphery of a clause, whether the material is a *wh*-phrase, as in (4), or a complementizer, as in (5). This generalization holds of 'Rikssvenska', the standard Swedish spoken in Sweden,[2] but does not hold of all dialects of Swedish. We will return to this point below.

Engdahl's generalization must be updated slightly in light of the adoption of the functional category C^0 instead of COMP. It is not an option to make Engdahl's claim about COMP a claim about C^0 instead, such that a resumptive occurs after an overt complementizer. This would wrongly exclude *wh*-phrases as in (4), since these constitute material in SpecCP, not in C^0. The descriptive content of Engdahl's generalization holds, though: if the bottom of an unbounded dependency immediately follows overt material in the left periphery of CP, then a resumptive pronoun is required. The upshot of the generalization, given general structural facts about Swedish grammar, is that an unbounded dependency into a subject position that immediately follows overt material at the left periphery of CP must be a binder-resumptive dependency.

Many propositional complement verbs in Swedish, such as *säga* ('say') and *tro* ('think/believe'), can take a bare clausal complement that lacks a complementizer, as in English. The subject of a bare complement cannot be realized as a resumptive pronoun:

(7) [Vilken elev]$_i$ trodde ingen __$_i$ skulle fuska?
which student thought no one __ would cheat
'Which student did no one think would cheat?'
(Engdahl, 1982: 166, ~(65a))

[1] I have left out the part of this rule that concerns gaps and slightly modified the wording of the remainder as a result of the omission.

[2] A separate standard, 'Finlandssvenska', exists in mainland Finland, where there is a Swedish-speaking minority.

(8) *[Vilken elev]$_i$ trodde ingen han$_i$ skulle fuska?
which student thought no one he would cheat
(Engdahl, 1982: 166, ~(65b))

If these verbs take a complement with a complementizer, a resumptive is necessary, in Rikssvenska.

(9) [Vilken elev]$_i$ trodde ingen att han$_i$ skulle fuska?
which student thought no one that he would cheat
'Which student did no one think that (he) would cheat?'
(Engdahl, 1982: 166, ~(65c))

This data indicates that the resumptive-licensing information must somehow be associated with left-peripheral material in CP and cannot be directly associated with complement clauses or with verbs that take complement clauses.

The information that licenses resumption must be optional, because left-peripheral material in CP may be present in the absence of a binder-resumptive dependency:

(10) Jag undrar [$_{CP}$ hur ofta [$_{C'}$ Pelle/han fuskar]].
I wonder how often Pelle/he cheats
'I wonder how often Pelle/he cheats.'

(11) Jag undrar [$_{CP}$ [$_{C'}$ om Pelle/han fuskar]].
I wonder if Pelle/he cheats
'I wonder if Pelle/he cheats.'

If the licenser for resumption were obligatory, occurrence of left-peripheral material in CP would require a resumptive pronoun.

The complementizers *om* ('if') and *att* ('that') occur with resumptive pronouns, as shown in (5) and (9) respectively. In colloquial speech it is also possible for the complementizer *som* to co-occur with material in SpecCP. Alongside sentences like (12) we find ones like (13):

(12) Jag undrar hur ofta Pelle fuskar.
I wonder how often Pelle cheats
'I wonder how often Pelle cheats.'

(13) %Jag undrar hur ofta som Pelle fuskar.
I wonder how often that Pelle cheats
'I wonder how often Pelle cheats.'

Some speakers have prescriptive biases against *wh*-material in SpecCP of a CP headed by *som*, but such examples are quite common.

In some dialects, the complementizer *att* can occur in the same position:

(14) %Jag undrar hur ofta att Pelle fuskar.
I wonder how often that Pelle cheats
'I wonder how often Pelle cheats.'

Examples (12–14) indicate that colloquial Swedish does not disallow the co-occurrence of material in SpecCP with an overt complementizer (i.e., it does not obey the 'Doubly-Filled COMP Filter'; Chomsky and Lasnik, 1977; Chomsky, 1981).

Swedish does not allow a resumptive pronoun as the highest subject of a clause:

(15) *Jag känner mannen som han sjunger.
I know man.DEF that he sings.

(16) *Vilken man han sjunger?
which man he sings.

Swedish allows only an embedded subject resumptive as the base of a binder-resumptive dependency. The language thus exhibits the effects of the Highest Subject Restriction (HSR), like Irish, Hebrew, Arabic, and Welsh (McCloskey, 1990; Shlonsky, 1992; Willis, 2000), The effect of the HSR is particularly conspicuous in Irish, since the highest subject is the *only* position from which a resumptive pronoun is blocked (McCloskey, 1990) and in Palestinian Arabic, since the highest subject is not just the only position from which a resumptive pronoun is blocked, but also the only position in which a gap rather than a resumptive is allowed (Shlonsky, 1992); see chapter 2.

The HSR in Swedish can be captured as for Irish (see chapter 7), with the following constraint:

(17) $(\uparrow_\sigma \text{ANTECEDENT}) \neq ((\text{SUBJECT} \uparrow) \text{ UDF})_\sigma$

The constraint has the effect that a subject cannot be locally bound by an unbounded dependency function in its clause. This follows McCloskey (1990) in treating the HSR as an anti-locality effect on anaphoric binding of a subject resumptive pronoun.

9.1.1 *Dialectal Variation: Both Gaps and Resumptives after Complementizers*

The dialect of Swedish spoken on the Åland Islands shows interesting variation with respect to resumptive pronouns. The Åland Islands are situated at the base of the Gulf of Bothnia, in the Baltic Sea, between Sweden and Finland. They are part of Finland, but the majority native language, by far, is Swedish. However, the dialect of Swedish spoken on the Islands, 'Ålandssvenska', is distinct from both Rikssvenska, the Swedish standard spoken in Sweden, and Finlandssvenska, the Swedish standard spoken on the Finnish mainland.

The basic generalization about the Scandinavian languages in the literature (Engdahl, 1982, 1985; Maling and Zaenen, 1982) is that either (1) they allow gaps following complementizers (there is no 'COMP-trace' effect), but disallow filled-COMP resumptives of the kind we have been looking at, as in Danish, Icelandic, and Norwegian or (2) they disallow gaps following complementizers (there is a 'COMP-trace' effect), but allow filled-COMP resumptives, as in Swedish. Speakers of Finlandssvenska deviate from the pattern slightly in allowing a gap after the complementizer *att*, but requiring a resumptive pronoun after all other complementizers or *wh*-phrases at the left periphery of CP (Anders Holmberg, p.c.).[3] This all seems to make a lot of sense from the perspective of whatever grammatical constraint blocks gaps following complementizers (Perlmutter, 1968; Bresnan, 1972; Chomsky and Lasnik, 1977, among many others; see Asudeh, 2009 for a recent LFG treatment and further references).

It would also seem to give excellent support to Last Resort theories of resumptive pronouns, which claim that resumptives occur specifically in order to avoid violations of independent grammatical principles, such as the 'COMP-trace' filter or the Empty Category Principle (Chomsky, 1981). Prominent examples include the theories of Shlonsky (1992) and Aoun et al. (2001). In fact, the Scandinavian languages seem to show much clearer support for such accounts than the languages that they have actually been applied to (Hebrew and Arabic). For example, in Hebrew unbounded dependencies, direct objects can be gaps or resumptive pronouns, which requires some special manoeuvring for Last Resort theories (Shlonsky, 1992). This is dubious if the resumptive is there by last resort: gaps in direct object position occur quite freely cross-linguistically, so only very peculiar and parochial grammatical constraints would block them.

Ålandssvenska is unlike the other Scandinavian languages in allowing both gaps and resumptive pronouns immediately after complementizers. The following are therefore both possible:

[3] Anders Holmberg also informs me (p.c.) that some Fenno-Swedes from the Finnish mainland speak a dialect that patterns like the non-Swedish Scandinavian languages in allowing gaps following overt complementizers and disallowing resumptives.

(18) Vem undrar du om _ fuskar?
who wonder you if _ cheats
'Who do you wonder if cheats?'

(19) Vem undrar du om han fuskar?
who wonder you if he cheats
'Who do you wonder if (he) cheats?'

Many speakers also allow either gaps or resumptives after left-peripheral *wh*-phrases:

(20) Vem undrar du hur ofta _ fuskar?
who wonder you how often _ cheats
'Who do you wonder how often cheats?'

(21) Vem undrar du hur ofta hon fuskar?
who wonder you how often she cheats
'Who do you wonder how often (she) cheats?'

For some speakers, gaps are only allowed after complementizers, and resumptive pronouns are obligatory after left-peripheral *wh*-phrases. For other speakers, resumptive pronouns are not permitted after complementizers, but are obligatory after left-peripheral *wh*-phrases.

It is hard to see how the Ålandssvenska facts could be naturally accommodated in a Last Resort theory. There is no constraint against subject extraction after left-peripheral material in CP, yet resumptive pronouns are also sanctioned, for the same speakers. The resumptive pronouns thus do not seem to be a last resort. A Last Resort theory might attempt to postulate that the complementizers in Ålandssvenska are systematically ambiguous between homophonous alternants, one of which leads to last resort insertion of a resumptive pronoun and the other of which does not. This is Shlonsky's (1992) proposal for the optionality of resumptives and gaps in Hebrew direct objects. He proposes that the Hebrew complementizer *she* is ambiguous between two homophonous alternants. There is little independent evidence for this in Hebrew, but matters become even worse in Ålandssvenska, since here at least two or three complementizers would have to be ambiguous between homophonous alternants, without independent justification. Furthermore, there is still the matter of the speakers who allow gaps and resumptives after left-peripheral *wh*-phrases; it is not feasible to assume a similar ambiguity in the productive sub-grammar of *wh*-phrases.

Another option might be to claim that speakers of Ålandssvenska are bi-dialectal between the Swedish and Finnish dialects of Swedish and that they control two grammars, one that allows resumptive pronouns after left-peripheral material in CP, but disallows gaps following complementizers (like Rikssvenska), and one that allows gaps following complementizers, but disallows left-peripheral material (like Finlandssvenska). It would be difficult to find independent evidence for this proposal, but, more importantly, it lacks any explanatory force. Why do the speakers not instead disallow both options? Such languages exist: English does not allow either option robustly.

In contrast, on the present account, as in other non-transderivational accounts, all that needs to be said is that the grammars of speakers of Ålandssvenska license resumptives in subject position and do not contain a constraint against a gap following left-peripheral material in CP. The speakers who allow gaps after complementizers, but nowhere else, only have the constraint with respect to left-peripheral *wh*-phrases. This is entirely expected, given that complementizers in many languages do not give rise to the effect and that it is generally stronger with *wh*-phrases.

9.1.2 *Swedish Resumptives as Syntactically Inactive Ordinary Pronouns*

The following phenomena have been used as evidence that Swedish resumptive pronouns are syntactically gap-like (Zaenen et al., 1981; Engdahl, 1982, 1985; Sells, 1984): islands, weak crossover, across-the-board extraction (ATB extraction), reconstruction, and parasitic gaps. I show in this section that, although there are issues with some of this evidence, as a whole it supports a theory in which Swedish resumptives are treated as gap-like in some respects, but not in all respects. In particular, Swedish resumptives must be treated as ordinary pronouns in their lexical contributions, including the contribution of a pronominal meaning, and they must be realized in c-structure. The difference between syntactically active resumptives, as in Irish and Hebrew, and syntactically inactive resumptives, as in Swedish and Vata, concerns f-structure. Swedish resumptives are, like gaps, equated with the UDF that represents the top of the unbounded dependency at f-structure; i.e. the binder and the resumptive are token-identical at f-structure. The pattern of data for Swedish, which still needs much more investigation, is shown in Table 9.1.

Swedish is generally quite permissive about extraction from islands, except for left-branch islands and subject islands (Engdahl, 1982, 1997). Engdahl (1985: 10) notes that island violations that are judged to be ungrammatical are not improved by resumptives:

TABLE 9.1. Some properties of Swedish resumptives.

Grammatically Licensed	Yes
Island-Sensitive	Yes?
Weak Crossover Violation	%
Licenses Reconstruction	No
Licenses ATB Extraction	Yes
Licenses Parasitic Gaps	Yes

(22) ?*Vilken bil$_j$ åt du lunch med [$_{NP}$ någon$_i$ [$_{S'}$ som t_i körde
which car ate you lunch with someone that drove
t_j/* <u>den</u>]]?
__/* it
'Which car did you have lunch with someone who drove it?'
(Engdahl, 1985: 10, (16))

Engdahl (1985) mentions that the example is judged as worse with a resumptive than with a gap. However, this resumptive is not a true grammatically licensed resumptive, since it is not a subject that occurs after left-peripheral material in CP. Much more work could be done on testing resumptives in islands in Swedish, but the island evidence cannot at present be considered very strong.

Engdahl (1985: 9) presents examples like the following to show that Swedish resumptives do not suppress weak crossover effects:

(23) *mannen$_i$ som$_i$ hans$_i$ mor tyckte bäst om __$_i$
the.man that his mother liked best
'the man who his mother liked best' (Engdahl, 1985: 9, (13a))

(24) *Vem$_i$ tyckte hans$_i$ mor bäst om __$_i$?
who liked his mother best
'Who did his mother like best?' (Engdahl, 1985: 9, (13b))

However, it should be clear that the pronouns in these examples are only coincidentally resumptive, because the theory that is assumed uses co-indexation to represent binding and understands resumptive pronouns to be operator-bound. But these pronouns are in fact not the base of the unbounded dependency, which is a gap. In other words, these examples do not contain resumptive pronouns.

We must instead consider examples where the base of the unbounded dependency follows left-peripheral CP material, since this is the only environment in which a grammatically licensed Swedish resumptive occurs:

(25) %Vilken elev$_i$ undrar hans$_i$ lärare om han$_i$ fuskar?
which student wonders his teacher if he cheats
'Which student does his teacher wonder if (he) cheats?'

(26) %Vilken elev$_i$ undrar hans$_i$ lärare varför han$_i$ fuskar?
which student wonders his teacher why he cheats
'Which student does his teacher wonder why (he) cheats?'

(27) %Jag känner en elev som hennes lärare undrar om hon fuskar.
I know a student that her teacher wonders if she cheats
'I know a student who her teacher wonders if (she) cheats.'

Some speakers accept such examples, while others reject them. As is common with weak crossover judgements, there is some speaker uncertainty and variation here. For some speakers the judgements are quite robust, though.

The weak crossover evidence casts doubt on any analysis in which the Swedish resumptive is just some kind of phonological realization of a gap. If the resumptive is a gap in syntax and weak crossover is derived from a syntactic relation, then there cannot be a relevant difference between actual gaps and resumptives qua phonologically realized gaps. In contrast, existing LFG theories of weak crossover (Bresnan, 1994, 1995, 2001; Dalrymple et al., 2001, 2007; Falk, 2001) potentially predict the distinction between gaps and syntactically inactive resumptives. LFG analyses of weak crossover are based on a notion of syntactic prominence, derived from a hierarchy of f-structural grammatical functions, and a notion of linear prominence, derived from the f-structural relation of f-precedence (Kaplan, 1989; Bresnan, 1995, 2001; Dalrymple, 2001), which is ultimately derived from standard tree-based precedence in c-structure, based on the c-structure to f-structure mapping. If the Swedish resumptive is present in c-structure, this affects the f-precedence relation. If the grammar of Swedish is sensitive to linear prominence the distinction between gaps and resumptives potentially follows.

Another phenomenon relevant to establishing the nature of Swedish resumptives is across-the-board extraction from a coordinate structure (Zaenen et al., 1981; Sells, 1984; Engdahl, 1985). Swedish normally respects the condition that extraction from a coordinate structure must extract from all conjuncts, 'across the board' (Williams, 1978), but apparent extraction out of a single conjunct is allowed if the other conjunct contains a resumptive pronoun:

(28) Där borta går en man som jag ofta träffar _ men inte minns
There goes a man that I often meet _ but not remember
vad han heter.
what he is called
'There goes a man that I often meet but don't remember what he is called.' (Zaenen et al., 1981: 681, (9))

This resumptive is a true grammatically licensed resumptive; it is a subject immediately following a *wh*-phrase in SpecCP. The standard LFG theory of coordination (Kaplan and Maxwell, 1988) is based on f-structure and derives the ATB constraint (see Dalrymple, 2001, and references therein). If the Swedish resumptive is not present in f-structure, then the LFG theory of coordination correctly predicts that it should not block ATB extraction.

In Asudeh (2004), I suggested that the ATB facts could be derivable even if Swedish resumptive pronouns were present in f-structure, based on the analysis of Asudeh and Crouch (2002*a*), which seeks to model, in Glue Semantics, Kehler's discourse parallelism theory of ATB exceptions (Kehler, 2002). On balance, the treatment suggested here is preferable, because it needs only to assume the simpler, general LFG analysis of coordination. Also, Steedman (2007) has argued against the kinds of analyses put forward by Kehler (2002) and Asudeh and Crouch (2002*a*) for ATB exceptions. Most importantly, (28) is not the kind of asymmetrical or temporally sequential coordination that is typical of ATB exceptions (see Kehler, 2002, and references therein), as in the following example from Ross (1967):

(29) What did you go to the store and buy?

The coordination in example (28) is not asymmetrical in this way. It just states two things about the man in question. Some evidence comes from the fact that swapping the order of coordinated phrases in asymmetrical coordination leads to infelicity, but this is not the case for (28) if the order of the coordination is reversed.

Another instance of a true subject resumptive behaving like a gap is in licensing of parasitic gaps:

(30) Det var den fången$_i$ som läkarna inte kunde avgöra om han$_i$
it was that prisoner that the.doctors not could decide if he
verkligen var sjuk utan att tala med P$_i$ personligen.
really was ill without to talk with P in person
'This is the prisoner that the doctors couldn't detemine if he really was ill without talking to in person.' (Engdahl, 1985: 7, (8))

As with ATB extraction, it is not clear that the phenomenon of parasitic gaps is narrowly syntactic. In Asudeh (2004: 273–276), I briefly sketched an analysis of parasitic gaps, following work by Steedman (1987, 1996) and Nissenbaum (2000), based on the theory of coordination of Asudeh and Crouch (2002*a*), where the latter is a polymorphic treatment of coordination of the kind that is common in Categorial Grammar (Steedman, 1985, 2000; Carpenter, 1997: 177ff.).

The upshot of the analysis in Asudeh (2004) is that semantic composition of adjunct parasitic gap examples, such as (30), proceeds successfully whether the licenser of the parasitic gap is a gap or a resumptive pronoun, provided that the resumptive pronoun is consumed by a manager resource as usual. However, the analysis leaves open the question of the precise licensing mechanism for parasitic gaps. In LFG, syntactic aspects of parasitic gap licensing must be captured at f-structure, because that is where unbounded dependencies are represented (Dalrymple and King, 2000; Alsina, 2008; Falk, 2010). If Swedish resumptives are syntactically inactive and are therefore represented equivalently to gaps at f-structure, then it follows that, all else being equal, they should license parasitic gaps equivalently to gaps.

Lastly, let us turn to reconstruction. I use this term purely pretheoretically to refer to the empirical phenomenon in which the top of an unbounded dependency behaves as if it were in its base position for the purposes of binding or scope. Zaenen et al. (1981) provide the following Swedish example. The sentence is grammatical, even though the reflexive is in a fronted constituent and would only meet syntactic requirements on binding if the fronted constituent occupies its base position in f-structure:

(31) Vilken av $sina_i$ flickvänner tror du att $Kalle_i$ inte längre träffar _ ?
which of his girlfriends think you that Kalle no longer sees
'Which of his girlfriends do you think that Kalle no longer sees?'
(Zaenen et al., 1981: 680, (5))

The grammaticality of this sentence follows automatically on theories of filler-gap dependencies that enforce token identity between the filler and the gap. In such theories, there is no need for any kind of reconstruction operation, because the filler simultaneously appear in both positions (Asudeh, 2011*c*). Two such constraint-based theories are the functional equality theory in LFG (Kaplan and Zaenen, 1989), adopted here, and the structure-sharing theory in Head-Driven Phrase Structure Grammar (Bouma et al., 2001). Derivational approaches that posit multidominance possibly derive the same effect (Nunes, 2001, 2004; Gärtner, 2002; Johnson, 2010).

Zaenen et al. (1981) also provide data that seems to show that Swedish resumptive pronouns permit reconstruction:

(32) Vilken av sina$_i$ flickvänner undrade du om det att Kalle$_i$ inte längre
which of his girlfriends wondered you if it that Kalle no longer
fick träffa <u>henne</u>$_i$ kunde ligga bakom hans dåliga humör?
sees her could lie behind his bad mood
'Which of his girlfriends do you think the fact that Kalle no longer gets to see (her) could be behind his bad mood?'
(Zaenen et al., 1981: 680, (6))

If a resumptive pronoun is a pronoun in the syntax, it should block reconstruction. In LFG-theoretic terms, the functional equality that normally derives reconstruction effects should be blocked by the uniqueness of the independent PRED features of the binder and the resumptive.

Two noticeable properties of this example are: (1) the resumptive pronoun is not the grammatically licensed kind and (2) the resumptive is in fact optional:

(33) Vilken av sina$_i$ flickvänner undrade du om det att Kalle$_i$ inte längre
which of his girlfriends wondered you if it that Kalle no longer
fick träffa __$_i$ kunde ligga bakom hans dåliga humör?
sees __ could lie behind his bad mood
'Which of his girlfriends do you think the fact that Kalle no longer gets to see could be behind his bad mood?'

Speakers vary as to whether they consider this sentence completely well-formed, but none of my informants rejected it outright. The pronoun arguably makes the sentence easier to process; we will return to this in chapter 11.

Reconstruction for binding of reflexives cannot be used to test true Swedish resumptives for reconstruction, since there is no way to test reconstruction of the reflexive possessor in subject position without incurring an independent binding-theoretic violation based on the locality requirements that the possessive reflexive places on its antecedent. The only option is to test for scope reconstruction. The required kind of examples are the following, where the reconstruction point is represented as a centred dot (·):

(34) Which student did every teacher say · cheated?

If reconstruction is possible, the *wh*-phrase should be able to take narrow scope with respect to the universal and a pair-list answer should be grammatical. If reconstruction is not possible, the *wh*-phrase must take wide scope and only an individual or a function on individuals should be possible as an answer.

The Swedish question corresponding to (34) with a gap at the reconstruction site, following no left-peripheral CP material, allows all three kinds of answer:

(35) Vilken elev tror varje lärare _ fuskar?
Which student tror every teacher _ cheats
'Which student does every teacher think cheats?'
a. Pelle
b. Hans mest begåvade elev
'His most gifted student'
c. Andersson, Alfons; Boberg, Benny; Cornelius, Conny

Similarly, a post-complementizer gap in Ålandssvenska allows all three answers:

(36) Vilken elev undrar varje lärare om _ fuskar?
Which student wonders every teacher if _ cheats
'Which student does every teacher wonder if (he) cheats?'
a. Pelle
b. Hans mest begåvade elev
'His most gifted student'
c. Andersson, Alfons; Boberg, Benny; Cornelius, Conny

This is what we would expect, since a gap should allow both wide scope and narrow scope for the quantifier.

In contrast, a resumptive pronoun does not seem to allow scope reconstruction, since the pair-list answer is no longer available:

(37) Vilken elev undrar varje lärare om han fuskar?
Which student wonders every teacher if he cheats
'Which student does every teacher wonder if (he) cheats?'
a. Pelle
b. Hans mest begåvade elev
'His most gifted student'
c. #Andersson, Alfons; Boberg, Benny; Cornelius, Conny

It is possible, however, that the pair-list answer is unavailable for independent reasons, having to do with general constraints on pronominal interpretation. We return to this general issue in the following section.

9.1.2.1 *Summary* This section reviewed evidence from islands, weak crossover, across-the-board extraction, parasitic gaps, and reconstruction, regarding the syntactic status of Swedish resumptive pronouns. The evidence is complex, but on balance it suggests that Swedish resumptives do share some qualities with gaps, as summarized in Table 9.1. It would be premature, however, to conclude that Swedish resumptives are underlyingly gaps, but with phonological content. An alternative analysis is that it is not the pronoun itself that is special, but rather the relation between the binder and resumptive. This can be captured in LFG-theoretic terms if Swedish resumptives are ordinary pronouns lexically and at c-structure, but are represented like gaps at f-structure. This will be the sort of analysis that I pursue in section 9.3, but first let us consider further certain problems with the suggestion that Swedish resumptives are spelled out traces or some such thing.

9.1.3 *Further Evidence against Resumptive Pronouns as Underlying Gaps*

On the standard assumption that lexical specification affects morphological exponence, McCloskey's Generalization that resumptive pronouns are, cross-linguistically, ordinary pronouns in their form would be completely surprising if resumptive pronouns are underlyingly gaps or have lexical specifications of any sort that distinguish them as resumptives. However, it may be possible to advance a special pronoun theory of resumption under certain theoretical assumptions about morphological exponence (Halle and Marantz, 1993; Elbourne, 2002; Boeckx, 2003; Kratzer, 2009). Some theories could posit that resumptives are special underlyingly, as suggested for Swedish by McCloskey (2006), yet potentially derive the fact that they just happen to have the form of ordinary pronouns. This move depends on separating phonological realization from lexical specification. The basic idea would be, for example, that a gap in the syntax is somehow morphophonologically realized as an ordinary pronoun.

There is a simple argument against this view. If a resumptive pronoun is anything other than an ordinary pronoun upon insertion and its phonology goes one way but its semantics goes the other, as in the typical branching Phonetic Form/Logical Form model of P&P Theory and the Minimalist Program, then no matter what form the pronoun has, it should be interpreted as the underlying thing. However, resumptive pronouns have restrictions on their interpretation that correlate precisely with restrictions on the interpretation of ordinary pronouns, as discussed in chapter 2. If the resumptive pronoun were not underlyingly an ordinary pronoun, this would be unexpected, even on a theory that allows identical exponence. Furthermore, gaps were shown to have crucially different possibilities for interpretation that are not shared by resumptive pronouns. Once again, if a resumptive pronoun were underlyingly a gap, even on a theory that allows proper exponence, this would be unexpected. Therefore, resumptive pronouns must be ordinary pronouns, even in theories that have a looser fit between lexical specification and exponence.

Swedish is the language that has provided the most persuasive evidence for an underlying gap view of resumptives (Engdahl, 1985). However, there is evidence that this view is untenable even for Swedish and that true Swedish resumptives—those in subject position after material at the left periphery of CP—are just ordinary pronouns rather than underlying gaps. We have already seen that resumptive pronouns, unlike gaps, do not necessarily give rise to weak crossover effects and do not permit syntactic reconstruction for scope. Further evidence comes from interpretation of Swedish resumptives according to the specificity diagnostic of Doron (1982). Doron shows that Hebrew resumptives cannot support non-specific readings, although gaps can. Sells (1984, 1987) shows that this follows from general properties of ordinary pronouns, which cannot refer to a concept antecedent, of which non-specifics are an instance. This follows for type-theoretic reasons, since concepts are intensional ⟨*s*,*e*⟩ types, but pronouns need type *e* antecedents.

Swedish resumptive pronouns are equally incapable of taking a non-specific antecedent, as shown by the following example:

(38) Kalle letar efter en bok som han inte vet hur den slutar.
Kalle looks for a book that he not knows how it ends
'Kalle is looking for a book that he does not know how (it) ends.'

This example can only mean that Kalle is looking for a certain book whose ending is unknown to him. It cannot mean that he will settle for any book so long as its ending is unknown to him.

If the resumptive pronoun were underlyingly a gap, then the non-specific reading should be possible, since sentences like the following allow it:

(39) Kalle kommer att hitta boken som han letar efter __.
Kalle comes to find book.DEF that he looks for __
'Kalle will find the book that he is looking for.'

This sentence allows both the non-specific reading where Kalle is looking for a book with certain properties but he does not have a particular one in mind (e.g., he is looking for a thick one or one with an ending he does not know about) and the specific reading (e.g., he is looking for *A Confederacy of Dunces*).[4]

Similarly, in the Ålandssvenska dialect which allows gaps after left-peripheral material in CP, the minimal pair for (38) with a gap allows both non-specific and specific readings:

(40) Kalle letar efter en bok som han inte vet hur _ slutar.
Kalle looks for a book that he not knows how _ ends
'Kalle is looking for a book that he does not know how ends.'

If Swedish resumptives were underlyingly gaps, it would be unexpected that they not receive an identical range of interpretation to gaps, as evidenced by weak crossover, scope reconstruction, and the specificity test. Even if the resumptive's exponence as an ordinary pronoun could be made to follow, its interpretation should be that of the underlying object. In sum, Swedish does not provide evidence for a 'spelled out gap' theory of resumption. Such theories are untenable on both theoretical and empirical grounds.

9.2 Licensing and Integrating Syntactically Inactive Resumptives

The licensing mechanism for syntactically inactive resumptives is the same as the licensing mechanism for syntactically active resumptives in the Resource Management Theory of Resumption. Syntactically inactive resumptives are ordinary pronouns lexically and therefore contribute pronominal meaning constructors. The pronominal meaning constructor is a surplus resource. In order for resource-sensitive semantic composition to succeed, this surplus resource must be consumed. The consumer of the pronominal resource is a manager resource, which identifies the pronoun through the mechanism of pronominal binding.

In Swedish, as in Hebrew, resumptives are licensed by the complementizer system as a whole, rather than by a particular complementizer, as in Irish. Information that is common to all complementizers is associated with the

[4] Some speakers seem to allow the non-specific interpretation of examples like (38). Even for these speakers, the specific reading is highly preferred. This could also be the case with the equivalent English and Hebrew examples investigated by Sells (1984, 1987), as discussed for Hebrew by Erteschik-Shir (1992). Further work needs to be done on specificity and resumption, but the data nevertheless support my argument, because *any* difference of interpretation between resumptive pronouns and gaps would be completely unexpected if the pronominal form of the resumptive were solely a matter of exponence and the resumptive were underlyingly a gap.

morphological feature +COMP, as discussed in chapter 8. The licensing component of the analysis of Hebrew can therefore be carried over to Swedish (with one modification to which I return below):

(41) +COMP, C^0 $\left(\begin{array}{l} \%RP = (\uparrow \textsc{subj}) \\ (\uparrow \textsc{udf})_\sigma = (\%RP_\sigma\ \textsc{antecedent}) \\ @MR(\%RP) \\ @RELABEL(\%RP) \end{array} \right)$

The resumptive licensing information is optional, since the complementizers in question occur in the absence of resumption. The one difference between this entry and the corresponding entry in (4) of chapter 8 is in the first line. The complementizer only licenses a local subject, since resumptives in Swedish occur only after left-peripheral material in CP. This contrasts with Hebrew and Irish, in which the resumptive may be an embedded grammatical function.

The left-peripheral material that licenses resumption need not be a complementizer. It can be a *wh*-phrase in SpecCP. One possible lexical solution for the SpecCP cases might be to associate the manager resource with the *wh*-phrase that immediately precedes the resumptive, presumably with the *wh*-word in particular. This is problematic for a number of reasons. First, *wh*-words can be embedded in a variety of ways inside the *wh*-phrase. In order to access the SUBJ of its CP the *wh*-word would have to reach outside the constituent in which it occurs. Furthermore, there will be no single kind of equation that can be used for all *wh*-words and there would be considerable heterogeneity in how the manager resources are specified. For example, *vilken* ('which'), *vem* ('who'), and *hur* ('how') would all require different sorts of equations, since they are embedded differently in f-structures. Second, on a related note, the manager resources contributed by *wh*-words would be quite different from those contributed by complementizers, because the latter are contributed by a functional head that maps to the main f-structure for the clause and can be specified straightforwardly in terms of (↑ SUBJ). Third, a manager resource contributed by a *wh*-word would result in a situation in which an argument or an adjunct, the grammatical function of the *wh*-phrase, affects another, more syntactically prominent argument, the SUBJECT. This sort of grammatical constraint on a coargument would be somewhat unusual, since it is normally the head that constrains the arguments in its clause. Fourth, due to the differences in how distinct *wh*-words would specify their manager resources, the prospects seem slim for adding the manager resources to the lexical entries for *wh*-words via a general lexical mechanism. The manager resources would have to be added to lexical entries for individual *wh*-words. But this makes an incorrect empirical prediction. If manager resources are associated with the lexical entries for individual *wh*-words (or perhaps classes of *wh*-words), then there could be variation among dialects as to which lexical entries for *wh*-words have manager resources. Dialect A might have a lexical item for *vilken* ('which') that has a manager resource, while Dialect B has a lexical item for *vilken* that lacks a manager resource. Dialect A would allow a resumptive pronoun after a fronted *vilken*-phrase, while Dialect B would not. There does not seem to be any such dialect variation.

The solution is to instead posit a null complementizer, as in the analysis of Hebrew. The lexical entry for the null complementizer is as follows:

(42) $\emptyset$+COMP, C^0 $\quad (\uparrow \text{UDF})_\sigma =_c ((\uparrow \text{SUBJ})_\sigma \text{ ANTECEDENT})$

The null complementizer bears the feature +COMP and therefore inherits the information in (41). It adds a constraining equation that performs two roles. First, because the equation mentions (↑ UDF), the complementizer's f-structure must contain an unbounded dependency function in order for the constraint to be satisfied. The UDF is contributed through SpecCP, which ensures that the null complementizer occurs with material in SpecCP. Second, the constraint requires that UDF in the complementizer's f-structure bind the SUBJ of the same f-structure, which entails that the subject is a resumptive pronoun. The null complementizer therefore only occurs with material in SpecCP that precedes a resumptive pronoun.

Syntactically active and syntactically inactive resumptives share the resource-logical licensing mechanism of manager resources, but differ with respect to their syntactic status. The gap-like nature of syntactically inactive resumptives is captured by extending the functional equality integration mechanism for filler-gap dependencies to SIRS. This requires modification of the functional equality mechanism, because resumptives, as ordinary pronouns, contribute a PRED feature to their f-structure. This would normally result in a Consistency violation. The restriction operator (Kaplan and Wedekind, 1993) is used to set aside the PRED feature in the functional equality. The basic form of the resulting functional equality, which integrates the UDF at the top of the unbounded dependency, is as follows:

(43)
$$(\uparrow \text{UDF})\backslash\text{PRED} = (\uparrow \text{GF}^{*} \underset{((\rightarrow \text{PRED}) = (\uparrow \text{UDF PRED}))}{\text{GF}})\backslash\text{PRED}$$

The unbounded nature of the dependency is captured through GF*, the body of the unbounded dependency, which allows the dependency to pass through zero or more grammatical functions. The body can be restricted appropriately to capture constraints on extraction (Dalrymple, 2001: 390–408). The same functional equality applies to filler-gap dependencies and binder-resumptive dependencies. It therefore follows that resumptive pronouns will be subject to the same constraints as gaps. The material that contributes to UDF lexically contributes a PRED. The restriction operator sets this PRED aside for the functional equality so that binders and resumptives can contribute to the same f-structure. However, a gap does not independently contribute a PRED, so there is an optional off-path constraint that states that the lexically provided PRED of the UDF is the PRED of the f-structure that is the shared value of both the UDF and the gap GF. This ensures that the gap GF satisfies the general f-structural well-formedness criterion of Completeness, which requires arguments to have PRED features. The off-path constraint is optional, since it does not apply if GF is a resumptive pronoun subject. In that instance, it would reinstate the Consistency violation caused by the lexically provided PREDs of the binder and the resumptive pronoun.

The functional equality (43) results in f-structure (44b) for the subject gap example (44a) and f-structure (45b) for the corresponding subject resumptive example (45a).

(44) a. Vem$_i$ trodde Maria _$_i$ skulle fuska?
who thought Maria _ would cheat
'Who did Maria think would cheat?'

b. 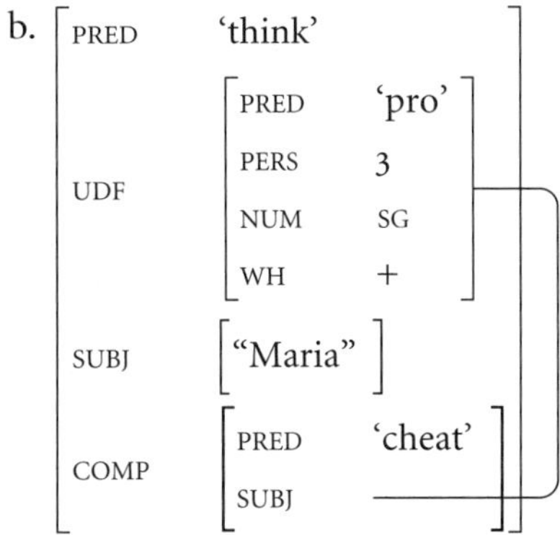

(45) a. Vem$_i$ trodde Maria att han$_i$ skulle fuska?
who thought Maria that he would cheat
'Who did Maria think that (he) would cheat?'

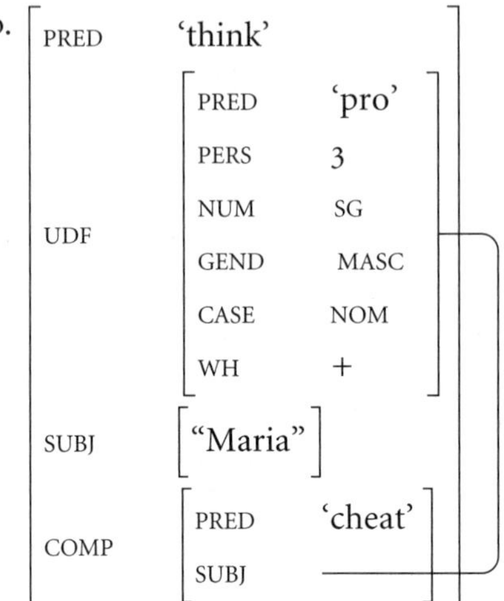

The only differences between the two f-structures are the gender feature, GEND MASC, the case feature, CASE NOM, and the *wh* feature, WH +. The last of these features is contributed by the *wh*-phrase and the others by the personal pronoun, since the personal pronoun is marked for gender and case, but the *wh*-pronoun *vem* is not. The pronoun's gender and case are therefore contributed to the common f-structure for the UDF and resumptive, but these features are absent in the common f-structure for the UDF and the gap.

9.3 Analysis

Swedish pronouns, resumptive or otherwise, are given a uniform treatment. The pronoun *han* ('he') serves as an example:

(46) *han*, D^0 $(\uparrow \text{PRED}) = \text{`pro'}$
$(\uparrow \text{PERSON}) = 3$
$(\uparrow \text{NUMBER}) = \text{SG}$
$(\uparrow \text{GENDER}) = \text{MASC}$
$(\uparrow \text{CASE}) = \text{NOM}$
$(\uparrow_\sigma \text{ANTECEDENT}) \multimap ((\uparrow_\sigma \text{ANTECEDENT}) \otimes \uparrow_\sigma)$

The pronoun is an ordinary pronoun. It lexically specifies standard pronominal information: the feature PRED 'pro', agreement features, a case feature, and a standard pronominal meaning constructor.

Let us see how the analysis treats the following example, which is a simplified version of (9):

(47) [Vilken elev]$_i$ trodde Maria att <u>han</u>$_i$ skulle fuska?
which student thought Maria that he would cheat
'Which student did Maria think that (he) would cheat?'

The c-structure and f-structure of this example are shown in (48) and (49). Notice that the finite verb is generated in C^0. This is a common LFG analysis of Germanic verb-second (Bresnan, 2001; Sells, 2001; Toivonen, 2003). A small fragment covering this example is presented in appendix C.

(48)

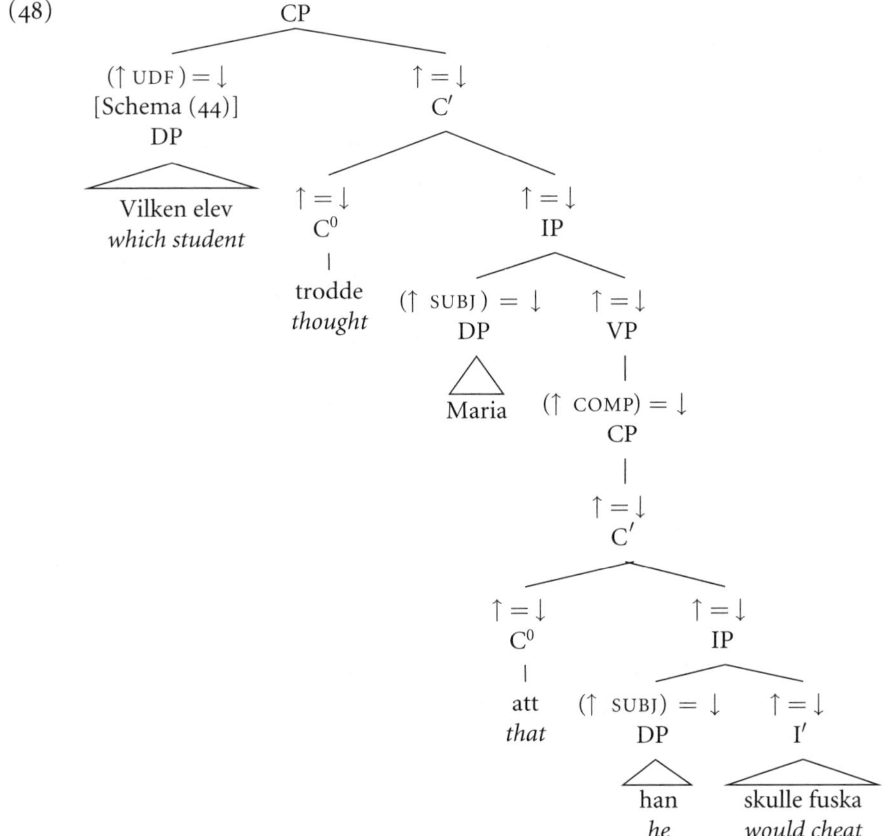

(49)

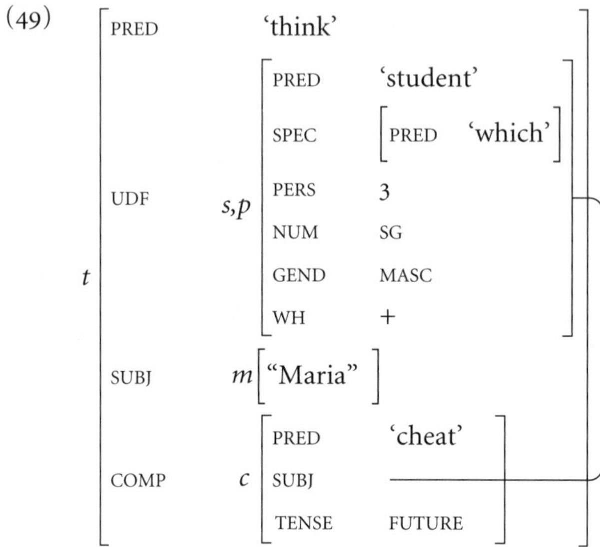

The following premises are contributed by the lexical items and SpecCP, as instantiated by the f-structure and semantic structure above (I have taken a shortcut by precombining the *wh*-determiner and its noun):

(50)

1. $\forall X.[(s \multimap X) \multimap X]$ — Lex. **vilken elev ('which student')**
2. $[s \multimap (s \otimes p)] \multimap (s \multimap s)$ — Lex. **+comp (MR)**
3. $(p \multimap t) \multimap (s \multimap t)$ — Lex. **+comp (RELABEL**
4. $m \multimap c \multimap t$ — Lex. **trodde ('thought')**
5. m — Lex. **Maria**
6. $s \multimap (s \otimes p)$ — Lex. **han ('he')**
7. $p \multimap c$ — Lex. **fuska ('cheat')**

The premises construct the proof in Figure 9.1.

9.4 Discussion

The grammatically licensed resumptives of Swedish, which occur after left-peripheral material in CP, have been analysed as syntactically inactive resumptives. They are ordinary pronouns lexically and are present in c-structure, but they are not present in f-structure as entities distinct from their binder. Restricted functional equality results in the binder and the resumptive contributing to the same f-structure, such that the UDF of the binder and GF of the resumptive share a single, token-identical value. The properties that Swedish resumptives share with gaps are derived from the fact that the same functional

(47) [Vilken elev]$_i$ trodde Maria att han$_i$ skulle fuska?
which student thought Maria that he would cheat
'Which student did Maria think that (he) would cheat?'

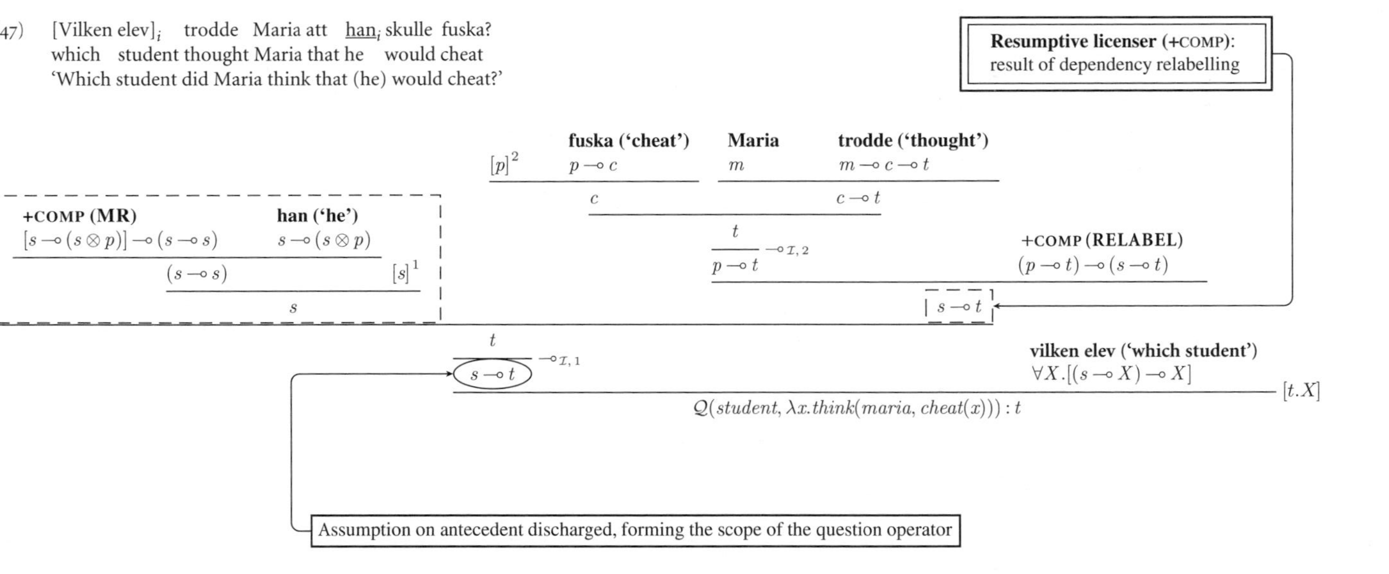

FIGURE 9.1. Proof for a Swedish binder-resumptive dependency.

equality also applies to filler-gap unbounded dependencies and from the fact that gaps and syntactically inactive resumptives are represented equivalently in f-structure, as token-identical to an unbounded dependency function.

The formal operation of restriction has an important further consequence with respect to the form-identity generalization that the top of a filler-gap dependency has case appropriate to the base of the dependency, whereas the top of a binder-resumptive dependency has case independently of the base and appears with 'default case' (Merchant, 2001: 132). The only features that restriction sets aside are those that are explicitly restricted. In the case of the unbounded dependency functional equality in (43), this is only the PRED feature. This means that any other features will be contributed to the common f-structure as usual. This resulted, for example, in gender and case features in f-structure (45b), which represents the syntactically inactive binder-resumptive example (45a), that were absent from f-structure (44b), which represents the corresponding gap example (44a), since the gap contributes no information and the *wh*-pronoun, *vem*, in the examples does not contribute its own values for these features. However, it also means that any features that are not restricted but which have distinct values will result in the usual violation of Consistency. It therefore follows that a case-marked filler can participate in a filler-gap dependency if and only if its case value is also appropriate for the base of the dependency. It also follows that a case-marked filler can participate in a syntactically inactive binder-resumptive dependency if and only if it has the same case as the resumptive pronoun; otherwise, the binder must be underspecified for case information, i.e. have default case. The form-identity generalization is thus predicted.

This prediction is unfortunately difficult to test for Swedish. The unmarked case for pronouns in Swedish seems to be nominative. Nominative is the case for post-copular pronouns:

(51) Det är jag/* mig | du/* dig | hon/* henne
it is I/me | you.NOM/you.ACC | she/her
'It is me/you/her.'

The Tarzan test similarly indicates that nominative is the default:

(52) Jag Tarzan. Du Jane.
I.NOM Tarzan. You.NOM Jane.
'Me Tarzan. You Jane.'

(53) *Mig Tarzan. Dig Jane.
I.ACC Tarzan. You.ACC Jane.

The form-identity prediction is best tested by looking at resumptives that do not have default case, but the grammatically licensed resumptives in Swedish only occur in the default case of nominative, because they are always subjects.

Lastly, this analysis of Swedish captures a further fact about interpretation of resumptives. The theory posits only one kind of underlying pronoun in both resumptive and non-resumptive uses. McCloskey's Generalization is therefore captured in the strongest possible terms, since there is no way in the theory for the same underlying thing to be formally realized in distinct ways. This also entails that Swedish resumptives must have the same intrinsic interpretive possibilities as ordinary pronouns. That is, resumptives share constraints on pronominal interpretation that are captured lexically or type-theoretically, such as constraints on potential antecedents. This prediction is correct, given the evidence from reconstruction and specificity, which shows that Swedish resumptives are interpreted like pronouns and are not interpreted like gaps.

9.5 Conclusion

Grammatically licensed resumptives in Swedish, which occur following left-peripheral material in CP, have been analysed as syntactically inactive resumptives (SIRS). Syntactically inactive resumptives are ordinary pronouns lexically, which maintains McCloskey's generalization that resumptive pronouns are cross-linguistically ordinary pronouns in their form. The generalization follows automatically in this analysis, because there is just one kind of pronoun, whether in resumptive or non-resumptive uses. As ordinary pronouns, Swedish resumptives contribute pronominal meaning constructors. The resumptive licensing mechanism of the Resource Management Theory of Resumption, manager resources, therefore license Swedish resumptives. Resource-logical semantic composition offers a unification of the distinct kinds of resumptives as discussed in detail in Asudeh (2011*c*). Syntactically active resumptives, as in Irish and Hebrew, and syntactically inactive resumptives, as in Swedish, and Vata, equally constitute surplus resources that must be consumed in order for resource-logical composition to succeed.

However, syntactically active resumptives and syntactically inactive resumptives have distinct syntactic properties. Various syntactic phenomena that are associated with gaps—islands, weak crossover, across-the-board extraction, parasitic gaps, and reconstruction—indicate, when taken as a whole, that Swedish subject resumptives share properties with gaps. Given McCloskey's Generalization, it is difficult to maintain that Swedish resumptives are underlyingly gaps, but are phonologically realized as ordinary pronouns. This would be pure coincidence, under many theories of exponence. Furthermore, Swedish resumptives are not interpreted completely equivalently to gaps. This means that they could not be underlyingly gaps, even on theories that do not treat exponence as a lexical property. These theories expect that phonological exponence operates independently of semantic interpretation, and therefore could not explain the distinct interpretive properties.

In the Resource Management Theory of Resumption, syntactically inactive resumptives are present in c-structure, but are absent as independent entities at f-structure, where the binder and the resumptive are equated in a single f-structure. In contrast, a syntactically active resumptive occupies an f-structure that is independent from that of its binder. The contrast is shown in Table 6.2. F-structure therefore provides a common representational basis for syntactically inactive resumptives and gaps, which are also equated with the top of the unbounded dependency at f-structure. The f-structural equality for gaps and syntactically inactive resumptives is derived from a single functional equation that is common to both filler-gap dependencies and syntactically inactive binder-resumptive dependencies. It follows that any constraints on the functional equality would apply to both gaps and resumptives.

Functional equality is not normally possible in a binder-resumptive dependency, because the binder and the resumptive contribute PRED features which are unique and cannot be equated without causing a Consistency violation. Syntactically active resumptives therefore satisfy the Extended Coherence Condition through binding. The restriction operation is used to modify the the equation for unbounded dependencies such that syntactically inactive resumptives can satisty the Extended Coherence Condition equivalently to gaps, through functional equality. Syntactically active and syntactically inactive resumptives are thus unified through licensing but differentiated in how

TABLE 9.2. A comparison of the resumptive pronoun systems of Irish, Hebrew, and Swedish.

		Resumptive licenser				Binding	
	HSR	**Form**	**Category**	**C-structure Position**	**Local to**	**Antecedent**	**Resumptive**
Irish	Yes	*aN*	$\hat{\text{C}}$	Top	UDF	UDF	GF^{+}
Hebrew	Yes	+COMP	C^0	Top	UDF	UDF	GF^{+}
Swedish	Yes	+COMP	C^0	Bottom	SUBJ	UDF	SUBJ

they are integrated in f-structure. The commonalities between the two kinds of resumptives flow from the licensing commonality and the difference from the integration distinction.

Table 9.2 compares the resumptive pronoun systems of Irish, Hebrew, and Swedish. In all three languages, the Highest Subject Restriction holds on resumptive pronouns. In all three languages, it is the complementizer system that licenses resumptive pronouns in unbounded dependencies. In Irish, it is the particular complementizer *aN*, which has the non-projecting category $\hat{C}$. In Hebrew and Swedish, it is complementizers, in general, that license unbounded dependency resumption. The information is therefore associated with a morphological feature, +COMP, that is associated with all complementizers, which have the projecting category C^0. In Irish and Hebrew, the licenser for the resumptive pronoun is local to the top of the c-structure correspondent of the unbounded dependency, i.e. local to the position of the UDF, but in Swedish the licenser is at the bottom, since it must be locally sensitive to whether there is material in SpecCP or not. Thus, Swedish resumptive licensers are local to the position of the SUBJ. The restricted distribution of Swedish resumptives is also reflected in the binding relation, where the UDF can bind only a SUBJ resumptive pronoun, as per the lexical specification for +COMP in (41).

10

Vata

Resumptive pronouns in Vata, as in Swedish, pattern like gaps with respect to certain diagnostics, particularly with respect to weak crossover and islands. This chapter develops an analysis of Vata resumptives as syntactically inactive resumptives, which are nonetheless licensed semantically like syntactically active resumptives, as found in Irish and Hebrew. The Resource Management Theory of Resumption thus achieves a unification between Vata resumptives and other resumptives.[1] Section 10.1 reviews some of the key resumptive pronoun data in Vata. Section 10.2 provides an analysis along the same lines as those in previous chapters. Section 10.3 concludes.

10.1 Resumptive Pronouns in Vata

The base of an unbounded dependency in Vata must be a resumptive pronoun, if it is a subject, and a gap otherwise (Koopman, 1982; Koopman and Sportiche, 1982). The situation for subjects, whether highest or embedded, is shown in (1). The situation for objects is shown in (2).

(1) a. àl5́ ɔ̱/* __ lē sȧká lȧ
who he/* __ eat rice WH
'Who is eating rice?' (Koopman, 1982: 128, (1a))

b. àl5́ ǹ gūgū nā ɔ̱/* __ yì lȧ
who you think that he/* __ arrive WH
'Who do you think arrived?' (Koopman, 1982: 128, (4a))

(2) a. yī kòfi lė́ __/* mí lȧ
what Kofi eat __/* it WH
'What is Kofi eating?' (Koopman, 1982: 128, (1b))

b. àl5́ ǹ gūgū nā wȧ yɛ̇̀ __/* mɔ̀ yé lȧ
who you think that they see __/him PART WH
'Who do you think they saw?' (Koopman, 1982: 128, (4b))

[1] Some aspects of the analysis in this chapter are presented in Asudeh (2011*c*), but this chapter develops the analysis further, in light of the previous three chapters.

The Highest Subject Restriction apparently does not hold in Vata, as shown by example (1a). I am not aware of any explanation of this cross-linguistic variation, but it would be an interesting area for future research.

In contrast to resumptive pronouns in Irish and Hebrew, Vata resumptive pronouns behave like gaps with respect to weak crossover (Koopman and Sportiche, 1982) and islands (Koopman and Sportiche, 1986). The sensitivity of Vata resumptives to weak crossover is shown in (3) and (4) and their island-sensitivity is shown for *wh*-islands in (5) and (6).

(3) *àlɔ́$_i$ ɔ̍$_i$ nɔ́ gùgù nā ɔ̱̀$_i$ mlì la̍
who$_i$ his$_i$ mother think that he$_i$ left WH
'Who did his mother think left?'
(Koopman and Sportiche, 1982: 22, (10a))

(4) *àlɔ́$_i$ ǹ yra̍ ɔ̍$_i$ nɔ́ nā ɔ̱̀$_i$ mlì la̍
who$_i$ you tell his$_i$ mother that he$_i$ left WH
'Who did you tell his mother left?'
(Koopman and Sportiche, 1982: 22, (10b))

(5) *àIÓ ǹ nI̍ [zĒ mĒmĖ` gbU̍ Ò̱ dI̍` -ɓȮ *t* mÉ] yì
who you NEG-A reason it-it for he-R cut REL it know
la̍
WH
'Who don't you know why he cut it?'
(Koopman and Sportiche, 1986: 161, (19a))

(6) *àIÓ ǹ nyla̍ nyni̍ nā Ò̱ dI̍ mÉ la̍
who you wonder NA he-R cut it WH
'Who do you wonder whether he cut it?'
(Koopman and Sportiche, 1986: 161, (19b))

Vata resumptives, despite being overt elements, (1) cannot occur in islands and (2) give rise to weak crossover effects. Whether or not weak crossover and islands are considered narrowly syntactic phenomena (as opposed to being entirely or in part matters of processing), these diagnostics separate syntactically active resumptives, as in Irish and Hebrew, from syntactically inactive resumptives, as in Vata. There must be some difference in the grammars of the languages that leads to the distinction.

10.1.1 *Vata Resumptives are not Special Pronouns*

Vata pronouns initially seem to have a distinct tone in their resumptive function, which would be a challenge to McCloskey's Generalization and probably to ordinary pronoun theories of resumption, depending on other assumptions. Resumptive pronouns have low tone (ɔ̀, ì, ...) instead of mid-high tone (ɔ́, í, ...) (Koopman and Sportiche, 1982):

(7) àlɔ́ ɔ̠̀ mlì lá
who he left WH
'Who left?' (Koopman and Sportiche, 1982: 23, (14a))

(8) ɔ́ mlì
he left
'He left.' (Koopman and Sportiche, 1982: 23, (14b))

Vata resumptives thus seem to show a case of special morphological marking of a pronoun in its resumptive function. This marking and the fact that Vata resumptives display gap-like behaviour initially seem to indicate that Vata resumptives are (1) special pronouns and (2) somehow lexically like gaps and unlike other pronouns.

However, the low tone marking in fact indicates that the pronoun is bound by a *wh*-operator, rather than just signalling resumption. Since resumptive pronouns are operator-bound, it follows that they receive the tone as well, but there are non-resumptive cases of operator-bound low tone pronouns. Koopman and Sportiche (1982: 24) note:

> [A] low tone pronoun may also occur in a position which is, informally speaking, neither too close, nor too far from the site of a *wh*-element provided that it is coindexed with a *wh*-trace, or a low tone pronoun [+*wh*].

The following example is an illustration:

(9) àlɔ́$_i$ ɔ̠̀ gūgū nā ɔ́$_j$ / * ɔ́$_i$ / ɔ̀$_i$ ní yà lá
who$_i$ he$_i$ think that he-ɔ́$_j$ / * he-ɔ́$_i$ / he-ɔ̀$_i$ NEG healthy WH
'Who thinks he is sick?' (Koopman and Sportiche, 1982: 24, (15a))

The upper low tone ɔ̀ ('he') is the obligatory subject resumptive. The lower low tone ɔ̀ is not a resumptive, but rather a pronoun bound by the same *wh*-phrase that binds the subject resumptive. A mid-high tone ɔ́ in this position is ungrammatical on the *wh*-bound reading. A pronoun with this tonal marking can only be understood as disjoint from the *wh*-phrase.

Non-resumptive instances of low tone pronouns as in (9) do not cause weak crossover violations:

(10) àlɔ́$_i$ ɔ̠̀$_i$ yrá ɔ̀$_i$ nɔ́ nā ɔ̀$_i$ mlì lá
who$_i$ he tell his$_i$ mother that he$_i$ left WH
'Who told his mother that he left?'
(Koopman and Sportiche, 1982: 24, (16))

The low tone pronoun in the embedded clause may be bound by the pronoun ɔ́ ('his') without a weak crossover violation; (10) contrasts with (4). It is not surprising that there is no weak crossover effect in (10), because it is the matrix subject that is extracted and the matrix subject is not in a weak crossover configuration with ɔ́, because the subject is not commanded by the pronoun. Another way of looking at it is that the embedded low tone pronoun in (10) is not the base of an unbounded dependency, so it should have nothing to do with weak crossover. This shows that the low tone marking is not indicative of a resumptive pronoun being a spelled out variable, but is actually a more general phenomenon. The low tone marks subjects that are bound by a *wh*-operator. Despite initial appearances, Vata does not constitute an exception to McCloskey's Generalization.

10.2 Analysis

Syntactically inactive resumptives like Vata's are puzzling because they behave like gaps syntactically, but seem to be morpholexically identical to other pronouns. A natural explanation of the lack of a morpholexical distinction is that there is no underlying distinction between the resumptives and other pronouns. In chapter 6, I argued that the gap-like behaviour can then be explained, in the context of LFG's theory of unbounded dependencies, if the binder-resumptive dependency involves functional equality at f-structure. This would normally result in a Consistency violation due to the distinct PRED values of the binder and the resumptive. As demonstrated for Swedish in the previous chapter, the solution is provided by the restriction operator, which allows the functional equality to be established by restricting out the problematic PRED features. The analysis of Vata in this chapter thus builds on the analysis of Swedish in the previous chapter.

Vata pronouns, resumptive or otherwise, are given a uniform treatment. The pronoun ɔ ('he') serves as an example:

(11) ɔ, D^0 $(\uparrow \text{PRED}) = \text{`pro'}$
$(\uparrow \text{PERSON}) = 3$
$(\uparrow \text{NUMBER}) = \text{SG}$
$(\uparrow \text{GENDER}) = \text{MASC}$
$(\uparrow_\sigma \text{ANTECEDENT}) \multimap ((\uparrow_\sigma \text{ANTECEDENT}) \otimes \uparrow_\sigma)$
@DEFAULT-TONE
@WH-TONE

The pronoun lexically specifies the usual pronominal information: agreement features, the feature PRED 'pro', and a standard pronominal meaning constructor. It also invokes two tone templates that are common to all personal pronouns in the language.

The tone templates invoked in (11) are defined as follows:

(12) DEFAULT-TONE = $\{ (\rho^{-1}(*)$ TONE$) \mid (\rho^{-1}(*)$ TONE = MID-HIGH$) \}$

(13) WH-TONE =
$\{ \neg[($SUBJ $\uparrow) \wedge (\uparrow_{\sigma}$ ANTECEDENT TYPE$) =$ WH-OP$] \mid$
$(\rho^{-1}(*)$ TONE$) =$ LOW $\}$

The variable $*$ stands for the current c-structure node (Dalrymple, 2001: 118), as discussed in chapter 3. The notation $\rho^{-1}(*)$ indicates the element in prosodic structure that corresponds to the c-structure node designated by $*$. The DEFAULT-TONE template, (12), requires that the pronoun have a TONE specification at prosodic structure. Unless specified otherwise, the value of TONE is MID-HIGH, as in ɔ̋. The WH-TONE template, (13), states that if the pronoun is a subject and is bound by a *wh*-operator, then it must have LOW TONE, overriding the default in (12). This accounts for the data in (9) and (10).

The lexical entry in (11) is the only specification for ɔ and is not particular to the pronoun in a resumptive function. Importantly, the pronoun has a PRED feature and a standard pronominal meaning constructor. The PRED feature means that the pronoun cannot be straightforwardly functionally equated with a UDF, because the unique PREDS of the UDF and the pronoun lead to a Consistency violation. The contribution of the meaning constructor has the consequence that a resumptive use of the pronoun constitutes a surplus resource. The resource surplus is once again resolved using a manager resource, which licenses the resumptive. Vata resumptives are thus unified with the resumptives of Irish, Hebrew and Swedish. Resumptive pronouns—whether syntactically active, as in Irish and Hebrew, or syntactically inactive, as in Swedish and Vata—require manager resources in order to be licensed.

The obvious candidate for the lexical element that licenses resumptives in (1) and other relevant *wh*-question examples is the question particle *la̍*. However, Vata resumptives also occur in focus constructions (clefts) and relative clauses, which do not contain the particle *la̍*. These other constructions show the same pattern of resumption: resumptives pronouns occur obligatorily in subject extraction and only occur in subject extraction. A focus construction contrast is shown in (14) and a relative clause contrast in (15).

(14) a. kɔ̍` mɔ́ *(ɔ̀) lē sa̍ká
man PRON *(he) eat rice
'It is the man who is eating rice.' (Koopman, 1982: 128, (2a))

b. sàká má kɔ̀ lè (*ma)
rice PRON man eat (*it)
'It is rice the man is eating.' (Koopman, 1982: 128, (2b))

(15) a. kɔ̀ mɔ̄mɔ̀ *(ɔ̀) lē ɓɔ̀ sàká
man REL.PRON *(he) eat REL rice
'the man who is eating rice' (Koopman, 1982: 128, (3a))

b. sàká mɔ̄mɔ̀ kɔ̀ lè ɓɔ̀ (*má)
rice REL.PRON man eat REL (*it)
'the rice the man is eating' (Koopman, 1982: 128, (3b))

The question particle does not occur in focus constructions and relative clause constructions, which nevertheless contain subject resumptives. Therefore, the question particle per se cannot be the lexical licenser for Vata resumptives.

This suggests that Vata, like Hebrew, has a more abstract realization of resumptive licensing than Irish, in which resumption is associated with a certain complementizer, *aN*. In Asudeh (2011*c*), I suggest a solution to the Vata licensing problem, but leave it unresolved whether the licensing information is associated with a structural position or a lexical item. However, we might instead seek to maintain McCloskey's conjecture that the lexicon is the locus of variation for resumption (McCloskey, 2002: 205). Two lexical solutions then suggest themselves. One is to postulate a null complementizer. This is more problematic in the case of Vata than in Hebrew and Swedish, though. In the latter two languages the null complementizer was postulated as a member of a paradigm of complementizers, all of whom license resumption. In contrast, in Vata the licenser would always be a null element, which is substantially less compelling. The other lexical solution that suggests itself is to assume that the left-peripheral focus and relative clause particles and the right-peripheral question particles all share some morphological feature. The morphosyntax of Vata has not been as well studied as that of Hebrew, Irish, and Swedish, so I will gloss over the exact nature of the morphological feature and the category or categories that it is associated with. The lexical information that licenses resumptives is then as follows, with +WH representing a *wh* morphological feature common to the elements in question and X^0 representing some syntactic category or categories:

(16)
$$+\textsc{wh},\quad X^0 \quad \left(\begin{array}{l} \%RP = (\uparrow \textsc{gf}^{*}\ \textsc{subj}) \\ (\uparrow \textsc{udf})_\sigma = (\%RP_\sigma\ \textsc{antecedent}) \\ @MR(\%RP) \\ @RELABEL(\%RP) \end{array}\right)$$

If the relevant elements—the question particle, the focus pronoun and the relative pronoun—could be succesfully analysed as complementizers, then +WH could be reanalysed as +COMP and X^0 as C^0, as in Hebrew and Swedish. The left- and right-peripheral status of the elements is promising in this regard, but further work needs to be done to support such a reanalysis. A challenge to this kind of analysis would be the apparent agreement between the base of the unbounded dependency and the focus pronoun or relative pronoun.

There is one principal difference between the lexical entry (16) and the sorts of entries already encountered for Irish, Hebrew, and Swedish. In Vata, resumptives must be subjects, so the path that is associated with the local name %RP, which identifies the resumptive pronoun, obligatorily ends in the grammatical function SUBJ, although the path can pass through zero or more other GFs and is therefore unbounded.

Thus far the analysis of Vata is by and large like that of syntactically active resumptives, which does not yet capture the difference in syntactic behaviour in Vata's gap-like, syntactically inactive resumptives. The final part of the analysis of Vata requires modification of the functional equality equation that integrates the UDF at the top of the dependency and the GF at the base:

(17) $(\uparrow \text{UDF})\backslash\text{PRED} =$
$(\uparrow \;\text{CF}^* \;\{\; \underset{(\rightarrow\,\text{PRED}) = (\uparrow\,\text{UDF PRED})}{[\text{GF} - \text{SUBJ}]} \;\mid\; \text{SUBJ}\backslash\text{PRED} \;\})$

The unbounded nature of the dependency is captured through CF*, the body of the unbounded dependency, which allows the dependency to pass through zero or more complement functions (COMP or XCOMP). The same functional equality integrates filler-gap dependencies, through the [GF – SUBJ] option, and binder-resumptive dependencies, through the SUBJ option. Constraints on extraction would be captured as specifications on the body of the dependency, CF*, which is shared by both kinds of dependencies. It therefore automatically follows that any constraints on extraction would apply to gaps and resumptive pronouns alike. For example, if island constraints are represented syntactically (Dalrymple, 2001: 390–408), the resumptive dependency inherits all island constraints.

The restriction operator is used to set aside the feature PRED in the functional equality in (17). However, the lexical items that correspond to the UDF and SUBJ are syntactically inserted with their full lexical information intact, including PRED. The restricted functional equality sets the PRED features of the UDF and SUBJ aside when equating their f-structures. This allows the resumptive pronoun SUBJ and the *wh*-element that is the UDF (*wh*-phrase, focus pronoun or relative pronon) to contribute to a single f-structure without causing a Consistency violation. This effectively creates an f-structure that is indistinguishable from what would have been the case if the SUBJ had been a gap, in which case the UDF would have provided the token-identical value for the two separate attributes SUBJ and UDF. The result of this kind of unbounded dependency relation is that the top of the dependency, e.g. a *wh*-phrase, must agree with a resumptive pronoun, but it does so by actually being equated with the pronominal f-structure. Agreement between the binder and resumptive thus follows automatically.

The part of the UDF functional schema (17) that is appropriate for an unbounded dependency that terminates in a non-subject, which must be a gap, is picked out by [GF − SUBJ]. The off-path constraint on [GF − SUBJ] states that the lexically specified PRED of the UDF is the PRED of the non-subject GF in all other cases. Otherwise the non-subject gap would be identified with a UDF that has its PRED restricted out, which would ultimately lead to an ill-formed f-structure. The off-path constraint in fact entails that a non-subject base is fully identified with the UDF. It allows gapped GFs to satisfy all constraints on f-structural well-formedness by sharing a value with the UDF function, just as in filler-gap dependencies in other languages.

The c-structure and f-structure for the simple resumptive example (18) are shown in (19) and (20):

(18) àlɔ́ ɔ̰̀ mlì lá
who he left *wh*
'Who left?' (Koopman and Sportiche, 1982: 23, (14a))

(19)

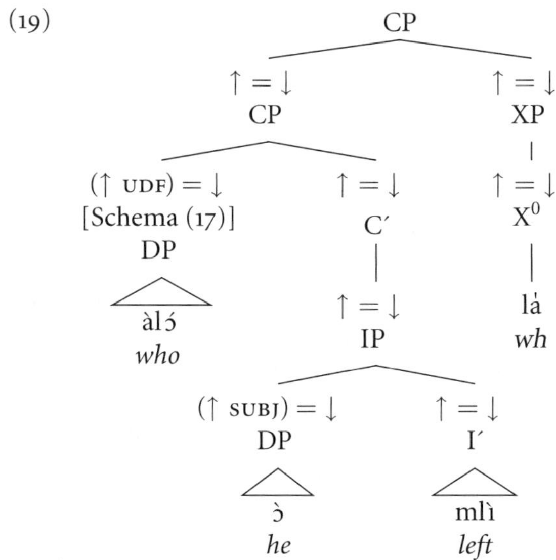

(20) 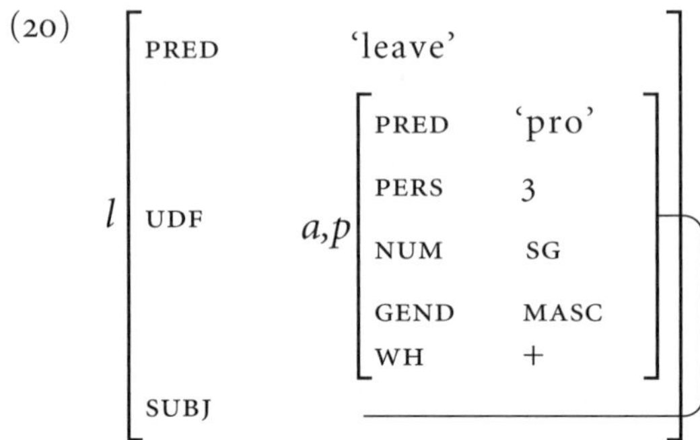

This f-structure is the same as what would have resulted if the pronoun were a gap, but there is no reference to 'underlying' gaps in the analysis, nor is there an alternative derivation with a gap instead of the resumptive. The resumptive pronoun is lexically an ordinary pronoun and is realized in c-structure.

Weak crossover is normally analysed in LFG in terms of linear prominence, based on the f-precedence relation derived from precedence in c-structure, and syntactic prominence, based on a hierarchy of f-structural grammatical functions (Bresnan, 1995, 2001; Dalrymple et al., 2001, 2007; Falk, 2001). Languages differ as to whether binding requires both syntactic prominence and linear prominence (e.g., English) or if either prominence relation on its own is sufficient (e.g., German). The Vata resumptive in c-structure affects the linear prominence condition but not the syntactic prominence condition, which is defined in terms of grammatical functions at f-structure, without reference to c-structure. If linear prominence is not relevant to Vata weak crossover, then the resumptive should not alleviate a weak crossover violation, since there is no f-structural distinction between gaps and resumptives. Reconstruction of the filler in the resumptive site is similarly predicted, because the f-structure of the UDF is token-identical to the f-structure of the pronoun. Across-the-board extraction and parasitic gaps are also predicted to be grammatical, all else being equal (that is, to the extent that the grammar independently licenses them).

The fact that schema (17) restricts out the PRED of a SUBJ that is the base of an unbounded dependency entails that a gap is ungrammatical as a SUBJ, since the gap will not independently contribute a PRED and the f-structure will therefore fail to satisfy Completeness and Coherence. However, this does not in itself entail that the SUBJ must be a pronoun, as opposed to any other contentful nominal that could independently occur in the position. But, as discussed in chapter 6, RMTR's specification of manager resources in terms of a pronominal meaning constructor and the feature ANTECEDENT entails that only a pronoun will satisfy the manager resource.

(18) `àlɔ́ ɔ̀ mlì là
who he left *wh*
'Who left?'

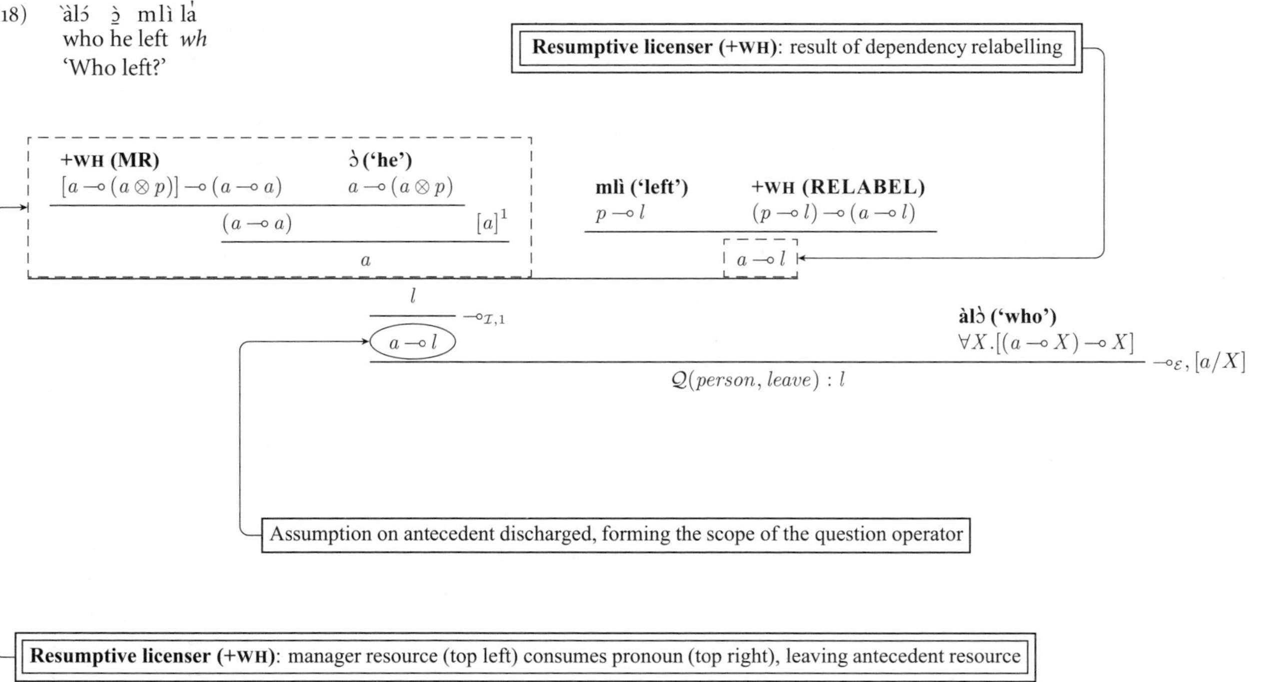

FIGURE 10.1. Proof for a Vata binder-resumptive dependency.

The obligatoriness of the resumptive is immediately explained if we assume that Vata resumption is licensed by a manager resource, like Irish, Hebrew, and Swedish. The pronoun is lexically just an ordinary pronoun, so it contributes a pronominal meaning constructor. The manager resource binds the subject (matrix or embedded) and removes its meaning constructor. The manager resource can only be satisfied if it actually finds a pronoun to consume. The end result is that a pronoun must be syntactically inserted as usual—and is therefore present in c-structure, despite its inactivity in f-structure—in order for the meaning constructor of the pronoun to satisfy the manager resource.

The following premises are contributed by the lexical items in (18), as instantiated by f-structure (20):[2]

(21)

1.	$\forall X.[(a \multimap X) \multimap X]$	Lex. **àlɔ́ ('who')**
2.	$[a \multimap (a \otimes p)] \multimap (a \multimap a)$	Lex. **+wh (MR)**
3.	$(p \multimap l) \multimap (a \multimap l)$	Lex. **+wh (RELABEL)**
4.	$a \multimap (a \otimes p)$	Lex. **ɔ̀ ('he')**
5.	$p \multimap l$	Lex. **mlì ('left')**

The proof that the premises construct is shown in Figure 10.1.

10.3 Conclusion

Vata resumptives constitute another instance of syntactically inactive resumptives, as also found in Swedish. The resumptive pronouns of both Swedish and Vata are nevertheless fully grammatically licensed: there are mechanisms in Vata and Swedish grammars for integrating the resumptives syntactically and semantically. The syntactic mechanism is functional equality, which is particular to syntactically inactive resumptives, in opposition to syntactically active resumptives, as found in Irish and Hebrew. This syntactic difference explains why Vata resumptives behave like gaps with respect to diagnostics such as islands and weak crossover. The restriction operator is used in the functional schema for unbounded dependencies, (17), such that equality between the f-structures of the binder and the resumptive is possible. This would otherwise be impossible due to the uniqueness of the distinct PRED features. The use of restriction in this way allows the pronouns to nevertheless be treated as completely ordinary pronouns in their lexical information and in c-structure, maintaining the ordinary pronoun theory of resumption, based on McCloskey's Generalization, in the Resource Management Theory of Resumption.

[2] I make the simplifying assumption here that the *wh*-particle is expletive (Mycock, 2004, 2006).

TABLE 10.1. A comparison of the resumptive pronoun systems of Irish, Hebrew, Swedish, and Vata.

		Resumptive licenser				Binding	
	HSR	**Form**	**Category**	**C-structure Position**	**Local to**	**Antecedent**	**Resumptive**
Irish	Yes	*aN*	$\hat{C}$	Top	UDF	UDF	GF^{+}
Hebrew	Yes	+COMP	C^0	Top	UDF	UDF	GF^{+}
Swedish	Yes	+COMP	C^0	Bottom	SUBJ	UDF	SUBJ
Vata	No	+WH	X^0	Top	UDF	UDF	GF^{*} SUBJ

The Resource Sensitivity Hypothesis then entails that the resumptive pronoun, as an ordinary pronoun, constitutes a surplus resource for semantic composition. The semantic mechanism for dealing with this surplus in Vata and Swedish grammars, just like in Irish and Hebrew grammars, is a manager resource. The Resource Management Theory of Resumption therefore achieves a theoretically novel and empirically well-supported unification of syntactically active resumptives and syntactically inactive resumptives, which have previously been treated heterogeneously (McCloskey, 2006). Furthermore, this was accomplished without treating Vata or Swedish resumptives as special pronouns or in any way crucially distinct from the kinds of pronouns found in Irish and Hebrew.

Table 10.1 compares the resumptive pronouns systems of Irish, Hebrew, Swedish, and Vata. Unlike the first three languages, Vata does not exhibit the Highest Subject Restriction. This difference is currently unexplained and points to an avenue for potentially important future work. Like Hebrew and Swedish, Vata licenses resumptives through a morphological feature, since there does not seem to be a single lexical item that licenses resumptives, as in Irish. However, it is not yet clear what the exact nature of the morphological feature +WH is and what the categorial status of the items that bear it is. It seems promising to pursue an analysis in which the items are complementizers, and the feature is +COMP, given the clause peripheral status of the likely candidates (the question particle and the focus and relative pronouns). In Vata, as is the case for Irish and Hebrew, but not Swedish, the licenser for the resumptive pronoun is at the top of the c-structure, i.e. it is c-structurally local to the position of the UDF. However, like Swedish, the resumptive pronoun is restricted to subjects, although not necessarily a subject local to the licenser, hence GF^{*} SUBJ. This is reflected in the binding relation, where the UDF can bind only a SUBJ resumptive pronoun.

Part V

Other Kinds of Resumption

11

Resumption and Processing

This chapter presents a processing model for resumptive pronouns that are not fully grammatically licensed. I thus distinguish between true grammatically licensed resumptive pronouns ('true resumptives') which are fully licensed according to the Resource Management Theory of Resumption, and 'processor resumptives', which are not licensed by the grammar. I argue that the latter arise through normal constraints on production and can be accommodated and interpreted, under certain circumstances, in parsing.[1]

Section 11.1 presents the general processing model. Section 11.2 considers how processor resumptives in English, also known as *intrusive pronouns* (Sells, 1984), are produced in the first place. It is argued that they are not licensed by the grammar at all, but arise from incremental production. Section 11.3 concerns parsing and interpretation of processor resumptives. I identify three major kinds of processor resumptives: complexity resumptives, island resumptives, and COMP resumptives. Much of the section is devoted to considerations of the interpretation of processor resumptives. The last part of section 11.3 returns to the matter of certain Swedish resumptive pronouns that were claimed not to be true grammatically licensed resumptives in chapter 9 and were therefore left aside until now.

11.1 The Processing Model

The processing model makes the following assumptions:

1. Production and parsing are incremental.
2. Incremental production and parsing attempt to construct *locally* well-formed structures.
3. Global well-formedness applies only to the output of production and parsing.

[1] This processing model is also discussed in Asudeh (2011*a*,*b*), but the main concerns of those papers are consequences of the model, rather than the model itself.

4. Production and parsing are constrained by memory limitations based on complexity factors, including distance, structural complexity, and intersecting interpretations of unbounded dependencies (Kimball, 1973; Dickey, 1996; Lewis, 1996; Gibson, 1998; among others).

This processing model is based on ideas that are supported by the psycholinguistics literature. However, the model is purely theoretical and has not been tested experimentally. Nevertheless, the model makes sense of attested experimental results and patterns of data that have been discussed in the theoretical literature based on native speaker intuitions. The model has been developed only with respect to unbounded dependencies, particularly binder-resumptive dependencies, and is not claimed to be a general processing model, although the assumptions above are general and not specific to resumption or unbounded dependencies.

The main questions that a model of resumptive processing must answer are:

1. How do speakers of languages that have no true resumptives, such as English, produce processor resumptives?
2. Why do speakers of languages without grammatically licensed resumptives produce processor resumptives?
3. Why do speakers of languages without grammatically licensed resumptives who produce processor resumptives reject sentences with processor resumptives as ill-formed?
4. Why do speakers prefer some sentences with processor resumptives to sentences where the resumptive is absent?
5. How do speakers interpret processor resumptives?
6. If a language has true resumptives, how does this aspect of its grammar affect processor resumptives? In particular:
   (a) Can a language have both kinds of resumptives and, if so, under what conditions?
   (b) Will processor resumptives take on different characteristics in a language that also has true resumptives?

These questions will be taken up throughout the remainder of this chapter.

11.2 Production

Work by Levelt (particularly Levelt, 1989) has been influential in the psycholinguistic study of sentence production, which has historically received less attention than sentence comprehension in psycholinguistics. One of Levelt's key points is that production is incremental (Kempen and Hoenkamp, 1987;

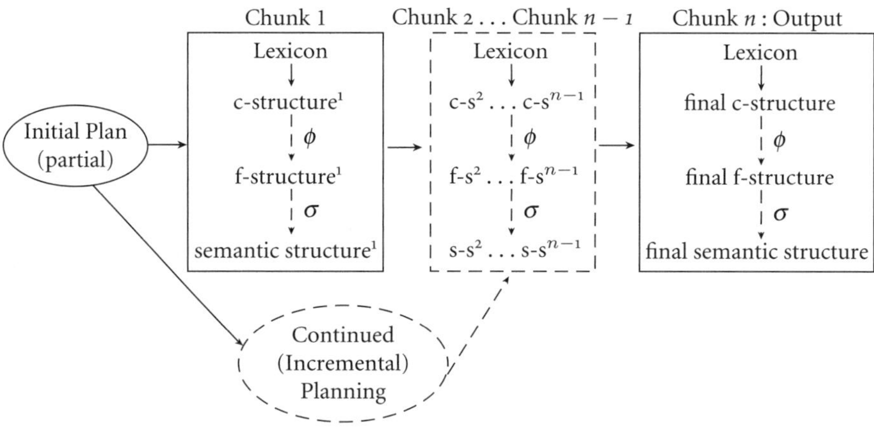

FIGURE 11.1. The production model.

Levelt, 1989, 1999), even in a serial production model. A simplified production model, based on Levelt (1989), is shown in Figure 11.1.

Incrementality in the model stems from the ability of LFG grammars to model fragments (Bresnan, 2001: 79–81). The need to deal with fragments has long been recognized in the theory (Kaplan and Bresnan, 1982) and fragments are also implemented in the major computational treatment of the theory (Crouch et al., 2011). Bresnan points out that, although LFG grammars can characterize the internal structural relations of sentence fragments, not all fragments receive analyses that are informative. The idea is that this matches our intuitions about the informativeness of fragments.

Bresnan contrasts the fragment in (1) with the fragment in (2).

(1) [Speaker A:] And he agrees?
[Speaker B:] — seems to.
Fragment: *seems to*

(2) The one he should be spoken to by, for God's sake, is his mother.
Fragment: *to by for*

Bresnan shows that the first fragment constructs an informative partial c-structure and f-structure. These form proper subparts of the c-structure and f-structure for a full sentence like *He seems to agree*. In contrast, the second fragment constructs only three unrelated structures. Bresnan (2001: 81) notes that the ability to construct informative fragments stems from the fact that the main predicator or head of a c-structure/f-structure, e.g. *seems* in (1), contributes subcategorization information, which results in a suitable subject and complement having to be present in f-structure to satisfy Completeness, and agreement information about its subject.

11.2.1 *Production of English Resumptives*

Kroch (1981) considers the problem of English resumptive elements in an incremental model of speech production that generates a filler before planning of the sentence has been completed. As production proceeds, the speaker ends up in a situation where the intended base position of the filler-gap dependency is in an island or would violate the 'COMP-trace' filter/Empty Category Principle (ECP). A nominal is inserted to avoid the island or ECP violation. Kroch (1981) does not specifically postulate that the inserted element is a pronoun, since he notes that insertion of an epithet is also possible:

(3) There was one prisoner that we didn't understand why the guy was even in jail. (Kroch, 1981: 129, (13a))

The essence of Kroch's proposal is that some nominal, typically a pronoun, is inserted to avoid a grammatical violation due to poor planning in production. However, subsequent psycholinguistic evidence calls into question Kroch's contention that insertion of a resumptive is due to poor planning.

Ferreira and Swets tested the production of resumptive pronouns in *wh*-islands by native speakers of English (Swets and Ferreira, 2003; Ferreira and Swets, 2005). They used a self-paced experimental design in which subjects were required to complete, in full sentences, partial descriptions that were presented with a picture array. Target sentences were sentences like the following, which contains a resumptive pronoun:

(4) This is a donkey that I don't know where it lives

Two kinds of control sentences were also elicited. The first kind controlled for surface length:

(5) This is a donkey that doesn't know where it lives.

The second kind controlled for length of the *wh*-dependency without an island violation:

(6) This is a donkey that I didn't say lives in Brazil.

Ferreira and Swets carried out two versions of the production experiment. In one experiment, participants were under pressure to begin speaking quickly due to a deadline procedure (Ferreira and Swets, 2002). In the other experiment, participants were not under pressure to begin speaking quickly (there was no deadline).

If the resumptive pronouns in *wh*-islands are due to lack of planning, as in the Kroch (1981) theory, then speakers should plan the utterance in the no-deadline experiment such that they avoid both the island violation and the resumptive pronoun. For example, a participant could construct the following sentence instead of (4):

(7) This is a donkey and I don't know where it lives.

Experimental participants in fact overwhelmingly produced island violations like (4) in both experiments.

In the no-deadline experiment, participants could take as much time as they needed to plan their utterance before speaking and typically took over 2 seconds to begin. Nevertheless, 47.3% of the targets produced for the *wh*-island condition consisted of an island containing a resumptive, as in (4). Experimental participants did not use the extra time in the no-deadline experiment to plan an utterance that avoids a resumptive pronoun. This casts serious doubt on Kroch's proposal that resumptive elements arise from poor planning, since they arise even when the conditions permit relatively careful planning. As for the deadline experiment, the proportion of sentences with resumptives in islands actually went *down* to 39.4%. The results for the deadline experiment contained a big increase in alternative well-formed sentences that were not targets, like *I don't know where this donkey lives.*

These results are all the more striking, because Ferreira and Swets also ran two grammaticality judgement experiments on the same population—one with auditory presentation of stimuli and the other with written presentation—that showed that participants rated resumptive sentences, like (4), as worse than corresponding controls, like (5). Participants were asked to rate the sentences on a forced scale of 1 ('perfect') to 5 ('awful'). In the auditory presentation, resumptive sentences received average ratings of 3.0, while control sentences received average ratings of 1.7, a significant difference. Similarly, in the written presentation, resumptive sentences received average ratings of 3.3, while control sentence received average ratings of 1.9, again a significant difference. These results are in accord with the independent experimental findings of McDaniel and Cowart (1999), Alexopoulou and Keller (2002, 2007), and Heestand et al. (2011), which show that resumptive pronouns result in degraded acceptability. The Ferreira and Swets results are particularly noteworthy, because they show that the same population both produces resumptives, even in the absence of deadline pressure, and yet rates them as worse than controls, and as fairly close to the bottom of the acceptability scale.

Swets and Ferreira (2003) conclude that speakers plan to produce sentences with resumptives in islands, despite rating them as quite ungrammatical. They sketch a solution for generating the island-resumptive sentences in Tree-Adjoining Grammar (TAG; Joshi et al., 1975; Kroch and Joshi, 1985; Frank, 2002). They speculate that the reason that the resumptive sentences are rejected despite being produced is that "the production and comprehension systems may set different parameters for accepting these structures". The upshot of the proposal is that the elementary trees required for producing the island-resumptives are part of the grammar and that the grammar therefore treats island-resumptive sentences as well-formed, in terms of production. This is tantamount to claiming that there are different grammars for production and comprehension, which is problematic, since grammars are normally construed as systems of knowledge (Chomsky, 1965, 1986) and should therefore be non-directional (Asudeh, 2011*a*). Moreover, although grammatical forms may be rejected for processing reasons, as in the case of centre embedding (Chomsky and Miller, 1963), such forms are normally also not readily produced, unlike these resumptives (Asudeh, 2011*b*).

Creswell (2002) also considers the problems raised by the production of English resumptives in islands from a Tree-Adjoining Grammar perspective. Creswell arrives at the same conclusion as Ferreira and Swets—that the grammar produces the island-resumptive structures—but for theoretical reasons. Creswell notes that the TAG theory of Frank (2002) does not permit generation of the trees necessary for island violations. She observes that TAG-based models of incremental production (Ferreira, 2000; Frank and Badecker, 2001) cannot support Kroch's (1981) solution for the island-resumptive structures:

> In this model of production where we assume that a speaker only has grammatical resources with which to work, we cannot use Kroch's (1981) explanation of the appearance of resumptive pronouns in island-violation contexts. The resources needed to produce the island-violating structures are not available in the grammar that licenses the set of tree building blocks. On the face of it then, it seems that the existence of resumptive pronouns in island violating contexts would prove devastating for this model of sentence production. Based on the assumptions that 1) the processing system has only grammatically-licensed trees with which to create larger structures and 2) the structures needed to extract from island-violation contexts are not grammatically-licensed, speakers could not be remedying violations that should not even be created given their underlying grammars. (Creswell, 2002: 103)

Creswell solves the theoretical problem by proposing that the grammars of English speakers must independently have the resources required to form island-resumptive structures.

Creswell's argument is based on the observation that resumptive pronouns in English also occur in relative clauses that are not islands, as in the following examples from Prince (1990), which are attested examples produced by native speakers:

(8) You get a rack that the bike will sit on it. (Prince, 1990: (15d))

(9) I have a friend who she does all the platters. (Prince, 1990: (4c))

Examples like these, although attested, are generally judged as ungrammatical by English speakers, including in controlled experiments (McDaniel and Cowart, 1999; Alexopoulou and Keller, 2002, 2007; Swets and Ferreira, 2003; Ferreira and Swets, 2005; Heestand et al., 2011). Prince (1990) analyses this kind of resumptive as a discourse pronoun, as opposed to a bound pronoun. This is essentially also what Sells (1984) proposes for English resumptive pronouns (i.e., intrusive pronouns). Erteschik-Shir (1992) also develops a very similar theory for Hebrew processor resumptives, although she intends some aspects of her theory to also apply to true resumptives.

In other attested examples, the resumptive element is a non-coreferential pronoun or even a full NP that serves a similar discourse function (Prince, 1990). This is further evidence that the resumptive pronouns are discourse pronouns, since they can be substituted with elements that cannot be bound, as in the following examples (Prince, 1990: (34a–d)):

(10) I had a handout and notes from her talk that that was lost too.

(11) He's got this lifelong friend who he takes money from the parish to give to this lifelong friend.

(12) I have a manager, Joe Scandolo, who we've been together over twenty years.

(13) You assigned me to a paper which I don't know anything about the subject.

In (10), the resumptive is a singular deictic pronoun that does not seem to even properly agree in number with its plural antecedent. In (11), the antecedent itself is repeated. In (12), the resumptive is a discourse pronoun, since its antecedent is comprised of the discourse markers for the speaker and for

Joe Scandolo, which are not in the right syntactic configuration to bind the pronoun. In example (13), the resumptive element is a relational noun that takes as its implicit argument the antecedent *a paper*; relational nouns cannot normally function resumptively (Asudeh, 2005*b*).

The question remains of how to properly explain English resumptives. The claim that they are in fact grammatically licensed is not satisfying, since there is considerable evidence that speakers do not find them grammatical; some of this evidence was reviewed above and more will be reviewed in section 11.3. The solution proposed here incorporates elements of the analyses given by Kroch (1981), Creswell (2002), and Ferreira and Swets (Swets and Ferreira, 2003; Ferreira and Swets, 2005) into the production model given above, but it is ultimately significantly different from these previous proposals. The key insight is that resumptive elements are not grammatically licensed, which explains why speakers deem them ungrammatical. Resumptives nevertheless arise as a result of the production system, as in the account of Kroch (1981), but as a result of incremental production of locally well-formed structures, not of poor planning.

Levelt (1989: 258) characterizes the production system as follows, based on a consideration of various experimental results.

> Taken together, these findings are supportive of the notion that the rhythm of grammatical encoding follows the semantic joints of a message—its function/argument structure—rather than syntactic joints. It is the partitioning of the message to be expressed that a speaker is attending to, and this (co-)determines the rhythm of grammatical encoding.

The "function/argument structure" mentioned here encodes planning units at the 'message level' (Levelt, 1989). This is a rough thematic structure, similar to the structures of Conceptual Semantics (Jackendoff, 1990, 1997, 2002, 2007).

The present proposal is based on the Levelt (1989) theory and works as follows. In initial planning of an utterance, a speaker forms a message that identifies the event or state, a basic predicate about the event or state, the predicate's arguments and their rough thematic relation to each other. The speaker also decides what sort of utterance s/he wants to make: a declarative statement, a question, a command, etc. The rough thematic structure unfolds through the incremental construction of fragments of grammatical structure. These fragments are added to the grammatical structure with which the speaker initiates the implementation of the message plan, which can also be incrementally augmented and modified. Incremental grammatical production proceeds by forming and adding new chunks based on the function/argument structure of heads, which is lexically encoded and which will, in general, be closely related to the function/argument structure of the planning unit. Importantly, each new chunk of grammatical representation must be *locally* grammatical in order to be generated. This leads to incremental generation of a grammatical structure that satisfies local grammaticality requirements at each incremental step. However, the end result does not necessarily satisfy global grammaticality requirements.

The interaction of the incremental production model with the theory of unbounded dependencies is crucial to explaining processor resumptives. The aspect of the LFG theory of unbounded dependencies that is most immediately relevant is that the unbounded dependency is launched at the top of the dependency (Asudeh, 2011*a*). This is formalized with an outside-in equation (Kaplan and Zaenen, 1989), which roughly constitutes a kind of downward search for a gap, in the case of a filler-gap dependency. Island constraints and other constraints on extraction, if they are part of the syntax, are stated by modifying the path or by stating off-path constraints on the path. For example, $\neg$ ($\rightarrow$ SUBJ) would be used to indicate that the path cannot reach inside a SUBJECT grammatical function. LFG is a declarative theory of grammar, so there is no real directionality in the theory at all, with respect to statements of grammatical well-formedness, just declarative constraint statements. There is therefore no literal downward search for a gap in the grammar. However, production and parsing are irreducibly directional, because each must start with the material that is to be produced or interpreted first. It is uncontroversial that production and parsing must go in the direction of the speech stream, not in the opposite direction.

The top-down theory of unbounded dependencies and the directionality of processing have an important consequence for the construction of locally well-formed grammatical representations. In constructing the chunk that contains the unbounded dependency in production, the top of the unbounded dependency contributes the outside-in equation that functionally equates the filler and an empty grammatical function corresponding to the gap, thus integrating filler and gap. However, what is pretheoretically called a gap does not correspond to any sort of marker in any of the local structures—the gap is just an absence. This has an important implication for incremental construction of fragments. The outside-in function contributed by the filler is unbounded and defines a path through f-structure material that is still being incrementally constructed. The grammar cannot integrate the filler into a local f-structure under construction if all grammatical functions are locally filled. However,

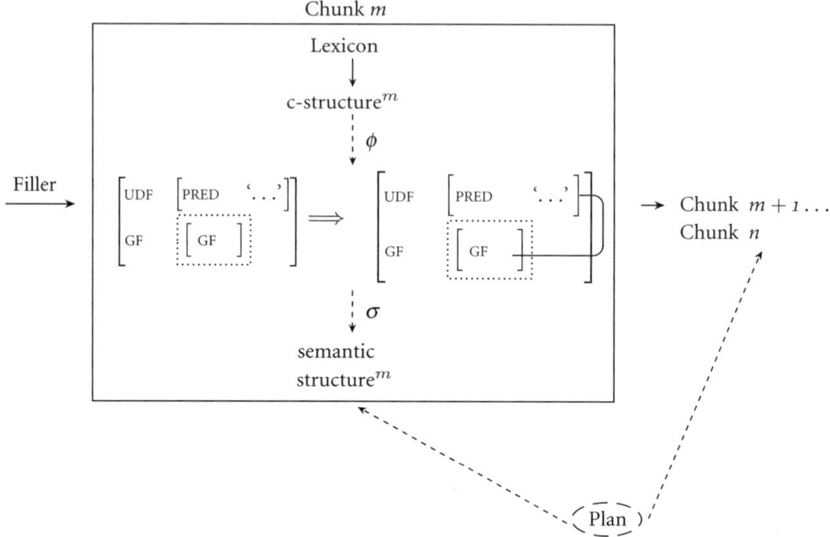

FIGURE 11.2. Local well-formedness satisfied by integration of a filler.

the integration site could be in the next chunk of f-structure that is yet to be constructed or in a subsequent chunk,[2] except in the case of islands, to which we will return shortly. It is therefore reasonable, in an incremental model of production and parsing, to assume that, at each incremental step, the grammar builds a local structure and then attempts integration of the filler.

In constructing a chunk, the production system can do one of two things with each grammatical function. It can leave the GF empty, in which case a filler must be functionally equated with this GF before moving on to the next chunk, or else the local structure would not be locally well-formed. Alternatively, the production system can posit lexical material, such as a nominal, that will add its information to the GF in question, provided it is consistent with the other specifications of the local structure. For example, in English, if the GF in question is an OBJECT and the lexical material to be inserted is a pronoun, an accusative pronoun must be inserted. The lexical material must also be consistent with the current message plan. If this second option is chosen, the filler is not integrated, but the local structure is well-formed. The filler searches for a gap further down its path, i.e. in a subsequent chunk.

[2] It is important to keep in mind that it is properties of the grammar, not the processor, that are currently under discussion.

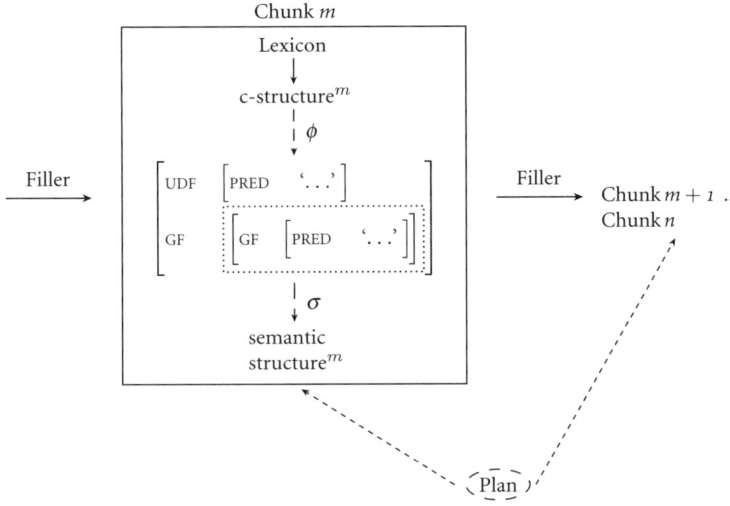

FIGURE 11.3. Local well-formedness satisfied by insertion of lexical material.

The two situations are outlined in Figures 11.2 and 11.3. Figure 11.2 shows what happens if the filler is locally integrated. Figure 11.3 shows what happens if lexical material is instead inserted and the filler is passed through the local structure rather than being integrated. The second pattern is the crucial one for explaining how an ungrammatical resumptive element is generated instead of a gap.

Let us see how this theory accounts for the following Prince (1990) example:

(14) You get a rack that the bike will sit on it.

This example is particularly appropriate, because it is syntactically simple. Not only does this makes it suitable for illustrative purposes, it also underscores the fact that this account does not depend on a notion of complexity to explain the production of processor resumptives.

Production starts as in (15). The local structure being constructed is indicated by the dashed box. The planned message is represented informally, in its entirety. The claim is not that entire utterances are generally planned in advance, which would no longer be a Levelt-style model, but the findings of Ferreira and Swets indicate that the production system plans far enough in advance to include a message of this length and complexity in the initial plan.

(15)

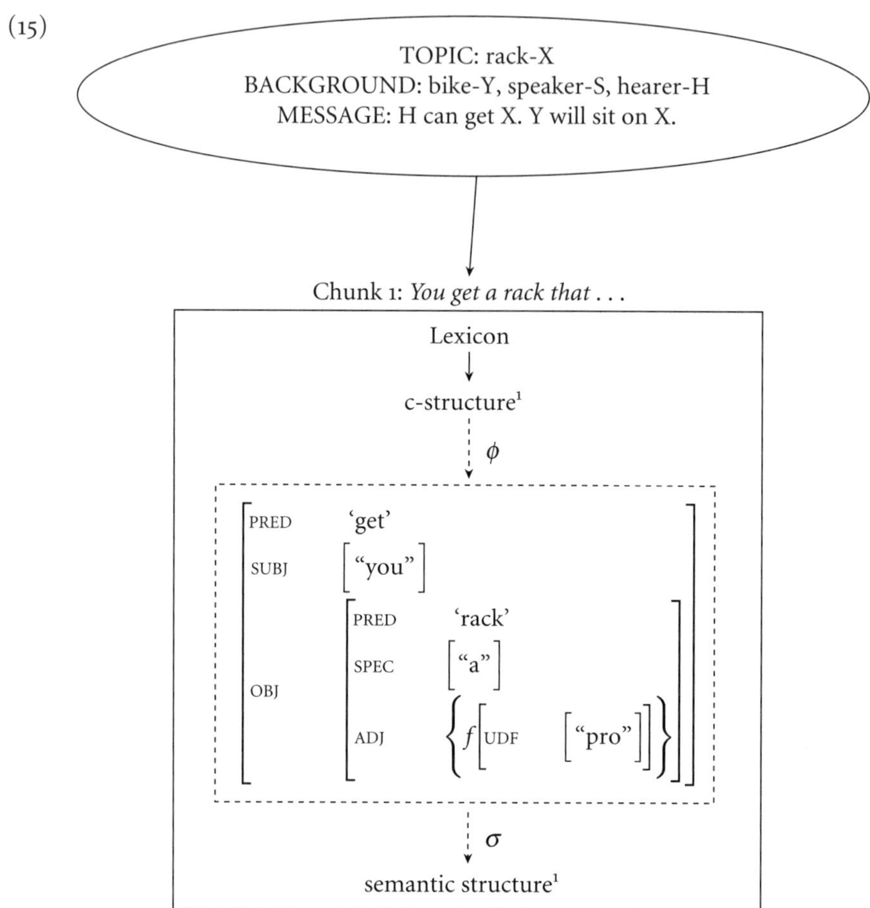

The first fragment that is constructed is made up of the head *get* and its arguments. I have assumed that relative clause construction also begins at this stage. This is not crucial, although it seems reasonable, given that the complementizer can be prosodically grouped with the relative head. This chunk is locally well-formed, since both the SUBJECT and OBJECT of *get* are locally filled.

An unbounded dependency has been launched due to the relative clause. This is represented by the UDF, abbreviated as "pro", in the innermost f-structure *f* in (15). The functional uncertainty that is initiated by the relative clause is carried over to construction of the next chunk. The details of the functional uncertainty equation need not concern us at this point (for details, see chapter 3; for a fuller discussion, see Dalrymple, 2001: 404), but will become relevant in the discussion of islands below. What needs to be represented at this point is how much of the path has been encountered. The chunk under construction contains the f-structure where the dependency was launched, which is arbitrarily labelled *f*. The up arrow metavariable in the outside-in functional uncertainty is set to *f*. The path encountered so far is therefore (*f* ...), where the ellipsis indicates material yet to be discovered.

The production system must now choose one of the options in Figures 11.2 and 11.3 in constructing the next chunk. If the first option is chosen, the filler is integrated into the local structure and the relative clause is produced with a gap:

(16) You get a rack that the bike will sit on.

The construction of the local structure is shown here:

(17)

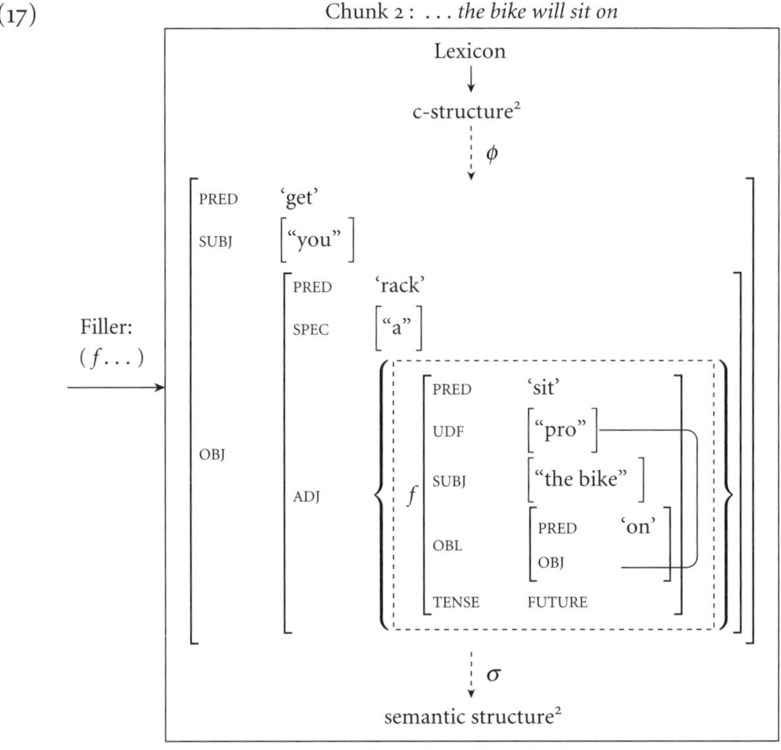

✓ **Locally well-formed**

The filler is integrated in this chunk. This satisfies both the demands of the filler and the local demand that the OBJECT must be integrated into the f-structure.

The overall production of the sentence is sketched here:

(18)

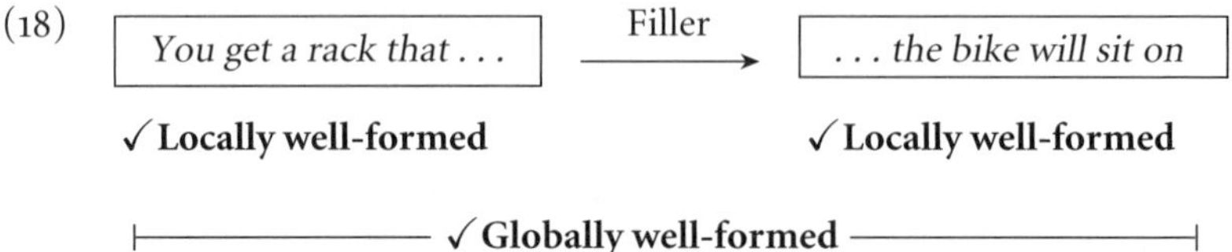

Each of the local structures is well-formed and consistent with the plan. The result is also globally well-formed.

Alternatively, the production system could construct Chunk 2 by choosing the option in Figure 11.3 of inserting lexical material that is consistent with the plan, rather than leaving the OBJECT of the preposition empty for integration with the filler. In that case, the Prince example (14) is produced instead. The local structure under construction is again indicated by the dashed box. The pronoun *it* has been inserted as the prepositional object.

(19)

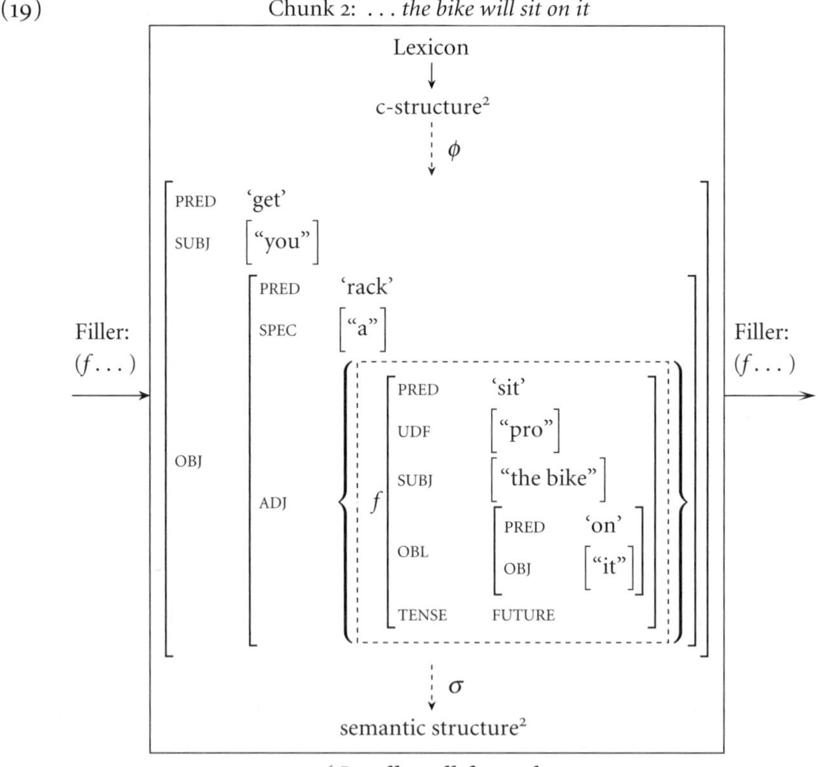

The production system passes the filler on and attempts to continue, but the filler can no longer be integrated. There is no remaining structure to be produced and insertion of the filler in the structure produced so far is impossible.

The situation is sketched here:

(20)

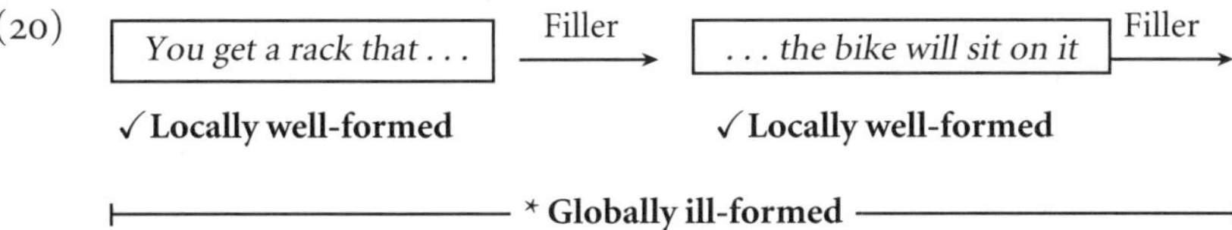

The grammar ultimately fails to sanction the structure that has been attempted. However, due to incremental production, the ungrammatical sentence has been produced, i.e. uttered. Each stage of producing (14) is locally grammatical. The overall result of production is, however, globally ungrammatical and is perceived as such by native speakers.

This account of production requires the grammar to incrementally generate locally well-formed structures. The incremental construction of grammatical structure starts from an initial plan and continues in tandem with incremental planning. The question arises of whether the option of inserting lexical material for local well-formedness, which leads to the construction of sentences like *You get a rack that the bike will sit on it*, is constrained at all. It is indeed non-trivially constrained by at least two factors and resumptive sentences are therefore not pure speech errors. First, insertion of lexical material is constrained by constraints that apply to the local structure in question. For example, in producing the sentence *You get a rack that the bike will sit on it*, insertion of a pronoun as the object of *on* is locally licensed by the rule that constructs PPs, the lexical requirements of *on*, which require an OBJECT, the independent fact that the OBJECT of *on* must be realized as a nominal, and so on. If local grammatical well-formedness is a criterion, then speakers could not instead produce utterances like *You get a rack that the bike will sit it*, except as actual speech errors. Second, the kinds of things that can be inserted are constrained by the message plan itself. For example, if the speaker wants to say something about a rack, then s/he must select a lexical item that is consistent with that plan, such as a personal pronoun (e.g., *it*), a deictic pronoun (e.g., *that*), a name or definite description that refers to the rack (e.g., *the rack*), or an epithet (e.g., *the damn thing*).

Consistency with the message plan is also what prevents production of examples like the following (Creswell, 2002: 106, (11–12)):

(21) the police officer who John prefers spinach

(22) the smell that my mom is baking bread

Bare nouns like *spinach* do not have the correct semantic properties to be used referentially. A plan to say something about a police officer would not lead to insertion of *spinach*. Creswell (2002: 106) also notes that sentences like the second one are grammatical in Japanese and Korean and contends that the pragmatic discourse conditions that determine the discourse relation between the relative head and the material in the relative clause are subject to some cross-linguistic variation. This is variation in *grammars* though, not variation in the production system.

Now let us consider resumptives in islands, as in the Swets and Ferreira (2003) donkey example, repeated in (23), or the attested example in (24).[3]

(23) This is a donkey that I don't know where it lives. (Swets and Ferreira, 2003)

(24) You have the top 20% that are just doing incredible service, and then you have the group in the middle that a high percentage of those are giving you a good day's work ... (Creswell, 2002: 102, (4d))

The main distinction between these cases and the case examined in detail above is that the island prevents local integration of the filler.

[3] Example (24) is available at http://web.archive.org/web/20041217051431/http://www.ssa.gov/history/WEIKEL.html; retrieved 5/8/2010.

Let us examine example (23) in detail. Production starts as follows:

(25)

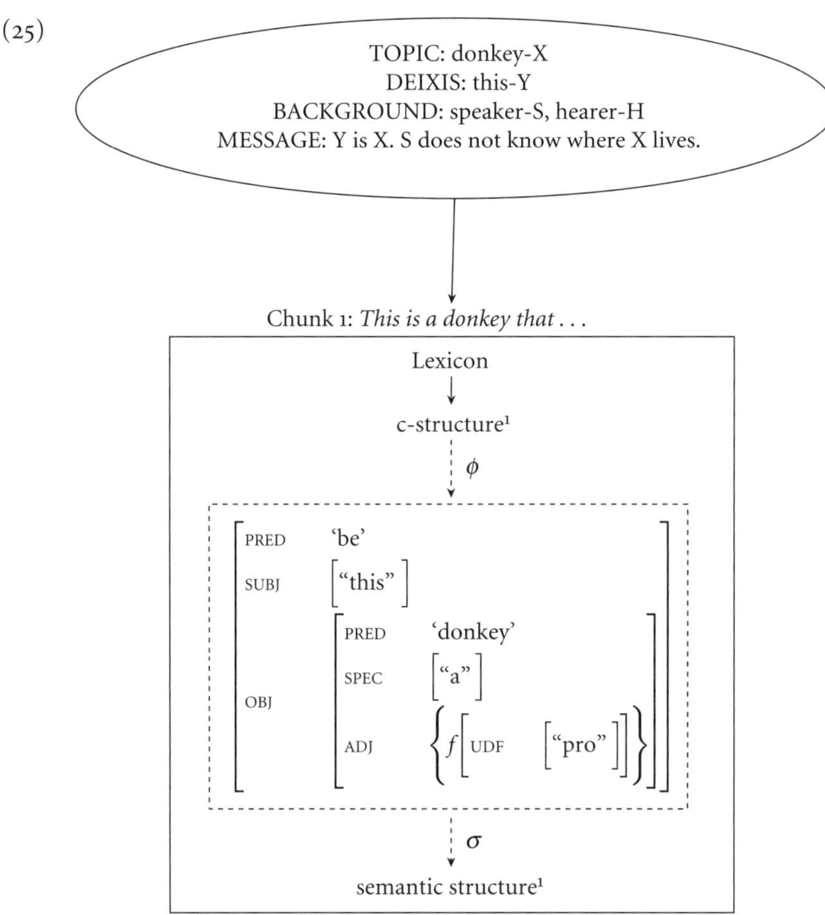

I have again assumed that the relative clause unbounded dependency is initiated in this first chunk, but this is not crucial.

Constraints on extraction in LFG are stated as constraints on the f-structure path between the top and bottom of the dependency. These constraints are captured by (1) limiting the grammatical functions that the path may pass through or (2) limiting the environments of these grammatical functions through off-path constraints (see chapter 3; for further details on this kind of functional uncertainty, see Dalrymple, 2001: 389ff.). Let us assume that the *wh*-island constraint is stated as an off-path equation to the effect that the functional uncertainty cannot pass through a COMP that contains a UDF.

A simplified version of the functional uncertainty that the relative clause initiates is shown here:

(26) $(\uparrow \text{UDF}) = (\ \underset{\neg(\rightarrow \text{UDF})}{\uparrow \text{COMP}^*}\ \ \text{GF}\ )$

The equation states that the grammatical function to be equated with the relative clause UDF can be found by going through zero or more COMP f-structures, but none of the COMP f-structures may itself contain an UDF. Upon construction of the first chunk, the relative clause UDF has not been integrated and the beginning of the path has been instantiated to one COMP.

The next chunk is the remainder of the sentence, but again nothing hinges on this. The partial local structure, indicated by the dotted box, is constructed:

(27)

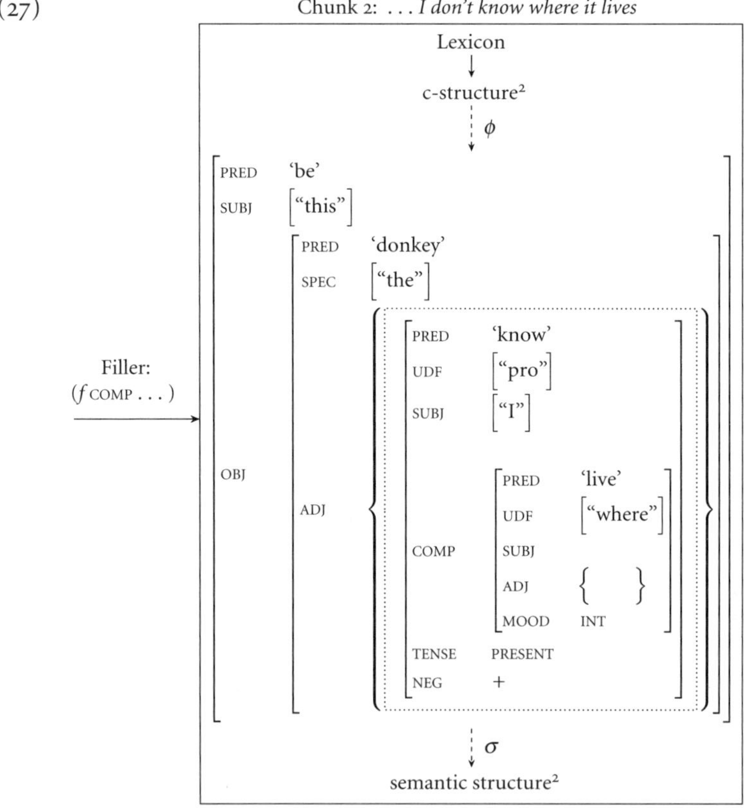

At this point, the production system has not integrated the relative clause unbounded dependency, but has now postulated a new unbounded dependency for the free relative.

The option of integrating the first unbounded dependency by positing a gap for the most deeply embedded SUBJ, as in Figure 11.2, is not possible. The presence of the embedded UDF means that there is no way to locally satisfy the upper UDF's functional uncertainty equation. As soon as a COMP containing a UDF is encountered, satisfaction is impossible. The result is that the only way to construct a locally well-formed f-structure is the option in Figure 11.3 of inserting some lexical material that is consistent with the plan (i.e., something that refers to the donkey). The filler does not pass through the chunk, though, because there is no way for it to do so and satisfy its equation. The new unbounded dependency also needs to be integrated, but this can be done using the filler integration option in Figure 11.2.

The final local structure is shown here in the dashed box:

(28)

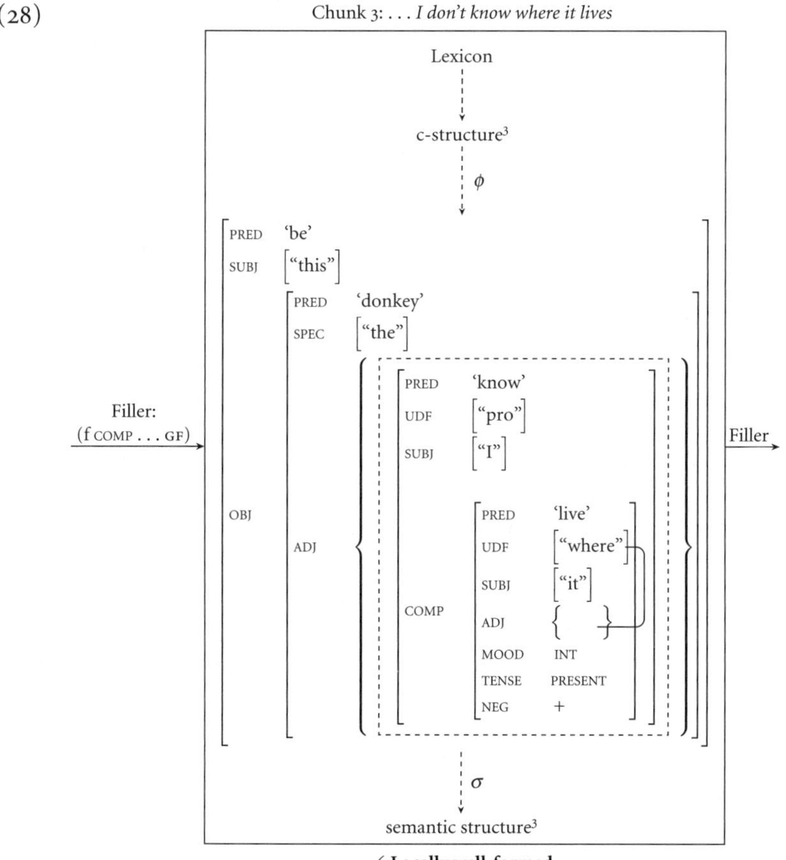

✓ **Locally well-formed**

There is no way for the filler to be integrated, because the local structure is an island.

The overall situation is sketched here:

(29)
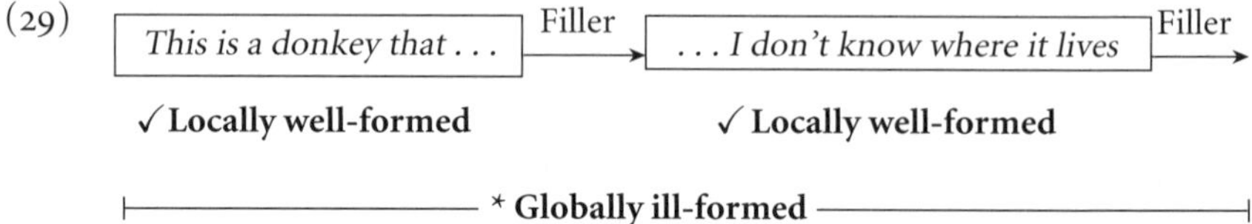

The grammar again ultimately fails to sanction the structure that has been attempted. However, the sentence is produced due to incremental production. For the sake of argument, I have assumed that the island constraint is captured syntactically, but the account would seem to work equally well if island constraints are captured as processing factors (Deane, 1991; Kluender, 1991; Kluender and Kutas, 1993; Kluender, 1998, 2004; Hofmeister and Sag, 2010; Sag, 2010), so long as the option of local integration of the filler is impossible or dispreferred.

11.2.2 *Summary and Discussion*

A production model that is based on incremental planning and production accounts for the production of both resumptives in non-islands, as in (30), and resumptives in islands, as in (31).

(30) You get a rack that the bike will sit on it.

(31) This is a donkey that I don't know where it lives.

The ability of LFG to define locally well-formed fragments (Bresnan, 2001) was the basis for incremental construction of structure. Fragments are also fundamental to the Tree-Adjoining Grammar analyses offered by Creswell (2002) and Swets and Ferreira (2003). The filler-driven theory of unbounded-dependencies provided the basis for the assumption that local structures are constructed before filler-integration is attempted.

Some of the questions posed at the beginning of section 11.1 can now be answered.

1. **Q.** How do speakers of languages that have no gramatically licensed resumptives produce processor resumptives?
   A. Processor resumptives are produced through incremental construction of locally well-formed structures.
2. **Q.** Why do speakers of languages without gramatically licensed resumptives produce processor resumptives?

A. Processor resumptives are produced in an attempt to construct locally well-formed structures that are consistent with the message plan.

3. **Q.** Why do speakers of languages without grammatically licensed resumptives who produce processor resumptives reject sentences with processor resumptives as ill-formed?
A. Sentences containing processor resumptives result from incremental production of locally well-formed structures, but are rejected because the sentences are globally ill-formed according to the grammar.

This account is similar to that of Kroch (1981), in denying a formal grammatical treatment of the phenomenon and instead localizing in the production system the phenomenon of producing resumptive pronouns that are not underlyingly grammatically licensed. However, Kroch's theory depended on lack of planning, while this theory does not. The findings of Ferreira and Swets (Swets and Ferreira, 2003; Ferreira and Swets, 2005), particularly in the no-deadline experiment, indicate that processor resumptives are not purely due to poor planning. The production theory presented here explains how resumptives could be produced in accordance with a plan, despite not being grammatically licensed.

This also sets the theory apart from those of Creswell (2002) and Swets and Ferreira (2003), who propose that the resumptives are actually grammatically licensed. This fails to explain native speakers' judgements that the resulting forms are not actually grammatical and substantial experimental evidence that backs up these judgements, to be reviewed in the next section. Although there are grammatical forms that are nevertheless perceived to be ungrammatical, such as centre embeddings, the sort of explanation that is offered for those cases cannot be readily extended to these cases. The basic explanation for the perceived ungrammaticality of centre embedding is that it arises because the sentences are hard to parse (see Gibson, 1998, for an overview). But there is no metric of parsing complexity that would account for the perceived ungrammaticality of a simple Prince example like (30). A proponent of the view that such examples are grammatical might be tempted to claim that they are perceived as ungrammatical precisely because the corresponding gap sentence is grammatical. This would constitute a transderivational explanation of a sort that has been proposed for syntactic resumptives (Shlonsky, 1992; Aoun et al., 2001; Pesetsky, 1998). There are two problems with this view, even setting general problems of transderivationality aside. The first is that if resumptive pronouns in English are grammatically generated and if they are avoided due to corresponding sentences with gaps, then there is no explanation for the fact that languages with true resumptive pronouns allow their resumptives to occur where gaps occur, in some but not all environments, without loss of perceived grammaticality. Second, the island examples without the resumptive pronoun are not perceived as grammatical and neither are the sentences with the resumptive pronoun (McDaniel and Cowart, 1999; Alexopoulou and Keller, 2002, 2007; Swets and Ferreira, 2003; Ferreira and Swets, 2005; Heestand et al., 2011).

Creswell (2002) notes that she is forced to adopt the view that English resumptives are generated grammatically rather than through production as a result of the theory of islands in Tree-Adjoining Grammar that she adopts (Frank, 2002). What is the difference between LFG, on the one hand, and TAG and other relevantly similar theories, on the other, that avoids the need to postulate that processor resumptives are underlyingly grammatical? The key difference is how the theories handle island constraints, to the extent that these should form part of syntactic theory. In the TAG theory of Frank (2002: 199ff.), islands are defined internally to the island, as in the 'phase' theory of the Minimalist Program (Chomsky, 2000, 2001) and the subjacency approach of Principles and Parameters Theory (Chomsky, 1986). In approaches that define islands internally, there is something ill-formed about the local structure that constitutes the island. This can mean that the relevant sort of structure cannot be constructed in the first place, as in TAG. Or it can mean that the relevant sort of structure is constructed, but there is no way for the filler to exit it, due to a phase boundary (MP) or a bounding node (P&P). In contrast, islands in LFG can be defined externally to the island, through constraints on outside-in functional uncertainty (Kaplan and Zaenen, 1989; Dalrymple, 2001). This means that the structure that constitutes the island is not necessarily ill-formed *locally*. The difference between islands being defined internally or externally is deeply related to whether the grammar treats filler-gap dependencies as gap-driven or filler-driven (Asudeh, 2011*a*). The production model that I have proposed could therefore likely be adapted to other theories that have a filler-driven approach to filler-gap dependencies, such as Categorial Grammar (Steedman, 1987; Morrill, 1994), or to theories that have a mixed system, such as Head-Driven Phrase Structure Grammar (Pollard and Sag, 1994; Bouma et al., 2001) and Sign-Based Construction Grammar (Sag, 2010).

11.3 Parsing and Interpretation

The parsing model is shown in Figure 11.4. The general assumptions of the processing model, which apply to both production and parsing, are once again the following:

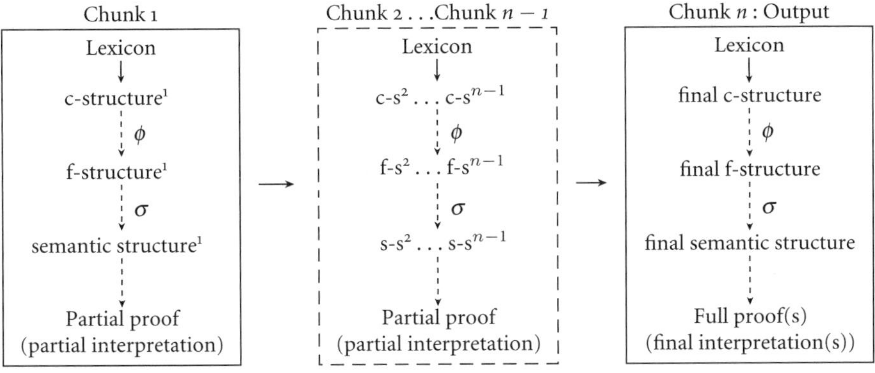

FIGURE 11.4. The parsing/interpretation model.

1. Production and parsing are incremental.
2. Incremental production and parsing attempt to construct locally well-formed structures.
3. Global well-formedness applies only to the output of production and parsing.
4. Production and parsing are constrained by memory limitations based on complexity factors, including distance, structural complexity, and intersecting interpretations of unbounded dependencies.

With respect to parsing in particular, the model also makes the following independently motivated assumptions:

1. Parsing of unbounded dependencies is filler-driven (Frazier, 1987; Frazier and Flores d'Arcais, 1989).
2. The result of incremental parsing is incrementally interpreted (Frazier, 1999).
3. Unsuccessful parsing results in reanalysis.

There are three principal factors that have been identified in the theoretical literature as ameliorating English processor resumptives. These are listed below with representative examples. In each case, the first example is meant to be better than the second. A variety of grammaticality judgements are found for processor resumptive examples in the literature, but these have been corroborated by experimental work only to a limited degree (McDaniel and Cowart, 1999; Alexopoulou and Keller, 2002, 2007; Swets and Ferreira, 2003; Ferreira and Swets, 2005; Heestand et al., 2011). In order not to prejudice judgements by providing the absolute judgements found in much of the theoretical literature on processor resumptives, I use a relational notation for the grammaticality of the paired examples: the first example is prefixed with ‘>’ (‘better’) and the second example with ‘<’ (‘worse’).

(32) **Distance**
(e.g., Erteschik-Shir, 1992)
a. > This is the girl that Peter said that John thinks that yesterday his mother had given some cakes to her.
b. < This is the girl that John likes her.
(Erteschik-Shir, 1992: 89, (4), (1))

(33) **Islands**
(e.g., Ross, 1967; Sells, 1984)
a. *Weak island*
i. > I’d like to meet the linguist that Mary couldn’t remember if she had seen him before.
ii. < I’d like to meet the linguist that Mary couldn’t remember if she had seen __ before. (Sells, 1984: 11, (9a))
b. *Strong island*
i. > I’d like to meet the linguist that Peter knows a psychologist that works with her.
ii. < I’d like to meet the linguist that Peter knows a psychologist that works with __ .

(34) **Avoidance of ‘COMP-trace’**
(e.g., Ross, 1967; Kroch, 1981; Sells, 1984; Swets and Ferreira, 2003)
a. > This is a donkey that I wonder where it lives.
b. < This is a donkey that I wonder where __ lives.

For convenience I will refer to these respectively as ‘complexity resumptives’,[4] ‘island resumptives’, and ‘COMP resumptives’. This does not imply that they will be handled heterogeneously by the theory. They are all treated as processor resumptives and any differences between them fall out of independently motivated aspects of the grammar or the processing model. Thus, these are purely descriptive labels. There is a connection between islands and ‘COMP-trace’ violations in which COMP is a *wh*-phrase, for example. However, I take the COMP resumptives to involve not just an island violation but also a violation of whatever additional grammatical constraints govern COMP-trace. Erteschik-Shir (1992: 90) has also

[4] Erteschik-Shir (1992) calls these “distance-resumptives”, but the notion of distance does not really capture all the relevant cases.

observed that there is an interaction between complexity and avoidance of islands and COMP-trace violations, to the effect that island/COMP-trace repair is improved if there is greater distance between the resumptive pronoun and its antecedent, where distance is one measure of complexity.

11.3.1 *Island Resumptives and COMP Resumptives*

Let us first look at the second and third classes. What these classes have in common is that the corresponding sentence with a gap violates some grammatical constraint or an independent processing constraint. The assumptions of the processing theory that are relevant here are the following:

1. Parsing is incremental.
2. Incremental parsing constructs locally well-formed structures.
3. Incremental parsing is incrementally interpreted.

Incremental interpretation will in particular be the key to explaining the properties of island resumptives.

Turning to a specific example, let us consider first a simplified version of a weak island example:

(35) I met the linguist that Kate forgot if Thora had seen him.

An unbounded dependency is initiated by the grammar when relative clause construction begins with the word *that*. This unbounded dependency is described in terms of an outside-in functional uncertainty. For the sake of simplicity, I assume that an island is marked with a feature UD, mnemonic for unbounded dependency, that has the value −. The functional uncertainty equation would have the off-path equation $(\rightarrow \text{UD}) \neq -$ on the grammatical function COMP. This will mean that the unbounded dependency cannot be functionally equated to a grammatical function inside a COMP that contains the feature UD with value −.

Assuming that the complementizer *if* contributes $(\uparrow \text{UD}) = -$, as soon as the parser encounters the complementizer it has reached a weak island. At this point the functional uncertainty associated with the unbounded dependency cannot be satisfied and there is no way to integrate the filler. The only way for local well-formedness to be satisfied is if all local arguments are occupied by lexical material. This in fact turns out to be the case, since the embedded COMP corresponds to *if Thora had seen him*. The local f-structure for the COMP is shown here:

(36)

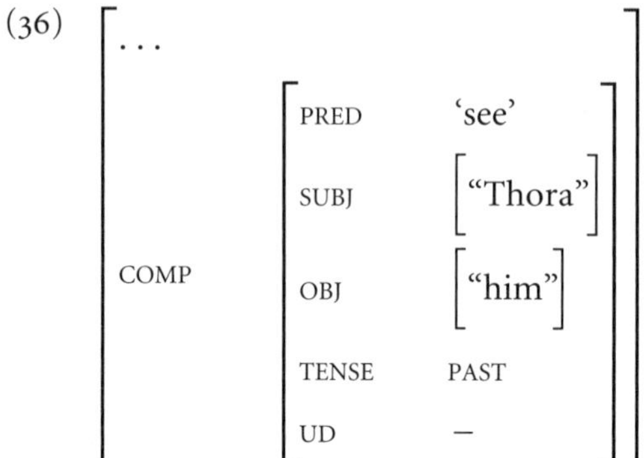

The overall parsing situation is shown here:

(37)

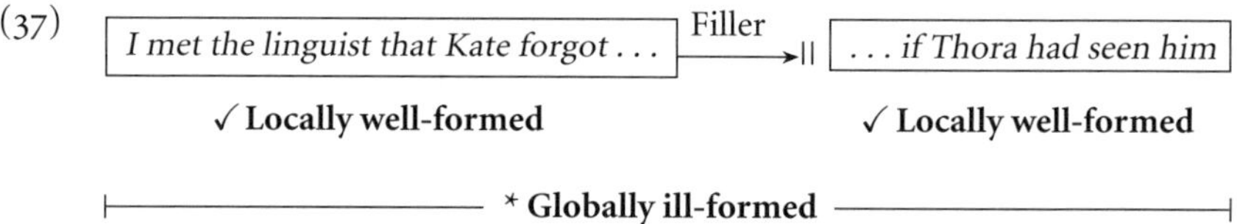

The sentence is syntactically ill-formed, since the filler cannot be integrated due to the weak island. However, the structures that have been incrementally constructed are locally well-formed. The structure containing the island is locally well-formed because of the presence of the processor resumptive, which fills the gap with lexical material. The same observations apply to island resumptives in strong islands and COMP resumptives.

Incremental parsing is accompanied by incremental interpretation in this model. Parsing has now accumulated the following resources, which have been lexically contributed by the words that have been encountered:

(38)

1.	$speaker : i$	Lex. **I**
2.	$\lambda x \lambda y.meet(x, y) : i \multimap l \multimap m$	Lex. **met**
3.	$\lambda P.\iota y[P(y)] : (v \multimap r) \multimap l$	Lex. **the**
4.	$ling : v \multimap r$	Lex. **linguist**
5.	$kate : k$	Lex. **Kate**
6.	$\lambda x \lambda p.forget(x, p) : k \multimap s \multimap f$	Lex. **forgot**
7.	$thora : t$	Lex. **Thora**
8.	$\lambda x \lambda y.see(x, y) : t \multimap p \multimap s$	Lex. **seen**
9.	$\lambda z.z \times z : l \multimap (l \otimes p)$	Lex. **him**

I have left out the relative clause resource purposefully, because the relative clause has not been integrated syntactically and therefore cannot be properly interpreted. The relevance of this will be discussed shortly. The determiner *the* has been assigned its *iota* meaning rather than its generalized quantifier meaning (Partee, 1986), so that *the linguist* will be a type *e* individual. The significance of this will also be discussed shortly. Lastly, I have left out a meaning for the complementizer *if*, purely for simplicity.

Incremental interpretation on these premises can accomplish a great deal, but it will not yield a well-formed Glue derivation ending in an atomic linear logic term with associated sentential semantics. Figure 11.5 illustrates the interpretation that is computed. The result of incremental interpretation is a multiplicative conjunction of two type *t* resources:

(39) $meet(speaker, \iota y[linguist(y)]) \times forget(kate, see(thora, \iota y[linguist(y)])) : m \otimes f$

The multiplicative conjunction corresponds to a product pair in the meaning language, which is, importantly, a *pair* of meanings corresponding to a conjunction of type *t* resources, not a conjunction of meanings corresponding to a single *t* resource. The function contributed by the pronoun is a type $\langle e, e \times e \rangle$ function. This means that the same type *e* argument is simultaneously added to both parts of the product pair. There is no way to have different type *e* arguments in each member of the pair.

The proof in Figure 11.5 does not meet the criterion for a successful Glue derivation of sentential meaning in two respects. First, the result is a type $\langle t \times t \rangle$ multiplicative conjunction of linear logic atoms, not a type *t* atom. The result is therefore not an appropriate semantics for sentential meaning, although a $\langle t \times t \rangle$ atom could potentially correspond to the semantics for a sub-sentential constituent. Second, and more importantly, the proof is not a well-formed Glue derivation because the proof is not a well-formed linear logic proof. In order to arrive at the proof in Figure 11.5, the premise corresponding to the unbounded dependency (the relative clause premise) was set aside. But this means that not all resources have been consumed in constructing the derivation.

Despite not being a well-formed derivation and not being a valid meaning for a sentence, the proof is crucially *informative*. The first member of the pair in the result states that the speaker met the linguist. The second member, leaving tense, aspect, and mood aside, states that Kate forgot if Thora had seen the (same) linguist. Although this is not a conjunction, it contains some of the essential information that successful construction of the restrictive relative clause would create, which is shown here:[5]

[5] It is tempting to say that (39) and (40) have similar truth conditions, but this would be an error, since (39) does not have truth conditions.

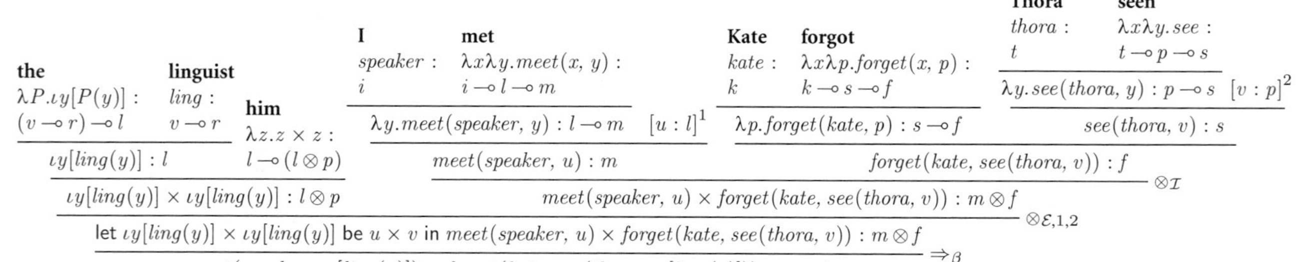

FIGURE 11.5. Partial interpretation of a processor resumptive example (lower type antecedent).

(40) $meet(speaker, \iota y[linguist(y) \wedge forget(kate, see(thora, y))]) : m$

The essential difference between (39) and (40) is that the former does not restrict the reference of the linguist.

The example above serves as a particularly simple illustration of incremental interpretation, because analysing *the linguist* in terms of the iota operator, ι, gives a reasonable semantics in the static framework. However, we might want to assume a dynamic framework, in order to, for example, also adopt a type *e* denotation for indefinites (Kamp, 1981; Heim, 1982). Dynamic Glue Semantics is very briefly discussed in chapter 4. However, I will not, at this point, move to a dynamic framework, because it would add complexity that is not really necessary, since processor resumptives are clause-bounded, like true resumptives. However, I will help myself to a notion that is fundamental to dynamic frameworks; namely, that certain discourse referents are globally available (those corresponding to noun phrases for which the *lower* type-shift is well-defined, i.e. names, indefinites, and definites; Partee, 1986), while others are available only within the scope of their contributor.

Presupposing the availability of discourse referents in a limited dynamic framework, the incrementally constructed partial semantics for the island resumptive we have been looking at would get a representation like (41), where *s*, *y*, *k*, and *t* are discourse referents contributed by *I*, *the linguist*, *Kate*, and *Thora*, respectively.[6]

(41) $[\, s, y, k, t \mid meet(s, \iota y[linguist(y)]) \times forget(k, see(t, \iota y[linguist(y)]))] : m \otimes f$

An indefinite example like (42) would get a partial interpretation as in (43):

(42) I met a linguist that Kate forgot if Thora had seen <u>him</u>.

(43) $[\, s, y, k, t \mid meet(s, linguist(y)) \times forget(k, see(t, linguist(y)))] : m \otimes f$

In sum, a sentence containing a processor resumptive is both syntactically and semantically ill-formed. However, definite and indefinite antecedents of processor resumptives lead to incremental construction of an informative partial interpretation that contains much of the essential content that a completely successful, compositional interpretation would contain, but that is nevertheless distinct from a full interpretation that properly integrates the restrictive relative clause.

This provides the basis for an explanation of Sells's (1984: 11–12) observation that processor resumptives, which he calls 'intrusive pronouns', do not allow

[6] I retain ι to mark the definite.

$$\dfrac{k \qquad \dfrac{\dfrac{\forall X.[(g \multimap X) \multimap X\,] \qquad \dfrac{\dfrac{\dfrac{\dfrac{[k]^1 \quad k \multimap l \multimap t}{l \multimap t} \qquad \dfrac{[h]^2 \quad \dfrac{j \quad j \multimap h \multimap l}{h \multimap l}}{l}}{t} \qquad \dfrac{[k]^3 \quad k \multimap (k \otimes h)}{k \otimes h}}{t}\otimes\mathcal{E},1,2 \qquad t \multimap g \multimap s}{g \multimap s}}{s}}{k \multimap s}\multimap\mathcal{I},3}{s}$$

FIGURE 11.6. Proof structure for a coreferential pronominal interpretation, *Every girl said Kate$_i$ thinks John likes her$_i$.*

bound variable readings. The following version of the weak island example, with *the linguist* replaced by *every linguist*, indeed seems markedly worse and Sells (1984: 12, (9b)) assigns the sentence a star:[7]

(44) *I met every linguist that Kate forgot if Thora had seen him.

The theory of anaphora assumed here is variable-free, so it is important to establish what the equivalent of a bound-variable reading is on this theory.

In order to receive a bound reading, a pronoun must make an assumption on its antecedent that is discharged within the scope of a scope-taking element. To be discharged within the scope of a scope-taking element means to be discharged in a contiguous sub-proof that extends from the assumption to the point at which the scope dependency is discharged (see the discussion of 'audit trails' by Crouch and van Genabith, 1999: 160ff.). This is illustrated by the following sentence, which is ambiguous between a bound reading, where *her* gets its interpretation from *every girl*, and a coreferential reading, where *her* takes the name *Kate* as its antecedent:

(45) Every girl said Kate thinks John likes her.

The two readings are shown in Figure 11.6, where the antecedent is *Kate*, and in Figure 11.7, where the antecedent is *every girl*. The proof in Figure 11.6 is somewhat more indirect than it needs to be, for expository purposes. In the bound reading in Figure 11.7, the assumption on the antecedent is discharged within the scope of *every girl*, but in Figure 11.6 it is not. The more direct proof that can be constructed for Figure 11.6 would make no assumption on *k* at all, allowing the pronoun to take the name directly as its antecedent.

[7] The actual sentence from Sells (1984) is: *I'd like to meet every linguist that Mary couldn't remember if she had seen him before.*

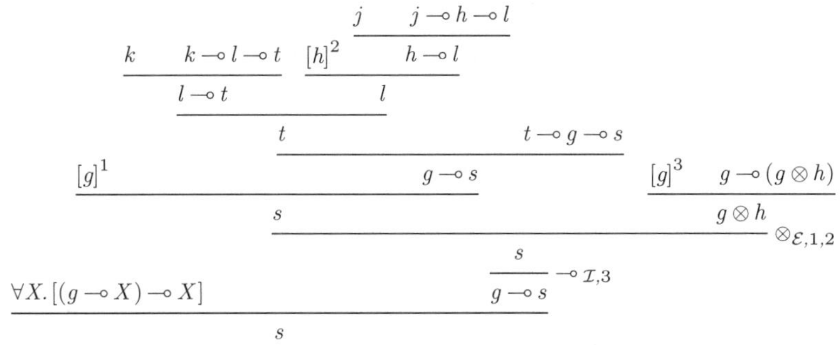

$$j \quad j \multimap h \multimap l$$
$$k \quad k \multimap l \multimap t \quad [h]^2 \quad h \multimap l$$
$$l \multimap t \quad l$$
$$t \quad t \multimap g \multimap s$$
$$[g]^1 \quad g \multimap s \quad [g]^3 \quad g \multimap (g \otimes h)$$
$$s \quad g \otimes h$$
$$\otimes_{\mathcal{E},1,2}$$
$$s$$
$$\forall X.[(g \multimap X) \multimap X] \quad g \multimap s \ \multimap_{\mathcal{I},3}$$
$$s$$

FIGURE 11.7. Proof structure for a bound pronominal interpretation, *Every girl$_i$ said Kate thinks John likes her$_i$*.

Now let us return to (44). The noun phrase *every linguist*, unlike *the linguist*, cannot take a type *e* meaning, because *every linguist* cannot undergo the *lower* type-shift operation to a type *e* meaning (Partee, 1986). Therefore the premise contributed by *every linguist* must be of the generalized quantifier type $\langle\langle e, t\rangle, t, \rangle$ as in (46), and cannot have the type *e* that *the linguist* received above.

(46) $\lambda S.every(linguist, S) : \forall X.[(l \multimap X) \multimap X]$

This means that *every linguist* must be a scope-taking element and that a pronoun that takes it as an antecedent must be a bound variable.

Figure 11.8 is a partial proof for example (44), without the addition of the resource for *every linguist*. The argument *l* of the pronominal resource must be introduced by assumption now, because there is no *l* that corresponds to a type *e* individual and the pronoun must therefore receive a bound interpretation. The result of incremental interpretation at this stage is:

(47) $meet(speaker, x) \times forget(kate, see(thora, x)) : m \otimes f$

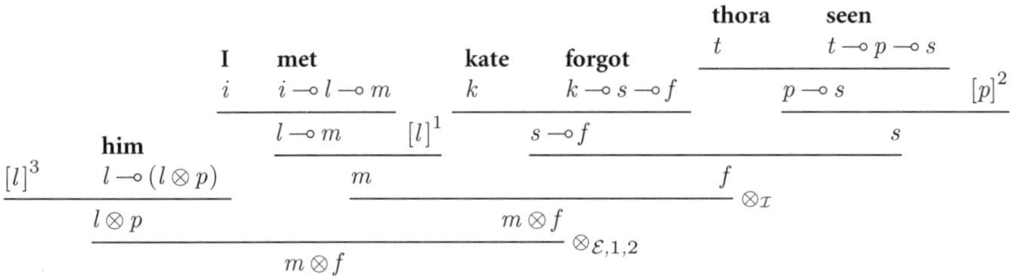

thora t **seen** $t \multimap p \multimap s$

I i **met** $i \multimap l \multimap m$ **kate** k **forgot** $k \multimap s \multimap f$ $p \multimap s$ $[p]^2$

$l \multimap m$ $[l]^1$ $s \multimap f$ s

$[l]^3$ **him** $l \multimap (l \otimes p)$ m f $\otimes_{\mathcal{I}}$

$l \otimes p$ $m \otimes f$ $\otimes_{\mathcal{E},1,2}$

$m \otimes f$

FIGURE 11.8. Partial interpretation of a processor resumptive example (higher type antecedent).

The first member of the product pair states that the speaker met something that the variable x picks out. The second member of the pair states that Kate forgot if Thora had seen something that a different variable x picks out. Also, since the theory is variable-free, there is no assignment function that could interpret free variables (whatever that would mean in this case).

Furthermore, it is impossible to add *every linguist* to the incremental interpretation. The linear logic term for the quantified noun phrase is $\forall X.[(l \multimap X) \multimap X]$, which requires a dependency of the form $l \multimap X$. However, there is no such dependency available. Discharging the assumption on l results in the following:

(48) $\lambda x.meet(s, x) \times forget(kate, see(thora, x)) : l \multimap (m \otimes f)$

There is no single type t linear logic atom that can instantiate X in the term for *every linguist*. Therefore, incremental interpretation ends up with an uninformative conjunction and the conjunction does not say anything about every linguist. In sum, the impossibility of a bound reading for a processor resumptive/intrusive pronoun is a reflection of the fact that, if it is a bound variable, incremental interpretation cannot assign an informative meaning to the relative clause.

If a processor resumptive cannot receive a bound interpretation, then the interpretation must be some 'other interpretation' (Sells, 1984: 9ff.). Chao and Sells (1983) argue that the other interpretation in question, for intrusive pronouns with indefinite or definite relative heads as antecedents, which I have argued leads to informative partial interpretation, is the E-type interpretation defended by Evans (1980). Sells (1984: 454) abandons this approach for two reasons. The first is that the work of Heim (1982) and Kamp (1981) in dynamic semantics undermined Chao and Sells's claim that E-type pronouns involve a special mechanism for pronominal interpretation, which was crucial to their approach, because a single dynamic method for interpreting pronouns subsumed E-type interpretations. The second reason was that Sells (1984) reads Heim (1982: 25–33) as having shown that the then standard approach to E-type interpretation makes certain false predictions.

Heim (1982) in fact only claims that the E-type account has trouble with indefinite antecedents. Also, she does not claim that the E-type account makes false predictions, but rather something more subtle: she shows that the E-type account fails to make a certain valid prediction and that the assumptions necessary to make the prediction on an E-type account are not obviously consistent with other predictions of the account. In her own words:

> Recall that I have attributed to Evans two assumptions which are independent of each other: (a) the assumption that certain anaphoric pronouns mean the same thing as

> certain definite descriptions, and (b) the assumption that definite descriptions are to be analyzed in a certain way, which involves predicting uniqueness-implications for singular definite descriptions. As it turns out upon closer investigation of the facts, it is (b) and not (a) that we should question ... Heim (1982: 31–32)

Heim argues that the task of properly accounting for definite descriptions in E-type pronominal reference to indefinites boils down to the task of accounting for pronouns with indefinite antecedents. However, this is somewhat irrelevant to the present approach, which does not rest on the assumption of any special mechanism for E-type interpretation and could equally countenance various alternatives for E-type interpretation (Heim, 1990; Elbourne, 2005).

The overall picture is the following. Incremental processing of processor resumptives, gives rise to incremental interpretation. The result of incremental interpretation is only partial, since the processor resumptive is not properly grammatically licensed and integrated. However, if the antecedent of the processor resumptive is a definite or indefinite, the partial interpretation is nevertheless informative and contains much of the essential information of an equivalent fully interpreted restrictive relative clause. In contrast, if the antecedent of the processor resumptive is a quantified noun phrase, the partial interpretation is not informative, since a bound variable reading is impossible. One candidate for the interpretation of the processor resumptive in the informative partial interpretations is an E-type interpretation.

We have thus far only considered quantificational antecedents to processor resumptives in relative clauses, but the observation that bound variable interpretations of processor resumptives lead to uninformative partial interpretations applies to scope-taking elements in general, and therefore also applies to *wh*-questions. Chao and Sells (1983) present two kinds of data that indicates that processor resumptives in questions are not bound variables. The first kind concerns the inability to provide list answers to English resumptive *wh*-questions. List answers are perfectly well-formed for English *wh*-questions in which the *wh*-dependency terminates in a gap rather than a resumptive. The resumptive case is shown here:

(49) Q: Who did you say you'd forgotten whether <u>she</u> had paid her fees?
A: Abby
#A: Abby, Buffy, and Connie (Sells, 1984: 475, ~(169))

The E-type interpretation for *she* must be something like *the female person* and the question is querying the identity of this person. The impossibility of answering with a list then follows from the fact that *Abby, Buffy, and Connie* is not a female person, but rather an aggregate of such persons.

The second kind of data that Chao and Sells (1983) consider concerns functional questions (Engdahl, 1986). They note that English resumptive *wh*-questions cannot be understood as functional questions and that a functional answer is therefore impossible:

(50) Q: Which woman does no Englishman even wonder if she will make a good wife?
A: Margaret Thatcher.
#A: The one his mother likes best.
(Sells, 1984: 477, ~(173))

A standard analysis of functional questions is that the gap is a free variable of type $\langle e, e \rangle$, a function from individuals to individuals, rather than of the type *e* of an individual (Engdahl, 1986).[8] In contrast, the processor resumptive is assigned an E-type interpretation. The E-type pronoun is therefore just the wrong sort of thing and does not allow a functional reading of the question. The only interpretation that the definite description in the answer can get is a bizarre '(putatively) lucky woman/conspiracy of mothers' reading where all the English mothers have decided on a single woman as being the best.

11.3.1.1 *Summary* Island resumptives and COMP resumptives are treated as ungrammatical on this theory, but they can allow informative partial interpretations, if the antecedent is a definite or indefinite and the pronoun can receive an E-type interpretation. This result follows from the usual grammatical analysis of the relevant constructions and the assumption that incremental parsing is incrementally interpreted, although the actual incrementality of the interpretation has not played a role here per se.

11.3.2 *Complexity Resumptives*

The key difference between complexity resumptives and island and COMP resumptives is that, in the case of complexity resumptives, the equivalent sentence with a gap instead of the processor resumptive is grammatically well-formed. Erteschik-Shir (1992: 89, (1–4)) offers the following examples (the judgements are hers):

(51) This is the girl that John likes __ /* her.

(52) This is the girl that Peter said that John likes __ /?? her.

(53) This is the girl that Peter said that John thinks that Bob likes __ /? her.

(54) This is the girl that Peter said that John thinks that yesterday his mother had given some cakes to ? __ /her.

[8] See Jacobson (1999: 149ff.) for a variable-free and trace-free alternative to the standard analysis.

These examples illustrate that (1) as the distance between the filler and the gap site increases, a gap becomes less acceptable and (2) as the distance between the filler and the processor resumptive increases, the resumptive becomes more acceptable. The cut-off point for both is variable across speakers. Resumptive sentences like the first example are rejected quite strongly, though, and the experimental literature, which is considered below, confirms this.

The features of the parsing model that are relevant to explaining complexity resumptives are the following:

1. Parsing of unbounded dependencies is filler-driven.
   (Frazier, 1987; Frazier and Flores d'Arcais, 1989)
2. Parsing is limited by short-term memory.
   (Kimball, 1973; Dickey, 1996; Lewis, 1996; Gibson, 1998)
3. Unsuccessful parsing results in reanalysis.

Point 1 bears a little elaboration. I assume something like the Active Filler Strategy (AFS; Frazier, 1987; Frazier and Flores d'Arcais, 1989), but the model need not be exactly the AFS model. Rather, there are two particular properties of the AFS that are relevant here. The first is that the search for a gap begins when the filler is encountered rather than when a 'missing argument' (i.e., gap or putative trace) is encountered.[9] This is in concord with the underlying LFG theory, since a filler is described in terms of an outside-in functional uncertainty that is initiated when the filler is encountered.

The second component of the AFS is that the parser attempts to stick the filler in as soon as possible. Here is the formulation of the AFS by Frazier and Flores d'Arcais (1989: 332, (3)):[10]

(55) **Active Filler Strategy**
Assign an identified filler as soon as possible; i.e. rank the option of a gap above the option of a lexical noun phrase within the domain of an identified filler.

Favouring a gap over lexical material in parsing will be particularly important.

[9] The AFS does not require traces, but it is also consistent with a theory of grammar that has traces. With respect to such theories, the AFS just states that the trace itself is not what drives parsing of a filler-gap unbounded dependency. Pickering and Barry (1991) make the even stronger argument that traces are not psychologically real. Further discussion is offered by Gibson and Hickok (1993) and Pickering (1993).

[10] Gibson (1998: 54ff.) argues that the AFS effects can be derived from his Syntactic Prediction Locality Theory (SPLT).

The AFS, together with the fact that English does not have true resumptives, is sufficient to explain the striking ungrammaticality of short-distance resumptives:[11]

(56) * This is the girl that John likes her.

According to the AFS, a search for a gap is initiated as soon as the clause begins. The first potential gap site is the subject of the relative clause. This gap site is occupied by lexical material (*John*) and the parser must therefore engage in reanalysis.[12] Reanalysis results in continued search for a gap. The second gap site is the object of *like*. The parser integrates the active filler here. At this point the sentence is syntactically complete and incremental interpretation can construct a full interpretation for the sentence. Then the pronoun *her* is encountered and the parser cannot do anything with this word. No causal link should be inferred between the grammaticality of *This is the girl that John likes* and the ungrammaticality of *This is the girl that John likes her*. The sentence with the resumptive is not ungrammatical on this theory *because* the version with the gap is grammatical. It is just a matter of the parsing system and there is no transderivationality required to state that the resumptive sentence is out.

The assumption that the parser is limited by short-term memory becomes relevant for longer sentences, where resumptives improve:

(57) This is the girl that Peter said that John thinks that yesterday his mother had given some cakes to her.

This assumption is not a controversial one and has previously formed the basis of a parsing model of resumptive pronouns by Dickey (1996), who discusses the issue of memory limitations in parsing in some detail. Dickey's model is principally meant to address the amelioration effect of a resumptive versus a gap and it does not address the issue of reanalysis or the issue of general ill-formedness of processor resumptives in English, which has been established experimentally in the meantime (McDaniel and Cowart, 1999; Alexopoulou and Keller, 2002, 2007; Swets and Ferreira, 2003; Ferreira and Swets, 2005; Heestand et al., 2011).

[11] As mentioned above, in the discussion of the similar attested Prince (1990) example (8), English speakers normally judge such sentences to be ungrammatical (McDaniel and Cowart, 1999; Alexopoulou and Keller, 2002, 2007; Swets and Ferreira, 2003; Ferreira and Swets, 2005; Heestand et al., 2011).

[12] A key piece of evidence in favour of filler-driven models is that subject relatives are processed faster than object relatives, since there is no need to revise the parser's first attempt (for discussion and references, see Gibson, 1998: 54ff.).

The proposal, specifically with respect to complexity resumptives, is the following:

1. A resumptive pronoun reactivates a filler that is no longer active (due to memory limitations).
2. This results in reanalysis of the local structure that the pronoun appears in.
3. If reanalysis succeeds in integrating the filler, the pronoun is removed by the parser.

On the model developed here, the perceived deterioration of a gap as distance gets larger follows from incremental construction of locally well-formed structures. If a filler is no longer being posited, then the gap will be initially perceived as an illicitly missing argument.

The reanalysis that is posited here seems quite radical in that it actually removes the linguistic contribution of a word. Reanalysis typically concerns revising syntactic assumptions based on ambiguity (Frazier and Clifton, 1996). However, the fact that the proposed parsing operation is destructive is not in itself radical, because reanalysis always entails the destruction of posited grammatical material and its replacement with new material (otherwise it would just be more analysis, not *re*analysis). Despite its unconventional nature, the current proposal really just is the usual sort of remove-and-replace reanalysis. Furthermore, there seems to be no alternative prospect to removal of the pronoun. Any syntactic formulation to the effect that the pronoun is underlyingly a gap, etc., would have to explain why the short examples are ill-formed. It might be tempting to attempt a transderivational (e.g., Last Resort) explanation to the effect that the short examples with a pronoun are ill-formed because a short example with a gap is well-formed, but the long examples with a gap are also well-formed. A syntactic account would therefore have to make reference to distance or node counts, or some such thing. As Erteschik-Shir (1992: 90) points out, "distance is not a syntactically well-defined notion". Syntactic operations are either unbounded or they are local.

The question arises of why the pronoun is permitted in the first place. The answer is the same as in the other cases of processor resumptives. The parser is trying to build locally well-formed structures and a gap does not meet this requirement. In the case of island resumptives and COMP resumptives, this was due to the impossibility of integrating the filler. In the case of complexity resumptives, it is due to the fact that, when the resumptive is encountered, there is no filler to integrate, it having dropped out of memory. The difference between the present case and the other two is that, after reanalysis, there is no problem in integrating the filler, since there is no grammatical constraint against integration in the position of the complexity resumptive. The various kinds of processor resumptive are not entirely independent, though. For example, an island resumptive that is also sufficiently far from, or in a sufficiently complex embedding relation to, its filler counts both as a complexity resumptive and as an island resumptive. In this case, though, reanalysis of the filler is not successful because it cannot be integrated in the island. Similarly, if the language in question does not have the relevant sort of constraint on extraction—i.e. the integration site is not an island in the language—then the processor resumptive in question is just a complexity resumptive and not an island resumptive. In this case, the sentence will be perceived as grammatical if the filler is no longer active; reactivation of the filler will result in successful reanalysis that removes the pronoun. The same comments apply to the interaction of complexity resumptives and COMP resumptives.

11.3.2.1 *Interim Summary* Complexity resumptives, island resumptives, and COMP resumptives share the property of allowing construction of locally well-formed structures. In the latter two cases, it is impossible to construct a locally well-formed structure otherwise, due to impossibility of integrating a filler. In the complexity resumptive case, the filler has become inactive due to memory limitations. The parser is therefore not positing a gap when the resumptive is encountered and the resumptive meets the parser's expectations, allowing construction of a locally well-formed structure. In finding its antecedent, the pronoun reactivates the filler. The reactivation leads to reanalysis with respect to the filler and the pronoun and attempted integration of the filler. Whether this integration is successful or not depends on the syntactic structure in which the pronoun occurs. If the filler can be successfully integrated in this structure, according to the grammatical constraints of the language in question, then the filler is integrated and reanalysis is completed by removing the pronoun. If the filler cannot be integrated in the structure according to the grammatical constraints of the language, then the filler is not integrated and the pronoun functions as it does in the case of island resumptives and COMP resumptives. The sentence is ill-formed and leads to only partial interpretation.

The question arises of multiple potential antecedents for the pronoun, as in the following example:

(58) This is the girl that Peter said that Julia thinks that yesterday his brother had given some cakes to <u>her</u>.

The choice of antecedents is between *the girl* and *Julia*. If the pronoun takes *the girl* as its antecedent, upon reanalysis of the pronoun as a gap, a full interpretation is possible. If the pronoun takes *Julia* as its antecedent, then full interpretation is not possible. The sentence will result in an uninformative partial interpretation. Either the hearer will perceive it as ungrammatical or else another attempt at reanalysis will be made. The question boils down to the more general one of how a hearer recovers from misidentifying a pronominal antecedent.

11.3.2.2 *Complexity resumptives in Swedish* Chapter 9 concerned true (grammatically licensed) resumptives in Swedish, which are subjects that occur immediately following material in the left periphery of CP. Swedish resumptives have been observed in some other environments, but Engdahl (1982) argues that these all arise due to processing factors. These other environments can be characterized as follows:

1. Deep embedding (at least two clauses)

(59) I går såg jag [en film]$_i$ [$_{CP}$ som jag undrar om någon
Yesterday saw I a film that I wonder if anyone
minns [$_{CP}$ vem som regisserat _$_i$ / <u>den$_i$</u>]].
remembers who that directed _ / it.
'Yesterday I saw a film that I wonder if anyone knows who directed (it).' (Engdahl, 1982: 154, ~(12))

2. Sentential subjects

(60) [Vilken skådespelare]$_i$ var det att publiken inte kände igen
which actor was it that audience.DEF not recognize
_$_i$ / <u>honom$_i$</u> ganska konstigt?
_ / him rather strange
'Which actor was the fact that the audience did not recognize (him) rather strange?' (Engdahl, 1982: 165, (58))

3. Crossing dependencies

(61) [Den här presenten]$_i$ kan du säkert aldrig komma på vem$_j$ jag fick
this here present.DEF can you surely never come on who I got
<u>den$_i$</u> / * _$_i$ av _$_j$.
it / _ from _
'This present you'll never guess who I got (it) from.'
(Maling and Zaenen, 1982: 236, ~(13a))

All of these cases can be analysed as complexity resumptives in the present processing model.

The first case involves distance and is the sort of case that we have already encountered. Distance is not a well-defined syntactic notion: the fact that these resumptives become acceptable as they get further from their binders is itself an indication that they are governed by processing factors, not by grammatical factors. Swedish patterns like English with respect to complexity resumptives and distance. Engdahl (1982: 152–153) notes that while sentences like (59) are accepted by native speakers, short examples like the following are not:

(62) *Nobelpriset i medicin ska vi snart få reda på vem som fått det.
the.Nobel prize in medicine shall we soon find out who that got it
'The Nobel prize in medicine, we will soon find out who got (it).'
(Engdahl, 1982: 152, ~(4))

(63) *I går såg jag en film som jag redan glömt vem som regisserat den.
Yesteday saw I a film that I already forgot who that directed it
'Yesterday I saw a film that I already forget who directed (it).'
(Engdahl, 1982: 152, (5))

(64) *Vilken bok kunde ingen minnas vem som skrivit den?
Which book could nobody remember who that wrote it?
'Which book could nobody remember who wrote it?'
(Engdahl, 1982: 152, (6))

The corresponding gap examples are grammatical. Notice that this is extraction from an embedded question, which is ungrammatical in English, but grammatical in Swedish. Engdahl (1982: 154) notes that:

> Although one might occasionally hear a resumptive pronoun instead of a gap in a sentence with only two levels of embedding, as in [(62)–(64)], the general consensus among speakers of Swedish is that a gap is preferable.

This mirrors what Erteschik-Shir (1992) notes about English complexity resumptives: they start improving at around the second level of embedding and become quite good at the third. Lewis (1996) argues that two or three levels of embedding seems to be the significant cut-off point for a variety of parsing phenomena.

Resumptives in sentential subjects can also be profitably analysed as complexity resumptives, although the examples in question first have to be shown to be complex in the relevant sense. Engdahl (1982) observes that there is a strong tendency in Swedish to extrapose sentential subjects. She notes that (65) is "by far more natural" (Engdahl, 1982: 165) than (66):

(65) Det var konstigt att publiken inte kände igen Evert Taube.
it was strange that the.audience not recognize Evert Taube
'It was strange that the audience did not recognize Evert Taube.'
(Engdahl, 1982: 165, (57c))

(66) Det att publiken inte kände igen Evert Taube var konstigt.
it that the.audience not recognize Evert Taube was strange
'That the audience did not recognize Evert Taube was strange.'
(Engdahl, 1982: 165, (57b))

Engdahl goes on to note that extractions out of sentential subjects, as in (67), are quite unnatural, and that speakers greatly prefer (68) and even spontaneously produce such questions when asked about sentential subject extraction.

(67) Vilken skådespelare var det att publiken inte kände igen __
which actor was it that the.audience not recognize __
ganska konstigt?
rather strange
'Which actor was that the audience did not recognize rather strange?'
(Engdahl, 1982: 165, (58))

(68) Vilken skådespelare var det ganska konstigt att publiken inte
which actor was it rather strange that the.audience not
kände igen __ ?
recognize __
'Which actor was it rather strange that the audience did not recognize?'
(Engdahl, 1982: 165, (59))

Nevertheless, speakers do accept extraction from a non-extraposed sentential subject, as in (67), even if they would prefer to extrapose the sentential subject. On the reasonable assumption that sentential subject extraction out of a non-extraposed sentential subject counts as complex in the relevant sense, both the reticence of speakers in accepting gaps in this environment and the possibility of a complexity resumptive are explained. The assumption regarding the complexity of a gap in a non-extraposed sentential subject needs to be independently confirmed, but the general complexity of non-extraposed sentential subjects has been established in the psycholinguistic literature (Frazier 1985: 177, Gibson 1998: 53).

The last remaining environment is crossing dependencies (Engdahl, 1982; Maling and Zaenen, 1982). Engdahl (1982: 168) notes that although it had previously been claimed that syntactically interchangeable fillers must be interpreted in a nested fashion (the Nested Dependency Constraint; Fodor, 1978), this does not seem to be universally valid and the Scandinavian languages generally seem to allow non-nested readings, although in the case of multiple gaps nested readings are still preferred. The preference for nested readings is derivable from the Active Filler Strategy, if it is assumed that the most recent filler is the active filler. The difficulty of a crossing reading is then due to the necessity of reanalysis, since the filler that is integrated first is integrated in the wrong gap. In other words, the reading that is first available for (61) with multiple gaps is a strange reading in which the perceiver is being urged to guess who the speaker got from the present, rather than who the speaker got the present from. Engdahl (1982: 169–170) notes that if symmetric predicates are used, or if the gaps are of distinct kinds, then a resumptive is not necessary to get an intersecting reading. The following example is a case of gaps that are of distinct kinds:

(69) Sina föräldrar$_i$ är det lätt att glömma hur mycket$_j$ man är skyldig
SELF's parents is it easy too forget how much one owes
$\_\_{}_i$ $\_\_{}_j$
— —
'It is easy to forget how much one owes one's parents.'
(Engdahl, 1982: 169, (80))

In short, the crossing dependency case can also be explained as a complexity resumptive.

11.3.3 *Summary and Discussion*

Three kinds of processor resumptives have been proposed and investigated: island resumptives, COMP resumptives, and complexity resumptives. The parsing model offers explanations for all three phenomena. The basic outline of the model is repeated here:

1. Parsing is incremental.
2. Incremental parsing attempts to construct locally well-formed structures.
3. Global well-formedness applies only to the output of parsing.
4. Parsing is constrained by memory limitations based on complexity factors.
5. Parsing of unbounded dependencies is filler-driven.
6. The result of incremental parsing is incrementally interpreted.
7. Unsuccessful parsing results in reanalysis.

The components of the model are reasonable, from a psycholinguistic perspective, although their exact nature requires further theoretical and experimental investigation.

The remaining questions posed at the beginning of section 11.3 can now be answered.

> **Q.** Why do speakers of languages without grammatically licensed resumptives who produce processor resumptives reject sentences with processor resumptives as ill-formed?
> **A.** The sentences that speakers reject as ill-formed are those that involve island resumptives and complexity resumptives. They are rejected because they are underlyingly ungrammatical—i.e. they do not meet global well-formedness criteria—and receive only a partial interpretation.

COMP resumptives are the only case that have been experimentally demonstrated to be better than the corresponding gap sentence (McDaniel and Cowart, 1999). This is arguably because the gap incurs additional grammatical violations that the resumptive pronoun does not, since the relevant constraint ('COMP-trace'/ECP) by definition applies only to gaps.

The previous question is related to the following question:

> **Q.** Why do speakers prefer some sentences with processor resumptives to sentences where the resumptive is absent?
> **A.** The sentences that speakers prefer involve complexity resumptives in positions where gaps are licensed by the grammar. The resumptive pronoun reactivates the filler and the resumptive is reanalysed as a gap.

The sentences that speakers supposedly do not reject are those involving complexity resumptives. Erteschik-Shir (1992) discusses complexity resumptives having to do with distance and her judgements are that deeply embedded resumptives are well-formed. I also argued that the resumptive pronouns that do not fit the bill of true resumptives in Swedish are complexity resumptives. These resumptives are also perceived as grammatical. The theory expects this to be the case, because the structures underlying complexity resumptives, after reanalysis, are grammatical. This expectation has not been confirmed by experimental findings (see Alexopoulou and Keller, 2002, 2003, 2007), but it has not been disconfirmed either, since the relevant experiments did not test complexity resumptives that are embedded more than two clauses deep. Sentences containing complexity resumptives that are not particularly deeply embedded are not expected to be well-formed, if the filler is still active. However, Philip Hofmeister (p.c.) has informed me of unpublished results (Hofmeister and Norcliffe, in progress) for experiments that seem to show greater acceptability for resumptives than gaps in stimuli with a greater degree of complexity than those of Alexopoulou and Keller. These results would be in line with the theory of complexity resumptives that has been presented here.

The next question has to do with interpretation:

> **Q.** How do speakers interpret processor resumptives?
> **A.** Speakers interpret processor resumptives incrementally, using the normal grammar. Island resumptives and COMP resumptives are underlyingly ungrammatical and permit only partial interpretations. Complexity resumptives may be underlyingly grammatical, in which case they permit full interpretations, upon reanalysis.

If the antecedent of an island resumptive or COMP resumptive is a type *e* nominal, such as a definite or indefinite, the partial interpretation is informative. If the antecedent is a type $\langle\langle e, t\rangle, t\rangle$ antecedent, such as a quantifier or *wh*-operator, the partial interpretation is not informative. Informative interpretations are more acceptable than uninformative interpretations.

The remaining question has two parts:

> If a language has true resumptives, how does this aspect of its grammar affect processor resumptives? In particular:
>
> (a) **Q.** Can a language have both kinds of resumptives and, if so, under what conditions?
> **A.** Swedish has both true resumptives and processor resumptives. The conditions that govern its processor resumptives are just the same conditions that govern those in English. Swedish complexity resumptives yield to the general explanation of complexity resumptives. Island resumptives do not really arise, due to the general lack of islands in the language. There are no COMP resumptives, because in that environment Swedish has true resumptives.
>
> (b) **Q.** Will processor resumptives take on different characteristics in a language that also has true resumptives?
> **A.** Given the answer to part (a) of this question, the answer to this part of the question is negative at this stage of our understanding.

As for the general question of how true resumptives might affect processor resumptives, the language that offers the most promise of the ones discussed in this work would seem to be Irish, since it has the most comprehensive and robust grammatically licensed resumptive system. However, it is hard to see how Irish could have processor resumptives at all. Island resumptives and COMP resumptives are irrelevant, because the language has true resumptives in these environments. As for complexity resumptives, given the analysis of

Irish filler-gap dependencies in which the filler is equated between successively embedded complements, one wonders how complexity resumptives could possibly arise. The filler is integrated into each new clause, so it is hard to see how it could become inactive.

One possibility presents itself, though. It may be that the analysis presented in chapter 7 and the analysis of McCloskey (2002) is wrong in treating the Pattern 2 mixed chains as a grammatical phenomenon. Recall that this pattern has the form *aL* ... *aN* ... *Rpro*. The dependency is marked at the top by the filler-gap complementizer *aL* and at the bottom by the binder-resumptive complementizer *aN*. It may be that the pronoun at the bottom is actually a processor resumptives. However, both grammatical analyses derive this pattern from general properties of the language. There is no real reason to suppose that the resumptive pronoun in question is a processor resumptive and there is quite an array of Irish data that would seem to stand in the way of any such claim.

11.4 Conclusion

I have presented a processing model that explains several facets of the distribution of non-grammatically licensed resumptive pronouns, which I have called processor resumptives. The model is based on the following assumptions:

1. Production and parsing are incremental.
2. Incremental production and parsing attempt to construct locally well-formed structures.
3. Global well-formedness applies only to the output of production and parsing.
4. Production and parsing are constrained by memory limitations based on complexity factors.

These are all assumptions that are supported by the psycholinguistic literature, although the model itself has not yet been tested experimentally.

The processing model was further articulated as models of production and parsing. The production model explained how processor resumptives are produced, despite being rejected as ungrammatical by native speakers. The model was based on the notion of fragments in LFG, which allow a definition of locally well-formed structures. I argued that, in producing locally well-formed structures that are consistent with the production plan, speakers can insert pronouns and other nominals in positions where a filler ought to be integrated. This leads to local well-formedness, even though the overall result is global ill-formedness. However, since production is incremental, such productions can nevertheless be uttered. This accounted for examples like the following attested example from Prince (1990), in which a nominal occurs where a filler could be successfully integrated:

(70) You get a rack that the bike will sit on it.

Another option for the formation of locally well-formed structure is to integrate the filler, resulting in the fully locally and globally well-formed equivalent of this example without the resumptive. Psycholinguistic results have confirmed intuitions that examples such as (70) are ungrammatical, despite being attested.

The situation for the production of processor resumptives in islands, as originally discussed by Kroch (1981), is similar. The key difference is that the island blocks integration of the filler. This means that the only choice for constructing a locally well-formed structure is to insert, in the gap position in the island, a pronoun or other nominal that is consistent with the production plan and local well-formedness. This results in sentences like the following:

(71) This is a donkey that I don't know where it lives.

(72) There was one prisoner that we didn't understand why the guy was even in jail.

Locally well-formed structures are possible in these cases, because the theory of islands in LFG identifies islands externally to the island structure through constraints on outside-in functional uncertainty (Asudeh, 2011*a*). Theories which identify islands internally would have difficulty even generating the required local structure.

The parsing model explains how processor resumptives are parsed despite their ungrammaticality. Three major subclasses of processor resumptives were identified: island resumptives, COMP resumptives, and complexity resumptives. Island resumptives and COMP resumptives are underlyingly ungrammatical according to the model. This is corroborated by experimental findings. However, parsing of the relevant sentences leads to a partial interpretation that can nevertheless be informative. Whether the partial interpretation is informative depends on properties of the resumptive's binder or antecedent. If the resumptive is bound by an operator, e.g. a quantifier or *wh*-phrase, the resulting partial interpretation is uninformative. In contrast, if the resumptive is bound by a type *e* binder, such as a definite or indefinite, the partial interpretation is informative. This explains patterns of data that have been noticed in the literature on intrusive pronouns. I argued in support of Chao and Sells (1983) that the only interpretation that a processor resumptive can have is an E-type interpretation, which is independently impossible for many quantifiers. The E-type interpretation of operator-bound processor resumptives explains the impossibility of giving list answers to resumptive *wh*-questions.

The memory limitations that are assumed for parsing are instrumental in the model's explanation of complexity resumptives. I assumed a filler-driven model of unbounded dependency parsing, such as the Active Filler Strategy, in which the integration of an unbounded dependency is determined by the filler rather than by the gap. Complexity resumptives occur when a pronoun is encountered after the active filler has dropped out of working memory. When the pronoun finds its antecedent, the filler-gap dependency is reanalysed and the pronoun is removed. Complexity resumptives are therefore reanalysed as gaps. Whether the reanalysis results in well-formedness depends on whether the underlying structure is well-formed. In the typical 'distance resumptive' cases discussed by Erteschik-Shir (1992), the underlying structure is grammatical. Lastly, the theory of complexity resumptives provides an explanation of the non-grammatically licensed Swedish resumptives that were set aside at the beginning of chapter 9.

12

Copy Raising

This chapter shows how the Resource Management Theory of Resumption can unify resumptive pronouns in unbounded dependencies and copy pronouns in copy raising as instances of resumption. It has been pretheoretically observed that the two phenomena are related (McCloskey and Sells, 1988; Boeckx, 2003), but they have resisted a unified, formal analysis. Section 12.1 lays out the data for copy raising in English and shows that there are four distinct dialects or grammars. The nature of the complement and of expletive subjects in copy raising is also carefully considered. Section 12.2 extends RMTR to copy raising by parametrizing manager resources appropriately to take into account the fact that one kind of resumption involves unbounded dependencies, whereas the other does not; this is captured by whether the manager resources are instantiated in terms of an unbounded dependency function or a subject. Section 12.3 provides a detailed analysis of the pattern of data for one of the English dialects and section 12.4 illustrates how the other dialects can be captured by lexical variation. Section 12.5 shows how the analysis correctly predicts a scope generalization about copy raising. Section 12.6 concludes and considers prospects for extending the analysis to other languages.

12.1 English Copy Raising

True copy raising in English, as shown in (1), is limited to the verbs *seem* and *appear* with complements introduced by *like*, *as if*, or *as though*. The complements as a class will be referred to as *like*-complements.

(1) Harry seems/appears like/as if/as though he fell.

Many authors group similar subcategorizations of the perception verbs *look*, *sound*, *smell*, *taste*, and *feel* with copy raising. Early work on English copy raising conflated the two classes of verbs and this continues to be prevalent in more recent literature, as discussed below. Rogers (1971, 1972, 1973, 1974), in pioneering work on perceptual reports in English, proposed the transformation "Richard"[1] to account for the related construction with the perception verbs. However, these 'perceptual resemblance verbs' are distinct from copy raising (Asudeh, 2002*b*, 2004; Asudeh and Toivonen, 2007, 2012), for reasons that will become apparent shortly.

English speakers can be divided into four dialects, according to the results of questionnaire studies of 110 native speakers reported by Asudeh and Toivonen (2012).[2] The division is based on patterns of grammaticality judgements, on a forced three-point scale, for the following kinds of sentences, presented without context, mixed with grammatical and ungrammatical fillers:

(2) Alfred seems like he hurt Thora.

(3) Alfred seems like Madeline claimed that he hurt Thora.

(4) Alfred seems like Thora hurt him.

(5) Alfred seems like Thora's hurt.

In sentence (2), the copy pronoun is the highest subject in the complement introduced by *like*. In sentence (3), the copy pronoun is an embedded subject. In sentence (4), the copy pronoun is an object. Lastly, sentence (5) is an instance of the copy raising subcategorization of *seem*, i.e. *seem* with a non-expletive subject and a complement introduced by *like*, but with no copy pronoun in the complement.

The results are summarized in Table 12.1.[3] Dialect A is the least permissive variety. These speakers do not accept *seem/appear* with a non-expletive matrix subject and a *like*-complement and would reject all of (2–5). Dialect B is the next strictest variety. These speakers accept copy raising only if the copy pronoun is the highest subject in the complement introduced by *like/as if/as though*. Dialect B speakers would reject (3–5). In contrast, Dialect C speakers accept copy raising no matter where the copy pronoun occurs in the *like*-complement. These speakers would reject only (5). Lastly, Dialect D is the most permissive. These speakers accepted *seem/appear* with a non-expletive matrix subject and a *like*-complement but did not require a copy pronoun in the complement.

[1] The transformation involves doubling and copying. The initial observation of copy raising is sometimes attributed to Postal (1974: 268, fn.1), as in Horn (1981: 353–356).

[2] Similar data was also collected for Dutch, German, and Swedish, for a micro-comparative study. I only report the English results here. See Asudeh and Toivonen (2012) for the Swedish results. The surveys were designed and the data were collected and compiled by Ash Asudeh, Ida Toivonen, Ilka Ludwig, Anna Pucilowski, and Marie-Elaine van Egmond.

[3] Speakers were exhaustively assigned to four categories, so the column of proportions adds up to 100%.

TABLE 12.1. Variation for English copy raising.

	% of speakers (n = 110)	Description
Dialect A	6.35%	No copy raising subcategorization with non-expletive matrix subject
Dialect B	45.1%	True copy raising I—copy pronoun must be highest subject in complement of *like/as*
Dialect C	42.2%	True copy raising II—copy pronoun not necessarily highest subject
Dialect D	6.35%	Copy raising subcategorization with non-expletive matrix subject and no copy pronoun in complement

Copy raising also shows interesting variation with respect to expletives. The copy raising verbs *seem* and *appear* can take an expletive subject and a *like*-complement, as in (6). This is a key piece of evidence that copy raising can take a non-thematic subject and therefore really is a kind of raising (Rogers, 1974; Horn, 1981; Potsdam and Runner, 2001).

(6) a. It seems like Harry fell.
 b. It appears as if Alfred hurt Harry.

Even Dialect A speakers, who reject copy raising, accept examples like these. Table 12.2 summarizes the grammaticality patterns for the four dialects by sentence type.

A number of speakers also allow an expletive *there* to be the subject of copy raising, as in (7), even though the copy raising verb cannot otherwise take a *there* expletive subject, as shown in (8) and (9).

(7) a. %There seems like there's moisture in the engine.
 b. %There seem like there are two garden gnomes missing.

TABLE 12.2. Grammaticality patterns for English copy raising.

	Dialect			
Example	A	B	C	D
It seems like Harry fell.	✓	✓	✓	✓
Alfred seems like he hurt Thora.	*	✓	✓	✓
Alfred seems like Madeline claimed that he hurt Thora.	*	*	✓	✓
Alfred seems like Thora hurt him.	*	*	✓	✓
Alfred seems like Thora's hurt.	*	*	*	✓

(8) a. It seems like Harry's jumping.
    b. *There seems like Harry's jumping.

(9) a. It seems like it's raining.
    b. *There seems like it's raining.

These examples show that a matrix *there* expletive subject is licensed only by virtue of the embedded *there* expletive. This is further underscored by the fact that, at least for some speakers, the matrix expletive has the agreement features of the embedded expletive, as shown in (7).

Some of the theoretical literature has attempted to distinguish between copy raising with the copy pronoun in the highest subject of the complement to *like/as*, as in (2), and copy raising with the copy pronoun more deeply embedded, as in (3) and (4) (see, e.g., Rogers, 1974; Ura, 1998; Potsdam and Runner, 2001; and Landau, 2009, 2011). Landau (2009: 343) calls the highest subject kind "genuine copy raising" and the other variety "apparent copy raising". Potsdam and Runner (2001) treat highest subject copy raising as an instance of raising, with a non-thematic subject, and the other variety as an instance of control, with a thematic subject. In the following discussion, I will use Potsdam and Runner's more neutral terms, 'subject copy raising' and 'non-subject copy raising', rather than Landau's 'genuine copy raising' and 'apparent copy raising'.

Expletive data is put forward as a key piece of empirical evidence to distinguish between subject and non-subject copy raising, as in the following distinction (Potsdam and Runner, 2001; Landau, 2009):

(10) %There seems like there's gonna be a riot.

(11) *There seems like John expects there to be an election

This is meant to show that *seem* in (11) does not accept a non-thematic subject (Landau, 2009: 343). Potsdam and Runner (2001) analyse subject copy raising as a base-generated A-chain, which means that a single theta role is shared between the copy raising verb's subject and the copy pronoun, as in the standard A-movement analysis of raising. They analyse non-subject copy raising as co-indexation, i.e. an anaphoric relation, between two thematic arguments. Thus, for Potsdam and Runner (2001), subject copy raising involves a single thematic role, as in raising, whereas non-subject copy raising involves two thematic roles, as in control.

However, there are empirical and theoretical problems with positing a distinction between subject and non-subject copy raising along these lines (see also Asudeh and Toivonen, 2007, 2012, for additional arguments). First, if there is only a raising *seem*, and no control *seem*, then the ungrammaticality of (11) would follow regardless, since raising is a relation between a higher grammatical function and an embedded subject. There is no theoretical framework that would expect a raising relation to obtain between a matrix subject and the subject of a complement's complement, as in (11). Considerations of parsimony favour this explanation over the appeal to a thematic subject for non-subject copy raising, since the raising-only explanation does not need to posit an ambiguity between two kinds of copy raising. Second, if the matrix subject in non-subject copy raising is thematic, a copy pronoun should not be required at all. This in turn predicts that if a speaker accepts non-subject copy raising s/he should accept sentences like (5), in which there is a thematic subject for *seem* and a *like*-complement with no copy pronoun. But the data does not support this prediction at all: 45% of native English speakers surveyed allowed copy raising with a copy pronoun that is not the highest subject in the complement, as in examples (3) and (4), but only 6% of speakers accepted putative 'copy raising' with no copy pronoun.

Nevertheless, much of the theoretical literature has either implied or explicitly claimed that non-subject copy raising in fact does not require a copy pronoun (Heycock, 1994; Gisborne, 1996, 2010; Potsdam and Runner, 2001; Matushansky, 2002; Landau, 2009, 2011). Gisborne (1996, 2010: 281) contends that the apparent necessity for a copy pronoun stems from a requirement of *like/as if/as though*, which he correctly analyses as involving comparison, for something like "ease of comparison". In Gisborne's theory, a pronoun in the complement facilitates comparison, although exactly how is not clear. However, the data in the literature that is provided to establish the possibility of non-subject copy raising almost invariably does not contain the verbs *seem* or *appear*, but rather the perceptual resemblance verbs *look*, *sound*, *smell*, *taste*, and *feel*, which occur in the same subcategorization frame:

(12) This dessert looks/sounds/smells/tastes/feels like it contains Rice Krispies.

(13) Harry smells like he needs to be changed.

(14) Harry smells like somebody has given him a bath.

(15) It smells like Harry needs to be changed.

The only exception to this that I am aware of is two examples in Gisborne (2010: 280, (68a–b)).[4]

[4] The examples in question are:

(i) The room seems like something bad has happened.

(ii) When the Toilet Flush Valve Seems like Something Has Stretched, it Probably Has!

Gisborne (2010: 280) notes that the second example is in a headline from a Google hit.

However, perceptual resemblance verbs do not require copy pronouns at all:

(16) This pan looks/smells/tastes like Isak's just started to learn to cook.

(17) Your car looks/sounds like Swedish engineering has made many advances.

(18) Alfred smells like Isak has made pancakes.

Asudeh (2002*b*, 2004) and Asudeh and Toivonen (2007, 2012) argue that this is precisely the distinction between copy raising verbs and perceptual resemblance verbs. In contrast to *seem* and *appear*, the perceptual resemblance verbs are semantically contentful enough to take a thematic subject argument (Asudeh and Toivonen, 2012) and, with the possible exception of dialectal variation for *look*, do not otherwise support raising:

(19) %Alfred looks to be ready to go.

(20) %Alfred looks to have eaten chocolate.

(21) *Alfred sounds to have eaten chocolate.

(22) *Alfred smells to have eaten chocolate.

(23) *Alfred tastes to have eaten chocolate.

(24) *Alfred feels to have eaten chocolate.

One cannot provide putative evidence for the lack of necessity of copy pronouns in non-subject copy raising, or so-called apparent copy raising, by citing well-formed examples of perceptual resemblance verbs without copy pronouns in their complements, rather than the actual raising verbs *seem* and *appear*, given that perceptual resemblance verbs more generally do not behave like true copy raising verbs.

12.1.1 *Complements*

This section establishes some properties of complements to *seem* and *appear* that are introduced by *like*, *as if*, and *as though*. I argue that '*like*-complements' have the following properties: (1) they are arguments, not adjuncts, (2) they are prepositional phrases in c-structure, and (3) they are open complements at f-structure, i.e. XCOMPS.

Evidence from extraction, deletion, and coordination indicates that *like*-complements are arguments; further evidence is presented by Bender and Flickinger (1999). It is possible to extract from *like*-complements, as shown in (25), but not from *like*-phrases that are clearly adjuncts, as in (26) and (27):

(25) a. What did Alfred seem like he was ashamed of?
b. What did Alfred appear as though Thora had told him?
c. How does Isak seem like he enjoys drawing?

(26) a. Alfred slinked away like he was ashamed of his actions.
b. Alfred slinked away.
c. *What did Alfred slink away like he was ashamed of?

(27) a. Isak draws like he enjoys it a lot.
b. Isak draws.
c. *How much does Isak draw like he enjoys it?

Extraction is possible from the *like*-phrase that occurs with a copy raising verb, but not from a *like*-phrase that is an adjunct.

The fact that the *like*-phrase in (26) and (27) can be deleted, as demonstrated in (26b) and (27b), indicates that the phrase is an adjunct. In contrast to these adjuncts introduced by *like*, it is not possible to delete a copy raising verb's *like*-complement while preserving meaning. Deletion of a *like*-complement either leads to ungrammaticality, as in (28), or changes the meaning of the verb, as in (29).

(28) a. Alfred seemed like he was happy.
b. *Alfred seemed.

(29) a. Harry might appear as though he's tired.
b. ≠Harry might appear.

The verb *seem* is ungrammatical without a complement and intransitive *appear* has a different sense from copy raising *appear*.

Lastly, it is possible to coordinate the *like*-complement with another open complement, such as a predicative argument, as in (30), but it is impossible to coordinate an adjunct *like*-phrase with an argument, as shown in (31c).[5]

(30) a. Alfred seemed quite ashamed and like Thora had scolded him.
b. Harry appeared happy and as if he had just eaten a big meal.
c. Isak seemed under the weather and like he couldn't go to school.

[5] The examples in (30) are better with the *like*-complement as the second conjunct rather than the first. This likely has to do with effects of the sort found in heavy NP shift (Wasow, 2002).

(31) a. Thora put the ice cream in the freezer like she meant to eat it later.
b. Thora put the ice cream in the freezer and on the shelf.
c. *Thora put the ice cream in the freezer and like she meant to eat it later.

In sum, evidence from extraction, deletion, and coordination shows that *like*-complements to copy raising verbs are arguments.

If these complements are arguments, what is their categorial status? Two options have been proposed in the literature:

1. *Like*-complements are CPs: *like*, *as if*, and *as though* are complementizers. (Bender and Flickinger, 1999; Matushansky, 2002)
2. *Like*-complements are PPs:[6] *like* and *as* are prepositions. (Heycock, 1994; Potsdam and Runner, 2001; Huddleston and Pullum, 2002; Asudeh, 2002*b*, 2004; Asudeh and Toivonen, 2007, 2012)

Evidence favours the second option, in which *like* complements are headed by prepositions with clausal complements.

First, *like*-complements take the same pre-modifiers as prepositions, as shown in (32–33), and these cannot modify complementizers, as shown in (34).

(32) a. Isak put the book just on the shelf.
b. Isak appears just as though he has been swimming.

(33) a. Thora passed the ball almost to the sideline.
b. Thora seems almost like she's just woken up.

(34) a. *Isak thinks almost/just that he won.
b. *Isak wonders almost/just whether he won.
c. *Harry asked almost/just if he had been bad.
d. *Isak wanted almost/just for Harry to leave.

[6] Maling (1983) analyses *like* as an exceptional, transitive adjective (a fossil of a more general diachronic pattern). The present analysis could be modified to take this into account, by treating the *like*-complement as an AP. The costs and benefits of the two options are as follows. The benefits of treating the *like*-complement as an AP, headed by an adjectival *like* or *as* with c-structure category A, are that the comparative semantics of *like* and *as* is less surprising and *as*, in particular, could potentially be assimilated to the comparative *as*. However, the fact that *like* and *as* can independently occur with nominal arguments, as discussed below (i.e. that they are, to use Maling's term, *transitive* adjectives), would be a rather exceptional syntactic structure in synchronic English grammar. On the other hand, if *like* and *as* are synchronically analysed as instances of the category preposition, the fact that they directly take nominal arguments is immediately accounted for, but their comparative semantics must be treated as a remainder of their adjectival roots. I have chosen the latter option here, but the AP analysis could also work in the broader theory I am assuming, because what is important is that the category be one that can independently map to a predicative/open complement, and this is true of both PP and AP.

If *like* and *as* are prepositions, then the grammaticality of (32b) and (33b) is expected, but not if they are complementizers.

Second, *like* and *as* have the complementation patterns of prepositions. Both *like* and *as* independently occur with nominal complements (Gisborne, 2010: 270–272), as in the following examples:

(35) Alfred dressed like/as Charlie Chaplin.

(36) I'm wary of actors as directors.

(37) With transformations like these, who needs global rules?

It is thus more parsimonious to claim that *as* and *like* are prepositions that can either take nominal or clausal complements—compare, for example, *before* and *after*—than to postulate a distinction between a complementizer *as/like* and a preposition *as/like*.

Third, treating *as* as a preposition taking a clausal complement allows us to assimilate the occurrences of *if* and *though* in *as if* and *as though* to their normal complementizer uses:[7]

(38) Matts rarely drinks, though he enjoys the occasional beer.

(39) Thora wondered if she should leave early.

It therefore seems promising to analyse *as* in the copy raising complement as a preposition that takes a CP complement introduced by *if* or *though*, which are just normal complementizers.

Furthermore, treating *if* in *as if* as a complementizer explains the possibility of subjunctive mood with *as if*, as in (41), since the complementizer *if* generally licenses subjunctive mood, as in (40).

(40) If he were alive today, John Lennon would probably protest against the war.

(41) But the way the section was constructed, it seemed as if he were telling the party it was bigoted and no longer welcome at his convention.

(Peggy Noonan, 'Welcome to Hard Truths', *Time*, August 26, 1996. http://www.cnn.com/ALLPOLITICS/1996/analysis/time/9608/26/noonan.shtml; retrieved 22/08/2010).

The alternative is to postulate, less parsimoniously, that *if* and *as if* are both complementizers that independently license the subjunctive.

[7] Huddleston and Pullum (2002: 971) classify the subordinating conjunction *though* as a preposition rather than a complementizer. Similarly, they classify *as if* as a complex preposition and presumably would do the same for *as though*, although it is not found in their list. The main point is that *like*-complements are PPs headed by P^0 and on this point there is agreement between their classification and this account. In generative terms, it seems reasonable to assign *though* the category C^0.

The fourth kind of evidence comes from dialect variation.[8] Certain dialects of English permit a CP with an overt complementizer after *like* in a *like*-complement. Here are two attested examples:

(42) I had some interest in Bill Bradley but it seemed like that he totally catered to the pro-choice people on the abortion side and I thought that he supported some reconciliation on this issue as Tony Campolo and Jim Wallis have promoted.

(http://www.sojo.net/sojomail/index.cfm/action/sojomail/issue/031700.html; originally retrieved 29/02/2004. Retrieved from the Internet Archive, 22/08/2010[9])

(43) My bike barely missed him as he seemed like that he didn't even notice us.

(Douglas T., 'Drunken Apparition', *Paranormal Story Archives*, March 2002. http://paranormal.about.com/library/blstory_march02_01.htm; retrieved 22/08/2010)

If it is maintained that *like* is a complementizer, then the *like that* dialect would either have a double complementizer, in which case (1) it would have to be shown that the dialect independently allows 'Doubly-Filled COMP' violations (Chomsky and Lasnik, 1977), or (2) it would have to be the case that, in this dialect, *like* is not a complementizer, while in other dialects it is a complementizer. A more elegant explanation is possible if it is instead assumed that *like* is a preposition in both dialects. In the *like that* dialect, *like* takes a full clausal complement, a CP, whereas in other dialects it takes a bare clausal complement, an IP.

In conclusion, evidence from modification, complementation, complementizers, and dialect variation suggests that *like*-complements are prepositional phrases, headed by *like* or *as*. The preposition *as* in a *like*-complement takes a CP complement, introduced by the complementizer *if* or *though*, while *like* takes an IP or CP complement, depending on dialect.

12.1.2 *Expletive Subjects*

Copy raising verbs and perceptual resemblance verbs have interesting behaviour with respect to expletives:

[8] I thank Mary Dalrymple (p.c.) for bringing this to my attention.

[9] http://web.archive.org/web/20030104152027/http://www.sojo.net/sojomail/index.cfm/action/sojomail/issue/031700.html

(44) It seemed/looked/smelled like Harry needed a bath.

(45) It seemed/looked/smelled like it rained.

(46) It seemed/looked/smelled like there was a problem.

(47) % There seemed/looked/smelled like there was a problem.

(48) * There seemed/looked/smelled like it rained.

There are two noteworthy aspects here. First, as shown in examples (44–46), copy raising verbs (CRVs) and perceptual resemblance verbs (PRVs) can take expletive subjects and the expletive is *it*, as we would expect. Second, and more surprisingly, some dialects (including my own) allow these verbs to take a *there* expletive subject (47), but only if the complement of *like/as* is headed by a verb that independently licenses a *there* subject (48). Not only is it surprising that a verb such as *seem* takes an expletive subject with form *there* rather than *it*, it is also surprising that the verb apparently raises *there* not from its own complement, but rather from the complement of its complement. Since raising is a local operation, we would expect that the verb could raise only the subject of the *like*-complement; otherwise we would have to give up the locality of raising.

A more natural assumption is the following, which maintains the locality of raising, but has consequences for LFG's theory of open complements, as discussed further in the conclusion to this chapter:

(49) *Like* and *as* have raising alternants.

This means that *like* or *as*, the head of the *like*-complement, raises the expletive subject from its complement, and then the expletive is raised one step further by the CRV/PRV, which we know independently can raise the subject of its predicative complement. Thus, we have double raising, but each step is completely local.

12.2 Unifying Copy Raising and Resumption

For many native speakers of English, a copy pronoun is obligatory in the *like*-complement to a copy raising verb with a non-expletive subject, as shown in the following contrast:

(50) * Alfred seems like Thora has been baking.

(51) Thora seems like she has been baking.

More than 87% of native speakers in the survey reported by Asudeh and Toivonen (2012) require a copy pronoun in this construction. A narrow majority of these speakers, 52%, did not require the copy pronoun to be the subject of *as/like*'s complement and allowed it to be embedded more deeply. This dialect was referred to as Dialect C above and is the dialect that will be captured in the initial analysis in section 12.3. Section 12.4 demonstrates how to lexically capture variation in English copy raising.

From the perspective of resource-sensitive semantic composition, an obligatory copy pronoun is a kind of resumptive pronoun. The copy raising verb does not consume its non-expletive subject as an argument. The argument is instead consumed in the position of the copy pronoun. The copy pronoun itself is then a surplus resource. The Resource Management Theory of Resumption thus has the prospect of unifying copy pronouns with resumptive pronouns, bringing copy raising into the fold of resumption. This has hitherto proven elusive, although the connection between copy raising and resumption has previously been observed (e.g., McCloskey and Sells, 1988; Boeckx, 2003). For example, Boeckx (2003: 165–166, fn.1) conjectures that copy raising is the A-movement analog of A′-movement resumptive pronouns. The difference between copy raising and the kind of resumption that has been studied more extensively is that copy raising does not involve an unbounded dependency. The top of the copy raising dependency is not an operator and must be the local subject of the copy raising verb.

The unification between copy raising and resumption in RMTR is achieved if copy raising verbs contribute manager resources. Resource-sensitive semantic composition then dictates that there must be a copy pronoun for the manager resource to consume, otherwise the manager resource will be left over, creating a resource surplus. The manager resource in copy raising is specified in terms of a local SUBJECT, namely the subject of the copy raising verb, and not in terms of a UDF (unbounded dependency function) at the top of a binder-resumptive unbounded dependency. This means that manager resources effectively need to be parametrized such that they can be specified in terms of either a UDF or a SUBJ local to the licenser. The template for manager resources is therefore revised as follows:[10]

(52) $\mathrm{MR}_2(g, f) = \lambda P \lambda y.y : [g_\sigma \multimap (g_\sigma \otimes f_\sigma)] \multimap [g_\sigma \multimap g_\sigma]$

[10] In the computational treatment of templates (Crouch et al., 2011) from which the theoretical work on templates derives (Dalrymple *et al.*, 2004*b*; Asudeh et al., 2008), multiple arguments to templates are separated by spaces, but here I separate arguments to templates explicitly with commas.

F-structure f is the f-structure of the pronoun to be consumed and f-structure g is the f-structure of the UDF, in the case of unbounded dependency resumptives, or of the SUBJ, in the case of copy raising resumptives.

In order to avoid clutter, monadic templates are defined in terms of MR_2 as follows:

(53) $\text{MR}_s(f) = \text{MR}_2((\uparrow \textsc{subj}), f)$

(54) $\text{MR}_u(f) = \text{MR}_2((\uparrow \textsc{udf}), f)$

MR_s is thus a manager resource parametrized such that the antecedent of the surplus pronoun is the local SUBJECT; this kind of manager resource is appropriate for copy raising. MR_u is a manager resource parametrized such that the antecedent of the surplus pronoun is the local UDF; this kind of manager resource is appropriate for resumptives in unbounded dependencies and is the kind that was initially presented in chapter 6.

Let us define the previous, unsubscripted template, MR, in terms of MR_u:

(55) $\text{MR}(f) = \text{MR}_u(f)$

Thus, the template MR_u can be written without the subscript when there is no risk of confusion. This ensures backward compatibility: previous instances of MR in the book have exactly the same interpretation as before.

The dependency relabelling template, RELABEL, can be similarly parametrized:

(56) $\text{RELABEL}_2(g, f) = \lambda P.P : (f_\sigma \multimap \uparrow_\sigma) \multimap (g_\sigma \multimap \uparrow_\sigma)$

F-structure g is either the local SUBJ or the local UDF. F-structure f is once again the f-structure of the resumptive pronoun. The RELABEL template relabels a dependency on the resumptive pronoun as a dependency on the antecedent of the resumptive pronoun.

Monadic templates are defined in terms of RELABEL_2 as follows:

(57) $\text{RELABEL}_s(f) = \text{RELABEL}_2((\uparrow \textsc{subj}), f)$

(58) $\text{RELABEL}_u(f) = \text{RELABEL}_2((\uparrow \textsc{udf}), f)$

The previous, unsubscripted template, RELABEL, is defined in terms of RELABEL_u:

(59) $\text{RELABEL}(f) = \text{RELABEL}_u(f)$

Again, this ensures backward compatibility, since previous instances of RELABEL have the same interpretation as before.

Another lexical specification on the copy raising verb states that its subject must be the antecedent of a pronoun embedded in its complement:

(60) $(\uparrow \text{SUBJ})_\sigma = (\%\text{Copy}_\sigma\ \text{ANTECEDENT})$

This is just the usual kind of pronominal binding equation seen in previous chapters. The local name %Copy picks out the copy pronoun, as will become clearer from the lexical entries in section 12.3.

The normal, unbounded nature of pronominal binding explains the capacity for a copy raising verb in Dialect C to be satisfied even if the copy pronoun is not the subject of the complement of *like/as* or even a subject at all:

(61) Thora seems like the judges have finally announced that she won.

(62) Thora seemed like Alfred had scolded her.

(63) Thora seems like the assertion by Isak that Alfred suspects the motives behind the gift offended her dignity.

Any account that tries to assimilate copy raising to strictly local raising would have trouble accommodating these facts. However, the present account does not treat copy raising as an unbounded dependency. Its unbounded nature stems purely from the Resource Management Theory of Resumption. RMTR depends on pronominal binding, which is non-local. As discussed further in section 12.4 below, lexical variation in the specification of the copy pronoun—i.e. the definition of %Copy—accounts for the difference between Dialect B, in which the copy pronoun must be the highest subject in the complement of *like/as*, and Dialect C, in which the copy pronoun may be embedded more deeply and need not be a subject.

Finally, the account offers some preliminary explanation for the fact that copy raising is restricted to only the verbs *seem* and *appear* and cannot be arbitrarily extended to any raising verb:

(64) *Alfred tends like he won.

The *like*-complements to copy raising are open complements. In order to take a *like*-complement, a raising verb must independently allow an open complement, such as a predicative complement. Raising verbs such as *tend* do not:

(65) *Alfred tends happy.

In addition, since the manager resources that allow copy raising are properties of the lexical entries of *seem* and *appear*, only these raising verbs may license copy raising, as a matter of lexical specification. Thus, even if a raising verb takes an open complement, it licenses copy raising only if it contributes a manager resource.

12.3 Analysis

The analysis offered in this section accounts for Dialect C, in which the copy pronoun is obligatory but does not have to be the highest overt subject, i.e. the subject of the complement of *as* or *like*. Section 12.4 builds on this analysis and shows how adding or removing lexical constraints captures the following variation in English copy raising: (1) Dialect A does not have copy raising, but allows *seems like* with an expletive subject; (2) Dialect B has copy raising only with the copy pronoun as the subject of *as/like*'s complement; (3) Dialect D allows *seems like* with a non-expletive subject and no copy pronoun; and (4) there is also variation in whether expletive *there* subjects are grammatical, in addition to expletive *it* subjects.

Asudeh and Toivonen (2012) motivate an event semantics (Davidson, 1967; Parsons, 1990) for copy raising. Their reasons have to do with the analysis of the 'source of perception' in copy raising, which can be thought of roughly as the individual or event that gives rise to the appearance reported by a copy raising sentence. Asudeh and Toivonen (2007, 2012) analyse the source of perception in terms of a semantic role called PSOURCE (for 'perceptual source'). I will set this aspect of copy raising semantics aside, since the main topic of interest here is compositionality, given the surplus resource constituted by the copy pronoun. However, I will also now switch to a semantics with events, albeit for a different reason.

Events facilitate the analysis of the semantics of the expressions that introduce the complement to copy raising, *like/as if/as though*. Consider sentence (2), repeated here:

(66) Alfred seems like he hurt Thora.

A reasonable characterization of the meaning of *like* in this sentence is that there is a comparison between a state that seems to hold now (of which Alfred is the perceptual source, according to Asudeh and Toivonen, 2007, 2012) and an event of Alfred's having hurt Thora. The second argument of the comparison relation can also be a state, as in the following example:

(67) Alfred seems like he knows the answer.

Therefore, the generalization is that copy raising involves a comparison between a state of something seeming to be the case and an eventuality in the *like*-complement, where I follow Bach (1981) in adopting the term *eventuality* as a cover term for events and states.

Leaving tense and the source of perception aside, a target event semantics for (66) is:

(68) $\exists s.seem(s, \exists e.[(s \sim e) \wedge hurt(e, a, t)])$

I adopt variables $s, s', s'', \ldots,$ for states and variables $e, e', e'', \ldots,$ for events. I adopt an eventuality metavariable, ε, over state or event variables. All bound instances of ε in a formula must be resolved to the same state or event variable; Glue proofs below will involve an implicit resolution of this kind, marked as, e.g. $[e/\varepsilon]$. Further details of the types assumed here can be found in Asudeh and Toivonen (2012).

The interpretation in (68) introduces a similarity operator, $\sim$, which is defined as follows:

(69) For any two eventualities α and β, $\alpha \sim \beta$ is true if and only if there is a property P such that $P(\alpha)$ is true and $P(\beta)$ is true.

In other words, for two eventualities to be considered similar, they must share some property. For example, in the case of (66), if the state that seems to hold involves Alfred looking abashed and an event of hurting Thora has also involved Alfred looking abashed, then (66) is true. This similarity operator begins to capture the comparative nature of *like* and *as*, which is appealing, but this version is somewhat simplistic, since it does not allow for modification of the comparison relation or otherwise take degrees into account. The operator could be improved by building on the insights of Alrenga (2006, 2007).[11]

The similarity operator provides the basis for the following lexical entry for *like*, the head of the copy raising verb's complement:

(70) *like*, P^0 $(\uparrow \textsc{pred}) = \text{`like'}$

$\lambda P \lambda s.\exists \varepsilon.[(s \sim \varepsilon) \wedge P(\varepsilon)]$:

$[(\uparrow \mathrm{COMP}_\sigma\ \mathrm{EVENT}) \multimap (\uparrow \mathrm{COMP})_\sigma] \multimap$

$((\mathrm{XCOMP} \uparrow)_\sigma\ \mathrm{EVENT}) \multimap \uparrow_\sigma$

Following previous work by Fry (1999), Lev (2007), and Asudeh et al. (2008), I introduce a semantic structure resource, EVENT, as the linear logic term corresponding to the eventuality argument. The meaning constructor for *like*

[11] Copy raising also touches on questions of evidentiality, such that (66) involves something about Alfred providing evidence for the claim that he hurt Thora. This is arguably due to the source of perception, which has been set aside here; see Asudeh and Toivonen (2012) for further discussion of this issue.

thus consumes the property of eventualities corresponding to its complement, existentially closes the complement's eventuality argument, and produces a property of the copy raising verb's state argument. This property will then compose with the copy raising verb's meaning, as will become clear shortly.

The lexical entry in (70) is specific to *like* in copy raising, since other uses of *like* head adjuncts and, as a result, their meaning constructors would have to be specified somewhat differently. An avenue for future work is to attempt a generalization of the various kinds of *like*. I also assume for the sake of simplicity that *as if* and *as though* can be analysed using this meaning constructor, but a fuller treatment would perhaps have to countenance the additional compositional complexities of *as if* and *as though*. I leave this for future work.

The lexical entry for the *seems like/as though/as if* subcategorization of *seem* in Dialect C is given in (71). It uses two templates, which are defined in (72) and (73). The first template is a general template for raising predicates. The second template is a template for copy raising and is specific to this use of *seem* and the corresponding use of *appear*. The second template is optional, since the copy raising verb also occurs with an expletive subject and, in this case, does not require a copy in its complement.[12]

(71) $seem_{like}$, V^0 $(\uparrow \textsc{pred}) = \text{`seem'}$
@RAISING
(@CR($\uparrow$ $\textsc{gf}^+$))
$\lambda P \lambda s.seem(s, P(s))$:
$[(\uparrow_\sigma \textsc{event}) \multimap (\uparrow \textsc{xcomp})_\sigma] \multimap (\uparrow_\sigma \textsc{event}) \multimap \uparrow_\sigma$

(72) RAISING = $\{ (\uparrow \textsc{subj expletive}) =_c \textsc{it} \wedge \neg (\uparrow \textsc{xcomp}) \mid$
$(\uparrow \textsc{subj}) = (\uparrow \textsc{xcomp subj}) \}$

(73) CR(f) = %Copy = f
$(\uparrow \textsc{subj})_\sigma = (\%\text{Copy}_\sigma\ \textsc{antecedent})$
@MR_s(%Copy)
@$RELABEL_s$(%Copy)
$\lambda x \lambda P.P(x) : (\uparrow \textsc{subj})_\sigma \multimap [(\uparrow \textsc{subj})_\sigma \multimap \uparrow_\sigma] \multimap \uparrow_\sigma$

[12] Recall that multiple arguments to templates are separated by commas in my notation, not spaces, unlike in computational treatments of templates in LFG (Crouch et al., 2011); see footnote 10 above. This means that the CR template has one argument, ($\uparrow$ $\textsc{gf}^+$).

The meaning constructor in the lexical entry for the copy raising verb, (71), treats the meaning of the verb as a property of states that results from combining with the property of eventualities that is the meaning of its complement (the *like*-complement).

The first of the two templates called in (71), RAISING, is the general template for raising verbs. It states that either there is a constraint that the raising verb's SUBJ is constrained to be an expletive *it* and the verb has no XCOMP argument or else the raising verb's SUBJ is equated with the SUBJ of the raising verb's XCOMP, its open complement. The latter of these specifications is how 'raising' is effected in LFG (Bresnan, 1982*a*). In fact, there is no raising in the sense of NP-movement; rather, a matrix subject is equated with the implicit subject of an open complement (a predicative or infinitival complement). Otherwise, we get the expletive subcategorization, which is appropriate for a raising verb with an extraposed CP complement. The RAISING template effectively sets the raising option as a default, since a disjunction of a constraining equation[13] and a defining equation will always result in the defining equation taking effect if the constraining equation is unsatisfiable (Dalrymple *et al.*, 2004*b*: 205–206).

The second template called in (71), CR, is the copy raising template shown in (73). The first line of this template states that the local variable, %Copy, is equated with the argument of the template, *f*. This is the copy pronoun in the complement clause. The argument to the template, *f*, is passed in from the copy raising verb's lexical entry. In the case of Dialect C, which places no restriction on the grammatical function of the copy pronoun, this is just the unrestricted ($\uparrow$ GF$^+$), as indicated in the third line of (71). The second line of the CR template states that the antecedent of the copy pronoun is the semantic structure correspondent of the SUBJ of the f-structure to which the template contributes information—i.e. the subject of the copy raising verb, since it is the copy raising verb's lexical entry that calls the template. The third line of the template is an instance of the subject-parametrized manager resource, with %Copy as its argument. This results in an instance of a manager resource that seeks to consume the pronoun %Copy, whose antecedent is the copy raising verb's subject. The fourth line of the template is an instance of the subject-parametrized relabelling resource. This will relabel a dependency on the copy pronoun as a dependency on the copy raising verb's subject. The last line of the copy raising template is a meaning constructor that consumes the

[13] The conjunction of a constraining equation and negative existential equation, as in (72), is itself a constraining equation (Bresnan, 2001; Asudeh and Toivonen, 2009).

resource of the subject of the copy raising and an implication from the subject resource to the copy raising verb's resource, resulting in an instance of the copy raising verb's resource. On the meaning language side, this corresponds to saturating an argument of a property with the denotation of the copy raising verb's subject. It is this meaning constructor that has the effect of composing the copy raising verb's subject in place of the copy pronoun that has been consumed by the manager resource.

Before turning to the analysis of the copy raising sentence (66), let us look at the analysis of a simpler sentence in the event-enriched theory:

(74) Alfred consoled Thora.

The lexically contributed meaning constructors for the sentence are as follows, where *e* is the semantic structure EVENT argument of the verb *consoled*:

(75)
1. $a : a$ — Lex. **Alfred**
2. $\lambda y \lambda x \lambda e.console(e, x, y) : t \multimap a \multimap e \multimap c$ — Lex. **consoled**
3. $t : t$ — Lex. **Thora**

These premises construct the proof in (76):

(76)

$$\dfrac{\dfrac{\dfrac{\overset{\textbf{Thora}}{t : t} \quad \overset{\textbf{consoled}}{\lambda y \lambda x \lambda e.console(e, x, y) : t \multimap a \multimap e \multimap c}}{\lambda x \lambda e.console(e, x, t) : a \multimap e \multimap c} \quad \overset{\textbf{Alfred}}{a : a}}{\lambda e.console(e, a, t) : e \multimap c}}{\exists e.console(e, a, t) : c}\ \exists\varepsilon$$

The proof assumes that there is a generally available optional operation of existential closure of an eventuality variable, indicated by $\exists\varepsilon$; this is a standard assumption in event semantics.[14]

Returning to the copy raising example (66), the c-structure and f-structure are shown in (77) and (78).

[14] There are a number of ways this could be formalized. The relevant optional premise, $\lambda P.\exists\varepsilon.[P(\varepsilon)] : [\uparrow_\sigma \text{EVENT} \multimap \uparrow_\sigma] \multimap \uparrow_\sigma$, could be associated with matrix verbs, or with the root node of the tree.

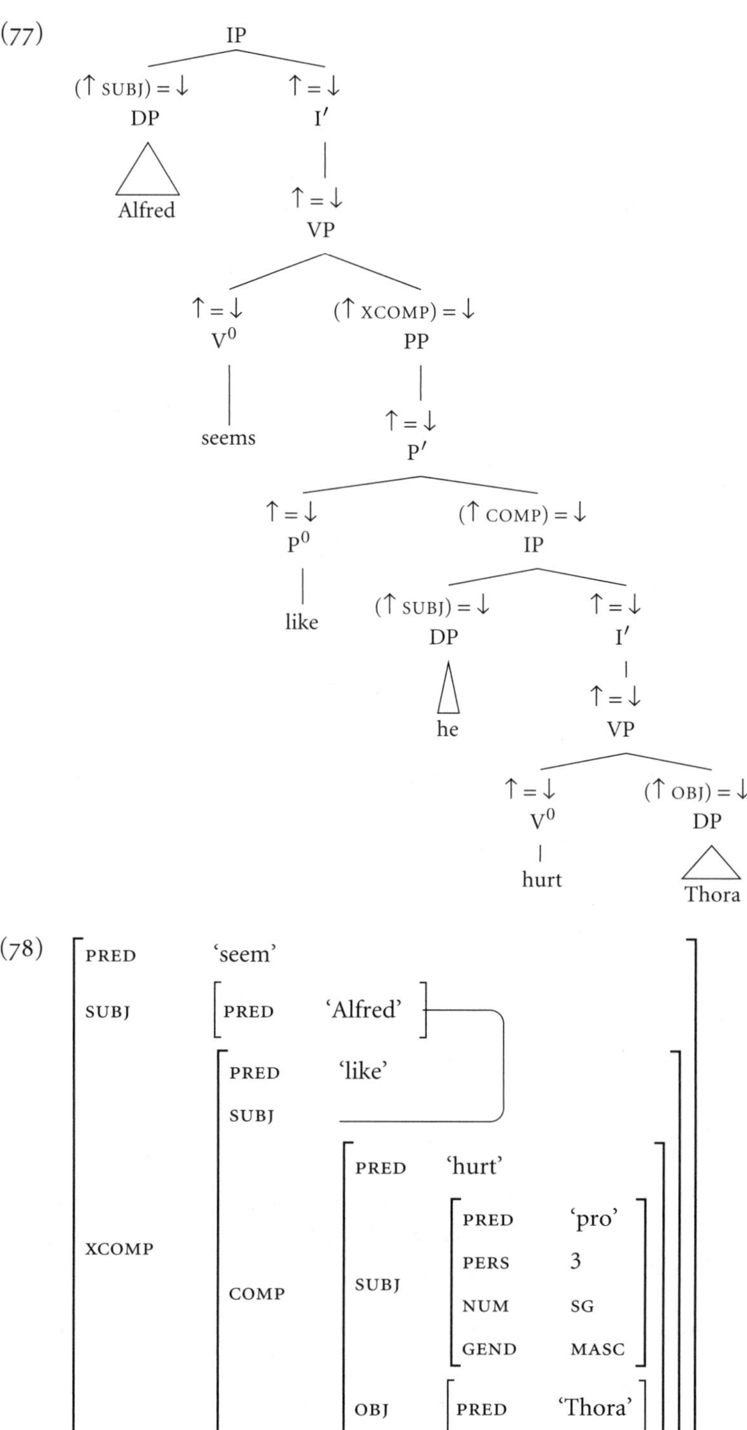
(77)
IP
(↑ SUBJ) = ↓
DP
Alfred
↑ = ↓
I′
↑ = ↓
VP
↑ = ↓
V0
seems
(↑ XCOMP) = ↓
PP
↑ = ↓
P′
↑ = ↓
P0
like
(↑ COMP) = ↓
IP
(↑ SUBJ) = ↓
DP
he
↑ = ↓
I′
↑ = ↓
VP
↑ = ↓
V0
hurt
(↑ OBJ) = ↓
DP
Thora
(78)
PRED 'seem'
SUBJ PRED 'Alfred'
XCOMP
PRED 'like'
SUBJ
COMP
PRED 'hurt'
SUBJ
PRED 'pro'
PERS 3
NUM SG
GEND MASC
OBJ PRED 'Thora'

This f-structure instantiates the following lexically contributed meaning constructors:

(79)
1. $a : a$ — Lex. **Alfred**
2. $\lambda P \lambda s.seem(s, P(s))$: $(e1 \multimap l) \multimap (e1 \multimap s)$ — Lex. **seems**
3. $\lambda x \lambda P.P(x)$: $a \multimap (a \multimap s) \multimap s$ — Lex. **seems (CR)**
4. $\lambda P \lambda y.y$: $[a \multimap (a \otimes p)] \multimap (a \multimap a)$ — Lex. **seems (CR: MR)**
5. $\lambda P.P$: $(p \multimap s) \multimap (a \multimap s)$ — Lex. **seems (CR: RELABEL)**
6. $\lambda P \lambda s'.\exists \varepsilon.[(s' \sim \varepsilon) \wedge P(\varepsilon)]$: $(e2 \multimap h) \multimap e1 \multimap l$ — Lex. **like**
7. $\lambda z.z \times z$: $a \multimap (a \otimes p)$ — Lex. **he**
8. $\lambda y \lambda x \lambda e'.hurt(e', x, y)$: $t \multimap p \multimap e2 \multimap h$ — Lex. **hurt**
9. $t : t$ — Lex. **Thora**

Figure 12.1 shows the proof constructed from these premises. Figure 12.2 also shows the meaning language side of the meaning constructors. The result of the proof is the target interpretation in (68): $\exists s.seem(s, \exists e.[(s \sim e) \wedge hurt(e, a, t)])$.

Next we turn to an expletive alternant, as in (80):

(80) It seems like Alfred hurt Thora.

If we take seriously the claim that the expletive variant, (80), has the same interpretation as the non-expletive variant,[15] (66), which is typically considered a key property of copy raising, then the target interpretation is the same as (68), repeated here:

(81) $\exists s.seem(s, \exists e.[(s \sim e) \wedge hurt(e, a, t)])$

The only real distinction here is that the denotation of *Alfred*, *a*, composes directly with the denotation of *hurt*, rather than being threaded through a manager resource and copy pronoun, as in the copy raising alternant.

[15] There is a slight complication here, because there is, in fact, a difference of interpretation between the expletive version and the non-explicit version once the source of perception is taken into account (Asudeh and Toivonen, 2012). However, in the event semantics analysis of Asudeh and Toivonen, the source of perception is a conjunct to the core interpretation, which is invariant across the two alternants.

(66) Alfred seems like he hurt Thora.

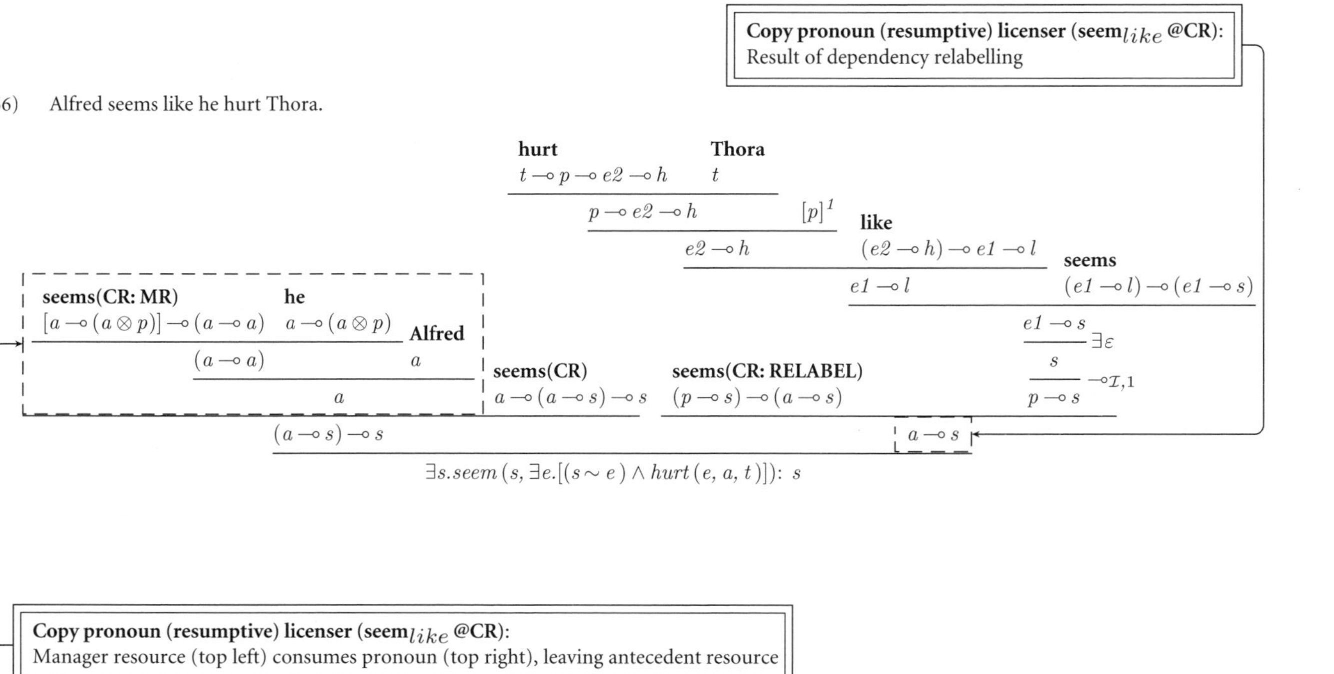

FIGURE 12.1. Proof for an English copy raising example.

(66) Alfred seems like he hurt Thora.

$$\dfrac{\dfrac{\textbf{hurt}\;\; \lambda y \lambda x \lambda e'.hurt(e', x, y) : t \multimap p \multimap e2 \multimap h \qquad \textbf{Thora}\;\; t : t}{\lambda x \lambda e', hurt(e', x, t) : p \multimap e2 \multimap h} \qquad [z : p]^{1}}{\lambda e'.hurt(e', z, t) : e2 \multimap h}$$

$$\dfrac{\lambda e'.hurt(e', z, t) : e2 \multimap h \qquad \textbf{like}\;\; \lambda P \lambda s'.\exists \varepsilon.[(s' \sim \varepsilon) \wedge P(\varepsilon)] : (e2 \multimap h) \multimap e1 \multimap l}{\lambda s'.\exists e.[(s' \sim e) \wedge hurt(e, z, t)] : e1 \multimap l}\,[e/\varepsilon]$$

$$\dfrac{\lambda s'.\exists e.[(s' \sim e) \wedge hurt(e, z, t)] : e1 \multimap l \qquad \textbf{seems}\;\; \lambda P \lambda s.seem(s, P(s)) : (e1 \multimap l) \multimap (e1 \multimap s)}{\lambda s.seem(s, \exists e.[(s \sim e) \wedge hurt(e, z, t)]) : e1 \multimap s}$$

$$\dfrac{\dfrac{\lambda s.seem(s, \exists e.[(s \sim e) \wedge hurt(e, z, t)]) : e1 \multimap s}{\exists s.[seem(s, \exists e.[(s \sim e) \wedge hurt(e, z, t)])] : s}\,\exists\varepsilon}{\lambda z.\exists s.[seem(s, \exists e.[(s \sim e) \wedge hurt(e, z, t)])] : p \multimap s}\multimap_{\mathcal{I},1}$$

$$\dfrac{\textbf{seems (CR: RELABEL)}\;\; \lambda P.P : (p \multimap s) \multimap (a \multimap s) \qquad \lambda z.\exists s.[seem(s, \exists e.[(s \sim e) \wedge hurt(e, z, t)])] : p \multimap s}{\lambda z.\exists s.[seem(s, \exists e.[(s \sim e) \wedge hurt(e, z, t)])] : a \multimap s}$$

$$\dfrac{\dfrac{\textbf{seems (CR: MR)}\;\; \lambda P \lambda y.y : [a \multimap (a \otimes p)] \multimap (a \multimap a) \qquad \textbf{he}\;\; \lambda z.z \times z : a \multimap (a \otimes p)}{\lambda y.y : (a \multimap a)} \qquad \textbf{Alfred}\;\; a : a}{a : a}$$

$$\dfrac{a : a \qquad \textbf{seems (CR)}\;\; \lambda x \lambda P.P(x) : a \multimap (a \multimap s) \multimap s}{\lambda P.P(a) : (a \multimap s) \multimap s}$$

$$\dfrac{\lambda P.P(a) : (a \multimap s) \multimap s \qquad \lambda z.\exists s.[seem(s, \exists e.[(s \sim e) \wedge hurt(e, z, t)])] : a \multimap s}{\exists s.seem(s, \exists e.[(s \sim e) \wedge hurt(e, a, t)]) : s}$$

FIGURE 12.2. Proof for an English copy raising example, with meaning language.

The c-structure and f-structure for (80) are shown in (82) and (83).

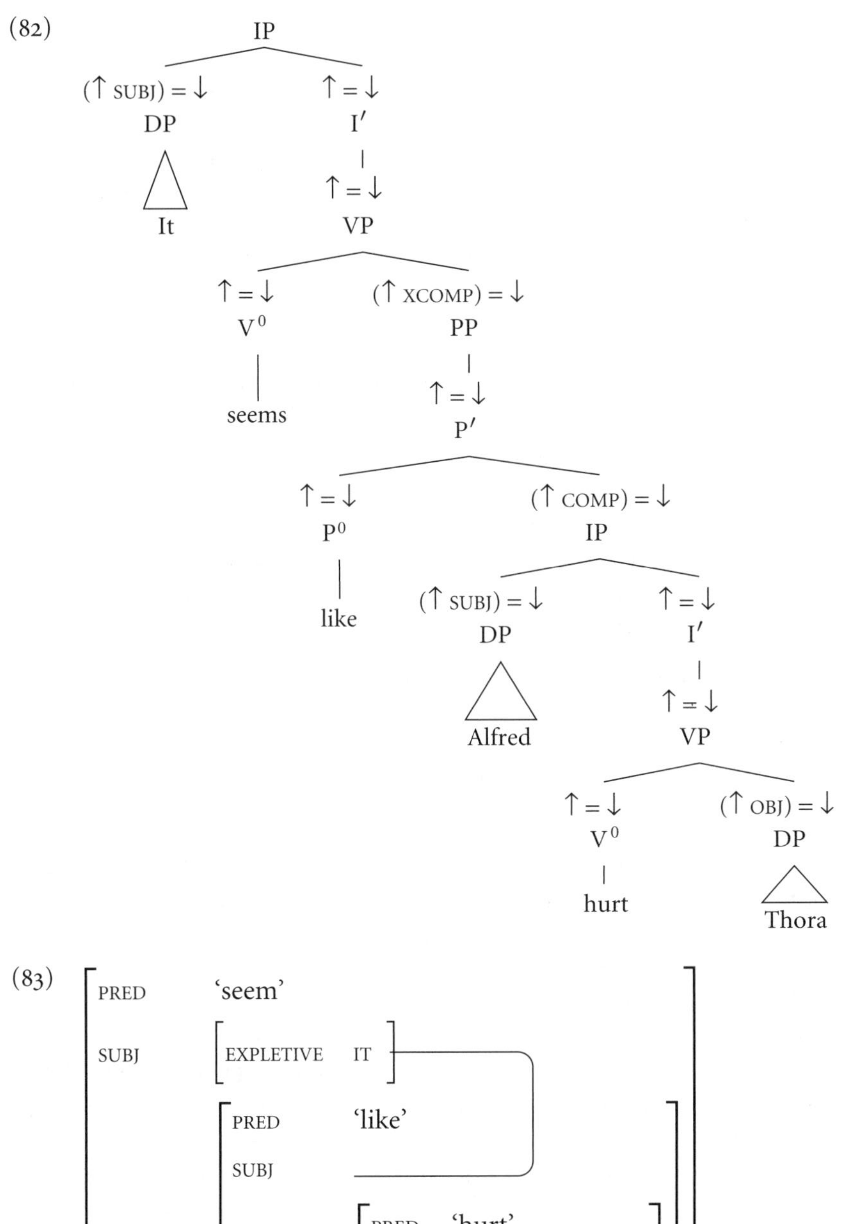

hurt $t \multimap a \multimap e2 \multimap h$ **Thora** t

$$a \multimap e2 \multimap h$$

Alfred a

$$e2 \multimap h$$

like $(e2 \multimap h) \multimap e1 \multimap l$

$$e1 \multimap l$$

seems $(e1 \multimap l) \multimap (e1 \multimap s)$

$$e1 \multimap s$$

$$\exists s.seem(s, \exists e.[(s \sim e) \wedge hurt(e, a, t)]): s \quad \exists\varepsilon$$

FIGURE 12.3. Proof for an expletive alternant example of English copy raising.

The c-structure and f-structure are largely the same as those for (66), except that the matrix subject is an expletive and the subject in the COMP is *Alfred*.

The key to the expletive interpretation is the optionality of the copy raising template, CR, in the lexical entry for the copy raising verb, (71). In the expletive variant, this template cannot be satisfied, since the manager resource cannot be satisfied, because the expletive variant does not contain a pronominal resource for the manager resource to consume. The lexically contributed meaning constructors for (80) are therefore the same as in (79), with the exception of the three premises that are contributed by the CR template and the premise contributed by the pronoun *he*:

(84)

1. $(e1 \multimap l) \multimap (e1 \multimap s)$ Lex. **seems**
2. $(e2 \multimap h) \multimap e1 \multimap l$ Lex. **like**
3. a Lex. **Alfred**
4. $t \multimap a \multimap e2 \multimap h$ Lex. **hurt**
5. t Lex. **Thora**

Figure 12.3 shows the proof constructed from these premises. Figure 12.4 also shows the meaning language side of the meaning constructors. The result of the proof is the target interpretation in (81): $\exists s.seem(s, \exists e.[(s \sim e) \wedge hurt(e, a, t)])$.

12.3.1 *Summary*

This section has presented an analysis of copy raising for Dialect C, the dialect of English in which a copy pronoun is obligatory but is not constrained with respect to where it can appear in the copy raising verb's complement. The analysis successfully unifies copy raising with other cases of resumption, as set out in section 12.2. The section demonstrated that the same set of lexical entries also correctly accounts for the expletive alternant of copy raising. In the next section, we turn to the dialectal variation in copy raising, also with respect to the nature of the expletive subject.

hurt
$\lambda y \lambda x \lambda e'.hurt(e', x, y)$:
$t \multimap a \multimap e2 \multimap h$

Thora
t :
t

$\lambda x \lambda e'.hurt(e', x, t)$:
$a \multimap e2 \multimap h$

Alfred
a :
a

$\lambda e'.hurt(e', a, t)$:
$e2 \multimap h$

like
$\lambda P \lambda s'.\exists \varepsilon.[(s' \sim \varepsilon) \wedge P(\varepsilon)]$:
$(e2 \multimap h) \multimap e1 \multimap l$

$[e/\varepsilon]$

$\lambda s'.\exists e.[(s' \sim e) \wedge hurt(e, a, t)]$:
$e1 \multimap l$

seems
$\lambda P \lambda s.seem(s, P(s))$:
$(e1 \multimap l) \multimap (e1 \multimap s)$

$\lambda s.\ seem\,(s, \exists e.[(s \sim e) \wedge hurt\,(e, a, t)])$:
$e1 \multimap s$

$\exists \varepsilon$

$\exists s.seem\,(s, \exists e.[(s \sim e) \wedge hurt\,(e, a, t)])$: s

FIGURE 12.4. Proof for an expletive alternant example of English copy raising, with meaning language.

12.4 Capturing Variation Lexically

The dialectal variation for copy raising, from surveys reported by Asudeh and Toivonen (2012), was summarized in Tables 12.1 and 12.2. Dialect B is like Dialect C in having copy raising, except that the copy pronoun must be the subject of the complement of *like/as*:

(85) **Dialect B: Restricted Copy Raising**
a. Alfred seems like he hurt Thora.
b. *Alfred seems like Thora hurt him.

The distinction between the two dialects is captured by restricting the argument of the copy raising template in the lexical entry of the copy raising verb as follows:

(86) *seem*$_{like}$, V^0
⋮
(@CR(↑ XCOMP COMP SUBJ))
⋮

The path is restricted such that the copy pronoun must be the SUBJ of the COMP of the copy raising verb's XCOMP. This is the highest overt subject, the subject of the complement of *like/as*. As indicated by the ellipses, the lexical entry is otherwise the same as the lexical entry for Dialect C in (71). Lastly, the CR template is again optional, which correctly allows Dialect B grammars to generate expletive-subject copy raising alternants, like *It seems like Alfred hurt Thora*, in the same way as in Dialect C.

Dialect A is even more strict than Dialect B. It does not have copy raising:

(87) **Dialect A: No Copy Raising**

a. *Alfred seems like he hurt Thora.

b. *Alfred seems like Thora hurt him.

This dialect is accounted for by deleting the CR template from the lexical entry for the copy raising verb. In other words, the lexical entries for Dialect A's copy raising verbs are just like those for Dialect C and Dialect B, except that there is no CR line. This correctly allows Dialect A grammars to generate expletive-subject copy raising alternants in the same way as in Dialect C, since these are generated when the optional CR template is absent.

Dialect D was the most permissive dialect, not requiring a copy pronoun at all with a copy raising verb:

(88) **Dialect D: No Copy Pronoun Required**

a. Alfred seems like Harry's hurt.

b. Alfred seems like Isak hurt Thora.

This dialect arguably has a modified interpretation for the copy raising subcategorization, such that the copy raising verb is in fact a control verb. Like Dialect A, this dialect lacks the CR template entirely. But unlike Dialects A–C, the putative copy raising verb is instead ambiguous, such that one reading is associated with a thematic subject, while the other reading is associated with the same raising meaning constructor as in (71) above. This ambiguity is somewhat unappealing, but is required to allow for the expletive alternation, as discussed further below. The meaning constructors are numbered in (89), for ease of subsequent reference.

(89) $seem_{like}$, V^0 $(\uparrow \text{PRED}) = \text{`seem'}$

@RAISING

$\{\ \lambda x \lambda P \lambda s.seem(s, x, P(s)) :$ ①

$(\uparrow \text{SUBJ})_\sigma \multimap [(\uparrow_\sigma \text{EVENT}) \multimap (\uparrow \text{XCOMP})_\sigma] \multimap (\uparrow_\sigma \text{EVENT}) \multimap \uparrow_\sigma$

$\lambda x \lambda P.P(x) :$ ②

$(\uparrow \text{SUBJ})_\sigma \multimap [(\uparrow \text{SUBJ}_\sigma) \multimap \uparrow_\sigma] \multimap \uparrow_\sigma \quad |$

$\lambda P \lambda s.seem(s, P(s)) :$ ③

$[(\uparrow_\sigma \text{EVENT}) \multimap (\uparrow \text{XCOMP})_\sigma] \multimap (\uparrow_\sigma \text{EVENT}) \multimap \uparrow_\sigma\ \}$

The first and second meaning constructors constitute one option for interpretation of the 'copy raising' verb in Dialect D, while the third meaning constructor constitutes the other.

The third meaning constructor in (89) is a raising meaning constructor, just as in (71). The second meaning constructor is the meaning constructor associated with the CR template in the other dialects. The first meaning constructor is the same as the meaning constructor for copy raising in the other dialects, except that the verb takes the matrix subject as an argument. Nevertheless, the verb invokes the RAISING template; i.e. it has the syntax of a raising verb, even though the matrix subject is an argument. This means that the relationship between the copy raising verb and its subject, in Dialect D, is like that of a subject control verb with that of its subject, rather than like that of a raising verb. This is, in effect, predicted by the standard LFG theory of functional control (Bresnan, 1982*a*), which posits the same syntactic relation of equality for raising and obligatory control, and LFG's grammatical architecture, which allows mismatches between levels of grammar (Kaplan and Bresnan, 1982; Kaplan, 1987, 1989), as discussed in chapter 3. Figure 12.5 shows a proof with meaning language for the Dialect D example (88b). Dialect D expletive examples are analysed exactly like the expletive examples in the other dialects, as previously illustrated in Figures 12.3 and 12.4.

The last aspect of dialectal variation to be captured concerns the nature of expletive subjects, which seems to cross-cut the four dialects. All speakers accept sentences like (90), and no speakers accept sentences like (91), but some speakers also accept sentences like (92):

(90) It seemed like there was a problem.

(91) *There seemed like it rained.

(92) %There seemed like there was a problem.

The existing lexical entries given in this section and the previous section generate (90) and correctly fail to generate (91), due to the RAISING template.

As discussed in section 12.1.2 above, the contrast between sentences like (91) and (92) indicates that the matrix expletive *there* is licensed only if there is an embedded expletive *there* in the *like*-complement. However, the f-structure projected by *like/as* itself has a SUBJ. In order to preserve the locality of raising, the lower *there* must be equated with this intervening subject position and the intervening subject position must then be equated with the matrix subject

(88b) Alfred seems like Isak hurt Thora.

hurt $\lambda y \lambda x \lambda e'.hurt(e', x, y) : t \multimap i \multimap e2 \multimap h$ **Thora** $t : t$

$$\frac{\lambda y \lambda x \lambda e'.hurt(e', x, y) : t \multimap i \multimap e2 \multimap h \qquad t : t}{\lambda x \lambda e'.hurt(e', x, t) : i \multimap e2 \multimap h}$$

Isak $i : i$

$$\frac{\lambda x \lambda e'.hurt(e', x, t) : i \multimap e2 \multimap h \qquad i : i}{\lambda e'.hurt(e', i, t) : e2 \multimap h}$$

like $\lambda P \lambda s'.\exists \varepsilon.[(s' \sim \varepsilon) \wedge P(\varepsilon)] : (e2 \multimap h) \multimap e1 \multimap l$

$$\frac{\lambda e'.hurt(e', i, t) : e2 \multimap h \qquad \lambda P \lambda s'.\exists \varepsilon.[(s' \sim \varepsilon) \wedge P(\varepsilon)] : (e2 \multimap h) \multimap e1 \multimap l}{\lambda s'.\exists e.[(s' \sim e) \wedge hurt(e, i, t)] : e1 \multimap l}\ [e/\varepsilon]$$

seems (Option 1) $\lambda x \lambda P \lambda s.seem(s, x, P(s)) : a \multimap (e1 \multimap l) \multimap (e1 \multimap s)$ $[z : a]^{1}$

$$\frac{\lambda x \lambda P \lambda s.seem(s, x, P(s)) : a \multimap (e1 \multimap l) \multimap (e1 \multimap s) \qquad [z : a]^{1}}{\lambda P \lambda s.seem(s, z, P(s)) : (e1 \multimap l) \multimap (e1 \multimap s)}$$

$$\frac{\lambda s'.\exists e.[(s' \sim e) \wedge hurt(e, i, t)] : e1 \multimap l \qquad \lambda P \lambda s.seem(s, z, P(s)) : (e1 \multimap l) \multimap (e1 \multimap s)}{\lambda s.seem(s, z, \exists e.[(s \sim e) \wedge hurt(e, i, t)]) : e1 \multimap s}$$

$$\frac{\lambda s.seem(s, z, \exists e.[(s \sim e) \wedge hurt(e, i, t)]) : e1 \multimap s}{\exists s.[seem(s, z, \exists e.[(s \sim e) \wedge hurt(e, i, t)])] : s}\ \exists \varepsilon$$

$$\frac{\exists s.[seem(s, z, \exists e.[(s \sim e) \wedge hurt(e, i, t)])] : s}{\lambda z.\ \exists s.[seem(s, z, \exists e.[(s \sim e) \wedge hurt(e, i, t)])] : a \multimap s}\ \multimap_{\mathcal{I},1}$$

Alfred $a : a$ **seems (Option 1)** $\lambda x \lambda P.P(x) : a \multimap (a \multimap s) \multimap s$

$$\frac{a : a \qquad \lambda x \lambda P.P(x) : a \multimap (a \multimap s) \multimap s}{\lambda P.P(a) : (a \multimap s) \multimap s}$$

$$\frac{\lambda P.P(a) : (a \multimap s) \multimap s \qquad \lambda z.\ \exists s.[seem(s, z, \exists e.[(s \sim e) \wedge hurt(e, i, t)])] : a \multimap s}{\exists s.seem(s, a, \exists e.[(s \sim e) \wedge hurt(e, i, t)]) : s}$$

FIGURE 12.5. Proof for English Dialect D 'copy raising', with meaning language.

position. This is shown in the following abbreviated f-structure for sentence (92).[16]

(93)

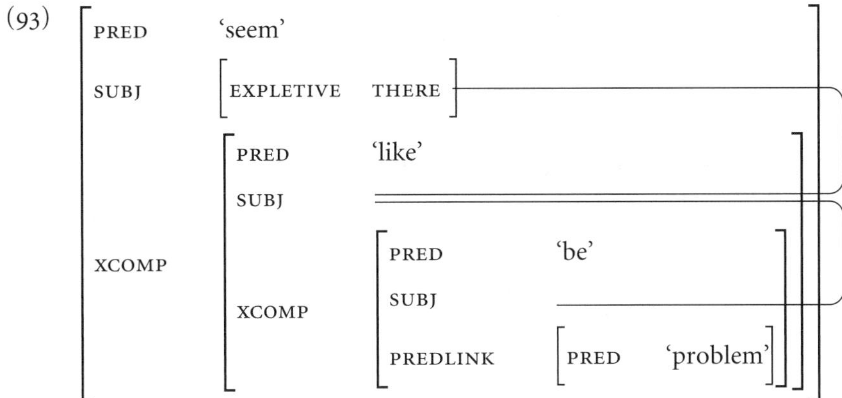

In other words, in order for the locality of raising to be preserved, *like* and *as* must therefore have raising alternants.

In dialects that allow (92), the lexical entry for *like/as* thus optionally calls the RAISING template:

(94) *like*, P^0 $(\uparrow \text{PRED}) = \text{`like'}$
(@RAISING)

%Complement = {XCOMP | COMP}
$\lambda P \lambda s. \exists \varepsilon. [(s \sim \varepsilon) \wedge P(\varepsilon)]$:
$[(\uparrow \%\text{Complement}_\sigma \text{ EVENT}) \multimap (\uparrow \%\text{Complement})_\sigma] \multimap$
$((\text{XCOMP} \uparrow)_\sigma \text{ EVENT}) \multimap \uparrow_\sigma$

The optional RAISING template, (72), can only be selected if both the subject of the copy raising verb and the subject of *like* are expletives, since the two subjects are equated by the copy raising verb. The first option in the template constrains the subject to be an expletive and states that there is no XCOMP, which is not possible. The second option, which is the raising option, equates the subject of *like* with that of its complement, but this subject is also equated with the matrix subject of the copy raising verb. If the two subjects are, by hypothesis, not expletives, there will be a Consistency violation due to distinct PRED features. Therefore, the addition of an optional RAISING template to

[16] The feature PREDLINK is sometimes used for closed copular complements (Butt et al., 1999; Dalrymple *et al.*, 2004*a*), as opposed to XCOMP, which is used for open copular complements. Open complements host their own SUBJ, which must be functionally controlled in order to satisfy Completeness, whereas closed complements do not have their own SUBJ. The PREDLINK function may be appropriate for at least some nominal complements to copulas (Dalrymple *et al.*, 2004*a*), but I use it here solely for simplification.

like does not affect the previous analyses in the chapter and has the effect of allowing doubled *there*-expletive subjects, in the grammars of speakers who allow this. Nothing more needs to be done to capture the variation in expletive subjects, but there are important implications of these facts, which are discussed further in the conclusion, section 12.6.

12.5 Further Consequences: Copy Raising and Scope

Copy raising verbs cannot take scope over their subjects, unlike raising verbs with infinitival complements. This observation, originally due to Lappin (1984), was extended to perceptual resemblance verbs by Potsdam and Runner (2001). The relevant data for copy raising is shown here:

(95) Every goblin seemed like he fainted.
every > seem
* *seem > every*

Copy raising only allows surface scope of the subject quantifier. Sentence (95) cannot mean that it seemed like every goblin fainted. It can only mean that every goblin is such that he seemed like he fainted; i.e. each goblin is involved in a distinct relation of semblance.

Contrast (95) with the related infinitival version:

(96) Every goblin seemed to faint.
every > seem
seem > every

This example has both a reading with *every goblin* taking wide scope over *seem* and one where the quantifier takes scope under *seem*.

The meaning constructor for *seem* with an infinitival complement or a finite *that*-complement is shown in (97). It is necessary to generalize over XCOMP, which is appropriate for infinitival raising, and COMP, which is appropriate for the *that*-complement. This is done by defining a complement meta-function, CF, using functional uncertainty(Dalrymple, 2001: 140): $\text{CF} \equiv \{\text{XCOMP}|\text{COMP}\}$.

(97) $\lambda p \lambda s.seem(s, p) : (\uparrow \text{CF})_\sigma \multimap (\uparrow_\sigma \text{EVENT}) \multimap \uparrow_\sigma$

This *seem* takes its complement function as its only argument, other than the eventuality argument. This means that the complement to standard raising, whether a finite *that*-clause or an infinitival clause, has the propositional type

t. I have shown in Asudeh (2005*a*: 488–489) that this allows both wide and narrow scope for quantificational subjects.[17]

The scope distinction between (95) and (96) is predicted from the interpretation of copy raising *seem*. The two relevant meaning constructors are shown in (98) and (99). The first is contributed by the copy raising verb directly, as in (71) above, and the second is contributed by the copy raising template, CR, as in (73) above. The meaning constructors are instantiated appropriately for (95), as per the usual mnemonic convention.

(98) $\lambda P \lambda s.seem(s, P(s)) : (e1 \multimap l) \multimap e1 \multimap s$ **copy raising *seem***

(99) $\lambda x \lambda P.P(x) : g \multimap (g \multimap s) \multimap s$ **copy raising *seem* (@CR)**

The crucial difference between copy raising *seem* and standard raising *seem*, as in (97), is that the copy raising verb, through the CR template, involves a dependency on the SUBJECT resource in the glue logic, whereas standard *seem* does not.

The quantifier *every goblin* contributes the following meaning constructor:

(100) $\lambda R \lambda S.every(R, S) : \forall X.[(g \multimap X) \multimap X]$

The quantifier can only take its scope by finding a dependency on g. There are thus two meaning constructors that are dependent on g: the quantifier's meaning constructor and the meaning constructor in (99).

The following are the lexically contributed meaning constructors for (95):

(101)

1. $\forall X.[(g \multimap X) \multimap X]$ Lex. **Every goblin**
2. $(e1 \multimap l) \multimap (e1 \multimap s)$ Lex. **seemed**
3. $g \multimap (g \multimap s) \multimap s$ Lex. **seemed (CR)**
4. $[g \multimap (g \otimes p)] \multimap (g \multimap g)$ Lex. **seemed (CR: MR)**
5. $(p \multimap s) \multimap (g \multimap s)$ Lex. **seemed (CR: RELABEL)**
6. $(e2 \multimap h) \multimap e1 \multimap l$ Lex. **like**
7. $g \multimap (g \otimes p)$ Lex. **he**
8. $p \multimap e2 \multimap f$ Lex. **fainted**

In this set of meaning constructors, there is one more meaning constructor that is dependent on g, the pronominal's meaning constructor, $g \multimap (g \otimes p)$. However, this will be removed by the manager resource. The quantifier's meaning constructor and the copy raising meaning constructor in (99) are thus the only two meaning constructors in play that depend on g.

[17] The analysis in Asudeh (2005*a*) does not assume an event semantics, but the result carries over straightforwardly, because it is not dependent on whether an event variable is present or not.

The only way for the quantifier to scope under *seem* is if it can take a dependency on g, $(g \multimap X)$, as its scope such that the dependency is not $g \multimap s$. However, the only dependency on g that can be constructed from these premises is $g \multimap s$, as in the following sub-proof:

(102)

$$\dfrac{\dfrac{\begin{array}{c}\textbf{seemed (CR: RELABEL)}\\ (p \multimap s) \multimap (a \multimap s)\end{array} \quad \dfrac{\dfrac{\dfrac{\dfrac{\dfrac{\begin{array}{c}\textbf{fainted}\\ p \multimap e2 \multimap f \quad [p]^{1}\end{array}}{e2 \multimap f} \quad \begin{array}{c}\textbf{like}\\ (e2 \multimap h) \multimap e1 \multimap l\end{array}}{e1 \multimap l} \quad \begin{array}{c}\textbf{seemed}\\ (e1 \multimap l) \multimap (e1 \multimap s)\end{array}}{e1 \multimap s}}{s}\,\exists\mathcal{E}}{p \multimap s}\,{\multimap_{\mathcal{I},1}}}{g \multimap s} \quad \begin{array}{c}\textbf{every goblin}\\ \forall X.[(g \multimap X) \multimap X]\end{array}}{s}\,[s/X]$$

This proof shows that the quantifier out-scopes *seem*, since it is necessarily introduced lower in the proof than the premise for *seem*. There are only two other potential dependencies that the quantifier could take scope over, $g \multimap f$ and $g \multimap l$, but there is no way to construct such dependencies, because there is no chain of implications such that $[g] \ldots f$ or $[g] \ldots l$. Furthermore, even if such a dependency could be constructed, the meaning constructor in (99) could not be satisfied, since it involves a dependency on $g \multimap s$ and the quantifier would have consumed the only such available dependency. This follows from the fact that the linear logic side of meaning constructor (99) is formally identical to that of a control verb, and it is an established result in Glue Semantics that such meaning constructors do not permit a quantifier subject to scope under them (Asudeh, 2005*a*).

The copy raising verb *seem* therefore, in principle, cannot out-scope the quantifier, because the only way to satisfy the quantifier's compositional requirement is if the quantifier out-scopes the verb. Figure 12.6 shows that a successful proof can be constructed in which the quantifier takes wide scope. Figure 12.7 shows the proof with the meaning language.

12.6 Conclusion

This chapter has extended the Resource Management Theory of Resumption to copy raising. This unification of the two kinds of resumption involves

(95) Every goblin seemed like he fainted.

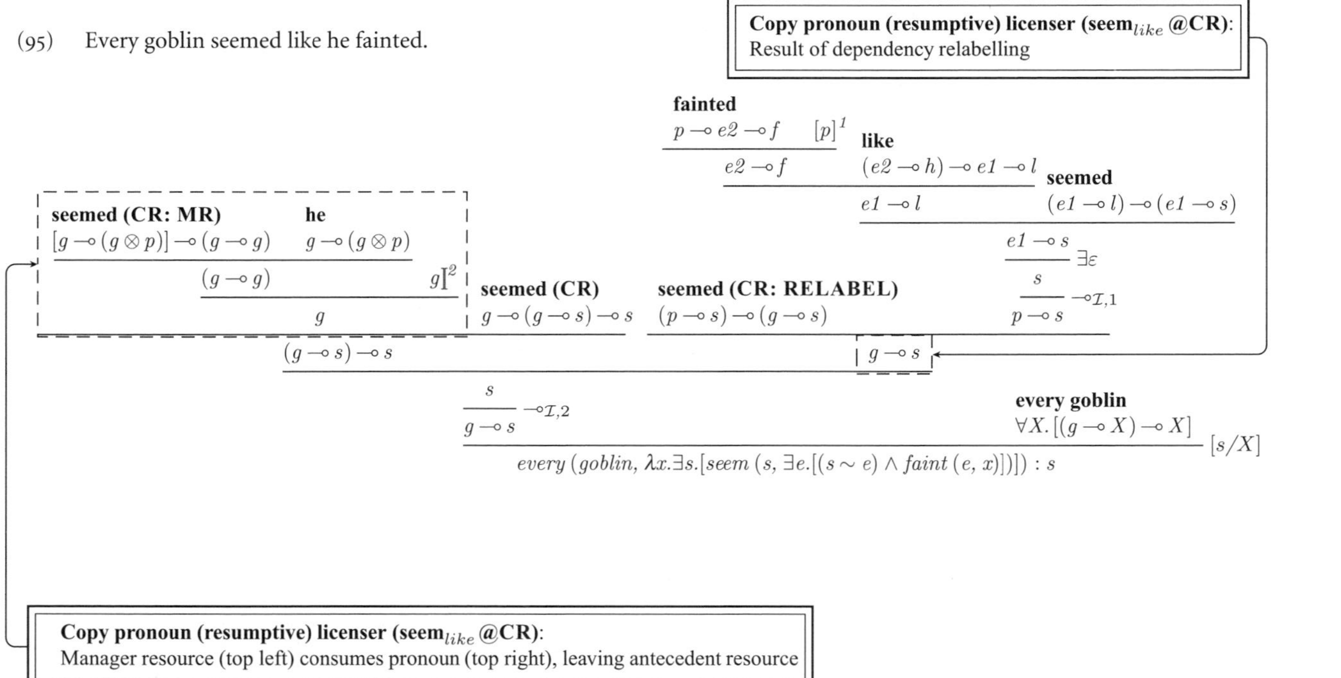

FIGURE 12.6. Proof for an English copy raising example with a quantifier subject.

(95) Every goblin seemed like he fainted.

fainted and $[z : p]^1$:

$$\frac{\lambda x\lambda e'.faint(e',x) : p \multimap e2 \multimap f \qquad [z:p]^{1}}{\lambda e'.faint(e',z) : e2 \multimap f}$$

like:

$$\frac{\lambda e'.faint(e',z) : e2 \multimap f \qquad \lambda P\lambda s'.\exists\varepsilon.[(s' \sim \varepsilon) \wedge P(\varepsilon)] : (e2 \multimap h) \multimap e1 \multimap l}{\lambda s'.\exists e.[(s' \sim e) \wedge faint(e,z)] : e1 \multimap l}\ [e/\varepsilon]$$

seemed:

$$\frac{\lambda s'.\exists e.[(s' \sim e) \wedge faint(e,z)] : e1 \multimap l \qquad \lambda P\lambda s, seem(s, P(s)) : (e1 \multimap l) \multimap (e1 \multimap s)}{\lambda s.seem(s, \exists e.[(s \sim e) \wedge faint(e,z)]) : e1 \multimap s}$$

$$\frac{\lambda s.seem(s, \exists e.[(s \sim e) \wedge faint(e,z)]) : e1 \multimap s}{\exists s.[seem(s, \exists e.[(s \sim e) \wedge faint(e,z)])] : s}\ \exists\varepsilon$$

$$\frac{\exists s.[seem(s, \exists e.[(s \sim e) \wedge faint(e,z)])] : s}{\lambda z.\exists s.[seem(s, \exists e.[(s \sim e) \wedge faint(e,z)])] : p \multimap s}\ \multimap_{\mathcal{I},1}$$

seemed (CR: MR) and **he**:

$$\frac{\lambda P\lambda y.y : [g \multimap (g \otimes p)] \multimap (g \multimap g) \qquad \lambda z.z \times z : g \multimap (g \otimes p)}{\lambda y.y : (g \multimap g)}$$

$$\frac{\lambda y.y : (g \multimap g) \qquad [x : g]^{2}}{x : g}$$

seemed (CR):

$$\frac{x : g \qquad \lambda y\lambda P.P(y) : g \multimap (g \multimap s) \multimap s}{\lambda P.P(x) : (g \multimap s) \multimap s}$$

seemed (CR: RELABEL):

$$\frac{\lambda P.P : (p \multimap s) \multimap (g \multimap s) \qquad \lambda z.\exists s.[seem(s, \exists e.[(s \sim e) \wedge faint(e,z)])] : p \multimap s}{\lambda z.\exists s.[seem(s, \exists e.[(s \sim e) \wedge faint(e,z)])] : g \multimap s}$$

$$\frac{\lambda P.P(x) : (g \multimap s) \multimap s \qquad \lambda z.\exists s.[seem(s, \exists e.[(s \sim e) \wedge faint(e,z)])] : g \multimap s}{\exists s.[seem(s, \exists e.[(s \sim e) \wedge faint(e,x)])] : s}$$

$$\frac{\exists s.[seem(s, \exists e.[(s \sim e) \wedge faint(e,x)])] : s}{\lambda x.\exists s.[seem(s, \exists e.[(s \sim e) \wedge faint(e,x)])] : g \multimap s}\ \multimap_{\mathcal{I},2}$$

every goblin:

$$\frac{\lambda x.\exists s.[seem(s, \exists e.[(s \sim e) \wedge faint(e,x)])] : g \multimap s \qquad \lambda S.every(goblin, S) : \forall X.[(g \multimap X) \multimap X]}{every(goblin, \lambda x.\exists s.[seem(s, \exists e.[(s \sim e) \wedge faint(e,x)])]) : s}\ [s/X]$$

FIGURE 12.7. Proof for an English copy raising example with a quantifier subject, with meaning language.

parametrizing the manager resource template, MR, and the dependency relabelling template, RELABEL, to either a local SUBJECT or a local UDF. The key aspect of the theory that generalizes resumption from unbounded dependencies to copy raising is the postulation of manager resources in the lexical entries of copy raising verbs. Thus, the mechanism that accounts for resumptive pronouns in unbounded dependencies also accounts for copy pronouns in copy raising. The analysis takes dialectal variation in English copy raising seriously. The variation between dialects is captured lexically. The analysis of copy raising also correctly predicts that the copy raising verb cannot take wide scope over its quantifier subject. Copy raising verbs were argued to be distinct from perceptual resemblance verbs, but the latter were not examined in detail. Further analysis of the perception verbs along the lines developed here can be found in Asudeh and Toivonen (2012).

A curious fact about copy raising verbs is that, for some speakers, they can raise expletives that they cannot otherwise take as subjects, as in (103).

(103) There seemed like there was a riot.

This was explained on the assumption that the prepositions *like* and *as* can exceptionally raise a subject from what would normally be a closed complement (e.g., *there was a riot*). The expletive *there* is raised from the complement of *like* or *as* to the subject of the preposition at f-structure and then raised again from that subject to the subject of the copy raising verb. Although it is convenient to describe the process using the procedural metaphor of 'raising', the theory is purely declarative. The expletive is therefore really just occupying three f-structural subject positions at once. The reason that the expletive is only realized in two c-structural positions follows from the general LFG assumption that lexical projections cannot take DPs in their specifiers at c-structure (Bresnan, 2001; Toivonen, 2001, 2003). Since the *like*-complement is a PP, it follows that the expletive in its subject position at f-structure is not realized in c-structure.

The behaviour of doubled *there* expletives challenges LFG's notion of open complements, because the finite, saturated complement to *like/as* would normally be expected to be a COMP, given LFG's standard structure-function mapping principles (Bresnan, 2001; Toivonen, 2001, 2003). However, unless we modify LFG's theory of functional control (Bresnan, 1982*a*), which has been a very stable part of the theory, there does not seem to be an alternative to calling the complement in question an XCOMP, in order that the lexical entry for *like/as* can use the RAISING template, which contains the normal functional control schema, ($\uparrow$ SUBJ) = (XCOMP SUBJ).

Doubled *there* expletives also challenge the adequacy of LFG's Subject Condition (Baker, 1983; Bresnan, 2001: 311):[18]

(104) **The Subject Condition**:
Every predicator must have a subject.

Since subjects are only defined at f-structure in LFG, the Subject Condition is a requirement that every f-structure predicator have a SUBJ grammatical function. If the double-raising analysis of the doubled *there* examples is correct, the overt distribution of expletives does not follow from the Subject Condition. In particular, there is no explanation of why it is impossible to have an expletive occupy the three positions at f-structure but only be realized in just the highest position:

(105) *There seems like is a problem.

At f-structure, the verb *is* does have a subject (the expletive), so the Subject Condition is satisfied. This points to the need for a c-structural correlate of the Subject Condition.

A version of the Subject Condition with a c-structural component could also explain the ungrammaticality of the following:

(106) *There seems there to be a problem.

In a sense, this sentence demonstrates the opposing problem to the problem in (105): the lower *there* is licensed at f-structure, but the c-structure position is not one that can normally host a subject. If the infinitival clause is analysed as an IP or CP, a c-structural Subject Condition, or a reference to TENSE at f-structure, seems necessary to block (106). Alternatively, if the infinitival clause is analysed as a VP (Pullum, 1982), the impossibility of (106) would follow from the standard assumption, mentioned above, that lexical categories cannot host subjects in their specifiers.[19]

A c-structural subject requirement would seem to mirror the structural requirement of checking an EPP feature in the Minimalist Program (Chomsky, 1995, 2000, 2001). There is thus some potentially interesting theoretical convergence. However, the EPP account is also challenged by the double *there* expletives. In particular, if the lower *there* checks its EPP feature in the lower

[18] The term 'predicator' in this principle is best understood as picking out any syntactic element that can serve a predicative function, such as verbs, but also heads of open, predicative complements, such as adjectives and certain prepositions and perhaps some nominals.

[19] Whatever the correct explanation of the ungrammaticality of (106) is, it should be clear that this type of sentence is a problem for the analysis of raising in general, not just for the analysis developed here.

clause, then there does not seem to be any way to raise it further to check an EPP feature in the upper clause. This indicates that the two *there* expletives are merged independently. But this does not explain why an upper *there* is licensed only if a lower *there* is present. Thus, the double expletive pattern is challenging for both theories and is a promising area for future work that might achieve a theoretical synthesis or at least form a further bridge between the two theories.

12.6.1 *Cross-Linguistic Prospects*

Copy raising is not just a quirk of English, but is actually quite widely attested cross-linguistically. It has been reported in such typologically diverse languages as Greek (Joseph, 1976; Perlmutter and Soames, 1979), Haitian Creole (Déprez, 1992), Hebrew (Lappin, 1984), Igbo (Ura, 1998), Irish (McCloskey and Sells, 1988), Persian (Darzi, 1996; Ghomeshi, 2001), Samoan (Chung, 1978), and Turkish (Moore, 1998).

Although I have only addressed copy raising in English, it should be apparent how the analysis could be extended to other languages and Asudeh and Toivonen (2012) present a careful comparative study of copy raising in English and Swedish, two closely related Germanic languages. The key aspect of any such cross-linguistic generalization of the analysis is that the copy raising verb contributes a manager resource that consumes a copy pronoun's resource. Other details may vary. For example, many languages do not have the equivalent of the English prepositions *like* and *as* in copy raising. Results of surveys conducted by Asudeh, Toivonen, Ludwig, Pucilowski, and van Egmond (reported in part in Asudeh and Toivonen, 2012; also see footnote 2 above) show that Dutch, English, German, and Swedish pattern somewhat differently to each other, with respect to the proportion of speakers that speak each of the four dialects discussed in this chapter (Dialects A–D), and other factors. Van Egmond (2004) investigates Dutch in more detail and finds that Dutch speakers also generally require a pronoun in copy raising, but the grammars of Dutch speakers otherwise pattern somewhat differently to those of English speakers. Much more work needs to be done on the typology of copy raising.

The resource management analysis of copy raising already shows potential in the analysis of copy raising in Irish, where it makes sense of an otherwise puzzling fact. Although Irish has the resumptive-sensitive complementizer *aN* and copy pronouns seem to be intuitively similar to resumptive pronouns, the neutral complementizer *go* is used to introduce the copy raising complement (McCloskey and Sells, 1988: 174–178):

(107) B'éigean daobhtha gur innis siad an scéal dó.
must to.them COMP told they the story to.him
'They must have told him the story.'
(McCloskey and Sells, 1988: 176, (65c))

(108) Ní cosuúil dó go gcuireann rud ar birth buaireamh air.
NEG.COP like to.him COMP puts thing any distress on.him
'Nothing seems to bother him.'
(McCloskey and Sells, 1988: 177, (68a))

The Resource Management Theory of Resumption correctly predicts that the neutral complementizer *go* must be used in Irish copy raising. The theory assumes that the copy raising verb contributes a manager resource. This licenses the copy pronoun in the complement and allows proper composition. The Irish resumptive-sensitive complementizer *aN* also contributes a manage resource. This is how the complementizer licenses resumptive pronouns in unbounded dependencies. But if both the copy raising verb and the complementizer *aN* were present, then there would be two manager resources contributed. It would not be possible to satisfy the needs of both manager resources with a single copy pronoun. Therefore, the resumptive-sensitive complementizer cannot be used in copy raising and the neutral complementizer must be used instead.

13

Conclusion

This book has presented a new theory of resumption, which is based on the theoretical hypothesis in (1) and the typological generalization in (2).

(1) **The Resource Sensitivity Hypothesis**
Natural language is resource-sensitive.

(2) **McCloskey's Generalization**
Resumptive pronouns are ordinary pronouns.

McCloskey's Generalization (McCloskey, 2002: 192) entails that resumptive pronouns are ordinary pronouns. As ordinary pronouns, resumptive pronouns constitute surplus resources for resource-sensitive semantic composition. The key issue of resumption is thus an issue of semantic composition. This was recognized independently in the early literature on resumption (McCloskey, 1979), but subsequently ceased to inform analyses of resumption in a deep way.

The Resource Sensitivity Hypothesis derives from Linguistic Resource Sensitivity, which in turn derives from Logical Resource Sensitivity. Resource logics, which are characterized by the absence of the structural rules of weakening and contraction, yield a useful perspective on linguistic combinatorics, including those of phonology, syntax, and semantics. All of these systems are equally resource-sensitive, in that no element of combination may be freely discarded or reused, but they are order-sensitive to differing degrees. Thus, the structural rule of commutativity, which enables reordering of premises in a proof, was also shown to be relevant. The fundamental operation of semantic composition, functional application, is not order-sensitive. The resource logic that is appropriate for characterizing semantic combinatorics is therefore linear logic, which is commutative.

Although resource logics alone give some insight into linguistic combinatorics, Logical Resource Sensitivity on its own is not linguistically illuminating. The relationship between Logical and Linguistic Resource Sensitivity is affected by the choice of logical connectives. If conjunction is present, Logical

Resource Sensitivity is no longer satisfactory for a characterization of linguistic combinatorics. Linguistic Resource Sensitivity can be regained in a system with conjunction by imposing on the resource logic proof a goal condition that is motivated by linguistic theory. Thus, Linguistic Resource Sensitivity is founded on Logical Resource Sensitivity but requires input from linguistic theory. Linguistic Resource Sensitivity for semantics and the syntax–semantics interface can be captured using Glue Semantics, which uses linear logic for semantic composition. A number of proposals in the literature constitute appeals to Resource Sensitivity and can possibly be eliminated, without losing their important insights.

The Resource Sensitivity Hypothesis is tested by cases of apparent resource deficit or resource surplus. As a case of resource surplus, resumptive pronouns thus constitute a key test of RSH. The Resource Management Theory of Resumption was offered as a solution. If a resumptive pronoun is an ordinary pronoun, maintaining McCloskey's Generalization, then it constitutes a surplus semantic resource. If RSH is correct, then there must be an additional consumer of the pronominal resource present. RMTR proposes *manager resources* as consumers of pronominal resources and, thus, licensers of resumption.

The Resource Management Theory of Resumption unifies resumption in two key respects:

1. Syntactically inactive resumptive pronouns, which are syntactically similar to gaps, and syntactically active resumptive pronouns, which are not syntactically similar to gaps, are equivalent with respect to semantic composition, since both classes equally constitute surplus resources and are licensed by manager resources.
2. Resumptive pronouns in unbounded dependencies and copy pronouns in copy raising are both instances of resumption, since they equally constitute surplus resources and are licensed by manager resources. The key distinction is that, in the former case, resumptive licensing is stated with respect to a local unbounded dependency function, whereas in the latter case it is stated with respect to a local subject.

RMTR was applied in detail to analyses of unbounded dependency resumption in Irish, Hebrew, Swedish, and Vata, and to copy raising resumption in English.

Following Chao and Sells (1983), Sells (1984), McCloskey (2006), and Asudeh (2004, 2011c), English resumptive pronouns were treated as a distinct, third kind of resumption which is not grammatically licensed. I presented a processing model for English resumptives, which I called processor resumptives. The model attempts to account both for their production and their parsing and interpretation. With respect to production, the model treats processor resumptives as a natural consequence of the attempt to construct locally well-formed structures and the prioritization of local well-formedness over global well-formedness. Processor resumptives are thus uttered in contexts in which they are appropriate for the underlying message plan and in which they lead to local well-formedness. With respect to parsing, sentences containing processor resumptives are perceived as ungrammatical, because they are not licensed by the grammar and are ill-formed. Thus, the production of processor resumptives is explained without assuming that they are underlyingly grammatical. Nevertheless, an ill-formed resumptive pronoun sentence may be perceived as more well-formed than a corresponding sentence with a gap, as in the case of complexity resumptives, if there is sufficient complexity in the sentence to render the equivalent sentence with a gap as even more difficult to process than the version with the unlicensed resumptive pronoun. Lastly, with respect to interpretation, processor resumptives partially support only a coreferential or E-type reading and do not support a bound interpretation. The reading is available for a lower type antecedent, such as a definite, but the bound interpretation is the only available option for a higher type antecedent, such as a quantifier. In both cases, since the sentence is underlyingly ill-formed, there is no full interpretation, but the partial interpretation in the case of the coreferential or E-type reading is more informative than the partial information in the case of the bound reading.

13.1 Predictions of the Resource Management Theory and the Processing Theory

This section presents some predictions of the Resource Management Theory of Resumption and of the processing theory, as well as predictions of the two theories taken together. The consequences of RMTR were discussed in depth in previous chapters, but they are mentioned again where appropriate, in order to better reveal the big picture.

13.1.1 *General Predictions*

True resumptives and processor resumptives alike are ordinary pronouns in the overall theory. A true resumptive is grammatically licensed by a manager resource. Processor resumptives are inserted through the usual grammatical means, in order to preserve local well-formedness. Complexity resumptives that are removed by successful reanalysis are also initially generated by the normal grammar. However, complexity resumptives could not be inserted in the first place if, for example, they did not have the right case or agreement information. In all cases, the simple insertion of the pronoun into local structure means that whatever grammatical constraints the pronoun brings with it must be satisfied or else modified independently. For syntactically active true resumptives, there is no modification beyond the licensing mechanism itself (i.e., the manager resource). For syntactically inactive true resumptives, the restriction operator is also necessary to permit proper syntactic integration.

The overall theory therefore makes the following general prediction:

(3) A resumptive pronoun's lexical information is preserved.

The term 'lexical information' is meant to encompass the form of the pronoun, any restrictions it places on binding, and whatever grammatical information it bears. Grammatical information includes agreement, case, and any conditions the pronoun places on its antecedent through lexical specification.

13.1.2 *Interpretation*

Since both true resumptives and processor resumptives are just ordinary pronouns, the following prediction is made.

(4) Resumptive pronouns are interpreted as ordinary pronouns.

True resumptives receive a bound interpretation. This is an intepretation that is available for other pronouns. Island resumptives and COMP resumptives receive a coreferential or E-type interpretation. These are also generally available pronominal interpretations. Complexity resumptives are not interpreted at all if successfully reanalysed and therefore satisfy this prediction vacuously.

A corollary of (3) and (4) is:

(5) True, grammatically licensed resumptives and processor resumptives alike block non-specific/*de dicto* readings.

Zimmermann (1993) shows that *de dicto* readings are contingent on properties of certain quantified NPs. Sells (1984, 1987) shows that pronouns in general cannot take these sorts of NPs as antecedents. It is therefore a lexical property of pronouns that they cannot take such antecedents and this is preserved under the current theory.

The theory correctly predicts that processor resumptives in English block the non-specific reading, as shown in (6–8) for island resumptives, COMP resumptives, and complexity resumptives, respectively.

(6) John is seeking a unicorn that Mary doubts if he will find it.

(7) John is seeking a unicorn that Mary knows that it will shy away from him.

(8) John is seeking a unicorn that Mary claimed Bill told Susan that no one except a fool would persist in the attempt to find it.

None of these sentences permit a non-specific/*de dicto* reading.

13.1.3 *Islands and 'COMP-trace' Effects*

The first prediction regarding islands concerns syntactically active resumptives:

(9) Syntactically active resumptives, which are grammatically licensed, are not island-sensitive and do not give rise to 'COMP-trace' effects.

This follows from the fact that grammatically licensed resumption in RMTR involves pronominal binding which is not island-sensitive and which does not give rise to 'COMP-trace' effects. This is a standard prediction made by most theories of resumptives for the simple reason that most theories treat resumption as a kind of binding, rather than a kind of movement (for an exception, see Boeckx, 2001, 2003). This prediction is confirmed by Irish and Hebrew.

The processing model also makes the following predictions:

(10) Island resumptives and COMP resumptives result in local well-formedness, but the resulting parse is globally ill-formed.

(11) Since island resumptives and COMP resumptives do not result in a globally well-formed, full parse, they result in only partial interpretations.

The second prediction has not been confirmed by experimental work, but the first prediction has been confirmed by a number of independent studies.

McDaniel and Cowart (1999) and Alexopoulou and Keller (2002, 2003, 2007) found that insertion of a resumptive pronoun does not improve the grammaticality of a weak island violation. These experiments were all carried out using similar methodologies that involved Magnitude Estimation (Bard et al., 1996; Cowart, 1997) for grammaticality judgements of written material. Magnitude Estimation allows subjects to construct their own scale and is an inherently relational measure of grammaticality, since subjects compare grammaticality of subsequent items to an initial item to which they have assigned an arbitrary value. Alexopoulou and Keller's experiments were carried out on the web using WebExp,[1] whereas McDaniel and Cowart's experiment was carried out using a scannable line-drawing method (Cowart, 1997: 74–75). McDaniel and Cowart's experiment was on English. Alexopoulou and Keller (2002) ran experiments for English and Greek that were methodologically identical and Alexopoulou and Keller (2003) ran a third, equivalent experiment for German. Alexopoulou and Keller (2007) report on all three experiments. In all of these experiments, island resumptives in weak islands were reported to be worse than grammatical controls and as bad as equivalent items with gaps. Alexopoulou and Keller (2002, 2003, 2007) ran items at both one level of embedding and two levels of embedding. A control was included at zero levels of embedding. The zero-embedding control did not contain an island, but it did contain a resumptive pronoun which was judged to be vastly worse than a gap. The weak island resumptives did not even improve at two levels of embedding. Complexity resumptives did not improve with embedding either, but it should be noted that two levels of embedding is not necessarily thought to be sufficient for parsing complexity to arise (Lewis, 1996). The theoretical literature also indicates that more embedding than this is required for distance to improve resumption (Erteschik-Shir, 1992). As noted in chapter 11, initial results of some thus-far unpublished experiments (Hofmeister and Norcliffe, in progress) show greater acceptability for resumptives than gaps in stimuli with a greater degree of complexity than those of Alexopoulou and Keller, which is in line with the theory of complexity resumptives that has been presented here. Lastly, as also discussed in chapter 11, Ferreira and Swets (2005) report on results of two forced-scale grammaticality judgement experiments, one with a visual presentation and the other with an auditory presentation, that show resumptives to be judged as worse than gaps in both modalities.

The case for strong islands is slightly murkier and perhaps therefore more interesting. Alexopoulou and Keller (2002, 2007) tested island resumptives in strong islands (but not in 'COMP-trace' positions). The following are samples of their items for strong islands at one level of embedding and at two levels of embedding:

(12) Who does Mary meet the people that will fire __ /<u>him</u>?

(13) Who does Jane think that Mary meets the people that will fire __ /<u>him</u>?

[1] Software and documentation available at `http://fordyce.inf.ed.ac.uk/`; retrieved 20/02/2011.

It must be noted that the use of the present tense in these example sounds quite odd in English, since it leads to a habitual interpretation that is hard to contextualize, but this feature was constant across items. The important point is that in both the English and Greek experiments resumptive pronouns failed to improve the grammaticality of strong island violations. There was no significant difference between the grammaticality of resumptives and gaps in either the one- or two-level embedding. All of the items were judged to be as bad as ones with a zero-level resumptive pronoun, as in the following example.

(14) *Who will we fire <u>him</u>?

This item got the worst ratings in both English and Greek and intuitions confirm its ungrammaticality in both languages.

In contrast, in the experiment on German (Alexopoulou and Keller, 2003, 2007), strong islands were the only condition in which resumptives became significantly better than gaps. However, it is a little hard to know what to make of this data. Resumptive pronouns in strong islands, whether at one or two levels of embedding, were not significantly better than zero-level resumptives, which are as bad in German as in English and Greek. What happened instead was that gaps became drastically bad in strong islands. But the gaps were still not significantly worse than the zero-level resumptives. Thus, although the gaps became worse than resumptives, all the data points are crowded together and if we take the zero-level resumptive as the gold standard of ungrammaticality for the experiment, resumptives and gaps alike were ungrammatical. The results show not so much that island resumptives improve strong islands in German, but rather that German speakers have extremely low tolerance for strong island violations.

The German results are all the more interesting, because they potentially have implications for the independent phenomenon of sluicing (see Merchant, 2001, and references therein). It has been claimed in the theoretical literature that "standard German seems not to possess the kind of resumptive strategy familiar from English ('intrusive' resumptives) at all" (Merchant, 2001: 139). I have argued that the English "resumptive strategy" is just a processing strategy and that the resulting sentences are ungrammatical and only partially interpretable. The experimental results uphold this. The examples that Merchant (2001) gives do not undermine this theoretical position, since all they show is that speakers of German, like speakers of English, resist resumptive pronouns. What would have to be shown is that speakers of German do not even build a partial interpretation for these sentences. That would be more problematic on this theory, but how to show the lack of partial interpretation is a difficult question. In turn, the present theory does not undermine Merchant's main point, which is that sluicing cannot be reduced to a binder-resumptive dependency. This result stands, because all that is necessary to establish it is that German does not allow resumption but allows sluicing, which Merchant (2001) demonstrates to be true. If German does allow resumptives in strong islands, then this undermines both the present theory, because this is predicted to be ungrammatical, and Merchant's theory, since German would after all have some kind of resumptive strategy (although any proponent of the resumptive analysis of sluicing would have to explain why the resumptive strategy is so marginal, while sluicing is not). However, in order to establish that German does have a resumptive strategy, it must be demonstrated that resumptives in strong islands are better than controls, not just better than gaps, and this has not been demonstrated.

In addition to testing weak-island resumptives, McDaniel and Cowart (1999) tested COMP resumptives. They found that COMP resumptives were in fact significantly better than gaps following a complementizer. The theory of processor resumptives developed here does not exactly predict this, but it does not necessarily conflict with the theory either. In order to predict this finding, the theory would have to be invested with a notion of degrees of grammaticality (Keller, 2000). At present, the theory merely predicts that complexity resumptives are ungrammatical, which McDaniel and Cowart's results generally confirm. Their findings can be accommodated in the current theory if we make the auxiliary assumptions that (1) in addition to any island violation that is common to COMP resumptives and corresponding gaps, a gap in the same position violates a further constraint, namely the 'COMP-trace' filter or its equivalent (see Asudeh, 2009, for a recent treatment and further references), and (2) additional violations result in additional ungrammaticality (having assumed degrees of grammaticality). This seems like a reasonable assumption and is what is generally independently assumed to be behind the observation that 'COMP-trace' violations in islands are worse than island violations on their own. The present theory undermines the assertion by McDaniel and Cowart (1999: B23) that their results "provide evidence for a framework like Minimalism that incorporates competition among derivations". There is no competition among derivations in the theory of grammar that I have been assuming and, if I am granted the assumption, which McDaniel and Cowart (1999) share, that gaps after overt complementizers violate additional grammatical constraints that do not apply to pronouns, then their pattern of data is predicted. Therefore, their results are compatible with both a framework that has competition among derivations and one that does not and fails to provide any evidence for the former kind of framework. In so far as a competition-based theory involves transderivationality, where transderivationality is an added theoretical assumption, their findings actually undermine competition-based theories, for reasons of parsimony, given that their results are also consistent with a theory that does not assume competition.

The processing theory also makes predictions about complexity resumptives with respect to islands and 'COMP-trace' effects:

(15) Complexity resumptives in an island or 'COMP-trace' configuration in a language that does not have grammatical constraints against the relevant configuration display the following characteristics:
  a. In short/non-complex dependencies where the filler is active, the complexity resumptive is ungrammatical.
  b. In long/complex dependencies where the filler is no longer active, the complexity resumptive leads to successful reanalysis and the sentence is grammatical.

These predictions have not been verified by experimental work to my knowledge, but there is evidence to this effect in the theoretical literature (Engdahl, 1985; Erteschik-Shir, 1992).

Prediction (15a) is verified by Swedish pairs like the following:

(16) Vilken tavla kände du faktiskt killen som målat?
which picture knew you in fact the.guy that painted
'Which painting did you actually know the guy who painted?'
(Engdahl, 1985: 10, (15))

(17) *Vilken tavla kände du faktiskt killen som målat <u>den</u>?
which picture knew you in fact the.guy that painted it
'Which painting did you actually know the guy who painted (it)?'
(Engdahl, 1985: 10, (15))

The first sentence is a short strong island violation that the grammar of Swedish allows. The corresponding sentence with a processor resumptive is ungrammatical.

Prediction (15b) is also verified by Swedish. I argued in chapter 11 that extraction out of a non-extraposed sentential subject in Swedish counts as complex. If the argument that these extractions are complex is correct, the theory correctly predicts that a resumptive pronoun is possible instead of a gap, as demonstrated by the following example:

(18) Vilken skådespelare var det att publiken inte kände igen honom
which actor was it that the.audience not recognize him
ganska konstigt?
rather strange
'(Which actor was that the audience did not recognize him rather strange?)'

(Engdahl, 1982: 165, (58))

In contrast to (17), this example is not perceived as ill-formed.

13.1.4 *Local Well-Formedness*

The experiments discussed in the previous section confirm the global ill-formedness of island resumptives and complexity resumptives, but they have nothing to say about local well-formedness, since they were all off-line experiments and therefore only accessed judgements of global well-formedness. The prediction of the processing theory is that, despite their global ill-formedness, sentences with processor resumptives contain only locally well-formed structures. The processing theory therefore makes the following prediction about the timing of on-line processing:

(19) If an on-line processing task measures local well-formedness, structures containing processor resumptives will do better on the measure than corresponding structures with gaps.

A simple self-paced reading task may be enough to demonstrate this. If self-paced reading can indeed be construed as a measure of local well-formedness and if participants take longer to initiate presentation of the next word after a gap than after a processor resumptive, the prediction above would be supported.[2]

13.1.5 *Weak Crossover*

The Resource Management Theory of Resumption predicts that, all else being equal, syntactically active resumptives do not cause weak crossover violations, but that syntactically active resumptives do. The processing theory makes the following prediction:

(20) Complexity resumptives can result in weak crossover violations.

If weak crossover is a diagnostic of gaps, then this follow due to the theory's claim that complexity resumptives are reanalysed as gaps.

[2] Self-paced reading may, in fact, be a measurement of global well-formedness up to each continuation point. If that is the case, it is not clearly an appropriate task to test this prediction.

Testing complexity resumptives for weak crossover is quite difficult. Since the sentences are independently long or otherwise complex, it is quite hard to bring out the weak crossover effect. The version of the following example with a gap is quite a bit worse than the version with a pronoun, but we know that this level of embedding leads to gaps being degraded anyway:

(21) > Who$_i$ did his$_i$ mother tell Mary that Nikki said that Thora suspects that Sarah saw him$_i$ yesterday.

(22) < Who$_i$ did his$_i$ mother tell Mary that Nikki said that Thora suspects that Sarah saw __$_i$ yesterday.

It also seems that example (21), repeated below as (24), is worse than a complexity resumptive example in which both pronouns are embedded quite low:

(23) > Who$_i$ did Alli tell Jo that Nikki said that Thora suspects that his$_i$ mother saw him$_i$ yesterday.

(24) < Who$_i$ did his$_i$ mother tell Mary that Nikki said that Thora suspects that Sarah saw him$_i$ yesterday.

If these judgements are upheld, it indicates that weak crossover violations are perceived quite early.

13.1.6 *Reconstruction*

The Resource Management Theory of Resumption predicts that syntactically active resumptives do not license reconstruction, but that syntactically inactive resumptives do, all else being equal. The processing theory makes the following additional predictions, based on the fact that complexity resumptives are reanalysed as gaps, but that island resumptives and COMP resumptives are not.

(25) Island resumptives and COMP resumptives block reconstruction.

(26) Complexity resumptives do not block reconstruction.

Safir (1986: 685) has claimed that English island resumptives do not allow reconstruction (Safir's judgement is given):

(27) ?* Michael Jackson, a picture of whom Mary wondered who would buy it, arrives tomorrow.

This is at least suggestive that the theory is on the right track.

The prediction for complexity resumptives was confirmed by the original reconstruction data from Zaenen et al. (1981), although reconstruction is not straightforward even for these cases:

(28) Vilken av sina$_i$ flickvänner undrade du om det att Kalle$_i$ inte längre
which of his girlfriends wondered you if it that Kalle no longer
fick träffa henne$_i$ kunde ligga bakom hans dåliga humör?
sees her could lie behind his bad mood
'Which of his girlfriends do you think the fact that Kalle no longer gets to see (her) could be behind his bad mood?'
(Zaenen et al., 1981: 680, (6))

The resumptive in this example is in a non-extraposed sentential subject. These resumptives were argued to be complexity resumptives, and the possibility of reconstruction is correctly predicted. Much more work needs to be done on the question of reconstruction for both grammatically licensed resumptives and processor resumptives.

13.1.7 *Parasitic Gaps and Across-the-Board Extraction*

RMTR predicts that syntactically active resumptives do not license parasitic gaps and ATB extraction, but that syntactically inactive resumptives license both, all else being equal. This does not mean that no other constraints can hold of these structures. For example, the fact that Hebrew syntactic resumptives do not robustly license parasitic gaps can be due to other aspects of its grammar, such as the Leftness Condition discussed by Sells (1984) and Demirdache (1991).

The processing theory makes the following predictions about parasitic gaps and ATB extraction:

(29) a. Island resumptives and COMP resumptives do not license parasitic gaps.
b. Island resumptives and COMP resumptives lead to ATB extraction violations.

(30) a. Complexity resumptives license parasitic gaps.
b. Complexity resumptives do not violate the constraint on ATB extraction.

Again, these predictions are due to the fact that complexity resumptives are reanalysed as grammatical gaps, whereas island resumptives and COMP resumptives cannot be reanalysed grammatically.

Turning first to parasitic gaps, prediction (29a) is hard to test, since these processor resumptives are ungrammatical anyway, but the following examples lend some initial plausibility:

(31) *Which cats do you forget if John deloused them without hurting P ?

(32) *What did you wonder if it repulsed John upon tasting P ?

The first of these is an attempt to license a parasitic gap by an island resumptive and the second by a COMP resumptive. Both examples seem quite bad.

Furthermore, a weak island with a gap—which is normally perceived as only weakly ungrammatical, as confirmed by experimental results (Alexopoulou and Keller, 2002, 2003, 2007)—marginally licenses a parasitic gap, whereas the same example with an island resumptive does not:

(33) > Which cake do you forget if John dropped __ before tasting P ?

(34) < Which cake do you forget if John dropped it before tasting P ?

Although these judgements need to be tested more systematically, they provide initial confirmation of prediction (29a).

Turning to ATB extraction, a weak-island gap is similarly better than a weak-island resumptive:

(35) > What show do you forget if Thora watches __ but dislikes P ?

(36) < What show do you forget if Thora watches it but dislikes P ?

Again, although these judgements need to be tested more systematically, they provide initial support for prediction (29b).

Prediction (30a), about complexity resumptives, does not initially seem to be supported, because a complexity resumptive does not seem to allow a parasitic gap in examples like the following:

(37) *What did Madeline tell Mary that Nikki said that Thora suspected that Sarah sold it after buying P ?

However, this could well be due to the adjunct being parsed with the material containing the complexity resumptive, in which case the parasitic gap is not perceived as having a proper host gap. If more material is added to the right of the complexity resumptive, the sentence becomes somewhat improved:

(38) ?What did Madeline tell Mary that Nikki said that Thora suspected that Sarah sold it to the scary man from Gloucester who frightens children after buying P ?

Nevertheless, it again seems that we need a better way to test such cases.

With respect to prediction (30b), ATB cases pattern similarly. They are bad if the ATB gap is parsed with the complexity resumptive, but improve with the addition of separating material:

(39) > Which book did Madeline tell Mary that Nikki said that Thora suspected that Sarah reads it repeatedly to the kids at Harry's preschool who are there on Thursdays, but still enjoys _ ?

(40) < Which book did Madeline tell Mary that Nikki said that Thora suspected that Sarah reads it repeatedly, but still enjoys _ ?

For reasons that I do not understand, I find the option without intervening material better for ATB extraction, as in (40), than for parasitic gaps, as in (37).

13.2 Alternative Approaches

A number of alternative approaches to resumption have been discussed in the main body of the book. This section provides some further discussion of those analyses and of some analyses that have not been mentioned explicitly yet.

There are a number of theories of resumption that can be characterized as transformational syntactic operator-binding theories; examples include the analyses of McCloskey (1979, 1990, 2002), Borer (1984), Sells (1984), Demirdache (1991), Pesetsky (1998), Boeckx (2001, 2003), and Alexopoulou (2006). The theory of McCloskey (2002) was discussed in detail In chapter 7. As McCloskey (2002) notes, the problem for this kind of theory is ensuring proper semantic composition. In particular, if the abstraction operation that the operator intitiates applies in intermediate positions, then the correct semantics is not derived. I argued in chapter 7 that the Irish mixed chain cases constitute a challenge for the operator-binding approach with respect to semantic composition, even if the intermediate traces can be handled somehow.

There are specific exemplars of transformational operator-binding theories that treat resumption as involving movement. Two salient examples are Pesetsky (1998) and Boeckx (2003). Movement analyses are challenged by the syntactically active resumptive pronouns, which are not island-sensitive, do not give rise to weak crossover effects, and do not license reconstruction, ATB extraction, or parasitic gaps. Boeckx (2003) is a movement treatment of resumptives that attempts to deal with the island issues. Boeckx (2003: 151–157) also makes some remarks about weak crossover and reconstruction. It may be that these arguments can be met by movement analyses. However, there is another reason to assume that resumption is not movement and that has to do with form-identity effects. Merchant (2001) notes that moved *wh*-operators can have non-default case if the extraction site is a gap. This is explained on the standard transformational assumption that Case is assigned in the base position of filler-gap dependencies or by the standard assumption in declarative constraint-based theories, like HPSG and LFG, that the head of the filler-gap dependency simultaneously occupies the top and bottom of the dependency. Merchant (2001: 136) observes that the binder in a binder-resumptive dependency, in contrast, cannot be case-marked (the "Case and resumptive-binding operator generalization"). If resumption is movement, the lack of case-marking is unexplained. This argument is pursued in detail by Merchant (2004).

A number of theories of resumptive pronouns invoke Last Resort mechanisms. Examples of such approaches include Shlonsky (1992), Pesetsky (1998), Aoun and Benmamoun (1998), Aoun et al. (2001), Willis (2000), and Alexopoulou (2006). The Swedish dialect data on Ålandssvenska, which was presented in chapter 9, undermines the empirical adequacy of these approaches. In the Ålandssvenska dialect of Swedish, there is no 'COMP-trace' filter, yet resumptive pronouns are also possible in the relevant positions. This is completely mysterious on a Last Resort account, which in general predicts that resumptive pronouns should occur only where gaps are blocked. This compounds the difficulty faced by such approaches with Hebrew, Irish, and Welsh, in which there are a variety of positions in which both resumptives and gaps occur. The Hebrew data lead Shlonsky (1992) to propose ambiguity in the Hebrew complementizer system. Such an account could be extended to the Swedish dialect facts, by stipulation, but it is not independently motivated. Similarly, in Irish both gaps and resumptive pronouns are also permitted in direct object positions and in embedded subject positions. Once again, an ambiguous licenser could be proposed. However, if the cost of maintaining Last Resort is the postulation of lexical ambiguity in language after language, then the cost is too great. Matters might be different if there were good theoretical reasons to assume Last Resort, but the principle in fact suffers serious theoretical drawbacks as well. In particular, it is a transderivational principle and has the problems of all such principles (Jacobson, 1998; Johnson and Lappin, 1997, 1999; Potts, 2001, 2002*b*; Pullum and Scholz, 2001). There thus seems to be very little empirical or theoretical motivation for Last Resort theories of resumption.

There are also a number of alternative non-transformational approaches to resumptive pronouns, including the GPSG accounts of Maling and Zaenen (1982) and Sells (1984), the HPSG accounts of Vaillette (2001, 2002), Assmann et al. (2010), Borsley (2010), the Dynamic Syntax accounts of Cann *et al.* (2005*a*,*b*), and the alternative LFG accounts of Zaenen (1983) and Falk (2002). Except for the Dynamic Syntax work and the GPSG account by Sells (1984), these approaches do not address the issue of semantic composition. The Dynamic Syntax analysis raises a number of concerns. First, Cann *et al.* (2005*a*) identify one possible locus of variation for resumption as differences in the tree construction operation *Merge*. This is a non-lexical point of variation, so the approach would seem to give up the hypothesis that whether a language has resumption or not depends on its lexical inventory, i.e. variation in resumption is lexical variation. A related point of concern is that the construction mechanism itself should be a strong candidate for a universal aspect of language, which means that we would not expect it to vary. Cann *et al.* (2005*a*,*b*) identify the relativizing element as another possible locus of variation. This would seem to be too narrow a locus, since it excludes other resumptive environments, notably *wh*-questions. The final locus of variation that they identify is the pronoun itself: certain pronouns do not make full semantic contributions. This loses the point of unification between syntactically active and syntactically inactive resumptive pronouns. It thus seems that there is no locus of variation for resumptive-licensing in the Dynamic Syntax account that is sufficiently general or empirically adequate. Lastly, Cann *et al.* (2005*a*,*b*) treat English resumptive pronouns as grammatically licensed, but this cannot explain the experimental results and patterns of intuitions reviewed in chapter 11. They propose that the explanation for the perceived ungrammaticality of English resumptive pronouns is that English also allows a gap in the relevant positions (Cann *et al.*, 2005*b*: 150). However, this runs afoul of the arguments above against Last Resort theories and also fails to explain why cases where English gaps are ungrammatical are still not fully grammatical with resumptives (Alexopoulou and Keller, 2007, among others).

The HPSG account of Vaillette (2001, 2002) is susceptible to some of the objections raised for movement-based analyses. Vaillette (2001, 2002) essentially generalizes the filler-gap mechanism of HPSG to cover resumptive pronouns. This fails to explain the asymmetries between filler-gap dependencies and binder-resumptive dependencies, although Vaillette addresses some of these points. A second drawback of Vaillette's approach is shared by the LFG account of Falk (2002). Both of these approaches treat resumptive pronouns as somehow different from ordinary pronouns. They are therefore special pronoun theories of resumption. On Vaillette's approach, resumptive pronouns have a feature RESUMP that stores their index and spreads like the SLASH feature of a gap. Non-resumptive pronouns lack the feature RESUMP or else have an empty RESUMP. On Falk's approach, pronouns can either provide a

PRED 'pro' to their f-structure or else provide an equation that is appropriate for resumption. These approaches suffer the drawbacks of special pronoun approaches. First, they cannot explain why the resumptive pronouns in question have the same morphological exponence as non-resumptive pronouns; i.e., there is no account of McCloskey's Generalization. Second, they cannot explain why resumptives are interpreted exactly like ordinary pronouns. Falk (2002) is aware of the issue of ordinary pronoun interpretation and his resumptive pronouns share the interpretation of ordinary pronouns. However, because of the underlying lexical difference between resumptives and non-resumptives, the similarity is arguably only coincidental. The subsequent HPSG analyses of Assmann et al. (2010) and Borsley (2010) do not treat resumptive pronouns as special pronouns, but they do not specify how the problem of semantic composition is to be resolved.

The transformational account of Boeckx (2003) is also a special pronoun theory, although this may not be immediately apparent. On this theory, pronouns are always the morphological realization of a D^0 with a null complement. However, resumptive pronouns are stranded by movement of their complement, which is their antecedent, whereas regular pronouns have a null complement in the sense of an absent complement. The complement to a resumptive pronoun is therefore a trace or copy of the antecedent, whereas the complement to a regular pronoun is just nothing. Boeckx (2003) thus conflates two senses of 'empty' that are architecturally distinct in the framework that he assumes. It is clear that the sense in which pronouns always have a null complement is only valid at Phonetic Form. At Logical Form there should be a difference between resumptive pronoun complements and regular pronoun complements. While Boeckx's theoretical assumptions possibly derive the equivalent PF/morphological exponence of resumptive and non-resumptive pronouns, the account fails to predict that the two kinds of pronouns are also interpreted equivalently.

13.3 Apparent Challenges to Resource Sensitivity

Vata has been explored as an example of a language with syntactically inactive resumptives, but it is also interesting due to its predicate cleft construction, in which a focused verb is repeated in its base form (Koopman, 1984):

(41) $\overline{\text{le}}$ à $\overline{\text{le}}$ sa̍ká
eat we eat rice
'We are really EATING rice.' or 'We are EATING rice.'
(Koopman, 1984: 38, (50a))

The focused, initial verb $\overline{le}$ is unmarked for tone (hence bearing mid tone). It occurs in a bare form without tense particles and cannot be accompanied by complements of the verb. It can, however, be inherently marked for aspect, as in the example above (Koopman, 1984: 38). Koopman treats focused Vata verbs as verbal equivalents of resumptive pronouns ("resumptive verbs").

A similar focus construction, which Cho and Kim (2003) call the "Echoed Verb Construction", occurs in Korean (Cho and Kim, 2003; Cho et al., 2004):

(42) John-i sakwa-lul [mek-ki-nun mek-ess-ciman], amwu-eykey-to
John-NOM apple-ACC eat-KI-CT eat-PAST-but, anyone-to-even
kwen-ha-ci anh-ass-ta
recommend-do-COMP NEG-PAST-DECL
'John ate the apples, but he didn't recommend them to anyone.'
(Cho et al., 2004: (1a))

There are clear similarities to the Vata example. Cho and Kim (2003) note that the focused verb (*mek-ki-nun* in this example) is not fully inflected, but is otherwise identical to the main verb it duplicates. In both cases, the focused verb is a morphologically impoverished copy of the main verb.

If the focused verb provides another instance of the main verb's meaning constructor for semantic composition, then this is both potentially a case of resource deficit, since there will not be enough argument resources for both the focused verb and the main verb, and of resource surplus, since the focused verb's resource is potentially not required for the basic compositional semantics of the sentence. However, an alternative analysis suggests itself in which the focused verb is a semantically bleached 'dummy' verb on a par with English *do*-support *do*. The lack of full morphology on the fronted verb indicates that it is not a full copy of the main verb, which makes a dummy verb analysis initially plausible.

The Vata construction lends further support to this sort of analysis. Koopman (1984: 158) observes that the basic generalization concerning which verbs in Vata can be clefted is that "any verb with a base form may occur in the predicate cleft construction". In particular, verbs that lack a base form cannot be predicate-clefted. By "base form", Koopman means that the root of the clefted verb can be the input to morphological processes. Furthermore, as noted above, the clefted verb bears the segmental form of the cleft target, but does not bear its tonal specification, taking only mid tone. In (41), the main verb happens to bear mid tone, but the main verb can bear a distinct tone, such as the mid-low tone in (43), while the clefted verb still bears default mid tone.

(43) l̄i Ọ́ lì sa̍ká
eat s/he ate rice
'S/he ATE rice.' (Koopman, 1984)

This example also illustrates the lack of tense on the focused verb. The morphological conditions on the Vata predicate cleft verb indicate that formation of the predicate-clefted verb is a lexical process, rather than a kind of syntactic copying. A lexical process is also plausible for the similar Korean construction. If we assume that the morphological process does not copy the semantics of the verb, i.e. its meaning constructor, then a dummy verb analysis based on sharing of partial information could be tenable.

The Vata and Korean phenomena bring up a number of important points. First, given the possibility of a dummy verb analysis, the constructions show that superficial similarity to resumption is not sufficient to warrant a literal resumption analysis. Second, the cases exemplify the kind of investigation that needs to be carried out to test the Resource Sensitivity Hypothesis, which is challenged by cases of apparent resource deficit or resource surplus. Third, the constructions show that it is important to be careful in investigating the hypothesis: it must be clearly demonstrable that the phenomenon involves extra or missing resources. In the kind of resumption examined in this book, this followed from the demonstration that resumptive pronouns and copy pronouns are ordinary pronouns and the necessity of removing these pronouns for successful semantic composition.

Another instance of apparently problematic 'syntactic doubling' (Barbiers, 2008*b*) concerns doubled *wh*-pronouns, as in the following examples (Barbiers, 2008*b*: 13, (22a–b)):

(44) **Wer** isch da gsi **wer**? (Swiss German)
who is there been who
'Who was there?'

(45) **Sa** alo magnà **che**? (Northern Italian)
what has-he eaten what
'What did he eat?'

If both instances of the *wh*-pronoun are semantically contentful, then there is a resource problem, since only one operator can consume the scope resource; see the discussion in chapter 5 of the ban on vacuous quantification.

However, there is reason to doubt that both copies of the *wh*-pronoun are fully contentful. The upper member of the dependency typically has fewer features (Barbiers et al., 2010), as attested by example (45) and the following contrast (Barbiers et al., 2010: 2–3):

(46) a. **Wie** denk je **die** ik gezien heb? (North-Holland Dutch)
who think you REL.PRON I seen have
'Who do you think I saw?'

b. ***Die** denk je **wie** ik gezien heb?
REL.PRON think you who I seen have

It therefore seems that the upper element is a marker or *wh*-expletive (Mycock, 2004, 2006). This is also consistent with the data from the Meran dialect of Tyrolean German that has been investigated by Alber (2008: 142, (1a–b)):[3]

(47) I kenn es Haus, **des** **wos** du glapsch, **des** **wos** die
I know the house REL.PRON C-REL you think REL.PRON C-REL the
Maria _ gekaaft hot.
Maria bough has
'I know the house which you think Maria bought.'

(48) **Wos** glapsch du, **wen** dass die Maria _ onruafn werd?
SCOPE MARKER think you whom C the Maria call will
'Whom do you think Maria will call?'

Alber also notes that the doubling structure alternates with a resumptive pronoun strategy, as shown by the contrast between (47) and the following example (Alber, 2008: 142, (2)):

(49) I kenn es Haus, des wos du glapch, _ dass die Marie 's
I know the house REL.PRON C-REL you think C the Maria it
gekaaft hat.
bought has
'I know the house which you think Maria bought (it).'

The resumptive pronoun version depends on the presence of the complementizer *dass*. This supports the general contention by McCloskey (2002), which the present work builds on, that resumption is lexically licensed and, at least typically, by complementizers. With respect to the doubling, Alber herself notes that, "doubling in Tyrolean A-bar movement is an instance of repetition of a semantically superfluous element". Therefore, it seems that syntactic doubling does not necessarily present a challenge to the Resource Management Theory of Resumption, and the Tyrolean resumptive case, in particular, seems to support the theory. However, if it could be shown that

[3] Alber translates (47) and (49) with a comma after the English *which*, following the German orthographic convention for relative clauses, but I have left the comma out, following the English convention, since these are intended as restrictive relative clauses.

there is a case of syntactic doubling in which both elements are contentful, that would constitute a true challenge to RMTR.

Turning back to the narrower case of apparently surplus pronominals, there are other examples that involve uses of pronouns that are initially similar to resumption. However, the pronouns in question are arguably not surplus to semantic composition. For example, consider *such that* relatives. These have an apparently saturated complement that often contains a pronoun that seems to be some kind of resumptive:

(50) Every polygon such that it has exactly three sides is a triangle.

However, is is not necessary for a *such that* relative to contain a pronoun (Pullum, 1985: 292, (1e)):

(51) The old crone had a manner such that even the children who saw her pass in the street would shudder and turn away.

In this sentence there is no anaphoric element in the relative clause that connects it to the relative head *a manner*. Since the connection between a *such that* relative and its relative head does not have to involve a pronoun, any case that involves a pronoun only coincidentally does so: the pronoun is not a resumptive.

Another example that initially seems like a case of pronominal resource surplus is the case of 'marked topics' (Huddleston and Pullum, 2002: 1409):

(52) As for caviar, I don't like it.

Once again, though, the pronoun is not obligatory and there need not be any anaphoric connection between the marked topic and the main clause:

(53) As for Best Picture, I can't stay up that late.

Like *such that* relatives, marked topics are not a real case of resource surplus. The resources contributed in these constructions are not surplus to composition of the phrases that they appear in and are thus not resumptive. This does not mean that the connection between the relative or marked topic and the element that it modifies is not a challenge for semantic composition — it clearly is.

A construction that is related to marked topics is left dislocation (Ross, 1967). In left dislocation an anaphoric link between the dislocated nominal and the main clause seems to be obligatory:

(54) The Academy, it doesn't reward understated performances often.

(55) *The Academy, Sean Penn pleased many voters despite his bad behaviour.

However, the anaphoric element in the main clause is not a bound pronoun. Although *Not many members of the Academy* can be a variable binder, as in (56), it cannot be left dislocated and bind a pronoun, as in (57).

(56) Not many members of the Academy said they voted for *Inception*.

(57) *Not many members of the Academy, they voted for *Inception*.

Resumptive pronouns are always bound pronouns. Therefore the anaphoric element in left dislocation is not a resumptive pronoun.

Furthermore, the anaphoric element need not be a conventional anaphoric element at all. For example, it can be a relational noun:

(58) The Smiths, neighbours never invite to parties.

The implicit argument of the relational noun is sufficient to establish the link between the main clause and the left-dislocated nominal. However, relational nouns cannot function resumptively (Asudeh, 2005*b*), even though their implicit arguments can be bound, as in (59):

(59) Most suburbanites know a neighbour.

The following Swedish contrast shows that relational nouns cannot be resumptives (Asudeh, 2005*b*: 378):

(60) Varje förortsbo som Maria vet att han arresterades försvann.
every suburbanite that Maria knew that he arrest.PASS vanished
'Every suburbanite who Maria knew that he was arrested vanished.'

(61) *Varje förortsbo som Maria vet att en granne arresterades
every suburbanite that Maria knew that a neighbour arrest.PASS
försvann.
vanished
'Every suburbanite who Maria knew that a neighbour was arrested vanished.'

Even though *en granne* ('a neighbour') appears in the position where true resumptives are licensed in Swedish, after material in the left periphery of CP, (61) is ungrammatical, whereas a resumptive in the same position is grammatical, as shown by (60).

There are therefore at least two compelling reasons to believe that the pronoun in the clause that hosts the left dislocation in (54) is not a resumptive pronoun. First, it is not a bound pronoun. Second, the linking element for left dislocation can be a relational noun and these cannot be resumptive, despite supporting bound readings. The resource contributed by the pronoun or other linking element in left dislocation constructions is consumed in the clause it occurs in and does not constitute a surplus resource.

In sum, verb-doubling focus constructions of the kind found in Vata and Korean, *wh*-doubling, *such that* relative clauses, marked topics, and left dislocations are all the kinds of candidate phenomena against which the Resource Sensitivity Hypothesis needs to be tested, but in none of these cases is there, in fact, a resource accounting problem, according to our current understanding. However, these are all good candidates for future work on Resource Sensitivity. I now turn to a consideration of some other candidate directions for extending this work.

13.4 Directions for Future Work

A direction for future work that immediately suggests itself is to investigate more languages in terms of the Resource Management Theory of Resumption, both with respect to unbounded dependency resumption and to copy raising resumption. Other languages that have been reported to have copy raising were mentioned in chapter 12. The analysis of resumptive pronouns should also be extended to data beyond Irish, Hebrew, Swedish, and Vata. Other African languages also have resumptive systems with properties that seem to make them good candidates for testing the theory of syntactically inactive resumptives. RMTR should be tested against data from these languages, which include Edo (Beermann et al., 2002), Igbo (Goldsmith, 1981; Sells, 1984), Swahili (Keach, 1980; Sells, 1984), and Yoruba (Carstens, 1987; Sonaiya, 1989; Cable, 2003). Yoruba is an especially good candidate, because, as in Vata, resumptive pronouns in this language do not seem to ameliorate weak crossover and island extractions, and thus seem to be another instance of syntactically inactive resumption.

Other directions for future work come from the analyses proposed in parts III and IV. The analysis of Irish identified two roles for the complementizers involved in unbounded dependencies. One was grounding of the unbounded dependency, the other was passing of the unbounded dependency. The filler-gap complementizer *aL* performs filler passing and grounding via functional equality, whereas the complementizer *aN* performs resumptive-binder passing and grounding via binding. This yields the classification of unbounded dependencies shown in Table 13.1. This classification was essentially motivated by the successive-cyclic effects observed for *aL* and by the

Table 13.1. A classification of unbounded dependencies with respect to grounding and passing.

	Grounding	**Passing**
Filler-gap dependency	Example: Irish *aL*	Example: Irish *aL*
Binder-resumptive dependency	Example: Irish *aN*	Example: Irish *aN*

analysis of mixed chains. It would be interesting to see whether the classification can be understood as a general typology of unbounded dependencies and whether such a typology yields new perspectives on other languages. First, more languages need to be investigated to see if the passing and grounding roles are fulfilled by complementizers or if other elements can serve the roles of the Irish complementizers. Second, the general typology needs to be investigated to check if passing and grounding effects hold for unbounded dependencies in other languages. For example, neither Swedish nor Hebrew was analysed as requiring a passing capacity. However, neither language was investigated in detail in these terms. The passing role of *aL* seems to have correlates in many languages—those that show some kind of successive-cyclic marking of extraction paths (for overviews and references, see Bouma et al. 2001 and McCloskey 2002).

As noted in chapter 7, the passing role of *aL* potentially explains several facts about the distribution of gaps in Irish. For example, it predicted the impossibility of extraction from prepositional object position without the appeal to an auxiliary notion of proper government (according to which Irish prepositions would not be proper governors). I noted that the extraction path specified in the lexical entries for both *aL* and *aN* might have to be further restricted by off-path constraints.

Another area of future work on Irish concerns mixed chains. The analysis was shown to predict the following extended mixed chain patterns:

(62) *aN* ... *go* ... *go* ... *aL* ... _ Pattern 1

(63) *aN* ... *aL* ... *aL* ... _ Pattern 1

(64) *aL* ... *aN* ... *go* ... *go* ... *Rpro* Pattern 2

(65) *aL* ... *aL* ... *aN* ... *Rpro* Pattern 2

(66) *aN* ... *aN* ... *go* ... *go* ... *Rpro* Pattern 3

(67) *aN* ... *go* ... *go* ... *aN* ... *Rpro* Pattern 3

Various combinations of these patterns and other patterns are also predicted. First, *aL* is predicted to repeat successive-cyclically if its lexical conditions on passing can be satisfied. Second, the lowermost *aN* is predicted to allow an unlimited number of following neutral *go* complementizers. However, all of these predictions are hard to test, because judgements for mixed chains strain the limits of speakers' grammatical competence (McCloskey, 1990: 195). Nevertheless, perhaps future work can reveal new ways to test longer mixed chains.

The analysis of resumptive pronouns in general appealed to a binding-theoretic Highest Subject Restriction (McCloskey, 1990). The HSR was argued to apply not just to Irish and Hebrew, as has previously been shown (Borer, 1984; McCloskey, 1990; Shlonsky, 1992), but also to Swedish. To my knowledge, although various proposals have been made for how to capture the effects of the HSR (for example, the one made here and the one made by McCloskey 1990), no proposal has been published that explains why the HSR should hold. It cannot be a universal, because it does not seem to hold in Vata (Koopman, 1982, 1984) or in Yoruba (Cable, 2003), which are both Niger-Congo languages. Comparative study of languages that do obey the HSR and languages that do not will hopefully reveal an explanation for what is otherwise essentially a stipulation, across theories.

The chapter on English copy raising analysed several aspects of the syntax and semantics of copy raising verbs. A lot of further work remains. In general, it is no small task to specify adequate interpretation for *like* and *as*. The general syntax and semantics of the word *like* is a topic that is worth pursuing in its own right (Lasersohn, 1995; Landman, 2006). *Like* can take both clausal and nominal complements and the phrases it heads can be either arguments or adjuncts. It will be quite challenging to provide a unified explanation of this behaviour.

The semantics of perceptual resemblance verbs is also interesting in its own right. Asudeh and Toivonen (2012) make an initial investigation into this area, but many interesting problems remain. For example, there is an intriguing ambiguity revealed in the same class of perception verbs when they have simple predicative complements. Consider the following sentence:

(68) The stranger smells bad.

The overwhelmingly favoured interpretation of this sentence is that the stranger's odour is unpleasant. However, it also has an additional reading that is swamped by the 'malodorous reading'. The other reading is that, according to the perceiver's sense of smell, the stranger is bad (i.e., malicious or evil). If the perceiver is a human being, this reading seems unlikely, since we are not in general capable of determining whether someone is good or bad according to their scent. But if the perceiver is a dog, for example, the reading becomes more readily available:

(69) That stranger smelled bad to the dog.

This sentence can mean either that the dog found the stranger malodorous or that the dog concluded that the stranger was a nasty customer. On one reading, the dog might simply wrinkle up his nose, on the other he might growl, etc. Similar ambiguities arise for the other perception verbs.

The two possible readings for (68) are further disambiguated if we use a predicative complement that can only readily be ascribed to sentient beings, such as *evil*. Consider the following alternative to (68):

(70) The stranger smells evil (to the dog).

Since it is strange to conceive of an odour as evil, this sentence only has the reading in which the predicate is ascribed to the subject, rather than to the subject's smell.

The two kinds of readings that are available for (68) are further distinguished by the following paraphrases:

(71) The stranger's smell is bad.

(72) The stranger smells like he is bad.

The first sentence can only mean that the stranger's smell is malodorous, since smells cannot be bad in the sense of maliciousness. The second sentence can only mean that the stranger himself is bad, but *according to smell*. The smell itself may not be particularly unpleasant. Suppose that we have reason to believe that strangers who smell like roses may be malicious, because we have been warned that there is a killer loose who uses rose perfume. Then *the stranger smells bad*, in the sense indicated by paraphrase (72), would not entail that his odour is bad.

The two readings of the perception verb can be represented with the same compositional semantics if a semantic head-switching analysis is adopted for one reading. The following two meaning constructors could, for example, represent the two readings for the verb *smell*, as in example (68):

(73) $\lambda x \lambda P.smell(x, P(odour(x))) : stranger \multimap (stranger \multimap bad) \multimap smell$

(74) $\lambda x \lambda P.P(odour(x)) : stranger \multimap (stranger \multimap bad) \multimap smell$

The ambiguity is entirely in the meaning language. In (73), *smells* is both the syntactic and semantic head of the sentence and is a $\langle e, \langle \langle e, t \rangle, t \rangle \rangle$ function.

In (74) *smells* is the syntactic head but its predicative complement (e.g., *bad*) is the semantic head. In both cases, the function *odour* is a type $\langle e, e \rangle$ function from individuals to their smells which applies to the subject.

The two alternative readings of (68) would be represented as:

(75) $smell(\iota x.[stranger(x)], bad(odour(\iota x.[stranger(x)]))) : s$

(76) $bad(odour(\iota x.[stranger(x)])) : s$

The first meaning is appropriate as the denotation for *The stranger smells bad* in the sense of 'the stranger seems like he is malicious, according to his odour'. The second is appropriate for *The stranger smells bad* in the sense of 'the stranger's scent is malodorous'. Further work is clearly required on this head-switching analysis.

Another avenue for future work that was identified with respect to copy raising concerned expletives. Double *there* expletives like the following are potentially problematic for both LFG's Subject Condition and for the EPP in the Minimalist Program:

(77) There seems like there's a party in the quad tonight.

The problem for LFG concerned ensuring c-structural realization of the shared expletive. The problem for Minimalism concerned establishing a link between the upper and lower instances of the expletive that explains why an upper *there* is not possible without a lower *there*. Future work on this phenomenon might be an opportunity for theoretical synthesis or at least further bridging between LFG and Minimalism.

Part VI

Appendices

APPENDIX A

Glue Semantics with Limited Multiplicative Intuitionistic Linear Logic

The glue logic is defined here in terms of a limited version of the multiplicative, modality-free fragment of intuitionistic linear logic, which I will call (MILL_l). The linear modalities, ! and ?, are absent, so the fragment is modality-free. Proofs terminate in a single conclusion, so the fragment is intuituionistic. Lastly, the fragment is limited, because it lacks a rule for universal introduction, since the rule is never used in this book—all universal quantifiers are specified in meaning constructors. A non-limited version of the fragment, with universal introduction, is presented in Asudeh (2005: 440–441).

The first section of this appendix defines the meaning language and types for the glue logic. The presentation follows Dalrymple et al. (1999*a*,*b*), Crouch and van Genabith (2000), and Asudeh (2005*b*). The second section presents Prawitz-style natural deduction proof rules for the linear logic fragment, following Crouch and van Genabith (2000), Benton et al. (1993), Troelstra (1992), Girard (1995), and Dalrymple et al. (1999*a*). The third section provides Curry-Howard term assignments for the proof rules; this follows presentations of Glue meaning language term assignments by Dalrymple et al. (1999*a*) and Crouch and van Genabith (2000), as well as more general presentations of Curry-Howard term assignments (Abramsky, 1993; Benton et al., 1993; Gallier, 1995).

A.1 The Glue Logic

⟨meaning⟩	::=	⟨meaning-const⟩	(constants)
	|	⟨meaning-var⟩	(variables)
	|	⟨meaning⟩(⟨meaning⟩)	(application)
	|	λ⟨meaning-var⟩.⟨meaning⟩	(abstraction)
	|	⟨meaning⟩ × ⟨meaning⟩	(product)
⟨type⟩	::=	⟨e-term⟩ | ⟨t-term⟩ ⟨t-var⟩	(atomic types)
	|	⟨type⟩ ⊸ ⟨type⟩	(linear implication)
	|	⟨type⟩ ⊗ ⟨type⟩	(multiplicative conjunction)
	|	∀⟨t-var⟩$_1$.⟨type⟩	(universal quantification over terms from ⟨type⟩)
⟨glue⟩	::=	⟨meaning⟩:⟨type⟩	

A.2 Proof Rules for MILL$_l$

	Elimination	Introduction
Implication ($\multimap$)	$\dfrac{\begin{matrix}\vdots & & \vdots\\ A & & A \multimap B\end{matrix}}{B}\multimap_{\mathcal{E}}$	$\dfrac{\begin{matrix}[A]^1\\ \vdots\\ B\end{matrix}}{A \multimap B}\multimap_{\mathcal{I},1}$
Conjunction ($\otimes$)	$\dfrac{\begin{matrix} & & [A]^1 \ [B]^2\\ \vdots & & \vdots\\ A \otimes B & & C\end{matrix}}{C}\otimes_{\mathcal{E},1,2}$	$\dfrac{\begin{matrix}\vdots & & \vdots\\ A & & B\end{matrix}}{A \otimes B}\otimes_{\mathcal{I}}$
Universal ($\forall$)	$\dfrac{\begin{matrix}\vdots\\ \forall x.A\end{matrix}}{A[c/x]}\forall_{\mathcal{E}}$ c free for x	

A.3 Meaning Language Term Assignments for MILL$_l$

	Elimination	Introduction
Implication ($\multimap$)	$\dfrac{\begin{matrix}\vdots & & \vdots\\ a : A & & f : A \multimap B\end{matrix}}{f(a) : B}\multimap_{\mathcal{E}}$	$\dfrac{\begin{matrix}[x : A]^1\\ \vdots\\ f : B\end{matrix}}{\lambda x.f : A \multimap B}\multimap_{\mathcal{I},1}$
Conjunction ($\otimes$)	$\dfrac{\begin{matrix} & & [x : A]^1 \ [y : B]^2\\ \vdots & & \vdots\\ a : A \otimes B & & f : C\end{matrix}}{\mathsf{let}\ a\ \mathsf{be}\ x \times y\ \mathsf{in}\ f : C}\otimes_{\mathcal{E},1,2}$	$\dfrac{\begin{matrix}\vdots & & \vdots\\ a : A & & b : B\end{matrix}}{a \times b : A \otimes B}\otimes_{\mathcal{I}}$
Universal ($\forall$)	$\dfrac{\begin{matrix}\vdots\\ t : \forall x.A\end{matrix}}{t : A[c/x]}\forall_{\mathcal{E}}$ c free for x	

APPENDIX B

A Fragment of Irish

Notes

- C-structure nodes are optional.
- The functional schema, $(\uparrow \textsc{pred fn}) =_c \text{pro}$, in (7) uses the decomposition of PRED proposed by Kaplan and Maxwell (1996) to specify that the rule element in question must be a pronoun (see Kaplan and Maxwell, 1996: 89, Crouch et al., 2011). The rule is used to generate right-peripheral pronouns (Chung and McCloskey 1987).
- The definite determiner is interpreted either as a generalized quantifier or as an iota operator, as is convenient. Nothing hinges on this.

B.1 C-structure Rules

(1)
$$\text{CP} \longrightarrow \left\{ \begin{array}{c} \text{XP} \\ (\uparrow \textsc{udf}) = \downarrow \end{array} \;\middle|\; \begin{array}{c} \epsilon \\ (\uparrow \textsc{udf pred}) = \text{`pro'} \\ (\textsc{adj} \in \uparrow) \\ \mathit{REL}_\sigma \end{array} \right\} \quad \begin{array}{c} \text{C}' \\ \uparrow = \downarrow \end{array}$$

(2)
$$\text{CP} \longrightarrow \begin{array}{c} \text{IP} \\ \uparrow = \downarrow \end{array}$$

(3)
$$\text{IP} \longrightarrow \begin{array}{c} \text{I}' \\ \uparrow = \downarrow \end{array}$$

(4)
$$\text{I}' \longrightarrow \begin{array}{c} \text{I}^0 \\ \uparrow = \downarrow \end{array} \quad \begin{array}{c} \text{S} \\ \uparrow = \downarrow \end{array}$$

(5)
$$\text{I}^0 \longrightarrow \begin{array}{c} \text{C}^0 \\ \uparrow = \downarrow \end{array} \quad \begin{array}{c} \text{I}^0 \\ (\uparrow \textsc{finite}) = + \end{array}$$

(6)
$$\text{S} \longrightarrow \begin{array}{c} \text{DP} \\ (\uparrow \textsc{subj}) = \downarrow \end{array} \quad \begin{array}{c} \text{XP} \\ \uparrow = \downarrow \end{array}$$

(7)
$$\text{V}' \longrightarrow \begin{array}{c} \text{V}^0 \\ \uparrow = \downarrow \\ (\uparrow \textsc{finite}) =_c - \end{array} \quad \begin{array}{c} \text{DP} \\ (\uparrow \textsc{obj}) = \downarrow \end{array} \quad \begin{array}{c} \text{CP} \\ (\uparrow \textsc{comp}) = \downarrow \end{array} \quad \begin{array}{c} \text{DP} \\ (\uparrow \textsc{obj}) = \downarrow \\ (\uparrow \textsc{pred fn}) =_c \text{pro} \end{array}$$

(8)
$$\text{D}' \longrightarrow \begin{array}{c} \text{D} \\ \uparrow = \downarrow \end{array} \quad \begin{array}{c} \text{NP} \\ \uparrow = \downarrow \end{array}$$

(9) NP $\longrightarrow$ NP CP
$\uparrow = \downarrow$ $\downarrow \in (\uparrow \text{ADJ})$

B.2 Templates

(10) $\text{MR}(f) = \lambda P \lambda y.y : [(\uparrow \text{UDF})_\sigma \multimap (\uparrow \text{UDF})_\sigma \otimes f_\sigma)] \multimap [(\uparrow \text{UDF})_\sigma \multimap (\uparrow \text{UDF})_\sigma]$

(11) $\text{RELABEL}(f) = \lambda P.P : (f_\sigma \multimap \uparrow_\sigma) \multimap ((\uparrow \text{UDF})_\sigma \multimap \uparrow_\sigma)$

B.3 Lexicon

(12) *an ('the')*, D^0
$(\uparrow \text{SPEC PRED}) = \text{'the'}$
$\lambda R \lambda S.the(R, S) :$
$[(\uparrow_\sigma \text{VAR}) \multimap (\uparrow_\sigma \text{RESTR})] \multimap \forall X.[(\uparrow_\sigma \multimap X) \multimap X]$

(13) *an ('the')*, D^0
$(\uparrow \text{SPEC PRED}) = \text{'the'}$
$\lambda P_\iota x.[P(x)] : [(\uparrow_\sigma \text{VAR}) \multimap (\uparrow_\sigma \text{RESTR})] \multimap \uparrow_\sigma$

(14) *rud ('thing')*, D^0
$(\uparrow \text{SPEC PRED}) = \text{'something'}$
$\lambda R \lambda S.some(R, S) :$
$[(\uparrow_\sigma \text{VAR}) \multimap (\uparrow_\sigma \text{RESTR})] \multimap \forall X.[(\uparrow_\sigma \multimap X) \multimap X]$
$thing : (\uparrow_\sigma \text{VAR}) \multimap (\uparrow_\sigma \text{RESTR})$

(15) *cén ('which')*, D^0
$(\uparrow \text{SPEC PRED}) = \text{'which'}$
$\lambda R \lambda S.Q(R, S) :$
$[(\uparrow_\sigma \text{VAR}) \multimap (\uparrow_\sigma \text{RESTR})] \multimap \forall X.[(\uparrow_\sigma \multimap X) \multimap X]$

(16) *mé ('I')*, D^0
$(\uparrow \text{PRED}) = \text{'pro'}$
$(\uparrow \text{PERS}) = 1$
$(\uparrow \text{NUM}) = \text{SG}$
$speaker : \uparrow_\sigma$

(17) *é ('him')*, D^0
$(\uparrow \text{PRED}) = \text{'pro'}$
$(\uparrow \text{PERS}) = 3$
$(\uparrow \text{NUM}) = \text{SG}$
$(\uparrow \text{GEND}) = \text{MASC}$
$\lambda z.z \times z : (\uparrow_\sigma \text{ANTECEDENT}) \multimap ((\uparrow_\sigma \text{ANT}) \otimes \uparrow_\sigma)$

(18) *siad ('they')*, D^0
$(\uparrow \text{PRED}) = \text{'pro'}$
$(\uparrow \text{PERS}) = 3$
$(\uparrow \text{NUM}) = \text{PL}$
$\lambda z.z \times z : (\uparrow_\sigma \text{ANTECEDENT}) \multimap ((\uparrow_\sigma \text{ANT}) \otimes \uparrow_\sigma)$

(19) *Aturnae an Stáit ('Attorney General')*, D^0 $(\uparrow \text{PRED}) = \text{`attorney-general'}$
$a\text{-}g : \uparrow_\sigma$

(20) *an aimsir ('the time')*, DP $(\uparrow \text{PRED}) = \text{`time'}$
$\iota x.[time(x)] : \uparrow_\sigma$

(21) *an t-airgead ('the money')*, DP $(\uparrow \text{PRED}) = \text{`money'}$
$\iota x.[money(x)] : \uparrow_\sigma$

(22) *t-úrscéal ('novel')*, N^0 $(\uparrow \text{PRED}) = \text{`novel'}$
$novel : (\uparrow_\sigma \text{ VAR}) \multimap (\uparrow_\sigma \text{ RESTR})$

(23) *fir ('men')*, N^0 $(\uparrow \text{PRED}) = \text{`man'}$
$(\uparrow \text{NUM}) = \text{PL}$
$man^* : (\uparrow_\sigma \text{ VAR}) \multimap (\uparrow_\sigma \text{ RESTR})$

(24) *bhean ('woman')*, N^0 $(\uparrow \text{PRED}) = \text{`woman'}$
$(\uparrow \text{NUM}) = \text{SG}$
$woman : (\uparrow_\sigma \text{ VAR}) \multimap (\uparrow_\sigma \text{ RESTR})$

(25) *mic léinn ('students')*, N^0 $(\uparrow \text{PRED}) = \text{`student'}$
$(\uparrow \text{NUM}) = \text{PL}$
$student^* : (\uparrow_\sigma \text{ VAR}) \multimap (\uparrow_\sigma \text{ RESTR})$

(26) *scríbhneoir ('writer')*, N^0 $(\uparrow \text{PRED}) = \text{`writer'}$
$writer : (\uparrow_\sigma \text{ VAR}) \multimap (\uparrow_\sigma \text{ RESTR})$

(27) *coinne ('expectation')*, N^0 $(\uparrow \text{PRED}) = \text{`expectation'}$
$expectation :$
$(\uparrow \text{ SUBJ OBJ})_\sigma \multimap (\uparrow \text{ COMP})_\sigma \multimap \uparrow_\sigma$

(28) *mheas ('thought')*, I^0 $(\uparrow \text{PRED}) = \text{`think'}$
$(\uparrow \text{FINITE}) = +$
$think : (\uparrow \text{SUBJ})_\sigma \multimap (\uparrow \text{COMP})_\sigma \multimap \uparrow_\sigma$

(29) *shíl ('thought')*, I^0 $(\uparrow \text{PRED}) = \text{`think'}$
$(\uparrow \text{FINITE}) = +$
$think : (\uparrow \text{SUBJ})_\sigma \multimap (\uparrow \text{COMP})_\sigma \multimap \uparrow_\sigma$

(30) *mholann ('praise')*, I^0 $(\uparrow \text{PRED}) = \text{`praise'}$
$(\uparrow \text{FINITE}) = +$
$praise : (\uparrow \text{SUBJ})_\sigma \multimap (\uparrow \text{OBJ})_\sigma \multimap \uparrow_\sigma$

(31) *thuig ('understood')*, I^0 $(\uparrow \text{PRED}) = \text{`understand'}$
$(\uparrow \text{FINITE}) = +$
$understand : (\uparrow \text{SUBJ})_\sigma \multimap (\uparrow \text{OBJ})_\sigma \multimap \uparrow_\sigma$

(32) *bhfaighinn ('get')*, I^0

$$\begin{array}{l}(\uparrow \text{PRED}) = \text{`get'}\\ (\uparrow \text{FINITE}) = +\\ (\uparrow \text{MOOD}) = \text{CONDITIONAL}\\ (\uparrow \text{SUBJ PRED}) = \text{`pro'}\\ (\uparrow \text{SUBJ PERS}) = 1\\ (\uparrow \text{SUBJ NUM}) = \text{SG}\\ (\uparrow \text{OBL PRED}) = \text{`from'}\\ (\uparrow \text{OBL OBJ PRED}) = \text{`pro'}\\ (\uparrow \text{OBL OBJ PERS}) = 1\\ (\uparrow \text{OBL OBJ NUM}) = \text{SG}\\ \textit{get-from}:\\ (\uparrow \text{SUBJ})_\sigma \multimap (\uparrow \text{OBJ})_\sigma \multimap (\uparrow \text{OBL OBJ})_\sigma \multimap \uparrow_\sigma\end{array}$$

(33) *choimhlíonfadh ('confirm')*, I^0

$$\begin{array}{l}(\uparrow \text{PRED}) = \text{`confirm'}\\ (\uparrow \text{FINITE}) = +\\ (\uparrow \text{MOOD}) = \text{CONDITIONAL}\\ \textit{confirm} : (\uparrow \text{SUBJ})_\sigma \multimap (\uparrow \text{OBJ})_\sigma \multimap \uparrow_\sigma\end{array}$$

(34) *raibh ('was')*, I^0

$$\begin{array}{l}(\uparrow \text{FINITE}) = +\\ (\uparrow \text{TENSE}) = \text{PAST}\\ (\uparrow \text{SUBJ PERS}) = 3\\ (\uparrow \text{SUBJ NUM}) = \text{SG}\\ \left(\begin{array}{l}(\uparrow \text{SUBJ}) = (\uparrow \text{XCOMP SUBJ})\\ \textit{be} : (\uparrow \text{XCOMP})_\sigma \multimap \uparrow_\sigma\end{array}\right)\end{array}$$

(35) *rabh ('were')*, I^0

$$\begin{array}{l}(\uparrow \text{FINITE}) = +\\ (\uparrow \text{TENSE}) = \text{PAST}\\ (\uparrow \text{SUBJ PERS}) = 3\\ (\uparrow \text{SUBJ NUM}) = \text{PL}\\ \left(\begin{array}{l}(\uparrow \text{SUBJ}) = (\uparrow \text{XCOMP SUBJ})\\ \textit{be} : (\uparrow \text{XCOMP})_\sigma \multimap \uparrow_\sigma\end{array}\right)\end{array}$$

(36) *ag súil ('hope')*, V^0

$$\begin{array}{l}(\uparrow \text{PRED}) = \text{`hope'}\\ (\uparrow \text{FINITE}) = -\\ (\uparrow \text{ASPECT}) = \text{PROGRESSIVE}\\ \textit{hope} : (\uparrow \text{SUBJ})_\sigma \multimap (\uparrow \text{COMP})_\sigma \multimap \uparrow_\sigma\end{array}$$

(37) *díleas ('loyal')*, A^0

$$\begin{array}{l}(\uparrow \text{PRED}) = \text{`loyal-to'}\\ \textit{loyal-to} : (\uparrow \text{SUBJ})_\sigma \multimap (\uparrow \text{OBL})_\sigma \multimap \uparrow_\sigma\end{array}$$

(38) *do'n Rí ('to-the King')*, PP

$$\begin{array}{l}(\uparrow \text{PRED}) = \text{`king'}\\ \iota x.[\textit{king}(x)] : \uparrow_\sigma\end{array}$$

(39) *agam ('at me')*, P^0 $(\uparrow \text{PRED}) = \text{'at'}$
$(\uparrow \text{OBJ PRED}) = \text{'pro'}$
$(\uparrow \text{OBJ PERS}) = 1$
$(\uparrow \text{OBJ NUM}) = \text{SG}$
$speaker : (\uparrow \text{OBJ})_\sigma$

(40) *uaithi ('from her')*, P^0 $(\uparrow \text{OBJ PRED}) = \text{'pro'}$
$(\uparrow \text{OBJ PERS}) = 1$
$(\uparrow \text{OBJ NUM}) = \text{SG}$
$(\uparrow \text{OBJ GEND}) = \text{FEM}$
$\lambda z.z \times z :$
$((\uparrow \text{OBJ})_\sigma \text{ ANT}) \multimap (((\uparrow \text{OBJ})_\sigma \text{ ANT}) \otimes (\uparrow \text{OBJ})_\sigma)$

(41) REL_σ, $\lambda P \lambda Q \lambda x.Q(x) \wedge P(x) :$
$[(\uparrow \text{UDF})_\sigma \multimap \uparrow_\sigma] \multimap$
$[[((\text{ADJ} \in \uparrow)_\sigma \text{VAR}) \multimap ((\text{ADJ} \in \uparrow)_\sigma \text{RESTR})] \multimap$
$[((\text{ADJ} \in \uparrow)_\sigma \text{VAR}) \multimap ((\text{ADJ} \in \uparrow)_\sigma \text{RESTR})]]$

(42) *go*, $\hat{\text{C}}$ $\neg(\uparrow \text{UDF})$

(43) *aL*, $\hat{\text{C}}$ $(\uparrow \text{UDF}) = (\uparrow \quad \text{COMP}^* \quad \text{GF})$
$(\rightarrow \text{UDF}) = (\uparrow \text{UDF})$

(44) *aN*, $\hat{\text{C}}$ $\%\text{Bound} = \; (\uparrow \text{GF}^* \; \{ \; \text{UDF} \; | \; [\text{GF} - \text{UDF}] \; \})$
$@\text{MR}(\rightarrow)$
$(\uparrow \text{UDF})_\sigma = (\%\text{Bound}_\sigma \text{ ANTECEDENT})$
$@\text{RELABEL}(\%\text{Bound})$

B.4 Examples

B.4.1 *Relative Clause Filler-Gap Dependency*

(45) an t-úrscéal aL mheas mé aL thuig mé __
the novel *aL* thought I *aL* understood I __
'the novel that I thought I understood' (McCloskey, 1979: 17, (42c))

(46)

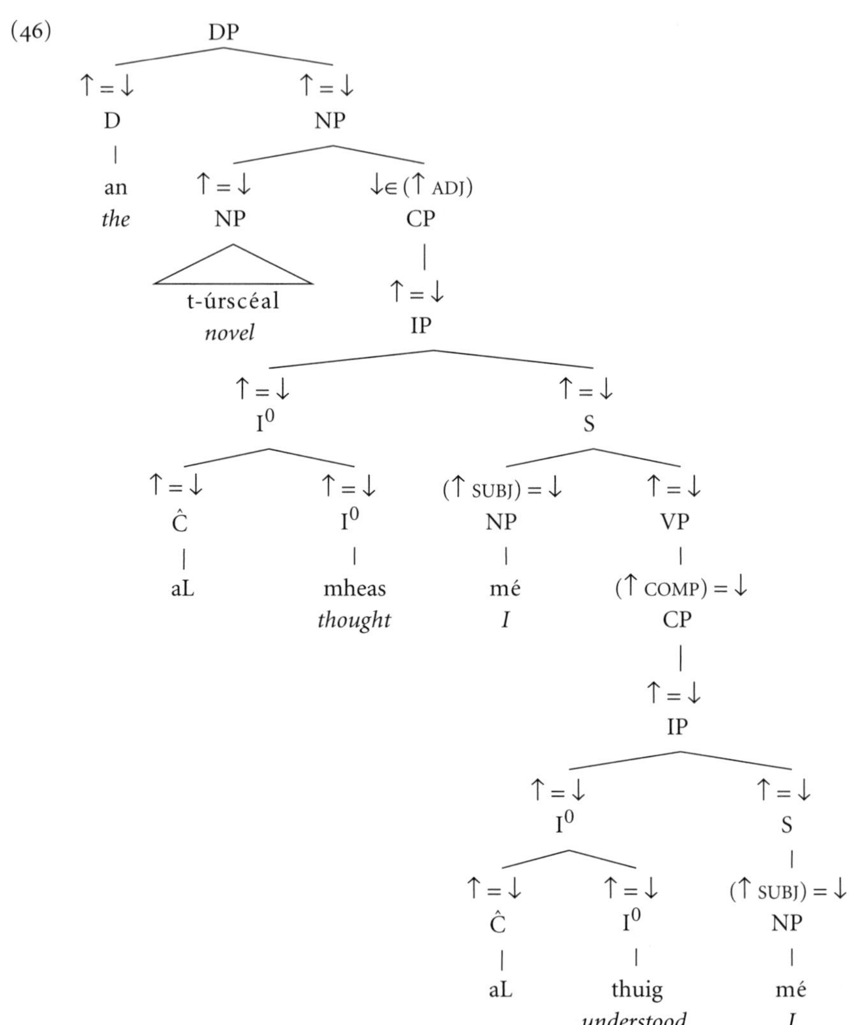

(47)

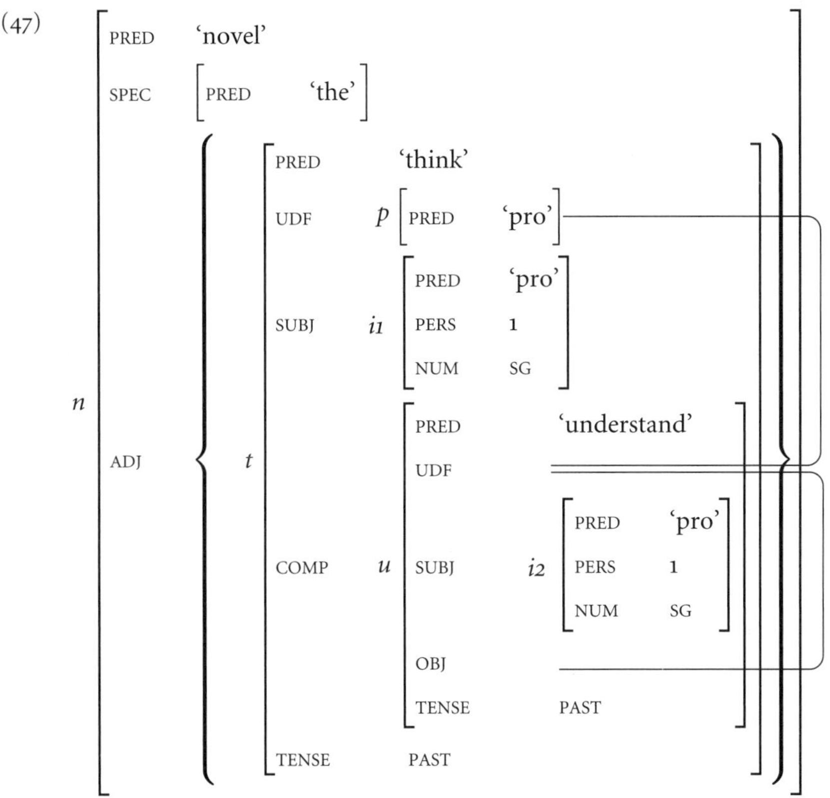

(48)

1. $\lambda R\lambda S.the(R, S)$:
   $(v \multimap r) \multimap \forall X.[(n \multimap X) \multimap X]$ — Lex. **an ('the')**
2. $novel : v \multimap r$ — Lex. **t-úrscéal ('novel')**
3. $think : i1 \multimap u \multimap t$ — Lex. **mheas ('thought')**
4. $speaker : i1$ — Lex. **mé ('I')**
5. $understand : i2 \multimap p \multimap u$ — Lex. **thuig ('understood')**
6. $speaker : i2$ — Lex. **mé ('I')**
7. $\lambda P\lambda Q\lambda x.Q(x) \wedge P(x)$:
   $(p \multimap t) \multimap [(v \multimap r) \multimap (v \multimap r)]$ — REL_σ

(49)

$$
\dfrac{
\begin{array}{l}\lambda R \lambda S.\mathit{the}(R, S) :\\ (v \multimap r) \multimap \forall X.[(n \multimap X) \multimap X]\end{array}
\quad
\dfrac{
\dfrac{
\dfrac{
\dfrac{
\dfrac{
\dfrac{
\dfrac{
\begin{array}{l}\mathit{speaker} :\\ i2\end{array}
\quad
\begin{array}{l}\mathit{understand} :\\ i2 \multimap p \multimap u\end{array}
}{
\begin{array}{l}\mathit{understand}(\mathit{speaker}) :\\ p \multimap u\end{array}
}\multimap_{\mathcal{E}}
\quad
[y : p]^{1}
}{
\begin{array}{l}\mathit{understand}(\mathit{speaker}, y) :\\ u\end{array}
}\multimap_{\mathcal{E}}
\quad
\dfrac{
\begin{array}{l}\mathit{speaker} :\\ i1\end{array}
\quad
\begin{array}{l}\mathit{think} :\\ i1 \multimap u \multimap t\end{array}
}{
\begin{array}{l}\mathit{think}(\mathit{speaker}) :\\ u \multimap t\end{array}
}\multimap_{\mathcal{E}}
}{
\begin{array}{l}\mathit{think}(\mathit{speaker}, \mathit{understand}(\mathit{speaker}, y)) :\\ t\end{array}
}\multimap_{\mathcal{E}}
}{
\begin{array}{l}\lambda y.\mathit{think}(\mathit{speaker}, \mathit{understand}(\mathit{speaker}, y)) :\\ p \multimap t\end{array}
}\multimap_{\mathcal{I},1}
\quad
\begin{array}{l}\lambda P \lambda Q \lambda z.Q(z) \wedge P(z) :\\ (p \multimap t) \multimap [(v \multimap r) \multimap (v \multimap r)]\end{array}
}{
\begin{array}{l}\lambda Q \lambda z.Q(z) \wedge \mathit{think}(\mathit{speaker}, \mathit{understand}(\mathit{speaker}, z)) :\\ (v \multimap r) \multimap (v \multimap r)\end{array}
}\multimap_{\mathcal{E}}
\quad
\begin{array}{l}\mathit{novel} :\\ v \multimap r\end{array}
}{
\begin{array}{l}\lambda z.\mathit{novel}(z) \wedge \mathit{think}(\mathit{speaker}, \mathit{understand}(\mathit{speaker}, z)) :\\ v \multimap r\end{array}
}\multimap_{\mathcal{E}}
}{}
}{
\lambda S.\mathit{the}(\lambda z.\mathit{novel} \wedge \mathit{think}(\mathit{speaker}, \mathit{understand}(\mathit{speaker}, z)), S) : \forall X.[(n \multimap X) \multimap X]
}\multimap_{\mathcal{E}}
$$

B.4.2 *Wh-Question Filler-Gap Dependency*

(50) Cén t-úrscéal aL mheas mé aL thuig mé _
which novel *aL* thought I *aL* understood I _
'Which novel did I think I understood?'

(McCloskey, 1979: 54, ~(10))

(51)

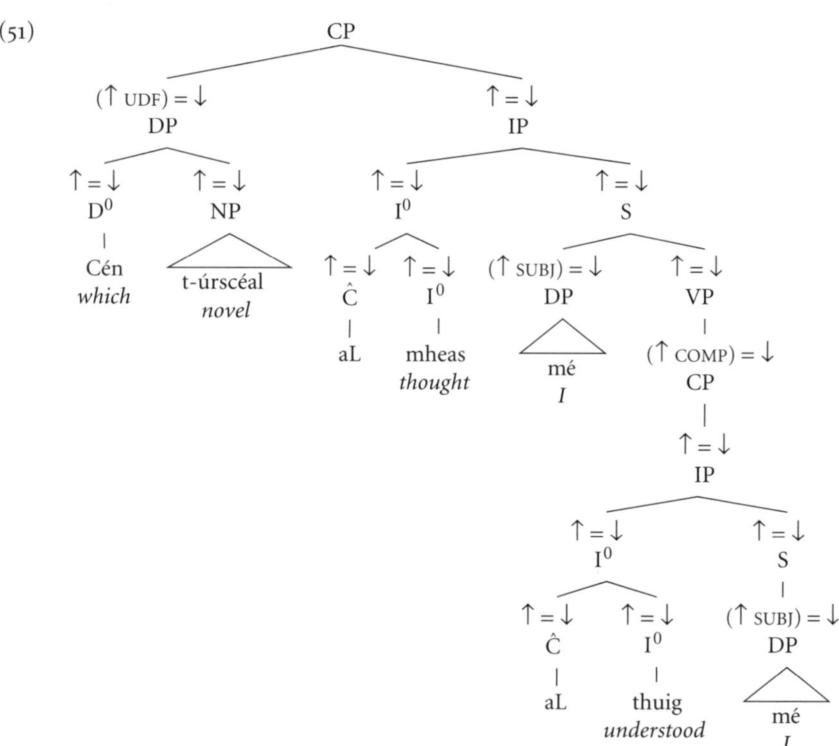

(52)

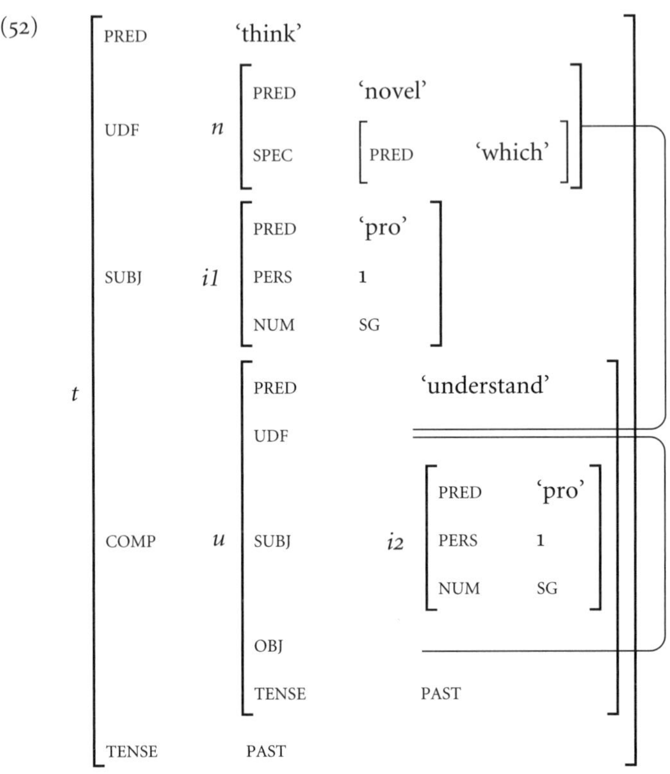

(53)

1.	$\lambda S.Q(novel, S)$: $\forall X.[(n \multimap X) \multimap X]$	Lex. **Cén t-úrscéal ('which novel')**
2.	$think : i1 \multimap u \multimap t$	Lex. **mheas ('thought')**
3.	$speaker : i1$	Lex. **mé ('I')**
4.	$understand : i2 \multimap n \multimap u$	Lex. **thuig ('understood')**
5.	$speaker : i2$	Lex. **mé ('I')**

(54)

$$\dfrac{\begin{array}{c}\lambda S.Q(novel, S) : \\ \forall X.[(n \multimap X) \multimap X]\end{array} \qquad \dfrac{\dfrac{\dfrac{\dfrac{\begin{array}{c}speaker : \\ i2\end{array} \quad \begin{array}{c}understand : \\ i2 \multimap n \multimap u\end{array}}{\begin{array}{c}understand(speaker) : \\ n \multimap u\end{array}}\multimap_{\mathcal{E}} \quad [y : n]^{1}}{\begin{array}{c}understand(speaker, y) : \\ u\end{array}}\multimap_{\mathcal{E}} \quad \dfrac{\begin{array}{c}speaker : \\ i1\end{array} \quad \begin{array}{c}think : \\ i1 \multimap u \multimap t\end{array}}{\begin{array}{c}think(speaker) : \\ u \multimap t\end{array}}\multimap_{\mathcal{E}}}{\begin{array}{c}think(speaker, understand(speaker, y)) : \\ t\end{array}}\multimap_{\mathcal{E}}}{\begin{array}{c}\lambda y.think(speaker, understand(speaker, y)) : \\ n \multimap t\end{array}}\multimap_{\mathcal{I},1}}{Q(novel, \lambda y.think(speaker, understand(speaker, y))) : t}\multimap_{\mathcal{E}}, \forall_{\mathcal{E}}, [t/X]$$

B.4.3 *Binder-Resumptive Dependency*

(55) fir ar shíl Aturnae an Stáit go rabh siad díleas do'n Rí
men *aN* thought Attorney the State *go* were they loyal to-the King
'men that the Attorney General thought were loyal to the King'
(McCloskey, 2002: 190, (16))

(56)

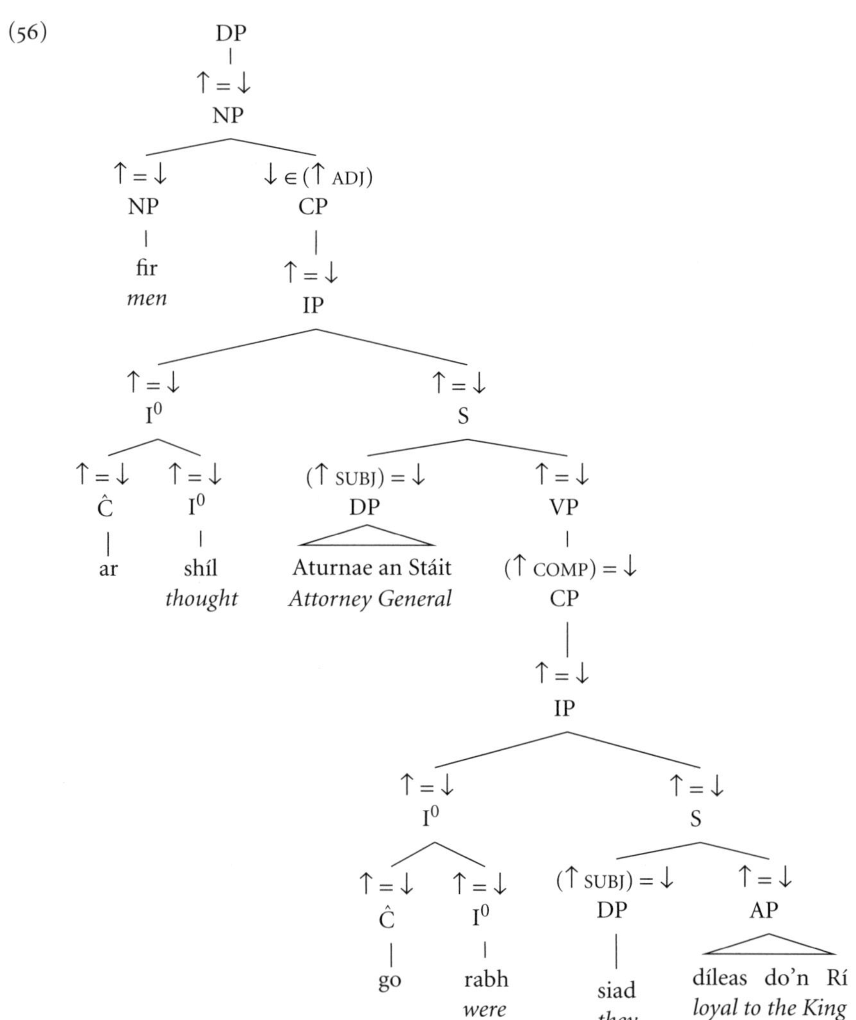

(57)

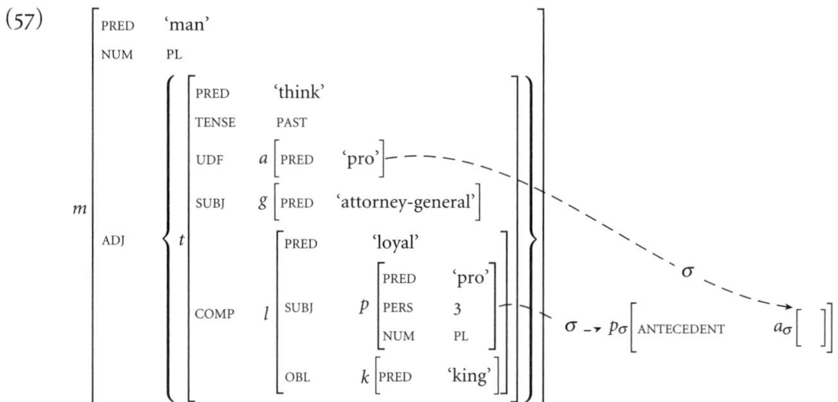

(58)

1.	$man^{*} : v \multimap r$	Lex. **fir ('men')**
2.	$\lambda P \lambda Q \lambda z.Q(z) \wedge P(z) :$ $(a \multimap t) \multimap [(v \multimap r) \multimap (v \multimap r)]$	REL_{σ}
3.	$\lambda P \lambda x.x :$ $[a \multimap (a \otimes p)] \multimap (a \multimap a)]$	Lex. **ar (aN, MR)**
4.	$\lambda P.P : (p \multimap t) \multimap (a \multimap t)$	Lex. **ar (aN, RELABEL)**
5.	$think : g \multimap l \multimap t$	Lex. **shíl ('thought')**
6.	$a\text{-}g : g$	Lex. **Aturnae an Stáit ('Attorney General')**
7.	$\lambda z.z \times z : a \multimap (a \otimes p)$	Lex. **siad ('they')**
8.	$loyal\text{-}to : k \multimap p \multimap l$	Lex. **díleas ('loyal')**
9.	$\iota x.[king(x)] : k$	Lex. **do'n Rí ('to-the King')**

(59)

$$\frac{\iota x.[\mathit{king}(x)] : k \qquad \mathit{loyal\text{-}to} : k \multimap p \multimap l}{\mathit{loyal\text{-}to}(\iota x.[\mathit{king}(x)]) : p \multimap l}$$

$$\frac{\mathit{loyal\text{-}to}(\iota x.[\mathit{king}(x)]) : p \multimap l \qquad [z : p]^2}{\mathit{loyal\text{-}to}(z, \iota x.[\mathit{king}(x)]) : l}$$

$$\frac{\mathit{a\text{-}g} : g \qquad \mathit{think} : g \multimap l \multimap t}{\mathit{think}(\mathit{a\text{-}g}) : l \multimap t}$$

$$\frac{\mathit{loyal\text{-}to}(z, \iota x.[\mathit{king}(x)]) : l \qquad \mathit{think}(\mathit{a\text{-}g}) : l \multimap t}{\mathit{think}(\mathit{a\text{-}g}, \mathit{loyal\text{-}to}(z, \iota x.[\mathit{king}(x)])) : t}$$

$$\frac{\mathit{think}(\mathit{a\text{-}g}, \mathit{loyal\text{-}to}(z, \iota x.[\mathit{king}(x)])) : t}{\lambda z.\mathit{think}(\mathit{a\text{-}g}, \mathit{loyal\text{-}to}(z, \iota x.[\mathit{king}(x)])) : p \multimap t} \multimap_{\mathcal{I},2}$$

$$\frac{\lambda z.\mathit{think}(\mathit{a\text{-}g}, \mathit{loyal\text{-}to}(z, \iota x.[\mathit{king}(x)])) : p \multimap t \qquad \lambda P.P : (p \multimap t) \multimap (a \multimap t)}{\lambda z.\mathit{think}(\mathit{a\text{-}g}, \mathit{loyal\text{-}to}(z, \iota x.[\mathit{king}(x)])) : a \multimap t} \multimap_{\mathcal{I},1}$$

$$\frac{\lambda P \lambda x.x : [a \multimap (a \otimes p)] \multimap (a \multimap a)] \qquad \lambda z.z \times z : a \multimap (a \otimes p)}{\lambda x.x : (a \multimap a)}$$

$$\frac{\lambda x.x : (a \multimap a) \qquad [y : a]^1}{y : a}$$

$$\frac{y : a \qquad \lambda z.\mathit{think}(\mathit{a\text{-}g}, \mathit{loyal\text{-}to}(z, \iota x.[\mathit{king}(x)])) : a \multimap t}{\mathit{think}(\mathit{a\text{-}g}, \mathit{loyal\text{-}to}(y, \iota x.[\mathit{king}(x)])) : t}$$

$$\frac{\mathit{think}(\mathit{a\text{-}g}, \mathit{loyal\text{-}to}(y, \iota x.[\mathit{king}(x)])) : t}{\lambda y.\mathit{think}(\mathit{a\text{-}g}, \mathit{loyal\text{-}to}(y, \iota x.[\mathit{king}(x)])) : a \multimap t} \multimap_{\mathcal{I},1}$$

$$\frac{\lambda y.\mathit{think}(\mathit{a\text{-}g}, \mathit{loyal\text{-}to}(y, \iota x.[\mathit{king}(x)])) : a \multimap t \qquad \lambda P \lambda Q \lambda z.Q(z) \wedge P(z) : (a \multimap t) \multimap [(v \multimap r) \multimap (v \multimap r)]}{\lambda Q \lambda z.Q(z) \wedge \mathit{think}(\mathit{a\text{-}g}, \mathit{loyal\text{-}to}(z, \iota x.[\mathit{king}(x)])) : (v \multimap r) \multimap (v \multimap r)}$$

$$\frac{\lambda Q \lambda z.Q(z) \wedge \mathit{think}(\mathit{a\text{-}g}, \mathit{loyal\text{-}to}(z, \iota x.[\mathit{king}(x)])) : (v \multimap r) \multimap (v \multimap r) \qquad \mathit{man}^* : v \multimap r}{\lambda z.\mathit{man}^*(z) \wedge \mathit{think}(\mathit{a\text{-}g}, \mathit{loyal\text{-}to}(z, \iota x.[\mathit{king}(x)])) : v \multimap r}$$

B.4.4 *Pattern 1*

(60) rud a raibh coinne agam a choimhlíonfadh _ an aimsir
thing *aN* was expectation at-me *aL* fulfil.COND _ the time
'something that I expected time would confirm'
(McCloskey, 2002: 196, ~(28))

(61)

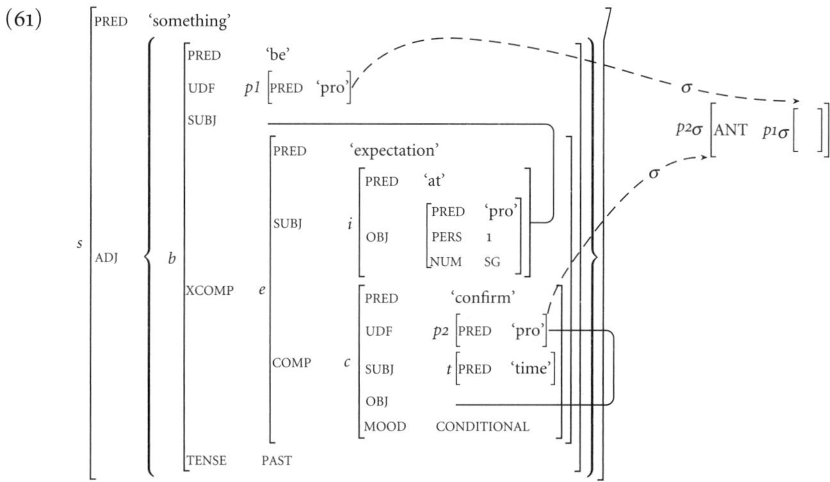

(62)

1. $\lambda R \lambda S.some(R, S)$: $(v \multimap r) \multimap \forall X.[(s \multimap X) \multimap X]$ — Lex. **rud ('thing')**
2. $thing : v \multimap r$ — Lex. **rud ('thing')**
3. $\lambda P \lambda Q \lambda y.Q(y) \wedge P(y)$: $(p1 \multimap b) \multimap [(v \multimap r) \multimap (v \multimap r)]$ — REL_σ
4. $\lambda P.P : (p2 \multimap b) \multimap (p1 \multimap b)]$ — Lex. **a (aN)**
5. $be : e \multimap b$ — Lex. **raibh ('was')**
6. $expectation : i \multimap c \multimap e$ — Lex. **coinne ('expectation')**
7. $speaker : i$ — Lex. **agam ('at-me')**
8. $confirm : t \multimap p2 \multimap c$ — Lex. **choimhlíonfadh ('confirm')**
9. $\iota z.[time(z)] : t$ — Lex. **an aimsir ('the time')**

(63)

$$\frac{\iota z.[\mathit{time}(z)] : t \qquad \mathit{confirm} : t \multimap p2 \multimap c}{\mathit{confirm}(\iota z.[\mathit{time}(z)]) : p2 \multimap c}$$

$$\frac{\mathit{confirm}(\iota z.[\mathit{time}(z)]) : p2 \multimap c \qquad [x : p2]^{1}}{\mathit{confirm}(\iota z.[\mathit{time}(z)], x) : c}$$

$$\frac{\mathit{expectation} : i \multimap c \multimap e \qquad \mathit{speaker} : i}{\mathit{expectation}(\mathit{speaker}) : c \multimap e}$$

$$\frac{\mathit{confirm}(\iota z.[\mathit{time}(z)], x) : c \qquad \mathit{expectation}(\mathit{speaker}) : c \multimap e}{\mathit{expectation}(\mathit{speaker}, \mathit{confirm}(\iota z.[\mathit{time}(z)], x)) : e}$$

$$\frac{\mathit{expectation}(\mathit{speaker}, \mathit{confirm}(\iota z.[\mathit{time}(z)], x)) : e \qquad \mathit{be} : e \multimap b}{\mathit{be}(\mathit{expectation}(\mathit{speaker}, \mathit{confirm}(\iota z.[\mathit{time}(z)], x))) : b}$$

$$\frac{\mathit{be}(\mathit{expectation}(\mathit{speaker}, \mathit{confirm}(\iota z.[\mathit{time}(z)], x))) : b}{\lambda x.\mathit{be}(\mathit{expectation}(\mathit{speaker}, \mathit{confirm}(\iota z.[\mathit{time}(z)], x))) : p2 \multimap b} \multimap_{\mathcal{I},1}$$

$$\frac{\lambda x.\mathit{be}(\mathit{expectation}(\mathit{speaker}, \mathit{confirm}(\iota z.[\mathit{time}(z)], x))) : p2 \multimap b \qquad \lambda P.P : (p2 \multimap b) \multimap (p1 \multimap b)}{\lambda x.\mathit{be}(\mathit{expectation}(\mathit{speaker}, \mathit{confirm}(\iota z.[\mathit{time}(z)], x))) : p1 \multimap b}$$

$$\frac{\lambda x.\mathit{be}(\mathit{expectation}(\mathit{speaker}, \mathit{confirm}(\iota z.[\mathit{time}(z)], x))) : p1 \multimap b \qquad \lambda P \lambda Q \lambda y.Q(y) \wedge P(y) : (p1 \multimap b) \multimap [(v \multimap r) \multimap (v \multimap r)]}{\lambda Q \lambda y.Q(y) \wedge \mathit{be}(\mathit{expectation}(\mathit{speaker}, \mathit{confirm}(\iota z.[\mathit{time}(z)], y))) : (v \multimap r) \multimap (v \multimap r)}$$

$$\frac{\lambda Q \lambda y.Q(y) \wedge \mathit{be}(\mathit{expectation}(\mathit{speaker}, \mathit{confirm}(\iota z.[\mathit{time}(z)], y))) : (v \multimap r) \multimap (v \multimap r) \qquad \mathit{thing} : v \multimap r}{\lambda y.\mathit{thing}(y) \wedge \mathit{be}(\mathit{expectation}(\mathit{speaker}, \mathit{confirm}(\iota z.[\mathit{time}(z)], y))) : v \multimap r}$$

$$\frac{\lambda R \lambda S.\mathit{some}(R, S) : (v \multimap r) \multimap \forall X.[(s \multimap X) \multimap X] \qquad \lambda y.\mathit{thing}(y) \wedge \mathit{be}(\mathit{expectation}(\mathit{speaker}, \mathit{confirm}(\iota z.[\mathit{time}(z)], y))) : v \multimap r}{\lambda S.\mathit{some}(\lambda y.\mathit{thing}(y) \ \wedge \ \mathit{be}(\mathit{expectation}(\mathit{speaker}, \mathit{confirm}(\iota z.[\mathit{time}(z)], y))), S) : \forall X.[(s \multimap X) \multimap X]}$$

B.4.5 *Pattern 3*

(64) an bhean a raibh mé ag súil a bhfaighinn an t-airgead
the woman *aN* was I hope.PROG *aN* get.COND.1SG the money
<u>uaithi</u>
from-her
'the woman that I was hoping that I would get the money from (her)'
(McCloskey, 2002: 199, ~(41))

(65)

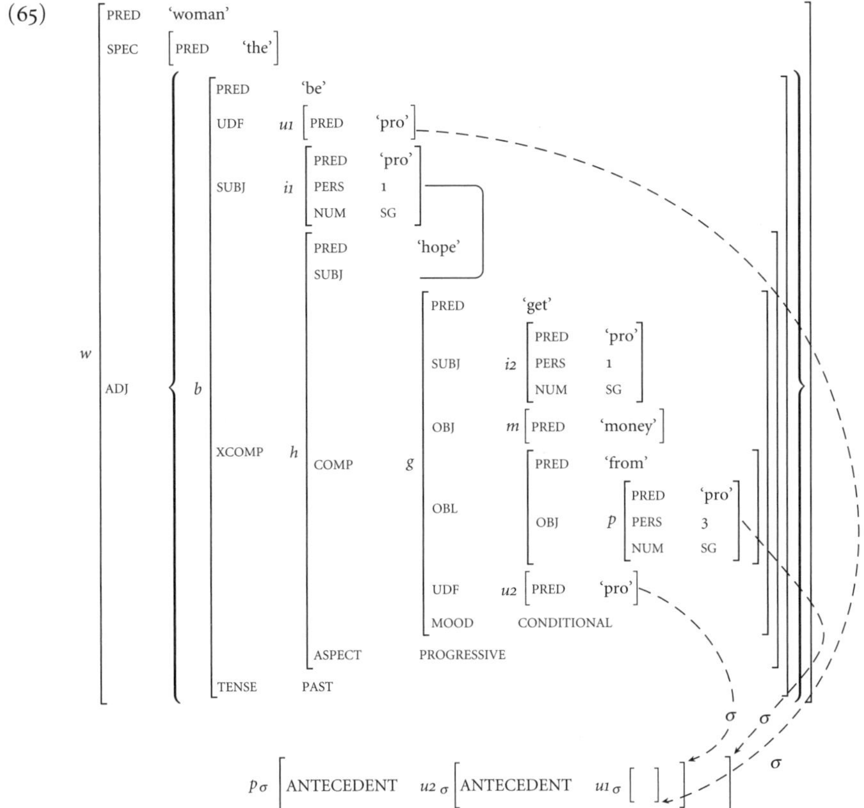

(66)

1.	$\lambda R \lambda S.the(R, S)$: $(v \multimap r) \multimap \forall X.[(w \multimap X) \multimap X]$	Lex. **an ('the')**
2.	$woman : v \multimap r$	Lex. **bhean ('woman')**
3.	$\lambda P \lambda Q \lambda y.Q(y) \wedge P(y)$: $(u1 \multimap b) \multimap [(v \multimap r) \multimap (v \multimap r)]$	REL_σ
4.	$\lambda P.P : (u2 \multimap b) \multimap (u1 \multimap b)$	Lex. **a (aN, RELABEL)**
5.	$be : h \multimap b$	Lex. **raibh ('was')**
6.	$speaker : i1$	Lex. **mé ('I')**
7.	$hope : i1 \multimap g \multimap h$	Lex. **ag súil ('hope')**
8.	$\lambda P.P : (p \multimap g) \multimap (u2 \multimap g)$	Lex. **a (aN, RELABEL)**
9.	$\lambda P \lambda y.y$: $[u2 \multimap (u2 \otimes p)] \multimap (u2 \multimap u2)$	Lex. **a (aN, MR)**
10.	$get\text{-}from : i2 \multimap m \multimap p \multimap g$	Lex. **bhfaighinn ('get')**
11.	$speaker : i2$	Lex. **bhfaighinn ('get')**
12.	$\iota x.[money(x)] : m$	Lex. **an t-airgead ('the money')**
13.	$\lambda z.z \times z : u2 \multimap (u2 \otimes p)$	Lex. **uaithi ('from-her')**

(67)

$$\frac{\textit{get-from} : i2 \multimap m \multimap p \multimap g \qquad \textit{speaker} : i2}{\textit{get-from}(\textit{speaker}) : m \multimap p \multimap g}$$

$$\frac{\textit{get-from}(\textit{speaker}) : m \multimap p \multimap g \qquad \iota x.[\textit{money}(x)] : m}{\textit{get-from}(\textit{speaker}, \iota x.[\textit{money}(x)]) : p \multimap g}$$

$$\frac{\textit{get-from}(\textit{speaker}, \iota x.[\textit{money}(x)]) : p \multimap g \qquad \lambda P.P : (p \multimap g) \multimap (u2 \multimap g)}{\textit{get-from}(\textit{speaker}, \iota x.[\textit{money}(x)]) : u2 \multimap g}$$

$$\frac{\textit{speaker} : i1 \qquad \textit{hope} : i1 \multimap g \multimap h}{\textit{hope}(\textit{speaker}) : g \multimap h}$$

$$\frac{\textit{get-from}(\textit{speaker}, \iota x.[\textit{money}(x)]) : u2 \multimap g \qquad [y : u2]^1}{\textit{get-from}(\textit{speaker}, \iota x.[\textit{money}(x)], y) : g}$$

$$\frac{\textit{hope}(\textit{speaker}) : g \multimap h \qquad \textit{get-from}(\textit{speaker}, \iota x.[\textit{money}(x)], y) : g}{\textit{hope}(\textit{speaker}, \textit{get-from}(\textit{speaker}, \iota x.[\textit{money}(x)], y)) : h}$$

$$\frac{\textit{hope}(\textit{speaker}, \textit{get-from}(\textit{speaker}, \iota x.[\textit{money}(x)], y)) : h \qquad \textit{be} : h \multimap b}{\textit{be}(\textit{hope}(\textit{speaker}, \textit{get-from}(\textit{speaker}, \iota x.[\textit{money}(x)], y))) : b}$$

$$\frac{\textit{be}(\textit{hope}(\textit{speaker}, \textit{get-from}(\textit{speaker}, \iota x.[\textit{money}(x)], y))) : b}{\lambda y.\textit{be}(\textit{hope}(\textit{speaker}, \textit{get-from}(\textit{speaker}, \iota x.[\textit{money}(x)], y))) : u2 \multimap b} \multimap_{\mathcal{I},1}$$

$$\frac{\lambda z.z \times z : u2 \multimap (u2 \otimes p) \qquad \lambda P \lambda y.y : [u2 \multimap (u2 \otimes p)] \multimap (u2 \multimap u2)}{\lambda y.y : u2 \multimap u2}$$

$$\frac{[z : u2]^2 \qquad \lambda y.y : u2 \multimap u2}{z : u2}$$

$$\frac{\lambda y.\textit{be}(\textit{hope}(\textit{speaker}, \textit{get-from}(\textit{speaker}, \iota x.[\textit{money}(x)], y))) : u2 \multimap b \qquad z : u2}{\textit{be}(\textit{hope}(\textit{speaker}, \textit{get-from}(\textit{speaker}, \iota x.[\textit{money}(x)], z))) : b}$$

$$\frac{\textit{be}(\textit{hope}(\textit{speaker}, \textit{get-from}(\textit{speaker}, \iota x.[\textit{money}(x)], z))) : b}{\lambda z.\textit{be}(\textit{hope}(\textit{speaker}, \textit{get-from}(\textit{speaker}, \iota x.[\textit{money}(x)], z))) : u2 \multimap b} \multimap_{\mathcal{I},2}$$

$$\frac{\lambda P.P : (u2 \multimap b) \multimap (u1 \multimap b) \qquad \lambda z.\textit{be}(\textit{hope}(\textit{speaker}, \textit{get-from}(\textit{speaker}, \iota x.[\textit{money}(x)], z))) : u2 \multimap b}{\lambda z.\textit{be}(\textit{hope}(\textit{speaker}, \textit{get-from}(\textit{speaker}, \iota x.[\textit{money}(x)], z))) : u1 \multimap b}$$

$$\frac{\lambda z.\textit{be}(\textit{hope}(\textit{speaker}, \textit{get-from}(\textit{speaker}, \iota x.[\textit{money}(x)], z))) : u1 \multimap b \qquad \lambda P \lambda Q \lambda y.Q(y) \wedge P(y) : (u1 \multimap b) \multimap [(v \multimap r) \multimap (v \multimap r)]}{\lambda Q \lambda y.Q(y) \wedge \textit{be}(\textit{hope}(\textit{speaker}, \textit{get-from}(\textit{speaker}, \iota x.[\textit{money}(x)], y))) : (v \multimap r) \multimap (v \multimap r)}$$

$$\frac{\textit{woman} : v \multimap r \qquad \lambda Q \lambda y.Q(y) \wedge \textit{be}(\textit{hope}(\textit{speaker}, \textit{get-from}(\textit{speaker}, \iota x.[\textit{money}(x)], y))) : (v \multimap r) \multimap (v \multimap r)}{\lambda y.\textit{woman}(y) \wedge \textit{be}(\textit{hope}(\textit{speaker}, \textit{get-from}(\textit{speaker}, \iota x.[\textit{money}(x)], y))) : v \multimap r}$$

$$\frac{\lambda R \lambda S.\textit{the}(R, S) : (v \multimap r) \multimap \forall X.[(w \multimap X) \multimap X] \qquad \lambda y.\textit{woman}(y) \wedge \textit{be}(\textit{hope}(\textit{speaker}, \textit{get-from}(\textit{speaker}, \iota x.[\textit{money}(x)], y))) : v \multimap r}{\lambda S.\textit{the}(\lambda y.\textit{woman}(y) \wedge \textit{be}(\textit{hope}(\textit{speaker}, \textit{get-from}(\textit{speaker}, \iota x.[\textit{money}(x)], y))), S) : \forall X.[(w \multimap X) \multimap X]}$$

APPENDIX C

A Fragment of Swedish

Note

- C-structure nodes are optional.

C.1 C-structure Rules

(1) $\text{CP} \longrightarrow \left\{ \begin{array}{c} \text{XP} \\ (\uparrow \textsc{udf}) = \downarrow \\ \\ (\uparrow \textsc{udf})\backslash\textsc{pred} = \\ (\uparrow \textsc{gf}^* \end{array} \middle| \begin{array}{c} \epsilon \\ (\uparrow \textsc{udf pred}) = \text{`pro'} \\ (\textsc{adj} \in \uparrow) \\ REL_\sigma \\ \\ \textsc{gf} \end{array} \right\} \begin{array}{c} \text{C}' \\ \uparrow = \downarrow \end{array}$

$)\backslash\textsc{pred}$

$(\ (\rightarrow \textsc{pred}) = (\uparrow \textsc{udf pred})\ )$

(2) $\text{C}' \longrightarrow \begin{array}{c} \text{C}^0 \\ \uparrow = \downarrow \end{array} \quad \begin{array}{c} \text{IP} \\ \uparrow = \downarrow \end{array}$

(3) $\text{IP} \longrightarrow \begin{array}{c} \text{DP} \\ (\uparrow \textsc{subj}) = \downarrow \end{array} \quad \begin{array}{c} \text{I}' \\ \uparrow = \downarrow \end{array}$

(4) $\text{I}' \longrightarrow \begin{array}{c} \text{I}^0 \\ \uparrow = \downarrow \end{array} \quad \begin{array}{c} \text{VP} \\ \uparrow = \downarrow \end{array}$

(5) $\text{VP} \longrightarrow \begin{array}{c} \text{V}' \\ \uparrow = \downarrow \end{array} \quad \begin{array}{c} \text{DP} \\ (\uparrow \textsc{obj}) = \downarrow \end{array} \quad \begin{array}{c} \text{CP} \\ (\uparrow \textsc{comp}) = \downarrow \end{array}$

C.2 Templates

(6) $\text{MR}(f) \quad = \quad \lambda P \lambda y.y : [(\uparrow \textsc{udf})_\sigma \multimap (\uparrow \textsc{udf})_\sigma \otimes f_\sigma)] \multimap [(\uparrow \textsc{udf})_\sigma \multimap (\uparrow \textsc{udf})_\sigma]$

(7) $\text{RELABEL}(f) = \lambda P.P : (f_\sigma \multimap \uparrow_\sigma) \multimap ((\uparrow \textsc{udf})_\sigma \multimap \uparrow_\sigma)$

C.3 Lexicon

(8) *vilken ('which')*, D^0 $(\uparrow \text{SPEC PRED}) = \text{`which'}$
$\lambda R \lambda S.Q(R, S) :$
$[(\uparrow_\sigma \text{ VAR}) \multimap (\uparrow_\sigma \text{ RESTR})] \multimap \forall X.[(\uparrow_\sigma \multimap X) \multimap X]$

(9) *han ('he')*, D^0 $(\uparrow \text{PRED}) = \text{`pro'}$
$(\uparrow \text{PERS}) = 3$
$(\uparrow \text{NUM}) = \text{SG}$
$(\uparrow \text{GEND}) = \text{MASC}$
$(\uparrow \text{CASE}) = \text{NOM}$
$\lambda z.z \times z : (\uparrow_\sigma \text{ ANTECEDENT}) \multimap ((\uparrow_\sigma \text{ ANT}) \otimes \uparrow_\sigma)$

(10) *Maria*, D^0 $(\uparrow \text{PRED}) = \text{`Maria'}$
$maria : \uparrow_\sigma$

(11) *elev ('student')*, N^0 $(\uparrow \text{PRED}) = \text{`student'}$
$(\uparrow \text{NUM}) = \text{SG}$
$student : (\uparrow_\sigma \text{ VAR}) \multimap (\uparrow_\sigma \text{ RESTR})$

(12) *skulle ('would')*, I^0 $(\uparrow \text{TENSE}) = \text{FUTURE}$
$(\uparrow \text{MOOD}) = \text{IRREALIS}$
$(\uparrow \text{FINITE}) = +$

(13) *fuska ('cheat')*, V^0 $(\uparrow \text{PRED}) = \text{`cheat'}$
$(\uparrow \text{FINITE}) = -$
$cheat : (\uparrow \text{SUBJ})_\sigma \multimap \uparrow_\sigma$

(14) *trodde ('thought')*, C^0 $(\uparrow \text{PRED}) = \text{`think'}$
$(\uparrow \text{FINITE}) = +$
$(\uparrow \text{TENSE}) = \text{PAST}$
$think : (\uparrow \text{SUBJ})_\sigma \multimap (\uparrow \text{COMP})_\sigma \multimap \uparrow_\sigma$

(15) *att*+COMP *('that')*, C^0

(16) +COMP, C^0
$$\left(\begin{array}{l} \%RP = (\uparrow \text{SUBJ}) \\ (\uparrow \text{UDF})_\sigma = (\%RP_\sigma \text{ ANTECEDENT}) \\ @MR(\%RP) \\ @RELABEL(\%RP) \end{array} \right)$$

C.4 Example

(17) [Vilken elev]$_i$ trodde Maria att han$_i$ skulle fuska?
which student thought Maria that he would cheat
'Which student did Maria think that (he) would cheat?'

(18)

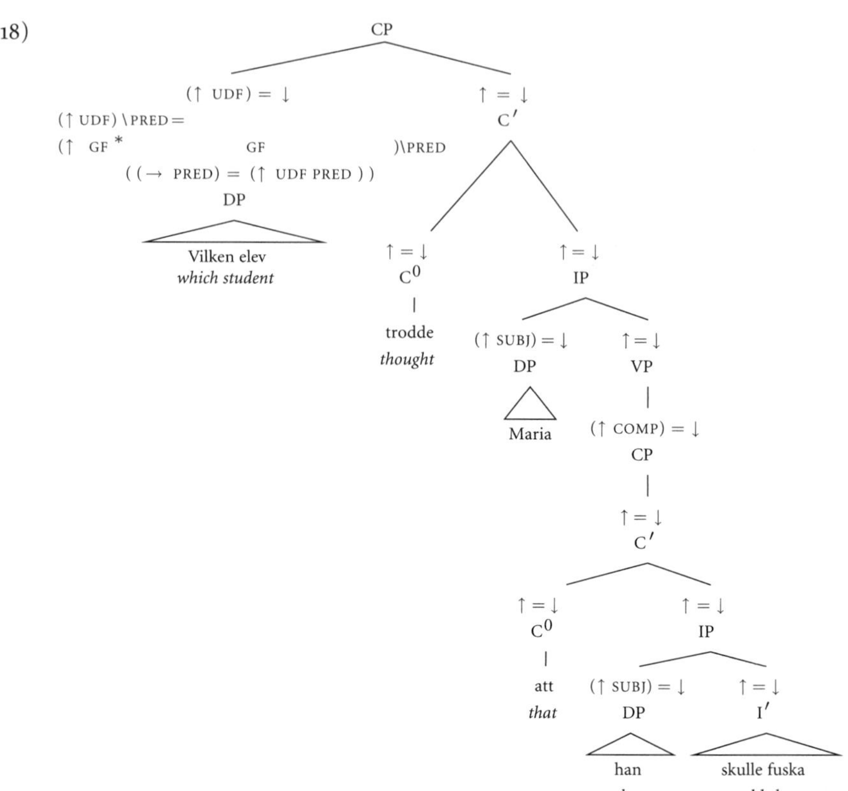

(19)

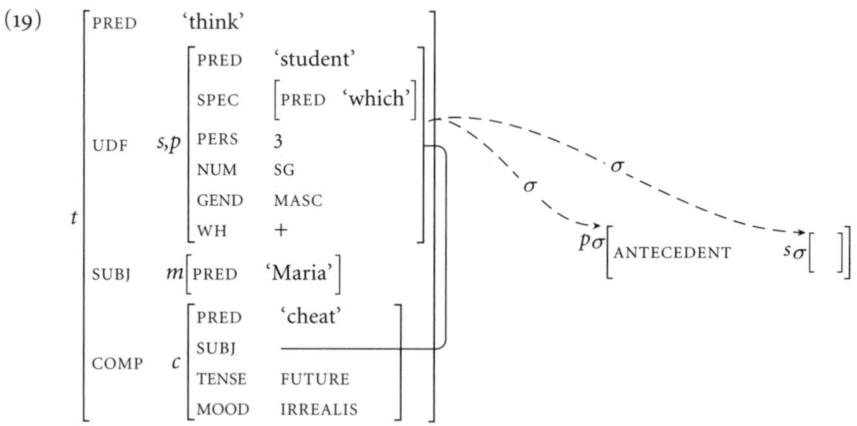

(20)

1. $\lambda S.Q(student, S)$: $\forall X.[(s \multimap X) \multimap X]$ — Lex. **vilken elev ('which student')**
2. $\lambda P \lambda y.y : [s \multimap (s \otimes p)] \multimap (s \multimap s)$ — Lex. +COMP **(MR)**
3. $\lambda P.P : (p \multimap t) \multimap (s \multimap t)$ — Lex. +COMP **(RELABEL)**
4. $think : m \multimap c \multimap t$ — Lex. **trodde ('thought')**
5. $maria : m$ — Lex. **Maria**
6. $\lambda z.z \times z : s \multimap (s \otimes p)$ — Lex. **han ('he')**
7. $cheat : p \multimap c$ — Lex. **fuska ('cheat')**

(21)

$$
\dfrac{
\dfrac{
\dfrac{
\dfrac{
\begin{array}{c}\lambda P\lambda y.y :\\ [s \multimap (s \otimes p)] \multimap (s \multimap s)\end{array}
\quad
\begin{array}{c}\lambda z.z \times z :\\ s \multimap (s \otimes p)\end{array}
}{\lambda y.y : (s \multimap s)}
\quad [x : s]^1
}{x : s}
\quad
\dfrac{
\dfrac{
\dfrac{
\dfrac{[y : p]^2 \quad \begin{array}{c}\mathit{cheat} :\\ p \multimap c\end{array}}{\mathit{cheat}(y) : c}
\quad
\dfrac{\begin{array}{c}\mathit{maria} :\\ m\end{array} \quad \begin{array}{c}\mathit{think} :\\ m \multimap c \multimap t\end{array}}{\mathit{think}(\mathit{maria}) : c \multimap t}
}{\mathit{think}(\mathit{maria}, \mathit{cheat}(y)) : t}
{\scriptstyle \multimap_{\mathcal{I},2}}
}{\lambda y.\mathit{think}(\mathit{maria}, \mathit{cheat}(y)) : p \multimap t}
\quad
\begin{array}{c}\lambda P.P :\\ (p \multimap t) \multimap (s \multimap t)\end{array}
}{\lambda y.\mathit{think}(\mathit{maria}, \mathit{cheat}(y)) : s \multimap t}
}{\mathit{think}(\mathit{maria}, \mathit{cheat}(x)) : t}
{\scriptstyle \multimap_{\mathcal{I},1}}
}{\lambda x.\mathit{think}(\mathit{maria}, \mathit{cheat}(x)) : s \multimap t}
\quad
\begin{array}{c}\lambda S.Q(\mathit{student}, S) :\\ \forall X.[(s \multimap X) \multimap X]\end{array}
}{\mathcal{Q}(\mathit{student}, \lambda x.\mathit{think}(\mathit{maria}, \mathit{cheat}(x))) : t}
\; [t/X]
$$

Bibliography

Abney, Steven P. 1987. The English Noun Phrase in its Sentential Aspect. PhD thesis, MIT.

Abramsky, Samson. 1993. Computational Interpretations of Linear Logic. *Theoretical Computer Science* 111: 3–57.

Adger, David. 2011. Bare Resumptives. In Rouveret 2011, 343–366.

Adger, David, and Gillian Ramchand. 2005. Merge and Move: *Wh*-Dependencies Revisited. *Linguistic Inquiry* 36: 161–193.

Ajdukiewicz, Kazimierz. 1935. Die syntaktische Konnexität. *Studia Philosophica* 1: 1–27. Translated as Ajdukiewicz (1967).

——. 1967. Syntactic Connexion. In Storrs McCall, ed., *Polish Logic, 1920–1939*, 207–231. Oxford: Clarendon Press. Translation of Ajdukiewicz (1935).

Alber, Birgit. 2008. Tyrolean A-bar Movement: Doubling and Resumptive Pronoun Structures. In Barbiers 2008*a*, 141–170.

Alexopoulou, Theodora. 2006. Resumption in Relative Clauses. *Natural Language and Linguistic Theory* 24: 57–111.

Alexopoulou, Theodora, and Frank Keller. 2002. Resumption and Locality: A Crosslinguistic Experimental Study. In Andronis et al. 2002, 1–14.

——. 2003. Linguistic Complexity, Locality, and Resumption. In *Proceedings of the 22nd West Coast Conference on Formal Linguistics*, 15–28. Somerville, MA: Cascadilla Press.

——. 2007. Locality, Cyclicity, and Resumption: At the Interface between the Grammar and the Human Sentence Processor. *Language* 83: 110–160.

Alrenga, Peter. 2006. Scalar (Non-)Identity and Similarity. In *Proceedings of the 25th West Coast Conference on Formal Linguistics*, 49–57. Somerville, MA: Cascadilla Press.

——. 2007. Comparisons of Similarity and Difference. PhD thesis, University of California, Santa Cruz.

Alsina, Alex. 2008. A Theory of Structure-Sharing: Focusing on Long-distance Dependencies and Parasitic Gaps. In Butt and King 2008, 5–25.

Anderson, Alan Ross, and Nuel D. Belnap. 1975. *Entailment: The Logic of Relevance and Necessity*, vol. I. Princeton: Princeton University Press. With contributions by J. Michael Dunn and Robert K. Meyer.

Andrews, Avery D. 1990. Unification and Morphological Blocking. *Natural Language and Linguistic Theory* 8: 507–557.

——. 2004. Glue Logic vs. Spreading Architecture in LFG. In Christo Moskovsky, ed., *Proceedings of the 2003 Conference of the Australian Linguistic Society*. http://www.als.asn.au/proceedings/als2003.html.

——. 2007. Input and Glue in OT-LFG. In Zaenen et al. 2007.

——. 2008. The Role of PRED in LFG+Glue. In Butt and King 2008, 46–67.

——. 2011. Propositional Glue and the Projection Architecture of LFG. *Linguistics and Philosophy* 33: 141–170.

Andronis, Mary, Erin Debenport, Anne Pycha, and Keiko Yoshimura, eds. 2002. *CLS 38: The Main Session*, vol. 1, Chicago, IL. Chicago Linguistic Society.

Aoun, Joseph, and Elabbas Benmamoun. 1998. Minimality, Reconstruction, and PF Movement. *Linguistic Inquiry* 29: 569–597.

Aoun, Joseph, Lina Choueiri, and Norbert Hornstein. 2001. Resumption, Movement, and Derivational Economy. *Linguistic Inquiry* 32: 371–403.

Assmann, Anke, Fabian Heck, Johannes Hein, Stefan Keine, and Gereon Müller. 2010. Does Chain Hybridization in Irish Support Movement-Based Approaches to Long-Distance Dependencies? In Müller 2010, 27–46.

Asudeh, Ash. 2000. Functional Identity and Resource-Sensitivity in Control. In Butt and King 2000, 2–24.

——. 2002*a*. A Resource-Sensitive Semantics for Equi and Raising. In David Beaver, Stefan Kaufmann, Brady Clark, and Luis Casillas, eds., *The Construction of Meaning*, 1–21. Stanford, CA: CSLI Publications.

——. 2002*b*. Richard III. In Andronis et al. 2002, 31–46.

——. 2002*c*. The Syntax of Preverbal Particles and Adjunction in Irish. In Butt and King 2002, 1–18.

——. 2004. Resumption as Resource Management. PhD thesis, Stanford University.

——. 2005*a*. Control and Semantic Resource Sensitivity. *Journal of Linguistics* 41: 465–511.

——. 2005*b*. Relational Nouns, Pronouns, and Resumption. *Linguistics and Philosophy* 28: 375–446.

——. 2006. Direct Compositionality and the Architecture of LFG. In Miriam Butt, Mary Dalrymple, and Tracy Holloway King, eds., *Intelligent Linguistic Architectures: Variations on Themes by Ronald M. Kaplan*, 363–387. Stanford, CA: CSLI Publications.

——. 2009. Adjacency and Locality: A Constraint-Based Analysis of Complementizer-Adjacent Extraction. In Butt and King 2009, 106–126.

——. 2011*a*. Directionality in Uncertainty and the Production of Ungrammatical Sentences. Ms., Carleton University and University of Oxford. To appear in Chesi (Forthcoming).

——. 2011*b*. Local Grammaticality in Syntactic Production. In Emily M. Bender and Jennifer E. Arnold, eds., *Language from a Cognitive Perspective*, 51–79. Stanford, CA: CSLI Publications.

——. 2011*c*. Towards a Unified Theory of Resumption. In Rouveret 2011, 121–187.

Asudeh, Ash, and Richard Crouch. 2002*a*. Coordination and Parallelism in Glue Semantics: Integrating Discourse Cohesion and the Element Constraint. In Butt and King 2002, 19–39.

Asudeh, Ash, and Richard Crouch. 2002*b*. Derivational Parallelism and Ellipsis Parallelism. In Line Mikkelsen and Christopher Potts, eds., *Proceedings of the 21st West Coast Conference on Formal Linguistics*, 1–14. Somerville, MA: Cascadilla Press.

——. 2002*c*. Glue Semantics for HPSG. In van Eynde et al. 2002, 1–19.

Asudeh, Ash, Mary Dalrymple, and Ida Toivonen. 2008 Constructions with Lexical Integrity: Templates as the Lexicon-Syntax Interface. In Butt and King 2008, 68–88.

Asudeh, Ash, and Ida Toivonen. 2007. Copy Raising and Its Consequences for Perception Reports. In Zaenen et al. 2007, 49–67.

——. 2009. Lexical-Functional Grammar. In Heine and Narrog 2009, 425–458.

——. 2012. Copy Raising and Perception. *Natural Language and Linguistic Theory.* (Forthcoming.)

Austin, Peter, and Joan Bresnan. 1996. Non-Configurationality in Australian Aboriginal languages. *Natural Language and Linguistic Theory* 14: 215–268.

Bach, Emmon. 1981. On Time, Tense, and Aspect: An Essay on English Metaphysics. In Peter Cole, ed., *Radical Pragmatics*, 62–81. New York: Academic Press.

Bach, Emmon, and Robin Cooper. 1978. The NP-S Analysis of Relative Clauses and Compositional Semantics. *Linguistics and Philosophy* 2: 145–150.

Baker, Mark. 1983. Objects, Themes, and Lexical Rules in Italian. In Lori S. Levin, Malka Rappaport, and Annie Zaenen, eds., *Papers in Lexical-Functional Grammar*, 1–45. Bloomington, IN: Indiana University Linguistics Club.

Baldridge, Jason. 2002. Lexically Specified Derivational Control in Combinatory Categorial Grammar. PhD thesis, University of Edinburgh.

Bar-Hillel, Yehoshua. 1953. A Quasi-Arithmetical Notation for Syntactic Description. *Language* 29: 47–58.

Barbiers, Sjef, ed. 2008*a*. *Microvariation in Syntactic Doubling*, vol. 36 of *Syntax and Semantics*. Bingley: Emerald Group Publishing.

Barbiers, Sjef. 2008*b*. Microvariation in Syntactic Doubling—An Introduction. In Barbiers 2008*a*, 1–34.

Barbiers, Sjef, Olaf Koeneman, and Marika Lekakou. 2010. Syntactic Doubling and the Structure of *Wh*-Chains. *Journal of Linguistics* 46: 1–46.

Bard, Ellen Gurman, Dan Robertson, and Antonella Sorace. 1996. Magnitude Estimation of Linguistic Acceptability. *Language* 72: 32–68.

Barss, Andrew. 1986. Chains and Anaphoric Dependence. PhD thesis, MIT.

——. 2001. Syntactic Reconstruction Effects. In Mark Baltin and Chris Collins, eds., *Handbook of Contemporary Syntactic Theory*, 670–696. Oxford: Blackwell.

Beermann, Dorothee, Lars Hellan, and Ota Ogie. 2002. Extraction in Edo. Ms., NTNU, Trondheim, Norway.

Beesley, Kenneth R., and Lauri Karttunen. 2003. *Finite State Morphology*. Stanford, CA: CSLI Publications.

Bender, Emily, and Dan Flickinger. 1999. Diachronic Evidence for Extended Argument Structure. In Bouma et al. 1999, 3–19.

Benton, Nick, Gavin Bierman, Valeria de Paiva, and Martin Hyland. 1993. A Term Calculus for Intuitionistic Linear Logic. In *Proceedings of the First International Conference on Typed Lambda Calculus*, vol. 664 of *Lecture Notes in Computer Science*, 75–90. Berlin: Springer Verlag.

Bittner, Maria, and Kenneth Hale. 1996. The Structural Determination of Case and Agreement. *Linguistic Inquiry* 27: 1–68.

Boeckx, Cedric. 2001. Mechanisms of Chain Formation. PhD thesis, University of Connecticut.

——. 2003. *Islands and Chains: Resumption as Derivational Residue*. Amsterdam: John Benjamins.

Bögel, Tina, Miriam Butt, Ronald M. Kaplan, Tracy Holloway King, and John T. Maxwell III. 2009. Prosodic Phonology in LFG: A New Proposal. In Butt and King 2009, 146–166.

Bögel, Tina, Miriam Butt, and Sebastian Sulger. 2008. Urdu Ezafe and the Morphology-Syntax Interface. In Butt and King 2008, 129–149.

Bögel, Tina, Tracy Holloway King, Ronald M. Kaplan, John T. Maxwell III, and Miriam Butt. 2010, 106–126. Second Position Clitics and the Prosody-Syntax Interface. In Miriam Butt and Tracy Holloway King, eds., *Proceedings of the LFG10 Conference*. Stanford, CA: CSLI Publications.

Bolinger, Dwight. 1977. *Meaning and Form*. London: Longman.

Borer, Hagit. 1981. Parametric Variation in Clitic Constructions. PhD thesis, MIT.

——. 1984. Restrictive Relatives in Modern Hebrew. *Natural Language and Linguistic Theory* 2: 219–260.

Borsley, Robert D. 2010. An HPSG Approach to Welsh Unbounded Dependencies. In Müller 2010, 80–100.

Bos, Johan, Elsbeth Mastenbroek, Scott McGlashan, Sebastian Millies, and Manfred Pinkal. 1994. A Compositional DRS-Based Formalism for NLP Applications. Verbmobil Report 59, Universität des Saarlandes, Germany.

Bouma, Gosse, Erhard W. Hinrichs, Geert-Jan M. Kruijff, and Richard T. Oehrle, eds. 1999. *Constraints and Resources in Natural Language Syntax and Semantics*. Stanford, CA: CSLI Publications.

Bouma, Gosse, Robert Malouf, and Ivan A. Sag. 2001. Satisfying Constraints on Extraction and Adjunction. *Natural Language and Linguistic Theory* 19: 1–65.

Brame, Michael. 1982. The Head-Selector Theory of Lexical Specifications and the Nonexistence of Coarse Categories. *Linguistic Analysis* 10: 321–325.

Bresnan, Joan. 1972. Theory of Complementation in English Syntax. PhD thesis, MIT. Reprinted as Bresnan (1979).

——. 1978. A Realistic Transformational Grammar. In Morris Halle, Joan Bresnan, and George A. Miller, eds., *Linguistic Theory and Psychological Reality*, 1–59. Cambridge, MA: MIT Press.

——. 1979. *Theory of Complementation in English Syntax*. New York: Garland.

——. 1982*a*. Control and Complementation. *Linguistic Inquiry* 13: 343–434.

Bresnan, Joan, ed. 1982*b*. *The Mental Representation of Grammatical Relations*. Cambridge, MA: MIT Press.

Bresnan, Joan. 1994. Linear Order vs. Syntactic Rank: Evidence from Weak Crossover. In Katie Beals, Jeannette Denton, Bob Knippen, Lynette Melnar, Hisami Suzuki, and Erika Zeinfeld, eds., *CLS 30-1: Papers from the Thirtieth Regional Meeting of the Chicago Linguistic Society*, 57–89. Chicago, IL: Chicago Linguistic Society.

——. 1995. Linear Order, Syntactic Rank, and Empty Categories: On Weak Crossover. In Dalrymple et al. 1995, 241–274.

——. 2001. *Lexical-Functional Syntax*. Oxford: Blackwell.

Bresnan, Joan, Ash Asudeh, Ida Toivonen, and Stephen Wechsler. 2012. *Lexical-Functional Syntax*, 2nd edn. Oxford: Wiley-Blackwell. (Forthcoming).

Bresnan, Joan, and Jonni M. Kanerva. 1989. Locative Inversion in Chicheŵa: A Case Study of Factorization in Grammar. *Linguistic Inquiry* 20: 1–50.

Bresnan, Joan, and Sam A. Mchombo. 1987. Topic, Pronoun, and Agreement in Chicheŵa. *Language* 63: 741–782.

Browning, Marguerite. 1987. Null Operator Constructions. PhD thesis, MIT.

Butt, Miriam, Mary Dalrymple, and Anette Frank. 1997. An Architecture for Linking Theory in LFG. In Butt and King 1997.

Butt, Miriam, and Tracy Holloway King, eds. 1996. *Proceedings of the LFG96 Conference*. Stanford, CA: CSLI Publications.

——. 1997. *Proceedings of the LFG97 Conference*. Stanford, CA: CSLI Publications.

Butt, Miriam, and Tracy Holloway King. 1998. Interfacing Phonology with LFG. In Miriam Butt and Tracy Holloway King, eds., *Proceedings of the LFG98 Conference*. Stanford, CA: CSLI Publications.

Butt, Miriam, and Tracy Holloway King, eds. 2000. *Proceedings of the LFG00 Conference*. Stanford, CA: CSLI Publications.

——. 2001. *Proceedings of the LFG01 Conference*. Stanford, CA: CSLI Publications.

——. 2002. *Proceedings of the LFG02 Conference*. Stanford, CA: CSLI Publications.

——. 2004*a*. *Proceedings of the LFG04 Conference*. Stanford, CA: CSLI Publications.

Butt, Miriam, and Tracy Holloway King. 2004*b*. The Status of Case. In Veneeta Dayal and Anoop Mahajan, eds., *Clause Structure in South Asian Languages*, 153–198. Dordrecht: Kluwer.

Butt, Miriam, and Tracy Holloway King, eds. 2006. *Lexical Semantics in LFG*. Stanford, CA: CSLI Publications.

——. 2008. *Proceedings of the LFG08 Conference*. Stanford, CA: CSLI Publications.

——. 2009. *Proceedings of the LFG09 Conference*. Stanford, CA: CSLI Publications.

Butt, Miriam, Tracy Holloway King, María-Eugenia Niño, and Frédérique Segond. 1999. *A Grammar Writer's Cookbook*. Stanford, CA: CSLI Publications.

Butt, Miriam, María-Eugenia Niño, and Frédérique Segond. 1996. Multilingual Processing of Auxiliaries within LFG. In Dafydd Gibbon, ed., *Natural Language Processing and Speech Technology: Results of the 3rd KONVENS Conference*, 111–122. Berlin: Mouton de Gruyter. Reprinted in Sadler and Spencer (2004: 11–22).

Cable, Seth. 2003. Resumption and Weak Crossover in Yoruba. Ms., MIT.

Cann, Ronnie, Tami Kaplan, and Ruth Kempson. 2005*a*. Data at the Syntax-Pragmatics Interface: Resumptive Pronouns in English. *Lingua* 115: 1551–1577.

Cann, Ronnie, Ruth Kempson, and Lutz Marten. 2005*b*. *The Dynamics of Language: An Introduction*. Amsterdam: Elsevier.

Carlson, Gregory N. 1977. Reference to Kinds in English. PhD thesis, University of Massachusetts, Amherst.

Carpenter, Bob. 1997. *Type-Logical Semantics*. Cambridge, MA: MIT Press.

Carstens, Victoria. 1987. Extraction Asymmetries in Yoruba. In David Odden, ed., *Current Approaches to African Linguistics*, vol. 4, 61–72. Dordrecht, Foris.

Chao, Wynn, and Peter Sells. 1983. On the Interpretation of Resumptive Pronouns. In Sells and Jones 1983, 47–61.

Chesi, Cristiano, ed. Forthcoming. *Directions in Derivations*. Amsterdam: Elsevier.

Cho, Sae-Youn, and Jong-Bok Kim. 2003. Echoed Verb Constructions in Korean: A Construction-Based HPSG Analysis. *Ene* 27: 661–681.

Cho, Sae-Youn, Jong-Bok Kim, and Peter Sells. 2004. Contrastive Verb Constructions in Korean. In Susumu Kuno, Ik-Hawn Lee, John Whitman, Joan Maling, Young-Se Kang, and Young-Joo Kim, eds., *Harvard Studies in Korean Linguistics X*, 360–371. Department of Linguistics, Harvard University.

Choi, Hye-Won. 1997. Information Structure, Phrase Structure, and Their Interface. In Butt and King 1997.

——. 1999. *Optimizing Structure in Context: Scrambling and Information Structure*. Stanford, CA: CSLI Publications. Revised version of 1996 Stanford University doctoral thesis.

Chomsky, Noam. 1965. *Aspects of the Theory of Syntax*. Cambridge, MA: MIT Press.

——. 1970. Remarks on Nominalization. In Roderick A. Jacobs and Peter S. Rosenbaum, eds., *Readings in English Transformational Grammar*, 184–221. Waltham, MA: Ginn and Company.

——. 1981. *Lectures on Government and Binding*. Dordrecht: Foris.

——. 1982. *Some Concepts and Consequences of the Theory of Government and Binding*. Cambridge, MA: MIT Press.

——. 1986. *Knowledge of Language: Its Nature, Origin, and Use*. New York: Praeger.

——. 1993. A Minimalist Program for Linguistic Theory. In Hale and Keyser 1993, 1–52. Reprinted as chapter 3 of Chomsky (1995).

——. 1995. *The Minimalist Program*. Cambridge, MA: MIT Press.

——. 2000. Minimalist Inquiries: The Framework. In Roger Martin, David Michaels, and Juan Uriagereka, eds., *Step by Step: Essays on Minimalist Syntax in Honor of Howard Lasnik*, 89–155. Cambridge, MA: MIT Press.

——. 2001. Derivation by Phase. In Michael Kenstowicz, ed., *Ken Hale: A Life in Language*, 1–50. Cambridge, MA: MIT Press.

Chomsky, Noam, and Howard Lasnik. 1977. Filters and Control. *Linguistic Inquiry* 8: 425–504.

Chomsky, Noam, and George Miller. 1963. Introduction to the Formal Analysis of Natural Languages. In R. Duncan Luce, Robert R. Bush, and Eugene Galanter, eds., *The Handbook of Mathematical Psychology*, vol. 2, 269–321. New York: Wiley.

Chung, Sandra. 1978. *Case Marking and Grammatical Relations in Polynesian*. Austin, TX: University of Texas Press.

Chung, Sandra, and James McCloskey. 1987. Government, Barriers, and Small Clauses in Modern Irish. *Linguistic Inquiry* 18: 173–237.

Cinque, Guglielmo. 1990. *Types of A-bar Dependencies*. Cambridge, MA: MIT Press.

Cooper, Robin. 1975. Montague's Semantic Theory and Transformational Syntax. PhD thesis, University of Massachusetts, Amherst.

——. 1983. *Quantification and Syntactic Theory*. Dordrecht: Reidel.

Cowart, Wayne. 1997. *Experimental Syntax: Applying Objective Methods to Sentence Judgments*. Thousand Oaks, CA: Sage Publications.

Creswell, Cassandre. 2002. Resumptive Pronouns, Wh-island Violations, and Sentence Production. In *Proceedings of the Sixth International Workshop on Tree Adjoining Grammar and Related Frameworks (TAG+ 6)*, 101–109. Universitá di Venezia.

Crouch, Richard, Mary Dalrymple, Ronald M. Kaplan, Tracy King, John T. Maxwell III, and Paula Newman. 2011. *XLE Documentation*. Palo Alto Research Center (PARC), Palo Alto, CA.

Crouch, Richard, and Tracy Holloway King. 2006. Semantics via F-structure Rewriting. In Miriam Butt and Tracy Holloway King, eds., *Proceedings of the LFG06 Conference*, 145–165. Stanford, CA: CSLI Publications.

Crouch, Richard, and Josef van Genabith. 1999. Context Change, Underspecification, and the Structure of Glue Language Derivations. In Dalrymple 1999, 117–189.

——. 2000. Linear Logic for Lingists. Ms., PARC and Dublin City University.

Curry, Haskell B., and Robert Feys. 1958. *Combinatory Logic*, vol. 1. Amsterdam: North-Holland.

——. 1995. The Basic Theory of Functionality. Analogies with Propositional Algebra. In de Groote 1995, 9–13. Reprint of Curry and Feys (1958: chapter 9, section E).

Dalrymple, Mary. 1993. *The Syntax of Anaphoric Binding*. Stanford, CA: CSLI Publications.

Dalrymple, Mary, ed. 1999. *Semantics and Syntax in Lexical Functional Grammar: The Resource Logic Approach*. Cambridge, MA: MIT Press.

Dalrymple, Mary. 2001. *Lexical Functional Grammar*. San Diego, CA: Academic Press.

——. 2006. Lexical Functional Grammar. In Keith Brown, ed., *Encyclopedia of Language and Linguistics*, 2nd edn., 82–94. Amsterdam: Elsevier.

Dalrymple, Mary, John Lamping, and Vijay Saraswat. 1993. LFG Semantics via Constraints. In *Proceedings of the Sixth Meeting of the European ACL*, 97–105. European Chapter of the Association for Computational Linguistics, University of Utrecht.

Dalrymple, Mary, Ronald M. Kaplan, John T. Maxwell III, and Annie Zaenen, eds. 1995. *Formal Issues in Lexical-Functional Grammar*. Stanford, CA: CSLI Publications.

Dalrymple, Mary, Vaneet Gupta, John Lamping, and Vijay Saraswat. 1999*a*. Relating Resource-Based Semantics to Categorial Semantics. In Dalrymple 1999, 261–280.

Dalrymple, Mary, John Lamping, Fernando Pereira, and Vijay Saraswat. 1999*b*. Overview and Introduction. In Dalrymple 1999, 1–38.

——. 1999*c*. Quantification, Anaphora, and Intensionality. In Dalrymple 1999, 39–89.

Dalrymple, Mary, and Tracy Holloway King. 2000. Missing-Object Constructions: Lexical and Constructional Variation. In Butt and King 2000, 82–103.

Dalrymple, Mary, Ronald M. Kaplan, and Tracy Holloway King. 2001. Weak Crossover and the Absence of Traces. In Butt and King 2001, 66–82.

Dalrymple, Mary, Helge Dyvik, and Tracy Holloway King. 2004*a*. Copular Complements: Closed or Open. In Butt and King 2004*a*, 188–198.

Dalrymple, Mary, Ronald M. Kaplan, and Tracy Holloway King. 2004*b*. Linguistic Generalizations over Descriptions. In Butt and King 2004*a*, 199–208.

——. 2007. The Absence of Traces: Evidence from Weak Crossover. In Zaenen et al. 2007, 85–102.

Dalrymple, Mary, and Irina Nikolaeva. 2011. *Objects and Information Structure*. Cambridge: Cambridge University Press.

Darzi, Ali. 1996. Word Order, NP-Movements, and Opacity Conditions in Persian. PhD thesis, University of Illinois at Urbana-Champaign.

Davidson, Donald. 1967. The Logical Form of Action Sentences. In Nicholas Rescher, ed., *The Logic of Decision and Action*, 81–95. Pittsburgh, PA: University of Pittsburgh Press. Reprinted in Davidson (1980: 105–122).

——. 1980. *Essays on Actions and Events*. Oxford: Clarendon Press.

de Groote, Philippe, ed. 1995. *The Curry-Howard Isomorphism*, vol. 8 of *Cahiers du Centre de Logique*. Louvain-la-neuve, Belgium: Academia.

Deane, Paul. 1991. Limits to Attention: A Cognitive Theory of Island Phenomena. *Cognitive Linguistics* 2: 1–62.

Demirdache, Hamida. 1991. Resumptive Chains in Restrictive Relatives, Appositives, and Dislocation Structures. PhD thesis, MIT.

Déprez, Viviane. 1992. Raising Constructions in Haitian Creole. *Natural Language and Linguistic Theory* 10: 191–231.

Dickey, Michael Walsh. 1996. Constraints on the Sentence Processor and the Distribution of Resumptive Pronouns. In Michael Walsh Dickey and Susanne Tunstall, eds., *Linguistics in the Laboratory*, vol. 19 of *UMOP*, 157–192. Amherst, MA: GLSA.

Doron, Edit. 1982. On the Syntax and Semantics of Resumptive Pronouns. In *Texas Linguistic Forum* 19, 1–48.

Duffield, Nigel. 1995. *Particles and Projections in Irish Syntax*. Dordrecht: Kluwer.

Elbourne, Paul. 2002. Situations and Individuals. PhD thesis, MIT.

——. 2005. *Situations and Individuals*. Cambridge, MA: MIT Press.

Embick, David, and Rolf Noyer. 2007. Distributed Morphology and the Syntax–Morphology Interface. In Ramchand and Reiss 2007, 289–324.

Emms, Martin. 1990. Polymorphic Quantifiers. In *Studies in Categorial Grammar*, no. 5 in Edinburgh Working Papers in Cognitive Science, 65–111. Edinburgh: Centre for Cognitive Science.

Engdahl, Elisabet. 1980. The Syntax and Semantics of Questions in Swedish. PhD thesis, University of Massachusetts.

——. 1982. Restrictions on Unbounded Dependencies in Swedish. In Elisabet Engdahl and Eva Ejerhed, eds., *Readings on Unbounded Dependencies in Scandinavian Languages*, 151–174. Stockholm: Almquist and Wiksell International.

——. 1985. Parasitic Gaps, Resumptive Pronouns, and Subject Extractions. *Linguistics* 23: 3–44.

——. 1986. *Constituent Questions*. Dordrecht: Reidel.

——. 1997. Relative Clause Extractions in Context. *Working Papers in Scandinavian Syntax* 60: 51–79.

Erteschik-Shir, Nomi. 1992. Resumptive Pronouns in Islands. In Goodluck and Rochemont 1992, 89–108.

Evans, Gareth. 1980. Pronouns. *Linguistic Inquiry* 11: 337–362. Reprinted in Evans (1985: 214–248).

——. 1985. *Collected Papers*. Edited by Antonia Phillips. Oxford: Clarendon Press.

Everaert, Martin, and Henk van Riemsdijk, eds. 2006. *The Blackwell Companion to Syntax*. Oxford: Blackwell.

Falk, Yehuda N. 2001. *Lexical-Functional Grammar: An Introduction to Parallel Constraint-Based Syntax*. Stanford, CA: CSLI Publications.

——. 2002. Resumptive Pronouns in LFG. In Butt and King 2002, 154–173.

——. 2007. Do We Wanna (or Hafta) Have Empty Categories? In Miriam Butt and Tracy Holloway King, eds., *Proceedings of LFG07 Conference*, 184–197. Stanford, CA: CSLI Publications.

——. 2010. Multiple-Gap Constructions. Ms., The Hebrew University of Jerusalem.

Fassi-Fehri, Abdelkader. 1988. Agreement in Arabic, Binding, and Coherence. In Michael Barlow and Charles A. Ferguson, eds., *Agreement in Natural Language: Approaches, Theories, Descriptions*, 107–158. Stanford, CA: CSLI Publications.

Ferreira, Fernanda. 2000. Syntax in Language Production: An Approach Using Tree-adjoining Grammars. In Linda Wheeldon, ed., *Aspects of Language Production*, 291–330. Philadelphia, PA: Psychology Press.

Ferreira, Fernanda, and Benjamin Swets. 2002. How Incremental Is Language Production? Evidence from the Production of Utterances Requiring the Computation of Arithmetic Sums. *Journal of Memory and Language* 46: 57–84.

——. 2005. The Production and Comprehension of Resumptive Pronouns in Relative Clause 'Island' Contexts. In Anne Cutler, ed., *Twenty-first Century Psycholinguistics: Four Cornerstones*, 263–278. Mahway, NJ: Lawrence Erlbaum Associates.

Finer, Daniel. 1997. Contrasting A′-Dependencies in Selayarese. *Natural Language and Linguistic Theory* 15: 677–728.

Fodor, Janet Dean. 1978. Parsing Strategies and Constraints on Transformations. *Linguistic Inquiry* 9: 427–473.

Fox, Danny. 2000. *Economy and Semantic Interpretation*. Cambridge, MA: MIT Press.

Frank, Anette, and Josef van Genabith. 2001. LL-based Semantics Construction for LTAG—And What It Teaches Us About the Relation Between LFG and LTAG. In Butt and King 2001, 104–126.

Frank, Anette, and Annie Zaenen. 2002. Tense in LFG: Syntax and Morphology. In Hans Kamp and Uwe Reyle, eds., *How We Say WHEN It Happens: Contributions to the Theory of Temporal Reference in Natural Language*. Tübingen: Niemeyer. Reprinted in Sadler and Spencer (2004: 23–65).

Frank, Robert. 2002. *Phrase Structure Composition and Syntactic Dependencies*. Cambridge, MA: MIT Press.

Frank, Robert, and William Badecker. 2001. Modeling Syntactic Encoding with Incremental Tree-adjoining Grammar. Presented at the CUNY Sentence Processing Conference, University of Pennsylvania, March 15th. University of Pennsylvania.

Frazier, Lyn. 1985. Syntactic Complexity. In David Dowty, Lauri Karttunen, and Arnold Zwicky, eds., *Natural Language Parsing: Psychological, Computational, and Theoretical Perspectives*, 129–189. Cambridge: Cambridge University Press.

——. 1987. Syntactic Processing: Evidence from Dutch. *Natural Language and Linguistic Theory* 5: 519–560.

——. 1999. *On Sentence Interpretation*. Dordrecht: Kluwer.

Frazier, Lyn, and Charles Clifton Jr. 1996. *Construal*. Cambridge, MA: MIT Press.

Frazier, Lyn, and Giovanni B. Flores d'Arcais. 1989. Filler Driven Parsing: A Study of Gap Filling in Dutch. *Journal of Memory and Language* 28: 331–344.

Frege, Gottlob. 1891/1952. Function and Concept. In P. T. Geach and Max Black, eds., *Translations from the Philosophical Writings of Gottlob Frege*, 22–41. Translated by P. T. Geach. Oxford: Blackwell.

Fry, John. 1999. Resource-logical Event Semantics for LFG. Presented at LFG99, University of Manchester.

Fujii, Tomohiro. 2005. Cycle, Linearization of Chains, and Multiple Case Checking. In Sylvia Blaho, Luis Vicente, and Erik Schoorlemmer, eds., *Proceedings of Console XIII*, 39–65. Student Organization of Linguistics in Europe, University of Leiden.

——. 2007. Cyclic Chain Reduction. In Norbert Corver and Jairo Nunes, eds., *The Copy Theory of Movement*, 291–326. Amsterdam: John Benjamins.

Gallier, Jean. 1995. On the Correspondence between Proofs and λ-terms. In de Groote 1995, 55–138.

Gamut, L. T. F. 1991. *Introduction to Logic*, vol. 1 of *Logic, Language, and Meaning*. Chicago, IL: University of Chicago Press.

Gärtner, Hans-Martin. 2002. *Generalized Transformations and Beyond: Reflections on Minimalist Syntax*. Berlin: Akademie-Verlag.

Gazdar, Gerald, Ewan Klein, Geoffrey K. Pullum, and Ivan A. Sag. 1985. *Generalized Phrase Structure Grammar*. Cambridge, MA: Harvard University Press.

Ghomeshi, Jila. 2001. Control and Thematic Agreement. *Canadian Journal of Linguistics* 46: 9–40.

Gibson, Edward. 1998. Linguistic Complexity: Locality and Syntactic Dependencies. *Cognition* 68: 1–76.

Gibson, Edward, and Gregory Hickok. 1993. Sentence Processing with Empty Categories. *Language and Cognitive Processes* 8: 147–161.

Girard, Jean-Yves. 1987. Linear Logic. *Theoretical Computer Science* 50: 1–102.

——. 1989. *Proofs and Types*, vol. 7 of *Cambridge Tracts in Theoretical Computer Science*. Translated and expanded by Yves Lafont and Paul Taylor. Cambridge: Cambridge University Press.

——. 1995. Linear Logic: A Survey. In de Groote 1995, 193–255.

Gisborne, Nikolas. 1996. English Perception Verbs. PhD thesis, University College London.

——. 2010. *The Event Structure of Perception Verbs*. Oxford: Oxford University Press.

Gisborne, Nikolas, and Jasper Holmes. 2007. A History of English Evidential Verbs of Appearance. *English Language and Linguistics* 11: 1–29.

Goble, Lou, ed. 2001. *The Blackwell Guide to Philosophical Logic*. Oxford: Blackwell.

Goldsmith, John. 1981. The Structure of *Wh*-Questions in Igbo. *Linguistic Analysis* 7: 367–393.

Goodluck, Helen, and Michael Rochemont, eds. 1992. *Island Constraints: Theory, Acquisition, and Processing*. Dordrecht: Kluwer.

Gregory, Howard. 2001. Relevance Semantics: An Approach to Intensionality. In Dick de Jongh, Henk Zeevat, and Marie Nilsenová, eds., *Proceedings of the 4th International Tbilisi Symposium on Language, Logic, and Computation*, 205–20. Department of Language Modelling, Georgian Academy of Sciences, Tbilisi, Georgia. Amsterdam: ILLC Scientific Publications.

——. 2002. Relevance Logic and Natural Language Semantics. In Gerhard Jäger, Paola Monachesi, Gerald Penn, and Shuly Wintner, eds., *Proceedings of Formal Grammar 2002*, 53–63.

Grimshaw, Jane. 1998. Locality and Extended Projection. In Peter Coopmans, Martin Everaert, and Jane Grimshaw, eds., *Lexical Specification and Insertion*, 115–133. Mahwah, NJ: Lawrence Erlbaum Associates.

Grosu, Alexander. 1973. On the Nonunitary Nature of the Coordinate Structure Constraint. *Linguistic Inquiry* 4: 88–92.

Gruber, Jeffrey S. 1965. Studies in Lexical Relations. PhD thesis, MIT.

Hale, Kenneth. 1980. *On the Position of Warlpiri in a Typology of the Base*. Bloomington, IN: Indiana University Linguistics Club.

——. 1983. Warlpiri and the Grammar of Non-Configurational Languages. *Natural Language and Linguistic Theory* 1: 5–74.

Hale, Kenneth, and Samuel Jay Keyser, eds. 1993. *The View from Building 20*. Cambridge, MA: MIT Press.

Halle, Morris, and Alec Marantz. 1993. Distributed Morphology and the Pieces of Inflection. In Hale and Keyser 1993, 111–176.

Halvorsen, Per-Kristian. 1983. Semantics for Lexical-Functional Grammar. *Linguistic Inquiry* 14: 567–615.

Halvorsen, Per-Kristian, and Ronald M. Kaplan. 1988. Projections and Semantic Description in Lexical-Functional Grammar. In *Proceedings of the International Conference on Fifth Generation Computer Systems*, 1116–1122. Institute for New Generation Systems, Tokyo. Reprinted in Dalrymple et al. (1995: 279–292).

Heestand, Dustin, Ming Xiang, and Maria Polinsky. 2011. Resumption Still does not Rescue Islands. *Linguistic Inquiry* 42: 138–152.

Heim, Irene. 1982. The Semantics of Definite and Indefinite Noun Phrases. PhD thesis, University of Massachusetts, Amherst.

——. 1990. E-Type Pronouns and Donkey Anaphora. *Linguistics and Philosophy* 13: 137–177.

Heim, Irene, and Angelika Kratzer. 1998. *Semantics in Generative Grammar*. Oxford: Blackwell.

Heine, Bernd, and Heiko Narrog, eds. 2009. *The Oxford Handbook of Linguistic Analysis*. Oxford: Oxford University Press.

Hepple, Mark. 1990. The Grammar and Processing of Order and Dependency: A Categorial Approach. PhD thesis, University of Edinburgh.

Heycock, Caroline. 1994. *Layers of Predication*. New York: Garland.

Higginbotham, James. 1983. Logical Form, Binding, and Nominals. *Linguistic Inquiry* 14: 395–420.

——. 1985. On Semantics. *Linguistic Inquiry* 16: 547–594.

Hindley, J. Roger, and Jonathan P. Seldin. 1986. *Introduction to Combinators and λ-Calculus*, vol. 1 of *London Mathematical Society Student Texts*. Cambridge: Cambridge University Press.

Hodges, Wilfrid. 2001. Classical Logic I—First-Order Logic. In Goble 2001, 9–32.

Hofmeister, Philip, and Elisabeth Norcliffe. In progress. Do Resumptive Pronouns Aid Sentence Comprehension? Ms., University of California, San Diego, and Max Planck Institute for Psycholinguistics.

Hofmeister, Philip, and Ivan A. Sag. 2010. Cognitive Constraints and Island Effects. *Language* 86: 366–415.

Horn, Laurence R. 1981. A Pragmatic Approach to Certain Ambiguities. *Linguistics and Philosophy* 4: 321–358.

Howard, William A. 1980. The Formulae-as-Types Notion of Construction. In Jonathan P. Seldin and J. Roger Hindley, eds., *To H. B. Curry: Essays on Combinatory Logic, Lambda Calculus, and Formalism*, 479–490. London: Academic Press. Circulated in unpublished form from 1969. Reprinted in de Groote (1995: 15–26).

Huddleston, Rodney, and Geoffrey K. Pullum. 2002. *The Cambridge Grammar of the English Language*. Cambridge: Cambridge University Press.

Jackendoff, Ray. 1972. *Semantic Interpretation in Generative Grammar*. Cambridge, MA: MIT Press.

——. 1977. *$\bar{X}$ Syntax: A Study of Phrase Structure*. Cambridge, MA: MIT Press.

——. 1990. *Semantic Structures*. Cambridge, MA: MIT Press.

——. 1997. *The Architecture of the Language Faculty*. Cambridge, MA: MIT Press.

Jackendoff, Ray. 2002. *Foundations of Language: Brain, Meaning, Grammar, Evolution.* Oxford: Oxford University Press.

——. 2007. *Language, Consciousness, Culture: Essays on Mental Structure.* Cambridge, MA: MIT Press.

Jacobson, Pauline. 1998. Where (If Anywhere) is Transderivationality Located? In McNally and Culicover 1998, 303–366.

——. 1999. Towards a Variable-Free Semantics. *Linguistics and Philosophy* 22: 117–184.

Jäger, Gerhard. 2003. Resource Sharing in Type Logical Grammar. In Kruijff and Oehrle 2003*b*, 97–121.

——. 2005. *Anaphora and Type Logical Grammar*. Dordrecht: Springer.

Johnson, David, and Shalom Lappin. 1997. A Critique of the Minimalist Program. *Linguistics and Philosophy* 20: 273–333.

——. 1999. *Local Constraints vs. Economy*. Stanford, CA: CSLI Publications.

Johnson, Kyle. 2010. Determiners and Movement. In Raffaella Folli and Christiane Ulbrich, eds., *Interfaces in Linguistics: New Research Perspectives*, 30–55. Oxford: Oxford University Press.

Johnson, Mark. 1999*a*. A Resource Sensitive Reinterpretation of Lexical Functional Grammar. *Journal of Logic, Language, and Information* 8: 45–81.

——. 1999*b*. Type-driven Semantic Interpretation and Feature Dependencies in R-LFG. In Dalrymple 1999, 359–388.

Joseph, Brian D. 1976. Raising in Modern Greek: A Copying Process. In Jorge Hankamer and Judith Aissen, eds., *Harvard Studies in Syntax and Semantics*, vol. 2, 241–281. Cambridge, MA: Harvard University, Department of Linguistics.

Joshi, Aravind K., Leon S. Levy, and Masako Takahashi. 1975. Tree Adjunct Grammars. *Journal of Computer and System Sciences* 10: 136–163.

Kamp, Hans. 1981. A Theory of Truth and Semantic Representation. In Jeroen Groenendijk, Theo M. B. Janssen, and Martin Stokhof, eds., *Formal Methods in the Study of Language*, 277–322. Amsterdam: Mathematical Centre Tracts.

Kaplan, Ronald M. 1987. Three Seductions of Computational Psycholinguistics. In Peter Whitelock, Mary McGee Wood, Harold L. Somers, Rod Johnson, and Paul Bennett, eds., *Linguistic Theory and Computer Applications*, 149–181. London: Academic Press. Reprinted in Dalrymple et al. (1995: 339–367).

——. 1989. The Formal Architecture of Lexical-Functional Grammar. In Chu-Ren Huang and Keh-Jiann Chen, eds., *Proceedings of ROCLING II*, 3–18. Reprinted in Dalrymple et al. (1995: 7–27).

Kaplan, Ronald M., and Joan Bresnan. 1982. Lexical-Functional Grammar: A Formal System for Grammatical Representation. In Bresnan 1982*b*, 173–281. Reprinted in Dalrymple et al. (1995: 29–135).

Kaplan, Ronald M., and John T. Maxwell III. 1988. Constituent Coordination in Lexical-Functional Grammar. In *Proceedings of COLING-88*, vol. 1. Budapest. Reprinted in Dalrymple et al. (1995: 199–214).

——. 1996. LFG Grammar Writer's Workbench. Tech. Rep., PARC, Palo Alto, CA. ftp://ftp.parc.xerox.com/pub/lfg/lfgmanual.ps; retrieved 28/02/2011.

Kaplan, Ronald M., and Jürgen Wedekind. 1993. Restriction and Correspondence-Based Translation. In *Proceedings of the 6th Meeting of the EACL*. European Chapter of the Association of Computational Linguistics, University of Utrecht.

Kaplan, Ronald M., and Annie Zaenen. 1989. Long-Distance Dependencies, Constituent Structure, and Functional Uncertainty. In Mark Baltin and Anthony Kroch, eds., *Alternative Conceptions of Phrase Structure*, 17–42. Chicago, IL: University of Chicago Press. Reprinted in Dalrymple et al. (1995: 137–165).

Karimi, Simin. 2003. *Word Order and Scrambling*. Oxford: Blackwell.

Karttunen, Lauri. 2003. Computing with Realizational Morphology. In *Proceedings of the 4th International Conference on Computational Linguistics and Intelligent Text Processing*, 203–214. Berlin: Springer-Verlag.

Kayne, Richard S. 1994. *The Antisymmetry of Syntax*. Cambridge, MA: MIT Press.

Keach, Camillia N. 1980. The Syntax and Interpretation of the Relative Clause Construction in Swahili. PhD thesis, University of Massachusetts, Amherst.

Keenan, Edward L., and Bernard Comrie. 1977. Noun Phrase Accessibility and Universal Grammar. *Linguistic Inquiry* 8: 63–99.

Kehler, Andrew. 2002. *Coherence, Reference, and the Theory of Grammar*. Stanford, CA: CSLI Publications.

Kehler, Andrew, Mary Dalrymple, John Lamping, and Vijay Saraswat. 1999. Resource Sharing in Glue Language Semantics. In Dalrymple 1999, 191–208.

Keller, Frank. 2000. Gradience in Grammar: Experimental and Computational Aspects of Degrees of Grammaticality. PhD thesis, University of Edinburgh.

Kempen, Gerard, and Edward Hoenkamp. 1987. An Incremental Procedural Grammar for Sentence Formulation. *Cognitive Science* 11: 201–258.

Kennedy, Christopher. 1997. Antecedent Contained Deletion and the Syntax of Quantification. *Linguistic Inquiry* 28: 662–688.

Kimball, John. 1973. Seven Principles of Surface Structure Parsing in Natural Language. *Cognition* 2: 15–47.

King, Tracy Holloway. 1995. *Configuring Topic and Focus in Russian*. Stanford, CA: CSLI Publications.

——. 1997. Focus Domains and Information Structure. In Butt and King 1997.

King, Tracy Holloway, and Annie Zaenen. 2004. F-structures, Information Structure, and Discourse Structure. Presented at the *Winter School in LFG and Computational Linguistics*, University of Canterbury, Christchurch, New Zealand.

Klein, Ewan, and Ivan A. Sag. 1985. Type-Driven Translation. *Linguistics and Philosophy* 8: 163–201.

Kluender, Robert. 1991. Cognitive Constraints on Variables in Syntax. PhD thesis, University of California, San Diego.

——. 1998. On the Distinction between Strong and Weak Islands: A Processing Perspective. In McNally and Culicover 1998, 241–279.

——. 2004. Are Subject Islands Subject to a Processing Account? In Vineeta Chand, Ann Kelleher, Angelo J. Rodriguez, and Benjamin Schmeiser, eds., *Proceedings of the 23rd West Coast Conference on Formal Linguistics*, 475–499. Somerville, MA: Cascadilla Press.

Kluender, Robert, and Marta Kutas. 1993. Bridging the Gap: Evidence from ERPs on the Processing of Unbounded Dependencies. *Journal of Cognitive Neuroscience* 5: 196–214.

Kokkonidis, Miltiadis. 2005. Why Glue a Donkey to an F-structure When You Can Constrain and Bind it Instead? In Miriam Butt and Tracy Holloway King, eds., *Proceedings of the LFG05 Conference*, 238–252. Stanford, CA: CSLI Publications.

——. 2006. A Glue/λ-DRT Treatment of Resumptive Pronouns. In Janneke Huitink and Sophia Katrenko, eds., *Proceedings of the Eleventh ESSLLI Student Session*, 51–62. Málaga, Spain.

——. 2008. First-Order Glue. *Journal of Logic, Language and Information* 17: 43–68.

Koopman, Hilda. 1982. Control from COMP and Comparative Syntax. *Linguistic Review* 2: 365–391. Reprinted in Koopman (2000: 126–150).

——. 1984. *The Syntax of Verbs: From Verb Movement Rules in the Kru Languages to Universal Grammar*. Dordrecht: Foris.

——. 2000. *The Syntax of Specifiers and Heads*. London: Routledge.

Koopman, Hilda, and Dominique Sportiche. 1982. Variables and the Bijection Principle. *Linguistic Review* 2: 139–160. Reprinted in Koopman (2000: 19–39).

——. 1986. A Note on Long Extraction in Vata and the ECP. *Natural Language and Linguistic Theory* 4: 357–374. Reprinted in Koopman (2000: 151–166).

Kratzer, Angelika. 1995. Stage-Level and Individual-Level Predicates. In Gregory N. Carlson and Francis Jeffry Pelletier, eds., *The Generic Book*, 125–175. Chicago, IL: University of Chicago Press.

——. 2009. Making a Pronoun: Fake Indexicals as Windows into the Properties of Pronouns. *Linguistic Inquiry* 40: 187–237.

Kroch, Anthony S. 1981. On the Role of Resumptive Pronouns in Amnestying Island Constraint Violations. In *Papers from the 17th Regional Meeting of the Chicago Linguistic Society*, 125–135. Chicago, IL: Chicago Linguistic Society.

Kroch, Anthony S., and Aravind K. Joshi. 1985. The Linguistic Relevance of Tree Adjoining Grammar. Tech. Rep. MS-CIS-85-16, Department of Computer and Information Sciences, University of Pennsylvania.

Kroeger, Paul. 1993. *Phrase Structure and Grammatical Relations in Tagalog*. Stanford, CA: CSLI Publications.

Kruijff, Geert-Jan M., and Richard T. Oehrle. 2003*a*. Introduction. In Kruijff and Oehrle 2003*b*, xi–xxii.

Kruijff, Geert-Jan M., and Richard T. Oehrle, eds. 2003*b*. *Resource-Sensitivity, Binding, and Anaphora*. Dordrecht: Kluwer.

Kuhn, Jonas. 2001. Resource Sensitivity in the Syntax-Semantics Interface and the German Split NP Construction. In W. Detmar Meurers and Tibor Kiss, eds., *Constraint-Based Approaches to Germanic Syntax*. Stanford, CA: CSLI Publications, 75–117.

Lambek, Joachim. 1958. The Mathematics of Sentence Structure. *American Mathematical Monthly* 65: 154–170.

Lamontagne, Greg, and Lisa Travis. 1986. The Case Filter and the ECP. In Eithne Guilfoyle, ed., *McGill Working Papers in Linguistics*, vol. 3. Department of Linguistics, McGill University.

——. 1987. The Syntax of Adjacency. In Megan Crowhurst, ed., *Proceedings of the 6th West Coast Conference on Formal Linguistics*, 173–185. Stanford, CA: CSLI Publications.

Landau, Idan. 2009. This Construction Looks Like a Copy is Optional. *Linguistic Inquiry* 40: 343–346.

——. 2011. Predication vs. Aboutness in Copy Raising. *Natural Language and Linguistic Theory*, 29: 779–813.

Landman, Meredith L. 2006. Variables in Natural Language. PhD thesis, University of Massachusetts, Amherst.

Lappin, Shalom. 1983. Theta-Roles and NP Movement. In Sells and Jones 1983, 121–128.

——. 1984. Predication and Raising. In Charles Jones and Peter Sells, eds., *Proceedings of NELS 14*, 236–252. Amherst, MA: GLSA.

Lasersohn, Peter. 1995. Sounds Like *Like*. *Linguistic Analysis* 25: 70–77.

Lev, Iddo. 2007. Packed Computation of Exact Meaning Representations. PhD thesis, Stanford University.

Levelt, Willem J. M. 1989. *Speaking: From Intention to Articulation*. Cambridge, MA: MIT Press.

——. 1999. Producing Spoken Language: A Blueprint of the Speaker. In Colin M. Brown and Peter Hagoort, eds., *The Neurocognition of Language*, 83–122. Oxford: Oxford University Press.

Levine, Robert, and Ivan A. Sag. 2003. *WH*-Nonmovement. *Gengo Kenkyu* 2003: 171–219.

Lewis, Richard L. 1996. Interference in Short-Term Memory: The Magical Number Two (or Three) in Sentence Processing. *Journal of Psycholinguistic Research* 25: 93–115.

Maling, Joan. 1983. Transitive Adjectives: A Case of Categorial Reanalysis. In Frank Heny and Barry Richards, eds., *Linguistic Categories: Auxiliaries and Related Puzzles*, 253–289. Dordrecht: Foris.

Maling, Joan, and Annie Zaenen. 1982. A Phrase Structure Account of Scandinavian Extraction Phenomena. In Pauline Jacobson and Geoffrey K. Pullum, eds., *The Nature of Syntactic Representation*, 229–282. Dordrecht: Reidel.

Marsh, William, and Barbara H. Partee. 1984. How Non-Context Free is Variable Binding? In Mark Cobler, Susannah MacKaye, and Michael Wescoat, eds., *Proceedings of the 3rd West Coast Conference on Formal Linguistics*, 179–190. Stanford, CA: Stanford Linguistics Association.

Matushansky, Ora. 2002. Tipping the Scales: The Syntax of Scalarity in the Complement of *Seem*. *Syntax* 5: 219–276.

McCloskey, James. 1979. *Transformational Syntax and Model Theoretic Semantics: A Case-Study in Modern Irish*. Dordrecht: Reidel.

——. 1985. The Modern Irish Double Relative and Syntactic Binding. *Ériu* 36: 46–84.

McCloskey, James. 1986. Inflection and Conjunction in Modern Irish. *Natural Language and Linguistic Theory* 4: 245–281.

——. 1990. Resumptive Pronouns, Ā-Binding and Levels of Representation in Irish. In Randall Hendrick, ed., *Syntax of the Modern Celtic languages*, vol. 23 of *Syntax and Semantics*, 199–248. San Diego, CA: Academic Press.

——. 1996. On the Scope of Verb Movement in Irish. *Natural Language and Linguistic Theory* 14: 47–104.

——. 2001. The Morphosyntax of WH-Extraction in Irish. *Journal of Linguistics* 37: 67–100.

——. 2002. Resumption, Successive Cyclicity, and the Locality of Operations. In Samuel David Epstein and T. Daniel Seeley, eds., *Derivation and Explanation in the Minimalist Program*, 184–226. Oxford: Blackwell.

——. 2006. Resumption. In Everaert and Riemsdijk 2006, 94–117.

McCloskey, James, and Kenneth Hale. 1984. On the Syntax of Person-Number Inflection in Modern Irish. *Natural Language and Linguistic Theory* 1: 487–533.

McCloskey, James, and Peter Sells. 1988. Control and A-Chains in Modern Irish. *Natural Language and Linguistic Theory* 6: 143–189.

McDaniel, Dana, and Wayne Cowart. 1999. Experimental Evidence for a Minimalist Account of English Resumptive Pronouns. *Cognition* 70: B15–B24.

McNally, Louise, and Peter W. Culicover, eds. 1998. *The Limits of Syntax*. San Diego, CA: Academic Press.

Merchant, Jason. 2001. *The Syntax of Silence*. Oxford: Oxford University Press.

——. 2004. Resumptivity and Non-Movement. *Studies in Greek Linguistics* 24: 471–481.

Michaelis, Laura. 2010. Sign-Based Construction Grammar. In Heine and Narrog 2009, 139–158.

Montague, Richard. 1970. English as a Formal Language. In Bruno Visentini et al., eds., *Linguaggi nella Societá e nella Tecnica*, 189–224. Milan: Edizioni di Communità. Reprinted in Montague (1974: 188–221).

——. 1973. The Proper Treatment of Quantification in Ordinary English. In Jaakko Hintikka, Julian Moravcsik, and Patrick Suppes, eds., *Approaches to Language*, 221–242. Dordrecht: Reidel. Reprinted in Montague (1974: 247–270).

——. 1974. *Formal Philosophy: Selected Papers of Richard Montague*. Edited and with an introduction by Richmond H. Thomason. New Haven, CT: Yale University Press.

Moore, John. 1998. Turkish Copy-Raising and A-Chain Locality. *Natural Language and Linguistic Theory* 16: 149–189.

Moortgat, Michael. 1997. Categorial Type Logics. In Johan van Benthem and Alice ter Meulen, eds., *Handbook of Logic and Language*, 93–177. Cambridge, MA: MIT Press. Co-published with Elsevier Science B.V., Amsterdam.

——. 1999. Constants of Grammatical Reasoning. In Bouma et al. 1999, 199–219.

Morrill, Glyn V. 1994. *Type Logical Grammar*. Dordrecht: Kluwer.

——. 2009. Categorial Grammar. In Heine and Narrog 2009, 67–86.

——. 2011. *Categorial Grammar: Logical Syntax, Semantics, and Processing*. Oxford: Oxford University Press.

Müller, Stefan, ed. 2010. *Proceedings of the HPSG10 Conference*. Stanford, CA: CSLI Publications.

Muskens, Reinhard. 1994. Categorial Grammar and Discourse Representation Theory. In *Proceedings of the 15th International Conference on Computational Linguistics (COLING94)*, 508–514. Kyoto.

Mycock, Louise. 2004. The *Wh*-Expletive Construction. In Butt and King 2004*a*, 370–390.

——. 2006. The Typology of Constituent Questions: A Lexical-Functional Grammar Analysis of 'Wh'-Questions. PhD thesis, University of Manchester.

Nissenbaum, Jonathan. 2000. Investigations of Covert Phrase Movement. PhD thesis, MIT.

Noonan, Máire. 1997. Functional Architecture and Wh-movement: Irish as a Case in Point. *Canadian Journal of Linguistics* 42: 111–139.

Nunes, Jairo. 2001. Sideward Movement. *Linguistic Inquiry* 32: 303–344.

——. 2004. *Linearization of Chains and Sideward Movement*. Cambridge, MA: MIT Press.

O'Connor, Robert. 2006. Information Structure in Lexical-Functional Grammar: The Discourse-Prosody Interface. PhD thesis, University of Manchester.

Oehrle, Richard T. 2003. Resource-Sensitivity—A Brief Guide. In Kruijff and Oehrle 2003*b*, 231–255.

Ouhalla, Jamal. 2001. Parasitic Gaps and Resumptive Pronouns. In Peter W. Culicover and Paul M. Postal, eds., *Parasitic Gaps*, 147–179. Cambridge, MA: MIT Press.

Parsons, Terence. 1990. *Events in the Semantics of English: A Study in Subatomic Semantics*. Cambridge, MA: MIT Press.

Partee, Barbara H. 1970. Negation, Conjunction, and Quantifiers: Syntax vs. Semantics. *Foundations of Language* 6: 153–165.

——. 1975. Montague Grammar and Transformational Grammar. *Linguistic Inquiry* 6: 203–300.

——. 1986. Noun Phrase Interpretation and Type-Shifting Principles. In Jeroen Groenendijk, Dick de Jongh, and Martin Stokhof, eds., *Studies in Discourse Representation Theory and the Theory of Generalized Quantifiers*, vol. 8 of GRASS, 115–143. Dordrecht: Foris. Reprinted in Partee (2004: 203–230).

——. 2004. *Compositionality in Formal Semantics: Selected Papers by Barbara H. Partee*. Oxford: Blackwell.

Partee, Barbara H., Alice ter Meulen, and Robert E. Wall. 1993. *Mathematical Methods in Linguistics*. Dordrecht: Kluwer.

Perlmutter, David M. 1968. Deep and Surface Structure Constraints in Syntax. PhD thesis, MIT. Reprinted as Perlmutter (1971).

——. 1971. *Deep and Surface Structure Constraints in Syntax*. New York: Holt, Rinehart, and Winston.

Perlmutter, David M., and Scott Soames. 1979. *Syntactic Argumentation and the Structure of English*. Berkeley, CA: University of California Press.

Pesetsky, David. 1987. *Wh*-in-situ: Movement and Unselective Binding. In Eric Reuland and Alice ter Meulen, eds., *The Representation of (In)definiteness*, 98–129. Cambridge, MA: MIT Press.

——. 1998. Some Optimality Principles of Sentence Pronunciation. In Pilar Barbosa, Danny Fox, Paul Hagstrom, Martha McGinnis, and David Pesetsky, eds., *Is the Best Good Enough?*, 337–383. Cambridge, MA: MIT Press.

Pickering, Martin. 1993. Direct Association and Sentence Processing: A Reply to Gorrell and to Gibson and Hickok. *Language and Cognitive Processes* 8: 163–196.

Pickering, Martin, and Guy Barry. 1991. Sentence Processing Without Empty Categories. *Language and Cognitive Processes* 6: 229–259.

Pollard, Carl, and Ivan A. Sag. 1987. *Information-Based Syntax and Semantics*. Stanford, CA: CSLI Publications.

——. 1994. *Head-Driven Phrase Structure Grammar*. Chicago, IL and Stanford, CA: The University of Chicago Press and CSLI Publications.

Postal, Paul M. 1974. *On Raising: One Rule of English Grammar and its Theoretical Implications*. Cambridge, MA: MIT Press.

Potsdam, Eric, and Jeffrey T. Runner. 2001. Richard Returns: Copy Raising and its Implications. In Mary Andronis, Chris Ball, Heidi Elston, and Sylvain Neuvel, eds., *CLS 37: The Main Session*, vol. 1, 453–468. Chicago, IL: Chicago Linguistic Society.

Potts, Christopher. 2001. Three Kinds of Transderivational Constraint. In Séamas Mac Bhloscaidh, ed., *Syntax and Semantics at Santa Cruz*, vol. 3, 21–40. Santa Cruz, CA: Linguistics Research Center, University of California, Santa Cruz.

——. 2002*a*. Comparative Economy Conditions in Natural Language Syntax. Paper presented at the *North American Summer School in Logic, Language, and Information 1*, Workshop on Model-Theoretic Syntax, Stanford University.

——. 2002*b*. No Vacuous Quantification Constraints in Syntax. In Masako Hirotani, ed., *Proceedings of the North East Linguistic Society* 32, 451–470. Amherst, MA: GLSA.

——. 2003. The Logic of Conventional Implicatures. PhD thesis, University of California, Santa Cruz.

——. 2005. *The Logic of Conventional Implicatures*. Oxford: Oxford University Press.

Prawitz, Dag. 1965. *Natural Deduction: A Proof-theoretical Study*. Stockholm: Almquist and Wiksell.

Prince, Ellen. 1990. Syntax and Discourse: A Look at Resumptive Pronouns. In Kira Hall, Jean-Pierre Koenig, Michael Meacham, Sondra Reinman, and Laurel Sutton, eds., *Proceedings of the Sixteenth Annual Meeting of the Berkeley Linguistics Society*, 482–497. Berkeley, CA: Berkeley Linguistics Society.

Pullum, Geoffrey K. 1982. Syncategorematicity and English Infinitival *To*. *Glossa* 16: 181–215.

——. 1985. *Such that* Clauses and the Context-Freeness of English. *Linguistic Inquiry* 16: 291–298.

Pullum, Geoffrey K., and Barbara C. Scholz. 2001. On the Distinction between Model-Theoretic and Generative-Enumerative Syntactic Frameworks. In Philippe de Groote, Glyn Morrill, and Christian Retoré, eds., *Logical Aspects of Computational Linguistics: 4th International Conference, LACL 2001*, 17–43. Berlin: Springer.

Ramchand, Gillian, and Charles Reiss, eds. 2007. *The Oxford Handbook of Linguistic Interfaces*. Oxford: Oxford University Press.

Read, Stephen. 1988. *Relevant Logic: A Philosophical Examination of Inference*. Oxford: Blackwell.

Restall, Greg. 2000. *An Introduction to Substructural Logics*. London: Routledge.

Retoré, Christian, and Edward Stabler. 2004. Generative Grammars in Resource Logics. *Research on Language and Computation* 2: 3–25.

Rizzi, Luigi. 1990. *Relativized Minimality*. Cambridge, MA: MIT Press.

——. 1996. Residual Verb Second and the *Wh*-Criterion. In Adriana Belletti and Luigi Rizzi, eds., *Parameters and Functional Heads: Essays in Comparative Syntax*, 63–90. Oxford: Oxford University Press.

Rogers, Andy. 1971. Three Kinds of Physical Perception Verbs. In *Papers from the Seventh Regional Meeting of the Chicago Linguistic Society*, 206–222. Chicago: Chicago Linguistic Society.

——. 1972. Another Look at Flip Perception Verbs. In *Papers from the Eighth Regional Meeting of the Chicago Linguistic Society*, 303–315. Chicago: Chicago Linguistic Society.

——. 1973. Physical Perception Verbs in English: A Study in Lexical Relatedness. PhD thesis, UCLA.

——. 1974. A Transderivational Constraint on Richard? In *Papers from the Tenth Regional Meeting of the Chicago Linguistic Society*, 551–558. Chicago: Chicago Linguistic Society.

Ross, John R. 1967. Constraints on Variables in Syntax. PhD thesis, MIT.

Rouveret, Alain, ed. 2011. *Resumptive Pronouns at the Interfaces*. Amsterdam: John Benjamins.

Sadler, Louisa, and Andrew Spencer, eds. 2004. *Projecting Morphology*. Stanford, CA: CLSI Publications.

Safir, Ken. 1986. Relative Clauses in a Theory of Binding and Levels. *Linguistic Inquiry* 17: 663–689.

——. 2004*a*. *The Syntax of Anaphora*. Oxford: Oxford University Press.

——. 2004*b*. *The Syntax of (In)dependence*. Cambridge, MA: MIT Press.

Sag, Ivan A. 2010. English Filler-Gap Constructions. *Language* 86: 486–545.

Sells, Peter. 1984. Syntax and Semantics of Resumptive Pronouns. PhD thesis, University of Massachusetts, Amherst.

——. 1987. Binding Resumptive Pronouns. *Linguistics and Philosophy* 10: 261–298.

——. 2001. *Structure, Alignment, and Optimality in Swedish*. Stanford, CA: CSLI Publications.

Sells, Peter, and Charles Jones, eds. 1983. *Proceedings of NELS 13*. Amherst, MA: GLSA.

Shan, Chung-Chieh, and Chris Barker. 2006. Explaining Crossover and Superiority as Left-to-Right Evaluation. *Linguistics and Philosophy* 29: 91–134.

Shapiro, Stewart. 2001. Classical Logic II—Higher-Order Logic. In Goble 2001, 33–54.

Sharvit, Yael. 1999. Resumptive Pronouns in Relative Clauses. *Natural Language and Linguistic Theory* 17: 587–612.

Shieber, Stuart M. 1985. Evidence Against the Context-Freeness of Natural Language. *Linguistics and Philosophy* 8: 333–343.

Shlonsky, Ur. 1992. Resumptive Pronouns as a Last Resort. *Linguistic Inquiry* 23: 443–468.

Siddiqi, Daniel. 2009. *Syntax Within the Word: Economy, Allomorphy, and Argument Selection in Distributed Morphology*. Amsterdam: John Benjamins.

Simpson, Jane. 1983. Aspects of Warlpiri Morphology and Syntax. PhD thesis, MIT.

——. 1991. *Warlpiri Morpho-Syntax: A Lexicalist Approach*. Dordrecht: Kluwer.

Sonaiya, Remi. 1989. *Wh*-Movement and Proper Government in Yoruba. In Paul Newman and Robert D. Botne, eds., *Current Approaches to African Linguistics*, vol. 5. Dordrecht: Foris.

Sportiche, Dominique. 2006. Reconstruction, Binding, and Scope. In Everaert and Riemsdijk 2006, 35–93.

Steedman, Mark. 1985. Dependency and Coordination in the Grammar of Dutch and English. *Language* 61: 523–568.

——. 1987. Combinatory Grammars and Parasitic Gaps. *Natural Language and Linguistic Theory* 5: 403–440.

——. 1996. *Surface Structure and Interpretation*. Cambridge, MA: MIT Press.

——. 2000. *The Syntactic Process*. Cambridge, MA: MIT Press.

——. 2007. On "The Computation". In Ramchand and Reiss 2007, 575–611.

Stevens, Stanley Smith. 1956. The Direct Estimation of Sensory Magnitudes—Loudness. *American Journal of Psychology* 69: 1–25.

——. 1975. *Psychophysics: Introduction to its Perceptual, Neural, and Social Prospects*. New York: John Wiley.

Stump, Gregory T. 2001. *Inflectional Morphology: A Theory of Paradigm Structure*. Cambridge: Cambridge University Press.

Svenonius, Peter, ed. 2002. *Subjects, Expletives, and the EPP*. Oxford: Oxford University Press.

Swets, Benjamin, and Fernanda Ferreira. 2003. The Effect of Time Pressure on the Production of Resumptive Pronoun Relative Clauses. Poster presented at the *Sixteenth Annual CUNY Conference on Human Sentence Processing*.

Toivonen, Ida. 2001. The Phrase Structure of Non-Projecting Words. PhD thesis, Stanford University.

——. 2003. *Non-Projecting Words: A Case Study of Swedish Verbal Particles*. Dordrecht: Kluwer.

Troelstra, Anne Sjerp. 1992. *Lectures on Linear Logic*. Stanford, CA: CSLI Publications.

Ura, Hiroyuki. 1998. Checking, Economy, and Copy-Raising in Igbo. *Linguistic Analysis* 28: 67–88.

Vaillette, Nathan. 2001. Hebrew Relative Clauses in HPSG. In Dan Flickinger and Andreas Kathol, eds., *Proceedings of the 7th International HPSG Conference*, 305–324. Stanford, CA: CSLI Publications.

——. 2002. Irish Gaps and Resumptive Pronouns in HPSG. In van Eynde et al. 2002, 284–299.

van Benthem, Johan. 1991. *Language in Action: Categories, Lambdas, and Dynamic Logic*. Amsterdam: North-Holland. Reprinted in 1995 by the MIT Press, Cambridge, MA.

van Dalen, Dirk. 2001. Intuitionistic Logic. In Goble 2001, 224–257.

van Egmond, Marie-Elaine. 2004. Copy Raising in Dutch. Undergraduate thesis, University of Canterbury.

van Eynde, Frank, Lars Hellan, and Dorothee Beermann, eds. 2002. *Proceedings of the 8th International HPSG Conference*. Stanford, CA: CSLI Publications.

van Genabith, Josef, and Richard Crouch. 1999*a*. Dynamic and Underspecified Semantics for LFG. In Dalrymple 1999, 209–260.

——. 1999*b*. How to Glue a Donkey to an F-structure. In Harry Bunt and Reinhard Muskens, eds., *Computing Meaning*, vol. 1, 129–148. Dordrecht: Kluwer.

Vermaat, Willemijn. 2005. *The Logic of Variation: A Cross-Linguistic Account of* Wh-*Question Formation*. Utrecht: LOT.

Wasow, Thomas. 2002. *Postverbal Behavior*. Stanford, CA: CSLI Publications.

Wheeler, Deirdre. 1988. Consequences of Some Categorially-Motivated Phonological Assumptions. In Richard T. Oehrle, Emmon Bach, and Deirdre Wheeler, eds., *Categorial Grammars and Natural Language Structures*, 467–488. Dordrecht: Reidel.

Williams, Edwin. 1978. Across-the-Board Rule Application. *Linguistic Inquiry* 9: 31–43.

Willis, David. 2000. On the Distribution of Resumptive Pronouns and *Wh*-Trace in Welsh. *Journal of Linguistics* 36: 531–573.

Wood, Mary McGee. 1993. *Categorial Grammars*. London: Routledge.

Zaenen, Annie. 1980. Extraction Rules in Icelandic. PhD thesis, Harvard University. Reprinted as Zaenen (1985).

——. 1983. On Syntactic Binding. *Linguistic Inquiry* 14: 469–504.

——. 1985. *Extraction Rules in Icelandic*. New York: Garland.

Zaenen, Annie, Elisabet Engdahl, and Joan Maling. 1981. Resumptive Pronouns can be Syntactically Bound. *Linguistic Inquiry* 12: 679–682.

Zaenen, Annie, and Ronald M. Kaplan. 1995. Formal Devices for Linguistic Generalizations: West Germanic Word Order in LFG. In Dalrymple et al. 1995, 215–239.

Zaenen, Annie, Jane Simpson, Tracy Holloway King, Jane Grimshaw, Joan Maling, and Christopher Manning, eds. 2007. *Architectures, Rules, and Preferences: Variations on Themes by Joan W. Bresnan*. Stanford, CA: CSLI Publications.

Zec, Draga. 1987. On Obligatory Control in Clausal Complements. In Masayo Iida, Stephen Wechsler, and Draga Zec, eds., *Working Papers in Grammatical Theory and Discourse Structure*, vol. I: *Interactions of Morphology, Syntax, and Discourse*, 139–168. Stanford, CA: CSLI Publications.

Zimmermann, Thomas Ede. 1993. On the Proper Treatment of Opacity in Certain Verbs. *Natural Language Semantics* 1: 149–179.

Author Index

Subject Index

OXFORD STUDIES IN THEORETICAL LINGUISTICS

PUBLISHED

1 The Syntax of Silence
Sluicing, Islands, and the Theory of Ellipsis
by Jason Merchant

2 Questions and Answers in Embedded Contexts
by Utpal Lahiri

3 Phonetics, Phonology, and Cognition
edited by Jacques Durand and Bernard Laks

4 At the Syntax-Pragmatics Interface
Concept Formation and Verbal Underspecification in Dynamic Syntax
by Lutz Marten

5 The Unaccusativity Puzzle
Explorations of the Syntax-Lexicon Interface
edited by Artemis Alexiadou, Elena Anagnostopoulou, and Martin Everaert

6 Beyond Morphology
Interface Conditions on Word Formation
by Peter Ackema and Ad Neeleman

7 The Logic of Conventional Implicatures
by Christopher Potts

8 Paradigms of Phonological Theory
edited by Laura Downing, T. Alan Hall, and Renate Raffelsiefen

9 The Verbal Complex in Romance
by Paola Monachesi

10 The Syntax of Aspect
Deriving Thematic and Aspectual Interpretation
Edited by Nomi Erteschik-Shir and Tova Rapoport

11 Aspects of the Theory of Clitics
by Stephen Anderson

12 Canonical Forms in Prosodic Morphology
by Laura J. Downing

13 Aspect and Reference Time
by Olga Borik

14 Direct Compositionality
edited by Chris Barker and Pauline Jacobson

15 A Natural History of Infixation
by Alan C. L. Yu

16 Phi-Theory
Phi-Features Across Interfaces and Modules
edited by Daniel Harbour, David Adger, and Susana Béjar

17 French Dislocation: Interpretation, Syntax, Acquisition
by Cécile De Cat

18 Inflectional Identity
edited by Asaf Bachrach and Andrew Nevins

19 Lexical Plurals
by Paolo Acquaviva

20 Adjectives and Adverbs
Syntax, Semantics, and Discourse
Edited by Louise McNally and Christopher Kennedy

21 InterPhases
Phase-Theoretic Investigations of Linguistic Interfaces
edited by Kleanthes Grohmann

22 Negation in Gapping
by Sophie Repp

23 A Derivational Syntax for Information Structure
by Luis López

24 Quantification, Definiteness, and Nominalization
edited by Anastasia Giannakidou and Monika Rathert

25 The Syntax of Sentential Stress
by Arsalan Kahnemuyipour

26 Tense, Aspect, and Indexicality
by James Higginbotham

27 Lexical Semantics, Syntax and Event Structure
edited by Malka Rappaport Hovav, Edit Doron and Ivy Sichel

28 About the Speaker
Towards a Syntax of Indexicality
by Alessandra Giorgi

29 The Sound Patterns of Syntax
edited by Nomi Erteschik-Shir and Lisa Rochman

30 The Complementizer Phase
edited by Phoevos Panagiotidis

31 Interfaces in Linguistics
New Research Perspectives
edited by Raffaella Folli and Christiane Ulbrich

32 Negative Indefinites
by Doris Penka

33 Events, Phrases, and Questions
by Robert Truswell

34 Dissolving Binding Theory
by Johan Rooryck and Guido Vanden Wyngaerd

35 The Logic of Pronominal Resumption
by Ash Asudeh

36 Modals and Conditionals
by Angelika Kratzer

37 The Theta System
Argument Structure at the Interface
edited by Martin Everaert, Marijana Marelj, and Tal Siloni

38 Sluicing in Cross-Linguistic Perspective
Edited by Jason Merchant and Andrew Simpson

39 Telicity, Change, and State
A Cross-Categorial View of Event Structure
edited by Violeta Demonte and Louise McNally

40 Ways of Structure Building
edited by Myriam Uribe-Etxebarria and Vidal Valmala

41 The Morphology and Phonology of Exponence
edited by Jochen Trommer

Published in association with the series
The Oxford Handbook of Linguistic Interfaces
edited by Gillian Ramchand and Charles Reiss

In preparation

The Syntax of Roots and the Roots of Syntax
Edited by Artemis Alexiadou, Hagit Borer, and Florian Schäfer

External Arguments in Transitivity Alternations
by Artemis Alexiadou, Elena Anagnostopoulou, and Florian Schäfer

Semantic Continuations
Scope, Binding, and Other Semantic Side Effects
by Chris Barker and Chung-Chieh Shan

Phi Syntax: A Theory of Agreement
by Susana Béjar

Stratal Optimality Theory
by Ricardo Bermúdez Otero

Diagnosing Syntax
edited by Lisa Lai-Shen Cheng and Norbert Corver

Phonology in Phonetics
by Abigail Cohn

Generality and Exception
by Ivan Garcia-Alvarez

Strategies of Quantification
edited by Kook-Hee Gil, Stephen Harlow, and George Tsoulas

The Indefiniteness and Focusing of Wh-words
by Andreas Haida

Genericity
edited by Alda Mari, Claire Beyssade, and Fabio Del Prete

The Count Mass Distinction: A Cross-Linguistic Perspective
edited by Diane Massam

The Semantics of Evaluativity
by Jessica Rett

Computing Optimality
by Jason Riggle

Nonverbal Predications
by Isabelle Roy

Null Subject Languages
by Evi Sifaki and Ioanna Sitaridou

Gradience in Split Intransitivity
by Antonella Sorace